Hong Kong Media Law

A Guide for Journalists and Media Professionals

Expanded Second Edition

HKU Press Law Series

The aim of the series is to publish new works on all major aspects of Hong Kong's law and legal system, as well as the law of China and other jurisdictions, in order to provide an understanding of current issues in law and related disciplines.

Also in the series:

Contract Law in Hong Kong (*Expanded Second Edition*)
Michael J. Fisher and Desmond G. Greenwood

Corporate Governance and Financial Reform in China's Transition Economy
Leng Jing

Criminal Law in Hong Kong
Michael Jackson

Hong Kong Commercial Law: Current Issues and Developments
Edited by Charles D. Booth

Hong Kong Legal Principles: Important Topics for Students and Professionals (*Second Edition*)
Stephen D. Mau

Hong Kong's Constitutional Debate: Conflict Over Interpretation
Edited by Johannes M. M. Chan, H. L. Fu and Yash Ghai

Hong Kong's New Constitutional Order: The Resumption of Chinese Sovereignty and the Basic Law (*Second Edition*)
Yash Ghai

Law, Morality and the Private Domain
Raymond Wacks

Legal Research: A Guide for Hong Kong Students
Jill Cottrell

National Security and Fundamental Freedoms: Hong Kong's Article 23 under Scrutiny
Edited by Fu Hualing, Carole J. Petersen and Simon N. M. Young

The New Legal Order in Hong Kong
Edited by Raymond Wacks

Shipping and Logistics Law: Principles and Practice in Hong Kong
Felix W. H. Chan, Jimmy J. M. Ng, Bobby K. Y. Wong

Understanding Chinese Company Law (*Second Edition*)
Gu MinKang

Hong Kong Media Law

A Guide for Journalists and Media Professionals

Expanded Second Edition

Doreen Weisenhaus
with contributions by Rick Glofcheski and Yan Mei Ning

香港大學出版社
HONG KONG UNIVERSITY PRESS

Hong Kong University Press
The University of Hong Kong
Pokfulam Road
Hong Kong
www.hkupress.org

Expanded Second Edition, 2014

ISBN 978-988-8208-25-8 *(Hardback)*
ISBN 978-988-8208-09-8 *(Paperback)*

British Library Cataloguing-in-Publication Data
A catalogue record for this book is available from the British Library.

10 9 8 7 6 5 4 3 2 1

Printed and bound by Paramount Printing Co., Ltd. in Hong Kong, China

Reviews for the first edition of *Hong Kong Media Law: A Guide for Journalists and Media Professionals*

"This book deserves to be the first port of call for anyone seeking guidance on free speech and media law in Hong Kong . . . That the book fulfills a felt need is beyond doubt."

—*The Commonwealth Lawyer*, London

"The book is truly the first of its kind in the recent past (and) a singularly important addition to the increasing body of country-specific media law books in Asia . . . *Hong Kong Media Law* covers all the key topics in the area of communication law . . . The scholarly merit of the book is substantial."

—Kyu Ho Youm, *Communications Lawyer*, American Bar Association

"An accessible guide to media law in Hong Kong and China . . . particularly useful for correspondents who have recently arrived in Hong Kong or China and are trying to get their bearings . . . (and) there is a lot here of interest to non-journalists, whether they are citizens trying to understand the peculiarities of Hong Kong's copyright laws, public figures confronting the paparazzi or just people who are curious about the mechanics of Hong Kong's broadcast regulations."

—Chris Dillon, *The Correspondent*, Foreign Correspondents Club Hong Kong

"Weisenhaus brings both a pragmatic and scholarly perspective to her subject . . . For scholars or legal practitioners interested in a concise summary of the law, *Hong Kong Media Law* is a useful resource. For journalists who plan to go to Beijing to cover the Olympics, it is a necessity."

—Jane Kirtley, *Journalism and Mass Communication Quarterly*, US

"This is an important book that goes a long way to filling a serious vacuum as far as the Hong Kong media is concerned. If it helps educate Hong Kong journalists and editors enough for them to feel more confident in publishing articles about even the most litigious subjects without fear of losing the resulting court case, the book will also play its part in protecting press freedom in Hong Kong."

—Danny Gittings, *Hong Kong Law Journal*

"A valuable resource for journalists and media professionals, to be read, kept and referred to."

—Kenneth Leung, *Chinese Journal of Communication*, Hong Kong

"This hefty well-researched book fills an important gap in media law studies in the Asia-Pacific region . . . The material is authoritative and fresh."

—Madanmohan Rao, *Media Asia*, Singapore

"Weisenhaus' book highlights loopholes in Hong Kong's legal system and its lack of protection for press freedom, compared to some Western democracies. For example, Hong Kong's Code on Access to Information is not only not statutory, but is full of exemptions, allowing for Hong Kong's government to be secretive."

—*World Press Freedom Review*, International Press Institute

"What is interesting about *Hong Kong Media Law* is that it traces the way that Hong Kong legislature and courts no longer simply adopt UK legislation or precedents. The book looks at the question of the directions in which Hong Kong will go in the future."

—The Hon. Judith Gibson, New South Wales District Court, Australia
Media and Arts Law Review, Melbourne

With much love, to Jake and Gene for a thousand days

Contents

Foreword

When the first edition of *Hong Kong Media Law* came onto the shelves it met a long outstanding and pressing need. For the first time, all those involved in the communications industry, including the lawyers who advise them, had available in a single published text an authoritative guide — set out in clear and concise terms — to the highways and byways of the otherwise almost impenetrable landscape of statutes, regulations and court-made jurisprudence governing the media law of Hong Kong.

Now, in a span of just a few years with the need being just as great, if not greater, the second edition is with us. But why should there be such a need? It is common wisdom that the Law moves with the speed of a tectonic plate. Surely law books remain good for a couple of decades at least?

Perhaps, when judges learnt their Latin using quill pens dipped into ink wells, time (and all that it encompassed) moved at a more leisurely pace. Not today. It is a statement of the obvious that the communications industry in all its aspects is evolving with dizzying speed. The DNA of the industry appears to reconstitute itself into something intrinsically new almost every year. Nor can the communications industry be said to be of just peripheral interest to the man on the street. It is no longer encompassed in the paper and ink of a broadsheet to be read on the train. Today, in Hong Kong and indeed globally, every second person on the street, if not reading hardcopy, is in some way or another communicating by electronic means.

The media industry dominates society, not simply within borders but globally. And whether the Law wishes it or not it must keep pace. It cannot sit on its throne like King Canute defying the tide to come in. It is for that reason that judges, who get their grandchildren to connect them to the Internet, must seek today, for example, to redefine the laws of defamation to accommodate the transitory, often radical language appearing on an increasing number of Internet chat sites.

It is primarily this rush to the future, I think, that propels the need for the second edition of this admirable text.

There is, however, in my opinion, a second reason. It is said that our present century is the 'Asian Century'. The base reason for that description may lie in the awe-inspiring economic development of so many of the Asian powers, of China and India especially. But it does not end there. It is not confined to the bleak reality of endless factories and the lung-staining pall of unrestrained advancement.

Asian societies are changing; they too are reconstituting their DNA, and with that change there comes an increasing awareness of human rights, of the fundamental societal values that make life worth living and of the demand — for increasingly it is exactly that, a *demand* — that those who govern us be answerable for their actions. And at the centre of all this change lies Hong Kong.

Whatever the naysayers may have said in past years, Hong Kong remains cosmopolitan, energetic, increasingly outspoken in respect of its political desires. The rule of law is entrenched here, the courts remain fiercely independent. Hong Kong is one of the true hubs of the world. It is also in all respects, whatever your cultural background or ethnic origins, a good place to live. In the result, Hong Kong not only has a fearless and diverse local media industry, it is increasingly a centre for the media industry internationally.

All that is to the good. But as everybody in the media industry knows, even though in Hong Kong our Constitution guarantees freedom of speech, freedom of the press and of publication, that freedom is not absolute. In this regard, Hong Kong is no different from any other modern society that espouses to be open and democratic. In all such societies there is a constant tension between guaranteed rights and lawfully imposed obligations and at the end of the day those rights and obligations must be weighed in the scales of the Law. That requirement to weigh rights and obligations, however, places complexity upon complexity.

That is why, at the beginning of this foreword, I spoke of the need for an authoritative guide to the highways and byways of the otherwise almost impenetrable landscape of our statutes, regulations and court-made jurisprudence governing media law, a landscape that, like Asia itself, is increasingly the subject of seismic change.

A guide, of course, is really no guide at all, except perhaps for the esoteric few, if it too is impenetrable. That was one of the reasons why, in my view, the first edition of *Hong Kong Media Law* earned such distinction. While comprehensive and rich in detail it was an essentially practical publication, of equal benefit to the student studying the subject, to the lawyer in his office and to working journalists. I am delighted to say that the second addition excels in these respects in equal measure. The seismic changes of which I have spoken have made it necessary to make a number of very substantial changes to the first edition. This is not simply therefore the first edition with a few added footnotes. It covers much new ground, doing so with admirable academic rigour.

I can foresee future editions of this text; I have no doubt that it will become a staple work in our libraries and offices, remaining equally rich in detail and clear in structure, no doubt a burden for its author but much more so a boon for its readers.

Michael Hartmann GBS
Non-Permanent Judge of the Court of Final Appeal, Hong Kong

Preface

In 2011 when I began putting together the updates for this second edition of *Hong Kong Media Law: A Guide for Journalists and Media Professionals*, I did not think it would take long for compiling and analyzing the several years of developments since the book first appeared in 2007. I was wrong.

More than 200 new cases, laws and regulations later, this expanded second edition is finally ready for publication. The new content, representing at least 40 percent of the book, includes analyses of major media law developments in Hong Kong in defamation, privacy, obscenity, copyright, media regulation and more, but also of significant global developments, particularly involving the Internet and social media, including cases and laws in key areas from more than 20 jurisdictions. This edition also includes an expanded examination of the increasingly volatile situation in mainland China, where developments have special significance for Hong Kong and foreign journalists working there. In addition to the updates and analyses, the second edition features improved chapter structure (including new chapters on obscenity and media regulation) and organization to consolidate related material. It also offers additional resources such as a listing of useful organizations, online publications and websites with regular updates on the intersections between the law, journalism and freedom of expression. For readers who want to follow continuing updates for *Hong Kong Media Law*, please visit the book website at http://medialaw.hk.

The inaugural edition of *Hong Kong Media Law*, the first English-language book of its kind, debuted on the tenth anniversary of the 1997 handover of the British territory to the People's Republic of China. It was a milestone that offered those of us in Hong Kong and the rest of the world an opportunity to reflect on the changes for media and press freedom leading up to the handover and during the initial decade of Chinese sovereignty under the "One Country, Two Systems" regime. In that time, a series of controversial interactions between the law and a robust media began to suggest the emergence of a Hong Kong-specific jurisprudence within an inherited colonial common law system. By 2013, well into Hong Kong's second decade as a Special Administrative Region, that jurisprudence by the courts was further evolved and included a growing commitment to freedom of expression that the Hong Kong government often did not seem to share. The media's coverage sometimes seemed to provoke a disproportionate hostility by a government that already makes it difficult for journalists to do their jobs. By showing where Hong Kong came from and where it is today, the hope is that this expanded second edition gives a glimpse of what Hong Kong media law might look like by the handover's twentieth anniversary in 2017.

I want to give special thanks again to my colleagues Yan Mei Ning for her comprehensive and tireless updates and major revisions for her chapters, especially involving media regulation and obscenity law, and Rick Glofcheski, a leading scholar on Hong Kong tort law, who took over the revisions for the defamation chapter from Jill Cottrell, now retired from HKU; Jill lives in Nairobi and works with the Katiba Institute, an NGO devoted to implementation of the 2010 Kenyan Constitution through litigation, civic education and comments on proposed legislation and public debate. I remain grateful for her contribution of that critical chapter to the first edition.

I also want to thank Professor Ying Chan, director of the Journalism and Media Studies Centre, a source of wise counsel, support and encouragement. I am deeply appreciative of the Hon. Justice Michael Hartmann, who retired from the Court of Appeal in 2012 and is now serving as a non-permanent justice on the Court of Final Appeal, for providing a new foreword and for continuing to inspire another generation of young journalists on the importance of a free press in a system of open justice.

Once more I am indebted to the legal scholars, practitioners and others who generously shared their knowledge and expertise by reviewing chapter manuscripts for accuracy and context (but I alone am responsible for any errors or omissions). They include: Robert Balin, partner, Davis Wright Tremaine LLP, New York; Cliff Buddle, former senior legal editor and current special projects editor, *South China Morning Post;* Chan Pui-king, honorary lecturer at JMSC and former editor-in-chief, *Next Magazine*; Dr. Fu Hualing, professor at the Faculty of Law, University of Hong Kong, a specialist on Chinese criminal justice and co-author of *Media Law in the PRC* (1996); Dr. Fu King-wa, assistant professor at the JMSC who has done groundbreaking work on access to information in Hong Kong; Graham Greenleaf, professor of law at the University of New South Wales and founder of *Privacy Law and Policy Reporter*, Alice Lee, associate professor, Faculty of Law, HKU, and co-author of *Intellectual Property Law and Practice in Hong Kong* (2010); Jared Margolis, director, IPI Associates Ltd, Hong Kong, and co-author of *Intellectual Property Rights: Hong Kong and the People's Republic of China*, 2nd ed. (2003); Simon N. M. Young, barrister and professor, Faculty of Law, HKU, and co-editor, *Hong Kong's Court of Final Appeal: The Development of the Law in China's Hong Kong* (2013) and Peter K. Yu, who holds the Kern Family Chair in Intellectual Property Law and is founder of the Intellectual Property Law Center, Drake University Law School, US.

My appreciation also goes to Vivian Kwok for updating Appendix B, the useful guide on searching court records she and Chan Pui-king provided for the first edition; and to the journalists I have interviewed for this book, who shared their sometimes harrowing experiences, particularly those reporting on the Mainland, including several former students with their own successful journalism careers — Ng Tze-wei, who has reported on mainland legal affairs since 2007, Sky Canaves and Zhuang Pinghui.

And I am especially grateful to my son, Jake Mustain, who provided invaluable research assistance; my husband Gene Mustain, editor extraordinaire; and other family members and friends, including Violet Mustain, Lisa Rasmussen, Michele Galen, Lisa Belkin, Trish Brandt, Lori Webb and Tiffany Montoya, for their support and love throughout.

Doreen Weisenhaus
December 2013

Contributor's Acknowledgments:

Dr. Yan would like to express her sincere gratitude to Dr. P. Y. Lo and Mr. Desmond Chan for their valuable comments on her chapters.

The Author and Contributors

Doreen Weisenhaus, BS Journalism, JD (Northwestern, US) is director of the Media Law Project at the Journalism and Media Studies Centre at the University of Hong Kong and an associate professor, teaching media law and ethics since 2000. She is a former prosecutor as well as a former city editor of *The New York Times*, law and politics editor of *The New York Times Magazine*, and editor-in-chief of *The National Law Journal*, a leading publication for lawyers in the US that won several major journalism awards during her tenure. Her research interests include international press freedom, media ownership and worldwide trends in media law, regulation and policy. She is working on books on media law developments in China and Asia as well as globally.

Contributors

Rick Glofcheski, BA (Wilfrid Laurier, Canada), LLB (Windsor, Canada), LLM (Cambridge), is a professor in the Faculty of Law at the University of Hong Kong. His primary areas of teaching and research are tort law, labour and employment law and teaching and learning in higher education. He is the general editor of *Hong Kong Law Journal*. He is the author of *Tort Law in Hong Kong*, third edition (2012), and the author and co-editor of *Employment Law and Practice in Hong Kong* (2010). In 2011, he was selected for the inaugural University Distinguished Teaching Award (2010), and the inaugural Hong Kong-wide University Grants Committee Teaching Excellence Award, in recognition of outstanding teaching and his leadership and contributions to the advancement of teaching and learning.

Yan Mei Ning (甄美玲), BA (HKU), LLB (London, external), LLM (Queen's, Belfast), PhD in Law (Essex), has been an associate professor at Shantou University Law School in China since September 2011, teaching media law, law and government in Hong Kong, and IP law. She has also taught at Shantou University Cheung Kong School of Journalism and Communication (2008–2011) and Hong Kong Baptist University Department of Journalism (1999–2008), and was a journalist in Hong Kong for fourteen years before joining academia.

Key Milestones and Developments for Press Freedom in Hong Kong

1985 The People's Republic of China and the United Kingdom ratify the Joint Declaration on the Question of Hong Kong, setting the stage for the eventual end of colonial rule and a transfer of Hong Kong to Chinese sovereignty in 1997.

1987 The Control of Publications Consolidation Ordinance is repealed, bringing an end to harsh colonial rules on local print media.

The Control of Obscene and Indecent Articles Ordinance (COIAO) is enacted; it aims to reduce objectionable newsstand publications and access by juveniles to indecent material.

1989 The Law Reform Commission (LRC) appoints a sub-committee on privacy to carry out a comprehensive review of law relating to privacy and to make recommendations for legislation protecting individual privacy rights.

1991 The Bill of Rights Ordinance is enacted to establish various fundamental rights, enforceable by the courts, including protection for freedom of expression.

1994 Hong Kong journalist Xi Yang, a reporter for the *Ming Pao* newspaper, is convicted in the PRC of disclosing state secrets and is sentenced to 12 years in prison. (He is released in 1997.)

The Court of Appeal applies the "newspaper rule", a common law rule protecting sources in libel cases, to a Hong Kong case in rejecting a request for the names of the author and editors of an article in a pre-trial defamation action. *John Sham v Eastweek Publisher Ltd.* [1995] 1 HKC 264.

1995 The Court of Appeal sets aside as excessive the first jury award for libel damages in Hong Kong of HK$2.4 million against a magazine. *Cheung Ng Sheong Steven v Eastweek Publisher Ltd.* [1995] 3 HKC 601.

Apple Daily newspaper debuts in Hong Kong, bringing a market-driven style of journalism.

The Hong Kong government rejects calls for a Freedom of Information law and institutes an administrative Code on Access to Information.

The Personal Data (Privacy) Ordinance (PDPO) is passed. It protects an individual's personal data, but provides "news activity" exemptions for reporting.

Legislative provisions in the Interpretation and General Clauses Ordinance (IGCO) to govern the search and seizure of journalistic materials are enacted.

1996 The Legislative Council amends the Prevention of Bribery Ordinance to offer greater protection to journalists. This comes after a highly controversial prosecution against *Ming Pao* for a 1994 article about ongoing investigations conducted by the Independent Commission Against Corruption (ICAC).

1997 On 1 July, the PRC resumes authority for Hong Kong. The Basic Law goes into effect, extending Constitutional protection for freedom of speech, of the press and of publication.

1998 The Court of Final Appeal, Hong Kong's highest court, overturns an Obscene Articles Tribunal's classification of a newspaper's photographs and articles as indecent and illegally distributed, saying that the tribunal is under a duty to give reasons and that the reasons given are inadequate. *Oriental Daily Publisher v Commissioner for Television and Entertainment Licensing* [1998] 4 HKC 505.

In what becomes known as the "Chan Kin Hong Incident", Hong Kong media extensively cover the suicide-homicide of a woman and her two children. A newspaper publishes a front-page photograph of the widower posing with prostitutes, but later apologizes for its role. The incident leads to calls for legislative proposals against media intrusion.

1999 A media company is fined HK$5 million and one of its editors is sentenced to four months in prison for contempt of court ("scandalizing the court") for publishing articles sharply criticizing two judges and for a paparazzi-style campaign against one of the judges. *Wong Yeung Ng v Secretary for Justice* [1999] 2 HKLRD 293.

Consultation papers issued by the LRC's sub-committee on privacy recommend the establishment of a statutory press council and new privacy laws to regulate the media.

In investigating a reporter bribery case, authorities search a newspaper's premises and seize documents and journalistic materials. (A court challenge to the search warrants is later rejected. *Apple Daily v Commissioner of the Independent Commission Against Corruption* [2000] 1 HKC 295.)

2000 In a landmark defamation case, the Court of Final Appeal expands the defence of fair comment, affirms the Constitutional guarantee of freedom of speech and of expression and urges lower courts developing the common law "not to adopt a narrow approach". *Cheng v Tse* [2000] 3 HKLRD 418.

The Court of Appeal holds that a photograph taken of an unidentified woman in the street without her consent and used for a magazine article criticizing her fashion sense was not a violation of data privacy law. *Eastweek v Privacy Commissioner* [2000] 1 HKC 692.

The Hong Kong Press Council, the first self-regulatory body for the print media, is established to handle public complaints.

The Broadcasting Ordinance is enacted, replacing the Television Ordinance.

2002 In the "Chater Garden Incident", police handcuff and arrest two journalists after they refuse to enter and stay in a designated press area, leading the media to call for better access in covering protests.

Eastweek magazine publishes nude photographs of actress Carina Lau under duress taken a decade earlier when she was kidnapped, prompting community protests and questions over obscenity standards; the magazine's owner shuts down the publication. The incident launches multiple legal proceedings.

The Hong Kong government introduces proposals for Article 23 laws on sedition, subversion, theft of state secrets, treason and secession.

The debut of *Metropolitan Daily*, Hong Kong's first free newspaper, spurs the introduction of other free dailies, increasing the competition of the already active print market.

2003 On 1 July, more than 500,000 people, including many journalists, march in protest of the Article 23 legislation. The government withdraws its proposals.

2004 The ICAC raids seven newsrooms in an attempt to uncover sources for news stories that revealed the identity of a witness in the government witness protection programme. The Court of First Instance upholds a newspaper's challenge of the search warrants. The Court of Appeal dismisses the government's appeal, but states it would have allowed the appeal had it had the necessary jurisdiction. *So Wing Keung v Sing Tao Ltd & Another* [2005] 2 HKLRD 11. (A trial against lawyers accused of attempting to disclose the witness' identity to reporters is held in 2006.)

The Law Reform Commission releases two reports recommending a statutory press commission and new civil privacy laws.

2005 In the first Hong Kong decision to consider the UK's *Reynolds* privilege in a defamation case, a Court of First Instance rules in favour of a newspaper relying on the defence after being sued for an article in its readers' complaint column about unsatisfactory services provided by a local business. *Cutting de Heart v Sun News Ltd* [2005] 3 HKLRD 133.

In a major policy shift, the Hong Kong Judiciary expands public access to in-chamber hearings in civil proceedings in the High Court, District Court, Lands Tribunal and Family Court, providing greater access to journalists.

A Hong Kong man becomes the first person in the world convicted for distributing copyright-protected movies on the Internet using BitTorrent technology. *HKSAR v Chan Nai Ming* [2005] 4 HKLRD 142. (The Court of Final Appeal later confirms the conviction. *Chan Nai Ming v HKSAR* [2007] 2 HKLRD 486.)

2006 The Court of First Instance orders the government to enact "corrective" legislation for its covert surveillance practices. The Interception of Communication and Surveillance Ordinance is passed, allowing covert surveillance by authorities on journalists, lawyers and other professions.

Published covert photographs of singer Gillian Chung undressing after a concert are classified as indecent. Chung files a breach of confidence suit against the magazine that published the photographs and obtains an injunction against further publication. The incident renews calls for more media regulation.

South China Morning Post reporter Magdalen Chow testifies under immunity in the trial of barrister Kevin Egan, who was convicted of attempting to disclose the identity of a participant in the witness protection programme. (The Court of Appeal later overturns Egan's conviction. *Secretary for Justice v Kevin Egan* (2008) CACC 248/2006.)

The Hong Kong government proposes the merger of the Broadcasting Authority and the Telecommunications Authority into a unified regulator, the Communications Authority.

The LRC's subcommittee on privacy issues a report — the last of its six reports on privacy — calling for new criminal laws against covert surveillance by government and private parties.

Hong Kong reporter Ching Cheong is convicted in the PRC on spying charges and is sentenced to five years in prison. (He is released in 2008 and returns to Hong Kong.)

In December, the PRC government announces the relaxation of some reporting restrictions against foreign, Hong Kong and Macau reporters in the run-up to the 2008 Olympics in Beijing.

2007 An investigation by the Ombudsman's office concludes that government officials breached the Code on Access to Information when they repeatedly denied a request by a university researcher for information on railway suicide incidents.

The Privacy Commissioner determines that a reporter's IP address, which a PRC subsidiary of Yahoo! Hong Kong turned over to mainland authorities, is not personal data. The PRC reporter, Shi Tao, was sentenced in 2005 to ten years in prison for emailing Communist Party instructions on Tiananmen Square anniversary news coverage to a foreign website. (The Administrative Appeals Board later agrees the IP address is not personal data. *Shi Tao v Privacy Commissioner for Personal Data* [2008] 3 HKLRD 332, AAB. Shi Tao is released from prison in 2013.)

2008 In January, a media frenzy erupts over the online publishing of intimate sexual photographs involving Hong Kong pop star Edison Chen and numerous female celebrities. The reproduction of the photos in mainstream media, police crackdowns and prosecutions trigger questions on freedom of expression and regulation of online pornography. By October, the government initiates its first round of public consultation for reviewing COIAO.

In the second Hong Kong case to consider the *Reynolds* privilege (now known as the public interest defence), a Court of First Instance finds the defence not proved and orders Asia Times Online to pay HK$1.3 million to a Pakistani businessman for defaming him in an online article. *Abdul Razzak Yaqoob v Asia Times Online Ltd.* [2008] 4 HKLRD 911.

A Court of First Instance rules that the Broadcasting Authority's censure of public broadcaster RTHK's programme on same-sex couples who want legalized marriage was "an impermissible restriction on freedom of speech". *Cho Man Kit v Broadcasting Authority* (2008) HCAL 69/2007.

Hong Kong becomes the 50th jurisdiction to localize Creative Commons, a supplemental licensing scheme to facilitate the public distribution of copyright-protected works.

Post-Olympics, China extends the relaxed reporting rules for foreign journalists covering the 2008 Olympics, but not for Hong Kong and Macau reporters.

2009 China issues new reporting rules for Hong Kong and Macau journalists reporting on the mainland that are more restrictive than those for foreign journalists.

The Ombudsman's office substantiates a complaint by *Apple Daily* that had tried unsuccessfully to obtain Hong Kong government test results of food samples from mainland China after a deadly, tainted baby-formula scandal there.

Becoming the first journalist jailed under Hong Kong's obscenity law, an editor is sentenced to five months for the 2002 publication of the Carina Lau nude photographs.

Macau's legislature approves a National Security Law, its own version of Article 23 implementation, heightening fears that its action would prompt a second attempt by Hong Kong authorities.

2010 The Court of Final Appeal's first Chief Justice, the Hon. Andrew Li Kwok Nang, who served since 1997, steps down. He is widely viewed as having successfully established the CFA as a respected and moderate court, which issued the landmark *Cheng v Tse*. The Hon. Geoffrey Ma Tao-li, then Chief Judge of the High Court, is appointed to replace him.

After a year-long review, the Ombudsman's office concludes that the Hong Kong government has done little to increase public awareness of the 15-year-old Code on Access to Information or to train officers in how to respond to information requests.

The PRC amends and strengthens its state secrets law, particularly involving the Internet.

2011 In Hong Kong's first disability vilification claim, a court rejects a claim by a mental patient against *The Sun* newspaper for a satirical commentary about the plight of the mentally ill. *Tung Lai Lam v Oriental Press Group* [2011] 2 HKC 294.

"Jasmine Revolution"-style protests in mainland China prompt restrictions and detentions of foreign and Hong Kong journalists trying to cover the events.

The Hong Kong government proposes amendments to the Copyright Ordinance to deal with Internet and digital issues, including measures to add criminal sanctions for unauthorized public communication of copyrighted works, and to establish a "safe harbour" for ISPs to limit liability, provided they assist in combatting online piracy. Many Internet users raise concerns the bill would limit creative derivative works, calling it "the Article 23 of the Internet". (The bill is later withdrawn.)

A visit to Hong Kong by then-Vice Premier Li Keqiang prompts immense controversy over how local police handled security, including imposing restrictions on the media.

The Broadcasting Authority imposes its largest fine to date — HK$300,000 — on Asia Television (ATV), one of two terrestrial stations in Hong Kong, for erroneously reporting that former Chinese leader Jiang Zemin had died.

The Constitutional and Mainland Affairs Bureau releases a consultation paper on stalking, inviting comments on such questions as whether to create a criminal offence or provide a specific newsgathering defence. (The bureau had announced earlier it would consider LRC reports on privacy reforms in stages, starting first with stalking.)

2012 Hong Kong courts issue two judgments concluding that website forum hosts are generally to be considered "subsidiary publishers", and not primary publishers, of defamatory comments that appear in online forums, suggesting that ISPs might be eligible for the defence of innocent dissemination. *Oriental Press Group Ltd v Fevaworks Solutions* [2012] 1 HKLRD 848; *Oriental Press Group Ltd v Inmediahk.net Ltd* [2012] 2 HKLRD 1004.

The Court of Final Appeal greatly reduces the libel damages awarded at trial in two decisions that clarified and revised some of the principles for damage awards, thus ensuring that they are likely to be more modest in the future. *Blakeney-Williams v Cathay Pacific Airways Ltd* (2012) 15 HKCFAR 261, and *Oriental Daily Publisher Ltd v Ming Pao Holdings Ltd.* (2012) 15 HKCFAR 299.

The Legislative Council amends the PDPO, restricting the direct marketing and sale of personal data. A new criminal offence to prohibit unauthorized disclosure of personal data with the intention to gain or to cause loss or psychological harm to the data subject is particularly troubling for journalists.

The Privacy Commissioner finds against two magazines for contravening the PDPO in publishing photographs of celebrities in their homes taken covertly with telephoto lenses, rejecting the publications' public-interest claims.

The Communications Authority is established as a unified regulatory body overseeing the telecommunications and broadcasting sectors.

The government conducts a second round of public consultation over COIAO.

The Court of Final Appeal quashes the convictions of several legislators and activists prosecuted for participating in a public forum broadcast without a licence by the activist group Citizens' Radio, which unsuccessfully challenged the constitutionality of the government's licensing scheme. *HKSAR v Wong Yuk Man & Others* [2012] HKCFA 68. (Defendants who operate Citizens' Radio were earlier convicted and fined.)

The PRC's Criminal Procedure Law is extensively amended with potential consequences for journalists who might be detained as they report on the Mainland.

2013 In January, the Ombudsman's office and the Law Reform Commission announce separate reviews into Hong Kong's access of information regime and the related government records management system. The two reviews are to include comparative analyses of FOI laws and record management and archival systems internationally.

After intense public criticism, including from journalists, the government withdraws a controversial legislative proposal to limit public access to personal data on company directors, such as home addresses and personal identity information.

The Court of Final Appeal confirms the availability of the innocent dissemination defence to an Internet Service Provider. *Oriental Press Group Ltd v Fevaworks Solutions Ltd,* [2013] 5 HKC 253.

In a third Hong Kong defamation case to consider the public interest defence, a court finds the defence not proved in an editorial in the *Ming Pao* newspaper and upholds a jury's fine of HK$500,000. *Pui Kwun Kay v Ming Pao Holdings Ltd,* HCA (2013) 854/2009.

The ICAC makes its first request for a production order for journalistic material under s 84 of the IGCO.

The Communications Authority releases an investigation report on ATV, orders the resignation of its executive director for allowing an investor to improperly exercise control over the station and fines ATV HK$1 million. A month later, the CA for the first time determines that a TV licensee (TVB) has violated anti-competition restrictions.

Table of Cases

India

Inter-American Court of Human Rights

Jamaica

New Zealand

People's Republic of China

Guangzhou Huaqiao Real Estate Development Co v China Reform Magazine (Tianhe Dist. People's Ct., Guangzhou, 2004): 224
New Express Daily v The Journalist Monthly (Tianhe Dist. People's Ct., Guangzhou, 2010): 223
Shi Tao (Intermediate People's Ct., Changsha, Hunan Province, 2005): 213n39
Zhao Yan (Second Intermediate People's Ct., Beijing, 2006): 212n36
Zhao Zhengui v Ministry of Health (First Intermediate People's Ct., Beijing, 2012): 219n55

Scotland
Shetland Times Ltd v Dr. Jonathan Wills [1997] SLT 669: 243

Singapore
Attorney General v Shadrake [2010] SGHC 327: 86n41
Attorney General v Shadrake [2011] SGCA 26: 86n41

South Africa
Independent News v Minister of Intelligence [2008] ZACC 6: 72n3

United Kingdom
Ashworth Hospital Authority v MGN [2002] UKHL 29: 193
Attorney General v Fraill [2011] EWCA CRIM 1570: 83
Attorney General v MGN Ltd [2002] EWHC 907: 79
Attorney General v New Statesman and Nation Publishing Co. Ltd [1980] 2 WLR 246: 81
Branson v Bower [2002] 2 WLR 452: 17n8
Byrne v Deane [1937] 1 KB 818: 40
Campbell v Mirror Group Newspapers Ltd [2002] EWCA Civ 1373: 115
Campbell v Mirror Group Newspapers Ltd [2004] UKHL 22: 114–116, 118–119
Cairns v Modi [2012] EWCA Civ 1382: 39, 62
Charleston v News Group Newspapers Ltd [1995] 2 AC 65: 34
Coco v Clark [1969] RPC 41: 114, 119
Derbyshire County Council v Times Newspapers Ltd [1993] AC 534: 41
Douglas v Hello! [2003] EWHC 786: 114
Douglas v Hello! [2005] EWCA Civ 595: 115–116
Duke of Brunswick v Harmer [1849] 14 QB 154: 38
El Naschie v Macmillan Publishers Ltd (t/a Nature Publishing Group) [2012] EWHC 1809: 17n8
Flood v Times Newspapers Ltd [2012] 2 WLR 760: 40, 57
Galloway v Telegraph Group [2005] EMLR 7: 55
Goldsmith v Bhoyrul [1997] 4 All ER 268: 41
Guardian News and Media Ltd v City of Westminster Magistrates Court (2012) EWCA Civ 420: 72
Jameel v Wall Street Journal Europe [2006] 3 WLR 642: 55–56
John v MGN Ltd [1997] QB 58: 63
Joseph v Spiller [2011] 1 AC 852: 17n8, 58

United States

Table of Legislation

India

International treaties, covenants and agreements

Late Developments

The following developments occurred after the chapter texts were finalized.

Chapter 4
Journalists can tweet, email or text live reports from courts

In January 2014, the Hong Kong Judiciary announced it would begin permitting live text-based communications from court. The move allows journalists to tweet, email or text live reports using a court-provided WiFi network. Mobile phones, tablet computers and similar devices used for communication must be switched to "flight mode" and disconnected from 3G and 4G telecommunications networks, which the Judiciary says interfere with its recording system. The action came three years after British courts began permitting live text-based communications. Full text of the guidance can be found at http://legalref.judiciary.gov.hk/doc/npd/eng/PD32.htm. For background on this development, see pages 83–84 of this chapter.

Chapter 5
Privacy commissioner's rulings upheld in covert photos cases

The Administrative Appeals Board (AAB) has upheld rulings by the Privacy Commissioner of Hong Kong against two magazines for publishing covert photographs taken of several celebrities from inside their homes that were secretly obtained from the outside with the use of telephoto lenses and other camera equipment. The AAB affirmed the Privacy Commissioner's rejection of the magazines' public-interest claims and upheld the commissioner's directive that the magazines develop privacy guidelines for covert photos. *Face Magazine Ltd v Privacy Commissioner for Personal Data* (2014) AAB 5/2012 and *Sudden Weekly Ltd v Privacy Commissioner for Personal Data* (2014) AAB 6/2012. For details on the cases, see page 108.

Chapter 9
PRC state secrets implementing regulations released

In February 2014, the Chinese government released its long-awaited new Implementation Regulations for its State Secrets Law, revised in 2010. Issued by the State Council and effective on 1 March 2014, the regulations instructed PRC officials to avoid labelling as state secrets information and documents that should be made available to the public. The regulations offered little clarity as to what constituted a state secret even as they addressed the need to enhance secrecy protection systems; thus, the impact of the regulations was not immediately clear. The State Secrets Implementation Procedures issued in 1990 were repealed. Chinese-language text of the regulations can be found at: http://politics.people.com.cn/n/2014/0203/c1024-24276690.html. For more discussion of state secrets, see pages 205–207.

Chapter 12
Regulatory disparities continue for broadcast, mobile and Internet television

Hong Kong Television Network (HKTVN) announced in late 2013 it had acquired China Mobile Hong Kong's mobile television licence for HK$142 million, and that it would launch its free television service on the mobile television platform. The deal remained uncertain in early 2014 as parent company China Mobile, the largest mobile service provider in mainland China, conducted a probe into this transaction by its Hong Kong subsidiary to see if it complied with mainland regulations on state assets. The move by HKTVN to acquire a mobile television licence after it failed to obtain a free terrestrial television licence vividly illustrated the problematic regulatory disparities in Hong Kong among conventional terrestrial television, mobile television and television on the Internet. For details, see pages 279–280 and 302–303.

Additional updates

For more updates, visit the website for *Hong Kong Media Law* at: http://medialaw.hk.

1

Overview

Doreen Weisenhaus

1. Introduction

An anti-corruption agency raids seven newsrooms. The government considers far-reaching national security legislation with serious implications for journalists. Covert surveillance and other privacy laws impacting paparazzi and the media are proposed. An editor is jailed for contempt of court.

These events and others in Hong Kong in the first decade after the 1997 return of the former British colony to Chinese sovereignty demonstrated the volatility of media law developments in one of two Special Administrative Regions (SAR) of the People's Republic of China (PRC). Yet, in 2007, on the tenth anniversary of the handover, it was clear that Hong Kong still enjoyed freedom of expression and that its exceptionally large, diverse and rambunctious media operated in an environment considered one of the world's freest, the only one of its kind within the PRC.

By 2013, well into Hong Kong's second decade as an SAR, another round of attention-getting developments continue to show an ever-changing legal landscape for the media and freedom of expression. These include an online publication ordered to pay HK$1.3 million in a defamation case, the first journalist jailed under obscenity law, a celebrity nude photo scandal raising questions about privacy and free speech rights and the prosecution of rogue radio broadcasters challenging the constitutionality of a government licensing scheme.

In Hong Kong, as in other common law jurisdictions, there is no single written set of rules for what comprises media law. Much depends on precedent, custom, equity, statutes and a constitution — and the range of issues can include freedom of expression, defamation, privacy, reporting restrictions, contempt of court, official secrets, access to information, protection of journalistic sources, obscenity, copyright, broadcast regulations and more.

After 1997, Hong Kong's judges no longer had to automatically apply British common law to issues that arose. They often still do, but they also draw from other jurisdictions as well as fashion their own interpretations, often looking to Hong Kong's own constitution, the Basic Law. A study of more than 40 constitutional rights cases decided by Hong Kong's highest court, the Court of Final Appeal (CFA), from 1999 to 2009 document a "robust, liberal and mainstream approach" to protecting fundamental rights, including presumption of innocence, legal certainty and protection against arbitrary imprisonment, freedom to travel and freedom of expression and assembly.[1] Hong Kong's unique arrangement that allows judges from other common law jurisdictions to serve on the CFA ensures an international perspective and influence in shaping its jurisprudence.

This open and robust climate evolved during more than 150 years of British rule, which gave Hong Kong its independent legal system, a freewheeling capitalism that nurtured its teeming media market, and a healthy respect for personal freedom and expression. British rule, however, also bequeathed a legacy of harsh laws regarding defamation, official secrets, sedition and reporting on court proceedings that make it sometimes hard — and sometimes risky — for journalists to do their jobs.

In recent years, the UK has instituted legal reforms to enhance freedom of expression for many aspects of media law, including new legislation on defamation, a Freedom of Information act (FOI) and the repeal of sedition, criminal libel and scandalizing the court offences. Its libel reform in 2013,[2] in particular, makes it harder for parties to sue, strengthens available defences and is expected to end the UK's reputation as a magnet for "libel tourism". Other commonwealth countries also have modernized their laws to extend protections. They include New Zealand, which repealed its official secrets and sedition laws, enacted FOI legislation and added more safeguards to its obscenity regime.

Meanwhile, Hong Kong has mostly remained frozen in time with many antiquated media laws inherited from another era. In other words, the UK and other countries have moved on while Hong Kong lags behind in providing adequate legislative protection for freedom of expression and the press. It remains, for example, one of the few developed jurisdictions in the world without a FOI law to mandate public release of government-generated information and documents, a gap noted more recently in March 2013 by the United Nations Human Rights Committee monitoring Hong Kong's compliance with the International Covenant on Civil and Political Rights.[3] (For more details, see this book's Chapter 2 The Legal System, section 3.4 International treaties and agreements.)

Some fear though that if the Hong Kong government did try to change its laws, it might be tempted to step backward rather than forward and impose new restrictions on the media and free speech. Indeed, since 2002, the government has introduced several controversial bills and withdrawn them after encountering immense public opposition, including proposed national security laws as mandated by Article 23 of the Basic Law. It has, however, announced a renewed interest in pursuing additional privacy proposals after having amended

1. Simon Young, "Constitutional Rights in Hong Kong's Court of Final Appeal", *Chinese (Taiwan) Yearbook of International Law and Affairs* [2011] v. 27 pp. 67–96. See also, Simon N. M. Young and Yash Ghai (eds.), *Hong Kong's Court of Final Appeal: The Development of the Law in China's Hong Kong* (Cambridge: Cambridge University Press, 2013).

2. Enacted three years after a bill introduced by Lord Anthony Lester.

3. "Concluding Observations on the Third Periodic Report of Hong Kong, China", UN Human Rights Committee, adopted 26 March 2013 (CCPR/C/SR2974).

the Personal Data (Privacy) Ordinance in 2012, which added a worrisome new criminal offence prohibiting disclosure of personal data resulting in psychological harm, and has concluded a second consultation on obscenity law.

The political winds that blow in from the mainland also make journalists and others worry about the years ahead. They first began expressing concern about the influences the mainland would exert on journalistic attitudes and practice in Hong Kong in the early 1980s, when Chinese and British officials were negotiating and signing the deal that set the timetable for China's resumption of sovereignty. Those concerns about the impact of the handover on press freedoms heightened after the pro-democracy crackdown in Tiananmen Square and elsewhere in China in 1989.

In the years since the handover, those winds from the mainland have grown stronger, despite the "one country, two systems" principle that is supposed to govern relations between the mainland and Hong Kong. The turbulence has brought the PRC's repeated intervention in constitutional matters in the SAR,[4] the mainland conviction of a Hong Kong-based reporter on spying allegations, mistreatment of Hong Kong journalists reporting across the border, anxiety over pending national security laws expected to be introduced by Hong Kong's newest Chief Executive C. Y. Leung, who took office in 2012, and a rising perception that the PRC's central government is escalating its efforts to influence key institutions in the city, including the media. More than eight in ten Hong Kong journalists surveyed in 2012 say they think press freedom has eroded,[5] a conclusion echoed by Freedom House, a US-based non-government organization, which rates the SAR's press freedom status as "partly free".[6] Thus, concern persists both within and beyond Hong Kong over the degree of its press freedom and the eventual contour of its media-law landscape, partly because of uncertainty about how much of a role the mainland will have in shaping (if not controlling) it.

2. Hong Kong media's unique role

Despite the mounting concerns about the future, the Hong Kong media still play a uniquely important and powerful role. Their traditional government-watchdog role is made even more significant by the SAR's limited democracy. As of 2013, only half of Hong Kong's 70 legislators are elected by universal suffrage. Its Chief Executive is elected by a predominantly pro-government election committee, comprised of 1,200 individuals, with approval from the one-party mainland government in Beijing. Universal suffrage is anticipated in 2017 for the Chief Executive election and in 2020 for the Legislative Council elections.[7] Until that happens, the

4. For details, see section 3.1.1 Relationship with the PRC, Chapter 2 The Legal System, of this book.

5. Survey results found in "New Leader Raises Fears: Challenges for Freedom of Expression in Hong Kong", Hong Kong Journalists Association, 2012 annual report.

6. Freedom of the Press 2013, http://www.freedomhouse.org.

7. In December 2013, the Hong Kong government launched a five-month election consultation to collect views on details of arrangements for the 2017 election of the Chief Executive, as well as

media continues to serve as a "parliament-in-print",[8] which they have done since Hong Kong's days as a British colony. They help preserve rule of law by keeping a vigilant eye on key institutions such as the executive government and the judiciary.

The media's special watchdog role is made more complicated by a long history of partisanship often tied to political developments in mainland China. Over the years, Hong Kong has been a politically volatile refuge for Chinese, including many journalists, caught in one upheaval or another on the mainland — from those challenging the Qing dynasty in the late nineteenth century to those fleeing the Communist Party in 1949 and the excesses of the Cultural Revolution of the 1960s and early 1970s. And many newspapers reflected those partisan views with competing political factions operating their own publications in Hong Kong. But during the 1970s, more commercial, less politically connected newspapers began to proliferate. Today, while several Beijing-supported newspapers remain, most of the Chinese-language market is dominated by privately owned or publicly traded media companies, in a community more than 95 percent Chinese. Dozens of local daily newspapers, hundreds of magazines and a growing number of broadcasting or cable outlets with news departments serve a population of 7 million.[9] A number of newspapers still reflect political views, usually those of their owners.

For example, the *Apple Daily* newspaper, part of Next Media Ltd[10] founded in the 1990s by entrepreneur Jimmy Lai, is unabashedly pro-democratic and champions universal suffrage for Hong Kong. *Apple Daily* also brought to Hong Kong a more flamboyant kind of journalism featuring big, colourful pictures and graphics and bold headlines that were soon embraced by many other news organizations. As *Apple Daily* became one of the most-read newspapers, along with its highly popular sister publication *Next Magazine*, with their stories about celebrities, scandals, car crashes and morbid deaths, such coverage became more prevalent in the other newspapers and magazines and set a different agenda for many news organizations in their competition for readers and viewers. The advent of free daily newspapers, beginning with *Metropolitan Daily* in 2002, increased the competitive nature of the already active print market. The free dailies now reach more than three million readers.

What then also became more prevalent was community concern and criticism over the increasingly aggressive news coverage and camera-wielding paparazzi. Public discussions arose over issues of privacy, responsible reporting and journalistic standards. Each new perceived media excess brought more calls by some policymakers and legislators for increased regulation and new laws to rein in what

---

for the forming of the Legislative Council in 2016, ahead of the expected 2020 elections.

8. Richard Cullen, "Freedom of the Press and the Rule of Law", in Steve Tsang (ed.), *Independence and the Rule of Law in Hong Kong* (Hong Kong: Hong Kong University Press 2001), p. 158.

9. Hong Kong also is one of the largest centres for international media operations in Asia.

10. Next Media Ltd. also expanded into the Taiwan market in the 2000s. One innovation that has drawn international interest and controversy is the media company's computer-animated dramatizations of current news stories, posted online at http://www.nma.com. Its 2009 animated video on Tiger Woods' marital problems drew millions of viewers.

they considered irresponsible newsgathering practices. Many in the journalism profession argued that the answer was more and better self-regulation.

But as the stakes have risen in more politically volatile times, maturing media have also risen to meet the challenges. For example, the past decade has seen largely responsible and thorough coverage of the Severe Acute Respiratory Syndrome health crisis and the debate around the first attempt to pass Article 23 legislation, a controversy that saw 500,000 people march in protest in 2003, leading the government to withdraw its proposals and, some say, Hong Kong's first Chief Executive, Tung Chee-hwa, to resign.

More recently, the media have contributed extensive reporting on the PRC's melamine-tainted dairy scandal, forcing the Hong Kong government to release its food sample testing of mainland products; the candidates for the 2012 Legislative Council and Chief Executive elections, with almost daily revelations, including of conflicts of interest and illegal building structures on properties of candidates; the contentious debate over national education and a spending scandal involving a former chief of Hong Kong's anti-corruption agency. Some say Hong Kong journalists are even having an impact on developments on the mainland as evidenced by their reporting of the reaction to the jailing of former food safety worker-turned-milk-scandal activist Zhao Lianhai in 2010. As Cliff Buddle, a senior Hong Kong editor, observed:[11]

> The support for Zhao came not just from the media, but across the political spectrum, including Hong Kong deputies to the National People's Congress. In a rare, if not unprecedented move, Xinhua responded publicly and directly to these Hong Kong concerns, defending the sentence. It is reasonable to believe that the subsequent release of Zhao on medical parole had much to do with the outrage his sentence had sparked in Hong Kong. In this respect, the Hong Kong media may find that by providing a platform for discussion of such cases, it can help shape events on the other side of the border.

3. Freedom of expression and of the press in Hong Kong

The legal guarantees for freedom of expression in Hong Kong are contained in the Basic Law and in the Bill of Rights Ordinance.[12] Article 27 of the Basic Law states:

> Hong Kong residents shall have freedom of speech, of the press and of publication; freedom of association, of assembly, of procession and of demonstration, and the right and freedom to form and join trade unions, and to strike.

Article 39 of the Basic Law mandates that provisions of the International Covenant on Civil and Political Rights (ICCPR), a 1966 United Nations treaty based on the Universal Declaration of Human Rights, are to be part of Hong Kong law. The ICCPR was ratified by the United Kingdom and extended to Hong

11. Interview with Cliff Buddle, *South China Morning Post,* Hong Kong's leading English-language newspaper, conducted by this author, 19 January 2013.
12. For more discussion, see Po Jen Yap, "Freedom of Expression", in J. Chan and C. L. Lim (eds), *Law of the Hong Kong Constitution* (Hong Kong: Sweet and Maxwell 2011).

Kong in 1976. According to Article 39, Hong Kong is required to enact laws to give effect to the ICCPR; local ordinances must be consistent with it.[13]

The Hong Kong Bill of Rights Ordinance (BORO), enacted in 1991 in the aftermath of the Tiananmen Square crackdown, incorporated verbatim numerous articles in the ICCPR. The BORO's Article 16, where freedom of expression guarantees are described, is identical to ICCPR's Article 19, which provides:

> (1) Everyone shall have the right to hold opinions without interference.
> (2) Everyone shall have the right to freedom of expression; this right shall include freedom to seek, receive and impart information and ideas of all kinds, regardless of frontiers, either orally, in writing or in print, in the form of art, or through any other media of his choice.
> (3) The exercise of the rights provided for in paragraph 2 . . . carries with it special duties and responsibilities. It may therefore be subject to certain restrictions, but these shall be only such as are provided by law and are necessary:
> (a) For respect of the rights or reputations of others; or
> (b) For protection of national security or of public order, public health or morals.

This means that Hong Kong law can restrict press freedom but only where reasonably necessary to respect the rights or reputations of others and to protect national security, public order, public health or morals.

Article 27 of the Basic Law separates freedom of speech and of the press. What is the difference? Freedom of speech and the broader concept of freedom of expression (which can include non-speech activities such as demonstrating) are long established and relate more to the right of individuals to speak and express freely without government restraint — a right that promotes the free exchange of ideas necessary for self-rule and individual autonomy. In a leading Hong Kong case on freedom of expression, then Chief Justice Andrew Li stated:

> Freedom of expression is a fundamental freedom in a democratic society. It lies at the heart of civil society and of Hong Kong's system and way of life. The courts must give a generous interpretation to its constitutional guarantee. This freedom includes the freedom to express ideas which the majority may find disagreeable or offensive and the freedom to criticise governmental institutions and the conduct of public officials.[14]

But in that 1999 case, the Court of Final Appeal upheld the constitutionality of Hong Kong laws that forbade one form of expression — desecration of Hong Kong and PRC flags. It concluded that legitimate and necessary interests existed in bolstering protection of these symbols in the early period after Chinese resumption of sovereignty over its Special Administrative Region.[15]

---

13. For more on Hong Kong's compliance with ICCPR, see Chapter 2 of this book.
14. *HKSAR v Ng Kung Siu* [1999] 2 HKCFAR 442, 464.
15. See Yap, note 12; Raymond Wacks, "Our Flagging Rights" (2000) 39(1) *Hong Kong Law Journal* 1; Johannes Chan, "Basic Law and Constitutional Review: The First Decade," (2007) 37 *Hong Kong Law Journal* 407.

The concept of freedom of the press is different from general free speech rights in that it can refer to protections for established media as they carry out their fundamental duties and functions.[16] One important issue to freedom of the press, for example, is protection of journalistic news sources. Other issues can arise in how journalists report the news and cover major institutions and in the type of medium they use, such as broadcasts, which are subject to additional restrictions.

4. This book

In a practical context, this book describes key media law developments in Hong Kong and internationally affecting the profession of journalism. It examines the issues journalists face in the day-to-day activities of reporting, editing, publishing, broadcasting, posting on the Internet or using social media, but it is also useful for those outside the profession who are actively writing, blogging, tweeting and so on.

Here are brief summaries of each chapter:

Chapter 2 (The Legal System): Before learning about media law, it is helpful for journalists to first learn about the law in general, the courts and the roles people play in them, and other aspects of the legal system, including in the context of Hong Kong's increasingly complicated relationship with the People's Republic of China. For many journalists and those without legal training or background, the law can seem intimidating, but some principles can help make it more understandable and accessible.

Chapter 3 (Defamation): Probably no issue looms larger for working journalists than defamation, particularly in Hong Kong, with its British legal legacy that has been particularly harsh on media defendants. Since 1997, Hong Kong courts have continued to follow and apply UK case law principles, and have recognized new developments in the UK, such as the *Reynolds* public-interest defence and the *Godfrey v Demon* extension of the subordinate publisher defence to Internet service providers. At the same time, Hong Kong courts have developed some of their own jurisprudence, including, for example, in regard to the meaning of malice in the defence of fair comment (now known as honest comment), a reform that has been adopted elsewhere in the Commonwealth. The Internet and the need to find the right balance between free speech and protection of reputation continue to drive developments in defamation. The chapter provides an extensive overview of defamation, including definitions of defamation, examining when criticism crosses the line into defamation, who can sue or be sued, the roles malice, motive and mistake play into libel cases, available defences and how damages are assessed and a discussion of the UK's major libel reform.

Chapter 4 (Court Reporting and Contempt of Court): While Chapter 2 describes some general concepts about law, legal systems and the courts, this chapter delves more deeply into the issues facing Hong Kong media in their

16. See Johannes Chan, "Freedom of the Press: The First Ten Years in the Hong Kong Special Administrative Region" (2007) 15(2) *Asia Pacific Law Review* 163.

coverage of court cases. The right to a fair trial versus the right of the press to cover a trial is one of the most important and enduring conflicts in any jurisdiction. Journalists must contend with reporting restrictions and the possibility of contempt of court liability should they run afoul of the restrictions. The use of the Internet, social media and other digital tools by today's journalists and the public raise new questions about what is permissible in the courtroom.

Chapter 5 (Privacy): The newsgathering practices of journalists, especially aggressive coverage of the private lives of individuals, in Hong Kong and worldwide, continue to come under intense criticism in an ongoing debate about privacy rights versus press freedom. While Hong Kong imposes minimal restrictions on the media regarding privacy intrusion, journalists should be aware that some aspects of privacy are protected through the Basic Law, local legislation such as the Personal Data (Privacy) Ordinance (Cap 486), amended in 2012, and civil actions. Over the years, other privacy laws have been proposed, but not enacted, to exert additional controls over the media. But recent developments, such as a new criminal offence prohibiting disclosure of personal data resulting in psychological harm and the government's renewed interest in considering additional legislation, might begin to alter the privacy picture. This chapter summarizes both current and proposed laws in Hong Kong, as well as developments in the UK, European Court of Human Rights and elsewhere.

Chapter 6 (Access to Information): This chapter focuses on laws and regulations that affect how certain government information and proceedings are required to be made available and open to the public and, by extension, journalists. It analyzes Hong Kong's limited administrative Code on Access to Information, comparing it with more expansive Freedom of Information laws available in other jurisdictions, and examines the impact of a secret government on the operation of a free press. The chapter also explains how the *absence* of other laws, such as archival laws to require the maintenance of public records and so-called sunshine laws to mandate open meetings for governmental bodies, further hampers the abilities of the public and the media to access government-held information.

Chapter 7 (Official Secrets and Sedition): While Chapter 6 focuses on access to government-generated information and the barriers that prevent much public access, this chapter centres on a specific category of prohibited government information known as "official secrets". In this post-Wikileaks era, what laws would guide the Hong Kong government? The chapter also examines the Article 23 national security proposals considered in Hong Kong in 2002–03 that would have greatly altered existing laws on official secrets and on sedition as well as have introduced new laws on subversion and secession. Can lessons be drawn from neighbouring SAR Macau's implementation of Article 23 in 2009 and from other countries' use — or repeal — of their national security laws?

Chapter 8 (Other Restrictions on Newsgathering and Reporting): This chapter explores additional restrictions on journalistic newsgathering and reporting. It discusses whether journalists have any special rights of access — or face any restrictions — to places and events and how they should respond to police use of press-only areas at public demonstrations and events and examines the rise in tension between the police and media. It elaborates on restrictions on reporting on elections and ongoing criminal investigations and on bans against disability and racial vilifications. It also addresses protection of journalistic material and sources.

Chapter 9 (Reporting on the Mainland): When Hong Kong and foreign journalists based in Hong Kong travel to the mainland for reporting, they are often covering stories that PRC authorities consider sensitive. This chapter focuses on some key laws, regulations and rules that these journalists face in an increasingly hostile and sometimes violent reporting environment, including revised reporting restrictions, implemented after the 2008 Olympics, and amended state secrets laws, and what they should do if restrained from their reporting or detained on the mainland. It also examines developments in defamation, privacy and Open Government Information (OGI) laws and regulations.

Chapter 10 (Copyright): In the Internet and multimedia age, copyright issues have become more important to journalists across all media platforms. Journalists today need to understand the concepts of copyright and their implications, particularly as more countries focus on enforcement. Awareness of copyright is vital in two key regards. The first is in acknowledging the copyright of other people's work that might affect newsgathering, writing and news production. The second is in protecting a journalist's own work. This chapter also looks at special copyright issues involving the Internet, including linking, social media such as Facebook and Twitter, attempts by the Hong Kong government to regulate the digital environment and the alternative licensing scheme, Creative Commons.

Chapter 11 (Obscenity and Indecency): Hong Kong's obscenity law not only regulates adult magazines and audio-visual materials, but also polices the city's mainstream print media. Indeed, criminal prosecutions of Hong Kong newspapers and magazines arise mainly from the publication of indecent or obscene content. Like its counterparts in many parts of the world, Hong Kong's obscenity law has stirred controversy and caused uncertainty to the daily operations of the local press. The rising popularity of online content compounds the situation. This chapter analyzes the current statutory regime, cases and controversies, including the impact of the Edison Chen photo scandal that made news worldwide, and public consultations to revamp the law.

Chapter 12 (Media Regulation in the Age of Convergence): Hong Kong media regulation broadly follows that of Western countries. Media operate freely subject to general media laws such as defamation, contempt of court, copyright and obscenity. In general, except in emergencies, the government does not engage in prior restraint, censorship or control of journalists' activity. But significant differences exist in the government's treatment of different media, with print and online media, unlike broadcast media, largely left to self-regulation. Today's media convergence, however, makes separate regimes for different media unwieldy since many print and broadcast media, for instance, have their own websites and online presence. This chapter outlines the existing regulation and self-regulation of print, broadcasting and online media in Hong Kong, with a focus on content regulation and some overview on media ownership and fair competition.

Additional Resources: This book also includes a glossary of legal terms, lists of cases and legislation referred to in the text, a chronology of key milestones and developments for press freedom, and five appendices — Excerpts of Key Statutes and Regulations (Appendix A), Searching for Public Records of Courts (Appendix B), Judicial Practice Directions: Hearings in Chambers in Civil Proceedings (Appendix C), the Code on Access to Information (Appendix D) and Useful Organizations, Online Publications and Websites, particularly helpful for timely updates on developments concerning the intersection between the law, journalism and freedom of expression, both in Hong Kong and mainland China (Appendix E).

5. Conclusion

This book summarizes and analyzes within local and international contexts the media laws, regulations, issues and developments for working journalists and other interested parties. As pointed out at the outset of this introduction, the media-law terrain is intricate. Assessing the degree to which press freedom is protected or threatened in the environment that exists today or which can be projected for the future is a complex undertaking. It is clear that an increasingly aggressive and secretive Hong Kong government keeps a tight rein on access to information and proceedings and that tensions and conflicts have escalated between it and the media. But so far, no new major laws restricting the press have been passed since the handover and no media organization has been shut down or blatantly censored for political reasons by the government. If such attempts are made in the future, the media might have a strong ally: the courts.

Time and again, in at least a dozen decisions over the past twenty years, the courts have ruled favourably for the press or for free speech, whether they are expanding the right to comment on a matter of public interest, accepting the public-interest defence for responsible journalism or upholding the right to take news photographs on the street.

As the Hon. Kemal Bokhary said to the Hong Kong Journalists Association in 2012 before his retirement as a permanent judge on the CFA:[17]

> How do I reconcile a controlled media with a free one? Quite simply, I do not. They are irreconcilable. A controlled media is not a free one . . . Between the media and the judiciary there is also a great similarity — especially in Hong Kong. Free speech is the lifeblood of the media. Judicial independence is the

17. Speech at 2012 annual dinner for Hong Kong Journalists Association. After his October 2012 retirement, Bokhary continues to serve as an occasional non-permanent judge on the Court of Final Appeal.

> lifeblood of the judiciary. The media must never engage in self-censorship. If it comes in, it is the end of the media as we know it. For the judiciary, the equivalent of self-censorship is seeking an interpretation to avoid a reinterpretation. Beyond that similarity, there is symbiosis. The judiciary protects the media, and the media protects the judiciary.

Because of the economic and political pressures, including from the mainland, that some media owners or managers face or accept, willingly or unwillingly, many journalists acknowledge the reality of self-censorship[18] in some newsrooms even as they embrace Bokhary's message: free speech is the lifeblood of the media.

If efforts are made to stem this lifeblood, the greatest defence against them may be journalists themselves and their ability to raise public consciousness when press freedom is threatened. They have demonstrated this many times in recent years through protest marches, signature and advertisement campaigns and the education efforts of their professional organizations. These efforts have worked, and they may have to work again.

18. The Hong Kong Journalists Association (HKJA) has conducted periodic surveys on self-censorship. A survey the HKJA conducted in 2012 showed that almost 80 percent of respondents thought that self-censorship had worsened since 2005 and that more than one in three reported that they or their supervisors had practised self-censorship in the previous twelve months. The most prevalent forms of self-censorship reported were downplaying issues and information unfavourable to advertisers (40.3 percent), to the PRC government (37 percent), or to media owners or their interests (34.5 percent). See also Anne Cheung, *Self-Censorship and the Struggle for Press Freedom in Hong Kong* (The Hague, Netherlands; New York: Kluwer International 2003).

2

The Legal System

Doreen Weisenhaus

FREQUENTLY ASKED QUESTIONS

1. What is "the rule of law" and "separation of powers"? (See sections 2 and 3.1)
2. What is meant by "common law"? (See section 3.2)
3. How do laws get changed? (See sections 3 and 5)
4. How are courts structured and what kinds of cases do different courts handle? (See section 4.3)
5. How is a jury trial different from a judge trial? (See section 4.2)
6. What is the relationship between the laws of Hong Kong and the People's Republic of China? (See section 3.1.1)

1. Introduction

Before journalists can learn about media law, they need to know something about the law in general, the courts and the roles people play in them, and other aspects of the legal system, including what makes it work. For many journalists and those without legal training or background, learning about law can seem intimidating, but some principles can help make it more understandable and accessible. This chapter summarizes several basic concepts.

2. What is law and the rule of law?

> Law is a collection of rules, principles, standards and concepts whose end is the regulation of human behaviour.
>
> — Peter Wesley-Smith[1]

In other words, law is a set of binding rules to govern action or conduct. Most law is administered by governmental and quasi-governmental parties, such as civil servants, police and statutory corporations, but the final arbiters of disputes usually are the courts, which apply the set of rules to reach an outcome. The type of law they apply, and how, depends on the legal system of that country or territory.

1. Peter Wesley-Smith, *An Introduction to the Hong Kong Legal System*, 3rd ed. (Hong Kong: Oxford University Press 1998), p. 12.

The public often hears that Hong Kong has "the rule of law". A recent dramatic example occurred in June 2013 when US whistleblower Edward Snowden famously fled to Hong Kong because, he said, he had "faith in Hong Kong's rule of law".[2] At its most basic level, rule of law means that law has been developed through established procedures and administered in ways to prevent its arbitrary application against individuals. To be effective, the rule of law depends on several guiding principles, including transparency (the laws are clear and readily available), impartiality (the laws are applied without bias by independent judges), and equality (everyone is equal under the law regardless of position or status in society).

Rule *by* law, on the other hand, can mean that law is more an instrument of government power, wielded without the same level of fairness and equality as provided under the rule of law. The result can be that some are outside the law, such as leaders who make laws but are themselves not subject to them, or that the laws allow arbitrary use of power.

The rule of law has long played an important role in Hong Kong's development and success. In 1997, after the People's Republic of China resumed sovereignty over Hong Kong, the rule of law was guaranteed in the Basic Law (BL), its "mini" constitution, under the "one country, two systems" principle that governs Hong Kong as a Special Administrative Region (SAR) of the PRC. Thus, individuals here continue to be able to seek protection of the courts against unjust governmental actions and assert their rights as provided by law. They also are able to rely on the legal system to resolve private disputes.

3. Legal systems and sources of law

What kind of legal system does Hong Kong have and what are its sources of law? The rule of law means law is to be applied fairly, with certainty and so on, but *what* law is applied and through what mechanism? In Hong Kong, the major sources of law include the Basic Law, common law, rules of equity, and legislation.[3] International law also imposes legal obligations on Hong Kong and can influence the interpretation and application of domestic law.

3.1 Constitutional: The Basic Law

For many jurisdictions, including Hong Kong, the most significant source of law is their constitution. Like other constitutions, Hong Kong's Basic Law establishes the essential political and legal principles, prescribes the powers and duties of the government and guarantees specific rights for its citizens.[4]

2. Lana Lam, "Whistle-blower Edward Snowden Tells SCMP: 'Let Hong Kong People Decide my Fate", *South China Morning Post*, 15 June 2013.

3. Basic Law, Article 8: "The laws previously in force in Hong Kong, that is, the common law, rules of equity, ordinances, subordinate legislation and customary law shall be maintained, except for any that contravene this Law, and subject to any amendment by the legislature of the Hong Kong Special Administrative Region."

4. http://www.basiclaw.gov.hk/en/basiclawtext/index.html.

For example, the Basic Law authorizes Hong Kong to: maintain its "capitalist system and way of life . . . for 50 years" (Article 5), have "independent judicial power" (Articles 19, 85), continue "the principle of trial by jury" (Article 86), and provide residents with "freedom of speech, of the press and of publication; freedom of association, of assembly, of procession and of demonstration; and the right and freedom to form and join trade unions, and to strike" (Article 27).

In defining the powers and duties of government, the Basic Law delineates the separation of power among the three branches of government in Hong Kong — executive (Articles 43–65), legislative (Articles 66–79) and judicial (Articles 80–96). Among the many functions and responsibilities listed for the three branches, the Chief Executive decides on government policies and issues executive orders (Article 48 (4)), the Legislative Council enacts laws and approves government budgets (Article 73 (1) and (2)), and the Judiciary administers the courts and adjudicates cases in accordance with applicable law (Article 84).

The Basic Law states that it is to be superior law, meaning that no other Hong Kong law can conflict with it (Articles 8, 11).

3.1.1 **Relationship with the PRC**

As mentioned, the Basic Law establishes the authority and rights for the SAR, but it also defines the relationship between Hong Kong and the PRC. For example, the Standing Committee of the National People's Congress (NPCSC) has the sole authority to amend the Basic Law (Article 159). The Basic Law guarantees Hong Kong a "high degree of autonomy" from the Central People's Government and the right to "enjoy executive, legislative and independent judicial power, including that of final adjudication" (Article 2). But the Basic Law also acknowledges that some matters are outside the authority of the SAR government, such as defence and foreign affairs, which are controlled by the Central People's Government (Articles 12–23). National laws of the PRC are not to be applied in Hong Kong "except for those listed in Annex III to this Law" and those listed "shall be applied locally by way of promulgation or legislation by the Region". These deal mainly with defence and foreign affairs (Article 18).

But it is the power of the NPCSC to interpret the Basic Law (Article 158) that has raised probably the most concern about Hong Kong's independence in the years since the handover to Chinese sovereignty. The interpretation has been carried out four times by the NPCSC between 1999 and 2011 — when dealing with mainlanders' right of abode in Hong Kong, electoral development, the length of the term of the Chief Executive and the issue of state immunity in a legal action.[5]

5. In March 2012, the Court of Appeal overturned a lower court ruling that would have allowed foreign domestic workers to qualify for right of abode after working seven years in Hong Kong. In the appeal before the Court of Final Appeal, the government asked the court to refer a question of interpretation to the NPCSC to resolve the issue. This request led to public criticisms that the government was trying to exert pressure on the court. In March 2013, the CFA declined to refer the question and ruled against the domestic workers. *Vallejos v Commissioner of Registration* [2013] 4 HKC 239.

The first case came in 1999 after the Chief Executive asked the NPCSC to re-interpret a ruling by the Court of Final Appeal, *Ng Ka-Ling & Others v Director of Immigration*, 1 HKLRD 315, which had held that mainlanders with at least one parent living in Hong Kong could become residents too. The re-interpretation in effect overturned the ruling by the Court of Final Appeal.

The other interpretations involved:

- A unilateral decision by the NPCSC in 2004 to interpret key provisions of the Basic Law to prohibit universal suffrage in Hong Kong for elections in 2007 and 2008.
- A question about the length of the term of the Chief Executive who replaced a predecessor resigning before the end of his term. In 2005, then-Chief Executive Tung Chee-hwa resigned, with two years remaining in his second five-year term. As provided in Article 53, Donald Tsang, Chief Secretary for Administration, became acting Chief Executive until a new Chief Executive could be elected by an 800-member election committee.[6] At the time, many Hong Kong legal experts said that, based on Article 46, a new Chief Executive should serve five years. But the NPCSC held that the person elected to replace Tung would serve only the two remaining years before running again (if he chose to) for a new five-year term. Elected by the committee, Tsang served out the two years of Tung's term and was elected again to his own five-year term until 2012. He could not run for another term as restricted by Article 46 of the Basic Law.
- A decision as to whether absolute state immunity should prevail in a commercial civil case. In 2011, the Court of Final Appeal, at the government's suggestion, asked for the interpretation of Articles 13(1) and 19 in a case involving a US company that sued the Democratic Republic of Congo in a Hong Kong court for a commercial payment. The Congolese government claimed state immunity from the action, a privilege recognized by the PRC but not previously in colonial Hong Kong, which denied state immunity in commercial cases. The NPCSC determined that the rules or policies on state immunity is an act of state involving foreign affairs, and thus concluded its policy prevailed. *Democratic Republic of Congo v FG Hemisphere* [2011] 4 HKC 151.

Another aspect of the Basic Law that directly involves the relationship between Hong Kong and the PRC is Article 23, which requires Hong Kong to pass laws that relate to national security (e.g. treason, secession, sedition, theft of state secrets and subversion). An attempt to enact Article 23 legislation in 2002–2003 resulted in a protest rally by 500,000 Hong Kong people and the government withdrew its proposals. (For a detailed discussion, see Chapter 7 Official Secrets and Sedition.)

For the most part, however, the Basic Law focuses on Hong Kong's powers and rights but does not provide many specifics for how they are to be applied.

6. The election committee was expanded to 1,200 members for the 2012 Chief Executive election.

For these, Hong Kong turns to other sources of law, primarily common law and legislation.

3.2 Common law

The term "common law" can be confusing because it is used interchangeably to refer to different things. It can refer to the legal system Hong Kong has, to the decided cases in its courts (called **case law**) and to similar cases in other countries with the same legal system.[7]

Common law originally referred to law "common" to the English kingdom dating back hundreds of years. As there were no enacted laws to govern the far-flung parts of the kingdom, legal principles evolved as judges made decisions affecting people's relationships with the state and with each other. These principles established legal rules, which other judges generally followed, a concept known as **precedent**.

The legacy of this historical development is that common law as it is practised today relies on a system of case precedent from higher courts, which is not limited to decisions in any one place but can refer to case law from any jurisdiction with the common law system.

As a former British colony, Hong Kong inherited the use of common law and thus can rely on precedents from the UK and other countries and territories that also were formerly under British rule. Before 1997, Hong Kong was required to follow the common law of England. Now, courts "may" refer to precedents of other common law jurisdictions (BL, Article 84). So while Hong Kong courts will generally look to UK cases for guidance, they also can look to cases from such nations as Australia, Canada, New Zealand, or even the US, as well as from the European Court of Human Rights.

To sum up, common law in Hong Kong is non-legislative "judge-made" law that relies on precedent — the previous rulings of its higher courts — and can refer to those from other similar jurisdictions. But the law is not static. It can evolve in incremental ways as courts apply different facts to the legal rules and fashion variations on established principles to reflect changing circumstances in their own communities.

One such case was *Cheng v Tse* [2000] 3 HKLRD 418, a landmark decision that greatly expanded the use of the fair comment defence in defamation cases in Hong Kong and has been cited and/or referred to by courts in the UK and other commonwealth countries.[8] (For more details, see Chapter 3 Defamation.) In *Cheng v Tse*, the Court of Final Appeal set out what it considered to be important

7. Wesley-Smith, p. 37.

8. For example, *Branson v Bower* [2002] 2 WLR 452; *Joseph v Spiller* [2011] 1 AC 852; *El Naschie v Macmillan Publishers Ltd (t/a Nature Publishing Group)* [2012] EWHC 1809. See further Young and Ghai (eds.), *Hong Kong's Court of Final Appeal: The Development of the Law in China's Hong Kong* (Cambridge: Cambridge University Press, 2013), Chapters 13 (Mason), 15 (Young), 20 (Glofcheski), and 22 (Lo).

values in Hong Kong and endorsed an approach for lower courts to follow in later cases (emphasis added):

> The freedom of speech (or of expression) is a freedom that is essential to Hong Kong's civil society. It is constitutionally guaranteed by the Basic Law. *The right of fair comment is a most important element in the freedom of speech.* In a society which greatly values the freedom of speech and safeguards it by a constitutional guarantee, *it is right that the court when considering and developing the common law should not adopt a narrow approach.*

Uniquely, Hong Kong can invite judges from other common law jurisdictions to participate in the rulings of its highest court, the Court of Final Appeal (BL, Article 82). For example, Lord Nicholls, who served on the House of Lords, the highest court in the UK (1994–2007) before the establishment of a Supreme Court there in 2009, was also a non-permanent member of Hong Kong's Court of Final Appeal (1998–2004). In addition to writing the lead opinion for *Cheng v Tse,* he also authored the lead opinion for *Reynolds v Times Newspaper* [2001] 2 AC 127, a landmark UK case that set out a ten-part test for responsible journalism.

3.2.1 Relationship with equity

Equity is a separate collection of principles, developed and originally administered in a separate system of courts, which, and to some extent still is, less rigid than the common law because it relies on more general concepts of fairness and even though it is now mostly administered in the same courts.

3.2.2 Contrast with civil law

Common law is one of two major legal systems in the world; the second is the civil law (or civil code) system. Other systems, to a lesser degree, are based on religious law like Sharia (Islamic law), or customary law,[9] deriving from local customs. Some countries have a combination of systems.

In a civil law system, every law is codified (written into law) by the legislature, resulting in an extensive set of rules (a civil code), which judges apply and interpret. Thus, the key difference between the two systems is that in civil law, legislation is the only binding source of law, with the courts basing their rulings on code provisions and not on case precedent. In contrast, in common law, court decisions are also legally binding, with judges playing a bigger role as they interpret legal doctrines and legislation.

The civil law system originated in the law of the Roman Empire, but it did not firmly take root until the nineteenth century when a major movement for codification led nations to adopt this system. It was accepted throughout Continental Europe, with Germany and France as leading examples. Germany's civil code, in particular, influenced a number of Asian countries — such as Japan, South Korea,

9. Hong Kong also observes some Chinese customary law, as guaranteed by Article 8 of the Basic Law, but it is not considered of great significance or influence and mostly affects some land issues in the New Territories.

China and Taiwan — in the formulation of their civil codes. Today, a majority of the world's countries, including much of Latin America, use the civil law system.

Many think that the two systems are experiencing a convergence with the line between them becoming less distinct. Civil law countries increasingly recognize the important role courts can play (and courts, after all, are likely to follow their own prior rulings). Common law nations are enacting more legislation. Precedent allows some flexibility and adaptability, but its strongest characteristic, stability, also means that it can offer only gradual change. Legislation often provides a more rapid response to shifting legal needs.

3.3 Legislation

In Hong Kong, the primary legislation is law enacted by the Legislative Council (LegCo) in the form of **ordinances**. As a general rule, the executive branch of the government is mostly responsible for drafting and introducing **bills**, which are proposed laws. This often happens after a process known as a public consultation, which can be conducted by various government departments in which they solicit public views on proposed legislation. A LegCo member may also introduce a bill, known as a **private member's bill**, but in a limited way. It cannot involve public expenditure, changes to the political structure, or the operation of the government, without the approval of the Chief Executive. This effectively means that private member's bills of any significance will need the government's approval if they are to go forward.

After a bill is introduced in LegCo, it goes through three readings and can be studied by a committee, which can make related amendments. The bulk of the debate and amendments occur during the second reading phase.

If a motion to read the bill a third time is passed, then the bill will be considered law after it is signed and put into effect by the Chief Executive. According to Annex II of the Basic Law, a government bill requires a simple majority vote of LegCo members present to be considered passed. But bills or amendments to government bills introduced by individual members need a majority vote both from directly elected members and from members representing functional constituencies (professional, business and special interest groups). As of 2013, there are thirty-five members for each of the two groups of lawmakers.

About a hundred ordinances are enacted into law annually. In addition, **subsidiary legislation** may be needed to supplement an ordinance, providing rules and bylaws to assist in making it work, and these are delegated generally to the executive branch. Typically, several hundred pieces of subsidiary legislation are passed each year.

3.4 International treaties and agreements

More than 200 international treaties and agreements, ranging from the World Trade Organization — Agreement on Trade Related Aspects of Intellectual Property Rights to the International Convention for the Suppression of Terrorist

Bombings, have been applied to Hong Kong.[10] But a treaty is not considered part of Hong Kong's local law unless legislation places it into effect.

Fifteen United Nations human rights treaties apply to Hong Kong. A prominent example is the International Covenant on Civil and Political Rights (ICCPR), a UN treaty based on the Universal Declaration of Human Rights, which was ratified by the UK and extended to Hong Kong in 1976. The Basic Law embraces the ICCPR by mandating that Hong Kong enact laws to give effect to it (BL, Article 39). The Hong Kong Bill of Rights Ordinance (Cap 383), enacted in 1991, incorporated verbatim numerous articles of ICCPR, such as provisions protecting individual privacy against government action (BORO, Article 14, and ICCPR, Article 17 (1)). The Hong Kong government is required to make periodic reports on how ICCPR rights are being implemented to the UN Human Rights Committee (HRC), a body that monitors such implementation. In 2011, the HKSAR submitted its third report.[11] The Hong Kong Journalists Association submitted to the HRC its own report, stating that the Hong Kong government has failed to implement sufficient aspects of ICCPR to protect freedom of expression and the rights of journalists, including, for example, not enacting a Freedom of Information law (see Chapter 6 Access to Information). In March 2013, the HRC held hearings and issued its concluding observations, expressing concern for, among other specifics, the NPCSC's re-interpretations of the Basic Law that could "weaken and undermine rule of law and independence of judiciary", "the lack of a clear plan to institute universal suffrage", and the absence of independent bodies or mechanisms to monitor human rights violations or police misconduct.[12] The fourth periodic report is due in 2018.

An international treaty or agreement also can indirectly impact Hong Kong law when a Hong Kong court refers to it to help interpret legislation or develop principles in common law.

4. The Judiciary

The Judiciary, consisting of Hong Kong's courts and its judges, is responsible for the administration of justice in Hong Kong, handling all criminal and civil cases. As the third branch of government (after the executive and legislative branches), it "shall exercise judicial power independently, free from any interference" (BL, Article 85).

---

10. For a list of all treaties and international agreements in force and applicable to Hong Kong, see: http://www.legislation.gov.hk/interlaw.htm.
11. A copy of the report can be found at: http://www.cmab.gov.hk/en/issues/prc_4.htm.
12. CCPR/C/SR2974, adopted 26 March 2013. Text of the concluding observations can be found at: http://www.cmab.gov.hk/doc/en/documents/policy_responsibilities/the_rights_of_the_individuals/Advance_Version_2013_ICCPR_e.pdf.

4.1 Judges and magistrates

Judges and magistrates are appointed by the Chief Executive or Chief Justice, with recommendations from the Judicial Officers Recommendation Commission, which includes the Chief Justice, the Secretary for Justice, judges, lawyers and non-lawyers. Members of the Judiciary are immune from legal action in the performance of their judicial functions (BL, Article 85). Mandatory retirement age for all judges (except non-permanent judges of the Court of Final Appeal) and magistrates is 65.

4.2 Juries

Trial by jury is guaranteed by the Basic Law (Article 86) and is available for the most serious criminal cases, such as murder, rape, armed robbery and certain drug and commercial fraud cases, and in civil actions for defamation. The purpose of a jury is for members of the community to evaluate and judge the evidence against a defendant. Jurors are expected to give fair deliberations to the individual on trial and to assure the community that justice is done.

The jury's basic job, then, is to decide the result of a case. For example, based on the evidence presented in a criminal case, was the defendant guilty? A judge, on the other hand, decides which evidence a jury will hear and what law is appropriate. (When there is no jury, the judge also decides the result.) In Hong Kong, all jury trials consist of seven jurors, except where the court orders that the jury have nine (Jury Ordinance, Cap 3, s 3). A civil trial verdict is reached by a majority vote. In a criminal case, five out of seven jurors must reach a verdict, or seven when there are nine jurors (JO, s 24). A jury of five can be used in some death inquests in Coroner's Court (Coroner Ordinance, Cap 504, s 23).

To qualify as a juror, a person must be between twenty-one and sixty-five years old, of sound mind and of good character, have sufficient knowledge of the language of the court proceedings (Chinese or English) and have no disabilities, such as hearing or visual impairments, that would interfere with the duties of being a juror (JO s 4).

Some persons may be excused from jury service, as listed in the exemptions in Jury Ordinance (s 5). They include judges, police, clergy, full-time students, doctors, and even "editors of daily newspapers in Hong Kong and such members of their staffs in respect of whom the Registrar is satisfied that jury service would disrupt the publication of such newspapers" (s 5(1)(f)).

4.3 Hong Kong courts

The courts in Hong Kong are the Court of Final Appeal, the High Court (the Court of Appeal and the Court of First Instance), the District Court, the Magistrates' Courts, the Coroner's Court, and the Juvenile Court. Also, several tribunals have authority to resolve disputes involving lands, labour, small claims and obscene articles.

Each court has its own registry, which is responsible for filing documents, listing cases for hearing and assisting the judges and judicial officers (see Appendix B of this book, "Searching for Public Records of Courts").

4.3.1 **The Court of Final Appeal**

The Court of Final Appeal (CFA) is Hong Kong's highest court and hears appeals on criminal and civil rulings from the High Court, which consists of the Court of First Instance and the Court of Appeal (BL, Article 82 and Court of Final Appeal Ordinance (CFAO), Cap 484).[13]

An appeal is heard by a panel of five, which typically includes the Chief Justice, three permanent judges, and one non-permanent Hong Kong judge or a judge from another common law jurisdiction.

The CFA may "confirm, reverse or vary the decision of the court from which the appeal lies or may remit the matter with its opinion . . . to that court, or may make such other order in the matter . . . as it thinks fit" (CFAO, s 17(1)).

Appeals are generally not automatic; the CFA must grant permission (unless the civil appeal concerns an amount more than HK$1 million). It issues about 30 substantive decisions annually.

The CFA's first Chief Justice, the Hon. Andrew Li Kwok Nang, was appointed[14] in 1997; he stepped down in 2010. Serving during the court's critical first 13 years, Li was widely viewed as having successfully established the CFA as a respected and moderate court.[15] Appointed to replace him was the Hon. Geoffrey Ma Tao-li, then Chief Judge of the High Court.

4.3.2 **High Court (Court of Appeal and the Court of First Instance)**

The High Court is divided into two parts: the Court of Appeal and the Court of First Instance (High Court Ordinance, Cap 4).

The **Court of Appeal** hears appeals of all civil and criminal cases from the Court of First Instance and the District Court. It also handles appeals from the Lands Tribunal.

The **Court of First Instance** serves as both an appeals court and a trial court. It hears appeals of criminal cases from the Magistrates' Courts and civil cases from the Labour Tribunal, the Small Claims Tribunal and the Obscene Articles Tribunal. It tries, with a jury, the most serious criminal offences — murder, manslaughter, rape, armed robbery, complex commercial frauds, and some drug offences. It has unlimited jurisdiction for civil matters, including bankruptcy, breach of contract, torts, matrimonial disputes, intellectual property, personal injury, probate, and

---

13. For an in-depth study, see Young and Ghai (eds.), *Hong Kong's Court of Final Appeal*, supra, note 8.
14. The Chief Justice must be a Chinese citizen and a permanent resident of Hong Kong with no right of abode in any foreign country (Court of Final Appeal Ordinance, Cap 484, s 6).
15. For an excellent review of the constitutional cases handled by the Court of Final Appeal from 1999 to 2009, see Young, "Constitutional Rights in Hong Kong's Court of Final Appeal", 27 *Chinese (Taiwan) Yearbook of International Laws and Affairs* 67–96 (2011).

injunctions. It is also the court for lodging requests for **judicial reviews** — i.e. challenges to administrative actions of government officials and agencies or the constitutionality of legislation or executive acts as contrary to the Basic Law — are first filed.

4.3.3 District Court

The District Court tries serious criminal cases except murder, manslaughter, and rape. The maximum term of imprisonment it can impose is seven years and there are no jury trials. This court also hears civil disputes of claims between HK$50,000 and HK$1 million (District Court Ordinance, Cap 336).

4.3.4 Magistrates' Courts

Magistrates' Courts handle a wide variety of criminal offences (Magistrates Ordinance, Cap 227). Most prevalent are the more minor crimes known as **summary offences**, which do not have jury trials, and those **indictable offences**, normally tried before a jury, which in certain circumstances can be disposed of summarily (by the magistrate alone). Maximum penalties in a Magistrates' Court is normally two years in prison and a fine of HK$100,000, but some ordinances allow sentences of up to three years in prison.

More serious indictable offences are referred to the District Court or the Court of First Instance, the latter sometimes after a **committal proceeding** in which the magistrate determines whether there is sufficient evidence to commit for trial. Bail hearings are also held in Magistrates' Courts.

Special Magistrates hear minor offences, such as hawking, speeding and littering, which do not have jail terms and have a maximum fine of HK$50,000.

The **Juvenile Court**, as part of the Magistrates' Courts, hears criminal charges (except homicide) against persons under sixteen years old. It also issues care and protection orders for persons under the age of eighteen.

4.3.5 Other courts and tribunals

The **Coroner's Court** conducts inquests into the causes and circumstances of unexpected deaths and can order a police investigation into a death. It can grant orders for burials and to remove dead bodies outside Hong Kong (Coroner's Ordinance, Cap 504).

The **Lands Tribunal** makes orders for possession of premises and determines how much compensation the government and others must pay to people whose land is seized or devalued because of public or private developments. It also hears matters governed by the Building Management Ordinance (Cap 344) and handles appeals from decisions by the Commissioner of Rating and Valuation and the Director of Housing. Its rulings can be appealed directly to the Court of Appeal (Lands Tribunal Ordinance, Cap 17).

The **Labour Tribunal** settles money disputes between employees and employers, such as claims for wages, sickness allowance, maternity leave, severance and so on. It also deals with claims arising from breach of employment contracts (Labour Tribunal Ordinance, Cap 25).

The **Small Claims Tribunal** hears money claims not exceeding HK$50,000. The main types of claims are debts, service charges, property damage and consumer complaints. Individuals represent themselves; lawyers are not allowed (Small Claims Tribunal Ordinance, Cap 338).

The **Obscene Articles Tribunal** classifies articles into three categories (Class I: neither obscene nor indecent; Class II: indecent; or Class III: obscene) and it will determine as part of a criminal trial whether an article referred to it is obscene or indecent (Control of Obscene and Indecent Articles Ordinance, Cap 390) (see Chapter 11 Obscenity and Indecency).

5. The Law Reform Commission

Established in 1980, the Law Reform Commission (LRC) is a government-appointed body whose lawyer and non-lawyer members conduct studies on aspects of law at the request of the Secretary for Justice or the Chief Justice with a view to recommending changes in the law. The LRC has published more than sixty reports covering subjects from sale of goods to divorce, with about half resulting in legislation, but only a half dozen new laws have resulted from LRC reports since 1997.[16]

The typical procedure is for the LRC to establish a sub-committee to examine a specific topic or project. A consultation paper is published, setting out the sub-committee's preliminary recommendations and inviting public responses and proposals. Following public consultation, the LRC prepares a final report that is submitted to the relevant government policy bureau. The bureau decides whether to pass the recommendations on to LegCo, which then decides whether the LRC's proposals should be made law. Some of the LRC's most controversial reports came in 2004 when it proposed new laws on privacy and media intrusion (see Chapter 5 Privacy).

6. The legal profession

The legal profession in Hong Kong consists of two groups of lawyers — barristers and solicitors — and is regulated by the Legal Practitioners Ordinance (LPO, Cap 159).

Barristers are specialists in advocacy, litigation, and legal advice and have the right to appear in any court in Hong Kong. They are hired through a solicitor or the Department of Justice, **Legal Aid** (which provides legal representation for committal proceedings in Magistrates' Courts and criminal/civil cases in District Court, High Court and the Court of Final Appeal and some tribunals), or the **Duty**

16. See: http://www.hkreform.gov.hk.

Lawyer Service (which provides lawyers for criminal defendants in Magistrates' Courts, Juvenile Court or Coroner's Court).

They must comply with a professional Code of Conduct. A complaint of misconduct is investigated by the Bar Council of the Hong Kong Bar Association, which can refer a case for disciplinary action to the Barristers Disciplinary Tribunal. A practising barrister may apply to be designated a Senior Counsel (known as Queen's Counsel before 1997).

Solicitors can deal with most legal matters, including giving legal advice, drafting documents and registering companies and property sales. In the past, solicitors were restricted to only representing clients in courts below the Court of First Instance. In 2010, the LPO was amended to permit solicitors with five years' experience to apply to an assessment board for the right to appear as a solicitor-advocate before the High Court and the Court of Final Appeal. The change, implemented in 2013, was recommended as a way to lower costs so a person did not have to hire two lawyers to go to court.[17] A solicitor is allowed to practise in a law firm or partnership, whereas a barrister must maintain a sole practice in a set of chambers. The Law Society establishes standards of conduct, monitors solicitors, and investigates complaints.

17. Solicitor-advocates, however, are not permitted to wear the traditional horsehair wigs worn by judges and barristers in the higher courts. Patsy Moy, "Top Hong Kong Judge Refuses to Let Solicitors Wear Wigs in Higher Courts", *South China Morning Post*, 26 April 2013.

3

Defamation

Rick Glofcheski

FREQUENTLY ASKED QUESTIONS

Questions about the media's "fault"

1. Are the media liable only if they *intended* to defame someone? (See sections 3, 7.1 and 13)
2. Are the media liable even if they innocently failed to realize that what they said might be read in a defamatory way? (See section 2.2.2)
3. Are the media liable for publishing what others have authored, such as letters to the editor? (See section 12.4)

Questions about the meaning of words and what is "defamatory"

4. Words may have different meanings to different people at different times; how will a court respond to the different possible meanings? (See sections 2.2 and 2.3.3)
5. Suppose that most people in Hong Kong would take no exception to something said or published, but a particular group has an unusual view and does think it is defamatory? (See section 2.3.3(2))
6. Is it defamatory to make a statement that would cause other people to pity a person or to laugh at a person? (See section 2.3.2–3)

Questions about unidentified people being "defamed"

7. Is there liability even if there is no mention of the name of the person who might complain about what was published? (See section 3.2)
8. Suppose no name is mentioned but there is a cartoon that could be thought to represent someone? (See section 2.2.3)
9. What happens if the name of a person is invented for the purposes of a story, but in fact there was such a person? (See section 3.1)

Questions about who can sue and what they must prove

10. Can anyone — including governments, companies, public figures, or the press — sue for defamation? (See section 5)
11. Can people sue for defamation even if their reputations have not been affected or they have not suffered any ill effects? (See section 7.3)

Questions about excuses and defences for the media

12. Is it acceptable to publish the truth even if it is damaging to someone's reputation? (See section 9)
13. Must a statement be shown to be true in order to escape liability? (See section 9.1)
14. What are the consequences of unsuccessfully arguing to the court that a statement was true? (See section 9.1)
15. Is it acceptable to use information from a respectable source? (See sections 9.1 and 11.4.2)
16. Is there any protection for reporting or commenting on events of political or other public importance? (See sections 10.4, 11.2–4 and 12)
17. How does the law protect freedom of speech? Is there a right to free speech in Hong Kong? (See sections 1.4 and 11–13)
18. How does the law of defamation apply to publications on the Internet? (See sections 1.3, 1.5, 4.1, 4.3, 6.8, 16.2, 16.3 and 18)

1. Introduction

The law of defamation (or libel and slander) is something that worries journalists and others involved in the media, and with good reason. It has some unpredictable qualities, and can result in the media having to pay very heavy damages to persons who are the subject of news reporting.

1.1 Overview

Defamation is concerned with damage to reputation. The underlying idea is that, as a result of something written or said, people in society will think less of the individual, company, or institution that has been attacked or criticized. The very nature of words makes this a problematic area of the law. The subtlety of meaning of language is its charm for many whose business is words, but sometimes there is room for disagreement over what the words mean, and whether that meaning would damage someone's reputation. Another difficulty lies in the idea of reputation — in whose eyes and what sort of reputation? Finally, this area of the law has some curious and technical rules and distinctions. This chapter will discuss what must be proved by someone who is claiming that his or her reputation has been damaged by something said or written by another, what defences may be raised, especially for the media, and what the consequences are of a court finding that a reputation has been damaged (in particular, how much might have to be paid as compensation).

The law of defamation is about the reputation of people and organizations — not the reputation of goods. Statements about the quality of a product cannot be defamation (unless there is some added or implied criticism of the competence or honesty of a person or of a body). There is a tort which can be committed by an attack on the quality of goods — "malicious falsehood" — but actions for it are rare, and it is much more difficult to prove than defamation. There can be no successful action if a deliberate falsehood cannot be proved.

1.2 Technicalities (why the law is so odd)

The main reason why the law has some curious rules has to do with history. The rules were developed piecemeal by the courts, rather than as a coherent whole by Parliament (the English equivalent of the Legislative Council in Hong Kong), and were developed by different courts over a long period. Some were difficult to fit with developments, such as the radio, and are proving perhaps even more difficult to fit with the Internet! Some of them are the result of genuine efforts by the courts to produce a fair outcome. Other complications arise because defamation actions can be tried by jury — ordinary people whose understanding of the law is limited.

1.3 Interests

Free speech is essential for a society aspiring to democratic values, but the right to be free of false attacks on one's character also warrants the law's attention. In *Yaqoob v Asia Times Online Ltd* [2008] 4 HKLRD 911, a case concerning an online news reporting service, the judge asked the question: "How does the court strike a balance between the individual's right to have his good reputation protected and the public's right to be told of serious potential wrongdoing [and, it might be added, the individual's right to free speech]?" This balance is the central issue raised by defamation, and the dilemma has become more, rather than less, acute with the Internet and its potential for instantaneous, worldwide distribution.

However, this idea of "balance" has its problems. First, it suggests that public interest is all on one side (freedom of expression) and private interest (in reputation) is on the other side — an over-simplification. Second, it may also suggest that there is always some compromise to be reached — but the value of free discussion will quite often outweigh other interests. Balance may not be needed.

1.4 The Basic Law and the Bill of Rights

These days, the values of free speech are very often expressed in constitutions. The most famous is the First Amendment to the Constitution of the US, which states: "Congress shall make no law abridging freedom of speech or of the press". This is the basis for the very wide protection of free speech in that country. Hong Kong has its own constitution — the Basic Law, which states: "Hong Kong residents shall have freedom of speech, of the press and of publication" (Article 27). And the Basic Law recognizes (in Article 39) the continued application of the International Covenant on Civil and Political Rights (ICCPR), which provides:

> Article 17
>
> 1. No one shall be subjected to arbitrary or unlawful interference with his privacy, family, home or correspondence, nor to unlawful attacks on his honour and reputation.
> 2. Everyone has the right to the protection of the law against such interference or attacks.

Article 19

1. Everyone shall have the right to hold opinions without interference.
2. Everyone shall have the right to freedom of expression; this right shall include freedom to seek, receive and impart information and ideas of all kinds, regardless of frontiers, either orally, in writing or in print, in the form of art, or through any other media of his choice.

Hong Kong's Bill of Rights Ordinance is identical in wording to the ICCPR. Ultimately the courts may decide, if there is any dispute, what "unlawful attacks" are, and what the protection of reputation and of free speech requires. So far there have been few cases on this in Hong Kong. New cases coming out of the courts of the UK must take into account the European Convention for the Protection of Human Rights and Fundamental Freedoms, now part of its national law. This is not identical to the ICCPR, but the basic concerns are similar. There is still a tendency for English cases to influence the courts in Hong Kong.

1.5 The Defamation Ordinance and the courts

The Defamation Ordinance (Cap 21), enacted in Hong Kong in 1887, is not a document which sets out all the law about defamation. Most of the law is actually laid down in decisions of the courts — the common law. The Defamation Ordinance contains certain changes to that law, changes that developed over a period of more than a hundred years in England, and were copied in Hong Kong. Some of these changes are of special concern to the press, as they give protection against lawsuits in some situations. Other provisions are intended to iron out rather minor problems in the law. There have been very few amendments in recent years that change the law substantially, most changes being piecemeal and of a housekeeping nature, such as acknowledging the change of sovereignty in 1997 and updating cross-references to other ordinances. However, it is unlikely that the law can resist significant change much longer, in particular because the Internet's widespread use by almost everyone as a forum for the expression of views is exerting pressure to liberalize the law of defamation.

It is incorrect to say that someone has "brought an action under the Defamation Ordinance". The ordinance does not give the right to sue; that right comes from the common law. The Defamation Ordinance is very similar to the English Acts of Parliament, which have changed the law of defamation, but it does not include changes made in that country since 1996. So one should be careful when reading about the English law of defamation — anything that is said about the UK's 1996 and 2013 Defamation Acts will probably not apply in Hong Kong.

Predicting exactly how a court might rule on defamation in a particular case is not often possible. Therefore, this chapter is written in the usual style of a lawyer; it tends to say "the courts would probably decide" in anticipating how courts might decide. Sometimes lawyers may say something like "the plaintiff would have to show the court" to mean that this is what the party would have to convince the court about.

1.6 Crime and tort

Torts are wrongs for which it is possible to bring a civil action, usually claiming compensation. There are two torts of defamation: libel and slander. Libel is a defamatory statement in written form, and slander one in spoken form. The difference between libel and slander is actually a bit more complicated than that and will be explained in section 8 of this chapter. But first, the issues which arise in both of them will be examined. There is also a crime of criminal libel. Today this is of very little practical significance in Hong Kong, which is a good thing as it could be a serious restriction on freedom of speech. More detail about the crime will be provided in section 17 of this chapter.

2. Defamatory meaning

This is the heart of the tort: defamation is making a statement which defames the plaintiff. To defame is to lower that person's reputation. The two main questions here are: (a) how does the court decide what the words mean; and (b) how does the court decide whether a statement is defamatory? The second question is also divided into a number of sub-issues.

2.1 Some Hong Kong examples

The following are some examples of statements that the Hong Kong courts have held to have a defamatory meaning:

- A university lecturer failed to deliver some of his lectures and refused to take part in a group photograph (*Cheung Ng Sheong Steven v Eastweek Publisher Ltd* [1995] 3 HKC 601)
- A newspaper publishing company was prone to sue in defamation every time it was mentioned by someone else in a way it did not like, in order to frighten people into keeping their mouths shut (*Eastern Express Publisher Ltd v Mo Man Ching Claudia* [1999] 4 HKC 425)
- "the objective of the school is to earn money rather than help the students" (*Top Express Consultants Ltd v Tai Lo Ngan Ying* (2003) DCCJ 4065/2002)
- A flat owner in a multi-storey building unlawfully refused to pay management fees (*Wong Sui Fung v Yip Siu Keung* (2003) HCA 5595/2000)
- A doctor (the speaker's political rival) was educated in a system that preferred quantity to quality (*Lee York Fai v Ho Hau Cheung* (2007) HCA 4305/2003)
- A law firm and its partners were involved in a lawsuit that cost owners of a housing estate unnecessary money when legal action was unnecessary (*Cheng Kar Foo Andrew and Others v Ho Sau Mo* HCA 284/2008 (Chinese judgment))

- A chairman of a trade union was using trade union money to fund her own education and was not fit to be the chairman of the union (*Kwan Siu Wa Becky v Marla Susilo* (2011) DCCJ 5396/2007)
- Terminated employees were unprofessional and not caring about the company's best interests or those of Hong Kong (*Blakeney-Williams v Cathay Pacific Airways Ltd* [2011] 1 HKLRD 901)
- A business partner was not the producer of a product but was merely a marketing company, responsible for liaising with the trade shows to find overseas buyers (*Yokview Co Ltd v Lo Ying Kit Henry* (2011) DCCJ 5136/2009)

In commenting on one of the impugned statements made against a group of newspapers in a recent case (*Oriental Press Group Ltd v Inmediahk.net Ltd* [2012] 2 HKLRD 1004) the judge said:

> To suggest that the plaintiff, being the ultimate owner of two newspapers in Hong Kong, hired someone to destroy or conceal news which contained facts was clearly to the plaintiff's discredit and tended to lower it in the estimation of others. The suggestion also had a tendency to damage the plaintiff in the way of its business. Newspapers thrive on credibility, and credibility is earned by reporting facts, not destroying or concealing them. The first Offending Words were an assault on the plaintiff's credibility.

2.2 The first question: Meaning

2.2.1 The basic rule

In a case that goes to court, the judge decides what the statement meant (except in the few cases that are tried by a jury). Judges say that they will decide on the meaning as it would appear to an ordinary, reasonable reader. Sometimes they mention "ordinary", sometimes "reasonable", sometimes both, or even "ordinary, reasonable *and* fair-minded people". This tends to imply that ordinary readers are not necessarily reasonable! However, the courts may sometimes expect too much of the ordinary reader. This may work to the advantage of the press, because the court may not recognize that the ordinary reader may see meanings in words which the judge, reading the statement in very different circumstances, does not. But the courts are a bit unpredictable. The judges will also take account of the type of publication or communication. A technical publication or a financial newspaper may have a rather different readership from a popular newspaper, and the "ordinary reader" in question will be the ordinary reader of that publication.

2.2.2 Hidden and double meanings

Double meanings (or several meanings) are not uncommon. Sometimes the double meaning is intended by the writer or speaker, and sometimes it is not. The double meaning may arise because of irony, or because a word has two meanings, or closely related meanings, or a slang meaning, or because of an intended pun, or because the statement explicitly or implicitly refers to some cultural or literary allusion, or simply because people would read something into them. An example of the last might be a statement that the police have been investigating a person: an English court once decided that the reader would think that this suggested the police *suspected* that the person had committed an offence (which is a defamatory statement) but not that the person was *guilty* (which would be a more serious defamatory statement).

Some double meanings are clear, or at least might come to the mind of the reader without having to know any special facts. In the example of the police investigating, it is common knowledge that one function of the police is to investigate crime. But some statements have a hidden meaning because of a special piece of knowledge. This might be the slang meaning of a word, or a literary allusion, or might be a fact not specifically stated. For example, if some people who read a statement that a certain person is "tone-deaf" knew that this person was a musician, the statement takes on a defamatory meaning. Such a statement made about a non-musician would probably not be defamatory.

Such a hidden meaning is called an "innuendo". (This word is used here in a wider sense than its everyday English usage.) If the hidden meaning will be clear only if the reader knows of some special fact or special language usage, this is called a "true innuendo", and the plaintiff must take care to prove that this special fact or usage is known to at least some readers. This is the tone-deaf musician situation.

If no special knowledge is required to perceive the hidden meaning, the task of convincing the court that there was defamation is easier. In one case, a court easily accepted that in Hong Kong a statement about "giving cakes" to the plaintiff implied corruption. It did not treat this as a true innuendo that required the plaintiff to prove a special meaning; it was an everyday meaning (*Far East Engineering Services Ltd v Choi Yau Chiu* (2005) HCA 2146/2004). But the boundary between the special and the everyday fact or usage is not so clear cut — when does a slang word become part of common speech? This is a problem for the lawyer, not the journalist, but the media should be aware that the surface meaning is not necessarily the only meaning. They should also be aware that the issue is not: "Did they *intend* the reader to see the second meaning?" The point is: "Would the ordinary/reasonable reader have seen it?"

2.2.3 **Cartoons**

Cartoons are a popular way of conveying messages. They do not raise any special legal issue. The question is the same: "What would the ordinary person have understood?" Sometimes it is necessary to show that those who saw the cartoon would have related the cartoon to the plaintiff because it showed a distinctive characteristic of the plaintiff, such as a bald head, a large stomach, or his bow-tie.

2.2.4 Newspaper headlines

In a newspaper the usual rule is that the article must be read as a whole. Thus, a headline, on the face of it defamatory, may be neutralized by the text (*Wong Wai Kay v Hong Kong Economic Journal Co Ltd* (2013) HCA 1385/2010). But it is not a hard and fast rule. As observed in *Charleston v News Group Newspapers Ltd* [1995] 2 AC 65, "It is plain that the eye-catching headline and the eye-catching photograph will first attract the reader's attention, precisely as they were intended to do, and equally plain that a significant number of readers will not trouble to read any further. This phenomenon must be well known to newspaper editors and publishers, who cannot, therefore, complain if they are held liable in damages for any libel thus published to the category of limited readers."

2.2.5 "Mere abuse"

Someone who hears abusive words spoken in the heat of the moment may not take them seriously. The courts take a similar view and may hold that words spoken in a quarrel would not have been taken seriously by the ordinary hearer and so would not injure the reputation of the person attacked. The court would take the circumstances into account: Was there a quarrel, or was this an argument calmly conducted? The courts take a different approach if the words are written, for it is assumed that people reflect more before they write. (This may fly in the face of experience, especially of those writing e-mails! But perhaps the courts are also saying that people *ought* to take more care before they write, and must take the consequences if they do not.) The approach is likely to be of little relevance to the media, with the possible exception of those broadcasting live events. What about the media *reporting* remarks made in a quarrel? Some courts have held that this does not attract the benefit of the "mere abuse" rule, so the media should be careful in such a situation.

2.3 The second question: Defamatory

2.3.1 Basic idea

Defamation is about people and their place in society, and about what others think of them. It is not about hurt feelings, but about reputations. A plaintiff complaining about a defamatory statement is saying: "After reading or hearing the statement, others would have thought less of me." Note the words "would have thought". The plaintiff is saying that this would have been the natural result of the statement, and does not have to prove that anyone actually did think less of him or her. Many statements are clearly defamatory. It would always be defamatory to say that someone is a thief (unless clearly meaning something like "he stole her heart"!). It is defamatory to suggest any form of dishonesty, immorality, or professional incompetence. Other statements will vary according to time and place. A book for the media in England (Crone: 7) suggests that the average person there would be unlikely to think less of an unmarried woman because of a statement that she spent the night in a hotel with her boyfriend. Would that be true in Hong Kong?

2.3.2 **Traditional descriptions of what constitutes defamation**

A great deal of judicial effort has been expended in trying to define exactly what defamation is. One of the early attempts to explain defamation described it as "something that leads the person affected to be regarded by others with hatred, ridicule, or contempt". Sometimes judges still use this, but more often they will describe defamation as something which "lowers another in the eyes of right-thinking members of society generally". People who are concerned whether something they are about to say or write might be defamatory should ask themselves: "Would people generally in Hong Kong think less of this person because of this statement?" If the answer is "yes" the statement is probably defamatory; otherwise not. Because defamation is about people's place in society, judges have sometimes suggested that defamation can include a statement which would tend to make others avoid the person about whom the statement is made. For example, a statement suggesting that an individual has a horrible infectious disease or some bodily condition leading to bad smell might be defamatory. The condition might be something for which others would — or ought to — pity, rather than despise or think less, of the individual. But the courts may decide that even such a statement is defamatory. This is a bit controversial. There is a good deal of disagreement, for example, on whether a court would, or should, hold that it is defamatory to say that a woman has been raped. A court in England in the 1930s did assume it was, but should a court do so today?

2.3.3 **Problem questions**

(1) Ridicule

Does laughing at other people necessarily mean thinking less of them? Unkind people might laugh at a very fat person, but this does not really mean that the person's reputation is lowered. Admittedly the person laughed at may feel embarrassment, but this is not the same as loss of reputation. Reputation involves a person's morals, personality, competence, or ability. And the last may depend on what that person aims to achieve. Maybe it is defamatory to say that an actor is ugly; but it may not be defamatory to say that another person is.

> In a Hong Kong case, the plaintiff complained that his photograph had been used in a film to represent the deceased husband of a character in the film. The son of the deceased character spoke to the photograph, asking his dead father to come and give his mother sexy dreams to keep her happy. The plaintiff said his friends laughed at him. The court held this was defamatory. *(Li Yau-wai, Eric v Genesis Films Ltd* [1987] HKLR 711)

Maybe the *Genesis* decision is a bit doubtful. On the other hand, ridicule might lead to lowered reputation, if things go too far.

(2) Different views in society

In different societies and at different times, people may think differently about statements. Perhaps people think differently now about those with a different religion, or about communists, or about homosexuals. The principle is clear: For cases of alleged defamation in Hong Kong, what would ordinary people in Hong Kong now think of someone of whom this statement was made? In a definition quoted earlier, defamation is something which "lowers another in the eyes of right-thinking members of society *generally*". There may be some people in society who have a peculiar view of certain characteristics or behaviour. Their unusual views cannot be allowed to dictate whether a statement is defamatory or not. This may have unfortunate consequences occasionally. For example, if a Muslim eats pork, other members of the same religion would think less of him or her. Most Hong Kong people would think that eating pork is perfectly natural. Muslims are a small minority in Hong Kong. If one person accuses a Muslim of eating pork, it would be very painful to the Muslim, but it would not be defamatory. However, looking at it a different way: the allegation is also a statement that the Muslim is a hypocrite, disloyal to religion. Not only Muslims would think less of such a person. In this way a court might agree that the statement was defamatory.

Sometimes the courts can find themselves in a dilemma. They may suspect that people do think less of others who are homosexual or of a certain race. But if they conclude that a statement that a person is "gay" or "black" is defamatory, they may feel that the judgment would give a sort of respectability to intolerance. So they would be reluctant to say that this is a view that would be held by "right-thinking members of society". A similar problem may occur in connection with illnesses: Is it defamatory to say that a person is HIV-positive? Logically it ought not to be, but maybe in reality it would cost that person their place in the community. Arguably, now that legislation against racial discrimination has been passed, the courts would have to say that racial intolerance is something of which right-thinking members of society disapprove.

3. Referring to the plaintiff

A person who complains of a statement must convince the court that the statement referred to him or her. However, it is not a requirement that the person who wrote, spoke, or published the words must have *intended* to refer to the plaintiff.

3.1 The plaintiff's name — but no intention

If the real name was used by accident or with no intention that any connection should be made, the question is simply: "What would the ordinary reader have thought?" Disclaimers sometimes put in novels and films, such as "no resemblance to any person living or dead is intended", would have no effect if the court thinks that people would have thought that the story was actually about a real person. If the real name of a person is used in the report of a court case, and the name is one which other(s) share, there is a risk that those others could sue for any statement which, while true about the person in the court case, is not true of them. The best approach for the press is to give enough detail that the identity of that particular person is clear. See section 13 below for a defence available under the Defamation Ordinance.

An example with a Hong Kong connection involves the famous author Somerset Maugham and his novel which was set partly in Hong Kong, *The Painted Veil.* The novel was partly about adultery. A couple by the same name as those in the novel filed a defamation case, so Maugham changed the name. Then the Assistant Colonial Secretary filed a case because in the novel the couple was the Assistant Colonial Secretary and his wife! Maugham then changed the name of the place!

Care should be taken to avoid the risk of other "accidental" connections with the wrong person. In an English case, a police officer sued when, in the course of a television programme about corruption, he was shown walking out of a police station, even though he was not accused of being involved in corruption (referred to in Crone: 10).

3.2 Names, no names, and nicknames

If the name used is a bit different from the person's real name or the name by which he or she is known, the person will have to show that others would have understood to whom the name refers. Sometimes no name is used, but the statement is understood to refer to a certain person, because of a physical description, connection with identified persons, a drawing, or some other way. In that case, the question is the same: "would the ordinary (perhaps the reasonable) reader have made the connection?" This is a case of "innuendo" mentioned earlier. A simple example would be where someone is known by a nickname which is not the "official" name; if defamed in a statement referring to the nickname, the person would have to prove that the nickname existed and would be known to readers.

3.3 Hidden meanings

Identities may be even more hidden. A famous example is where a photograph in a newspaper was captioned "General X and his fiancée". But General X already had a wife, not the lady in the picture! The real wife sued, saying that "if that was his fiancée, people would think I was not really his wife and that I had been 'living in sin' with him!" She won. This was an "innuendo", and one in which both the meaning and the fact that the real wife might be referred to were hidden.

There is an excellent Hong Kong example of a play on words.

> Lui Yau-wai complained that she had been accused of having a sexual affair. But the publication referred to a woman called Nui Mo Sheung. The affair was supposed to have been with an actor called "King of Big Stomach", who was said to have five stomachs. Ms Lui said this referred to Ng Wai-kwok. The connection between Ms Lui and "Ms Nui", and between "King of Big Stomach" and Mr Ng was made thus: Cantonese people often pronounce "nui" as "lui'; "mo" is the antonym (opposite in meaning) of "yau'; Ng as a name and ng as number 5 sound the same, as do the word for stomach and the name Wai! The court was convinced. *(Lok Kwai-fu v Y.C. Chan* [1978] HKLR 225)

3.4 Groups

"All lawyers are thieves." "All journalists are liars." Could any individual lawyer or journalist sue? Probably not, unless the statement was made in a place with only two or three lawyers or journalists. When an "obstetrician working at the Caritas Medical Centre" was mentioned critically, with no name, the plaintiff, who was one of only two obstetricians there, was found sufficiently referred to and could sue (*Sim Hok Gwan v Tin Tin Yat Po Ltd* [1981] HKLR 227). It is basically a matter of common sense — if the class of people is large, a reasonable person would not have thought that every individual was referred to. There have been some cases in which as many as ten people, all of whom could fit the description, have sued — as in an English case in which it was said that a policeman or policemen from a Criminal Investigation Department had raped a woman. There were ten officers who fit this description and they all sued successfully. Even if the group is larger, there may be something else which points a finger at one or two individuals.

> In a Hong Kong case, a newspaper said that a delegation of "elders of the securities industry" had gone to Beijing, and named the plaintiff as one. It also said that "most members" of the group were "tainted". It named no names in this connection, but the article also referred to an earlier period when "Seven Honourable Men", including the plaintiff, had been charged with corruption. The court said that a reasonable person would have little difficulty in making a connection between the plaintiff (who had actually been acquitted of the charge of corruption) and being "tainted". *(Sin Cho Chiu v Tin Tin Publication Development Ltd.* [2002] 1 HKLRD A21)

4. Publication

4.1 The basic rule

If the tort of defamation were simply about hurt feelings, it could be committed when the only communication was between the plaintiff and the defendant. However, publication requires that there be a communication to someone other than the person about whom the statement was made. After all, the tort is concerned with damage to reputation. Moreover, publication takes place each time when and where it is received. Each copy of a newspaper or book is a separate publication (*Duke of Brunswick v Harmer* [1849] 14 QB 154), as is each Internet download or "hit" (*Oriental Press Group Ltd v Fevaworks Solutions* Ltd [2012] 1 HKLRD 848; decision confirmed at [2013] 5 HKC 253). According to the "multiple publication rule", each such publication potentially gives rise to a fresh cause of action. The rule applies equally to the Internet (*Dow Jones & Co Inc v Gutnick* (2002) 210 CLR 575), although the position is different in some US states (see e.g. *Firth v State*, 747 NYS 2d 69 (2002)), and after recent reforms, in the UK (see section 18 below).

The burden is on the plaintiff to prove, by inference as well as by direct evidence (if any), the fact of publication and the extent of it. Can any presumptions be made regarding the Internet? In a recent Hong Kong case the court held that there is no presumption that material placed on a generally accessible website has been published to a substantial, albeit unquantifiable, number of persons (whether within the jurisdiction or elsewhere) (*Oriental Press Group Ltd v Inmediahk.net Ltd* [2012] 2 HKLRD 1004). On the other hand, in *Cairns v Modi* [2012] EWCA Civ 1382, a UK case concerning the social media tool Twitter, the court observed that "as a consequence of modern technology and communication systems . . . stories will have the capacity to 'go viral' more widely and more quickly than ever before". And in *John Raymond Luciw v Wolfgang Derler* (2013) HCA 2148/2011, a Hong Kong case involving the popular social media platform Facebook, the court found it "reasonable to infer that the dissemination of the defamation by the use of Facebook meant that the publication of the defamatory statements were both inside and outside Hong Kong". As this was Hong Kong's first defamation case concerning Facebook, it is worthwhile to consider more closely the court's explanation of the character of Facebook, the way it functions, and the implications for defamation litigation:

> 14. The "Facebook friend" to whom Mr Luciw sent a message has 201 "Facebook friends" herself. The settings for the Facebook page created by Mr Derler were such that the page had no restrictions upon access. Any of those 201 friends accessing her Facebook page would be able to link directly to the offending Facebook page without difficulty. It is not possible to say how many of them did this, but I infer that it is more likely than not that at least some of them did follow that link. The nature of the message posted by Mr Derler was such that it is inevitable that some would follow the link to find out who would post such a message.
>
> 15. Facebook has many millions of users and it is not unusual for Facebook users to look for people with similar interests, or by name, or simply to encounter a particular page and read the material on that page. By including details of Mr Luciw's employment it was easier for persons who knew him to locate the Facebook page if they wished to find out if Mr Luciw had a Facebook page. Asiaexpat.com [Mr Luciw's employer] is a well-known website in Hong Kong and throughout Asia. It has 15 different city/country sections covering virtually all of the countries in south-east Asia. It claims 950,000 visits per month and 400,000 registered users.
>
> 16. Facebook has become ubiquitous. It is quite common today for persons dealing with other persons to check to see whether or not they have a Facebook page. It would not be at all unusual; indeed it would be likely, that anyone dealing with Mr Luciw through Asiaexpat.com would check to see if he had a Facebook page. If they did so during August and September 2011, they would have gone to the page created by Mr Derler.

4.2 Unintended publication

Suppose an oral statement is overheard, or a remark made to one person is repeated to others. The basic rule is: "Should the person making the communication have foreseen that the communication might go further?" If so, he or she is liable. As such, someone who calls a press conference can hardly complain that what he or she said was published in the press. And a Hong Kong court said that it is a natural result of saying something in a meeting that it may appear in written form in the minutes (*Chan Chook Tim v Wong Kwok Hung* [2004] 1 HKC 18).

4.3 Publication by omission

Occasionally someone might be liable for failing to remove a publication. For example, someone who has responsibility for a notice board on which another person pins a defamatory notice could be liable as publisher if the notice is not removed within a reasonable time of learning of its existence (*Byrne v Deane* [1937] 1 KB 818). In the modern context, this is most likely to happen regarding Internet publications. In *Oriental Press Group Ltd v Fevaworks Solutions* Ltd [2013] 5 HKC 253, the defendants, the hosts of a popular Internet discussion forum, were found liable in respect of an anonymous posting which remained on the website for eight months following the plaintiffs' complaint and notification. The defendants were found liable not on the basis of the notice board analogy, but on the basis of their being subordinate publishers (section 6.6 below) with knowledge of the libel. The notice board analogy was rejected because, in the court's view, an Internet host plays an active role in the publication from the beginning. The defendants were found not liable for two other postings, having removed them from the website within one day of notification.

4.4 Repeat publication

The maker of a defamatory statement will be liable for its re-publication if the republication was authorized, intended or reasonably foreseeable (*McManus v Beckham* [2002] 1 WLR 2982), and so long as the substance and the sting of the original statement have not been altered (*Wan Chiu Ying v Tam Wai Chu* (2005) HCA 3479/2002; *Lee York Fai v Yue Shin Man* (2007) HCA 4305/2003).

Moreover, under what is known as the "repetition rule", a person who repeats a defamatory allegation first made by someone else is treated as if he had made the allegation himself, even if he attempts to distance himself from the allegation (*Oriental Press Group Ltd & Others v Ted Thomas* (1995) HCA 5217 of 1995; *Flood v Times Newspapers Ltd* [2012] 2 WLR 760). In *Oriental Daily Publisher Ltd v Ming Pao Holdings Ltd (No 1)* [2011] 3 HKLRD 393, the defendants — a newspaper and its proprietors — published stories about a person ("X") who called himself "Hong Kong Bin Laden". X made public allegations against the plaintiff newspaper publisher and proprietors accusing them of criminal intimidation against X, statements obviously defamatory of the plaintiff. In its report of these activities, the defendant included a photograph of X outside the High Court displaying a banner in which X accused the plaintiffs of forgery and false claims against X. The defendants were held liable for having repeated X's defamatory allegations. It was irrelevant that the defendants had not adopted the truth of X's allegations nor sought to justify them.

5. Who can sue

In the Hong Kong system almost anyone can sue for defamation, with some restrictions.

5.1 Government

In *Derbyshire County Council v Times Newspapers Ltd* [1993] AC 534 the then highest English court, the House of Lords, decided that government cannot sue for defamation (the actual case involved a local government to which the nearest Hong Kong equivalent would now be a District Council). The rationale is that governments have many other ways they can defend themselves against attack; it is not necessary for them to have the civil law of defamation available. Moreover, the chilling effect that libel actions may have on the media and free speech should not be underestimated.

5.2 Public figures, political parties, etc.

English courts have applied the same principle to political parties in the course of an election (*Goldsmith v Bhoyrul* [1997] 4 All ER 268). There has been no Hong Kong case directly on point. In the US, the right of public figures to sue was restricted in the landmark US Supreme Court decision in *New York Times Co. v Sullivan,* 376 U.S. 254 (1964), requiring the plaintiff to prove that the publisher knew that the statement was false or acted in reckless disregard of its truth or falsity. Most other countries have not gone so far. The US rule is based on the First Amendment to the Constitution (see section 1.4 in this chapter). As shown below, in Hong Kong, people who are attacked in public discussion of politics, etc. may have difficulty suing (see section 11 on qualified privilege and section 12 on honest comment).

The Bill of Rights applies to "public authorities": this means that public authorities must not infringe freedom of expression. In *Hong Kong Polytechnic University & Others v Next Magazine Publishing Ltd & Anor* [1997] 7 HKPLR 286 it was argued that this prevented a university from suing for defamation, because it is a public authority. The Court of Appeal did not accept the argument, ruling that a university was to be distinguished from public authorities as contemplated in *Derbyshire County Council v Times Newspapers Ltd.* They are not organs of government and do not participate in the governance of Hong Kong. Moreover, universities were particularly dependent on their reputation for survival. In *Lee York Fai v Yue Shin Man* (2007) HCA 4305/2003 the plaintiff, a candidate in an election, failed in his defamation action against an election rival not on the basis of his public or political status but because he was unable to prove that the allegedly defamatory statement referred to him. In the court's view the statement that election campaign guidelines were not being followed was made not of him but of his election campaign workers. The court said nothing about the plaintiff's standing to sue. On appeal, the Court of Appeal in dismissing the appeal also said nothing about the plaintiff's standing to sue ((2007) CACV 184/2007). More recently, controversy arose when the Chief Executive, C. Y. Leung, instructed lawyers to send a letter to a newspaper to retract an article allegedly defamatory of Leung in implying connections with triads (see C. Lee, "Chief Executive Demands Retraction of Defamatory Article", *South China Morning Post,* 8 February 2013). This move sparked an outcry from the media and some academics demanding that Leung withdraw his letter in order to avoid setting a bad precedent and the consequent chilling effect that might be felt by the press (see C. Lee and J. But, "Leung Unlikely to Win, Say Experts", *South China Morning Post,* 8 February 2013). No further developments have been reported on this incident, suggesting that the Chief Executive intends to let the matter rest.

5.3 **Companies and other bodies**

A company is not human. However, for most legal purposes, it is treated as a person. Does a company have the sort of reputation that can be protected by the law of defamation? The courts have decided that it does, and the law reports abound in decisions involving corporate plaintiffs. In Hong Kong, even newspapers regularly sue for defamation (see recently *Oriental Press Group Ltd v Inmediahk.net Ltd* [2012] 2 HKLRD 1004, and *Oriental Press Group Ltd v Fevaworks Solutions* Ltd [2013] 5 HKC 253 to name just a few). In *China Youth Development Ltd v Next Magazine Publishing Ltd & Others* (2000) HCA 6206/1994, a charity successfully sued for defamation. But a company cannot sue for a statement that does not affect its trading reputation. If the statement is about the company's individual employees or directors, the company will not be able to sue even if it has actually suffered concrete harm.

> A mission which ran a hospital sued for defamation but the court held that the statements referred to the doctors only and not the mission itself (despite a loss in donations suffered by the mission). (*The President in Hong Kong of the Basel Evangelical Missionary Society v The Hong Kong Sheng Po Co. Ltd.* (1909) 7 HKLR 170)
>
> Another court was prepared to accept that a statement critical of a university could be viewed as defamatory of its president, on the basis that accusations were implied against the president (decision overturned on other grounds by the Court of Appeal). (*Hong Kong Polytechnic University & Others v Next Magazine Publishing* [1997] HKLRD 102)

5.4 The dead

The law does not protect the reputations of people who have died. Hong Kong people might think this is not very respectful of the dead, but the idea is that once you are dead you no longer have any reputation that needs protecting. The action is thought to be so closely tied up with the personality of the individual person that if a person was alive when the statement was made but dies before or during the court action, the action also dies. This also applies if the person being sued dies. (Companies cannot die, of course.) If the statement also affects other living individuals in the sense that they are lowered in their reputations, they could sue.

6. Who can be sued?

The basic position is that anyone involved in the production and dissemination of a defamatory statement can be sued. The writer, the publisher, the printer, and the bookseller can all be sued. However, a special defence, innocent dissemination (section 6.6 below), may serve to relieve some of these persons of liability. Moreover, an employer may be vicariously liable for defamation by an employee acting in the course of employment. It does not follow that all persons involved in the publication will be sued. It is not worth suing someone who has no resources, and there may well be a reason — financial, political, or other — for suing a particular defendant.

6.1 Writers and speakers

Those who author or deliver a statement are the obvious defendants. However, it would be unusual to sue an actor who delivered a defamatory line written by a playwright. The principles are the same whatever the form of communication, including e-mails (for Hong Kong cases concerning email defamation see *Drummond v Kwaku* [2000] 1 HKLRD 604, *Emperor (China Concept) Investments Limited v SBI E-2 Capital Securities Limited & Another* [2005] 4 HKLRD L6, *Wang Lin Jia v Ng Kai Cheung* (2008) HCA 113/2008, and *Yokview Company Limited v Lo Ying Kit and Others* (2011) DCCJ 5136/2009).

6.2 Reporters

Someone (like a journalist) who reports what someone else has said is also liable, as is the original speaker (section 4.4 above). If the journalist *mis*reports what was said — and makes an innocent statement appear defamatory — the journalist but not the speaker could be liable.

6.3 Editors

Editors of newspapers have to take responsibility for everything printed, though they may not have read every word. Sub-editors would be among those responsible legally for the particular items they deal with.

6.4 Printers

Printers are in an odd position. In the past they had to read every word as they typeset it. Possibly they did not think about the sense, but concentrated on ensuring that they reproduced the text accurately. In Hong Kong, where many books are printed, perhaps by people who do not read the language in which they are printed, it could be a harsh approach to hold printers liable. Nonetheless, that is the theoretical position. As time has gone by and printing practices have changed, printers read less and less of what they produce. In England, the Defamation Act 1996 provides that printers are not liable for defamation just because they printed something, but there is no such enactment in Hong Kong.

6.5 Publishers

The publisher of a book, newspaper, or other publication would be liable for any defamation which it contains.

6.6 Booksellers, distributors and libraries

In principle anyone who sells a book or lends it to another person or spreads its contents is a publisher and can be liable for any defamation in it. But long ago the courts recognized that this may be unrealistic and may lead to unreasonable results. Booksellers, distributors and libraries have so many publications that they simply do not have time to read them all. The common law defence of innocent dissemination is available to such "subordinate publishers", if they merely assisted in the dissemination of the publication with no knowledge that it contained anything defamatory, and no reason to believe that it did. The burden of proving innocent dissemination is on the defendant. The courts will not accept the defence if there was a reason to suspect that the publication was defamatory. For example, a book about particularly scandalous events is quite likely to contain defamatory statements, and the sellers, libraries, etc. cannot hide behind innocent dissemination. The courts will also reject the defence where, as in *Chau Hoi Shuen v SEEC Media Group Ltd* (2012) HCA 1194/2010, the distributor's distribution system makes it effectively impossible for it to vet the publication before it is sent to subscribers. In that case the court rejected the innocent dissemination defence not only because the Hong Kong-based defendant failed to take care to identify possible libels from clues on the cover of the Beijing-based magazine it distributed in Hong Kong and overseas, but because the defendant's distribution system was such that the magazine was sent to subscribers before it even reached the defendant and thus before the defendant's staff could have had any opportunity to check the magazine's contents.

6.7 Broadcasting organizations

Broadcasting is another way of publishing and such organizations are also liable, even for an unscripted remark in a live broadcast (see e.g. M. Chow, "Jury Clears

Hosts But Finds Radio Firm Liable", *South China Morning Post*, 26 February 2000, summarizing a jury trial in which Commercial Radio was held liable for remarks made by a caller to its phone-in radio show).

6.8 Internet service providers (ISPs)

ISPs have a particular problem. The Internet seems to offer a great temptation to people to defame, especially in e-mails and in internet bulletin boards. An ISP which hosts a discussion forum may have had no or limited control over what was posted but is nonetheless a publisher. Some jurisdictions, including England, the US, and Australia, have introduced legislation to give protection to ISPs to varying degrees. In Hong Kong there has been no such legislation. However, recent Hong Kong case law confirms that ISPs will be eligible for the defence of innocent dissemination in the same way as booksellers and libraries, despite their more primary role as providers of the medium through which communications are published — see *Oriental Press Group Ltd v Inmediahk.net Ltd* [2012] 2 HKLRD 1004; and *Oriental Press Group Ltd v Fevaworks Solutions* Ltd [2013] 5 HKC 253. Hong Kong courts have not yet had to deal with cases involving internet search engines as defendants, but it is expected that similar leniency will be applied. In a recent UK case, the popular search engine Google was found not liable for "snippets" of defamatory comments that turned up in its search results, because its use was automated, requiring no human input (*Metropolitan International Schools Ltd. v Designtechnica Corp*, (2011) 1 WLR 1743; see also *Payam Tamiz v Google Inc* [2012] EMLR 24). A lawsuit challenging Google's search engine results as defamatory was filed in Hong Kong in mid-2012 and was pending as of late 2013 (*Yeung, Sau Shing, Albert v Google, Inc.* HCA 1383/2012).

7. What the plaintiff does *not* have to prove

Defamation is a serious problem for the media because of the things that a plaintiff does not have to prove in order to succeed. The basic rules have been developed by the courts, but there are some statutory provisions, mainly in the Defamation Ordinance, which provide some additional protection for the media (as discussed in section 13 below).

7.1 Intention

It is not necessary to show that the defendant *intended* to make a defamatory statement at all or intended to make it about the particular plaintiff.

7.2 Untruth

It is not necessary for the plaintiff to show that the statement was untrue. It is open to the defendant to try to argue that the statement was in fact true (see section 9 below). Given that plaintiffs are usually advised by their lawyers to give evidence in the case, they run the risk of being asked questions by the defendant's lawyer about whether the statement was true, and if it was they may get caught out.

7.3 Damage

All that the plaintiff has to show is that the statement would lower his or her reputation in the eyes of right-thinking people. It is not necessary to prove that a single person actually did believe it. Even if anyone did believe it, the plaintiff does not have to prove that this actually led to any loss of esteem or any other form of damage to reputation (though this is less true in the case of slander; see section 8.3 below).

8. Slander and libel

The difference between slander and libel is of limited interest to the media. This topic is included here for the sake of completeness.

8.1 The basic difference

A statement that is written and is defamatory is an example of libel. A statement that is spoken is slander. The logic to this distinction is that people should be more cautious or think twice before they write than before they speak. And things that are written are often more long-lasting than things which are merely spoken. The spoken word also has a more restricted circulation than the written in many circumstances; before modern methods of communication the spoken word could be communicated only to people within a few metres. So the courts would hold that a statue that is defamatory of the plaintiff is a form of libel — being equivalent more to writing than to speech. The distinction arises from English legal history as much as from logic. These days there are so many borderline situations that the distinction should be abolished. A number of countries have done so, but not Hong Kong. Some difficult cases are presented below; then the question "what difference does it make whether something is libel or slander" will be examined.

8.2 Difficult cases

8.2.1 Radio, film, recordings, etc.

The distinction between slander and libel developed in the days before modern means of communication. The radio was the first form of mass simultaneous communication, soon to be followed by television. Was this slander or libel? This is now dealt with by the Defamation Ordinance s 22 which reads:

> For the purposes of the law of libel and slander, the broadcasting of words shall be treated as publication in permanent form.

Defamation in a radio or television broadcast is therefore considered libel. It was long ago held that defamation in film was libel (*Youssoupoff v MGM* (1934) 50 TLR 581). And Internet publications have been repeatedly treated by the courts as libel, removing any controversy about that issue.

8.2.2 **Press conferences, performance, and dictation**

A press conference is an event at which words are spoken, but it has the purpose of generating printed or broadcast words. On the other hand, a lecture or a performed play often transforms the printed word into the spoken word. (A lecture probably does both — lecturers' written words are transformed into spoken words, then they are transformed into students' written notes.) Dictation to a secretary, or a shorthand writer in court or in the Legislative Council, transforms the spoken word into the written word. If these various statements are defamatory, are they libel or slander? These may be entertaining possibilities, but rarely give rise in practice to any problem. There have been cases in which the courts have held that a play is libel — if based on a written script — or that someone who gives a press conference is liable in libel for the resultant publication, since that is the purpose of a press conference. If faced with any of these issues, the journalist would be best advised to seek the opinion of a specialist. Incidentally, in the UK a stage play is libel (even if some words spoken in the course of the play are spontaneous and not scripted), because of an Act of Parliament, but there is no such law in Hong Kong.

8.3 **The implications**

What difference does it make whether something is libel or slander? The most important difference is that in the case of libel the plaintiff need not show that he or she suffered some actual damage from the libel. In the case of slander, such damage must be shown. But there are four exceptions to this rule. In the following cases, it is not necessary to show damage from the slander:

1. If the plaintiff is alleged to have committed a criminal offence: The offence must be one for which there is some physical punishment available, which these days means prison, not just a fine. Therefore a Hong Kong court decided that where a person said that another had been convicted of an unspecified offence, but had been bound over to keep the peace, there was no allegation of an offence that could be punished physically (*Chan Chook Tim v Wong Kwok Hung* [2004] 1 HKC 18).
2. If the plaintiff is alleged to have some terrible disease: Clearly venereal disease, leprosy, and perhaps smallpox are in this category; but there has been no decision about HIV/AIDS.
3. If the plaintiff is alleged to be unfit for his or her "business or calling": there is a slight extension of this category by virtue of s 23 of the Defamation Ordinance.
4. If a female plaintiff is alleged to be unchaste: This Victorian oddity might succumb to challenge under the Basic Law or other human rights legislation, because it penalizes statements about women only. Defamation Ordinance, s 21:

> Words spoken and published which impute unchastity or adultery to any woman or girl shall not require special damage to render them actionable.

It should also be noted that there is an offence of criminal libel (see section 5 of the Defamation Ordinance) but no criminal offence of slander.

9. The defence of "justification" (truth)

9.1 Basic idea

The purpose of defamation law is to protect reputations — deserved reputations. So if a defamatory statement is true, the plaintiff should not be able to sue. (If the person complaining decides to bring a criminal prosecution rather than a civil action, the rule is slightly different — see section 17, crime of defamatory libel, below.) Some people have suggested that the law is unsatisfactory and that a plaintiff should be required to prove that the statement complained of is untrue, but this suggestion has not really been taken up by lawmakers.

If the defendant sets out to prove that the spoken or written statement is true, it is not enough to show that someone else, however respectable, thought it was true. Even if the original statement was something like "It is rumoured that . . ." or "X says that . . ." it is not good enough to prove that indeed there was a rumour or X actually had said it. The reason is that by repeating the story or rumour, the defendant has given some support to the content of the statement, and so the defendant must prove that the content was true.

The fact that the statement is true must be proved "on a balance of probabilities". That is, the court must be satisfied that the statement was more likely than not true. If it is a serious allegation, especially if a criminal offence was mentioned, the evidence that it was true will have to be really convincing. The more serious the allegation, the more convincing the proof must be.

Suppose the statement made was that a person had committed a criminal offence, and he or she had actually been found guilty of the offence by a court. Could the issue be re-opened in a civil court through an action for defamation, with the plaintiff arguing that the conviction was wrong? The answer now is "no". Some years ago the law was changed to prevent this happening and to provide that a conviction is conclusive evidence of guilt (Evidence Ordinance (Cap 8), s 64(1)).

On the other hand, the Rehabilitation of Offenders Ordinance (Cap 297) prevents certain (relatively minor) previous convictions being brought up in court to prove a fact. Under this ordinance, if a person has been convicted in Hong Kong of an offence and not sentenced to imprisonment for more than three months or to a fine over HK$10,000, and it was a first conviction, and the person was not convicted for any further offence within three years, no evidence may be brought in any court to prove the conviction. If the offence was connected with being a member of a triad society, the person must have renounced membership in order for the conviction to lapse in this way (s 2). So the media could not use the fact of the conviction to show that the person actually committed the act. If the defamatory statement was that the person had been a triad member, for example, an offence which had lapsed under this ordinance could not be used to prove that the statement was true. The defendant must find some other evidence to prove it.

For the defence of justification to succeed, it is necessary to prove that what was actually said or written — and not something else, however, damaging — was actually true. If the statement was something like "Y beats his wife" and the defendant could not prove this was true, but could prove that Y murdered his child, this would not mean that "truth" of the statement was established.

It is a bit risky to rely on truth as a defence. If the defendant fails to prove that the statement was true, the court may increase the damages the defendant has to pay. The reason is that the defendant has not only defamed the plaintiff untruthfully, but has compounded this by insisting that the statement was true. In *Mak Shiu Tong v Yue Kwok Ying, Sekit & Another* [2005] 1 HKLRD 33, Ribeiro PJ made the point that justification involves a repetition of the alleged defamation, in effect, a further attack on the plaintiff, and if the defendant does not have reasonable evidence to support the plea of justification, an order to pay aggravated damages may be warranted. The principle was applied in *Lee Ching & Another v Lau May Ming* (2007) HCA 108/2005. The failed plea of justification was taken into account in awarding additional ("aggravated") damages in the amount of HK$200,000. However, the mere fact that a defendant sticks to a defence of justification and does not offer an apology does not mean that an award of aggravated damages is indicated. The decision, in good faith, to rely on justification and therefore to not offer an apology may be entirely reasonable on the facts of the case, as in *Blakeney-Williams v Cathay Pacific Airways Ltd* (2012) 15 HKCFAR 261.

There are only a few Hong Kong cases in which the defence of justification has been successful. Examples include *Khan v O'Dea* [1985] HKLR 237 and *Woo Tak Yan v Lam Sik Chuen* (2011) DCCJ 5381/2009 (both applying section 26 of the Defamation Ordinance) and *Drummond v Kwaku* [2000] 1 HKLRD 604. Another example, involving the media, is *Next Publications v Oriental Press Group Ltd* [2000] 2 HKC 557, where the judge held that the Oriental Press had, as alleged, deliberately quoted out of context.

9.2 **Problem cases — the sting**

If the statement in question is largely true but is inaccurate to some minor extent, can a defamatory action succeed? If there was basically one allegation and this is largely true, the court will ask, "Is the 'sting' of the statement true?" An English case involved a statement that a person had been to prison for three weeks, when in fact it was for two weeks only. The court accepted that this was essentially a true statement.

However, if the plaintiff is complaining of two or three separate statements, the situation is a bit more complicated. The Defamation Ordinance, s 26 states:

> In an action for libel or slander in respect of words containing two or more distinct charges against the plaintiff, a defence of justification shall not fail by reason only that the truth of every charge is not proved if the words not proved

> to be true do not materially injure the plaintiff's reputation having regard to the truth of the remaining charges.

In other words, when more than one statement was made, but only some were proved to be true, if the result is that the plaintiff's reputation is left seriously damaged by the statements that were true, so that the untrue statements do not cause any damage, the court will treat the whole as being true. In *Khan v O'Dea & Another* [1985] HKLR 237, some of the statements were found to be true. One was not, but the judge applied section 26 of the Defamation Ordinance in favour of the defendant. A similar result was reached in *Wong Sui Fung v Yip Siu-keung* (2003) HCA 5595/2000.

There is a twist to this: if the plaintiff chooses to sue only for the least serious allegation, knowing it could not be proved to be true, it would not be possible to argue that any other allegation made was true.

10. Situations where all statements are protected (absolute privilege)

There are a few people who have special protection. They can say what they want, in the course of their duties, without having any legal liability. It is not so much the office as the situation which gives this immunity. Some immunities apply to the media when reporting important public events. It is mainly the law and government to which this immunity applies, although not to all governmental or legal transactions. The immunity is known as "absolute privilege". In these situations freedom of speech has been given greater weight than protection of reputation. As stated by Judge Sakhrani in *Ng Chiu Mui v Shum Lik Keung* [2011] 5 HKLRD 88, where absolute privilege applies, no action will lie even where the defendant published the words with full knowledge of their falsity and even with the express intention of injuring the claimant.

10.1 Legislative Council

The privileges of Parliament were the result of historic battles with the monarchy, and the results of those battles benefit political debate and the members of the Legislative Council today. The Legislative Council (Powers and Privileges) Ordinance (Cap 382), s 3 states:

> There shall be freedom of speech and debate in the Council or proceedings before a committee, and such freedom of speech and debate shall not be liable to be questioned in any court or place outside the Council.

10.2 Courts and tribunals

Everything said in court — by the judge, a party, a witness, or a lawyer — is protected. Documents prepared for a court case, including letters between lawyers in the run-up to a court case, are also protected (*Wong Shiu Kee v Victor Chu* [2001] 2 HKC 589). The same applies to tribunals. Absolute privilege was accorded in *Ng Chiu Mui v Shum Lik Keung* [2011] 5 HKLRD 88 to the defendants, witnesses in a Securities and Futures Commission (SFC) investigation, who gave evidence in the investigation in which the plaintiffs were found guilty of improper conduct leading to their licence suspension.

10.3 High officers of state

Communications between very important public officers are given the same protection. These would probably include communications between the Chief Executive and a minister, or the Chief Executive and senior government officers in Beijing.

10.4 Reports

Section 13(1) of the Defamation Ordinance provides that a report in a newspaper of any court proceedings in Hong Kong will have this immunity, provided that the report is fair, accurate, and contemporaneous (meaning close in time to the proceedings which are reported). The ordinance uses the word "privileged", but English cases, which would almost certainly be followed in Hong Kong, have held that in this context this means *absolutely* privileged.

10.5 Other points

Some ordinances provide that statements in certain contexts are absolutely privileged; for example, the Ombudsman Ordinance (Cap 397) protects statements to the Ombudsman (s 18). Other ordinances say that statements in certain contexts cannot give rise to any defamation claim (which has the same effect); for example, publishing a disciplinary order under section 28 of the Architects Registration Ordinance (Cap 408).

11. Situations where statements are protected if no "malice" (qualified privilege)

In many situations there is some protection for statements, but this protection is lost if there was some improper reason for making the statement. So the privilege is not absolute, or complete, but "qualified". The importance of freedom of speech is balanced against other interests.

11.1 Everyday situations of qualified privilege

For the defence of qualified privilege to apply, a relationship between the person making the statement and the person receiving it must exist, in that the person receiving it has a legitimate interest in doing so, and the person making it has a duty (legal, social or moral only) to do so. Classic examples of activities that would attract qualified privilege include the writing of a job-related reference letter, the reporting of an offence to the police, as well as discussions at meetings of clubs and at management committees of building owners' corporations (an area of frequent defamation litigation in Hong Kong). A less obvious example would be circumstances in which a person defends himself or herself against attack. Here, the person making the statement does not have a duty to make the statement, but has a valid interest in doing so.

> A typical Hong Kong example of qualified privilege involved the management committee of a residential development. The plaintiff was the chair, and the defendant was asked by the owners of the flats to supervise some aspects of maintenance works being carried out on the development. The two had a disagreement over the work and the defendant circulated the committee members and owners with statements accusing the plaintiff of incompetence and dishonesty. The judge said that the committee members and owners had a duty and interest to receive the statements made by the defendant, who had a corresponding duty and interest to make them. (*Ho Ping Kwong v Chan Cordelia* [1989] 2 HKC 415)

In all such cases the privilege only covers communications to the person with the corresponding interest or duty to receive it. If the communication is made too widely, the privilege is said to have been exceeded.

11.2 **Reports in the press**

The courts have recognized a few situations where reports in the press are privileged. The clearest example would be a report in the press of a court case somewhere else in which people in Hong Kong would have a legitimate interest. Probably a report of a court case in mainland China which involved a Hong Kong person would be covered. Reports on cases in Hong Kong would have absolute privilege, as shown above (see section 10.4).

The category of protected reports has been much extended by the Defamation Ordinance s 14 and with the schedule, which provides that certain newspaper or broadcast reports have qualified privilege. There are two categories of report:

1. Reports of proceedings of Commonwealth courts and legislatures (it still refers just to the Commonwealth here, which means that reports of mainland court proceedings would have to rely on the common law privilege), of international organizations and courts, copies of registers kept under statute, and court notices. A provision that included "any proceedings before a court martial held outside Hong Kong" under UK law was amended in 2012 to such proceedings "of the Chinese Liberation Army held outside Hong Kong".
2. Reports of meetings or decisions of associations, boards, companies and lawful public meetings (which was held in a British case to include a press conference open to the public).

Reports of the second kind are privileged only "subject to explanation or contradiction". This means that the privilege is lost if the plaintiff asked the defendant to publish a statement explaining or contradicting the original report and the latter refused to do so or has done so inadequately. The original report must also be a fair and accurate account of the proceedings reported.

There is a particular situation of qualified privilege that is sometimes important for the press. If certain individuals have been attacked, and they choose to defend themselves, a defamatory statement they make in the course of that self-defence may be a "privileged" statement. The courts may recognize that some people may be rather vigorous when defending themselves.

> The wife of a man who had tried to commit suicide made certain allegations to the press against the institution he worked for. The principal of the institution replied and the situation was held to be privileged. (*Wan Chiu Ying v Tam Wai Chu* (2005) HCA 3479/2002)

11.3 **"Malice"**

The protection, or privilege, is qualified. It only applies if the statement was made without "malice". It is the plaintiff's responsibility to argue and prove that the statement was made maliciously. Malice here means an improper motive; a proper motive would be to communicate the information for the purposes the law envisages, for the benefit of the recipient or the protection of the communicator, etc. An improper motive might be an intention to hurt the person who is the subject of the statement (as in *Drummond v Kwaku* [2000] 1 HKLRD 604). If the plaintiff is to succeed in arguing that malice defeats the defence, it must be shown that malice motivated the statement. However, since the courts recognize that people may have mixed motives, they would require that the *dominant* factor is malice. In most situations if the plaintiff could prove that the defendant did not actually believe in the truth of what was said, this would show malice. But just being angry or even rude would not be malice (though being rude might be *evidence* that the person speaking or writing was actually malicious). In the *Cordelia Chan* case (section 11.1 above), the judge observed that the defendant was persistent and stubborn, and even irritating, intolerant, and over-suspicious among other characteristics, but he concluded that she was sincere, and not malicious in the sense of acting from a wrong motive.

Mere carelessness or unreasonable belief in the truth of the statement will not qualify as malice. In *Tsang Hon Chu v Wong Kwok Leung* (2005) DCCJ 3917/2003, a student's condemnation of the plaintiff's teaching was found to be inaccurately based on his poor recollection of events, but was nonetheless not treated as malice for the purposes of qualified privilege. On the other hand, recklessly making a statement, not caring whether it was true, was held to constitute malice on the part of the signators of a letter (all of whom were residential owners in the same block) in which the plaintiff, a member of their residents' sub-committee was defamed. The signators were found to have signed the letter either with knowledge of the errors it contained, or recklessly not caring about the truth or falsity of the allegations it contained (*Lee Man Kin v Wang Mei Chun & Others* (2005) HCA 2876/2003).

11.4 Public discussion of public affairs, politics, etc.

11.4.1 The issue

Democracy depends on public interest and participation, and these days much of this discussion takes places in the media. Expressions of opinion on matters of politics and public affairs, provided they are based on facts, will usually be protected by the defence discussed in section 12 below (honest comment), but what about statements which appear to be of fact? Would they have qualified privilege? There is one slightly curious rule in the Defamation Ordinance, s 28:

> A defamatory statement published by or on behalf of a candidate in any election to the Legislative Council or to a District Council shall not be deemed to be published on a privileged occasion on the ground that it is material to a question in issue in the election . . .

This is a rather unfortunate restriction of political discussion at election time, which was designed to reverse the effect of a particular court decision in England in 1948. It would not apply to media discussion because that would not be "by or on behalf of the candidate".

Generally the courts have taken the view that the media have no special privilege not enjoyed by ordinary citizens. Public or media discussion of public affairs, if it involves statements of fact, has not generally been given the protection of qualified privilege. It was felt that "interest", in the sense in which it is used in qualified privilege, could not be extended so widely. Recent cases in a number of countries have modified this approach.

11.4.2 Public interest defence

In many countries there has in recent years been a greater willingness to recognize the role of the news media and to protect from defamation lawsuits the timely dissemination of information of importance to the public, including, but not necessarily limited to, political issues. This has resulted in the introduction of a new defence, originally a variant of qualified privilege, but soon styled as the "public interest defence", in order to distinguish it from qualified privilege as conventionally understood, and also to underline its broad social function in protecting journalistic material of a minimum threshold of public importance.

In English law the introduction of the defence took place in *Reynolds v Times Newspapers Ltd* [2001] 2 AC 127. Albert Reynolds had recently resigned from his position as prime minister of the Republic of Ireland. *The Sunday Times* newspaper in London published an article about the resignation. Reynolds pleaded that the sting of the article was that he had lied to the Dáil [Irish Parliament] and his cabinet colleagues. The reasons for Reynolds' resignation were of public significance and interest in the United Kingdom because he was one of the chief architects of the Northern Ireland peace process. In the leading judgment Lord Nicholls (at the time also a non-permanent member of the Court of Final Appeal of Hong Kong) said that the question was, as in qualified privilege whether there existed the necessary duty and/or interest, but he thought it was simpler to say, "Was the public entitled to know the particular information?" Then the question was whether the report met the standard of responsible journalism. The court held that the following factors might be relevant to this question:

1. The seriousness of the allegation. The more serious the charge, the more the public is misinformed and the individual harmed, if the allegation is not true.
2. The nature of the information, and the extent to which the subject-matter is a matter of public concern.
3. The source of the information. Some informants have no direct knowledge of the events. Some have their own axes to grind, or are being paid for their stories.
4. The steps taken to verify the information.
5. The status of the information. The allegation may have already been the subject of an investigation which commands respect.
6. The urgency of the matter. News is often a perishable commodity.
7. Whether comment was sought from the plaintiff. He may have information others do not possess or have not disclosed. An approach to the plaintiff will not always be necessary.
8. Whether the article contained the gist of the plaintiff's side of the story.
9. The tone of the article. A newspaper can raise queries or call for an investigation. It need not adopt allegations as statements of fact.
10. The circumstances of the publication, including the timing.

This list of ten factors is not to be treated as exhaustive, and not all will be relevant to every case. Precisely what is covered by the new defence is evolving as the cases are decided by the courts. Allegations of serious misconduct or corruption on the part of public figures (as in *Reynolds*) are obvious examples where the defence can apply. In *Bonnick v Morris* [2003] 1 AC 300, a case from Jamaica, the court said, "The general tone of the article was restrained. [The plaintiff] was approached, and his comments were printed even-handedly beside those of the anonymous source. The article did not associate itself with one or other of the two divergent versions of the events." The defence was accepted.

However, in *Galloway v Telegraph Group* [2005] EMLR 7, a case brought by an English member of Parliament against a newspaper that alleged he had profited from the United Nations' "oil-for-food programme" in Iraq, the judge held that the paper had gone further than raising comments on the documents it relied on, had drawn its own conclusions and added its own comments and therefore the defence did not apply.

The House of Lords revisited the public interest defence in *Jameel v Wall Street Journal Europe* [2006] 3 WLR 642. In this case the defendant newspaper had published an article reporting that Saudi Arabian authorities were cooperating with US authorities in monitoring the bank accounts of certain prominent Saudis, including the claimants who were named in the article, for evidence that they supported terrorism. In allowing the defence the court revised the defence as introduced in

Reynolds in certain important aspects. The privilege does not require proof of a reciprocal duty/interest relationship in the conventional sense because, according to Lord Hoffmann, it is the subject matter, not the occasion, that is privileged: "If the publication is in the public interest, the duty and interest are taken to exist." Moreover, "there is no question of the privilege being defeated by proof of malice because the propriety of the conduct of the defendant is built into the conditions under which the material is privileged." What is important is whether the steps taken to gather and publish the information were responsible and fair. In this context, Lord Nicholls' ten non-exclusive factors identified in *Reynolds* "are not tests that the publication has to pass . . . but . . . must be applied in a practical and flexible manner."

In Hong Kong, the defence was first applied in *Cutting de Heart v Sun News Ltd & Another* [2005] 3 HKLRD 133, a case decided before *Jameel*. The case concerned an article published in the Readers' Complaints column of the defendant's newspaper about unsatisfactory hair treatment provided by the plaintiff's hair salon, and about the plaintiff's refusal to honour its "satisfaction guarantee". The article was held to be protected by the public interest defence, the court giving a wide reading to the meaning of "public interest" in *Reynolds v Times Newspapers Ltd.*

In *Yaqoob v Asia Times Online Ltd.* [2008] 4 HKLRD 911, an internet news service had published an article alleging money laundering, terrorist financing and drug trafficking by a prominent Pakistani businessman and his companies based in Dubai. The court found the defence not proved because, on consideration of Lord Nicholls' ten factors, the defendant had not engaged in responsible journalism. In particular, sources had not been adequately checked, and the journalist's faxed questions to the plaintiff did not provide a real opportunity for the plaintiff to comment on the allegations as envisioned in *Reynolds*; they were written casually, directed to a corporate fax number, and focused on the plaintiff's gold-trading rather than the allegations of illegal activity.

Subsequently, the scope of the public interest defence was further broadened by a decision of the Privy Council (the UK-based appeals court that serves as the final court of appeal for some former British colonies) hearing an appeal from Jamaica, *Seaga v Harper* [2009] 1 AC 1. The Privy Council extended the defence beyond the press and broadcasting media to publications of material of public interest by any person in any medium, so long as the conditions framed by Lord Nicholls in *Reynolds* for "responsible journalism" were satisfied. The Hong Kong Court of Appeal applied the defence to a press release in an employment dispute in *Blakeney-Williams v Cathay Pacific Airways Ltd.* A group of dismissed airline pilots sued their former employer alleging wrongful termination for their participation in trade union activities. The airline's press release asserted that the terminated pilots could not be relied upon to act in the best interests of the company, a defamatory statement. Its attempt to rely on the public interest defence was considered by the court, although the court preferred the term "responsible public dissemination" rather than "public interest defence". The privilege defence failed, however, because there was insufficient evidence to support the allegation and because the press release did not include the pilots' perspective or response.

The public interest defence was most recently considered by the Supreme Court of the United Kingdom (the court that replaced the House of Lords as the UK's highest court in 2009) in *Flood v Times Newspapers Ltd* [2012] 2 WLR 760, a case concerning the publication of an article in the defendant's newspaper alleging wrongful disclosure of information and corruption by a police officer. The court identified a distinction to be made between the standard of verification required in cases of "reportage", where the publication repeats allegations made by others, and cases of original allegation: "Reportage is a special, and relatively rare, form of *Reynolds* privilege. It arises where it is not the content of a reported allegation that is of public interest, but the fact that the allegation has been made. It protects the publisher if he has taken proper steps to verify the making of the allegation and provided that he does not adopt it." On the other hand, a more exacting verification standard is required for original allegations, in which case the "privilege will normally only be earned where the publisher has taken reasonable steps to satisfy himself that the allegation is true before he publishes it". The court also amplified the meaning of public interest. A distinction must be made between material the publication of which is *in* the public interest, and material that is merely of public interest, which is much wider. Lord Bingham's dicta in the Court of Appeal in *Reynolds* was cited approvingly: "By that we mean matters relating to the public life of the community and those who take part in it, including within the expression 'public life' activities such as the conduct of government and political life, elections . . . and public administration, but we use the expression more widely than that, to embrace matters such as (for instance) the governance of public bodies, institutions and companies which give rise to a public interest in disclosure, but excluding matters which are personal and private, such that there is no public interest in their disclosure."

Finally, the defence was considered again in Hong Kong in *Pui Kwan Kay v Ming Pao Holdings Ltd* (2013) HCA 854/2009, and once again it was rejected. The court found that the defendant newspaper failed to sufficiently verify what the plaintiff football promoter said at a post-press conference interview. Based on a news story about the interview by one of its reporters, the newspaper published an editorial that suggested the plaintiff had in the interview attempted to conceal his association with a football team suspected of match-fixing. The court ruled that the seriousness of the allegations and the format in which they appeared — an editorial as opposed to a news story — required the defendant to exercise greater care about the accuracy of the allegations. The court said that before publication the defendant should have reviewed articles in seven other newspapers to try and verify the accuracy of its own reporter's story. At a minimum, the defendant should have in its editorial alerted readers to the differing accounts in the other newspapers. Such requirements could be considered cumbersome because they seem to require an additional layer of verification with sources that may not be available or whose reliability cannot be independently tested, a burden that goes against the spirit of the defence as originally conceived.

12. Honest comment (formerly "fair comment")

This defence, formerly known as "fair comment", but re-styled because of recent developments in the leading Hong Kong case, *Cheng v Tse* [2000] 3 HKLRD 418, protects honest expressions of opinion on matters of public interest. It applies only to a comment, not a statement which purports to be one of fact. This is another important defence for the media but is not restricted to them.

12.1 The rationale

Matters in the public eye should be debated freely. This is a necessary condition for a free and democratic society, and is recognized in international human rights instruments and in the constitutions of most advanced nations.

12.2 The basic requirements

According to the Court of Final Appeal in *Cheng v Tse* [2000] 3 HKLRD 418, in order to rely on this defence the defendant must prove to the satisfaction of the court that:

1. The matter under discussion was one of public interest — [which is] "not to be confined within narrow limits". This includes matters like politics, education, religion, and also anything which is deliberately placed before the public such as literature, works of art, etc. In *Oriental Press Group v Next Publications* [2003] 1 HKLRD 751, the Court of Final Appeal was clear that the dealings in shares in a public company by the vice-chairman of the company was a matter of public interest.
2. The comment must be recognisable as comment, as distinct from an imputation of fact. This is not always easy to decide, for the same remark may be a statement of fact or a comment depending on the circumstances. If the imputation is one of fact, a ground of defence must be sought elsewhere, for example justification [i.e. the defence of truth].
3. The statement must be based on facts which are true or protected by privilege.
4. The facts on which the comment is based must either be stated, or referred to so the reader can make his own evaluation of the comment. However, it was subsequently held that the facts on which a comment is based need not be so particularized in the publication that readers or listeners are able to judge for themselves how far the comment was well founded because such a requirement would be unnecessarily stifling of free speech. According to Lord Phillips in *Joseph v Spiller* [2011] 1 AC 852, all that is required is that the comment "identify at least in general terms what it is that led the commentator to make the comment so that the reader can understand what the comment is about".
5. The comment must be "fair" but only in the sense that it must be a comment which could have been made by someone who was being honest.

It is not very easy for a defendant to satisfy all these requirements and many attempts to do so have failed because the underlying facts, if they existed, were not referred to, or the statement was not comment. In one important case the courts accepted that a statement made in a television programme was fair comment: "If every time other people mention about you only incidentally then you say you are not satisfied and want to sue, this is akin to frightening people into keeping their mouths shut." This was spoken of a media organization and based on the fact that it had brought a number of actions for defamation. *(Eastern Express Publisher Ltd. v Mo Man Ching Claudia* [1999] 4 HKC 425)

In another case the court decided that to say that the newspaper was acting pettily and was over-reacting, and that it was not being fair and balanced nor acting ethically, were statements of opinion, and met the requirements of fair comment. (*Oriental Daily Publisher Ltd v Ming Pao Holdings* [1999] 4 HKC 354)

12.3 The end of "malice"

It is often said that, like qualified privilege, a defence of fair comment will not succeed if the plaintiff can show that it was motivated by "malice". In *Cheng v Tse,* the Court of Final Appeal decided that malice in the context of fair comment means only one thing: that the person making the statement did not believe it to be true or justified. This is a significant expansion of the defence and an important development for press freedom. Provided that he or she did believe the statement, it makes no difference that the purpose in making it was spite, or desire for political or personal benefit, for example. For this reason the defence is no longer styled fair comment but honest comment. Interestingly, one of the members of the Court of Final Appeal in *Oriental Press Group v Next Publications* (see section 12.2 above) suggested that the defence of fair comment would still apply if the defendant had a belief in the truth of *one* of the possible meanings of the statement, even if the court held this was not the "right meaning". This approach if adopted by the courts would further strengthen freedom of expression.

12.4 Fair comment in which the media publish someone else's opinion

If the statement which is giving rise to complaint is contained in a letter from a reader or some other contribution which is not authored by the publisher, is the publisher still liable? The issue of genuine opinion of the publisher seems less relevant here. The *Cheng* case does not deal with this point. However, assuming that it satisfies the requirements of public interest, etc., including being a statement that could have been made fairly and honestly, the defence should still be available. But whose honest belief is relevant to the question of the *Cheng*-style malice? The legal position is not entirely clear. The courts could take the view that the media lose the defence if they knew that the opinion was not the genuine opinion of the person who wrote the letter. Or it could be lost if the plaintiff could prove that the media did not share the view. One day a court will have to decide this. It seems that the press would be unwise to publish a statement, however fair on its face, which they knew could be shown not to be the opinion of the writer.

13. Special statutory defences for the press

Certain special defences have been provided for the media in the Defamation Ordinance. The important sections are 4 and 25. Both the defences are rather complex and technical, and rarely used.

13.1 Section 4 of the Defamation Ordinance

This section applies only to newspapers, defined in section 2 to mean "any paper containing public news or observations thereon or consisting wholly or mainly of advertisements which is printed for sale and is published in Hong Kong either periodically or in parts or numbers at intervals not exceeding thirty-six days". This would not cover a free publication (which is not "for sale"), nor an Internet publication. By virtue of section 4 a newspaper which is sued for libel could argue that:

1. There was no "actual malice" which would mean no intention to injure, and no "gross negligence".
2. That a full apology for the libel was inserted in the newspaper before the action began, or at the earliest opportunity.

At the same time as it raises this defence, the newspaper must pay some money into court as "amends". If the plaintiff accepts the defence, he or she may take the money and that is the end of the case. Hong Kong courts have held that the amount of money must be as much as the court would give as damages. If the plaintiff refuses to accept the sum and fights on, and the court agrees that the sum was not enough, the plaintiff wins and gets the higher sum plus costs, that is, their legal fees. If the plaintiff insists on going to court and the defendant fails to prove that there was no "actual malice" and no "gross negligence", the defence fails anyway. But if the plaintiff insists on going to court, but is awarded no more than the payment into court and the court finds that the other elements of the defence are satisfied, the plaintiff loses the case.

A rare example of an attempt at relying on the defence is *Chu Siu Kuk Yuen, Jessie v Apply Daily Ltd* [2002] 1 HKLRD 1. The defendant newspaper printed an item (in Chinese) headed "Suspected to have cheated clients, building funds and second mortgage loan proceeds, Yuen Long female solicitor disappeared with 2 million", which proceeded to identify the plaintiff. The story was based on information received by a reporter to the effect that complaints had been made against an unnamed solicitor. Having ascertained that the police had visited a certain building in Yuen Long in connection with the complaint, the reporter leapt to the conclusion that the plaintiff was the solicitor in question. The court held that the reporter's "assumptions and deductions had been made too carelessly" and rejected the defence.

13.2 Section 25 of the Defamation Ordinance

This is a more modern defence known as "unintentional defamation". It has not yet been used in any Hong Kong case. It is not restricted to the media, and it does not involve considerations of malice and gross negligence, but applies if a statement was published "innocently". This is defined to mean that either:

(a) the publisher did not intend the statement to refer to the plaintiff and did not know of circumstances which would mean the statement might be understood to refer to him, *or*

(b) the statement did not seem to be defamatory, and the publisher did not know of circumstances which would mean the statement might be understood to be defamatory; the publisher exercised all reasonable care.

In either case, it really covers only hidden meaning situations: innuendoes, and only "true innuendoes". There is also a requirement of an offer of "amends" which in this case means an offer to publish an apology and, if it is not a newspaper, to notify recipients of the document that the statement was untrue. The requirements of this defence are still very technical and it has been replaced in England by a less demanding one.

14. Other issues

There are a few other defences, most of which are rarely raised.

14.1 Consent

If someone says "hit me", this is likely to be a defence to a civil action for the resultant blow. Similarly, if someone invites defamation, this may be held to be consent. This is unusual. But it would apply if the person defamed willingly agreed to a letter, which had so far been shown only to him or her, being communicated to others.

On the other hand, if a member made a defamatory remark in the Legislative Council and the person affected said, "I challenge you to repeat that remark outside the Council Chamber," — that is in a non-privileged situation — and the member did so, this would not be consent. The court would view this as a challenge and a threat, not as agreement to be further defamed.

14.2 Time limits

Actions for defamation cannot be brought after a certain time has elapsed. In Hong Kong an action for libel or slander cannot be brought more than six years after the publication (Limitation Ordinance (Cap 347) s 4(1)(a)). This is a longer period than in most countries. For example, in the United Kingdom, the relevant period is one year from the date of publication (Limitation Act 1980, s 4A), as it is in New South Wales (The Limitation Act 1969, s 148). In the US, it varies from one to three years (see Citizen Media Law Project at http://www.citmedialaw.org/legal-guide/state-law-defamation), and in Ontario, Canada, it is three months from when the publication came to the plaintiff's attention (Libel and Slander Act R.S.O. 1990, c. L.12, s 6).

15. Remedies

15.1 Damages

The main remedy the law provides for someone who has been defamed is a sum of money — referred to as damages. The purpose of an award of damages is to try to compensate for the loss, to put the person in the same position as though he or she had never been defamed. Of course, this is impossible. How can money compensate for a lost reputation? On the other hand, because in libel cases, and some slander cases, the plaintiff does not have to prove that any loss was actually suffered, there is a risk that the damages will be rather generous. The awards of damages have not been as high in Hong Kong as they have been in the UK.

Usually the damages are assessed by the judge. In general an appeals court will be slow to set aside an award of general damages made at trial, and will do so only where it regards the award as manifestly wrong, or where the award is vitiated by some error made by the judge in assessing damages. An example of such an error is where in assessing general damages the court takes into account awards made in cases that are not relevant or comparable to the one under consideration (as in *Blakeney-Williams v Cathay Pacific Airways Ltd* (2012) 15 HKCFAR 261 and *Oriental Daily Publisher Ltd v Ming Pao Holdings Ltd* (2012) 15 HKCFAR 299).

If the trial is by jury, then it is the responsibility of the jury to decide. If the amount awarded is very excessive, or very low, the Court of Appeal would be prepared to intervene on appeal. So in the case of *Cheung Ng Sheong Steven v Eastweek Publisher Ltd* [1995] 3 HKC 601, a jury had awarded the plaintiff HK$2.4 million. The Court of Appeal said this was very high and ordered a re-trial on the question of damages. Unlike in some countries, there is no power for the Hong Kong court to substitute its own sum for that awarded by the jury.

15.1.1 Regular damages

How do the courts decide on the appropriate amount? They will look at the seriousness of the allegation, the reach of the publication, and the status of the plaintiff. On this basis a newspaper with a big circulation would have to pay more damages than a smaller paper, or than a non-media defendant, all other things being equal. The "viral" nature of social media and its potential to "percolate" by way of the Internet can be taken into account in the assessment of damages (*Cairns v Modi*; *John Raymond Luciw v Wolfgang Derler* (see section 4.1 above)). Courts also will take into account whether the defendant seemed to have set out to hurt (malice) the plaintiff, and whether there was any apology (apology is specifically mentioned in the Defamation Ordinance, s 3). The absence of an apology was a factor in the determination of aggravated damages in *John Raymond Luciw v Wolfgang Derler* but interestingly, the obvious malice in the creation of a false Facebook page intended to suggest that the plaintiff was a paedophiliac was not — because malice was not pleaded. The courts will look at levels of damages in other cases of a similar nature in order to try to be consistent. If the plaintiff can actually prove concrete damage, such as loss of a job, then the damages can compensate for this. In the case of *Chu Siu Kuk Yuen, Jessie* (see section 13.1 above), the court awarded damages for mental distress and illness.

Some people perhaps do not deserve a good reputation. Is it possible to argue this in court? It can be done, but it is not easy to succeed in this argument. The court must be satisfied that the plaintiff had a generally bad reputation (not actual fault but *reputation*), that this was in the same area of life as the statement which is the subject of the action, and that the bad reputation existed at the time of the defamation and did not come into effect later. There seem to be no Hong Kong cases where this line of argument has been attempted.

Awards of damages have sometimes been criticized as being too high in comparison with those given for physical injuries to a person. It does seem rather strange if a lost reputation leads to higher damages than a lost leg. In England the courts will now take the levels of damages for personal injuries into account (*John v MGN Ltd* [1997] QB 58), but in Hong Kong the courts have refused to do this (see *Cheung Ng Sheong Steven v Eastweek Publisher Ltd*). Unfortunately, perhaps, they did this following older English case law, before the English courts changed their view.

Actual awards of damages vary considerably. In *Sin Cho Chiu v Tin Tin Publication Development Ltd* [2002] 1 HKLRD A21 (see section 3.4 above), the plaintiff received HK$3 million; but in *Li Wei v Brightec Ltd* [2001] 1 HKLRD A18, concerning an article the judge described as "scandalous", the plaintiff received only HK$150,000.

15.1.2 **When damages may be higher**

In some circumstances the plaintiff's injury may be seen to have been aggravated by the defendant's conduct, resulting in an award of "aggravated damages". Despite the specialized term, aggravated damages are also compensatory in function, but in this case "to compensate a claimant for the additional hurt he has suffered from the way in which the defendant has conducted himself and his case" (*John Raymond Luciw v Wolfgang Derler*). One example is a failed plea of justification, which will often be treated by the court as extending or exacerbating the original defamation (see section 9.1 above). To qualify for an award of aggravated damages, it is important that the plaintiff adduce some evidence as to injury to feelings. There is no basis for presuming aggravated pain and suffering in a given case: "that must be a matter of evidence, depending on the circumstances, such as the robustness or vulnerabilities of the plaintiffs in question" (*Oriental Daily Publisher Ltd v Ming Pao Holdings Ltd* (see section 15.1 above)).

Moreover, the mere fact that a defendant sticks to its defence of justification and does not offer an apology does not mean that an award of aggravated damages is indicated. The decision, in good faith, to rely on justification and therefore to not offer an apology may be entirely reasonable in the facts of the case, as in *Blakeney-Williams v Cathay Pacific Airways Ltd* (see section 11.4.2 above), where the Court of Final Appeal agreed with the Court of Appeal's decision to set aside the trial judge's award of aggravated damages.

The law also has a concept of punitive or exemplary damages (intended to punish or intended to make an example of). This idea is at odds with the basic notion of damages intended to compensate, and in the last few decades such damages have been awarded less often. The English courts would only give such increased damages in restricted circumstances: if there was abuse of public position or power, or the defendant set out deliberately to make a profit from the defamation. The Hong Kong courts seem to have ignored this point in a number of cases; presumably lawyers failed to bring it to their attention. Different countries take different views on this; for example, in New Zealand exemplary damages will be more often awarded than in England. The Hong Kong cases seem to be the result of oversight.

15.1.3 **When damages may be very small**

A lower amount of damages may be awarded where the credibility of the speaker is not very high, or where the impugned statement is a repeat publication (*Oriental Daily Publisher Ltd v Ming Pao Holdings Ltd* (see section 15.1 above)). Moreover, because the plaintiff does not have to show any actual damage, the court may sometimes feel that, though technically the plaintiff has won, the case has very little merit. It is possible for the court to award a very small sum of damages only. In *Ki Ping Ki & Another v Oriental Daily Publisher Ltd & Others* [1999] HKCA 422, the jury awarded only HK$1 damages.

15.2 **Injunction**

An injunction is a court order not to do something (exceptionally, it may be an order to do something positive). Failure to obey the order is a criminal offence.

15.2.1 **Regular injunctions**

An injunction may be awarded at the end of a defamation case if there is a real possibility of the defendant repeating the defamatory statement.

15.2.2 **Interim injunctions**

There is a greater reluctance to grant an interim or interlocutory injunction, to restrain the publication of a defamation which has not yet taken place. This is considered to be a very serious infringement on freedom of speech. The principles usually applied are that an interlocutory injunction will only be granted if it is clear that the statement is defamatory, that — if the defendant intends to argue that the statement was true — the plaintiff must satisfy the court that the words are untrue (by swearing an affidavit), and that there is no reason to take the view that the occasion of publication is or will be protected by privilege. See, for example, *Chan Shui Shing Andrew v Ironwing Holdings Ltd* [2001] 2 HKC 376.

16. Procedure and evidence

The technicalities of bringing or defending an action are not something the media need to worry about very much, since this is where the lawyers really come into their own. But a few points might be interesting or useful to know about.

16.1 Legal aid

Hong Kong has a scheme under which people who cannot afford to bring or defend a civil action may receive some financial assistance to do so. This does not apply to defamation. Neither the plaintiff nor the defendant may receive legal aid. As a result, generally speaking, defamation actions are brought only by the relatively wealthy.

16.2 Revealing sources

The media publish many things of which they are not the author, and depend on many sources of information not all of which are made public. Can the court order the media to reveal the source of information, so that someone can sue the originator? This is viewed as a serious risk for the press and the court will rarely order such disclosure. The Hong Kong Court of Appeal observed that the rule supported the "free flow of information" and refused to order that a newspaper disclose the source of its information in the early stages of an action (*John Sham Otherwise Known as Shum Kit-fun, John v Eastweek Publisher Ltd* [1994] 2 HKLR 381). But website operators cannot use this rule to refuse to disclose the names of people who make anonymous postings (*Oriental Press Group Ltd v Inmediahk.net Ltd* [2012] 2 HKLRD 1004).

16.3 Worldwide defamation

Technology has long made possible the widespread dissemination of information. A statement made or written in one place may be reported on the other side of the world, or a paper published in one country may appear somewhere else. And the Internet has introduced new possibilities for worldwide defamation. But not all countries have the same laws regarding the right to sue in defamation. For instance, the US seriously restricts the right to sue public figures (see section 5.2 above). It also restricts the right to sue Internet service providers (see Communications Decency Act 47 USC s 230), as does the UK, after reforms recently enacted there (see section 18 below). Hong Kong does not have such laws. In addition to differences in laws, the size of damages awards may vary across jurisdictions. In view of such differences, plaintiffs may be tempted to "shop around" for legal systems that favour them. Can they do this?

In order to bring an action for defamation in a jurisdiction where the plaintiff is not resident, the plaintiff must show that he or she has some connection with the place and a reputation to be protected there. It is also necessary to show that the publication was actually "published" — in the sense of being made public — there; it does not have to have originated there. In *Investasia Ltd and Another v Kodansha Co. Ltd and Another* [1999] 3 HKC 515, the court permitted the plaintiff to commence Hong Kong court proceedings against a Japanese defendant with no Hong Kong connection. The plaintiff was able to convince the court that the article had been published in Hong Kong (however few copies), that he was connected with Hong Kong in a number of ways, and had a reputation in Hong Kong to be protected.

In *Yaqoob v Asia Times Online Ltd.* [2008] 4 HKLRD 911, the defendant's online news service was based in Hong Kong but it was not clear whether the offending article, which concerned activities of the Dubai-based defendant, and was available online for just one day, had been downloaded in Hong Kong or only overseas. The court found that the article was probably downloaded in Hong Kong as well as overseas, but even on the assumption that the publication was downloaded only outside Hong Kong, the court held that it had jurisdiction to hear the case because the defendant corporation was based in Hong Kong.

In *Dow Jones & Co. Inc v Gutnick* [2002] 210 CLR 575, an Australian case, the plaintiff, a well-known businessman in the Australian state of Victoria, was permitted by the court to start an action in Victoria against a US company for an Internet defamation that originated in the US. It was held to have been published in Australia, even though it was available only by subscription there.

17. The crime of defamatory libel

Libel is also a crime, but slander is not. The Defamation Ordinance provides for this offence (sections 5 and 6) but says nothing about when there could be a prosecution. The Hong Kong courts might well apply the same principle as those in England — that the libel must be a serious one, "sufficiently serious to merit the use of the criminal law". The original purposes behind the offence seem to have included avoiding the risk that people would be tempted to respond with violence, but the ordinance says nothing about this. There have been very few cases in Hong Kong. There has been some criticism of the whole idea of bringing a criminal case for libel, because of the impact on freedom of speech.

17.1 How is it different from the tort?

There can be a prosecution for the offence even if the person defamed is dead. The other important difference is that truth alone is not a defence: publication must also have been in the public interest (Defamation Ordinance, s 6).

17.2 The special prosecution rule

According to section 18 of the Defamation Ordinance,

> No criminal prosecution shall be commenced against any proprietor, publisher, editor, or any person responsible for the publication of a newspaper without the approval of a judge.

Note that the same protection is not given to the individual journalists.

18. Changes in the law?

Substantial reforms of defamation law are required, if only so that the law remains consistent with expectations and popular practice. In England, the jurisdiction that carries the most influence in Hong Kong, a growing recognition that reforms were needed, and that alignment with defamation laws elsewhere was necessary if only to counter the problem of so-called "libel tourism", the Defamation Act 2013 was passed into law on 25 April 2013. It came into force on 1 January 2014, and applies to defamations committed after that date. The Act introduces greater protection for secondary publishers such as booksellers and for website operators in relation to material posted by users of sites which they host. The Act reforms the multiple publication rule that, as applied to online archives and other Internet publications, can keep libels actionable long after the expiry of limitation periods. The new law abolishes the presumption in favour of a jury trial in defamation cases, thereby significantly decreasing the cost and time to resolve claims. It introduces a requirement for a claimant to demonstrate that the published material has caused serious harm, in order to discourage trivial claims. It restricts the jurisdiction of English courts to hear cases involving foreign defendants. It replaces the common law defences of justification and fair comment with statutory versions that are easier to understand and apply, and that to some degree reflect developments in the case law, and it puts the *Reynolds* public interest defence on a statutory footing.

Hong Kong faces most of the same issues as were addressed in the Defamation Act 2013, but the government of the HKSAR has so far shown little interest in reforming its defamation laws. With change on the scale taking place in England and in other leading jurisdictions, Hong Kong is at risk of being left behind. Its laws will be unable to address the changes brought about by developments in communications technology, and the expectation, particularly in Hong Kong, of more open discussion of matters of public importance, driven both by the new technology but also by changing political conditions and social expectations in Hong Kong. Moreover, the developing body of case law from English courts that Hong Kong courts normally count on as a guide to the development of its law will no longer be applicable to Hong Kong. Thus, it is important that Hong Kong address these issues now. If it fails to do so, Hong Kong may well run the risk of becoming the next international centre for libel tourism!

19. Checklist for the media

Situation I: Are you about to publish something that may be defamatory?

1. Does it read on the face of the words as though it would lower the person referred to in the eyes of ordinary, reasonable Hong Kong people?
2. Is there some fact that is not obvious on the surface, but is or might be known to readers which would give it a meaning which is defamatory?
3. Is there some fact which would make the statement (if defamatory) be understood as referring to someone other than the person actually named?
4. If it is defamatory, are you sure you could prove that it is true?
5. If you are not sure, is the statement one which would have the benefit of some privilege?

a. Does the statement report (accurately and fairly) a current or recent court case?

b. Does the statement report proceedings in the Legislative Council?

c. Does the statement report some official announcement?

d. Does the statement constitute a defence to an attack in the media?

e. Is the statement on a matter of public importance which the public have a genuine interest in and which would meet the criteria suggested by Lord Nicholls in *Reynolds*?

f. Is it a comment?

g. If it is a comment, is it based on facts which are specified or clearly referred to?

h. Is it a comment on a matter of public interest?

i. Is it a statement that could be honestly and fairly made?

j. If it is the opinion of someone other than the media, is there any reason to believe it is not honestly believed?

k. If it is the opinion (e.g. of the editor), is it an opinion genuinely held?

Situation II: Have you received a complaint that something is defamatory?

1. Are you confident of being able to defend it on one of the bases referred to under questions 4 and 5 in Situation I above?
2. If not, can you credibly argue that you did not intend it to refer to the complainant or did not intend it to be defamatory (either of anyone or specifically of the complainant)?
3. If not, could you claim that you acted in good faith without any reason to believe it was defamatory?
4. Are you prepared to apologize?
5. If not, are you prepared to pay damages (realizing that even if you do apologize you may still have to pay)?
6. If not, are you prepared to bluff it out, hoping that the person complaining will lack the will or the means to sue?

4

Court Reporting and Contempt of Court

Doreen Weisenhaus

FREQUENTLY ASKED QUESTIONS

1. Do courts have to be open to the public? When are they allowed to close proceedings? (See section 2)
2. What are the reporting restrictions for journalists covering courts or other legal proceedings? What sanctions do they or their news organizations face if these restrictions are violated? (See sections 3–6 and 8)
3. Are journalists allowed to talk to jurors, even after a trial is over? (See section 3.4)
4. What is contempt of court? How is it triggered? (See section 3)
5. Who can be held liable for contempt? The reporter? The editor? The publisher? (See section 3.3)
6. What is "scandalizing the court"? (See section 3.6)
7. What special issues involving the Internet, social media and other technologies should reporters who cover the courts be aware of? (See section 3.5)

1. Introduction

As in other areas of law covered in this book, a constant balancing act exists between freedom of the press and individual interests. The right to a fair trial versus the right of the press to cover a trial is one of the most important and enduring conflicts. In courtrooms across Hong Kong, as the media began devoting more coverage to the courts, clashes with the judicial system were inevitable. These have resulted in more calls for the media to resist the sensationalizing of court coverage and for the courts to be more open.

Coverage of courts in Hong Kong is a fairly recent phenomenon. Until the early 1990s, the courts were not seen as a major source of news and were covered mostly by the two local English-language newspapers. But by the mid to late 1990s, when competition in the Chinese press heated up after the debut of the *Apple Daily* newspaper, other Hong Kong media discovered what media all over the world have — that trials, especially criminal ones, frequently have many of the elements of great storytelling: scandal, conflict, murder, sex, victims, and (alleged until proven guilty) villains. Now several dozen reporters regularly cover court cases throughout Hong Kong and many newspapers have regular features devoted to court coverage.

Despite their enthusiasm for court coverage, the media here recognize the difficulties of reporting on legal proceedings. As in many areas of law, Hong Kong inherited the UK's restrictive approach to coverage of court cases. Reporters face many prohibitions on the kinds of information they can report about pending cases, especially about criminal cases on trial or about to go on trial before a jury. When journalists run afoul of the restrictions, they can face contempt of court charges.

While contempt of court charges are not an everyday occurrence for the media in Hong Kong, they have happened often enough in recent years to be a threat. Journalists and media found in contempt have faced thousands of dollars in fines and, in one extreme case, prison time.

One positive development for the press in the coverage of court cases has been an increase in court transparency. In 2005, the Hong Kong Judiciary implemented a major policy change when it opened some court proceedings to journalists and the public that previously had been closed. But open proceedings for the media can still be subject to limits or bans on publication of information beyond the usual reporting restrictions, especially in high-profile cases. In one of Hong Kong's most famous recent murder prosecutions, a court allowed the media (although not the public) to attend a hearing in 2010 on the application of Nancy Kissel to halt a retrial for the murder of her husband, but barred journalists from reporting details until after the retrial verdict.[1]

Developments in the use of the Internet, social media and other technologies as they affect the courts — such as whether reporters should be allowed to twitter in real-time during trials or how to prevent jurors from doing online research on cases in which they are involved — have prompted some jurisdictions, including Hong Kong, to re-examine their practices, rules or laws.

2. The open justice principle

> Publicity is the very soul of justice. It is the keenest spur to exertion and the surest of all guards against improbity. It keeps the judge, while trying, under trial.
>
> —Jeremy Bentham

This quote from Bentham, the eighteenth-century philosopher, has been cited countless times to underscore the idea that justice must be seen to be done. This concept, known as the "open justice principle", is considered a cornerstone for many legal systems, including those in the UK, Canada, Australia, and Hong Kong. See *Scott v Scott* [1913] AC 417; *R v Chief Registrar of Friendly Societies* [1984] 1 QB 227; *Canadian Broadcasting Corp. v New Brunswick (Attorney General)* [1996] 3 SCR 480; *John Fairfax Group Pty Ltd v Local Court (NSW)* [1991] 26 ALD 471; *R v B Suttill, Esq, Magistrate, ex parte Asiaweek Ltd* [1984] HKC 474.

---

1. Nancy Kissel was convicted of murder in 2005 for poisoning her husband, Robert Kissel, with a drug-laced milkshake and bludgeoning him to death. The Court of Final Appeal overturned her conviction in 2010 for legal errors. *Kissel v HKSAR* [2010] 2 HKLRD 435. After a second trial, she was convicted again in 2011 and is serving a life sentence.

What the open justice principle means is that the administration of justice, including trials, derives its legitimacy from being conducted in public, and that the press, as representatives of the public, can help enforce this principle. The media keep the justice system under scrutiny by their monitoring of its operations and proceedings and thus, help keep it fair and honest.

In 2005, a Hong Kong district court cited this principle when it was asked to hear evidence *in camera* (in secret) from officers of the Independent Commission Against Corruption (ICAC), who claimed that their testimony would be too sensitive to give in open court. The judge granted the request by ICAC but said he did so reluctantly because hearing evidence in secret was an "extraordinary" action. According to the court, "There can be no doubt that it is a fundamental principle of our system of law in Hong Kong, as well as in many others, that proceedings should be conducted in a manner which affords the public and media free access to those proceedings (and) that there should only be a departure from this cardinal principle in exceptional and limited circumstances" *(HKSAR v Mo Yuk Ping* (2005) DCCC 367/2004).

The open justice principle is referred to in the Hong Kong Bill of Rights Ordinance (BORO), Article 10, which reproduced Article 14 of the International Covenant of Civil and Political Rights (ICCPR) (emphasis added):

> All persons shall be equal before the courts and tribunal. In the determination of any criminal charge against him, or of his rights and obligations in a suit at law, everyone shall be entitled to a *fair and public hearing* by a competent, independent and impartial tribunal established by law . . .

The BORO, Article 10, however, also sets out the special circumstances in which court proceedings may be closed. These include for reasons of morals, public order, national security, individual privacy or "to the extent strictly necessary" where such publicity would "prejudice the interests of justice". It states:

> The press and the public may be excluded from all or part of a trial for reasons of morals, public order (ordre public) or national security in a democratic society, or when the interest of the private lives of the parties so requires, or to the extent strictly necessary in the opinion of the court in special circumstances where publicity would prejudice the interests of justice . . .

Those circumstances are further discussed in section 123(1), Criminal Procedure Ordinance (Cap 221):

> Subject to the provisions of the Hong Kong Bill of Rights Ordinance, if it appears to a court that it is necessary to do so in the interests of justice or public order or security, the court may order that the whole of the proceedings before it in respect of any offence or, having regard to the reason of the making such order, any appropriate part of such proceedings shall take place in a closed court.

However, as BORO, Article 10, finally notes, even if parts of a court proceeding are closed, the court must make public any final decision except in certain cases involving children or divorce (emphasis added):

> . . . but *any judgment rendered in a criminal case or in a suit at law shall be made public* except where the interest of juvenile persons otherwise requires or the proceedings concern matrimonial disputes or the guardianship of children.

Obtaining those judgments and other court records is a key element to effective court reporting. Some records, such as writs of summons that initiate legal actions and judgments, are accessible to the media and the public.[2] But unlike in several other jurisdictions where broader public access to court records is available,[3] most court records in Hong Kong case files remain difficult to access. (For a detailed guide on what to look for and where, see Appendix B of this book, "Searching for Public Records of Courts".)

British journalists faced similar obstacles until a landmark Court of Appeal ruling in 2012 (*Guardian News and Media Ltd v City of Westminster Magistrates Court*, EWCA Civ 420) established a common law right for the media and the public to obtain documents used in court cases. The court held that, under the open justice principle, the presumption should be for access, particularly for "a proper journalistic purpose", but also held that a risk-of-harm assessment would be appropriate in a case-by-case basis.

In a significant development in July 2005, the Hong Kong Judiciary made major changes in granting public access to in-chamber hearings in civil proceedings in the High Court, the District Court, the Lands Tribunal and Family court (see Appendix C, "Judicial Practice Directions: Hearings in Chambers in Civil Proceedings").[4] Prior to this development, hundreds of these hearings every week were closed. The new rules meant that the previously secret hearings, involving a wide range of matters from applications to amend pleadings and other pre-trial motions to requests for legal aid, could be reported in the same way as hearings in open court.

Exceptions remained, however, for those hearings required by legislation to be closed or for those usually closed by reason of their nature, as allowed by Article 10 of BORO. These include adoption proceedings, matrimonial disputes, applications for injunctions and matters relating to disability, bankruptcy and intellectual property. For a full list, reporters should refer to Schedules 1 and 2 of Practice Direction 25.1[5] (see Appendix C).

---

2. Rules of the District Court (Cap 336H), Order 63 rule 4; Rules of the High Court (Cap 4A), Order 63 rule 4.
3. Public right of access to court cases has been recognized in Canada, *Dagenais v Canadian Broadcasting Corp.* [1994] 3SCR 835 and *R v Mentuck* [2001] 3 SCR 442; New Zealand, *Mafart v TVNZ* [2006] NZSC 33; South Africa, *Independent News v Minister of Intelligence* [2008] ZACC 6; and the US, *Nixon v Warner Communications Inc*, 435 US 589 (1978) and the Public Access to Court Electronic Records (PACER) system which permits access to most documents submitted electronically in federal court cases.
4. Practice Direction 25.1 (http://legalref.judiciary.gov.hk/doc/prac_dir/html/PD25.1.htm); Practice Direction 25.2 (http://legalref.judiciary.gov.hk/doc/prac_dir/html/PD25.2.htm).
5. Schedule 1 (http://legalref.judiciary.gov.hk/doc/prac_dir/pdf/PD25.1E_Sch1.pdf) and Schedule 2 (http://legalref.judiciary.gov.hk/doc/prac_dir/pdf/PD25.1E_Sch2.pdf).

The changes came eight years after a Judiciary working group, chaired by a senior judge, called for an overhaul of a system that had demonstrated a preference for privacy, possibly in breach of BORO. The changes did not make a large practical difference in the daily lives of reporters covering courts as the bulk of the now-open hearings continued to involve mostly non-newsworthy administrative matters. But even if such hearings did not result in immediate news stories, they gave journalists opportunities to glimpse pre-trial wrangling among the parties, which may provide insights to later coverage of trials.

Most important, the rules represented a major policy shift because they established a presumption for open proceedings. And in the courts' "daily cause list", a published schedule of court proceedings, the media are notified when a particular hearing is to be closed.[6]

Beyond physical access to the courts and legal proceedings is the issue of whether certain information arising out of cases can be made public. While reporters may be barred from attending *in camera* proceedings, it is not contempt to publish information relating to them, provided the information does not violate statutory restrictions nor has been expressly prohibited from publication by the court (Judicial Proceedings (Regulation of Reports) Ordinance, Cap 287, s 5).

One privilege for the media covering the courts is that news reports of court proceedings in Hong Kong are protected against defamation claims, provided they are fair, accurate, contemporaneous, and do not contain extraneous information from outside the proceedings (Defamation Ordinance, Cap 21, s 13 (1). For more details, see Chapter 3 Defamation). But journalists should be aware that reports relating to *in camera* or in-chambers proceedings might lose that privilege. Furthermore, contempt considerations mean that reporters have to be extra careful in their coverage as some information cannot be published or broadcast until after a case is over. Other information, such as the identity of a sex crime victim or certain details from a divorce, can never be published or broadcast (see sections 4–8 of this chapter).

3. Contempt of court

Contempt of court has been defined as the wrongful interference with the administration of justice. As noted below, it is restricted only to what is necessary for justice to be achieved:

> The law of contempt is restricted to what is necessary for the attainment of justice. Inherent in the law of contempt is a restriction on the right of freedom of speech. That freedom is a cardinal freedom. It is one which the law is there to uphold. The importance of the freedom of speech cannot be underestimated. Nevertheless, the right of freedom of speech and the due administration of law have synergistic qualities because without one the other cannot truly exist. (*Attorney General v Cheung Kim Hung* (1997) HKLRD 472)

6. http://www.judiciary.gov.hk/en/crt_lists/daily_caulist.htm.

Contempt of court can happen in a number of ways. The media most often get into trouble when they comment or report on current court cases beyond what is permitted by Hong Kong law, which in some instances can result in a jury trial collapsing. The purposes behind contempt of court actions are to protect the administration of justice and to prevent abuse of the judicial process. Its sanctions are not supposed to be invoked to protect the personal dignity of the court or its judges by preventing legitimate criticism of the legal system.

The source of law for contempt of court in Hong Kong is mostly common law with some statutory restrictions. In the UK, the media is governed by the 1981 Contempt of Court Act, which Hong Kong did not adopt. In 2012, the UK Law Reform Commission recommended changes in UK contempt laws to modernize and reflect digital and other developments,[7] and a year later the UK Parliament enacted one of the recommendations — abolishing the contempt offence of scandalising the court[8] (see sections 3.5 and 3.6).

3.1 Civil versus criminal contempt

Contempt of court can be either civil or criminal. A criminal contempt is concerned with protecting the public interest in the due administration of justice, whereas a civil contempt is concerned with protecting the private interest in the enforcement of court orders (*Secretary for Justice v Apple Daily Ltd & Another* [2000] 2 HKLRD 704). But the distinction between civil and criminal contempt can be misleading because both can result in jail sentences for violators. That is why the standard of proof in either civil or criminal contempt cases is the criminal standard of "beyond a reasonable doubt" instead of the civil standard of "preponderance of the evidence".

Civil contempt is generally to punish those who fail to comply with court orders, such as an injunction, non-publication order and disclosure of sources of information. The penalty is usually a fine, but jail can be an option. A typical case is one that occurred in 2004 involving an inheritance dispute in which a Hong Kong court sentenced a woman to a seven-day suspended jail sentence for failing to comply with a court order to reveal details of her mother's property to the two co-heirs.

The media are usually not involved in civil contempt actions, but they can be if they refuse, for example, to obey an injunction or a court order not to reveal certain information.

In the 1980s *Spycatcher* case, the British government tried to stop publication of a book by Peter Wright, a former MI5 operative who wrote about espionage activities of the British security services. The UK government obtained injunctions in the UK, Hong Kong, and Australia, but could not in the US, where the book was published. *The Sunday Times* of London and the *South China Morning Post* in Hong Kong then began printing book excerpts. Despite the book's publication in

7. "Contempt of Court", UK Law Reform Commission Consultation Paper No 209, 28 November 2012, and "Contempt of Court: Scandalising the Court", UK LRC Report No 335, 18 December 2012. Both can be found at: http://lawcommission.justice.gov.uk/areas/contempt.htm.
8. Crime and Courts Act 2013, s 33.

the US and elsewhere, the UK government was able to get injunctions in Hong Kong and the UK to stop further excerpts. Had the *South China Morning Post* or any other Hong Kong newspaper continued to publish excerpts, it could have been found in civil contempt (*Attorney General v South China Morning Post* [1988] 1 HKLR 143). In 1991, the European Court of Human Rights found that, once the book was published in the US, the injunctions violated freedom of expression (*The Sunday Times v The United Kingdom* (No 2) [1991] ECHR 50). More recently, a group of activists known as Citizens' Radio, who had been broadcasting sporadically without a licence since their application was turned down, were found in civil contempt for breaching an injunction in 2008 banning illegal broadcasting. They were ordered to pay HK$360,000 in fines and costs; see *Secretary for Justice v Ocean Technology* [2009] HKC 456. (For more on the Citizens' Radio cases, see Chapter 12 Media Regulation in the Age of Convergence.)

Criminal contempt can be grouped into several categories (described in detail in following sections):

1. contempt in the face of the court (involving words spoken or acts done in a court which might interfere with a case, such as the disruption of a proceeding);
2. wrongful interference with the due administration of justice in a particular case (usually by publication); and
3. "scandalizing the court".

Prosecutions for criminal contempt are brought by the Secretary for Justice, and judges have referred such cases for prosecution when they have observed what they believe to be improper conduct by the media. There have not been many prosecutions against the Hong Kong media for contempt, but several high-profile cases are noteworthy, including rare charges brought in 2013 against newspaper reporters (see section 3.3).

Journalists should be aware of the possibility for prosecution and that contempt of court is considered a "strict liability" offence. That means that it is not essential for the prosecution to prove that the media *intended* to interfere with the administration of justice or the courts, only that the act occurred. Intention is relevant only to any possible sentence imposed. For example, if there is no evidence of the media's intention to interfere with a case, then the result is usually just a fine, but courts have indicated that if intention to interfere is found, as it was in the "scandalizing the court" case involving *Oriental Daily News* in 1998 and 1999, then they would impose a jail sentence. Also, the prosecution does not need to prove that there was an actual interference with the administration of justice, only that there was a strong risk.

3.2 **Contempt in the face of the court**

Actions for contempt in the face of the court often try to assert control after a court proceeding has been disrupted. Situations can include a witness refusing to be sworn in or to give testimony,[9] a defendant yelling at a judge or opposing parties coming to blows in the courtroom.[10] In 2007, a defendant was sentenced to two months in jail for scolding a judge in a matrimonial case, using "extremely foul and highly insulting language" (*Secretary for Justice v Yau Chi Wah* [2007] 2 HKLRD 617). In another case, a defendant who threw a shoe at a government lawyer received a twenty-eight-day sentence.

Journalists can get into trouble for this type of contempt action if they disrupt proceedings or secretly tape record or photograph proceedings.[11] Increasingly though, cameras in the courtroom have gained acceptance by judiciaries in the US, UK, Canada, Brazil and others as long as they comply with certain standards.[12] Live streaming of court proceedings in addition to briefings on key cases and expansive court websites have contributed to a growing trend of judiciary communication with the public. Hong Kong, however, lags behind these developments.[13] Not only are cameras not permitted in any Hong Kong courts, it is even prohibited to do a sketch in a courtroom or in areas near the courtroom,[14] although someone can draw from memory what was witnessed in court. As a result, sketches rarely appear in Hong Kong newspapers. In some jurisdictions, these types of restrictions, such as the ban against audio recording of proceedings, can be lifted upon application to the court, which might permit limited use. For example, a UK court may, at its discretion, allow audio recording as an "aide-mémoire" as long as it is not used to broadcast or to brief witnesses.[15]

3.3 Wrongful interference in a particular case by publication

A contempt action for wrongful inference by the publishing of information frequently arises as a result of the media's coverage of a particular court case. These actions are to discourage "trial by media", which might jeopardize a fair trial. In *Attorney General v Cheung Kim Hung*, the court observed: "One of the most common

9. Criminal Procedure Ordinance (Cap 221), s 36.
10. Magistrate Ordinance (Cap 227), s 99; District Court Ordinance (Cap 336), s 20.
11. Summary Offences Ordinance (Cap 228), s 7. It is prohibited to take or attempt to take in court any photograph, or with a view to publication make or attempt to make in any court any portrait or sketch of a judge, juror, witness or party to any proceeding in court, in the building or precinct. Violators are subject to a HK$250 fine.
12. Section 47 of the Constitutional Reform Act 2005 permits cameras in the UK's Supreme Court, with live coverage available worldwide on the Sky News website since 2009. Proceedings in the Court of Appeal began to be broadcast in late 2013. The Supreme Court of Canada has permitted the broadcasting of oral arguments since the 1990s and the proceedings are now streamed live on the Internet as well. While the US Supreme Court does not permit cameras, courts in all 50 states and some federal courts allow them. The Brazilian Supreme Court also permits broadcasting of its justices' deliberations. See also Kyu Ho Youm, "Cameras in the Courtroom in the Twenty-First Century: The US Supreme Court Learning from Abroad?" *Brigham Young University Law Review* 2012.
13. Austin Chiu, "Courts in the Dark Ages When it Comes to Communications, Say Experts", *South China Morning Post*, 3 August 2013.
14. Summary Offences Ordinance (Cap 228), s 7.
15. Practice Direction (Criminal Proceedings: Consolidation) [2002] 1 WLR 2870 para 1.2.

forms (of wrongful interference) is the making of comments about current cases. Often this happens in newspapers in statements and observations about current cases."

For an act to be found in contempt, it must pose a serious risk of a real and substantial danger of prejudice to the conduct of a fair trial. The concern is about information that can affect a court's or jury's impartiality (such as publishing a confession) or that can make it difficult for determining the facts of a case (such as publishing information that might deter witnesses from coming forward). Thus, other examples of acts committed by the media that can bring potential contempt charges include commenting on the personal character of the accused or the merits of the case before the court, publishing photographs of a suspect when identification is an issue,[16] publishing contemporaneous news coverage that casts doubts on witnesses, publishing material not before the court (e.g. interviews of witnesses or a newspaper's own investigation), interfering with jurors and witnesses, or reporting on jury deliberations. In mid-2013, the Secretary for Justice asked the High Court to jail two editors and two reporters for *Apple Daily* and sister newspaper *Sharp Daily* for publishing an article and posting online a video of an interview with a defendant in a double homicide case after criminal proceedings had commenced.[17]

Criminal cases and those with juries present the most problems for the media, particularly if they publish information not available to jurors in a trial, who are viewed as being more easily influenced by extraneous material than by judges. In Hong Kong and the UK, courts are always looking to the vulnerability of a jury. It is presumed that those with more experience in the legal system, such as judges, are better able to disregard any news coverage of court cases as they are only supposed to consider the evidence presented in court, but that lay members of society, such as jurors, might not be able to do so.

In non-jury civil cases, the courts are concerned about publication that tends to deter parties from bringing or defending an action or to cause a party to abandon or compromise a case. Both criminal and civil cases also can trigger numerous statutory reporting restrictions designed to protect the individual privacy of victims, juveniles, defendants or other parties and to encourage victims and others to come forward (see section 4 in this chapter on statutory reporting restrictions).

Media representatives who can be held liable for contempt charges include the reporter, editor, publisher, owner, and even the printer, but typically in Hong Kong, only the editor and publisher are held liable in these cases. The *Apple Daily* and *Sharp Daily* cases are unusual in that writs were filed against the reporters as well.

Under the common law principle of *sub judice* ("before a court or judge"), a publication is considered likely to prejudice a fair trial if proceedings are said

16. In 2008, a court barred the media from publishing photographs that could identify a man accused of murdering three prostitutes who had not yet appeared in a police line-up. Anita Lam, "Photo Ban on Accused Sex Killer", *South China Morning Post*, 26 March 2008.

17. *Secretary for Justice v Cheung Kim Hung*, HCMP 1851/2013, and *Secretary for Justice v Wong Sau Kwan* HCMP 1890/2013.

to be "pending" or "imminent". In a criminal case, "pending" is usually after an arrest has been made or a warrant has been issued. "Imminent" is more difficult to define, but the principle comes into play when it becomes reasonably certain that a suspect will be charged and that court proceedings about the charge will take place.[18] For a civil case, "pending" can mean when a writ has been filed and proceedings can begin. This *sub judice* period for civil and criminal proceedings officially lasts until an appeal hearing is complete or the time has expired for an appeal notice.[19] But practically speaking, the Hong Kong media take a narrower view of this period and frequently do not limit their coverage until after a suspect has been formally charged. Once a verdict has been reached, the media often resume reporting and commenting until the appeals proceedings start.

Factors the court will consider when determining whether the media should be found in contempt include: the content of the article, the closeness of publication to the start of trial, the prominence of the article (is it front page with a large story and headline?), circulation (how many readers or viewers might have seen it?) and whether the case is an ongoing jury trial.[20]

Courts have particular concern over stories in the media that comment or report on the credibility or guilt of a defendant accused of a crime. Article 87 of the Basic Law, as well as Article 11 of the BORO, guarantee that the accused is presumed innocent until proven guilty.[21] But in a 1998 ruling in the case of notorious gangster Yip Kai-foon, the Court of Appeal held that sensational publicity surrounding his arrest did not prevent him from having a fair trial. Prejudicial publicity included a film allegedly based on Yip's life that portrayed him as a murderer and as committing crimes for which he had not been charged. The Court of Appeal said the jury had been sufficiently warned about reaching a verdict solely on the evidence presented before them. Yip was sentenced to 41 years in prison (see *HKSAR v Yip Kai-foon* [1999] 1 HKLRD 277).

More recent cases, however, involving less notorious criminals have been harsher to the media. In 2000, the *Apple Daily* newspaper was fined HK$100,000 and its editor-in-chief was found guilty of contempt for a story that reported that a man on trial for the murder of a young boy was a paedophile, a revelation that led to the collapse of the jury trial (*Secretary for Justice v Apple Daily Ltd & Another* [2000] 2 HKLRD 704).

In its 5 October 1999 edition, *Apple Daily* had published a story with the headline, "A Paedophiliac Vietnamese Male Is Suspected of Killing a 5-year-old Child". The trial was in its second day and prosecutors had not presented any evidence of the accused having committed sex crimes. The jury was dismissed. Four months later, a new trial resulted in the defendant's conviction and a life

18. *Report on Contempt of Court,* The Law Reform Commission of Hong Kong [1986], p. 25.
19. Ibid.
20. See *Attorney General v Cheung Kim Hung* [1997] HKLRD 472.
21. Article 87, Basic Law: ". . . Anyone who is lawfully arrested shall have the right to a fair trial by the judicial organs without delay and shall be presumed innocent until convicted by the judicial organs." Article 11, Bill of Rights Ordinance (Cap 383): "(1) Everyone charged with a criminal offence shall have the right to be presumed innocent until proved guilty according to law."

sentence. It turned out that he had previous convictions for sexual molestation, but that information was not presented at trial.

In general, the criminal record of a defendant may not be admissible at trial because it could prejudice the outcome and would not be considered evidence that the accused committed the crime in question. Furthermore, the story was relying on information that had been previously published in other newspapers some time before trial. This case should remind journalists that published information that might not bring contempt charges at an earlier point could become problematic if published near or during trial and that the media will not escape liability for merely repeating what has been published elsewhere.

In another case, a murder trial collapsed after fabricated and prejudicial witness statements were published in *The Sun* newspaper. The court found that *The Sun* had no intention to prejudice the trial and had not realized it was ongoing. But the judge said the article created potential for injustice, causing the trial to be postponed. The publisher was fined HK$150,000 and its editor, HK$30,000 (*Secretary for Justice v The Sun News Publisher Ltd* (2002) HCMP 6152/2001).

Lawyers and others at the time criticized the $150,000 penalty as too low to deter the media from such coverage. The prosecutor had sought a much higher fine. Similar cases in the UK have resulted in more substantial fines and the possibility that the media might be required to pay the costs of any new trial, which could run in the millions of dollars. In 2001, the publisher of the *Manchester Evening News* was fined £30,000 (HK$443,000) for violating a strict reporting ban against identifying the juvenile killers of two-year-old James Bulger (*Venables v News Group International* [2001] SJLB 279). In 2002, the *Sunday Mirror* was ordered to pay a fine of £75,000 (HK$1.1 million) plus legal costs for the collapse of a Leeds footballer trial after publishing an interview of a witness during trial (*Attorney General v MGN Ltd* [2002] EWHC 907).

As a result of a regulation added in 2004 under the UK's Courts Act 2003, third parties in the UK such as news organizations could be liable to pay for the costs of a collapsed criminal trial if they are considered to have committed serious misconduct, not necessarily at the level of contempt.[22] Hong Kong media have not faced this liability, although they can be held responsible for legal and court costs in civil cases.

In 2006, the publishers of *The Sun* newspaper and sister newspaper *Oriental Daily News* and their chief editors were fined HK$500,000 for contempt of court after publishing stories that resulted in the delay of a rape trial. The articles had been published in 2005, less than three weeks before the scheduled start of the trial of a Pakistani man accused of raping two English tourists.

The stories alleged that the defendant was involved in sexual assaults of other inmates at the Lai Chi Kok reception centre where he was being held awaiting trial. The Court of First Instance determined that the contempts were not deliberate or malicious, but stemmed from "negligence and insufficient supervision". The court concluded that the newspapers were not aware that the trial was imminent,

22. Costs in Criminal Cases (General) (Amendment) Regulations 2004.

but that they should have made attempts to find out when it was scheduled to start (*Secretary for Justice v The Sun News Publisher & Others* [2006] HKC 540).

Contempt of court cases usually result from media coverage of criminal cases, but they can also happen in civil cases, particularly when a jury is involved. In 1994, *Next Magazine* published a story that a plaintiff had spent HK$2.4 million in legal costs in pursuing a defamation case against rival magazine *Eastweek*, just before the jury was to decide the amount of damages. The jury decided in favour of the plaintiff and the damages awarded were the reported amount, HK$2.4 million. The Court of Appeal set aside the award as excessive (*Cheung Ng Sheong v Eastweek* [1995] 3 HKC 601). While the Court of Appeal did not find evidence that any juror actually saw the article, it said that the coincidence between the figure mentioned in the article and the amount awarded by the jury was "so remarkable" that it was difficult to believe that the sum in the *Next* article was not related to the jury award. It referred the matter to the Attorney General for prosecution, which the Department of Justice pursued.

At trial, a high court judge found the publisher of *Next Magazine* in contempt of court. The publication of the article posed a real risk, the court concluded, because the jury could have taken into account the extraneous information. The risk of the article coming to the attention of one or more of the jurors was high given the large circulation of Hong Kong's best-selling magazine (*Attorney General v Cheung Kim Hung* [1997] HKLRD 472).

In finding the magazine's actions in contempt, the court looked at the close timing of the story and similar amount awarded in damages by the jury. The court was concerned with the risk of prejudice, not whether the jury was actually affected. If this case had not been before a jury, then there likely would not have been a contempt prosecution. The only civil cases in Hong Kong that can have jury trials are defamation actions and this had been the first jury in a libel trial in decades.

The court also found that the law of contempt was a permissible restriction on the right to freedom of expression under the Bill of Rights.

Next Magazine was fined HK$25,000 and its editor, HK$5,000, plus *Next* was held liable for legal costs.[23] Had there been any evidence of intent on the part of the publication to influence the jury, the court said it would have considered jail time for one or more of the magazine's representatives. The court also noted that if the article had appeared *after* the jury verdict, it would not have found *Next* in contempt.

3.4 Interviewing former jurors?

While commenting on legal fees after a jury verdict would have been permissible, what about interviewing former jurors? As mentioned earlier in this chapter, reporters are clearly prohibited from talking to jurors *during* an ongoing trial,

23. Before the case could go back to court to determine costs, the parties settled for an undisclosed amount.

but what about *after* a trial? It has been the long-standing practice for Hong Kong reporters not to contact former jurors for fear of a contempt prosecution.

British common law has a long history in protecting the secrecy of jury deliberations. As a former colony, Hong Kong has followed this principle. The reasons given for this protection include ensuring the finality of a jury verdict and encouraging the free flow of discussion within a jury room. If defence lawyers were permitted to challenge jurors after a verdict, then no jury verdict would be final. And if jurors knew that their comments would be examined after a verdict, they might not feel free to openly discuss issues, evidence and so on.

In 1979, a UK magazine, *New Statesman*, published an interview with a former juror after a high-profile murder conspiracy trial ended in acquittals. The juror disclosed to the magazine how the jury had reacted to certain witnesses and evidence during deliberations, including that they could not accept the uncorroborated word of a prosecution witness who had agreed to accept money from a newspaper, the amount to be increased if there was a conviction. The UK government chose to prosecute the magazine that revealed the information (and not the newspaper that offered the money!).

The court, however, declined to hold *New Statesman* in contempt under common law, saying that while jury deliberations normally should be kept secret, not all revelations of such deliberations would constitute contempt. The court held that it is necessary to show in the light of the circumstances of a case, that such disclosure tended or would tend to imperil the finality of jury verdicts, or to affect adversely the attitude of future jurors and the quality of their verdicts and that the circumstances in this case did not warrant contempt (*Attorney General v New Statesman and Nation Publishing Co. Ltd* [1980] 2 WLR 246).

In 1981, the Parliament passed the UK Contempt of Court Act, which made it an offence for a journalist to "obtain, disclose or solicit any particulars of statements made, opinions expressed, arguments advanced or votes cast by members of a jury in the course of their deliberations in any legal proceedings". Hong Kong did not adopt the 1981 Act and thus does not have direct legislation on this issue.[24] Before the handover, it was thought that the Hong Kong Jury Ordinance (Cap 3) would have some bearing. Prior to 1997, the Jury Ordinance stated that whenever the ordinance was silent on any issue, UK law would prevail and in such case, it was arguable that the 1981 law prohibiting jury contact about deliberations would apply here.[25]

But now after the handover, Hong Kong relies on the common law on this issue and its strong presumption against talking to jurors. And as a rule, the Hong Kong media do not interview former jurors about deliberations although there apparently have been several examples in recent years of the press publishing jurors' generic comments about their feelings, particularly after a long trial, but not about deliberations.

24. Peter Duff, Mark Findlay, Carla Howarth, and Tsang-Fai Chan, *Juries: A Hong Kong Perspective* (Hong Kong: Hong Kong University Press 1992), p. 12.
25. Ibid., p. 13.

If a Hong Kong journalist were to reveal jury deliberations, even if it disclosed a miscarriage of justice, the results still might not turn out the same as the *New Statesman* case. It is not clear that the Hong Kong reporter would get the same break because, as the British court stated, it would depend on the circumstances in the specific case. Furthermore, as Hong Kong courts are no longer required post-handover to follow all UK precedents, they may choose not to apply that particular precedent and there is no Hong Kong case law on this point. To clarify this issue (and to establish clear media guidelines in covering court cases), the Hong Kong Law Reform Commission in 1986 recommended that Hong Kong enact its own ordinance similar to the 1981 UK Contempt of Court Act to expressly prohibit juror contact as it relates to deliberations,[26] but such law has not been passed.

But what if the media spoke to jurors about other issues besides deliberations? Noted media lawyers Geoffrey Robertson and Andrew Nicol advise reporters in the UK that, despite the Contempt Act, as long as they do not intentionally solicit information about jury deliberations in reaching verdicts, it would not be an offence to solicit or publish a juror's view on such things as "the desirability of a prosecution, the quality of the advocates, the sobriety of the judge or the attentiveness of the court usher".[27] Many journalists, however, might find those distinctions amounting to a slope too slippery to climb.

To be safe, the vast majority of Hong Kong journalists do not interview former jurors at all. And for the rare one who has, it was to talk to jurors only generally and not about deliberations. While the law has not been clearly settled in Hong Kong, the presumption and tradition against such juror contact is strong here and thus it is highly likely that a contempt prosecution would be brought against the media for revealing juror deliberations or for talking extensively to jurors, particularly in a high-profile case. How the case would be resolved is another question.

3.5 Internet, social media and technology

From online research by jurors on smart phones to "tweets" by journalists during trials, courts around the world are struggling over how to deal with the impact of a wired population.

One key concern is keeping prejudicial information about cases away from jurors and potential jurors. In the UK, a court requested two newspapers to voluntarily remove stories from their online archives in a high-profile case of a police officer accused of manslaughter. They did, but critics raised questions about the effectiveness of singling out mainstream media when information and comments about cases were often widely available elsewhere on the Internet via Google and social media such as Facebook and Twitter. And courts increasingly have turned their attention to jurors using online tools during trials. Since 2011, jurors in several UK cases were found guilty of contempt for conducting internet searches during jury deliberations and were sentenced to jail time. One juror had

26. *Report on Contempt of Court*, pp. 32–3, *supra*, see note 18.
27. *Robertson & Nicol on Media Law*, pp. 393–4.

also exchanged Facebook comments during the trial with a defendant who had already been acquitted. See *Attorney General v Fraill* [2011] EWCA CRIM 1570.

Citing alarm over these and other cases, the UK's Law Reform Commission in November 2012 issued a consultation paper[28] in which it recommended measures to reform the pre-Internet 1981 Contempt of Court Act. These proposals included giving courts authority to order newspapers and broadcasters to remove potentially prejudicial information from their websites and electronic archives and introducing a new criminal offence against jurors who conduct online research on cases. Consultation closed in early 2013 and a final report was expected in 2014.[29] Likewise, the New Zealand Law Reform Commission also was exploring how to revise its contempt and other laws to keep up with digital developments.[30] In California, a new law went into effect in 2012 that clarified that jurors cannot use the Internet or social media to research or disseminate information in cases or face contempt charges.[31] Jurors in the US have also gotten into trouble for sending "friend" requests to defendants, including a juror in Florida who received a three-day jail sentence for criminal contempt after he bragged on Facebook that he got dismissed because of his action.[32]

While there have been no similar developments to amend this area of law in Hong Kong, a court — in a matter raised by the Kissel case in 2010 — addressed the issue of whether pre-trial publicity presented such a risk of prejudice that a trial judge would not be able to adequately instruct a jury not to do its own online research. The court said that although Hong Kong had yet to formulate a standard judicial direction to instruct jurors to avoid Internet searches, it was confident that a trial judge could sufficiently "explain to a jury the rationale behind the direction in the context of the paramount importance of ensuring a fair trial for the defendant" (*HKSAR v Kissel* [2011] 3 HKLRD 1; see also *R v Thompson* [2011] 1 WLR 200). Currently, empanelled jurors are informed by the trial judge "they should not conduct their own online searches for information relating to the case they are trying", according to a Judiciary spokesperson.[33] "They are not prohibited from using communication devices outside the courtroom during the course of the trial but from the moment they are sent to the jury room to commence deliberations on their verdict they . . . will be required to surrender any communication devices to the court usher . . ."[34]

The media's use of technology in the courtroom has also come under examination and clarification in some jurisdictions. In the UK, for example, reporters

28. "Contempt of Court", UK Law Reform Commission, *supra*, see note 7.
29. For updates, check: http://lawcommission.justice.gov.uk/areas/contempt.htm.
30. "The News Media Meets 'New Media': Rights, Responsibilities and Regulation in the Digital Age", NZ Law Reform Commission, December 2011, tabled in New Zealand's Parliament, 26 March 2013.
31. 2011 Cal Laws Chap 181.
32. http://www.citmedialaw.org/blog/2012/us-first-juror-gets-jail-fallout-over-his-friending-defendant.
33. Reply by Florence Wong, Principal Information Officer for the Judiciary, 21 February 2013, in response to query by this author.
34. Ibid.

have been allowed to use their laptop computers and hand-held devices for live, text-based communications, including tweeting and blogging, since interim guidelines were issued in 2010. After a year, final guidelines removed the requirement that the media needed court permission for the practice, although members of the public still must apply to the court to use their devices. However, the guidelines cautioned journalists that the devices "should not cause a disturbance or distraction" and that the judge "always retains full discretion" to prohibit the text-based communications "in the interests of justice", such as "legal discussions in the absence of the jury (that) may appear on the internet and be seen by jury members."[35] Twitter and other text-based reporting have also been allowed in courtrooms in the US, Canada and Australia. In Hong Kong, mobile phones are required to be turned off inside courtrooms and, while laptops are permitted for "word processing purposes", they cannot be used for live, text-based communications, according to a Judiciary spokesperson.[36]

3.6 **Scandalizing the court**

> The constitutional right of free speech as contained in the Basic Law . . . is not an absolute right. Every civilized community is entitled to protect itself from *malicious conduct aimed at undermining the due administration of justice.* It is an important aspect of the preservation of the rule of law. Where the contemnor goes way beyond reasoned criticism of the judicial system and acts in bad faith, the guarantee of free speech cannot protect him from punishment. (*Wong Yeung Ng v Secretary for Justice* [1999] 2 HKLRD 293)

By far, the most controversial contempt of court case to date involving media misconduct in Hong Kong is the one that culminated in the landmark 1999 Court of Appeal ruling, *Wong Yeung Ng v Secretary for Justice,* and one of the rare times in a common law jurisdiction that a journalist had been imprisoned for criminal contempt of court. The case also introduced to Hong Kong a very old legal concept: scandalizing the court.

35. "Practice Guidance: The Use of Live Text-Based Forms of Communication (Including Twitter) from Court for the Purposes of Fair and Accurate Reporting", Lord Chief Justice, England and Wales, 14 December 2011, at: http://www.judiciary.gov.uk/publications-and-reports/guidance/2011/courtreporting.

36. When asked by this author about the source of restrictions not included in specific statutes and whether the Judiciary would reconsider lifting them in light of international developments, the Judiciary spokesperson replied on 22 March 2013: "Generally speaking, a court exercising judicial functions would rely on its inherent jurisdiction to regulate its proceedings . . . Currently, there are signage indicators displayed in court premises to remind court users of the prevailing restrictions . . . These would be reviewed from time to time to see if any updating is necessary. As part of this ongoing exercise, the Judiciary is now in the process of drawing up relevant guidelines for reference by court users. Once they are ready, they will be posted at suitable locations within court buildings . . . The intention is that these guidelines will also be uploaded onto the Judiciary website."

3.6.1 **Background/History**

Scandalizing the court is not directed to a particular case, but is aimed at protecting the judicial system as a continuing process by preserving public confidence in the due administration of justice. In general, criticism of the legal system or the Judiciary is not to be considered abuse, but historically, criminal liability has been found in situations in which the misconduct crossed the line into what was considered undue interference. Still, prosecutions in common law jurisdictions for the contempt offence of scandalizing the court have been infrequent.

The concept originated in the UK hundreds of years ago. In 1765, the court found in contempt a publisher of a pamphlet who said the chief justice had acted "officiously, arbitrarily and illegally" (*R v Almon* [1765] Wilm 243). Since then, apart from some cases in the nineteenth century, the concept was considered obsolete until *R v Gray* [1900] 2 QB 36. A journalist was found in contempt for describing a judge as "an impudent little man in horsehair, a microcosm of conceit and empty-headedness", even though the comments did not relate to a current case. Additional court cases occurred in the 1920s and 1930s (such as whether a birth control reformer would receive a fair trial from a Catholic judge). The last successful UK prosecution against the media for scandalizing the court was in 1931.

A number of common law countries have considered contempt cases involving scandalizing the court and have developed different approaches.

Some jurisdictions reject the concept outright or require a very high threshold that makes it difficult to bring a case. In Canada, the offence of scandalizing the court was found to be incompatible with the Canadian Charter of Rights and Freedoms unless there is a "clear, serious and immediate" danger to the administration of justice. Thus, the emphasis is on the danger to the administration of justice rather than to the danger of public confidence in it being undermined (*R v Kopyto* [1988] 47 DLR (4th) 213). The US does not recognize the offence of scandalizing the court at all. For other criminal contempt actions, there must be a clear and present danger of a court being influenced, intimidated, impeded, embarrassed or obstructed in the administration of justice.

Other countries, such as the UK and New Zealand, had endorsed the offence with a less onerous test — that publication creates a "real risk" that public confidence in the administration of justice will be undermined. No actual interference with the administration of justice has to be proved, only a determination that public confidence in the justice system might be damaged. But what is "real risk"? How is it to be measured or assessed? In New Zealand, the standard for "real risk" is that it is "distinct from a remote possibility that the conduct would undermine public confidence in the administration of justice" (see *Solicitor General v Radio Avon Ltd* [1978] 1 NZLR 225; *Solicitor General v Radio New Zealand* [1994] 1 NZLR 48).

When the Hong Kong courts endorsed the offence of scandalizing the court in the *Oriental Daily News* case in 1998 and 1999, they adopted the UK and New Zealand test of "real risk". However, since the Hong Kong case, the offense of scandalising the court in the UK has been abolished. While the UK government rejected an attempt to eliminate the offence of scandalizing the court when it revamped its law in the 1981 Contempt of Court Act, it reversed course after a more recent review of contempt laws.[37] In 2012, the UK's Law Reform Commission recommended eliminating the offence of scandalizing the court, concluding that it was an unnecessary infringement on freedom of expression and already in disuse as there had not been a prosecution since 1931.[38] (The government declined, for example, to prosecute the *Daily Mirror* in 1987 when the newspaper criticized a ruling by the House of Lords in the *Spycatcher* case by publishing upside down photographs of the judges with the headline: "YOU FOOLS!") The 2012 Law Reform Commission report pointed out that "a great deal of extreme abuse of judges exists, much of it online, and does not appear to be doing any harm".[39] The 2013 Crimes and Courts Act abolished the offence.[40] As noted by Lord Anthony Lester:

> Although abolishing this crime in this country will make very little difference because the law is entirely obsolete . . . it will send an important message across the common law world.[41]

3.6.2 The Hong Kong case: *Wong Yeung Ng v Secretary for Justice*

The boundaries of freedom of expression were at the centre of landmark contempt of court rulings involving the *Oriental Daily News*, Hong Kong's most popular newspaper. Wong Yeung Ng, a former chief editor, was convicted on two counts of contempt of court — for scandalizing the court and for wrongful interference in the administration of justice as a continuing process — and was sentenced to four months in prison. The Oriental Press Group was convicted on one count of scandalizing the court and was fined an unprecedented HK$5 million. It was the first prosecution and convictions in Hong Kong's legal history for such offences.

The contempt convictions were based on articles in December 1997 and January 1998 in the newspaper in which it sharply criticized the rulings in two legal cases to which it or a sister publication in the Oriental Press Group was a party and on a paparazzi-style campaign conducted in January 1998 against one of the judges involved in the cases.

37. Crime and Courts Act 2013, clause 22, section 33.
38. *Contempt of Court: Scandalising the Court*, UK Law Reform Commission Report, *supra*, see note 7.
39. Ibid.
40. The debate may be viewed at http://www.publications.parliament.uk/pa/ld201213/ldhansrd/text/121210-0001.htm#1212107000682.
41. Lord Lester, a member of Parliament who championed the change, was referring to a Singapore case in which author Alan Shadrake was found guilty of the offence of scandalizing the court for writing a book critical of Singapore's judicial system in death penalty cases and was sentenced to a fine and jail time. The Singaporean court that convicted Shadrake did however adopt the "real risk" test, rejecting the long-standing "inherent risk" standard (*Attorney General v Shadrake* [2010] SGHC 327), which was upheld by Singapore's Court of Appeal (*Shadrake v Attorney General* [2011] SGCA 26).

What prompted Oriental's actions?

In 1996, the Obscene Articles Tribunal had ruled against the *Oriental Daily News*, holding that several photographs of naked women it had published were indecent. The newspaper publisher appealed the tribunal's ruling to both the High Court and Court of Appeal, losing at both levels. In December 1997, the Court of Appeal refused to grant the publisher's request to take its case to the Court of Final Appeal.

Also, in 1996, Oriental Press Group sued the *Apple Daily* newspaper for breach of copyright after the latter reproduced without permission exclusive photographs its magazine, *Oriental Sunday Weekly*, had of a pregnant singer, Faye Wong. In April 1997, High Court Justice Rogers held that *Apple Daily* had violated *Oriental's* copyright for the photographs but granted only HK$8,001 in damages. Challenging the amount as insufficient, Oriental Press Group appealed. In September 1997, a three-judge panel of the Court of Appeal in an opinion written by Justice Gerald Godfrey dismissed the appeal (and later ordered that Oriental Press Group pay two-thirds of the costs of the appeal).

Justice Godfrey was critical of the Faye Wong photograph, saying that "public sentiment has turned . . . against those who are guilty of invasion of the privacy of public figures by taking their photographs for large sums which reflect the cupidity of the publishers and the prurience of their readers". He suggested that courts or legislatures may step in to withhold copyright protection for photographs that invaded the privacy of public figures. In January 1998, the same court turned down Oriental Press Group's request to appeal to the Court of Final Appeal.[42]

Contempt I: The articles and scandalizing the court

In seven articles published over a period of a month from December 1997 to January 1998, *Oriental Daily News* sharply criticized the Obscene Articles Tribunal and judges Rogers and Godfrey, accusing them of political persecution against the newspaper.[43] The articles described the tribunal and its members as "mangy yellow-skinned dogs" and the judges as "British white ghosts" and "white-skinned judges" or "pigs". The first article (with the headline "The Swinish White-Skinned Judges and the Canine Yellow-Skinned Tribunal") stated, "Oriental does not care if you are yellow-skinned or white or a pig or a dog. In our self-defence, we are determined to wipe you all out!" The article also said that if the judges ever "bother" the newspaper again they would "regret it".

Another article about Rogers and Godfrey and the Obscene Articles Tribunal, whose members were described as "stupid men and women who suffer from congenital mental retardation", issued a warning, "irrespective of race and status, effective action to restore full righteousness will be taken against those scrum bags and demons who oppress freedom of the press". Yet another article cited a reader's support for the newspaper having "torn off (the judges') designer briefs

42. The Court of Final Appeal eventually agreed to hear both cases.
43. The facts are according to the court rulings in the case.

that conceal their deficiencies and expose the ring worm, scabies and syphilis that they have hidden under their solemn black gowns".

The Court of First Instance found that, based on the common law, contempt of scandalizing the court was committed because there was a "real risk" that the articles would undermine public confidence in the due administration of justice in the minds of "at least some of the persons who were likely to have become aware of the particulars of the acts complained of" (*Secretary for Justice v The Oriental Press Group* [1998] 2 HKLRD 123). The editor appealed his conviction.

In affirming the lower court, the Court of Appeal held that the contempt of scandalizing the court was a "necessary" exemption to freedom of expression under Article 16 of the Bill of Rights Ordinance and the Basic Law (*Wong Yeung Ng v Secretary for Justice* [1999] 2 HKLRD 293). While acknowledging that the Judiciary are not immune from criticism, the court said:

> Sustained scurrilous, abusive attacks made in bad faith, or conduct which challenges the authority of the court, are not susceptible to reasoned answer. If they continue unchecked, they will almost certainly lead to interference with the administration of justice as a continuing process.

The court rejected the more stringent "real, substantial and imminent danger" test because of the unique circumstances of Hong Kong, including the relatively small size of its legal system and the easy way to communicate with a "very substantial proportion of the population". Real risk that the published articles would undermine public confidence in the administration of justice was satisfied, the court concluded, because of the duration, "abusive nature" and wide availability of the articles.

As a result of the court rulings, prosecutors have to prove three elements to sustain a conviction for the contempt of scandalizing the court:

1. that the statement or conduct was calculated to interfere with the administration of justice in the widest sense;
2. that it involved a real risk that the due administration of justice would be interfered with; and
3. that there was an intention or recklessness without regard for consequences to commit the acts that constituted the contempt.

Contempt II: The paparazzi pursuit and interference with the administration of justice as a continuing process

At about the same time *Oriental Daily News* ran the controversial articles, the newspaper also announced it would conduct a pursuit of Justice Godfrey because it said he had called the photographer who took the Faye Wong photograph a paparazzo (which the Court of Appeal said was erroneous). A team of reporters and photographers were assigned to follow Godfrey around the clock for three days in January 1998 to "educate" the judge on the true meaning of paparazzi. The newspaper published photographs and articles of its pursuit and advised the judge not "to take any false steps". Other media were invited to join in, which they did.

The Court of Appeal upheld the lower court's conviction of the editor for the newspaper's pursuit of Godfrey as an interference with the administration of justice as a continuing process. The appeals court accepted the finding that the real purpose was to take "revenge" and punish the judge for his earlier rulings.

The court rejected the argument that Godfrey would not have been influenced by the pursuit and therefore the actions were not a real risk that public confidence would be undermined. The court said that the issue was not whether Godfrey would be influenced but the wider question of whether the pursuit would lead to the undermining of public confidence. The actions created a "real risk" that confidence in the due administration of justice would be undermined, the court concluded, because the public might think that judges do not act independently or fairly for fear of punishment by those who have received adverse rulings.

What does it mean?

As a result of these cases, the Hong Kong courts imported the long-standing British prohibition (now obsolete) against severe criticism of the Judiciary as a way to bolster public confidence in the judicial system. Some observers believe timing was a significant factor, as the cases occurred soon after the handover when there were concerns about the future of the rule of law. While the examples cited here were extreme and not likely to be repeated, as always, it remains to be seen how any future cases would apply this now valid legal concept to the media in Hong Kong.

4. Statutory reporting restrictions: What you can and cannot report

Statutory reporting restrictions spell out other limitations for Hong Kong reporters covering legal cases. The rationales behind the restrictions are to protect privacy, fair trials and criminal investigations. Note that some restrictions are temporary until a case is over and others are permanent. Unless otherwise indicated, any journalist violating these restrictions can face a fine of up to HK$10,000 and a penalty of up to six months in jail, but usually only a fine is likely. (The full text of some of the following ordinance sections is provided in Appendix A.) In major cases, journalists should consider applying to the court for restrictions to be lifted.

4.1 Juvenile offenders

According to Juvenile Offenders Ordinance (Cap 226) s 20A, no person shall publish a written report or broadcast a report of any proceedings in a juvenile court or on appeal from a juvenile court revealing the name, address or school (or include any particulars that might lead to such identification) of any juvenile offender (defendant under 16 years of age). Publishing or broadcasting a photograph of a juvenile offender is also prohibited.

The court, however, in the interests of justice, has the discretion in a particular case to permit identification by issuing a court order. Persons who can be prosecuted for publication of prohibited information are any proprietor, editor, publisher or distributor. In the case of a broadcast of a prohibited report or picture, the persons liable will be anyone who transmit or provides the programme and anyone whose function corresponds to those of an editor of a newspaper or magazine.

4.2 Victims of certain sexual offences

According to Crimes Ordinance (Cap 200) s 156, after an allegation of a sexual offence has been made, "no matter likely to lead members of the public to identify any person as the complainant" shall be published or broadcast. The media are prohibited from using a detailed description that might identify the victim. If a case involves a child victim of sexual abuse, the media also cannot identify the parents as it might then identify the child.

4.3 Committal and bail proceedings

In general, all criminal cases begin in Magistrates' Court. More minor cases known as summary offences and some indictable offences are tried in this court and the proceedings generally can be reported. More serious indictable offences are referred to the District Court or the Court of First Instance, the latter sometimes after a **committal proceeding** in which the magistrate determines whether there is sufficient evidence to "commit the accused for trial". The committal proceeding is open but subject to many restrictions. Apart from the name of the defendant and the charges, most information is not to be published or broadcast until after trial or the magistrate has decided not to commit the accused for trial.

Magistrates Ordinance (Cap 227) s 87A (1) and (7):

> No person shall publish in Hong Kong a written report or broadcast in Hong Kong of any committal proceedings containing any matter *other than that permitted* . . .

The permissible information are:

1. the identity of the court and the name of the magistrate;
2. the names, addresses, occupations and ages of the parties and witnesses;
3. the offence with which the accused is charged;
4. the names of the lawyers;
5. the magistrate's decision to commit the accused for trial or any decision not to commit;
6. the charge on which a defendant is committed;
7. date and place of adjournment of a committal proceeding; and
8. whether legal aid was granted.

Those who may be held liable for violations of these provisions include the owner, editor, publisher, or distributor of a newspaper or magazine, or in the case of a broadcast report, any person who transmits or provides the programme in which the report is broadcast and any person whose functions correspond to those of the editor of a newspaper or magazine. Those responsible for violations could face fines of up to HK$10,000 and six months in jail (s 8).

The media are also limited as to what they can report on **bail application proceedings**, during which an arrested defendant applies in court to be released on bail. As this proceeding is usually the first court appearance for a defendant, the media often are interested in newsworthy cases. They can only publish: the defendant's name, the offence, the identity of the court and the name of the magistrate or judge and lawyers, whether bail was granted or not, bail conditions and information on an adjournment, if any. (Criminal Procedure Ordinance (Cap 221) s 9P(1))

4.4 Ongoing criminal investigations

According to Prevention of Bribery Ordinance (Cap 201) s 30, it is considered a violation to disclose the details, purpose and progress of investigations of ICAC cases. The purpose behind this restriction is to prevent the person being investigated from knowing about such an investigation. (For more details, see Chapter 8 Other Restrictions on Newsgathering and Reporting.) Violation of this restriction can result in a fine of up to HK$20,000 and up to one year in prison. Permissible facts that can be published or broadcast include:

1. that a warrant has been issued for a suspect's arrest;
2. when a suspect has actually been arrested with or without a warrant;
3. when ICAC forces a suspect to furnish detailed information about finances;
4. when ICAC serves a restraining order to prevent disposal of certain property;
5. when a suspect's residence has been searched under warrant; or
6. when ICAC confiscates a suspect's passport or other travel documents.

It is also a violation for any disclosure likely to prejudice a drug investigation, such as information that would reveal or suggest that authorities have been informed that property was purchased with proceeds of drug trafficking or was used or is intended to be used in connection with drug trafficking, or that would reveal or suggest the identity of a person making such a disclosure; see Drug Trafficking (Recovery of Proceeds) Ordinance (Cap 405, s 24). Similarly, anyone revealing information regarding property being funded by the proceeds of an indictable offence is prohibited by the Organized and Serious Crimes Ordinance (Cap 455, s 26).

4.5 Witness protection programme

Witness Protection Ordinance (Cap 564) s 17:

> (1) A person shall not, without lawful authority or reasonable excuse, disclose information —
>
> (a) about the identity or location of a person who is or has been a participant or who has been considered for inclusion in the witness protection programme; or
>
> (b) that compromises the security of such a person.

The potential penalty for violation of this ordinance is particularly harsh. If convicted, a journalist could face up to ten years in prison. This information received wide publicity in 2004 after the ICAC raided seven newsrooms in an attempt to uncover the sources for news stories that revealed the identity of a witness in the government protection programme when reporting on a habeas application. (For more on this case, see Chapter 8 Other Restrictions on Newsgathering and Reporting.)

4.6 **Proceedings for divorce or legal separation**

According to Judicial Proceedings (Regulation of Reports) Ordinance (Cap 287) s 3, the media are prohibited from publishing or broadcasting information relating to the dissolution or nullification of a marriage or legal separation except for the following information:

1. names, addresses and occupations of the parties and witnesses;
2. a concise statement of charges, defences and counter charges in support of which evidence has been given;
3. submission on any point of law arising in the proceedings and the court decision; or
4. summing up by the judge, finding of the jury, judgment, and observations made by the judge in giving judgment.

Violators can face a fine of up to HK$8,000 and up to four months in jail. But the media will not be held liable for contempt of court if they did not know or had no reason to suspect that the proceedings were pending or that such proceedings were imminent (s 4).

4.7 **Private court proceedings**

According to Judicial Proceedings (Regulation of Reports) Ordinance (Cap 287) s 5, it is not contempt of court to publish information relating to proceedings before any court sitting in private (*in camera* or in chambers) except when the proceedings are about:

1. the wardship or adoption of an infant or relating to the guardianship, custody, maintenance or upbringing of an infant or rights of access to;
2. where proceedings are brought under certain provisions of the Mental Health Ordinance (Cap 136);
3. when the court sits in private for reasons of national security;
4. where information relates to a secret process, discovery of an invention which is in issue in the proceedings; or
5. when the court expressly prohibits the publication of all information relating to a private proceeding.

4.8 Restrictions on reports of appeals

Criminal Procedure (Appeal Against Discharge) Rules (Cap 221F) rule 6:

(1) Unless the Court of Appeal, on the application of the respondent, otherwise directs, no person shall publish in Hong Kong a written report, or broadcast in Hong Kong a report, of any proceedings on an appeal containing any matter other than that permitted by paragraph (3).

(2) Notwithstanding paragraph (1), a report of proceedings on an appeal containing matter other than that permitted by paragraph (3) may be published where the Court of Appeal either disallows the appeal or allows the appeal but does not quash the acquittal of the respondent and order him to be tried.

(3) A report of proceedings on appeal may contain —

- (a) the identity of the court and the names of the judges thereof;
- (b) such details concerning the proceedings on the application under section 16 to which the appeal relates as may lawfully be published or broadcast in accordance with the Criminal Procedure (Applications under Section 16) Rules (Cap 221 sub. leg.);
- (c) the grounds of the appeal or a summary thereof;
- (d) the names of counsel and solicitors engaged in the proceedings;
- (e) any decision of the Court of Appeal on the disposal of the appeal and, in the event of the Court of Appeal determining that the respondent is to be tried, the charge upon which he is to be tried;
- (f) where the proceeding on appeal are adjourned, the date to which they are adjourned;
- (g) whether legal aid was granted to the respondent.

5. The identity of other crime victims?

Another restriction for the media, even though there is no statutory basis for it, is the occasional case in which a court bans the public identification of certain crime victims, such as those who were subject to blackmail, as a way of encouraging them to step forward.

In 2005, a district court judge barred the press from revealing the identity of a wealthy couple allegedly blackmailed in a kidnapping plot. As authority, the judge cited a Court of Appeal decision from earlier that year that recommended such an action. The Court of Appeal, in reviewing the sentence of a prostitute in a blackmailing scheme, recommended that the victims of blackmail not be identified. Acknowledging that its comments were not part of the appeal, the court said it "strongly disapproves of the general practice of identifying by name, address or in other ways the victims in such cases" and recommended that the Department of Justice discontinue the practice. The court said that identifying the victims was "great embarrassment" and would lead to them "being reluctant to come forward" (*HKSAR v Chen Wei-li* [2005] 2 HKC 174).

Two years later, another district judge ruled that publishing the identity of a senior government official who alleged he was being blackmailed by a former lover, a karaoke hostess, would be a contempt of court offence. When the case went to trial several months later, "Mr X" was allowed to testify behind a wooden screen in court and wear sunglasses and a surgical mask. The woman was convicted and sentenced to three years in prison (*HKSAR v Hui Wing* (DCCC 624/2007)). And in 2010, at the request of prosecutors in another blackmail case, a court barred the media from disclosing the names of a victim and witnesses in a blackmail case and also the name of the religious group they were members of and their occupations (*HKSAR v Chan Hok-yan*, (2011) HKDC 720). After the victim's name and photo were posted on a Facebook page, police launched an investigation to determine whether the court order had been violated but no one was apparently prosecuted for the disclosure.[44]

6. Additional broadcasting restrictions

In addition to the restrictions applicable to all journalists, the broadcast media also must comply with television and radio codes of practice that deal with court coverage.

These codes, overseen by the Communication Authority (CA), stipulate that news stories based on court proceedings must be presented fairly and accurately. In reports of ongoing criminal cases, the media are cautioned to avoid presentations likely to prejudice a fair trial including any pre-judgment of the issues in the case, such as the guilt or innocence of the accused; any discussion of the merits or facts of the case which may prejudice the relevant legal proceedings; any comment relating to the character or conduct of the accused; and any comment or report which tends to impair the impartiality of the court.

Even if the Secretary for Justice declines to prosecute for contempt of court, the CA can investigate complaints filed by the public. (For more on reporting restrictions for broadcast media, see Chapter 12.)

7. Future developments

In recent years, the government has brought relatively few contempt-related prosecutions against the media in Hong Kong. Some attribute this to more careful coverage by the media. Others say that prosecutors fear being accused of interfering with press freedom. Whichever, a maze of restrictions endures, and journalists covering the courts must stay aware of the potential consequences of violating some restrictions. However, the Internet, social media and other digital developments are impacting how courts around the world function. More judiciaries are acknowledging the challenges and inevitable changes that technology-dependent media and citizens bring to the courtroom. Developments such as cameras and tweets during legal proceedings are gaining acceptance, but other issues — such as whether reporting restrictions emanating from a pre-Internet era should continue — are still evolving. Whether and how Hong Kong addresses these developments in the future remain to be seen.

44. Austin Chiu, "Inquiry as Sex Blackmail Victim Named", *South China Morning Post*, 1 August 2010.

8. Court reporting checklist for journalists

As discussed in this chapter, journalists face numerous restrictions in covering court cases and other legal proceedings. To summarize some of the more sensitive areas of concern (relevant chapter sections are noted, as well as whether the ban is *permanent* or *temporary*), they should exercise caution when their coverage involves the following topics:

An arrest and committal proceeding (sections 3.3, 4.1, 4.2, 4.3, 4.4 and 5)
After a suspect has been arrested, a committal proceeding is held by a magistrate to determine whether there is sufficient evidence to "commit the accused for trial". An arrest signals the start of a criminal case and the committal proceedings are subject to many reporting restrictions. Most of the restrictions are *temporary* until after trial or the magistrate has decided not to commit the accused for trial. Some restrictions, such as the identification of a sex crime victim or a juvenile defendant, are *permanent.*

A claim of mistaken identity by the accused (sections 3.3, 4.1 and 4.3)
The media cannot run a photograph of the accused or comment on this issue. The prohibition is *temporary* and will end once the case concludes.

A criminal case (sections 3.3, 4.2–4.5 and 5)
Criminal cases trigger many reporting restrictions, with the more serious crimes likely to result in the selection of a jury. See chapter text and checklist for relevant issues, including any references for "committal and bail proceedings", "jury trial" and "ICAC criminal investigation".

A divorce or legal separation (sections 2 and 4.5)
These actions sharply limit what you can report, even after a case is over. *Permanent.*

An ICAC criminal investigation (sections 2, 4.4 and 4.7)
It is considered a violation to disclose the details, purpose and progress of investigations of ICAC cases until after an arrest or a warrant is issued. *Temporary.* Be aware of other problems arising out of ICAC probes, such as the involvement of a witness in government protection, as noted elsewhere.

In camera proceedings (sections 2 and 4.6)
You can report on what happened in closed *in camera* proceedings, but you must check that they do not involve one of several prohibited areas or that the court has banned publication. Also, the privilege for defamation might not apply to what you report.

A jury trial (sections 3.3, 3.4 and 4–6)
A case likely to involve a jury (serious criminal cases or civil defamation cases) presents the most reporting restrictions for the media. It can involve *permanent* and *temporary* bans.

A juvenile (sections 4.1, 4.2 and 4.6)
Whether a juvenile offender or a sex victim, a person under sixteen cannot be identified. Even if the child's name is not used, liability can still occur if other identifying information, such as the name of his school, is used. *Permanent.* You also cannot report about the wardship or adoption of an infant or relating to the guardianship, custody, maintenance or upbringing of an infant or rights of access to. *Permanent.*

Reporting counsel submissions (sections 2 and 3.3)
It can be risky to base a story on written submissions by prosecutors or counsel without knowing what is actually presented in court because counsel submissions often change in court. This can also affect the defamation privilege for reporting on court proceedings.

A victim of a sexual offence (section 4.2)
You cannot identify victims of sex crimes. *Permanent.*

Witness in the government witness protection programme (sections 2 and 4.7)
Do not identify the person ever! *Permanent.*

5

Privacy

Doreen Weisenhaus

FREQUENTLY ASKED QUESTIONS

1. What is the definition of "privacy"? What laws regulate it? (See sections 2–6)
2. Is there a "right to privacy" in Hong Kong? (See sections 1–3)
3. Do celebrities have more, less or the same protection for privacy rights than average citizens? (See sections 2, 4 and 6)
4. Are there special rules governing "paparazzi", photographers who specialize in photographs of celebrities? Do the media face any liability for using hidden cameras or microphones? Are journalists subject to covert surveillance and anti-stalking laws? (See sections 4–6, 7.2 and 7.5)
5. Can a journalist or photographer be sued over privacy intrusion? (See sections 4 and 6)
6. What kinds of privacy complaints can the Hong Kong government investigate? What sanctions, if any, can it impose? Can journalists claim public interest as a defence? (See sections 4–6)
7. Can the media handle privacy complaints by self-regulation? (See section 7)
8. What special privacy issues are raised concerning the Internet, social media and other technologies? (See sections 2, 4.2–4.4 and 6.1.2)

1. Introduction

The newsgathering practices of journalists have long been under public scrutiny. But media scandals and controversies of more recent vintage — from phone hacking to publication of nude photos of celebrities — have brought escalating criticism of their behaviour. For many, such actions and coverage have come to symbolize an unethical and unrestrained press; for others, however, they are instead symptoms of an increasingly competitive marketplace. In either case, the debate over privacy rights and press freedom that such scandals and controversies invariably provoke has intensified.

In many countries, the public, governments, lawmakers, and others have called for increased regulation, additional laws and/or judicial intervention to rein in what they consider to be excessive privacy intrusion by the media. Meanwhile, the journalism profession has urged more self-regulation. Efforts to define the relationship between the press and privacy rights for individuals have ranged from the Leveson Inquiry's proposals in 2012 seeking to revamp media regulation in the UK to anti-paparazzi legislation passed in California in 2010 to permit lawsuits against media outlets that publish photos obtained by unlawful invasion of privacy and decisions by the European Court of Human Rights on where to draw the line on permissible media intrusion in the private lives of public figures.

Presently in Hong Kong, where rambunctious media and paparazzi are a familiar phenomenon, there are minimal restrictions on the media regarding privacy intrusion. Hong Kong does not recognize a general right to privacy, but some aspects of privacy are protected through its constitution, the Basic Law; legislation such as the Bill of Rights Ordinance and the Personal Data (Privacy) Ordinance (PDPO), and civil actions under common law and equity such as breach of confidence. For example, the Privacy Commissioner invoked the PDPO in 2012 when finding against two magazines for publishing photographs of celebrities in their homes taken covertly with telephoto lenses. That same year, the PDPO was amended to prohibit the unauthorized disclosure of personal data that might cause psychological harm to the data subjects. (For more on PDPO, see section 4.)

But proposals with potentially far greater impact on the media also have been made. Between 1994 and 2006, the Law Reform Commission (LRC) of Hong Kong issued six reports recommending new legislation on various aspects of privacy. The first of these resulted in passage of PDPO in 1995. The other five reports covered stalking, covert surveillance, the interception of communications, media intrusion and publication of private facts.

The Hong Kong government and the Legislative Council began reviewing some of these proposals after controversies erupted in 2006 when a local magazine published covert photographs of popular singer Gillian Chung undressing backstage at a concert in Malaysia and again in 2008 following a media frenzy over the online publishing of nude photos of actor Edison Chen with various female entertainers and other celebrities (including Gillian Chung). In 2009, the Constitutional and Mainland Affairs Bureau announced it had "considered the LRC reports" and wanted to reconcile divergent community views on "the sensitive and controversial issue of how to strike a balance between protection of individual privacy rights and freedom of the media".[1] The Bureau said it would do so by handling the reports in stages, starting with stalking. A public consultation, which invited comments on such questions as whether to create a criminal offence or provide a specific newsgathering defence, ended in March 2012 (see section 7.2). In late 2013, the Bureau released a consultancy study it had commissioned that recommended a new criminal offence against stalking with exemptions for newsgathering for media organisations and activities "discussing or communicating matters that concern public affairs".[2] As of date of publication, however, no additional privacy legislation had been introduced. (For a more detailed discussion, see section 7.2 below.)

1. Administration's response, April 2009, http://www.hkreform.gov.hk/en/publications/subject.htm.
2. LC Paper No. CB(2)471/13–14(03).

2. History/Background

Legal protection for an individual's privacy has been developing for more than a century. Many trace the origins of privacy protection to an 1890 *Harvard Law Review* article, "The Right to Privacy", written by Samuel Warren and Louis Brandeis (the latter became a US Supreme Court justice). The authors, lamenting the impact of then-modern communications technology ("instantaneous photographs") and "newspaper enterprise" on individual privacy, argued that common law implicitly recognized a right to privacy. As authority, Warren and Brandeis cited English cases of breach of confidence, property, copyright and defamation. While they defined privacy as the "right to be left alone", little global consensus exists for an exact definition of privacy.[3] In one of the few Hong Kong cases to address this point, Justice Michael Hartmann wrote that "privacy is not the easiest concept to reduce to a legal definition", but said it referred to "that part of every person's life in which, without imposing on the rights and freedoms of others, personal autonomy may be expressed".[4]

The US has recognized four basic torts, or civil actions, for individuals to sue for privacy intrusion:

1. misappropriation of name or likeness for commercial purposes;
2. public disclosure of private facts;
3. unreasonable intrusion upon seclusion; and
4. putting someone in a false light in the public eye.

Individual states, however, vary widely over what privacy claims they accept and in what manner. For example, California accepts all four claims but New York only one (misappropriation of name or likeness for commercial purposes). No similar development of privacy law has occurred in Hong Kong. The tort of passing off protects commercial reputations (including of individuals) similar to the US misappropriation tort.

Despite these privacy protections in the US, its media still have much leeway. The general US rule is that the press can report about people involved in news events, voluntarily or involuntarily, or involved in matters of legitimate public interest that do not necessarily arise from news events.

Worldwide, privacy is an area of law still evolving, particularly as the Internet, social media and mobile and other technologies continue to impact development of the law, but current trends can be grouped into several categories. One is the role of government, both as a transgressor and as a protector of privacy rights. Many constitutions[5] and laws prohibit undue government interference with an

---

3. The UK Calcutt Committee on Privacy (1990) defined privacy as: "The right of the individual to be protected against intrusion into his personal life or affairs, or those of his family, by direct physical means or by publication of information."
4. *Democratic Party v Secretary for Justice* (2007) HCAL 84/2006.
5. For a comprehensive list of countries with privacy provisions in their constitutions, see Privacy International's "Privacy in Constitutions: The Data" (2012), at: https://www.privacyinternational.org/blog/privacy-in-constitutions-the-data.

individual's privacy. Hong Kong's Basic Law and Bill of Rights Ordinance have such provisions. But heightened concerns in the twenty-first century over terrorism, national security and high-tech crime have prompted more invasive government surveillance of individuals. The greater surveillance has sometimes come with new legislation, but more often not. The Internet search engine Google reported it received more than 42,000 government requests globally in 2012 for data on its users, with 447 requests coming from Hong Kong's law enforcement agencies, for which some data was provided in more than 30 percent of the requests.[6] Search engine Yahoo and social media websites Facebook and Twitter also have begun reporting data on government requests.[7] In response to a lawmaker's question, the Hong Kong government admitted in 2013 it made more than 14,000 data requests to ISPs over a three-year period.[8] The controversial Interception of Communications and Surveillance Ordinance, enacted in Hong Kong in 2006 amid much debate, has raised concern as law enforcement agencies have improperly intercepted calls to journalists and conducted covert surveillance against lawyers (see section 5).

More countries are adopting or refining data protection laws that also address how to protect private information. These laws go beyond placing restrictions on governments and can apply to any institution that collects personal data on individuals. Hong Kong was one of the first jurisdictions outside Europe to have a data protection law covering both the private and public sectors, but more recently, its government and others struggled with how to stem an increasing number of data breaches by their own agencies and private institutions that have resulted in the inadvertent release of personal data, ranging from hospital records to sensitive financial information. Governments, including Hong Kong's, were implementing more measures to prevent these data breaches as well as improper uses of data by private institutions, such as the sale of data without consent of the data subjects. Governments and courts are also responding to privacy concerns of users of Google, Facebook and other online social media as new privacy controls and features are debuted.

But for journalists and the media, the trend more likely to directly impact them is the increased willingness of individuals, especially celebrities in the UK and elsewhere in Europe, to sue for invasion of privacy or seek injunctions to prevent disclosure of personal information. Many jurisdictions such as Hong Kong already recognize the right to sue for breach of confidence, a civil action that protects confidential relationships and information. While Hong Kong celebrities generally have been reluctant to bring these actions, there have been some recent cases.

6. Google Transparency Report, at: http://www.google.com/transparencyreport/userdatarequests/.

7. http://info.yahoo.com/transparency-report/government-data-requests/; https://www.facebook.com/about/government_requests; https://transparency.twitter.com/information-requests/2013/jan-jun.

8. The government's disclosure can be found at: http://www.info.gov.hk/gia/general/201302/06/P201302060424.htm. For more on tracking government requests for data, see also *Hong Kong Transparency Report*, http://transparency.jmsc.hku.hk/.

And one of the most significant trends in recent years — the recognition of privacy as a "human right" that should be protected by law — continues to develop internationally, especially at the European Court of Human Rights. Since Hong Kong recognizes human rights principles in its Basic Law, such developments may eventually have impact here, but to date, there is little case law in Hong Kong, except in relation to the necessity for legislation controlling wiretapping.

3. Sources of law

While there is no general right to privacy in Hong Kong, numerous laws address privacy in some aspect. These include the Basic Law, ordinances and the common law.

3.1 Constitutional: The Basic Law

The Basic Law deals with privacy in several ways. Three articles directly address specific individual privacy.

Article 28 protects personal privacy, that is, the privacy of someone's body. It provides:

> The freedom of the person of Hong Kong residents shall be inviolable. No Hong Kong resident shall be subjected to arbitrary or unlawful arrest, detention or imprisonment. Arbitrary or unlawful search of the body of any resident or deprivation or restriction of the freedom of the person shall be prohibited . . .

Article 29 protects the privacy of where someone lives and "other premises". It states:

> The homes and other premises of Hong Kong residents shall be inviolable. Arbitrary or unlawful search of, or intrusion into, a resident's home or other premises shall be prohibited.

Article 30 prohibits interference with the privacy of people's communications such as mail, telephone calls and so on. It states:

> The freedom and privacy of communications of Hong Kong residents shall be protected by law. No department or individual may, on any grounds, infringe upon the freedom and privacy of communication of residents except that the relevant authorities may inspect communication in accordance with legal procedures.

These three articles apply to interference of individual privacy by both government and non-government parties, including the media, and are limited to the subject matters as described — privacy for the body, home and "other premises" and communications. (In 2005, the Hong Kong government was challenged as violating Article 30 for the covert surveillance practices of its law enforcement authorities, discussed in more detail in section 5 of this chapter.)

Article 39 of the Basic Law mandates that provisions of the International Covenant on Civil and Political Rights (ICCPR), a United Nations treaty based on the Universal Declaration of Human Rights, are to be part of Hong Kong law. The ICCPR was ratified by the UK and extended to Hong Kong in 1976. According to Article 39, Hong Kong is required to enact laws to give effect to the ICCPR; local ordinances must be consistent with it. The Hong Kong Bill of Rights Ordinance (BORO, Cap 383), enacted in 1991, incorporated verbatim numerous articles of ICCPR, including Article 17 (1), which prohibits arbitrary or unlawful interference with a person's privacy. Thus, BORO, Article 14, states:

> (1) No one shall be subjected to arbitrary or unlawful interference with his privacy, family, home or correspondence, nor to unlawful attacks on his honour and reputation.
>
> (2) Everyone has the right to the protection of the law against such interference or attacks.

Note that BORO's Article 14 provides for the right of individuals to be protected against *government action only.*[9] It does not apply to private actions, such as by the media.

Remember that Article 27 of the Basic Law, as well as Article 16 of BORO, as mandated by ICCPR, also protect freedom of expression and of the press (see Chapter 1 Overview). This means that Hong Kong law can only restrict press freedom where reasonably necessary to respect the rights or reputations of others.

3.2 Legislative

Hong Kong has several ordinances that deal with privacy matters, including the already discussed Hong Kong Bill of Rights Ordinance and the Personal Data (Privacy) Ordinance, which protects an individual's personal data. (For more on the latter, see section 4 in this chapter.) The Interception of Communication and Surveillance Ordinance (Cap 589) establishes a two-tier system of approval for covert surveillance and wiretapping by law enforcement agencies, in part in an effort to minimize unnecessary privacy intrusion in criminal investigations (see section 5).

Various other statutes restrict the media in their coverage of court cases and other legal proceedings. Typical is the Juvenile Offenders Ordinance (Cap 226), which prohibits journalists from revealing the name, address or school or publishing the photograph of any juvenile offender. Other laws with similar restrictions include the Criminal Procedure Ordinance (Cap 221), for victims of sexual offences and the Magistrates Ordinance (Cap 227), for people involved in committal proceedings. (For more details and discussion, see Chapter 4 Court Reporting and Contempt of Court.) Broadcast journalists also must comply with statutory codes of practice governing television and radio that address privacy concerns such as limits on how children can be interviewed and whether funerals can be covered (see Chapter 12 Media Regulation in the Age of Convergence).

9. BORO, Cap 383, section 7: "This Ordinance binds only — (a) the Government and all public authorities; and (b) any person acting on behalf of the Government or a public authority."

Numerous statutes regulate the availability of information provided in government registries such as land records (Land Registration Regulations, Cap 128A) and corporate information (Companies Ordinance, Cap 32), although controversy has arisen over how much private information should be disclosed about individual company directors. (For more discussion, see sections 3.4 and 6.3 in Chapter 6 Access to Information.)

And as mentioned, the LRC has recommended additional legislation to create civil and criminal liability for media misconduct (see section 7 of this chapter).

3.3 Common law

While Hong Kong's common law does not provide a general right to privacy, several civil actions under common law can protect some aspects of privacy. These include actions for breach of confidence, trespass to land, nuisance, breach of contract, defamation, and conversion, among others.

The law of trespass, for example, protects an individual's right to privacy in his or her home. Entering someone's property without permission or under false pretences or installing a camera or microphone on the premises can incur liability for trespass. (See more on trespass in Chapter 8 Other Restrictions on Newsgathering and Reporting.) A nuisance action could challenge harassing telephone calls or prolonged encampment outside a private residence. A breach of contract claim might try to enforce contract terms that forbid certain disclosures of information. A civil action taken against the media that directly relates to disclosure of private information is breach of confidence. (See section 6 in this chapter.)

4. Personal Data (Privacy) Ordinance

More than 100 jurisdictions have personal data privacy laws; Hong Kong's ordinance, enacted in 1995, was one of the first in Asia.[10] The Personal Data (Privacy) Ordinance (PDPO, Cap 486) protects "personal data", which is any representation of information relating to a living individual. A corporation is not protected under this statute. The law also requires that the data be recorded in a document or other permanent medium at some point when it is held by the organization dealing with the information.

The ordinance protects personal data, rather than personal privacy. In other words, it is concerned about how information about a person — name, address, financial situation, and so on — is collected and used, not whether someone's privacy has been invaded. Thus, privacy is a broader concept than information privacy or data protection, but these are part of the concept of privacy. As then Privacy Commissioner Roderick Woo stated in 2010:

> It is a fact that no universal definition of "privacy" has been found nor does the Ordinance attempt to define it. However, the term "personal data" is clearly defined. Primarily, the Ordinance regulates the proper collection, handling

10. Graham Greenleaf, "Sheherezade and the 101 Data Privacy Laws: Origins, Significance and Global Trajectories", *Journal of Law, Information & Science*, June 2013.

and other uses of an individual's personal data.[11]

Like in most countries with data protection laws, Hong Kong's PDPO applies to both the public and private sectors. Some countries, however, such as the US, restrict only the public sector; others such as India, Singapore and Malaysia have data laws applying only to the private sector.[12] The Office of the Privacy Commissioner for Personal Data oversees enforcement of the ordinance, investigates complaints and issues decisions and interpretations, which can be appealed to the Administrative Appeals Board (AAB) (Administrative Appeals Board Ordinance (Cap 422))[13] or to a court. The media, as data collectors, are subject to the PDPO, but the law also provides special exemptions and conditions for newsgathering activities.

In June 2012, the Legislative Council amended the PDPO; it was prompted by revelations that the issuer of the popular "Octopus" smart cards used for electronic payments for public transportation and retail stores had sold personal details of more than a million customers to business partners. The Personal Data (Privacy) (Amendment) Ordinance 2012 included provisions to restrict the use of personal data for direct marketing and prohibit the sale of such data without first informing the data subjects and providing an opportunity to opt-out. If data users failed to comply with these provisions, they could face fines of up to HK$500,000 and up to three years' imprisonment for direct marketing violations and fines of up to HK$1 million and up to five years' imprisonment for data sale violations. A grandfather provision permitted in some circumstances the continued use of personal data that had been used in direct marketing prior to passage of the new law.

A new criminal offence also was created to prohibit data users from disclosing personal data, without the consent of the data subject, with the intention to gain or to cause loss or psychological harm to the data subject. Violators could be fined up to HK$1 million and sentenced up to five years in jail (PDPO, s 64). Journalists have expressed alarm about this new offence, saying it exposes them to risks, despite an exemption for news activities and a public-interest defence (see section 4.2.1).

4.1 Data Protection Principles

The PDPO sets out six principles, known as Data Protection Principles (DPPs), to regulate the collection, accuracy, use, disclosure, and security of personal data by both the public and private sector. "Personal data" is broadly defined and includes all retrievable information, in any medium, that could identify an individual. In general, a data user cannot contravene a DPP unless permitted by the ordinance. The DPPs, as set out in Schedule 1 of the ordinance (a copy is provided in the

11. "Privacy Commissioner Responds to a Local Magazine's Editorial on Privacy Issues", 18 June 2010, http://www.pcpd.org.hk/.

12. Greenleaf, note 8.

13. The jurisdiction of the Administrative Appeals Board extends over certain administrative decisions made under the ordinances or regulations set out in the Schedule to the AAB Ordinance.

Appendix A of this book), establish that personal data can be collected only if it is relevant to the data user's activities and is done so in a lawful, fair manner. The following is a summary of the six principles:

DPP1: Purpose and manner of collection of personal data
The data cannot be collected unless it is for a lawful purpose directly related to the function or activity of the data user and is done in a lawful and fair manner and that the data subject is duly notified.

DPP2: Accuracy and duration of retention of personal data
All practicable steps need to be taken to ensure that the data are accurate in relation to their purpose and that they not be kept longer than necessary.

DPP3: Use of personal data
The data shall not be used for any purpose other than the purpose for which the data were to be used at the time of collection.

DPP4: Security of personal data
All practicable steps need to be taken to ensure that data are protected against unauthorized or accidental access, processing, erasure or other use.

DPP5: Information to be generally available
All practicable steps need to be taken to ensure that a person can ascertain a data user's policies and practices and be informed of the kind of personal data held and of the main purposes for which data are being held. (It is important to note here that DPP5 gives rights to people who are not "data subjects". Any person — particularly the media — have standing to demand information about how information systems work under DPP5. The media in Hong Kong, as elsewhere, have yet to realize this potential weapon for investigation.)

DPP6: Right of access to personal information and the right to correct
A data subject is entitled to ascertain whether a data user holds personal data and can request access to the personal data within a reasonable time, in a reasonable manner and for a fee, if any, that is not excessive. The data subject can also request corrections be made for inaccurate personal data.

4.2 The media and DPPs

While the Privacy Commissioner's Office (PCO) has conducted some formal investigations into complaints it has received against media organizations (see 4.2.2, 4.2.3 and 4.2.5), it generally prefers to resolve cases through mediation. If, however, the PCO does investigate a complaint against the media and concludes a breach has occurred and is likely to continue or be repeated, an enforcement notice may be issued to the offending journalist or news organization. Failure to respond to the notice could result in a maximum fine of HK$50,000 and/or imprisonment of up to two years. Between 1996 and 2012, the PCO received 11,690 complaints, with only a handful every year involving the media. Most cases substantiated by the PCO involved complaints against employers, property management companies and government and statutory bodies.[14] While the PDPO offers personal data protection for individuals, it also provides safeguards for press freedom.

4.2.1 Exemptions for "news activity" and a public-interest defence

PDPO s 61 allows for any data user involved in "news activity" to be exempt from DPP3 — which says data cannot be used for any purpose other than the purpose for which the data was to be used at the time of collection — if the use is for news activity and such disclosure is made by someone who has reasonable grounds to believe that the publishing or broadcasting is in the public interest (s 61 (2) (a) and (b)). "Public interest" is not defined in the ordinance.

PDPO s 61 also allows for any data user involved in "news activity" to be exempt from DPP6 (the right of the data subject to access personal information and the right to correct inaccurate data) and PDPO s 18(1)(b) (which requires data users to provide a copy of data they are holding to the data subject) until after the data is broadcast or published (s 61 (1) (a) and (b)). Thus, if reporters are merely gathering information about someone, they can do so and not be required to reveal what they have gathered or to release it to the person(s) they are gathering information about. If the data subject wants to invoke DPP6 — to find out what personal data the press is collecting on him — he is not able to ask for it before publication or broadcast. Also, the Privacy Commissioner will not initiate an investigation of a complaint until after publication or broadcast (PDPO s 61(b) (i) and (ii)).

These exemptions apply for personal data collected by data users whose business, in part or in whole, consists of "news activity" and for data used "solely for the purpose of that activity (or any directly related activity)" (PDPO s 61(1) (a) and (b)).

The definition of "news activity" includes the gathering of news, preparation or compiling of articles or programmes concerning news, observations on news or current events and the dissemination to the public of news or observations on news or current events (PDPO s 61(3) (a) and (b)).

Likewise, the new section 64 regarding offence for the unauthorized disclosure of personal data, effective in January 2013, provides identical exemption for "news activity" as defined in s 61(3) and public-interest defence. ("The person had reasonable grounds to believe that the publishing or broadcasting of the personal data was in the public interest", PDPO s 64(4)(d)(ii).) But to hold someone liable if the disclosure causes psychological harm or loss of money or other property raises concern among journalists because of the possibility of prosecution and the untested elements of the offence, such as: What would constitute "psychological harm"? And what disclosures would be considered in the "public interest"?

14. Anne Cheung, "An Evaluation of Personal Data Protection in Hong Kong Special Administrative Region (1995–2012)", *International Data Privacy Law*, 28 November 2012.

4.2.2 *Eastweek v Privacy Commissioner*

In one of the few Hong Kong court cases involving the media and the PDPO, the Court of Appeal in 2000 held that a photograph taken of an unidentified woman in the street without her consent and used for a magazine article criticizing her fashion sense was not a violation of data privacy law. In *Eastweek v Privacy Commissioner* [2000] 1 HKC 692, the court concluded that the common journalistic practice of running photographs of unidentified persons in public areas to illustrate a news article was not to be "unduly inhibited" by the PDPO.

The Court of Appeal held that personal data might be collected by means of a photograph, but that the first Data Protection Principle (DPP1) — data can only be collected for a lawful purpose and in a fair manner — was not engaged in this case. In order to be considered an act of personal data collection, the data user must be compiling information about an *identified* person. Because the woman was not identified by *Eastweek* magazine nor was it interested in discovering her identity, DDP1 was not violated.

In his opinion, Justice Ribeiro described this distinction as "potentially important and must be preserved if legitimate journalistic activity and particularly photo-journalism is not to be unduly inhibited by the Ordinance" and added:

> Thus, a newspaper may wish to publish photographs illustrating a social phenomenon in which, inevitably, persons whose identities are not known to the publisher and not considered relevant by him, will be identifiably depicted . . . [I]t is conceivable or even likely that some of the persons identifiable in the photographs may not welcome publication of their picture. Nevertheless, in none of those cases is the publisher or editor . . . seeking to collect personal data in relation to any of the persons . . . and . . . the taking of such and their use in such articles would not engage the data protection principle . . .

But the court made it clear that the media would be subject to the ordinance if they were collecting data about specific individuals, just not in this case:

> All sorts of reasons may exist for the media to collect personal data. For instance, one can envisage a newspaper engaged in investigative journalism compiling over a long period a dossier on a public official suspected of involvement in corrupt activity or of having financial interests which conflict with his public duties. To take a less dramatic example, a newspaper may build up files on well-known personalities for the purposes of writing their eventual obituaries. These are likely to be instances of personal data collection ad, subject to the express exemptions provided by s 61 and DPP1 (3) would fall within the scope of the Ordinance and the data protection principles. **If photographs formed part of the dossiers compiled, they too would become personal data subject to the statutory requirement.** (emphasis added)

A decade later, citing *Eastweek*, the Privacy Commissioner reached a similar conclusion in two cases involving surreptitious photographs taken of several celebrities inside their homes, as described in the next section.

4.2.3 Covert photos not in the public interest

In 2012, the PCO investigated the complaints of three television celebrities who objected to the publication of photographs of them from inside their homes that were secretly obtained from the outside with the use of camera equipment, including telephoto lenses and magnifiers. The two entertainment magazines that published the photos argued that it was in the public interest to show the private lives of these celebrities because they had denied certain aspects of them, such as whether they were "co-habitating".

While noting that "existing legislation does not clearly define and prohibit taking photos clandestinely", the PCO found that these photos constituted personal data and that the magazines had unfairly obtained them without the consent of the individuals, in violation of DPP1(2) (*Unfair Collection of Two Artistes' Personal Data by FACE Magazine Limited*, Report No. R12–9164, and *Unfair Collection of an Artiste's Personal Data by Sudden Weekly Limited*, Report No. R12–9159, 28 March 2012).

According to the findings, the photos were personal data that were knowingly taken of "identified" persons through "systematic surveillance" of them and "although DPP1(2) does not require media organizations to obtain the artistes' consent before collecting their personal data, they must take into account the artistes' reasonable expectation of privacy before doing do." In these cases, it was held that the individuals had a legitimately high expectation of privacy in their homes, which were not exposed to public view within normal viewing distances.

In rejecting the magazines' public-interest claims, the PCO observed that the articles "did not involve topics such as public affairs, people's livelihood or politics", but did stress that the ordinance "does not prohibit media organizations from taking candid photos of their targets". Enforcement notices were issued to both magazines to "rectify the situation". The magazines have appealed the notices to the Administrative Appeals Board.

The use of hidden or covert cameras is a popular practice in Hong Kong. In a survey this author conducted in 2003 of more than 400 Hong Kong journalists, nearly half of the respondents (46 percent) said they had used, or, if they were editors, had worked on stories that used hidden cameras or microphones. These practices were used most often for stories involving social problems (60 percent), followed by crime news (47 percent) and accident-and-disaster stories (31 percent).

4.2.4 The case of Shi Tao

In a controversial 2007 ruling involving DPP3 — that data cannot be used for any purpose other than the purpose for which it was collected — the PCO concluded that a reporter's IP (Internet Protocol) address,[15] which a PRC subsidiary of

15. According to Electronic Privacy Information Center (*http://www.epic.org*): "An IP address is a device's (typically a computer's) numerical address as expressed in the format specified in the Internet Protocol . . . In some circumstances, the IP address identifies a unique computer. In

Yahoo! Hong Kong turned over to mainland authorities in a state secrets criminal investigation, was not personal data. The PCO held that the IP address alone did not reveal the PRC reporter's identity and only disclosed details about the Chinese newspaper office where he worked (*The Disclosure of Email Subscriber's Personal Data by Email Service Provider to PRC Law Enforcement Agency*, Report No. R07–3619, 14 March 2007). The reporter was mainland journalist Shi Tao, who was alleged to have used his Yahoo! email account to send Communist Party instructions about how PRC media should handle the fifteenth anniversary of the June 4 Tiananmen Square riots to a foreign website. Shi was convicted and sentenced to 10 years in prison (He was released in 2013 after serving eight years of his sentence.) The Administrative Appeals Board agreed with the PCO that the disclosed information was not personal data and dismissed the appeal. The AAB also concluded that Shi had consented to the disclosure when he accepted Yahoo's terms of service. However, the AAB disagreed with the PCO's conclusion that Yahoo! Hong Kong did not control the information, finding that its mainland subsidiary was acting as "an agent" (*Shi Tao v Privacy Commissioner for Personal Data* [2008] 3 HKLRD 332, AAB). (For more on Shi's case, see Chapter 9 Reporting on the Mainland.)

How do other jurisdictions view IP addresses? The UK and most of Europe can consider IP addresses as personal data, particularly if individuals can be identified with other information, usually provided by the internet service provider. In 2011, the European Court of Justice ruled that IP addresses were "protected personal data", in a case examining whether ISPs could be required to monitor online activity for copyright violations (*Scarlet v SABAM.* ECJ No. C-70/10, 24 November 2011). US federal regulations do not provide uniform protection for IP addresses.[16]

4.2.5 The PCO and other complaints against the media

The PCO has investigated other complaints against the media. For details on these and other cases, refer to the office's website at http://www.pcpd.org.hk/english/casenotes/case_complaint.php). In several instances, the PCO has substantiated the complaints. They included:

- The PCO served an enforcement notice on a magazine, which published a story about an alleged mishandling of customers' data by a telecommunications company. To illustrate the article, the magazine had printed several contracts between the company and its customers, revealing their personal data; one customer filed a complaint with the PCO. The office found that news activity did not necessitate the disclosure of his data and amounted to a breach of DPP4 (that all practicable steps are taken to ensure that personal data held by a data user are protected against

other circumstances, such as when a network of computers connects to the Internet via a single Internet connection, it may not. An IP address for a computer is similar to a telephone number for a telephone."

16. http://epic.org/privacy/search_engine/.

unauthorized or accidental access, processing, erasure of other use). The enforcement notice directed the publisher to put into place a policy and procedures to prevent future similar disclosures.

- In another case involving DPP4, the PCO found against a newspaper, which had published the address of an assault victim. The victim had complained that the public release of the information was likely to cause serious harm since the assailant, who remained at large, had previously committed several assaults against the complainant and his family. The newspaper appealed to the Administrative Appeals Board, which reversed the PCO, saying that DPP4 related only to the security in the storage and transmission of data and that this published information was not "unauthorized or accidental" within the meaning of DPP4 (*Apple Daily v Privacy Commissioner for Personal Data* [1999] Appeal No. 5).
- In a 2001 case involving DPP3 (which prohibits data from being used for a purpose other than for what it was collected), a police officer complained that a newspaper disclosed in its website coverage of a criminal case a witness statement that contained his Hong Kong identity card number, officer number and Chinese name. The PCO said that display of this information was not in the public interest, finding the newspaper in breach of DPP3 and ordering it to remove the data from its website (Case No. 2001004).

4.3 Personal data in the public domain

In August 2013, the PCO again invoked DDP3 when it found that a smartphone application enabling targeted searches of litigation and bankruptcy records had "seriously invaded" personal privacy. The PCO issued an enforcement notice against a company that collated and provided the information to the app's developer to stop doing so, and the company agreed without contesting the order. The "Do No Evil" app had provided its users access to two million records collated from multiple public data registries. Many journalists, researchers and open-government advocates welcomed the app when it became available in 2012 because it greatly reduced the time and effort it took to access publicly available information from registries in different locations. The app could reveal a person's name, partial identity card number, address, specifics of civil or criminal charges and other details. After its inception, the app received about 200,000 search requests, which resulted in about 40,000 downloads.

The PCO began investigating the app's development and use after receiving 12 complaints as well as 60 inquiries and "expressions of concern". In its investigation report, the PCO said DDP3 means that personal data of the type that may appear in civil and criminal litigation as well as bankruptcy cases cannot be used for a "new purpose" without the permission of the data subject.[17] In support of its finding,

17. The PCO's investigation report (R13–9744) and details of the enforcement notice can be found at: http://www.pcpd.org.hk/english/publications/files/R13_9744_e.pdf.

the PCO cited a Court of Appeal ruling that held that DPP3 is aimed at the misuse of personal data and it "matters not" that the data involved has been published elsewhere or is publicly available; the ruling came in a case involving the website publications of an individual's full name, name of employer, job position and links to certain recorded conversations. *Re Hui Kee Chun* (2013) CACV 4/2012. In a guidance note, the PCO did list several exemptions that may be invoked by a data user when using personal data from the public domain for a new purpose, such as PDPO s 61 for news activity, but that the burden was on the data user who wishes to apply the exemption.[18]

4.4 The PCO and other Internet-related concerns

The PCO has issued several opinions, through case notes on complaints settled without enforcement actions, on other issues related to the Internet. They include:

- Internet Service Providers (ISPs) are not considered to be "data users", under section 2(1) of the PDPO when subscribers themselves circulate personal data on a website. For example, when subscribers use online chatrooms "to disseminate personal information to other Internet users, the data users . . . are the subscribers, not the ISPs". But if ISPs "collected, hold, process or use such data for their own purposes", such as sending electronic bills to their subscribers, they would be subject to the ordinance (Case No. 2008102).
- A statutorily regulated professional body is permitted to publish an online directory of the names, addresses and qualifications of its members, consistent with DPP3 (Case No. 200116).
- An email address is not personal data of a person simply because the name of that person is on a list of recipients (Case No. 2005016).

5. Covert surveillance

Hong Kong's regime of regulating the use of surveillance and interception of communication by its law enforcement agencies is complex and still evolving. In a 1996 consultation paper, the Law Reform Commission concluded that two ordinances — the Telecommunications Ordinance (Cap 106) and the Post Office Ordinance (Cap 98) — gave law enforcement agencies excessive powers to intercept personal communications in violation of the Basic Law because they did not provide sufficient protection for individual privacy. The LRC recommended that

18. "Guidance on Use of Personal Data Obtained from the Public Domain", August 2013, http://www.pcpd.org.hk/english/publications/files/GN_public_domain_e.pdf. For more on the US approach, see "Public Access to Court Records — Protecting Personal Sensitive Information", The American Bar Association Section of Individual Rights and Responsibilities, Princeton Center for Information Technology Policy, and the ABA Center for Continuing Legal Education, 17 March 2011, http://recap.s3.amazonaws.com/20110317_citp_abacle_Public_Access_to_Court_Records-Written_Materials.pdf.

interception of communications be prohibited unless the government received court approval for warrants for such interceptions.[19]

In 1997, the Legislative Council passed a private members bill, the Interception of Communication Ordinance (Cap 532), which prohibited the interception of communications by post or telecommunications (but not by emails) without court order unless the person consented or the act was allowable by law. The Hong Kong government, however, did not implement the ordinance, saying that some of the provisions would hamper law enforcement efforts, and thus the ordinance never took effect.

In 2005, the Independent Commission Against Corruption was challenged for its use of secret recordings in its investigations in two cases. One involved the installation of a hidden camera and bugging device in a restaurant; in the other, investigators used an informer to tape covertly a conversation between a defendant and his lawyer. While these acts did not directly involve the interception of telecommunications, they highlighted the lack of legislative authority for them. After two court rulings criticized the government practices as violations of fundamental rights, then Chief Executive Donald Tsang issued an executive order permitting this type of covert surveillance without prior court approval. In February 2006, the Court of First Instance declared Tsang's order and the surveillance practices as being constitutionally problematic and gave the government six months to enact "corrective legislation" (*Leung Kwok Hung & Another v Chief Executive of HKSAR* (2006) HCAL107/2005). After being rebuffed by the Court of Appeal,[20] the government introduced a bill in LegCo.

In August 2006, in a highly contested vote, LegCo passed the Interception of Communication and Surveillance Ordinance (ICSO, Cap 589),[21] which established a two-tier system of approval for covert surveillance and wiretapping by law enforcement agencies. The ordinance authorized the chief executive to appoint a Commissioner on Interception of Communications and Surveillance and a panel of three judges to oversee the process. Under the law, authorities must obtain the panel's permission before entering a premise to place or operate surveillance equipment. Security agency heads can approve less intrusive surveillance, such as monitoring email and telephone calls through servers and telecommunications switches, without going before a judge on the panel. These acts can still be reviewed later by the panel and the commissioner.

Critics said they feared that the law gave too much discretion to law enforcement agencies to conduct covert surveillance (such as wiretapping telephones, bugging homes and offices and monitoring email) of lawyers, journalists and other professions. The failure to pass any of the nearly 200 amendments to the bill by opposing lawmakers and the power of the legislature's president to refuse certain amendment proposals were the subject of a court challenge, which was

19. "Regulating the Interception of Communications", http://www.hkreform.gov.hk/reports/index.htm.

20. *Leung Kwok Hung & Another v Chief Executive of HKSAR* (2006) CACV 73 and 87/2006.

21. Section 33 of the Telecommunications Ordinance was amended and section 13 of the Post Office Ordinance was repealed with enactment of the ICSO.

rejected by the Court of First Instance (*Leung Kwok Hung v President of Legislative Council of HKSAR & Another* [2007] 1 HKLRD 387).

Since the law's enactment, the Commissioner on Interception of Communications and Surveillance has submitted annual reports on law enforcement activities under the ordinance, which have revealed numerous irregularities, including instances of the interception of journalistic materials such as phone calls. (For detailed discussion, see Chapter 8 Other Restrictions on Newsgathering and Reporting, section 7.2.) In 2011, the Hong Kong government began a comprehensive review of the ordinance. In mid-2013, the government reported to LegCo that it was preparing possible legislative amendments, which would include provisions to strengthen the Commissioner's oversight functions and clarify the powers of the panel judges and law enforcement.[22]

In 2006, the LRC also proposed regulation against non-government third parties, including journalists, recommending the creation of two criminal offences to prohibit the unlawful obtaining of personal information through intrusion into private premises and covert surveillance[23] (see section 7.5 below).

6. Breach of confidence

A breach of confidence claim challenges in court the unauthorized disclosure of confidential information. This civil action is based on the premise that when someone gives information to another person with the understanding that it is confidential — whether explicitly or by the nature of the relationship or by the private nature of the information — that person expects that information to remain so. If the receiving person to whom the information has been entrusted reveals that information without authorization, there is said to be a breach of confidence.

In *Li Yau-wai v Genesis Films Ltd* [1987] HKLR 711, Li agreed to let a film company photograph him for casting purposes only and instead his photograph was used as a comedic prop in a film. The court held that Genesis Films' disclosure to a larger audience amounted to breach of confidence. The more typical cases are about trade or commercial secrets or other types of similar confidential information. In another Hong Kong case, the Court of Appeal found a misuse of confidential information by a medical researcher who used a questionnaire that had been developed by a competing researcher (*Lam Tai Hing v Koo Chih Ling, Linda* [1993] 2 HKC 1). The court held that there was a duty of confidence regarding the questionnaire because of its unique nature, even if a relationship between the parties did not exist.

The plaintiff may also have an action against a third party to whom the information was disclosed, if the third party knew or should have known that the information was confidential. In breach of confidence cases involving the media, the press is often the third party that publishes confidential personal information that it has

22. LC Paper No. CB(2)1465/12–13(03).

23. The proposals can be found in the LRC's report, "Regulating the Interception of Communication", December 2006.

received. The plaintiff can seek damages for harm caused by the disclosure and/or an injunction to prevent publication or further publication of the information.

Traditionally, in a breach of confidence action, a plaintiff had to demonstrate three elements, as defined in the UK case, *Coco v Clark* [1969] RPC 41:

1. that the information had the necessary quality of confidence about it,
2. that the information was originally given under circumstances that obligated the second person to keep the information confidential, and
3. that the person under obligation of confidence disclosed or released the information without authority.

But this classic formulation of a breach of confidence action has evolved after a House of Lords ruling in 2004 in a case involving British model, Naomi Campbell (*Campbell v Mirror Group Newspapers* [2004] UKHL 22). Instead of relying on the existence of a confidential relationship, actions can now also be based on the misuse of private information. With an increased emphasis on the private nature of the information concerned and the potentially harmful effect its disclosure would have on the subject, the law imposed a duty of confidence when the media receives information it knows or should know could reasonably be regarded as confidential or private. In other words, what would a reasonable person of ordinary sensibilities feel if placed in the same position?

In defending against a breach of confidence claim, the media can argue that publishing the information exposes an inequity, or is otherwise in the public interest. Journalists can also argue that the information was not confidential as it was already in the public domain or that the owner of the information consented to its disclosure, or that it did not have "the necessary quality of confidence" (e.g. the information was trivial).

6.1 **UK cases against the media**

A number of breach of confidence cases[24] have been brought against the media in the UK, with varying degrees of success. The UK, like Hong Kong, does not have a general right to privacy, and, British courts have been hesitant to formulate a separate law of privacy. Instead, the courts there have preferred to extend the reach of breach of confidence claims to protect personal or private information. Several high-profile cases involving celebrities and the press have drawn some controversial boundaries regarding permissible media behaviour.

In *Douglas v Hello!*, a High Court judge in 2003 ruled that a magazine's unauthorized, published photographs of the wedding of film stars Michael Douglas and Catherine Zeta-Jones had been a breach of confidence (2003 EWHC 786). The couple had an exclusive publication contract with another magazine, *OK!*, which paid £1 million for their wedding images. A rival magazine, *Hello!*, published

24. The earliest case of breach of confidence was a British case in 1848 in which Prince Albert obtained an injunction against the unauthorized publishing of drawings and etchings made by himself and Queen Victoria. The court held that such private work could not be published without permission and the courts could intervene (*Prince Albert v Strange* 1 Mac. & G. 25).

other photographs that had been taken surreptitiously. The judge held that the photographs had the necessary quality of confidence and deserved protection as a trade secret. He rejected a separate privacy claim under the UK's Human Rights Act 1998, which recognizes principles safeguarding private and family life (Article 8) as well as freedom of expression (Article 10), saying that it was up to Parliament to pass new privacy laws.

Because their private subject matter had become a commercial transaction, Douglas and Zeta-Jones were not able to recover much in damages from *Hello!*, the third party that spoiled the deal. They were awarded less than £15,000 for distress and inconvenience. The high court did grant *OK!* £1 million in damages for lost sales from *Hello!*. But *OK!*'s award was overturned in 2005 by the Court of Appeal, which said that the couple's privacy and property rights over the photographs were personal and not transferable to *OK!* (*Douglas v Hello!* [2005] EWCA Civ 595). The case was appealed to the House of Lords.

Nonetheless, the Court of Appeal endorsed the extension of privacy protection in breach of confidence cases that resulted, in part, from a landmark decision a year earlier by the UK's highest court involving model Naomi Campbell.

6.1.1 **Is disclosure in the public interest?**

In 2004, in a 3–2 divided opinion, the House of Lords ruled that the *Daily Mirror* newspaper was wrong to publish photographs of fashion model Naomi Campbell on the street outside a Narcotics Anonymous meeting and certain details of her drug treatment (*Campbell v Mirror Group Newspapers* [2004] UKHL 22). Campbell had claimed breach of confidence, invasion of privacy and breach of the UK's Data Protection Act after the *Daily Mirror* published the photographs along with a generally positive article about her attendance at Narcotics Anonymous meetings.

The trial court had awarded modest damages to Campbell, ruling that the newspaper must have known that the information about the model's drug treatment was confidential. The Court of Appeal reversed the decision, holding that publication of Campbell's confidential information was justifiable in the public interest because Campbell had previously publicly stated that she did not use drugs (*Campbell v MGN* [2002] EWCA Civ 1373). The Court of Appeal said that journalists had to be given reasonable latitude in how they conveyed such information.

While the House of Lords held that the newspaper was justified on public interest grounds to report about her addiction and that she was receiving treatment, the three judges in the majority objected to publishing additional details about her treatment, including the surreptitious photographs. Even though Campbell did not bring her case under the Human Rights Act, the Lords said that in this instance Campbell's right to privacy under Article 8 (as protected by the breach of confidence action) outweighed the *Daily Mirror's* right to freedom of expression under Article 10, but again stopped short of creating a separate right to privacy. What the Lords did create, however, were new standards in breach of confidence cases for unlawful disclosure of private information.

6.1.2 **More human rights developments and the rise of injunctions**

A 2004 landmark decision by the European Court of Human Rights (ECHR) in Strasbourg, issued a month after the House of Lords *Campbell* ruling, further complicated matters for the media. That ECHR decision, involving Princess Caroline of Monaco and members of her family, began having far-reaching effects almost immediately.

The ECHR ruled that photographs appearing in German magazines of Princess Caroline and her family doing various activities in public, such as sunbathing, cycling and shopping, infringed their privacy. The court said there was no legitimate public interest in where Princess Caroline spent her holidays or what she did in her private life and that the publication of the pictures contradicted the right to respect for private and family life in Article 8 of the European Convention for the Protection of Human Rights and Fundamental Freedoms (*Von Hannover v Germany* [2004] ECHR 294).

As the European Convention on Human Rights has been incorporated into the UK's Human Rights Act, judges in the UK are obligated to take into account the judgments of the Strasbourg court. And they did so for the first time in the 2005 Court of Appeal decision in *Douglas v Hello!* The Court of Appeal said it would develop breach of confidence actions to "give effect to both Article 8 and Article 10 rights" and to take into account "Strasbourg jurisprudence" and decisions of the ECHR. The court noted the potential for invasive photographs to cause distress and the personal nature of privacy rights.[25] And in 2008, a UK court awarded £60,000 (US$92,000), the largest damages award to date for privacy intrusion, to Max Mosley, the former president of Formula One racing federation. Mosley sued the *News of the World* newspaper for publishing articles and a video alleging his involvement in Nazi-themed sadomasochistic sex acts with prostitutes (*Mosley v News Group Newspapers* [2008] EWHC 1777 (QB)).

UK courts also began granting more privacy injunctions requested by celebrities and others to prevent disclosure of embarrassing personal details such as extra-marital affairs. In some cases known as "super-injunctions", the media could not report even the existence of the gag order or its application. In 2009, controversy arose when the *Guardian* newspaper was prevented from reporting on comments made in Parliament to protect the identity of a private party.[26] While traditional media generally do not violate the injunctions, users of social media like Twitter increasingly have posted the banned information, raising questions as to whether such injunctions can be effective in the digital environment. In May

25. In 2007, the House of Lords in a 3–2 decision held that the Douglas–Zeta-Jones wedding photographs were confidential and under circumstances of confidence (wedding attendees were told not to take or communicate photographs) and that publication was detrimental to OK!. Lord Hoffman stated that the ruling was not about the Douglases' privacy as they were no longer parties to this particular appeal and only involved the commercial secret interests of OK! (see combined *Douglas v Hello!* judgment with *OBG Ltd v Allan* [2007] UKHL 21).

26. http://www.guardian.co.uk/media/2009/oct/12/guardian-gagged-from-reporting-parliament.

2011, a judicial committee report examining the phenomenon concluded, among other things, that super-injunctions were being issued too frequently and should be more time-limited.[27] Later that year, a judicial guidance was issued instructing courts to notify the media before a privacy gag order was granted on behalf of a public figure.[28]

Some say that the media should be required to warn people before publishing stories with personal revelations. After winning damages in his case against *News of the World*, Mosley asked the ECHR to require the media for such notification. The ECHR disagreed and rejected his request, citing the "chilling effect" of such a requirement and "significant doubts" as to its effectiveness (*Mosley v The United Kingdom* [2011] ECHR 774).

In a trio of cases in 2012 and 2013, the ECHR further clarified the balance between privacy (Article 8) and freedom of expression (Article 10) under the European Convention of Human Rights, pushing the pendulum back toward press rights.

In *Von Hannover v Germany No. 2* [2012] ECHR 228, the court rejected an application for an injunction by Princess Caroline against further publication of photographs of her and her husband on a ski trip and articles about the poor health of her father, Prince Rainier of Monaco; the court concluded that the material contributed to a debate on a matter of public interest (Prince Rainier's medical condition). In *Axel Springer AG v Germany* [2012] ECHR 227, the court held that there was a public interest in the publication of photographs and articles on the prosecution of drug charges against a television actor, especially because the information had been released by the prosecutor. And in *Von Hannover v Germany No. 3* [2013] ECHR 835, the court again rejected Princess Caroline's challenge to the publishing of a photograph — one of her and her husband on holiday that accompanied a magazine article on the trend of celebrities who rent out their vacation homes. In denying her appeal, the court reiterated the criteria set out in *Von Hannover No. 2* and *Axel Springer*, which included whether the information contributed to a debate of general interest, whether the person concerned was a public figure, the circumstances in which the photo was taken, and the content, form and consequences of publication. The ECHR noted that public figures could not claim protection of their private lives in the same way as lesser known individuals.

6.1.3 **Statutory right to privacy?**

For years, UK courts and government expressed their reluctance to declare a separate right to privacy. The British government has rejected repeated calls for

27. Owen Bowcott, "Superinjunctions Granted Too Readily", *The Guardian*, 20 May 2011, at: http://www.guardian.co.uk/law/2011/may/20/superinjunctions-granted-too-readily-judges-say.
28. "Super-injunction and Anonymised Injunction Data Collection and Practice Guidance for Non-Disclosure injunctions", Master of the Rolls, 29 July 2011, at: http://www.judiciary.gov.uk/publications-and-reports/guidance/2011/super-injunction-and-anonymised-inj-data-collection-and-guidance-non-disclosure-inj.

new statutory privacy laws, and instead endorsed self-regulation by the media industry. In 2003 the House of Lords dismissed an appeal by family members visiting a relative in prison who challenged strip searches of them as an invasion of privacy. The question of privacy "must wait for another day", the Lords said, and can only be achieved by Parliament passing new laws.[29] That "day" came in July 2011 with the convening of the Leveson Inquiry to probe ongoing revelations of widespread phone hacking of the royal family, celebrities and others by British media, most notably, News Corp.'s *News of the World*, the Rupert Murdoch-owned newspaper, which was shuttered after its role in the scandal became known. Expanding into a broader examination of the culture, practices and ethics of the press, the inquiry, led by Lord Justice Leveson, conducted months of public hearings with hundreds of witnesses. In November 2012, it released a 2,000-page report in the first phase of its inquiry, recommending, among other proposals, a new industry-led system of press regulation with an independent body set up by royal charter with authority to police the media with sanctions such as fines and power to order apologies and corrections. In 2013, however, the main political parties proposed a new regulatory body with authority to impose large fines to be set up by royal charter, which was approved by the Privy Council in October. The newspaper industry strongly opposed this development and has urged self regulation.[30] Part two of the Leveson inquiry was expected to continue after criminal investigations have concluded, possibly in 2014, but many doubt the inquiry will resume.

6.1.4 **Hong Kong developments**

In Hong Kong, soon after the Gillian Chung photographs taken backstage at a concert in Malaysia were published in 2006, her lawyers filed an action for breach of confidence, becoming the first local case to invoke the *Campbell* principle.[31] The court issued a preliminary injunction preventing further publication of the photographs, but the case settled and did not proceed to trial. More recently in February 2013, a Court of First Instance judge issued an interim injunction in a breach of confidence claim against a journalist, ordering her to remove from YouTube a video she produced ("The Life of a Hong Kong Tai Tai") featuring interviews of a Hong Kong woman and her husband, a local businessman.[32] The husband filed

29. *Wainwright v Home Office* [2003] 3 ALL ER 943. However, in 2006, the European Court of Human Rights held that Britain was found to have breached Article 13 of the Human Rights Convention by not providing a way in which the family could obtain compensation because of an absence of a tort of privacy in English law (*Wainwright v The United Kingdom* [2006] ECHR 807).

30. For current developments, see: http://www.theguardian.com/media/leveson-inquiry.

31. While the privacy claim did not proceed any further, the magazine, *Easy Finder*, was fined HK$30,000 for publishing an indecent article without proper wrapper and warnings in violation of the Control of Obscene and Indecent Articles Ordinance (Cap 390). For more discussion, see section 3.3 of Chapter 11 Obscenity and Indecency.

32. In addition to seeking the removal of the video, the writ also asked for an injunction to remove from the website: www.cnngo.com, a photograph of the couple accompanying an article the defendant wrote about golfers and golf courses.

the action, saying that he and his wife agreed to the interviews only to help the journalist, Lorea Solabarrieta, who was also a university student at the time, with a graduation project and did not consent for the interviews to be published or details of their personal lives to be disclosed. Solabarrieta said the couple agreed to the interviews without such restrictions.[33] In issuing the interlocutory injunction, the court said, "much of the factual dispute between the parties needs to be argued and resolved", especially to resolve "the context in which and the purpose for which information was elicited and provided".[34] The court noted, "both parties referred to the elements of an action for breach of confidence set out in *Coco v Clark* . . . as applied in *Li Yau-wai v Genesis Films*", making this case more a traditional breach of confidence claim, rather than along the lines of *Campbell* and the cases that followed. However way this case is resolved, Hong Kong courts in any future litigation will likely continue to look to breach of confidence cases in the UK. It also might seek guidance from the ECHR cases, even though Hong Kong is not required to as the UK is because Hong Kong has not incorporated the European Convention on Human Rights. In fact, some argue that Hong Kong's privacy provisions on non-government parties are more narrowly drawn. The real change then for the Hong Kong media might most likely come if Hong Kong enacts any new privacy legislation recommended by the LRC, which draws inspiration from many places, including Europe and the US.

7. Privacy proposals

Self-regulation versus more privacy controls is a battle in Hong Kong as well. Concern over the use of deception, hidden cameras and other aspects of more aggressive media, particularly those involving issues of privacy intrusion and Hong Kong's notorious "puppy packs" of paparazzi, has resulted in repeated calls for more regulation.

7.1 Privacy and the Law Reform Commission

In 1989, the LRC appointed the sub-committee on privacy to carry out a comprehensive review of law relating to privacy and to make recommendations for protecting individual privacy rights. Over the next seventeen years, the sub-committee issued five consultation papers and six final reports concerning privacy.[35] The sub-committee's 1994 report on the protection of personal data led to the Personal Data (Privacy) Ordinance of 1995 and the establishment of the Privacy Commission. In addition to ones on regulation of media intrusion and civil liability for invasion of privacy, it also released reports on interception

33. *Chor Ki Kwong David v Lorea Solabarrieta* [2013] HKCFI 209.

34. Ibid.

35. The final reports were: "Reform of the Law Relating to the Protection of Personal Data" (1994); "Regulating the Interception of Communications" (1996); "Stalking" (2000); Civil Liability for Invasion of Privacy" (2004); "Privacy and Media Intrusion" (2004); "Privacy: The Regulation of Covert Surveillance" (2006). They can be found at the government website: http://www.hkreform.gov.hk/reports/index.htm.

of communication (discussed above in section 3.2, "Legislative") and stalking. In March 2006, the sub-committee issued its final report on covert surveillance. In 2009, the Constitutional and Mainland Affairs Bureau announced it would handle the reports in stages "in consultation with relevant parties . . . with a view to reaching a general consensus within the community on the way forward having regard to the need to balance the legitimate interests of all parties concerned". The Bureau said it would tackle the stalking report first.[36]

7.2 **Stalking**

The LRC report on stalking, issued in 2000, recommended enactment of criminal offences and civil remedies, based on the UK's Protection from Harassment Act 1997 (PHA), which could have repercussions for journalists. The key proposed criminal offences would protect individuals from a "course of conduct" that the perpetrator knows or ought to know would cause the person alarm or distress, with maximum penalties ranging from 12 to 24 months. Defences would include that the conduct was pursued under lawful authority or for the purpose of preventing or detecting crime or that the conduct was reasonable in the particular circumstances. Persistent telephone calls or "door stepping", showing up at a private residence for an ambush interview, could amount to such an offence, unless journalists can show that their actions were reasonable. Journalists strongly opposed the proposed legislation, which was then shelved.

In December 2011, the Constitutional and Mainland Affairs Bureau announced it was ready to consider laws against stalking, based in part on the LRC's proposals of a decade earlier. The Bureau issued a consultation paper to seek public views on some of the more controversial recommendations such as whether stalking should be a criminal offence and whether journalists should be entitled to a special newsgathering defence. The consultation period ended March 2012 with the Bureau receiving more than 500 submissions, including from journalist/media organizations, legal professional associations and women's groups.[37]

The Hong Kong Journalists Association objected to the wide scope of the proposed law and vague definitions (e.g. "harassment" is not defined) and said legitimate newsgathering activities could be threatened by abuse of the law if enacted. The HKJA cited an example of an official with the North Korean consulate in Hong Kong who called police to help disperse journalists seeking comment on the death of North Korean leader Kim Jong Il. If, however, a law were to be enacted, the HKJA, the Hong Kong Press Council and other groups urged special exemptions for newsgathering.

The UK law on harassment, on which the Hong Kong proposals are based, has been applied against the media, mostly in civil actions against paparazzi, but in other cases as well. An injunction obtained by a power station against protesters

36. See note 1 above.

37. Results of the government's consultations can be found at: LC Paper No. CB(2)196/12–13(04). Other submissions came from the Hong Kong News Executives' Association, the Hong Kong Press Photographers Association and the Newspaper Society of Hong Kong.

also initially prohibited a photographer from covering the protest (*RWE npower plc v Carrol* [2007] EWHC 947 (QB)). Publishing newspaper articles can also be construed as "course of conduct" subject to civil penalties (*Thomas v News Group Newspapers Ltd* [2001] EWCA Civ 1233).[38] The UK law was amended in November 2012 to add more specific offences on stalking and stalking involving a fear of violence, with more detailed examples of conduct that would constitute stalking, including "physical following; contacting, or attempting to contact a person by any means (this may be through friends, work colleagues, family or technology); or, other intrusions into the victim's privacy such as loitering in a particular place or watching or spying on a person". Hong Kong's proposals did not include these offences.[39]

In December 2013, the Bureau submitted to the Legislative Council's Panel on Constitutional Affairs a consultancy study it had commissioned from the Centre for Comparative and Public Law at the University of Hong Kong, which examined anti-stalking laws in several other jurisdictions and recommended a new criminal offence against stalking that differed from the LRC's recommendations. The study suggested criminalizing a course of conduct, consisting of at least two acts in a list of four categories of prohibited acts, which causes a person "reasonably in all circumstances to fear for his safety or the safety of anyone known to him". The acts would include watching or loitering near the person, contacting a person directly or indirectly through various means, sending or delivering letters, emails or other objects and following, pursuing or accosting a person from place to place.

It offered several exemptions, including two to address the concerns of journalists and free speech advocates: 1) for activities of a person "gathering information for communication to the public if those activities are done pursuant to a contractual arrangement with a . . . media organisation", and 2) for activities of a person "carried out for the sole purpose of discussion or communication matters that concern public affairs".[40]

7.3 Media intrusion: Statutory press commission

In 1995, before the privacy sub-committee had examined stalking, it had focused on the issue of media intrusion. Three years later, the media's lurid coverage of a tragic story, the so-called Chan Kin Hong incident, propelled the idea of establishing a press council onto its agenda.

In 1998, the Hong Kong media covered the suicide of a woman who pushed her two young children out a window from a high-rise building and then jumped

---

38. For more discussion of UK media cases involving the Protection from Harassment Act 1997, see Andrew Scott, "Flash Flood or Slow Burn? Celebrities, Photographers and Protection from Harassment", 14(4) *Media and Arts Law Review* (Dec 2009) pp. 397–424.

39. For a list of countries with anti-stalking or anti-harassment laws, see https://www.stalkingriskprofile.com/what-is-stalking/stalking-legislation/international-legislation.

40. The jurisdictions studied were: UK, Canada, New Zealand, South Africa, Queensland and Victoria (Australia) and California and Nevada (US). For more details of the study's recommendations, see: http://www.cmab.gov.hk/en/issues/stalking.htm.

herself. Soon after the deaths, the *Apple Daily* newspaper published a front-page photograph showing her husband, Chan Kin Hong, with two prostitutes. It was later revealed that the newspaper had provided money for Chan in connection with the photograph, and after public outcry, the newspaper published a front-page apology. The incident led to heated public debate on press ethics, with some community groups organizing protests and newspaper boycotts.

In August 1999, the sub-committee issued its consultation paper, "The Regulation of Media Intrusion", which concluded, "there is no self-regulation on the industry level" and recommended setting up a press council with statutory powers to regulate the press. The council would handle complaints from the public and publish its findings. It would also have the power to impose large fines on any newspaper that failed to print an apology, correction or other matters that the council ordered. In November 1999, however, after much protest by the media, the Legislative Council voted overwhelmingly, 39–0, against the statutory press council as proposed. In the meantime, a voluntary Hong Kong Press Council was established in 2000 to regulate public complaints, but faced criticism because several of the city's largest newspapers refused to join.

In December 2004, the LRC issued its report, "Privacy and Media Intrusion", which toned down its earlier proposals. It still called for the creation of a statutory press commission, but one without the power to fine news organizations and any government role in the appointment of its members. But the print media would still be bound by a press privacy code and any publication deemed by the commission to have violated the code would be required to publish corrections and other findings or face possible court sanctions. (For more details on the report's proposals and the operation of the current press council, see section 2.2 in Chapter 12 Media Regulation in the Age of Convergence.)

7.4 Civil liability for invasion of privacy

Also in December 2004, the LRC released another report, "Civil Liability for Invasion of Privacy", which recommended the creation of separate civil actions for "intrusion upon the solitude or seclusion of another" and invasion of privacy based on public disclosure of private facts.

7.4.1 Tort 1: Intrusion upon the solitude or seclusion of another

The LRC recommended that any person who intentionally or recklessly intrudes, physically or otherwise, upon the solitude of another or into his private affairs or concerns in circumstances where that other has a reasonable expectation of privacy should be liable in tort, provided that the intrusion is seriously offensive or objectionable to a reasonable person of ordinary sensibilities. (Note that publication is not necessary for this intrusion to occur.)

While the 1999 consultation paper had also recommended this civil action, one of the biggest changes in the 2004 version was the addition of the words, "where that other has a reasonable expectation of privacy". This change means that liability would now be broadened to include intrusion in *public places* with privacy as a matter of degree that would be determined by whether there is a reasonable expectation of privacy. Although privacy expectations are less in a public place, this action would provide that a person nonetheless retains some legitimate expectation of privacy. The fact that the place is accessible to others or that a person may be visible to others does not preclude an expectation of privacy.

Physical intrusion could include if someone was intruded on in his or her home, office, guest room, or hospital room. Non-physical could be looking onto a person's private property or eavesdropping on private conversations or taking a photograph of another on a "private occasion". But generally if a photograph is taken in a public place in plain view in an area visible to the general public where there is no expectation of privacy, then intrusion will not have occurred.

What are "intrusions into private affairs or concerns of another"? These actions would include opening someone's mail; examining personal belongings like a diary or wallet; gaining access to bank accounts, medical records or computer data; conducting a body search; intercepting someone's communications, fixing a tracking device or keeping someone under surveillance.

Defences would include consent and if intrusion was necessary for and proportionate to the protection of the person or property of another; prevention of a crime or unlawful conduct, or protection of national security or other security. The 2004 report did not include a defence that had been recommended in 1999 — the defence of third-party interception done with the consent of one party, such as a person allowing the media to record his conversation with someone else. The 2004 report also explicitly stated that there would be *no public interest defence* for intrusion. The Hong Kong Journalists Association argued that it would be a serious impediment on investigative journalism to exclude a public interest defence.

7.4.2 **Tort 2: Unwarranted publicity given to an individual's private life**

The second proposed civil action for unwarranted publicity for someone's private life could be more ominous for Hong Kong's media. For this action, the LRC recommended that any person who gives publicity to a matter concerning the private life of another should be liable in tort provided that the publicity is of a kind that would be seriously offensive or objectionable to a reasonable person of ordinary sensibilities and he knows or ought to know in all the circumstances that the publicity would be seriously offensive or objectionable to such a person.

The factors that the courts should take into account[41] include whether the facts are "very intimate", whether the defendant used unlawful or intrusive means to collect the facts; the manner and extent of publication, the degree of harm to the plaintiff's "legitimate interests" and, alarmingly for journalists, "the motive of the defendant". This last factor was not explained or defined. What reasons or motives are allowed? And does a good motive negate the elements of the action?

41. These factors were taken from privacy law from Germany and France, both civil code countries considered to have some of the strictest privacy protections in the world.

What are "matters concerning an individual's private life"? Unlike the 1999 paper, the 2004 report rejected any categorization or definition of what facts are private. Instead, it stated that private life is a broad term not susceptible to exhaustive definition and that these categories are not fixed and may change over time. It cited various ECHR cases for a range of what is considered private. The problem with this, of course, is that there is no guidance for journalists as to the boundaries of what information may be published.

Defences to the proposed tort of unwarranted publicity offer varying degrees of media protection. They would include consent, lawful authority, privileged disclosure (publicity that would have been privileged in defamation cases), facts in the public domain, and public interest. The latter two especially are not strong media defences.

The attitude towards "reporting facts in the public domain" has been changing. The 1999 proposals recommended adopting the US standard of exempting the media from liability when they merely give further publicity to something that is already public (i.e. in public records, activities in public places or dealing business with the public). But the 2004 report rejected that recommendation for a far less generous one. It advocated that the mere fact that the information in question is open to public view or can be found in a public record should not preclude a plaintiff from obtaining relief, modelled roughly on French law.

Public interest can be used as a defence but its definition must be noted. The 2004 report recommended that it should be a defence "to show that the publicity was in the public interest". It rejected the broader language of the 1999 paper, which suggested a defence of "if the matter publicized was a matter of legitimate concern to the public". The LRC instead said that public interest should be narrowly defined — as the prevention, detection or investigation of crime or unlawful or seriously improper conduct; establishing whether the plaintiff was able to discharge his or her public or professional duties or was fit for public office or profession; the prevention of the public being materially misled by a public statement made by the plaintiff; or the protection of public health, safety, national security or security in respect of the Hong Kong SAR — and was proportionate to the legitimate aim pursued by the defendant.

Is it safe when dealing with "people of public interest"? The LRC said that being a public figure alone does not mean that a person's private life is in the public interest. Also, if someone is an *involuntary* public figure, the relationship between private facts disclosed and the matter of public interest must be substantial.

7.5 Journalists and covert surveillance

In 2006, the LRC proposed creation of two criminal offences to prohibit the unlawful obtaining of personal information through intrusion into private premises. The LRC made similar recommendations in a 1996 consultation paper that examined covert surveillance, mostly in the context of government conduct.[42]As noted earlier in this chapter, LegCo passed legislation regulating covert surveillance by law enforcement.

The first proposed offence would prohibit the "entering or remaining on private premises as a trespasser with intent to observe, overhear or obtain information". Private premises is defined as "any premises, or any part of premises, occupied or used by any person, however, temporarily, for residential purposes or otherwise as living accommodation" and would include a hotel room, or patient-sleeping areas of a hospital or nursing home, but not any common areas. Neither the use of a technical device nor covert actions would be required for this offence.

The second offence would make it a crime "to place, use, service or remove a sense-enhancing, transmitting or recording device (whether inside or outside private premises) with the intention of obtaining personal information relating to individuals inside the private premises in circumstances where those individuals would be considered to have a reasonable expectation of privacy".

Where the person is in plain view and is visible to the naked eye, the use of telephoto lenses or binoculars to record would not constitute an offence, but if what is observed could not be seen without the use of these devices, then an invasion of privacy has occurred, according to the proposal.

A permissible defence would be if the accused had an honest belief, and there were reasonable grounds for believing, that a serious crime had been or was being committed, that law enforcement would not investigate or prosecute the crime, that evidence could not be obtained by less intrusive means and that the purpose of the surveillance was the prevention or detection of the crime.

Journalists have expressed considerable concern over these proposals; they argue that privacy complaints against the media can be handled through existing remedies. The Hong Kong government has said it would carefully consider any impact on press freedom and did not have plans to introduce legislation on the covert surveillance proposals.[43]

7.6 The bottom line on the privacy proposals

The LRC recommendations are ambitious proposals to push Hong Kong to the forefront of privacy protection for individuals, at the expense of the media. The proposals draw on aspects of law from various jurisdictions, both common law countries, such as the US, and civil code nations, such as France and Germany, that result in the most restrictions upon the press. For example, while the LRC models the two torts of civil liability for privacy invasion in part on US privacy law, it did not propose the concurrent US protections that its media enjoy, such as the broader defences of public information, public interest or public figures. For these, the proposals tend to favour the harsher remedies from European jurisdictions. And some proposals — such as the LRC's on stalking — that look to the UK,

42. "Regulating Surveillance and the Interception of Communications", 1996.
43. "Results of Study of Matters Raised in the Annual Report to the Chief Executive by the Commissioner on Interception of Communications and Surveillance", LC Paper No. CB(2)351/10–11(01), 29 November 2010.

Hong Kong's legal predecessor, do not address excesses against the media. It was encouraging that the government commissioned a consultancy study to consider other approaches, but the fact that the Hong Kong government has stated it would systematically review and consider privacy proposals has alarmed Hong Kong's journalism community who continue to monitor the situation closely.

8. Privacy's future?

As of 2013, Hong Kong's media still faced relatively few privacy restrictions on what they can report, but recent developments — such as a new criminal offence prohibiting disclosure of personal data resulting in "psychological harm" and the government's renewed interest in considering privacy legislation — are troubling signs. Furthermore, the media should be aware that public pressure worldwide has been escalating for the protection of individual privacy rights with the courts and legislatures becoming increasingly active in expanding these rights. With such an environment, Hong Kong's laws regarding the media and privacy may change.

9. Privacy checklist for journalists (reporters and photographers)

As discussed in this chapter, Hong Kong's media still face several specific areas of concern. More detailed descriptions of some of these restrictions are included in Chapter 4 (Court Reporting and Contempt of Court), Chapter 8 (Other Restrictions on Newsgathering and Reporting), Chapter 10 (Copyright), and Chapter 11 (Obscenity and Indecency). A broadcast journalist should also consult the relevant statutory codes of practice in Chapter 12 (Media Regulation in the Age of Convergence). To summarize, as a journalist, you should be aware of potential liability when you:

Enter private property
Do not enter a private home unless its owner gives permission. Using false pretences to gain access is not acceptable.

Enter public areas
All public areas are not equal. Journalists can generally report from the street unless police impose restrictions, such as at crime scenes and disaster areas, and for reasons of public order, such as at public demonstrations. Hospitals and government properties also can limit access or restrict movement by journalists.

Take a photograph or video
It is generally permissible to take photographs or video of an individual from a public place such as a street, especially if the person's name or identity is not used, but restrictions can be placed on some public areas. Permission must be given for taking photographs or video inside a private place such as a home. Permission to enter someone's home does not equal consent to take a picture. Separate consent must be obtained. If a hidden camera is used, be prepared to defend its use on

public interest grounds. At no time can a photograph or video be taken inside a courtroom during a legal proceeding.

Collect data on a specific person
If you collect "data" on a specific individual, you are subject to the PDPO. A photograph is considered data.

Publish someone's personal materials
If the materials were not obtained by illegal means such as theft, the media could still face copyright violations if permission to publish was not obtained.

Publish information about a child or young person
A person who is under sixteen years old and is involved in a Juvenile Court case or custody hearing cannot be identified. For any other legal proceedings, watch out for any restrictions imposed. Even if the child's name is not used, liability can still occur if other identifying information, such as the name of the child's school, is used.

Record a telephone call with the person you are interviewing or listen to a person's telephone call with a third party
It is not a criminal offence to record your own telephone call with a person, even if that person was not notified of the recording. Nor is it an offence if someone gives you permission to listen to and/or record his or her telephone conversation with an unaware third party. The practices might run afoul of Article 30 of the Basic Law (which protects the privacy of personal communications) and the Personal Data (Privacy) Ordinance, but to date, no cases have been found against the media.

Publish a nude photograph
If the photograph was not obtained illegally, such as by theft, the media could still face obscenity or indecency charges, even if the person depicted in the photograph gave permission for its publication.

6

Access to Information

Doreen Weisenhaus

FREQUENTLY ASKED QUESTIONS

1. What is Hong Kong's "Code on Access to Information" and what government information is available under it? (See section 3)
2. If the government refuses to release accessible information, what remedies do journalists have? (See section 3.3)
3. How does this administrative Code on Access to Information differ from Freedom of Information laws in other jurisdictions? (See sections 2 and 7)
4. What other laws or regulations require release of public information? (See section 6)
5. Does Hong Kong require open meetings and public access for its governmental agencies and advisory bodies? (See sections 5–6)
6. Must government records be kept for a specific time period or under certain conditions? (See section 4)

1. Introduction

The Hong Kong government, like most modern governments, gathers and generates large amounts of recorded information. It documents its decisions, its operations and its dealings with the private and public sectors. It collects statistics and data on people, institutions and the economy. Whether and how it shares that information with its citizens are the subjects of much discussion and controversy.

This chapter focuses on laws and regulations that affect how certain government information and proceedings are made available to the public and, by extension, journalists. In particular, it examines Hong Kong's administrative Code on Access to Information and how it compares to access laws elsewhere. While the code requires public access to some government-held or produced information, it also expressly excludes disclosure of information across more than a dozen broad categories. The chapter also explains how the *absence* of other laws, such as archival laws to require the maintenance of public records and so-called sunshine laws to mandate open meetings for governmental bodies, further hampers the abilities of the public and the media to access government-held information.

Thus, the practical effect of the code — together with the highly restrictive Official Secrets Ordinance, described in Chapter 7, and the lack of archival and open meeting laws — is to cloak in secrecy much of even the ordinary work of the government.

2. History/Background

As a former colony, Hong Kong inherited the British government's penchant for secrecy. Journalists trying to report on the activities of the local administration face formidable barriers, from the Official Secrets Ordinance, which tightly controls the unauthorized obtaining or disclosing of official information, to the government's typical closed-door approach to the business of running Hong Kong.

Many societies try to combat government tendencies towards secrecy by enacting Freedom of Information (FOI) laws, also known as Right to Information (RTI) laws, which compel the public release of government documents and information. The first such law emerged in Sweden in 1766. Since then, more than 90 countries have adopted FOI laws, including the United States (1966), Australia (1982), New Zealand (1982) and Canada (1983). Most of the laws have been passed since 1990, with an increasing number from Asian countries such as Thailand (1997), South Korea (1998), Japan (2001), Pakistan (2002), India (2005), Taiwan (2005), Nepal (2007), Bangladesh (2009), Indonesia (2010) and Mongolia (2011). In 2007, China enacted its first national Open Government Information regulations, effective in 2008. (For more details, see Chapter 9 Reporting on the Mainland.) Furthermore, more than 60 countries have acknowledged constitutional status for the right to government information either directly in their constitutions (e.g. Mongolia, Pakistan and the Philippines) or through court decisions (India, Japan and South Korea).

The central premise of a FOI law is to establish the right for individuals to ask for records, documents or information held by public authorities and other governmental bodies. Persons making a request generally do not need to show a legal interest or provide a reason. According to a 2006 survey of FOI laws worldwide,[1] the majority of such laws allow anyone to ask for information, not just citizens of that country. Some permit anonymous requests to guard against the possibility of discriminatory or punitive actions by the government.

Recent trends include extending FOI laws to cover non-governmental bodies such as companies and NGOs that receive public money to do public projects. In 2001, for example, South Africa enacted one of the strongest FOI laws, which allows the obtaining of information from private entities if it is necessary to enforce individual rights. Because FOI laws also create an affirmative duty for governments to release certain categories of information, many also mandate that electronic versions of records be open and accessible.

FOI laws generally exempt certain sensitive information, such as that concerning national security and personal privacy, but most require that harm be shown before the information can be withheld. Some laws include a public-interest test, which permits disclosure even if harm may be caused if the public interest in releasing the information outweighs the harm. Since the September 11, 2001 terrorist attacks in the US, however, anti-terrorism measures worldwide have resulted

1. David Banisar, "Freedom of Information Around the World, 2006", freedominfo.org, Global Survey, July 2006, http://www.freedominfo.org/documents/global_survey20.pdf.

in governments restricting some previously available information and increasing the number of classified documents. Yet, a fundamental feature for FOI laws remains the availability of independent and judicial review in the courts after the denial of a request.

Governmental transparency and accountability are among the major policy concerns driving the movement. Laws often have been enacted following government scandals or power struggles between a legislature and a strong executive branch. In recent years, international bodies and organizations also have pushed nations to adopt FOI legislation to make financial systems more transparent, to reduce corruption and to implement human rights goals.

The Johannesburg Principles on National Security, Freedom of Expression and Access to Information, endorsed by the United Nations Commission on Human Rights, recommends a FOI law "to discourage governments from using the pretext of national security to place unjustified restrictions" on the exercise of the freedoms of expression and information.[2]

In a 2006 landmark ruling, the Inter-American Court of Human Rights held that individuals have a fundamental human right to access government information under the American Convention on Human Rights.[3] Likewise, the European Court of Human Rights has held in favour of NGOs, researchers and others seeking state-held information but stopped short of embracing an unlimited right of access.[4] And in 2011, the UN Human Rights Committee[5] endorsed a resolution that access to public information is a human right under Article 19 of the International Covenant on Civil and Political Rights. It stated that governments "should proactively put in the public domain Government information of public interest" and "make every effort to ensure easy, prompt, effective and practical access to such information".[6]

These developments add to perhaps the most potent argument for a FOI law, which is the recognition that for a society based on self-rule, its citizens must have real access to information so they can make sound decisions about their own governance. In Hong Kong, the struggle for that access has been ongoing for two decades.

In the early 1990s, the Hong Kong Journalists Association, lawmakers and others began calling for a FOI law. In 1994, independent legislator Christine

2. UN Doc. E/CN.4/1996/39 (1996). The principles were adopted in 1995 by a group of experts in international law, national security and human rights, convened at the University of Witwatersrand, Johannesburg, South Africa.

3. *Reyes v Chiles,* Inter-Am C.H.R (Ser. C) No 151 (2006); English translation: http://www.corteidh.or.cr/docs/casos/articulos/seriec_151_ing.doc.

4. *Gillberg v Sweden* [2012] ECHR 569, *Társaság A Szabadságjogokért (Hungarian Civil Liberties Union) v Hungary* [2009] ECHR 618.

5. The Human Rights Committee is a body that monitors implementation of the International Covenant on Civil and Political Rights by countries that are signatories. For more on Hong Kong's compliance with ICCPR, see Chapter 2 The Legal System.

6. General Comment 34. Text can be found at: http://www2.ohchr.org/english/bodies/hrc/docs/GC34.pdf.

Loh Kung-wai tried to introduce a private member's FOI bill. But then Governor Christopher Patten resisted these calls and instead in 1995 instituted an administrative Code on Access to Information. The code was much less favourable to those seeking public information than a FOI statute because it exempted many categories of information and did not come with force of law or provide for judicial review of any denials.

Events in Hong Kong at the time mirrored those in the UK. After similar debates, in 1994, British authorities implemented an administrative Code of Practice on Access to Government Information. Journalists there, like their Hong Kong counterparts, found the code of little practical use. But that is where the similarity ends. A change in government resulted in the passage of the UK Freedom of Information Act 2000, which went into effect in 2005. Hong Kong has not followed this more recent UK example or those of the increasing number of Asian countries adopting FOI legislation or recognizing right of access in their constitutions.

3. Code on Access to Information: What is it?

Instead, Hong Kong relies on its Code on Access to Information, which on its surface sounds promising. It requires Hong Kong government agencies to publish or make available a list of records held by that agency and to respond to requests for information in a timely fashion.

At the time it was established, the code did not encompass such government entities as the police and the offices of the Chief Secretary and the Financial Secretary and was amended in 1996 to include all government agencies and departments. (For the list of entities covered, see Appendix D of this book or the government website, http://www.access.gov.hk.) The code does not cover information held by courts and tribunals and hundreds of advisory and statutory boards and committees that help the government run its operations.

The code is divided into two parts. The first part explains what information the government can provide and how someone can apply for the information. The second part details the kinds of information government departments can choose not to release.

The Constitutional and Mainland Affairs Bureau[7] has oversight responsibility for code compliance. The code's text, as well as guidelines instructing departments how to respond to a request, can be found on the government website. What is considered a record covered under the code is described as follows:

> A record may include a document in writing and–
> (a) any book, map, plan, graph or drawing;
> (b) any photograph;
> (c) any label, marking or other writing which identifies or describes anything of which it forms part, or to which it is attached by any means whatsoever;
> (d) any diskette, tape, sound-track or other device in which sounds or other data (not being visual images) are embodied so as to be capable (with

7. Until 30 June 2007, the Home Affairs Bureau was responsible for administration of the code.

or without the aid of some other equipment) of being reproduced therefrom;

(e) any film, negative, tape, microfilm, microfiche, CD-ROM or other device in which one or more visual images are embodied so as to be capable (with or without the aid of some other equipment) of being reproduced therefrom; and

(f) anything whatsoever on which is marked any words, figures, letters or symbols which are capable of carrying a definite meaning to persons conversant with them.[8]

3.1 How to apply for information

The request can be made orally, in writing, by fax or email. The government provides an application form, which can be filled out in English or Chinese (http://www.access.gov.hk/en/annexc.htm). A sample of the form is also contained in Appendix D of this book.

The request can be sent to the designated Access to Information Officer, listed on each departmental website. Note that some departments charge fees for specific services provided to the public, such as those charged by the Land Registry for the search of land records. Charges should be "simple and inexpensive", according to government guidelines, and materials normally provided for free cannot be charged. A standard fee for photocopying is HK$1 per page.

The department is expected to try and respond to the request within 10 days, but if it cannot, it should respond by twenty-one days. In "exceptional circumstances" for complicated requests, it may take up to 51 days.

Information to be published or made available routinely include annual updates of details of organization and services; performance pledges and the extent to which they have been met; a list by category of kept records; a list of information either published or otherwise made available, whether free or for cost, and the procedures and charges for access to information not routinely published. The code does not require a department to acquire information not in its possession, create a record that does not exist, provide on request information already published or provide information available through an existing service for fee, although the department is encouraged to direct the person making the request to where the information might be obtained.

3.2 What information can be withheld

Part 2 of the code lists and defines categories of information whose disclosure *may* be withheld. Government guidelines point out the use of the word *may*, and not *shall*, meaning that departments are not prohibited from disclosing the information, provided they have considered whether the public interest in disclosure of such information outweighs any harm or prejudice that could result

8. Code on Access to Information, Annex B.

from disclosure and have obtained the necessary authority.[9] According to the guidelines:

> The approach to release of information under the Code should be positive; that is to say, departments should work on the basis that information requested **will** be released unless there is good reason to withhold disclosure under the provisions of Part 2 of the Code.[10] (emphasis in original text)

At the same time, departments are advised that they have the discretion to refuse to confirm or deny the existence of information, if necessary.

What is exempted from disclosure under the Code of Access to Information? A lot! The code has sixteen categories of exemptions that greatly limit its scope. They include:

1. defence and security
2. external affairs (such as dealing with foreign countries or territories)
3. immigration and nationality
4. law enforcement, legal proceedings and public safety
5. damage to the environment
6. management of the economy (such as regulation of financial markets, public utilities, land use, revenue or expenditure proposals and "discussion of possible proposals significant to the formulation or modification of the Government's policy on the economy")
7. management and operation of public service
8. internal discussions and advice
9. public employment and appointments
10. improper gain or advantage
11. research, statistics, analysis generated by the government
12. third-party commercial interests
13. privacy of individuals
14. business affairs (information including commercial, financial, scientific or technical confidences, trade secrets or intellectual property whose disclosure would harm the competitive or financial position of any person)
15. premature requests (information soon be published, or whose disclosure would be premature in relation to a planned announcement or publication)
16. legal restrictions (information whose disclosure is legally restricted by statute, common law or international agreement)

3.3 How to challenge

If journalists and members of the public think the department is taking too long, charging too much or wrongly denying a request, in part or in whole, they can ask a senior officer of the department to review the denial.

---

9. Guidelines on Interpretation and Application, para 2.1.1, Code on Access to Information, at: http://www.access.gov.hk/guidelines.pdf.
10. Ibid., para (vii).

If the request is again denied, they can go to the Office of the Ombudsman, which has taken an increasingly critical stance on how the Hong Kong government has complied with the code. This office can review government actions and substantiate a complaint, although it cannot force departments to disclose information (Ombudsman Ordinance (Cap 397) s 7). The code does not provide for judicial review of denied requests. (In theory, of course, any government action can be challenged in court, but in the case of a court challenge arising from a dispute under the code, the underlying merits of the denial cannot be addressed.)

3.4 The code's effectiveness

In the code's first fifteen years of operation (1995–2010), the government reported that it received 28,785 requests, of which 25,431 (88 percent) were met in full or in part and that 608 requests (2 percent) were refused. The remainder was referred to other organizations, withdrawn by applicants or still being processed.

Over the years, some government departments have made strides in providing and publicizing the information they have available. Probably among the most transparent of the government agencies under the code are the Lands Registry, which provides records of any parcel of land and house or apartment in Hong Kong (Land Registration Regulations, Cap 128A) and the Companies Registry, which hosts annual company reports with key information on directors, shareholders and more (Companies Ordinance, Cap 32). Both registries have been used, for example, to track the backgrounds of landowners, especially if ownership is held by a company or other business entity.[11] Many journalists feel that transparency appears to be the exception, rather than the rule, for many government agencies; they take a dim view of the code's value, pointing out that most requests under the code are from the public for simple information. In 1999, in the early years of the code, the Hong Kong Journalists Association tested it through various government agencies and found only one-third of 81 requested documents were available. Since then, the HKJA and others have concluded that access to public information has worsened.

Corporate governance advocate David Webb tried to use the code repeatedly to obtain directors' reports and audited financial statements — required by the Companies Ordinance — for the government-owned Hong Kong Cyberport Management Company Ltd and its subsidiaries.[12] Cyberport is a multi-billion-dollar high-tech development project on Hong Kong Island, which generated controversy after it became more known as an expensive residential development.

The government initially denied Webb's requests as "premature" because it was preparing a report on Cyberport to submit to the Legislative Council. Later, three

11. One of the leading experts on accessing public information in Hong Kong is Chan Pui-king, former editor-in-chief of *Next Magazine*. For more of her analysis on the code, see "Hong Kong's Code on Access to Information Turns 15 Years Old: Can the Right to Know Thrive Without a Law", 19 March 2010, at: http://www.freedominfo.org/2010/03/hong-kong-code-on-access-to-information-turns-15-years-old-can-the-right-to-know-thrive-without-a-law/.

12. See: http://www.webb-site.com/articles/cybersecrets.asp.

months after the first request, it declined to release the records because it said they contained "commercially sensitive information".

While the Ombudsman in 2005 ultimately supported the government's refusal on the commercial-confidentiality basis, it criticized the government's handling of the requests as against the "spirit of the code, which calls for an open and positive attitude" and suggested it apologize to Webb. The government did, and provided what it described as "sanitized accounts without the commercially sensitive information" to LegCo.

But in subsequent investigations, the Ombudsman's office has taken a decidedly stronger tone against the government's denials of information requests.

In 2007, the Ombudsman's office concluded that Transport and Housing Bureau officials breached the code when they repeatedly denied a request by Fu King-wa, a University of Hong Kong researcher for information on railway suicide incidents. After the ruling and 14 months after the initial request, the bureau released the information. In its finding, the Ombudsman said, "This case highlights the need for Government to raise the awareness of bureaux and departments regarding their obligations under the Code."[13]

In 2009, the Ombudsman's office substantiated a complaint by the *Apple Daily* newspaper that had tried unsuccessfully to obtain government test results of food samples from mainland China in the aftermath of a scandal in which infants consuming dairy products tainted with the chemical melamine suffered kidney stones and kidney failure, resulting in deaths and hospitalization. The Food, Environment and Health Department argued that disclosure of the melamine test results for products it already deemed safe would cause confusion for the public and harm relationships with food manufacturers, some of which might sue the Hong Kong government. The Ombudsman rejected these grounds as "not a valid reason for refusal under the Code" and advised that "the veracity of (the department's) findings on melamine levels is a complete defence to any action for libel brought by food manufacturers".[14]

And in a year-long broader review of government code compliance, the Ombudsman's office concluded in 2010 that the government had done little to raise public awareness of the code or to train officers in how to respond to information requests.[15] Government departments had demonstrated "considerable misunderstanding of the provisions and unfamiliarity with the procedural requirements of the Code after well over a decade of implementation", according to the Ombudsman's report. It cited examples of departments failing to give reasons, giving reasons not specified in the code or misusing reasons in their denials of information requests. It again advocated training, compliance monitoring and promoting of the code to the public.

---

13. OMB 2007/1987(I) 7 August 2007.
14. Direct Investigation Report, Effectiveness of Administration on Code of Access of Information, January 2010, at: http://ofomb.ombudsman.gov.hk/doc/DI189.pdf.
15. Ibid.

In January 2013, the Ombudsman's office announced it would again conduct another investigation into Hong Kong's access of information regime, but said it would also examine the government's records management and archival system. The review would include a comparative analysis of FOI regimes and record management systems of other jurisdictions around the world.

4. Lack of archival laws

In announcing a review of how Hong Kong manages its public records and archives, the Ombudsman joined a growing chorus of critics concerned that the code's effectiveness might also be hindered by Hong Kong's lack of archival laws, which are common in many countries that use them to require the retention and management of public record archives.

Access to Hong Kong's archives is subject to Public Records (Access) Rules 1996, which hold that most public records more than 30 years old are available for public use, and is managed by the Government Records Service (GRS), with the Public Records Office as the central repository.[16] But because this system is not protected by statutory authority, the non-binding administrative rules and guidelines to manage and provide access to records and archives are limited in range with few enforcement mechanisms. For example, many departments do not transfer records for archival, there are no penalties for rule violations and statutory bodies funded by public money, such as the Hospital Authority and the Trade Development Council, are not covered under the rules. By contrast, the UK's Public Records Act 1958 mandates that files 30 years old are automatically released by the National Archives.

The impact of the absence of an archival law was evident in 2011 when the government revealed it had destroyed 6 million sheets of records, 3.5 million from the Office of the Chief Executive and its policy bureaux alone, before its move to the new Central Government Complex in Tamar. These actions were described as "travesties of records and archives management" by Donald Brech, Hong Kong's first GRS director and a member of the Archives Action Group, composed of lawmakers, retired judges, professors and other advocates for an archives law who have drafted a public records bill.[17]

The bill proposed, among other provisions, to establish an archives authority with statutory powers to formulate records policy and procedures, to provide public access to records and archives and to penalize non-compliance. A motion debate on enacting an archives law was defeated in LegCo in November 2011.[18]

16. Established in 1989, the GRS maintains a website (http://www.grs.gov.hk/), which contains a copy of Public Records (Access) Rules 1996, at: http://www.grs.gov.hk/ws/english/engimages/publicforms/access.pdf.
17. http://www.archivesactiongroup.org/.
18. For more on the issue, see Christine Loh and Nick Frisch, *Memory Hole: Why Hong Kong Needs an Archives Law*, Civic Exchange, 24 November 2011, at: http://www.civic-exchange.org/wp/111124publicrecords_en/.

5. Open meetings

Coupled with the absence of meaningful access to, and archival of, official records is the absence of so-called sunshine laws, which require meetings of governmental agencies and advisory boards and committees to be open to the public and thus the media.

5.1 Advisory and statutory boards and committees

More than 450 advisory and statutory bodies (ASBs), with thousands of appointed members, are crucial in the development and governance of Hong Kong.

They include: [19]

Regulatory boards and bodies. They consist of registration boards regulating professions or trades (e.g. the Land Surveyors Registration Committee); licensing boards regulating the licensing of premises or equipment for a specific purpose or function (e.g. the Liquor Licensing Board); regulatory bodies regulating an industry or sector of the economy (e.g. the Securities and Futures Commission), and supervisory boards monitoring specific activities (e.g. the Electoral Affairs Commission).

Appeals boards. They perform a semi-judicial function by handling and adjudicating appeals to resolve disputes in certain areas between private citizens and the government or a public body set up by the government (e.g. the Licensing Appeals Board and Copyright Tribunal).

Non-department public bodies. They are non-commercial organizations that deliver public services with a high degree of autonomy (e.g. the Hospital Authority, Consumer Council and the Equal Opportunities Commission).

Public corporations. They are commercial entities set up by law to provide goods and services, typically created by the transferral of government assets to a corporate structure (e.g. the Kowloon-Canton Railway Corporation).

Advisory and management boards of trusts/funds and funding schemes. They are bodies set up to hold and control property for the benefit of named beneficiaries or for stated purposes (e.g. Board of Directors of the Widows and Orphans Pension Scheme).

Advisory committees. They provide ongoing information or professional expertise in particular areas or subjects and/or advise on the development of policies or the delivery of services (e.g. the Law Reform Commission).

Miscellaneous boards and committees (e.g. university councils, Independent Police Complaints Council).

Some ASBs such as certain tribunals and boards (e.g. the Copyright Tribunal, Securities and Futures Appeals Tribunal, Administrative Appeals Board) will hold hearings in public,[20] but most of the bodies, however, do not regularly hold open meetings or conduct press briefings afterward or do so at the discretion of the

19. http://www.info.gov.hk/cml/eng/cbc/index.htm.
20. Halsbury's Laws of Hong Kong [255.037].

particular body or its chairman.[21] A typical example of an important advisory body with little transparency or accountability was the Antiquities Advisory Board, a statutory body which advises the Antiquities Authority on heritage preservation and helps the Hong Kong government decide which buildings or structures should be declared monuments, thus ensuring legal protection against their demolition (Antiquities and Monuments Ordinance (Cap 53)). For 30 years, agendas, meeting schedules and minutes were not made public. Only after public outcry over controversial decisions not to give heritage status to such sites as the Star Ferry Pier were some meetings and documents made public in 2007. Now, the public can access the board's website for up-to-date information (http://www.aab.gov.hk).

Since 1996, LegCo has sought an overhaul of these advisory bodies and urged changes in transparency, appointments, handling conflicts of interests, compensation and public input. In 2003, the Home Affairs Bureau released a consultation paper ("Review of the Role and Functions of Public Sector Advisory and Statutory Bodies")[22] that said it would conduct a study on how to increase transparency and recommend other changes for statutory and advisory committees and bodies. Since then, the bureau has submitted a series of interim progress reports to LegCo's Panel on Home Affairs and has implemented some guidelines and principles for ASB appointments, such as limiting non-official members from serving more than six years in the same capacity on the same ASB or from sitting on more than six ASBs at a time, but as of late 2013, the administration had not released a final report nor appeared to have finished its review.[23]

5.2 Town planning bodies and records

One important advisory body, the Town Planning Board, has embraced more transparency and accountability, following passage in 2004 of amendments to the Town Planning Ordinance (Cap 131).

In 2005, the Town Planning Board, which makes key decisions about land use in Hong Kong, began allowing members of the public to view by closed circuit television parts of its proceedings. The public can now directly attend open meetings of the board and its committees, but are requested to register. The board also releases meeting minutes and the latest "Gist of Decisions", although these do not disclose what individual board members said or how they voted. Enquiry counters were established in the Sha Tin and North Point government offices to accommodate public access to planning documents. These allowed people to inspect planning applications, representations on draft plans and comments on representations. In addition, the hearings for the Town Planning Appeals Board are also public. Public information can be found on the Town Planning Board website (http://www.info.gov.hk/tpb).

21. Ibid.
22. The consultation paper can be found at: http://www.hab.gov.hk/file_manager/en/documents/whats_new/advisory_and_statutory_bodies/ASBmempaper.pdf.
23. For more details, copies of interim reports and government answers to LegCo questions, see: http://www.legco.gov.hk/database/english/data_ha/ha-review-advisory-statutory-bodies.htm.

Such transparency for advisory and statutory bodies remains rare. The proceedings and records for many of these bodies are not open to the public. Some maintain substantial websites, but many ASB websites contain minimal information such as membership lists.

6. Other public information and proceedings

As with the amendments that opened up the Town Planning Board, other laws, regulations and rules provide for some openness for public records and/or meetings in several categories. Examples include the courts, the Legislative Council, personal data and public health.

6.1 Courts

As detailed in Chapter 4 Court Reporting and Contempt of Court, the courts operate on the "open justice principle". This principle translates into a presumption that criminal and civil cases, especially trials, should be held in open court and has its basis in the Hong Kong Bill of Rights Ordinance, Article 10, that everyone is entitled to a "fair and public hearing". But as also noted, Article 10 states that court proceedings may be closed for reasons of morals, public order, national security, individual privacy or "to the extent strictly necessary" where such publicity would "prejudice the interests of justice". Even if parts of a court proceeding are closed, however, the court must make public any final decision except in certain cases involving children or divorce.

One positive development for the media in covering court cases has been an increase in court transparency. In 2005, the Hong Kong judiciary implemented a major policy change when it opened some in-chamber civil proceedings to journalists and the public (see Appendix C, "Judicial Practice Directions: Hearings in Chambers in Civil Proceedings").

The courts also have many public records, including writs of summons and judgments, but accessing them can be difficult as there is no one central registry. Journalists cannot access court files without approval from the court or the parties involved (see Appendix B, "Searching for Public Records of Courts"). A private company that compiled and collated litigation and bankruptcy records from multiple public registries and made them available to the public via a smartphone app was ordered to stop doing so in 2013 by Hong Kong's Office of the Privacy Commissioner for Personal Data as an improper use of personal data in the public domain. (For details, see section 4.3, Chapter 5 Privacy)

6.2 Legislative Council

6.2.1 Council meetings

Council meetings are generally open to members of the press and the public. But the president, chairman of a committee of the whole council, or chairman of a committee or subcommittee may order the removal from a meeting of any member of the press or of the public who behaves, or who appears likely to behave, in a disorderly manner (Rules of Procedure (Part N), Rule 86).

At a meeting of the council, a committee of the whole council, a committee or a subcommittee, a member may without notice at any time rise and move that members of the press and of the public withdraw, specifying whether the withdrawal is to be for the remainder of that day's meeting or during the consideration of certain business. The president or chairman of a committee or subcommittee shall then propose the question and the council, committee of the whole council, committee or subcommittee shall dispose of it before proceeding further with the business before it when the motion was moved. The president or chairman may at any time order members of the press and of the public to withdraw and that the doors of the Council Chamber be closed (Rules of Procedure (Part N), Rule 87).

When an order has been made by the council, committee of the whole council, committee or subcommittee, or by the president or chairman, members of the press and of the public shall withdraw from the Council Chamber or the committee room in which the committee or subcommittee is meeting, and the clerk shall ensure that the order is complied with (Rules of Procedure (Part N), Rule 88).

6.2.2 Press briefings and legislative records

Press briefings are normally not arranged after public meetings. For meetings held in private, the chairman and other members may hold press briefings, with the location arranged by the secretariat. The press is free to ask questions, take photographs or do filming during briefings (House Rule 27).

The Legislative Council library provides access to records, papers, reports and audio-visual recordings of open meetings; and inspection of members' claims for reimbursement of operating expenses and register of members' interests. Photocopying is self-service and available at a charge. LegCo also offers an online library catalogue and electronic versions for many of these records, research papers and other materials at its website (http://www.legco.gov.hk/general/english/library/index.html). LegCo conducted a public consultation in 2013 to determine if changes were needed in how it provided public access to its information and records.

6.3 Personal data

Under the Personal Data (Privacy) Ordinance (Cap 486), an individual, not a corporation, has the right to see any personal data collected and held by governmental and private bodies. The person can also request corrections be made to that data. The ordinance provides that the media can ask organizations how their information systems work, including policies and practices over the kinds of personal data held and the underlying purposes (see Chapter 5 Privacy).

Authorities often cite privacy considerations in refusing to release information to the media, but journalists can seek an opinion from the office of the Privacy Commissioner for Personal Data as to whether a specific situation falls under the personal data ordinance. For example, in 2011, the media requested clarity after the Fire Services Department declined to release addresses of people involved in incidents; the Privacy Commissioner issued an advisory that "disclosure of a room number or street number" of an individual did not constitute disclosure of personal data under the ordinance, even if the media are later able to ascertain the identity of the person involved from other sources.[24]

But in early 2013, Privacy Commissioner Allan Chiang Yam-wang said that he supported a proposed regulation by the Hong Kong government to limit public access to information on company directors, such as home addresses and personal identity information, after the Legislative Council approved an overhaul of the Companies Ordinance in 2012.[25] Various groups protested, including bankers, lawyers and the media, with more than 1,700 journalists signing a petition against the move. "The identity of a company's shareholders and directors contained in the documents are important reference for journalists to identify the persons who are being investigated," according to Chan Pui-king, former editor-in-chief of *Next Magazine.* If identifying information is not provided in future company documents, Chan said, "I don't think journalists could probe into any news issues of public interest like conflict of interest and corruption." In March 2013, the government announced it would withdraw the controversial proposal.[26]

6.4 **Public health**

The Food and Health Bureau, responsible for overall health care policy in Hong Kong, and the Department of Health, the government's health advisor and regulatory authority, are subject to the Code on Access to Information.

The Medical Registration Ordinance (Cap 161) requires all medical practitioners to register with the Medical Council of Hong Kong, which is responsible for maintaining the register of eligible doctors, administering the licensing examination, issuing guidelines and a professional code of conduct, exercising regulatory and disciplinary powers for the profession, and answering general enquiries from doctors and the public.

A list of registered doctors is available at the Medical Council's website (http://www.mchk.org.hk). Under the ordinance, all disciplinary inquiries by the Medical Council are held in public unless there are exceptional reasons. For years, no written record of hearings were available to the public, but in 2008, after articles in the *South China Morning Post* on the Medical Council's lack of transparency, the Medical Council began to publish its judgments on its website with the names of the doctors being disciplined. Judgments prior to 2008 are not posted.

The Chinese Medical Council of Hong Kong regulates Chinese medicine and Chinese medical health practitioners under the Chinese Medical Ordinance

24. "Response to Media Enquiries: Fire Services Department's Arrangement for Releasing Information to the Media", 3 October 2011, at: http://www.pcpd.org.hk/.
25. Danny Mok, "Privacy Chief Backs Law Changes", *South China Morning Post,* 14 January 2013.
26. Olga Wong and Patsy Moy, "Public Pressure Forces Shelving of Law That Hides Company Director Details", *South China Morning Post,* 29 March 2013.

(Cap 549). The council's website provides names of registered Chinese medical health practitioners who have successfully passed a certification examination and are permitted to prescribe Schedule 1 Chinese herbal medicines under the ordinance. It also publishes names of "listed" practitioners who are more limited in their practice. Also on its website, the Chinese Medical Council provides annual reports and periodic newsletters detailing activities of the council and the Chinese Medicine Practitioner Board, including summaries of disciplinary actions, but without specific names of practitioners who have been investigated or disciplined (http://www.cmchk.org.hk).

The Hospital Authority is a statutory body created in 1990 to manage all public hospitals in Hong Kong. The Hospital Authority Ordinance (Cap 113, s 4) mandates that the Hospital Authority is to "encourage public participation in the operation of the public hospitals system and to ensure accountability to the public for the management and control of the public hospitals system".

The Hospital Authority Board's meetings are open to the public; anyone wanting to attend must register first, with admission on a first-come basis. The monthly Administrative and Operational meetings are closed. Agendas, meeting minutes and papers are available to the public at Hospital Authority headquarters and on its website (http://www.ha.org.hk).

6.5 **Police and fire information**

The Hong Kong Police Force wields much discretion in how it releases, if at all, information on crimes, major incidents and other matters of potential interest to the media. While the Police Force Ordinance (Cap 232) establishes the department's duties and functions, it does not contain any provisions requiring the public release of information related to these duties and functions.

The department is subject to the Code on Access to Information and lists the categories of records it maintains, including operations, traffic, crime investigations, firearms licensing, convictions and personnel records. But, as previously noted, law enforcement is among the sixteen categories of exemptions.

Police relations with the media are detailed in department internal guidelines (*Force Procedures Manual*, Chapter 39, "Police Public and Media Relations", and *Major Incident Manual*, Chapter 11, "The Media and VIPs"). The guidelines advise officers to cooperate with the media and to provide "sufficient operational detail . . . in a timely manner". But they also caution against giving information that might interfere with an individual's privacy and an accused's right to a fair trial and that might subject victims and their families to "harassment from the media". The officers are to "release only brief, factual information, provided it will not hamper an investigation or prejudice the inquiry" and to "avoid speculative comment or opinion" ("Disclosure of Information to the Media", *Force Procedures Manual*, 39–03 (2) and (3)).

In criminal cases in which there has been an arrest, police are advised to release only "minimum information", such as (emphasis in original text):

(a) The victim/suspect's surname and part of any names, age, gender and area of residence (NO information which could directly or indirectly identify the person or his or her actual address/identity);
(b) The officer-in-charge of the investigation/enquiry;
(c) The time and approximate location of the crime/incident;
(d) General nature of the crime/incident and property involved; BUT
(e) Particulars of victims of sexual offences must NOT be released.

— "Criminal Cases", *Force Procedures Manual* 39–03 (11) (a)–(e)

In 2004, the police introduced a digital communications system to replace its analogue system. This technology had the practical effect of blocking the public's ability to monitor police communications, which had allowed journalists and others (without permission) to learn quickly about incidents. The police began issuing news alerts giving the nature and location of unfolding events, but the media complained that these failed to indicate their seriousness or other newsworthy details. The media also said the alerts often were delayed and appeared selective.

Over the years, the media discovered and complained that they were not being alerted to a number of significant crimes, accidents and other incidents, including violent attacks, indecent assaults and cases involving celebrities or government officials. For example, police did not report to the media when the son of a lawmaker was arrested for alleged drink-driving or when the car of a senior ambulance officer hit a pedestrian. In 2011 the Hong Kong Journalists Association (HKJA) issued a demand, signed by 1,602 journalists, professors and journalism students, that police release crime information in real time and meaningful detail. As a result, in November 2011, police issued new spot news guidelines,[27] which specified, among other things, that cases of blackmail, criminal intimidation, sexual offence and unlawful detention were being withheld. The department also revealed that it released details on only about one in five cases, citing the Code on Access to Information and privacy considerations.[28]

Further control of spot news coverage occurred in February 2012 when the Fire Services Department (FSD) also switched to a digital communications system. Within days of the new digital system, the HKJA reported that details of cases disseminated to the media plummeted to less than 10 percent of the average daily calls received by the FSD in 2011.[29] The FSD is also subject to the Code on Access to Information.

27. "Arrangements on Releasing Unforeseen Incident Information by the Police", Hong Kong Police Force, November 2011. The author notes that the Access to Information officer of the Hong Kong police department responded in 21 days to her request for a copy of these guidelines.
28. "New Leader Raises Fears: Challenges for Freedom of Expression in Hong Kong", 2012 Annual Report, Hong Kong Journalists Association.
29. Ibid.

7. The cost of a secret government

Despite the availability of some information, the limitations of the code, as well as the general preferred atmosphere of secrecy, deny the public timely and sufficient access to matters of obvious public importance. Occasional leaks in the media about information kept secret provide telling examples of the excessive reach of the existing administrative scheme. In some cases, the government released confidential documents after the media publicized their existence; in others, it did not. Below are some examples:

- A confidential study on the feasibility of the expansion of Central Government Offices, commissioned through the Government Property Agency in 1990, concluded that it would be more practical and cost effective to redevelop existing headquarters than to build a new headquarters on prime waterfront property known as the Tamar site. In February 2006, the *South China Morning Post* revealed the existence of the report, which the government initially refused to release until after LegCo threatened to force production of these documents. The report was released two months later. Regardless, the Central Government Complex at Tamar was built at a cost of HK$50 billion.
- A confidential government-paid consultancy report, as revealed by the *Hong Kong Economic Times* in 2005, questioned the feasibility of a controversial canopy design for key structures of the then-proposed West Kowloon Cultural District. Again after receiving pressure from LegCo members in the wake of news stories, the government released a portion of the information. It later withdrew its support for the canopy design. The West Kowloon Cultural District Authority, established in 2008[30] and endowed with HK$21 billion to develop the cultural hub, remains a target of criticism for its lack of transparency. The authority did not publish records of its board meetings on its website for more than two years and refused to reveal how much it charged third parties to rent land it leases from the government while awaiting construction of venues, citing the information as "commercially sensitive".
- Many documents and records related to the financial details and development of major projects by the government, such as Hong Kong Disneyland on Lantau Island and Cyberport, have never been released, despite repeated demands for disclosure.

While Hong Kong journalists are not unique in depending on confidential government information in their reporting, they have become frequent users. A survey of more than 400 local journalists in 2003 found that an overwhelming majority has used anonymous sources in their stories, involving mainly local government news. One-third of the respondents reported that they had used

30. West Kowloon Cultural District Authority Ordinance (Cap 601).

confidential government documents in the previous year. Only one in twelve said that journalists should never use confidential government documents in their stories.[31]

Leaked confidential government information is a fact of almost daily life in Hong Kong journalism. "In Hong Kong, you don't expect to be able to force the government to release internal documents," said one veteran journalist. "You need to get them by other means. Only after you get them, then you can get official confirmation."

Many in the media believe that the government itself has abused this process by its continued reliance on "off-the-record" briefings, in lieu of open press conferences, in which government officials ask not to be identified in exchange for discussion, often with selected journalists, of government actions and policies. In fact, many Hong Kong journalists now see tighter government control over public records and information in an increasing number of ways — including more limited access to news events and designated press areas (see Chapter 8 Other Restrictions on Newsgathering and Reporting) — as the most significant factor in what they see as erosion of press freedom.[32]

Despite repeated calls for a Freedom of Information law in Hong Kong, the government has declined to respond and remains one of the very few modern societies without such a law. As mentioned, the UK's FOI law went into effect in January 2005. The types of information the UK public now has access to include details of contracts awarded, information about decisions made by governmental bodies, meeting minutes and internal policies.

The UK government receives about 120,000 requests annually. Like most other countries with FOI laws, the UK government organizations found that the media represented just one group among many making requests; journalists make up only about 10 percent of the requests.[33] But what the media have uncovered has made headlines. One significant investigation was in 2009 when *The Telegraph* newspaper obtained information under FOI on expense reports of Parliament members, revealing inappropriate claims and resulting in several MPs being charged with fraud. Since then, MP expense accounts are routinely released. Other news articles published after information was released under FOI revealed:

- Foreign diplomats with foreign immunity who have been implicated in crimes including rapes, child abuse and murder while working in Britain.
- The number of patients who died in operations performed by every heart surgeon in the National Health Service.

31. Survey conducted by this author in 2003 of 422 journalists in 25 Hong Kong newsrooms. See D. Weisenhaus, "Newsgathering Practices: Hong Kong Journalists' Views and Uses of Controversial Techniques", *Global Media Journal*, Fall 2005, at: http://lass.purduecal.edu/cca/gmj/fa05/gmj-fa05-weisenhaus.htm.

32. Survey by the Hong Kong Journalists Association in April 2012, detailed in its 2012 Annual Report, *supra*, see note 28.

33. "Independent Review of the Impact of the Freedom of Information Act, A Report Prepared for the Department of Constitutional Affairs", Frontier Economics Ltd., October 2006.

- Casework data from the Crown Prosecution Service, indicating that criminal suspects were up to eight times more likely to go free in some parts of the UK than others.
- The amount of farming subsidies given to rich landowners and members of the royal family.
- The extent to which schools manipulated exam entries to improve school standing.

Likewise, elsewhere in Asia, successful FOI requests gained access to such information as government food subsidies for the poor being diverted to the black market for personal gain (India) and test scores for entrance exams for a state elementary school showing that some children who had failed the exam were being admitted over others who had passed (Thailand).[34]

8. Conclusion

The existing laws (or lack thereof) and practices regarding access to public information — and the retention and maintenance of records — affect Hong Kong citizens and journalists in many negative ways. They deny them timely and convenient access to information of public importance, both about the process of government and the development of Hong Kong. This denial of access tends to separate the governed from those who govern. This promotes distance and mistrust, which cannot be good for the development of a democratic society. A dramatic example of this came in late 2013 when the Hong Kong government refused to provide details for its decision to deny a television licence to a popular applicant, igniting large public demonstrations and demands for transparency.[35]

Such denial of access also has contributed to a media culture struggling for information that should be in the public domain, resulting in journalism that can be distorted or incomplete because journalists do not have the full picture of events. The public domain is the best place for ideas and issues to play out, and to rise and fall on their own merit. By failing to construct a legal infrastructure that facilitates access to information, the Hong Kong government has demonstrated so far its inability — or unwillingness — to match the public accountability efforts of other countries around the world and in Asia. But in January 2013, days after the Ombudsman's announcement of his latest investigation into access to information and archives regimes, Secretary for Justice Rimsky Yuen announced that the Law Reform Commission would conduct a comparative study of relevant laws internationally with a possible eye to reform in Hong Kong and cooperate with the Ombudsman's investigation. Whether those efforts result in new laws will be closely watched.

34. These and other examples can be found at: http://www.right2info.org/resources/foi-in-action.

35. See section 3.1 in Chapter 12 Media Regulation in the Age of Convergence of this book.

7

Official Secrets and Sedition

Doreen Weisenhaus

FREQUENTLY ASKED QUESTIONS

1. What is an "official secret"? (See section 2)
2. If journalists publish "official secrets" or other confidential government information, what possible sanctions do they face? (See section 2)
3. Can journalists invoke a public-interest defence or other defences for receiving or publishing "official secrets"? (See sections 2–3)
4. How might the law on official secrets change if and when Article 23 of the Basic Law is implemented? (See sections 3–3.1)
5. How would other laws mandated by Article 23 — on sedition, subversion, secession, and treason — affect journalists? What are Hong Kong's current laws on sedition? (See section 4)

1. Introduction

In 2010, the disclosure by the website Wikileaks of thousands of classified US documents about the wars in Iraq and Afghanistan — and subsequently hundreds of thousands of diplomatic cables — prompted coverage by many mainstream media and a worldwide discussion about how nations should respond.[1] More questions arose in 2013 when whistle-blower Edward Snowden was in Hong Kong after revealing widespread surveillance by the US government, including in Hong Kong and mainland China. Were any of the Hong Kong government's confidential documents or communications leaked and, if so, what were the legal implications? While Chapter 6 of this book focuses on public access to government-generated information and the roadblocks that substantially limit access, this chapter centres on a specific category of prohibited government information known as "official secrets", as detailed in Hong Kong's Official Secrets Ordinance (OSO, Cap 521).

1. Numerous books have been written about the Wikileaks phenomenon and the impact on the release of classified government documents, including: Andy Greenberg, *This Machine Kills Secrets: How Wikileaks, Cypherpunks and Hacktivists Aim to Free the World's Information* (New York: Dutton 2012); Charlie Beckett and James Ball, *Wikileaks: News in the Networked Era* (Malden, MA: Polity 2012); New York Times Staff, *Open Secrets: Wikileaks, War and American Diplomacy* (New York: Grove Press 2011).

The OSO is designed to prevent the public release of sensitive information about security and intelligence; defence; international relations, and information relating to the commission of offences and criminal investigations. The OSO is aimed primarily at sources — that is, those currently or formerly working for the government who might be in a position to provide information to the media — more than against journalists themselves. Thus, for the media, the law's greatest impact is the potential effect it has on the amount and type of information that might be released. But members of the media should also be aware that they too are vulnerable to prosecution under this ordinance.

When additional laws on national security — including theft of state secrets, sedition, subversion, secession and treason — as mandated by Article 23 of the Basic Law, are eventually implemented in the manner many people anticipate, an already secretive government is expected to become even more so and journalistic liability will likely increase. In the meantime, though, journalists must continue to be careful about violating present law; although prosecutions against the media have been rare, they can arise.

2. Official Secrets Ordinance

The OSO controls the unauthorized obtaining or disclosing of official information in several categories.

2.1 What are official secrets and who needs to keep them?

Under the ordinance, an official secret is defined as one of certain categories of sensitive government information that are given special protection and that generally relate to information whose disclosure might be prejudicial to the safety and interests of Hong Kong. The OSO protects government information via two main groups of offences: espionage (sections 3 to 6) and unlawful disclosure of protected information in categories relating to security and intelligence, defence, international relations and the commission of criminal offences and criminal investigations (sections 13 to 20).

The law mostly regulates the actions of those *inside* the government (members of security and intelligence services, public servants and government contractors) regarding the handling and disclosure of official secrets, but it also has implications for those *outside* the government (the public, including journalists).

2.2 History/Background

The current Official Secrets Ordinance (Cap 521) came into effect on 1 July 1997. Its origin, however, goes back many years earlier to the official secrets laws of the UK that were imposed in Hong Kong by the British colonial government. The UK's highly restrictive Official Secrets Act 1911, passed hastily in a period of public panic over national security before World War I, and its later amendments, were applicable in Hong Kong. After years of criticism over the law, the UK replaced part of the 1911 act that dealt with unlawful disclosure of specific information with the Official Secrets Act 1989; that law was applied to Hong Kong in 1992.[2]

Just before its return to Chinese sovereignty in 1997 as a Special Administrative Region under the "one country, two systems" regime, Hong Kong localized its law by passing its own Official Secrets Ordinance, which was closely modelled on the 1989 act. The British government was motivated in part by the 1994 conviction of Xi Yang, a Hong Kong reporter for the *Ming Pao* newspaper who was sentenced to twelve years in prison on the mainland for disclosing state secrets. Xi had written about the People's Bank of China's gold rates and plans to raise interest rates.

The British government wanted to avoid a legal lapse that might invite mainland intervention once Hong Kong became part of the People's Republic of China. But passage of Hong Kong's OSO was unpopular with local journalists who considered the law still overly harsh and feared it would suppress freedom of expression and the free flow of information after the handover. Under the OSO, journalists who received unauthorized, damaging information and disclosed it could face prosecution, even if the restricted information was already in the public domain. The law also did not provide a public-interest defence.

The OSO came under the public spotlight again in 2002–03 when the Hong Kong government attempted unsuccessfully to broaden the law's provisions in its proposals for national security legislation relating to Article 23 of the Basic Law. Article 23 mandated that Hong Kong had to pass laws dealing with theft of state secrets as well as treason, secession, sedition and subversion. Those proposals were withdrawn in 2003 after more than 500,000 Hong Kong people, including many journalists, marched in protest (see section 3 for more details). Since then, periodic calls for enactment of Article 23 legislation in Hong Kong have been raised, especially after neighbouring Macau, the Special Administration Region that came under Chinese sovereignty in 1999, passed its version of Article 23 laws in 2009 (see section 5 below). But local political leaders in Hong Kong have been reluctant to tackle the volatile topic, and as of late 2013, no new legislative proposals have been introduced.

2.3 Spying

Most countries have laws against spying. The concern over the UK's and by extension Hong Kong's laws against espionage focus on how expansive and overly broad these laws can be. Sections 3 to 6 of the OSO are based on the UK's 1911 Act and list the main espionage offences: spying (s 3), harbouring a spy (s 4), unauthorized use of uniforms, forgery and other acts related to spying (s 5), and unauthorized use of official documents in furtherance of spying (s 6).

2. Several other former colonies still retain official secrets laws they inherited from the UK, including India (Official Secrets Act 1923), Singapore (Official Secrets Act 1935, revised 2012) and Malaysia (Official Secrets Act 1972). In recent years, Malaysia has prosecuted several bloggers under OSA. Canada replaced its OSA with the Security of Information Act 2001. New Zealand repealed its secrets law in 1982 when it enacted the Official Information Act, its version of a freedom of information law.

In OSO s 3(1), an offence is committed, if, for a purpose prejudicial to the safety or interest of the People's Republic of China or Hong Kong, a person

(a) approaches, inspects, passes over or is in the neighbourhood of, or enters, a prohibited place;
(b) makes a sketch, plan, model or note that is calculated to be or might be or is intended to be directly or indirectly useful to an enemy; or
(c) obtains, collects, records or publishes, or communicates to any other person, any secret official code word or password, or any sketch, plan, model or note, or other document or information, that is likely to be or might be or is intended to be directly or indirectly useful to any enemy.

For journalists, section 3(1)(c) is the most problematic because it deals with the obtaining, publishing or otherwise communicating of secret official information. Also, the "prohibited place" mentioned in section 3(1)(a) is widely defined in section 2 to include any military establishment, factory, dockyard, camp, vessel or aircraft, railway or "telegraph, telephone, wireless or signal station or office" used by the government.

But prosecutions against journalists in connection with this offence are extremely rare. There have been none in Hong Kong and only one in the UK, the so-called "ABC" case in 1978. The case involved two journalists and a magazine article about signals intelligence and defence installations as well as an ex-soldier who had provided some of the information. Documents containing details on government surveillance systems were seized from the home of one of the journalists, Duncan Campbell, but it was later discovered that the information had come mostly from published sources, including government press releases. The government was forced to withdraw the spying charges against the journalists in mid-trial after the judge called the charges "oppressive".

For the Hong Kong government to win a case alleging this offence, it must prove that the obtaining or publishing of the secret information was for a "purpose prejudicial to the safety and interest" of Hong Kong and the PRC. Anyone convicted of an offence under OSO s 3 faces up to 14 years in prison. Conviction on an offence under OSO ss 4–6 can result in up to two years in prison. Based on prior case history and practice, and though Hong Kong is now under Chinese sovereignty, it appears unlikely that a journalist merely reporting official information without the intent to aid an enemy would be prosecuted for spying activities under OSO s 3. The more likely problems for the media would occur under other aspects of official secrets law that deal with unlawful disclosure. These are discussed next.

2.4 Unlawful disclosure (of what and by whom?)

As mentioned, most of the Official Secrets Ordinance is directed toward those with a current or former connection or relationship with the government. The law prohibits current and former government employees and contractors from disclosing, without authorization, information relating to four categories of official information (security and intelligence; defence; international relations, and information relating to the commission of offences and criminal investigations). But it may also be a crime for a journalist, who received the protected information by an unauthorized disclosure by a current government employee or contractor, to disclose that information. The penalties for conviction are up to two years in prison and a HK$500,000 fine.

The law is somewhat complicated because the culpability of those making the disclosures, what the prosecution needs to prove and the available defences all vary according to the kind of information disclosed and the person who discloses it. The next section will look at the four categories of protected information and the differing levels of liability. While the ordinance is quite clear about *who* is covered under it, its provisions are less clear about precisely what information is covered and under what circumstances; some of its terms are too broadly or vaguely defined.

2.4.1 Categories of protected information

The ordinance has several categories of protected government information. They are:

Security and intelligence

The persons facing the most restrictions are current or former members of government security and intelligence services or those notified they are subject to the same restrictions. They are prohibited from disclosing unauthorized information, documents or other articles relating to security or intelligence to which they had access because of their positions (OSO s 13). This includes making any statements about such information to any outsiders, including the press. The government does not have to prove that the disclosure was damaging, only that the disclosure occurred. The two defences available for persons in this category accused of disclosing prohibited information are that they did not know or had no reason to know that the information was related to security or intelligence (OSO s 13(3)) or that they had reasonably thought they were authorized to release the information (OSO s 21(4)).

The terms "security and intelligence" are not really defined in the ordinance except by OSO s 12(7):

> security or intelligence means the work of, or in support of, the security or intelligence services or any part of them, and references to information relating to security or intelligence include references to information held or transmitted by those services or by persons in support of them, or any part of them.

If a person is outside the security and intelligence services as a current or former "public servant" or government contractor, and makes an unauthorized disclosure on a security or intelligence matter that he or she came in contact with during the course of his or her work, then the government must also prove that the disclosure was damaging or likely to cause damage (OSO s 14). A public servant is defined as anyone who holds public office or is employed by the civil service or other part of government (OSO s 12(1)). A government contractor is not a public servant but someone who provides or is employed in the provision of goods or services to the government (OSO s12(2)).

One particular difficulty in Hong Kong is that there is no designated authority responsible for "security and intelligence". Hong Kong does not have an agency similar to those existing in the UK (MI5, which protects against internal national security risks, and MI6, which oversees espionage activities outside the country) or in the US (Central Intelligence Agency). Because of that, it is more difficult to determine who is engaging in security and intelligence services.

What is damaging? OSO s 14(2) says that a disclosure is damaging if it "causes damage to the work of, or any part of, the security or intelligence"; or that the information, document or article is of such a nature or falls within a class or description of information that its unauthorized disclosure would likely cause such damage.

Government employees or contractors not working for security or intelligence services have one additional defence to the two available for service members: that they did not know or had no reason to know the disclosed information would be damaging (OSO s 14(3)).

These same three defences also are available for current and former government workers and contractors in the next two categories, defence and international relations.

Defence

OSO s 15 prohibits current or former public employees or contractors from the unauthorized and damaging disclosure of information, documents or articles relating to defence. Defence is traditionally thought of as troops, plans, weapons and equipment. OSO s 12(1) broadly defines defence as:

> (a) the size, shape, organization, logistics, order of battle, deployment, operations, state of readiness and training of armed forces;
> (b) the weapons, stores or other equipment of the armed forces and the invention, development, production and operation of such equipment and research relating to it;
> (c) defence policy and strategy and military planning and intelligence;
> (d) plans and measures for the maintenance of essential supplies and services that are or would be needed in time of war.

A disclosure is considered damaging if it harms the capability of the armed forces to carry out its tasks; leads to loss of life or injury to anyone in the armed forces, or causes serious damage to equipment or installations. The disclosure must endanger the interests of Hong Kong or the PRC elsewhere, seriously obstruct the promotion or protection by Hong Kong or the PRC of those interests or endanger the safety of mainland nationals or Hong Kong permanent residents elsewhere (OSO s 15(2)). Those interests are not defined in the ordinance.

As mentioned, defences for current or former government employees or contractors charged with this offence are similar as for those charged with offences regarding security and intelligence who are not members of security and intelligence services: that they did not know or had no reason to know that the disclosed information related to defence or that it would be damaging or that they reasonably thought they had authority to release the information.

International relations

Section 16 prohibits current or former government employees or contractors from disclosing without authorization damaging information, documents or other articles, relating to international relations (meaning between Hong Kong or the PRC and another state or international organization) or information that is confidential and obtained from a foreign territory, state or an international organization.

To be damaging, the prosecution must prove the disclosure "endangers the interests" of Hong Kong or the PRC elsewhere, "seriously obstructs the promotion or protection" by the PRC or Hong Kong of those interests or "endangers" the safety of Chinese nationals or Hong Kong permanent residents elsewhere or that the information, documents or articles are of such a nature that their unauthorized disclosure would be likely to have any of these effects (OSO s 16(2)(a) and (b)).

Again, the OSO does not define what those interests are or what is precisely meant by the promotion and protection of those interests. Some guidance might be found in the 1988 White Paper by the Franks Committee, which made recommendations for reform that were incorporated in the UK's 1989 act. It said that:

> Exchanges between governments not amounting to negotiations are often on a confidential basis. One nation may entrust to a second nation or to its friends or allies information which it is on no account prepared to allow to go further. A breach of this trust could have a seriously adverse effect on relations between the countries concerned, which might extend well beyond the particular matter which leaked.[3]

As with the previous two categories of former and current public servants and contractors not with intelligence or security services, they have the defences of not knowing or not having reason to know that the disclosed information related to international relations or that the released information would be damaging or that they reasonably thought they had authority to release the information.

Crime and criminal investigations

OSO s 17 concerns disclosed information that is likely to result in a crime being committed, helping someone in legal custody to escape, or interfering in the prevention or detection of crimes or the arrests and prosecution of suspects. Again, these offences pertain to former and current public employees or contractors. Here, the government does not have to prove the likelihood of harm because

3. White Paper: Reform of Section 2 of the Official Secrets Act 1911 (1988), p. 50, para 130.

the information as described is, by its nature, likely to cause harm. In this case, one defence is slightly different from those available for the other categories. It is a defence that the accused did not know or had no reason to know that the disclosure would have any of the effects mentioned in OSO s 17 (that it would result in a crime being committed, etc.). The other two defences are similar: that the accused did not know or had no reason to believe that the information, document or article was related to the commission of crimes or criminal investigations and that he thought or had reason to think he was authorized to release the information.

As a general rule, the Hong Kong police do not rely on OSO s 17 to withhold information on crime investigations. Since Hong Kong does not have a Freedom of Information law requiring government departments to release information to the public, including the press (see Chapter 6 Access to Information), police officers simply tell reporters they cannot give details of investigations. Often, however, when officials wish to distribute certain information, they provide it anonymously "on background". As a result, many stories about crimes and accidents in Hong Kong newspapers use unnamed sources.

Several other Hong Kong ordinances, such as the Prevention of Bribery Ordinance, restrict the publishing of certain details in criminal investigations. (These ordinances are discussed in Chapter 8 Other Restrictions on Newsgathering and Reporting.)

Information entrusted in confidence to territories, States or international organizations

Section 20 bans unauthorized and damaging disclosures of information or documents relating to security or intelligence, defence or international relations that have been communicated in confidence by the Hong Kong or mainland governments to a territory or State or an international organization. In June 2013, questions were raised about potential liability under this section when whistle-blower Snowden, a former employee of a private security contractor and the US National Security Agency (NSA) who had fled the US for Hong Kong, disclosed details about American intelligence operations in China and Hong Kong.

Simon N.M. Young, a professor at the University of Hong Kong, warned that any surveillance that took place in Hong Kong as a result of information provided confidentially by the Chinese or Hong Kong governments might subject Snowden to criminal charges if he obtained possession of such information without authority and made the damaging disclosure knowing or having reasonable cause to believe that the information was communicated in confidence and the disclosure would be damaging.[4] According to Young:

> The meaning of 'damaging disclosure' is broad and includes when the information is of such a nature that its unauthorised disclosure would likely cause damage to the work of security and intelligence services.[5]

---

4. Simon Young, Media Advisory–Mr. Edward Snowden, 13 June 2013. http://www.law.hku.hk/ccpl/aboutthecentre/Update%20Snowden%2013%20June.pdf.
5. Ibid.

While in Hong Kong, Snowden was charged by US prosecutors with espionage and theft of government property. He left Hong Kong without incident for Russia, where he was granted temporary asylum. As of late 2013, he was apparently still in Russia at an undisclosed location.

2.4.2 Journalists and others outside government

Normally, as government outsiders, journalists are not subject to OSO ss 13–17, but if they induce a current or former government employee or contractor to release prohibited information or document, such as by paying money for it, they could be charged with conspiracy or aiding and abetting.

Beyond that issue, OSO s 18 is the most important provision of the OSO regarding the media as it specifically deals with non-government persons, including journalists. It also is the most complex. Basically, it prohibits those outside government who have come into possession of restricted information in the four protected categories (intelligence/security, defence, international relations, and criminal investigations) from revealing that information without lawful authority if they know or have reason to know that it is protected. But before a journalist is considered to have violated this section, certain circumstances must also exist:

1. that the journalist got the information from a government employee or contractor who did not have lawful authority to release it, or that the journalist was given the information in confidence by the government employee or contractor;
2. if the information came from a government contractor, that person also had to be a Chinese national or a Hong Kong permanent resident or the information had to be received in Hong Kong;
3. that the disclosure was damaging and the reporter knew or had reasonable cause to believe that it would be damaging.

In bringing a case against a member of the media or anyone else outside government, the prosecution has more of a burden of proof than in cases against government workers. One of the first hurdles for the prosecution is to prove the information came from someone working inside or for the government. Unlike the other sections, OSO s 18 involves only *current* public employees or contractors, not former ones.

Therefore, under existing law, if a reporter obtains sensitive government information (from an anonymous source, as often happens), a key inquiry in the newsroom typically is: Did it come from a current public employee? If not or there is no reasonable cause to believe it has come from a public servant or contractor, then even if the information is damaging, reporters and editors are not likely to face liability. If, however, the information or documents did come from a public employee or contractor, or there was reason to believe that it did, then the journalists could face liability if the government can also prove that the disclosure was damaging and the journalists had reason to believe that it would be harmful.

It is important to note that disclosure can be made indirectly to a journalist. OSO s 18 (2)(a) refers to circumstances in which prohibited information has come into a person's possession as a result of it having been "disclosed (whether to him or another) by a public servant or government contractor without lawful authority". Thus, sometimes the nature of the information will speak for itself that it must have come from a public servant, either directly or indirectly, and so it is unnecessary for the prosecution to prove that a journalist obtained the information directly from a public servant.

2.5 No public interest or prior publication defence

What about other defences for journalists? The OSO does not provide a public-interest defence, which in some jurisdictions exempts from prosecution reports on abuse of office, malfeasance or other acts of illegality by officials. A public-interest defence traditionally has been championed as an essential way to guard against government abuse. In 1997, when the British government was acting to localize the Official Secrets Act 1989 in Hong Kong, journalists and some lawmakers advocated such a defence, but it was not included when the law went into effect after the handover.

During the contentious debate in 2002–03, when the government proposed to revamp the laws in compliance with Article 23, it initially refused to offer a public-interest defence. After much opposition by the media, academics, human rights lawyers and others, the government eventually agreed to include this defence. (For details, see section 3 in this chapter on theft of state secrets and Article 23.) But because the legislative proposals were withdrawn before the law could be changed, there is no public-interest defence in the current OSO. And there is no guarantee that when Article 23 proposals are re-introduced they will include a public-interest defence.

In a key UK case in 2002, *R v Shayler* [2002] 1 AC 247, which involved the Official Secrets Act 1989, the House of Lords rejected a public-interest defence for David Shayler, a former MI5 operative who disclosed to a newspaper that the intelligence agency had kept secret files on some officials. The House of Lords also held that his right to freedom of expression pursuant to Article 10 of the European Convention for the Protection of Human Rights and Fundamental Freedoms as incorporated by the UK's Human Rights Act 1998 was not violated.

But the ruling did not address issues relating to persons who were not members of the security and intelligence services, namely the media, and thus the case did not resolve this issue relating to journalists. (Three of the five Lords specifically said that the decision did not involve the media's role.) The newspaper that published Shayler's disclosures, *The Mail on Sunday*, was not prosecuted in the case, even though it had paid £40,000 to Shayler to obtain and publish the information.

Two UK laws — the Public Interest Disclosure Act 1998, which protects public and private workers who blow the whistle on wrongdoing, and the Freedom of Information Act 2000 — have incorporated the concept of public interest in determining whether disclosure of protected information is allowed, but neither law applies to intelligence employees or information relating to national security.

A public-interest defence does exist in other Hong Kong laws. For example, the Prevention of Bribery Ordinance provides a "reasonable excuse" defence for disclosures that reveal "any unlawful activity, abuse of power, serious neglect of duty or other serious conduct" by any officers of the Independent Commission Against Crime.[6] Likewise, the Personal Data (Privacy) Ordinance permits exemption for disclosures "made by a person who has reasonable grounds to believe (and reasonably believes) that the publishing or broadcasting . . . of the data . . . is in the public interest".[7] (See Chapter 5 Privacy.)

Furthermore, the OSO does not specifically provide for a defence of prior publication, which would permit the use of protected information already published or otherwise in the public domain. This too was discussed during the Article 23 debate, but the government resisted explicit inclusion of the defence in its proposals, saying that harm could still occur with re-publication of sensitive information. While prior publication is not a defence *per se*, it may come through damaging disclosure on the basis that the disclosure is not damaging as the information has already been published elsewhere. This may not succeed in every instance, but at least this line of defence remains a possibility.

As a practical matter, what risks do journalists face from current official secrets laws? Even though the UK government has long had the power to go after journalists, it is usually reluctant to do so. In the Shayler case, while Shayler was paid a substantial amount of money by *The Mail on Sunday* for his disclosures, no one from the newspaper was prosecuted. But in prosecutions against current and former employees, the government might decide to go after journalists to uncover evidence relating to those investigations. And in fact, in 2011 UK police invoked the Official Secrets Act in an attempt to force reporters from the *Guardian* newspaper to disclose their sources and materials for articles relating to a phone-hacking scandal. Although police later dropped their action, the attempt prompted renewed calls to revamp the law and provide additional legal protection for journalists. Furthermore in 2013, after the *Guardian* began publishing articles based on leaked information provided by Snowden, the UK government threatened legal action against the newspaper unless it destroyed document copies in its computer hard drives. The newspaper did so, but stated it had other copies outside UK jurisdiction.[8]

To date, though, no UK journalist has been convicted of violating the 1989 Act; nor have there been any media convictions under the Official Secrets Ordinance in Hong Kong. But questions remain about what would happen if publication

6. Laws of Hong Kong, Prevention of Bribery Ordinance (Cap 201) s 30 (3)(a) and (b).
7. Laws of Hong Kong, Personal Data (Privacy) Ordinance (Cap 486) s 61 (2)(b).
8. Julian Borger, "NSA Files: Why the Guardian in London Destroyed Hard Drives of Leaked Files", *Guardian*, 20 August 2013. http://www.theguardian.com/world/2013/aug/20/nsa-snowden-files-drives-destroyed-london.

of leaks of national security information continues or escalates, or in the case of Hong Kong, when changes are implemented under Article 23.

3. Theft of state secrets and Article 23

Article 23 of the Basic Law requires the Hong Kong government to pass, at some future date, national security legislation. It states:

> The Hong Kong Special Administrative Region shall enact laws on its own to prohibit any act of treason, secession, sedition, subversion against the Central People's Government, or theft of state secrets, to prohibit foreign political organizations or bodies from conducting political activities in the Region, and to prohibit political organizations or bodies of the Region from establishing ties with foreign political organizations or bodies.

One of the main journalistic concerns about the government's initial attempt to enact Article 23 legislation was the prohibition of "theft of state secrets". Hong Kong had already inherited Britain's restrictive laws on official secrets, but would it now also inherit China's obsession with keeping state secrets?

During 2002–03, the Hong Kong government made its first attempt to amend the OSO with proposals it said would implement Article 23 requirements by introducing a bill that it hoped would be passed by the Legislative Council.[9] (For other aspects of Article 23 proposals that dealt with sedition, subversion, secession and treason, see section 4 of this chapter.) The government's proposals to change the OSO went beyond what was mandated by Article 23, by trying to expand the law in ways that were not necessary for national security.

Article 23 — in particular how it relates to "theft of state secrets" — has been one of the chief journalistic concerns in the transition to Chinese sovereignty. While journalists had their concerns about the OSO, derived as it is from British law, they were not sure how "theft of state secrets", a term for a crime more common on the mainland and inserted into Article 23, would manifest itself into Hong Kong law after the handover. The "one country, two systems" principle governing Hong Kong under Chinese sovereignty should mean that the law would be enforced under the current common law system that recognizes British-style official secrets laws, and not as interpreted by the mainland criminal system.

On the mainland, theft of state secrets is a well-known but vaguely defined crime that is frequently invoked against journalists, academics and others who obtain and use information across a broad range of categories considered sensitive by the PRC government. Information on oil reserves, national exam questions and growth figures are just some of the government information that has been deemed state secrets on the mainland. Despite the different legal systems of Hong Kong and the mainland, journalists and others in Hong Kong worry that some mainland legal traditions — how state secrets are interpreted and how alleged

9. For more background on Article 23, see Fu Hualing, Carole J. Peterson and Simon N. M. Young (eds.), *National Security and Fundamental Freedoms: Hong Kong's Article 23 Under Scrutiny* (Hong Kong: Hong Kong University Press 2005).

violations of state secrecy are prosecuted — might become part of Hong Kong's legal tradition as national security concerns are invariably intertwined with those of the mainland.

Hong Kong and overseas journalists and scholars already face dangers for reporting and research done on the mainland because of the vagueness of China's laws, including those on state secrets, as evidenced by the 1994 conviction of Xi Yang, the *Ming Pao* reporter,[10] and more recent cases. (For more on PRC state secrets and reporting risks, see Chapter 9 Reporting on the Mainland.)

In the first case of a Hong Kong reporter being charged with spying since the handover, Ching Cheong, a Hong Kong-based reporter for Singapore's *The Strait Times,* was detained and charged in 2005 for alleged spying for Taiwan and handling state secrets. Also in 2005, Guan Yi, a scientist for the University of Hong Kong, was warned that he might be revealing state secrets after he published some of his avian flu research from Guangdong Province in two international scientific journals. In 2004, Zhao Yan, a researcher for *The New York Times* was charged with "divulging state secrets" for allegedly providing advance details of former president Jiang Zemin's imminent resignation as China's military chief; the newspaper denied his involvement. Penalties for divulging state secrets and spying are much more severe on the mainland than official secrets laws in Hong Kong — they can include life imprisonment or even execution.

In 2006, both Ching and Zhao were convicted and sentenced to prison. Ching received a five-year prison term after a Beijing court found him guilty of passing state secrets and confidential military information contained in articles he reportedly wrote for a Taiwanese think tank that was alleged to be a front for Taiwanese intelligence agencies. In 2008, Ching was discharged from prison after serving half his sentence and returned to Hong Kong. In May 2012, he published a book, *My 1,000-Day Ordeal,* which chronicled his experience in custody but refrained from detailing the facts behind the charges for which he was convicted. Zhao was sentenced to three years for a fraud conviction after the state secrets charge was dropped. Released in 2008, Zhao remains a journalist and dissident living in New York. China's state secrets law was amended and strengthened in 2010; changes included prohibiting electronic transmission of state secrets and requiring internet service providers to help enforce potential leaks. (For more details, see Chapter 9 Reporting on the Mainland.)

3.1 The proposed Article 23 amendments

As mentioned, the OSO protects government information via two main groups of offences: espionage and unlawful disclosure of protected information. The Hong Kong government's proposed Article 23 amendments in 2002–03 sought to broaden the law regarding the second group, unlawful disclosure.

One proposed amendment would have added a fifth category of shielded information (in addition to the current ones of security and intelligence, defence,

10. After serving three years of his twelve-year sentence, Xi was released in 1997 just before the handover.

international relations, and information related to the commission of offences and criminal investigations). The new category would have been "information, document or other article that relates to any affairs concerning the Hong Kong Special Administrative Region which are, under the Basic Law, within the responsibility of the Central Authorities". Critics quickly and sharply attacked this proposed category as too broad. This information could include political and economic information such as the appointment of the Chief Executive and principal officials, changes in migration policy, negotiation of air service agreements, the establishment of consulates in Hong Kong, the implementation of relevant directives by the Chief Executive or even information on the Basic Law, such as opinions of members of the Basic Law Committee on a proposed interpretation.

A second amendment proposed to add a new offence: prohibiting the disclosure of information "acquired by means of illegal access" such as by computer hacking, theft, robbery, burglary or bribery. This new clause, had it been enacted, would have done much more than close what was described as a loophole in the OSO. It would have changed the very nature of how a journalist could be held liable. Prohibition against illegal access would have put the media on notice that it had to determine the legality of its source of information, rather than just whether it came from a public employee or contractor. In fact, for this offence, a prosecutor would not have to show a connection to a government employee or contractor at all, only that the reporter knew or had reason to believe that the protected information was obtained through illegal means. If a reporter tried to confirm information with the government and was told that the information was stolen or hacked, then he would be considered informed. If the reporter then disclosed the information, he could be prosecuted. Journalists instinctively know that information not officially released may well have been obtained and passed on illegally.

The unauthorized disclosure of information in this category would be considered "damaging", according to the proposal, if it "endangers national security" or is "likely to endanger national security". National security was defined as the "safeguarding of the territorial integrity and the independence of the People's Republic of China". Again, critics charged that what was likely to endanger national security would be hard to predict and that the language cast too wide a net. Without further refinements and clarifications, journalists and others warned, this section of the proposed legislation would greatly discourage those working in and for government from speaking to the press about any topic that has even the remotest connection to relations between the Hong Kong and PRC governments for fear of stumbling into prohibited areas.

In July 2003, just days after a massive anti-Article 23 rally in Hong Kong, the government reversed its position and agreed to introduce a public-interest defence. The defence would have allowed a disclosure if it revealed any unlawful activity, abuse of power, serious neglect of duty or other serious misconduct by any public official; or a serious threat to public order; public security, or the health or safety of the public. The disclosure could not exceed the extent that was necessary for revealing the matter and the public interest served by the disclosure outweighed the public interest served by not making that disclosure.

While welcoming the amendment, journalists, lawyers, and others considered the defence as proposed too narrow and still problematic. In particular, the necessity test mandated for such disclosures was vague and offered no guidance for working journalists. Also, the proposed requirement of a balancing test over which public interest should dominate — that served by disclosure versus that served by nondisclosure — was unduly complicated and further limited the scope of the defence.

In making their decision to publish information that they believe to be in the public interest, journalists would find it difficult to know what factors might be put forward later by the government for keeping certain information confidential.

4. Other Article 23 provisions: Sedition, secession and subversion

Article 23 also requires the enactment of laws against sedition, subversion and secession. While laws on subversion and secession do not exist in Hong Kong, sedition laws do. A centuries-old crime to curb dissent against the crown, sedition offences to criminalize speech likely to incite others to insurrection or public disorder were imported to Hong Kong soon after it became a British colony; prohibition of seditious content in newspapers and books followed by the early twentieth century.[11]

While the colonial government in Hong Kong did not often use its powers against the press, it did so in times of political strife, especially by invoking sedition. Two notable prosecutions were against pro-China publications in the *Ta Kung Pao* case, which happened soon after the Communist takeover in 1949, and in cases arising during the Hong Kong riots of 1967 that reflected the turbulence of the Cultural Revolution. After violence erupted in the wake of a squatter campfire in 1951, the editor and publisher of *Ta Kung Pao* were both tried and convicted of sedition for the reprint of a commentary the left-leaning Hong Kong newspaper published that accused the British government of suppressing the Chinese people (*Fei Yi Ming and Lee Tsung Ying v R* [1952] 36 HKLR 133). In 1967, three Chinese-language newspapers — *Tin Fung Daily*, *Afternoon News* and *Hong Kong Evening News* — were prosecuted after urging Hong Kong people, including local police of Chinese descent, to fight British repression.[12]

After undergoing numerous changes over the years, Hong Kong's sedition laws were consolidated into the Crimes Ordinance in 1971 and are now contained in sections 9–14. In 1996, many in the Legislative Council discussed repealing the "archaic" offence of sedition as "contrary to the development of democracy" because it "criminalizes speech or writing and may be used as a weapon against

11. For more on the history of sedition laws in Hong Kong, see Fu Hualing, "Past and Future Offences of Sedition in Hong Kong", *National Security and Fundamental Freedoms: Hong Kong's Article 23 Under Scrutiny* (Hong Kong: Hong Kong University Press 2005).
12. Ibid., p. 228.

legitimate criticism of the government".[13] Instead, LegCo approved an amendment to limit the scope of sedition and expand available defences.[14] But the scaled-down law, signed by the last colonial governor, Christopher Patten, just days before the handover, never went into effect.

The legal legacy is that current sedition laws that primarily pertain to the press remain exceptionally harsh. It is still a crime, for example, to publish anything that brings "into hatred or contempt or to excite disaffection against . . . the Government of Hong Kong" (s 9(1)(a)), promotes "feelings of ill-will and enmity between different classes of the population of Hong Kong" (s 9 (1)(e)), or incites "persons to violence" (s 9 (1)(f)). It is not necessary for the prosecution to prove that a person or publication intended to commit sedition or to incite violence. It is also a crime to possess a seditious publication (s 10 (2)) or handle one by printing, selling, distributing, displaying, reproducing or importing (s 10(1)(c) and (d)) (for full text, see Appendix A).

When the Hong Kong government reviewed sedition laws under the Article 23 framework, the most optimistic had hoped that it might consider eliminating these antiquated laws, noting that many modern countries, such as South Korea in its 1980s Democratic reforms, have done so. (More recently, the UK repealed its sedition laws in 2010,[15] and New Zealand did so in 2007,[16] although several former British colonies in Asia — Singapore, Malaysia, India and Bangladesh — have invoked sedition laws respectively against bloggers, cartoonists and a teacher who used Facebook to insult the prime minister.)[17] Most, however, did not expect sedition offences to be eliminated in Hong Kong — indeed, the language of Article 23 seems to require some sedition laws — but hoped they might be modernized and minimized, along more liberal, international standards, particularly those contained within the Johannesburg Principles on National Security, Freedom of Expression and Access to Information.[18] Johannesburg Principle 6 states that "expression may be punished as a threat to national security only if a government can demonstrate that: a) the expression is intended to incite imminent violence;

13. Ibid., p. 230, citing the Report of the Bills Committee on the Crimes (Amendment)(No. 2) Bill 1996: Paper for the House Committee meeting on 13 June 1997 (LegCo Paper No. CB(2)2638/96–97).

14. Ibid., pp. 230–231.

15. The common law offences of sedition and seditious libel (as well as criminal libel) were abolished by section 73 of the Coroners and Justice Act 2009, but sedition laws against aliens, Aliens Restriction (Amendment) Act 1919, s 3, remain.

16. New Zealand, Crimes (Repeal of Seditious Offenses) Amendment Act 2007. Its neighbour, Australia, enhanced its sedition laws in the Anti-Terrorism Act 2005, but in response to intense criticism that the enhanced laws would impact freedom of expression, it passed the National Security Amendment Act 2010 that replaced references to sedition with "urging violence".

17. Singapore: Sedition Act (1985); Malaysia: Sedition Ordinance (1948); India: Penal Code (1860), s 124A; Bangladesh: Penal Code (1860), s 124A. See also Doreen Weisenhaus, "Communication Law and Policy: Asia", *The International Encyclopedia of Communication*, edited by Wolfgang Donsbach (Malden, MA: Blackwell Publishing 2008); Blackwell Reference Online, revised 2012, http://www.communicationencyclopedia.com.

18. U.N. Doc E/CN.4/1996/39.

b) it is likely to incite such violence; and c) there is a direct and immediate connection between the expression and the likelihood or occurrence of such violence."

The government's proposed sedition legislation and amendments in 2003 did not adopt the Johannesburg principles. However, they did offer some significant improvements over existing laws, such as narrowing the definition of sedition to against those who "intentionally incites others" to commit treason, subversion or secession or "to engage in violent public disorder that would seriously endanger the stability of the People's Republic of China".[19] They also included a likelihood test: "the nature of the incitement and the circumstances in which the incitement is made are such that another person is likely to be induced to . . . commit the offence or to . . . engage in violent public disorder."[20] The new version did not grant the full protection provided under Johannesburg Principle 6, but it nonetheless would have made convictions more difficult to obtain.

The government's decision to drop possession of seditious publications as a crime was universally praised. But journalists and publishers remained dismayed at the continued retention of the offence of handling seditious publications, even though it was substantially liberalized to include a likelihood test and an intent requirement.[21] It was viewed as redundant to the main sedition offence and as targeting the publishing industry as a "clear threat to the fundamental freedoms to publish and to read".[22]

As for the crimes of subversion and secession, they are not specific offences in current law; the 2003 legislative bill proposed their inclusion. Under the bill, a person commits secession if he "withdraws any part of the People's Republic of China from its sovereignty by (a) using force or serious criminal means that seriously endangers the territorial integrity" of the PRC; or (b) "engaging in war".[23] For subversion, a person would be guilty if he (a) "disestablishes the basic system" of the PRC "as established by the Constitution" of the PRC; (b) "overthrows the Central People's Government; or (c) intimidates the Central People's Government by using force or serious criminal means that seriously endangers the stability" of the PRC or "by engaging in war".[24] The bill was problematic, by not providing a definition of "force" or making clear how one "intimidates" the Central People's Government. These changes would have affected the long-standing crimes of treason and "treasonable offences" (Crimes Ordinance s 2–3), which deal mostly with levying war and assisting public enemies at war.

19. National Security Bill, c 16
20. Paper No. 69, "Proposed Committee Stage Amendments to the National Security (Legislative Provisions) Bill", 3 June 2003, p. 3.
21. The Proposed s 9C defined "seditious publication" as one that is "likely to induce a person to commit an offence" of treason, subversion or secession. A person who handles such a publication "with intent to incite others" would be guilty of the offence.
22. 14 March 2003 submission to the HKSAR Government by the Geneva-based International Publishers Association, which represents publishers in more than 60 countries.
23. Proposed s 2 (B)(1).
24. Proposed s 2 (A)(1).

Journalists' fears were once again linked to coverage involving the political fault lines of China. Would publishing articles and editorials about separatist movements in Taiwan and Tibet lead to trouble if these proposals became law? For the substantive crimes of subversion or secession, it did not seem likely that mere journalism would meet the legal threshold. The proposed laws appeared to require some measure of open revolt or resistance to PRC authority. It was more likely that if a prosecution were to be brought against a journalist, it would be for inciting others (sedition) to commit treason, secession or subversion. It might also be possible for the press to get tangled up in the inchoate offences of attempting, aiding, abetting or conspiracy for subversion or secession.

5. Macau's passage of national security legislation

In October 2008, when the Macau government introduced a draft bill of a new national security law, concern arose 40 miles away in Hong Kong. Both municipalities shared a status as special administrative regions of the PRC with identical Article 23 mandates for enacting laws on treason, secession, sedition, subversion and theft of state secrets. Many in Hong Kong feared that Macau's action would inspire or provoke the Hong Kong government into a second attempt at implementing Article 23 national security legislation. Pro-democracy lawmakers from Hong Kong who planned to protest the Macau proposals and a photographer were blocked from entering Macau in the run-up to the vote.

After a public consultation period of just six weeks and little opposition or public response, Macau's legislature approved in February 2009 its National Security Law with offences punishable by sentences of up to 25 years.[25] Critics, both Hong Kong and international, objected to what they saw as flaws in the new legislation such as vague wording and worrisome procedural mechanisms. For example, the offence of subversion is defined as anyone using violence or "practising other grave illegal acts" to overthrow the Central People's Government; state secrets are defined as "documents, information or objects that must be kept secret and are classified as such in the fields of national defence, foreign relations and *other issues concerning the relationships between the Central Authorities and the Macau Special Administrative Region*" (emphasis added). The law also contains a provision that the judiciary could obtain from the Chief Executive or from central Chinese authorities certification that the "relevant documents, information or objects are classified as state secrets", permitting potentially arbitrary classification of such materials.

25. The text of the law in Chinese and Portuguese can be found on the Macau government website at: http://images.io.gov.mo/bo/i/2009/09/lei-2–2009.pdf. The unofficial English text of the draft bill submitted in December 2008 to the Macau legislature can be found on Amnesty International's website at: http://www.amnesty.org/en/library/info/ASA27/002/2009/en.

6. Conclusion

If and when Article 23 legislation is reintroduced in Hong Kong, journalists are likely to have many of the same concerns over any new proposals that relate to the same troublesome areas of sedition and theft of state secrets as well as secession, subversion and any expansion of powers for police and the Secretary for Security. Journalists also are apprehensive about whether the government will attempt to open up new ground in a later bill.

As the crimes of sedition, subversion, theft of state secrets and so on are essentially political in nature, journalists fear that the local Hong Kong government in applying these laws might be tempted to defer to the PRC when it comes to issues of national security. What role will China play when these issues arise again? The "one country, two systems" structure mandates two systems of law and governance for Hong Kong and the PRC. But what happens when one country is being protected by two systems? Which system dominates? In 2003, the Hong Kong government asserted that, of course, its system would prevail in Hong Kong. And it should as the content of Hong Kong's laws and legal safeguards are clearly different from what is available on the mainland. But how does the process unfold in a shifting relationship between Hong Kong and China and when it is China's security at stake? How will national security issues in a post-Wikileaks era further complicate the terrain? The "one country, two systems" formula is untested in this context and the boundaries in which the media can safely operate have yet to be fully drawn.

8

Other Restrictions on Newsgathering and Reporting

Yan Mei Ning

FREQUENTLY ASKED QUESTIONS

1. Do journalists have any special rights of access to places and events? (See section 2)
2. Do reporters need a press card? (See section 2.2.3)
3. Can the police prevent journalists from taking pictures in the street? (See section 2.2)
4. What obligations do journalists have when police establish press-only areas at public demonstrations? (See section 2.2)
5. Do journalists face criminal liability if, in the course of reporting, they lie in order to enter a private home or take another's belongings without permission? Can acting under a supervisor's order be a lawful excuse? (See sections 2.1 and 2.5)
6. Can journalists take pictures and report in hospitals without permission? (See section 2.4)
7. Do journalists face criminal liability when they enter unauthorized into border areas, military installations, or places under quarantine? (See sections 2.3 and 2.4)
8. Can press photographers freely take pictures of voters and their ballot papers? (See section 3.1)
9. Under what circumstances can law enforcement officers gain access to material held by journalists? What can journalists and media organizations do in response to such demands and operations? (See section 7)

1. Introduction

This chapter examines additional restrictions journalists face in their daily newsgathering and reporting. It also discusses the protection of journalistic material and sources.

2. The right of newsgathering

Newsworthy events may occur anywhere. Ideally, journalists need to be at the scene right away to report on a breaking news event. They also need to be familiar with laws and other restrictions that might affect such coverage, and come up with informed decisions and appropriate work plans for covering news events.

The right of newsgathering is encompassed in the right to media freedom and is vital for putting media freedom into practice. The right of newsgathering, however, is not explicitly protected in either the HKSAR Basic Law or the International Covenant on Civil and Political Rights, nor has the scope of the right of newsgathering ever been clearly defined by the courts.

As such, journalists are just ordinary citizens. With notable exceptions involving courts and legislatures, journalists do not enjoy greater privileges than ordinary citizens in their access to private or public places. Moreover, unlike law enforcement officers, journalists do not have any legally vested investigative powers.

2.1 Entry to private property

An aircraft or a bus may crash into the backyard of a house. Fires, thefts, and murders commonly occur on private premises. To gain entry to private property, journalists must seek permission from the owner or occupant. Otherwise, journalists can face civil actions for trespass — the wrongful interference with another person's possession of property. Trespass is actionable, regardless of whether damage was caused, and even if the journalist entered the private property inadvertently.

When the police conduct any arrest, search, or seizure on private property, they must be authorized by law or by court warrants. These powers are for the police only and cannot be extended to news reporting activities. Journalists must first obtain permission from the owner or occupant before they enter private premises. Until the 1990s, police officers would occasionally invite journalists to cover their operations inside targeted premises, but police guidelines no longer permit this practice.

Journalists who impersonate police or any other public officer to gain access to private premises face criminal penalties. In 2002, an editor and a photographer from *Eastweek* magazine entered a public housing unit to take photographs on the pretext that they were Housing Department staff checking the plumbing. They were subsequently convicted of falsely pretending to be public officers under the Summary Offences Ordinance (SOO, Cap 228) s 22, and both were given suspended prison sentences. They were found guilty despite their submission that they were merely acting upon the instructions of their supervisors and that no loss or damage had been caused by their actions *(HKSAR v Wong Chung Ki,* HCMA 653/2003).

Journalists gaining entry into private premises using pretexts that are not illegal, such as asking to use the washroom, are still liable for trespass if they do not confine their activities to those for which consent has been given. Even if they are granted permission to enter and carry out newsgathering activities on private property, the owner or occupant may withdraw consent at any time.

Shopping malls and office blocks are not considered public places but in fact are private property. The public can only visit these places for authorized purposes. Journalists often need to seek permission before carrying out newsgathering activities on these premises, particularly for filming purposes. Again, owners, occupiers, and the estate management may at any time withdraw their permission or stop any prohibited or unwelcome activities.

Some reporters sneak into buildings pretending to be visitors. Once discovered and told to leave, journalists are liable for trespass if they do not comply. Even if trespass was not detected at the time, damages could still be sought from the journalists and media organizations involved, though such legal action is uncommon. On the other hand, journalists must beware of estate management staff exceeding their authority. If a reporter has made an appointment to interview an occupant of an office block, for example, the doorman at the main entrance normally cannot refuse access.

2.2 Newsgathering in public places

Defining "public places" can be difficult. One commonly used definition, as in Public Order Ordinance (POO, Cap 245) s 2, refers to any place to which the public or sectors of the public are entitled or permitted to have access, whether by payment or not. Streets are the most obvious public places, where members of the public can have access most of the time (see SOO s 2 and Interpretation and General Clauses Ordinance (IGCO, Cap 1) s 3).

Generally speaking, journalists are free to cover any newsworthy event taking place in the street. This includes taking pictures. No prior permission is needed from the authorities for conducting such activities. Nonetheless, reporters may have to register in advance when reporting some events, even if they take place in public streets, for crowd control or security reasons.

2.2.1 Wide range of police powers to keep public order

The police are equipped with wide powers to keep public order. The Police Force Ordinance (PFO, Cap 232) s 10 stipulates that duties of the police force include the taking of lawful measures for a variety of purposes such as preserving the public peace and regulating processions and assemblies in public places. Disorderly behaviour and obstruction in public places and public meetings are prohibited (POO ss 17B, 50A). The police officers present are empowered to use necessary force to overcome resistance or make arrests (POO s 45).

In addition, the Offences Against the Person Ordinance (Cap 212) s 36(b) makes it an offence to assault, resist, or wilfully obstruct any police officer in the execution of his or her duty. PFO s 63 contains similar prohibitions and further stipulates that it is illegal to refuse assistance to any police officer, or to wilfully mislead any officer by giving false information with intent to defeat or delay the ends of justice.

These police powers, if wrongly exercised, can severely inhibit newsgathering activities in public places. Such dangers have grown in recent years amid a trend of heavy police deployment in connection with public demonstrations and visits by dignitaries. A vivid illustration was the tight security measures imposed in August

2011 by the police during a three-day visit by Li Keqiang, then Vice Premier of the People's Republic of China. The police action, including at a University of Hong Kong appearance by Li, attracted widespread criticism from numerous sectors of the community, including the press.

In another incident, two journalists from NOW TV complained that two plain-clothes policemen obstructed their filming by waving a hand in front of the camera and by holding down the camera. The policemen also refused to show their credentials upon request. Police Commissioner Andy Tsang Wai Hung later publicly explained that the two policemen had mistaken the camera for a dark "object" and their acts were simply natural responses to a misconception.

The Complaints Against Police Office (CAPO), an internal review unit within the Hong Kong Police Force, however, found the journalists' allegations against the two policemen substantiated, as unnecessary use of police authority, neglect of duty, misconduct, and impoliteness. The CAPO also ruled the search by a policewoman of another NOW TV reporter's trouser pockets and jacket without giving a reason as an unnecessary use of police authority. A complaint by the same reporter of police misconduct was upheld as well. A senior police officer had asked the reporter to move to another location and had threatened to block her from filming Li if she did not comply.

However, the police were apparently slow to learn from these adverse CAPO findings. In mid-2012, President Hu Jintao visited Hong Kong to commemorate the HKSAR's 15th anniversary. At one of Hu's public appearances, a reporter from the *Apple Daily* newspaper shouted a question about the 1989 Tiananmen crackdown to the president from a designated press area. The police immediately removed the reporter by force and detained him briefly. *Apple Daily* and the reporter later jointly filed a writ in the High Court claiming damages for false imprisonment.

2.2.2 **Designated press areas**

The police practice of setting up designated press areas has been a source of bitter complaint by journalists. Such areas confine the movements of journalists in their coverage of public events, protests, and demonstrations. The areas also block views and prevent journalists from reporting and photographing police actions. In particular, journalists encounter immense difficulties when the police begin to disperse protesters or when scuffles break out between protestors and police. Journalists have been arrested for venturing out of the designated press areas or for following protestors.

The problem of designated press areas was illustrated in 2002 by what has become known as the "Chater Garden Incident". Two journalists were handcuffed and arrested by the police after they refused to enter and stay in a designated press area while the police began dispersing a prolonged protest staged in Chater Garden, a public park near the then Legislative Council building in Central. The two journalists later lodged complaints with CAPO, which conducted an investigation into the incident and found no wrongdoing by the police.

This initial finding was rejected by the Independent Police Complaints Council (IPCC), an advisory body appointed by the HKSAR Chief Executive to monitor and review CAPO's handling of complaints. Eventually, CAPO substantiated the complaint against the use of handcuffs, noting that the policeman complained of did not fully take account of the situation and whether the use of handcuffs was necessary. But CAPO also concluded that the complaints of improper arrangement of the designated press area and over compelling journalists to stay inside the area were not substantiated. No reasons were given for these findings.

Although the police met with journalist organizations and denied accusations of inhibiting media freedom, the setting up of designated press areas has remained a routine practice. More recently, the problem has become acute outside the Central Government Liaison Office in Western District, where huge crowds of protestors gather from time to time. Journalists and media organizations complain that police arrangements there make filming and reporting extremely difficult.

Meanwhile, a reporter from Metro Broadcast lodged complaints with CAPO alleging that the locations of several designated press areas during Vice-Premier Li's visit in 2011 were too far away from event venues. The CAPO ruled that the location of the areas was appropriate, namely, providing the best camera view while not compromising security arrangements.

While the IPCC did not endorse CAPO's ruling, it noted that it was unable to confirm whether there could be more proper arrangements and found the complaints unsubstantiated. But CAPO did not agree and the IPCC therefore in late 2012 referred its views on these two complaints to the Chief Executive for further considerations.

In addition, the IPCC made several suggestions concerning the setting up of designated press areas. These include: the police should refrain from setting up designated press areas in places which are generally accessible to the public; if a designated press area is required, the police should, as far as practicable, consult reporters as to the desirable location without compromising the safety of dignitaries; and the police should inform the press in advance of the media arrangements so long as security operations are not compromised.

2.2.3 **The issuance of press cards**

The police published a report in early 2012 reviewing its operational arrangements during Vice-Premier Li's visit. The report highlighted the difficulty of identifying *bona fide* members of the press. It noted that a large number of media organizations, journalists, freelancers and staffers of websites, not part of the traditional press, cover public events in Hong Kong. The police therefore found it necessary to apply more stringent measures before allowing journalists to enter designated press areas, including checking their identity and searching their belongings. The report suggests exploring the possibility of a universal verification system for journalists. This proposal, however, was met with scepticism from the Hong Kong Journalists Association.

To facilitate newsgathering, most Hong Kong media organizations issue their own press cards, which serve as a form of identification for reporters. But these press cards are neither accredited nor required by the authorities. The government's Information Services Department, which handles government publicity and media relations, used to issue press cards to local reporters but stopped the practice in the 1970s. Nowadays, it would be considered an affront to media freedom if reporters were required to obtain press cards from the authorities or to show their own press cards before they could cover news or take photographs in a public street.

2.2.4 **Journalists on assignments**

Journalists are not above the law. Nor are they immune from arrest and prosecution. Getting reporting done in an efficient manner while at the same time avoiding harm and legal consequences presents immense challenges. Extreme care has to be taken by reporters at public events such as protests and demonstrations where obstructions and attacks from police and others are likely. Journalists need to be well aware of their rights and possible legal restrictions. It is also important for them to behave in a professional, restrained, and tactful manner in order to avoid confrontation or agitation. Journalists must refrain from quarrelling or fighting while covering any news event.

Under most circumstances, journalists are advised to obey the instructions of police officers at the scene. But journalists should also state any objections clearly and politely. In many instances, it would be helpful to contact senior police officers to persuade them to alter instructions given by lower-ranking officers.

If in doubt, journalists should consult superiors or seek legal advice. To guard against newsgathering rights being chipped away by the authorities, journalist organizations and media establishments need to lobby regularly and educate both the police and the public on the importance of the right of newsgathering, and organize media law and ethics training courses for journalists.

The above advices are also mostly applicable in dealing with privately employed security guards. In recent years, the increasing presence of security guards in newsgathering scenes has made the lives of journalists more difficult. Journalists and security guards often have different understandings of what public or private places are and what journalists can or cannot do on location. The situation becomes more complicated when clashes break out between the two parties. At least two photo-journalists were arrested and prosecuted on separate occasions in 2012 on charges of assaulting security guards.

2.3 **Restrictions of access to certain public places**

Many government-owned premises are not open to the public nor to newsgathering activities. The Hong Kong government can resort to the civil actions of trespass or nuisance to curb unwelcomed access or activity on government property. Moreover, SOO s 4(30) stipulates criminal sanctions for any trespass onto government-controlled or managed property. Any such actions can attract a fine of HK$500 or a prison term of three months.

According to POO s 36, the Chief Executive may issue an order to declare any place or area a closed area for the protection of national security, public safety, public order, or public health. Frontier areas and military installations have been declared closed areas, as was the location of the World Trade Organization Ministerial Conference for the duration of that conference in 2005. Any trespass onto these places attracts a higher fine of HK$5,000 and a prison term of two years. Persons visiting these closed areas must first obtain a permit unless they belong to specified categories of persons (see POO ss 37–39; Frontier Closed Area Order, Cap 245A; Military Installations Closed Areas Order, Cap 245B; Marine Closed Area (Consolidation) Order, Cap 245E; and Frontier Closed Area (Permission to Enter) Notice, Cap 245H).

In most cases, visits to military installations are pre-arranged and journalists are escorted throughout. In December 1996, seventeen media workers, including reporters, technicians, and drivers, were arrested and charged with crossing the Lok Ma Chau Control Point without a permit when they went to report on demonstrations held in the frontier closed area against the then Provisional Legislative Council, meetings of which were conducted across the border in Shenzhen. The prosecution was later dropped when the journalists agreed to be bound over.

Airports and ports have similar prohibitions against unauthorized entry into restricted areas. Persons other than *bona fide* airline passengers need permits for access to a restricted area in the airport; see Airport Authority Bylaw (AAB, Cap 483A) s 11. Moreover, the Airport Authority can limit access to or close any parts of the airport it deems necessary (AAB s 12). Entering or remaining in a restricted area without a permit is also prohibited in some ferry terminals such as those designated for Macau and mainland China-bound ferries. Again, this restriction does not apply to *bona fide* passengers (see Shipping and Port Control (Ferry Terminals) Regulations (Cap 313H) Regulations 12 and 23).

In 1974, eleven journalists were convicted and fined HK$200 each for entering a restricted area at Kai Tak Airport. They had followed a group of protesting relatives and friends of deported Vietnamese refugees onto the airport tarmac. In 1993, seven press photographers were arrested and prosecuted for entering a restricted area of Kai Tak Airport while covering a plane crash. The charges against these photographers were later withdrawn and written warnings were issued instead. Some media organizations have occasionally resorted to the practice of buying passenger tickets for their reporters to cover newsworthy events in restricted areas. Journalists on such assignments might run afoul of the requirement of being *bona fide* passengers if they return to the office without boarding a plane or ferry.

In conclusion, journalists must bear in mind that the occurrence of newsworthy events in itself does not make private property or restricted areas accessible to journalists. This mirrors the general practice in the United States and many Western countries that journalists do not have right of access to scenes of crime or disaster when the general public is excluded. This practice continues despite the complaints of media and journalists organizations that such exclusions infringe on the public's right to know. In addition to coverage of crimes and accidents, news organizations have carried out their own investigations to test the adequacy of security measures in places such as airports, military installations, or official residences of dignitaries. These activities are likely to attract civil or even criminal liability and should be carefully considered.

2.4 Restrictions on access for public health reasons

Access may also be restricted for public health reasons. Such laws and regulations do not target journalists, but they do have an impact on newsgathering. Hospitals under the Hospital Authority are deemed to be public places for the purposes of the SOO and POO (Hospital Authority Ordinance (Cap 113) s 22). Moreover, the Hospital Authority may make bylaws regulating the conduct of persons there (HAO s 21); when it closes any part of its hospitals to the public, no person may enter such part unless authorized (Hospital Authority Bylaws (HAB, Cap 113A) Bylaw 6(3)).

Taking photographs or videos of a patient without his or her consent is prohibited (HAB Bylaw 7(1)(f)). Also prohibited is the taking of photographs or videos of any ward without the consent of hospital staff, but consent will generally be given unless the act would cause annoyance or disturbance to a patient or be prejudicial to the medical treatment of a patient (HAB Bylaw 7(1)(g)). Violations of the above rules can attract a fine or a prison term (HAB Bylaw 10).

In late 2006, an Indonesian maid was jailed for four weeks for taking a video without the consent of Lydia Shum, a well-known actress (since deceased) who was receiving treatment in the intensive care unit of Queen Mary Hospital. The accused, who worked as a domestic helper for an editor of *Eastweek*, concealed a video-camera in her backpack. Upon arrest, the maid did not reveal her motive nor whether she was under instructions to carry out covert filming. The magazine distanced itself from the incident, saying it had no knowledge of the non-consensual filming and would not condone such an act.

Photographers and camera crews routinely take pictures of victims of crimes and accidents arriving at the hospital, without seeking the consent of victims or hospital staff. Although this practice has attracted criticism, it has been tolerated. On the other hand, journalists should note that it is an offence to wilfully obstruct any hospital staff in the lawful performance of their duties or hospital users in their lawful use of the hospital (HAB Bylaw 9). As such, whether newsgathering activities at public hospitals amount to obstruction depends to a large extent on the actual behaviour of the journalists involved. In the case of private hospitals, the management may resort to the civil actions of trespass and nuisance.

As Hong Kong has experienced outbreaks of infectious diseases such as bird flu and SARS in the past decade, journalists should also be familiar with the following provisions. First, any person entering or landing at a quarantine station without permission may be detained and kept in isolation at his or her own expense for a maximum of fourteen days, according to Quarantine and Prevention of Disease

Ordinance (QPDO, Cap 141, s 40). A quarantine station is any place where isolation is carried out and includes an infectious diseases hospital and any place declared by the Chief Executive in Council to be a quarantine station or a sanitary station. Second, no person, other than those specified, shall enter a place infected by animal and bird diseases without a special permit (see Public Health (Animals and Birds) Regulations, Cap 139A, Regulation 32).

In addition to laws governing access, journalists should be mindful of other legal consequences when working on enterprise or investigative stories. It is unlawful to obstruct or impede any health officers in the execution of their duties (QPDO s 9). Journalists would risk violating the provision if they, for example, tested the vigilance of health officers by falsely stating in a health declaration form that they had recent contact with a SARS patient. Furthermore, such a practice might contravene Crimes Ordinance (Cap 200) s 36, which prohibits various kinds of false statements made knowingly or wilfully in documents.

2.5 **Illegal practices**

Journalists should avoid using illegal means in their newsgathering activities. In recent years, two journalists were convicted of bribery and received prison sentences after being found in breach of the Prevention of Bribery Ordinance (POBO, Cap 201). In 2000, an *Apple Daily* reporter was convicted and jailed for ten months for paying two police officers on a monthly basis to obtain information about police operations and investigations. In 2003, a photographer from *Sudden Weekly* was jailed for three months for paying HK$300 to a security guard so he could sneak onto a movie filming location to take exclusive pictures. Again, under these circumstances, carrying out instructions from supervisors can never be a lawful excuse, and the journalist involved would be personally liable for the offences committed.

Meanwhile, journalists should also be aware that some common newsgathering techniques may be illegal. Some local newspapers and magazines publish personal photographs or private letters of victims of crimes or accidents or of people who have committed suicide. Journalists who obtained these photographs or letters without permission could be prosecuted for the offence of theft.

Another example occurred in the summer of 2002 after mass transit railway (MTR) passengers complained they were injured by train doors not shutting properly. Several media organizations rushed to conduct their own investigations by placing various objects between train doors. These experiments violated a law that prohibits tampering with or wilfully impeding or interfering with the operation of MTR trains, which can attract a fine of HK$5,000 and a prison term of six months (see Mass Transit Railway Bylaws, Cap 556B, Bylaw 28A).

To ensure smooth operations and safety, railway and ferry operators are empowered to make and enforce bylaws to prevent trespass or obstruction or to limit access if necessary (see, for example, Mass Transit Railway Ordinance, Cap 556, ss 34–35). No action has been taken against reporters so far, but this neither excuses nor affirms the legality of continuing the above practices. Journalists must carefully consider whether any major public interest justifies breaking the law, and whether they can face the consequences.

3. Restrictions on coverage of elections

Detailed rules have been devised to ensure orderly voting, vote counting, and the ballot secrecy in elections. These rules are not aimed at journalists but have a definite impact on newsgathering activities. As such, journalists covering elections should familiarize themselves with rules concerning who may enter a polling station and what constitutes an offence in a polling station, and who may be present at a vote-counting station and what constitutes an offence in a vote-counting station (Electoral Affairs Commission (Electoral Procedure) (District Councils) Regulation, Cap 541F, ss 47, 48, 68, 69 and 94; and Electoral Affairs Commission (Electoral Procedure)(Legislative Council) Regulation, Cap 541D, ss 44, 45, 68, 68(A), 96).

3.1 Photography at polling stations and exit polls

Press photographers, for example, should be mindful that it is unlawful to film or to take photographs within a polling station without the express permission of the officer(s) in charge of the polling station or any member of the Electoral Affairs Commission (EAC), the government body that oversees Hong Kong elections. It is also unlawful to induce a voter to display his or her ballot paper so that his or her choice is disclosed. The secrecy of the ballot is protected. A voter is not required to disclose who he or she has voted for in an election, and it is against the law for anyone to require, without lawful authority, a voter to disclose such information (District Councils Ordinance, Cap 547, s 48; Legislative Council Ordinance, Cap 542, s 60). Fines or jail terms of up to six months may be handed down for convictions on some of the offences.

Meanwhile, the EAC issues detailed guidelines (posted and updated regularly on its website: http://www.eac.gov.hk) governing the conducting and reporting of exit polls so as to protect ballot secrecy and to avoid unfair influence on elections. Media are requested not to announce results of exit polls or to make specific remarks or predictions on the performance of individual candidates before the close of polls so that voters' behaviour would not be unduly affected ("Guidelines on the Election-Related Activities in respect of the 2012 Legislative Council Election" issued by the EAC, Chapter 15).

Broadcasters are further reminded by the 2012 Guidelines to follow codes of practice on programme standards issued by the Broadcasting Authority (now the Communications Authority), which require news and current affairs programmes to be fair, objective, and impartial. In addition to the criminal sanctions provided in the District Councils and Legislative Council ordinances, the EAC may publicly reprimand or censure a news organization or broadcaster for any violations of the guidelines.

3.2 Specific rules for broadcasters

The Guidelines closely follow the traditional distinctions between broadcast and print media. Broadcasters are subject to much stricter regulation of their programme content in their coverage of elections. There are two important rules to be followed. To begin with, no unfair advantage should be offered to or obtained by any candidate over others regarding election campaigning. Secondly, the "fair and equal treatment" principle applies to all programmes that relate entirely or in part to an election.

When inviting a candidate to attend such a programme, a broadcaster should include in the invitation a notice that a similar invitation has been or will be made to other candidates of the same constituency. The broadcaster should retain a record of the date, time and content of the invitation and the notice until three months after the election. In the programme, each of the candidates contesting the same constituency has to be introduced and reported, and no favourable or unfavourable treatment can be given to any of them. Each candidate taking part in the programme must be given equal time to present his or her election platform. Moreover, care should be taken in multi-episode programmes to avoid any misunderstanding over the actual number of candidates contesting a constituency.

The above principles are also applicable to political parties and political organizations to which the candidate belongs and organizations authorized to have their names or emblems printed on a ballot paper. If a broadcaster invites a candidate from any such body to take part in a programme that is partially or entirely devoted to the election, invitations should also be extended to all other bodies with members contesting the election.

Broadcasters may organize election forums in their programmes. They have to ensure that the "fair and equal treatment" principle applies, meaning that all candidates in a constituency have to be invited, and each candidate taking part in the forum has equal time to present his election platform. However, these principles do not apply to programmes that are purely news reporting and are not related to candidates' participation in the election. Candidates may also take part as guests in current affairs or other programmes that are not election-related so long as their participation is pertinent. Once unfair or unequal treatment is detected, the EAC may, in addition to public reprimand or censure, notify the relevant authorities to take appropriate action.

3.3 Election advertisements and reporting

Hong Kong still imposes a broadcasting ban on political advertising (Broadcasting Ordinance schedules 4–7 and 2011 Radio Code of Practice on Advertising Standards para 28; see also section 5.3 of Chapter 12), and as a general rule, no election advertisements should appear in television or radio broadcasts. Broadcasters are urged to treat all candidates fairly and equally when making comments on or references to candidates in their programmes. Comments that promote or prejudice a candidate may be treated as election advertisements, and the EAC will refer such comments to the Communications Authority for appropriate action. Nonetheless, if there is fair and equal treatment to all candidates in the same constituency, the editorial line of the broadcaster or personal opinions of the programme presenter regarding individual candidates can be freely expressed so long as they are fair comments and are based on true facts. The Guidelines note that they do not seek to shackle the expression of such views.

Meanwhile, candidates may freely advertise in the print media. However, if such an advertisement takes the form of a news report, it must be clearly stated to be an election advertisement to avoid misunderstanding. Moreover, publishers should not offer unfair advantage to any candidate(s). Free publications promoting or prejudicing a particular candidate may be treated as election advertisements, subject to rules on election advertisements and expenses. This serves to prevent incidents similar to what happened in the 2007 Legislative Council by-election, when on the afternoon of the polling day, *Apple Daily* published a supplement that was widely regarded as a last-minute appeal for Anson Chan, a former HKSAR Chief Secretary participating in the by-election. The print media are urged to treat all candidates in a fair and equal manner. Once this baseline is met, a newspaper is free to express its support or disapproval of any candidate, as long as such views are fair comments and factually based.

Over the years, these election guidelines for media coverage have caused controversy due to their vague wording. Public reprimands and censure have been either disputed or largely ignored by the media. The EAC has continued to revise and update the guidelines to make them more workable. In May 2011, the EAC proposed extending the election guidelines to cover the online media as well. If implemented, online radio and television and the online versions of print media would all be regulated by the election guidelines. However, public opposition was so strong that the EAC withdrew the proposal.

4. The ban on disability and racial vilifications

Hong Kong is a pioneer in enacting a law against disability vilification. Enacted in 1995, Disability Discrimination Ordinance (DDO, Cap 487) s 46 prohibits disability vilification, stipulating that it is unlawful for a person, by an activity in public, to incite hatred towards, serious contempt for, or severe ridicule of, another person with a disability or members of a class of persons with a disability. "Activity in public" is given a wide meaning that includes any form of communications to the public such as writing, printing, broadcasting, etc., and the distribution or dissemination of any matter to the public. It is immaterial whether anyone is actually incited by the activity. Several defences, including fair reporting of an activity in public, are available.

The case of *Tung Lai Lam v Oriental Press Group Ltd & Anor* [2011] 2 HKC 294 involved Hong Kong's first disability vilification claim. It was brought by a mental patient against *The Sun* with legal assistance provided by the Equal Opportunities Commission. The plaintiff felt insulted, angered, and distressed after reading an article published by *The Sun* in 2007 about mental patients, and maintained that the article constituted disability vilification. The article, entitled "Hospital Authority's Plan Goes Insane, Crowded Wards Drive People Crazy", included statements about mentally ill patients chopping up their fathers, killing their mothers, and murdering their children, and complained that over-crowding in hospital wards had compounded madness. The plaintiff claimed HK$100,000 as damages for injury to feelings and another HK$50,000 as aggravated damages.

The court ruled the complaint unsubstantiated. The judge found that the article published by *The Sun* had neither targeted nor ridiculed people with mental illness but would be understood by ordinary reasonable readers to be a satirical commentary to vent dissatisfaction, anger, and criticism of the perceived incompetence of the Hospital Authority, with an underlying sympathy for the plight of mental patients in Hong Kong. Moreover, although the judge condemned the use of distasteful, insensitive, and derogatory wording in the article, he did not think the statements complained of would have the capacity to incite ordinary reasonable readers to have feelings of hatred towards, serious contempt of, or severe ridicule for people suffering from mental illness.

This court decision nevertheless sounded an alarm for journalists and news organizations, because it brought newspaper commentaries under the scrutiny of DDO s 46. Meanwhile, the Race Discrimination Ordinance (Cap 602), enacted more than a decade later than the DDO, contains a similar provision prohibiting vilification based on race (s 45). As discrimination is increasingly being taken more seriously in Hong Kong, journalists and news organizations should be more aware of potential liability in their commentaries and coverage.

5. Reporting or advertising?

In August 2012, *Apple Daily* and its printer were each fined HK$3,000 for publishing an article detailing a certain brand of cigar in its finance section in April. The article contained information about the cigar's brand name, the price, and the sales location. The Department of Health's Tobacco Control Office regarded the article not as a news report or feature but rather an advertisement, thus violating the Smoking (Public Health) Ordinance (Cap 371) s 11 which bans tobacco advertisements in newspapers. Indeed, the practice of newspapers and magazines to publish advertorials — advertising copy that looks like news reports or news features — is not only unethical but can at times attract criminal liability.

The Undesirable Medical Advertisements Ordinance (UMAO, Cap 231) aims to prevent the adverse effects of improper self-medication by members of the public, including incorrect or delayed treatment. In the UMAO, the term "advertisement" is widely defined and includes notices, posters, circulars, labels, wrappers, documents and announcements. As such, news articles or media interviews may be considered advertisement and come within the ambit of the ordinance.

UMAO s 3 prohibits or restricts the advertising of medicines, surgical appliances, or treatments for curing or preventing certain diseases or conditions. A new s 3B and schedule 4 regulating "orally consumed products", a term ambiguously defined, came into force in mid-2012. Six types of health claims for "orally consumed products", including regulating body sugar or blood pressure, are restricted. The maximum penalties for a contravention of the ordinance have also been increased to HK$50,000 and six months' imprisonment on first conviction and to HK$100,000 and twelve months imprisonment on subsequent conviction.

The Department of Health monitors medical and health advertisements in newspapers and magazines, and investigates complaints. In early 2012, the department noted that its trained staff screen on a regular basis some 20 local newspapers and magazines for any violations. Warning letters will first be sent to publishers and distributors for any advertisements that appear to have contravened the UMAO. If the warning is ignored and publication of advertisement(s) continues, the case will be referred to the police for investigation, and prosecution may be followed upon a review by the Director of Health.

When SARS struck Hong Kong in early 2003, the department issued nearly 200 warnings against medical advertisements claiming to have the effect of preventing or curing the disease. *The Sun*, insisting that it did not receive any warning, was fined HK$6,000. In 2005, more than 2,000 letters were sent to various media for alleged breaches of the ordinance, including 283 to *Oriental Daily News*, 269 to *The Sun* and 204 to *Apple Daily*. Also in 2005, fourteen prosecutions were directed at media organizations. The Department of Health refuted accusations of selective prosecutions targeting particular media organization(s), stressing standard monitoring procedures have been followed.

6. Restrictions on reporting criminal investigations

Journalists face additional reporting restrictions concerning criminal investigations. Organized and Serious Crimes Ordinance (Cap 455) s 26 stipulates that no person shall publish or broadcast any information that would reveal or suggest (a) that a person has disclosed to the authorities that any property has been funded by the proceeds of an indictable offence, or was used or is intended to be used in connection with an indictable offence; or (b) the identity of the person making the disclosure.

A similar provision can be found in Drug Trafficking (Recovery of Proceeds) Ordinance (Cap 405) s 26, which bans the publication or broadcast of any information that would reveal or suggest (a) that a person has disclosed to the authorities that any property is funded by drug trafficking proceeds, or was used or is intended to be used in connection with drug trafficking; or (b) the identity of the person making the disclosure. The prohibition in both ordinances is applicable to reports on all civil and criminal proceedings. The court or the magistrate, in the interests of justice, may by an order lift such reporting restrictions. Prosecutions for any breach of the restrictions can only be instigated with the consent of the Secretary for Justice.

6.1 Section 30 of the POBO

Reporting on criminal investigations of bribery and corruption are restricted by POBO s 30. It is illegal for a person, knowing or suspecting that an investigation of bribery or corruption offences is taking place, to disclose without lawful authority or reasonable excuse details of corruption investigations, including the identity of the person being investigated, unless one of several circumstances has occurred in relation to the person being investigated.

These circumstances are: an arrest warrant has been issued, the suspect has been arrested, the suspect's residence has been searched, he or she has been required to surrender travel documents or has been required to furnish a statutory declaration on property or expenditures, or a restraining order has been served on the suspect or any third party related to the case. Meanwhile, the term "reasonable excuse" includes a disclosure that reveals any unlawful activity, abuse of power, serious neglect of duty, or other serious misconduct by any officer of the Independent Commission Against Corruption (ICAC), the Hong Kong government's anti-corruption agency, or a serious threat to public order, the security of Hong Kong, or the health or safety of the public.

The current POBO s 30 is an amended version passed by the Legislative Council in 1996. It offers greater protection to journalists than the previous version by allowing more circumstances under which the ban on disclosure would be lifted and by specifying the kinds of public interest-related disclosures that would fall within the scope of "reasonable excuse". The law was amended after a highly controversial prosecution under the old s 30 involving the *Ming Pao* newspaper for a 1994 article about an ICAC investigation into allegations that property developers had colluded to suppress prices in a land auction (*Ming Pao Newspapers Ltd & Others v Attorney General* [1996] 6 HKPLR 103).

The old s 30 had long been criticized as too broad. Nonetheless, the Court of Appeal held that *Ming Pao* and its editors were liable, maintaining that the offence was a justified restriction on freedom of expression necessary for bribery investigations. *Ming Pao* took the case to the Privy Council (the UK-based court of final appeal for Hong Kong before the 1997 handover), which allowed the appeal on technical grounds, ruling that s 30 (as it was then written) would only apply when there was a suspect or an allegation of a bribery ordinance offence against a specified person. *Ming Pao* was not liable because its report was general and did not mention a specific suspect.

As the ICAC became very concerned about the Privy Council ruling, the administration proceeded to amend s 30 to make it applicable to all investigations, whether general or specific. Journalist organizations and some legislators opposed such a move, arguing that it would widen the scope of the provision. The current s 30 was eventually adopted as a compromise.

6.2 Section 17(1) of the Witness Protection Ordinance

The media in their reporting of criminal investigations are heavily restricted by yet another statutory provision — Witness Protection Ordinance (WPO, Cap 564) s 17(1). The section serves to protect witnesses whose personal safety or well-being may be at risk as a result of being witnesses. It stipulates that a person shall not, without lawful authority or reasonable excuse, disclose information: (a) about the identity or location of a person who is or has been a participant, or who has been considered for inclusion in the witness protection programme (WPP); or (b) that compromises the security of such a person. Contravention of the provision can attract a prison term of up to ten years.

On 24 July 2004, ICAC officers conducted the biggest ever search of Hong Kong media organizations, involving the premises of seven newspapers and the offices and homes of a number of journalists (see also section 7 of this chapter, "Protection of journalistic material"). A businessman and his secretary had been arrested by the ICAC and news reports revealed that the secretary had become a protected witness. The ICAC wanted to find out who leaked the WPP participant's identity to the press in violation of WPO s 17(1).

Senior Counsel Kevin Egan and solicitor Andrew Lam were later prosecuted for their alleged involvements in the disclosure. During the trial in 2006, it was revealed that the chief court reporter of the *South China Morning Post* (*SCMP*), Magdalen Chow, was arrested on the day of the ICAC search operation for breach of the WPO in connection with an article published in the *SCMP* (*HKSAR v Kanjanapas Chong Kwong, Derek & Others,* DCCC298/2005).

Immunity was offered to Chow and all other editorial staff of the *SCMP*. Chow appeared at trial as a prosecution witness. Upon Chow's evidence, the trial judge was satisfied that Egan, when answering Chow's enquiry, had effectively linked the secretary to the WPP. As a result, Egan was convicted for the offence of attempting to disclose to Chow, without lawful authority or reasonable excuse, information about the identity of a participant in the WPP. But Egan and Lam were acquitted of the offence of conspiracy to disclose information, without lawful authority or reasonable excuse, to journalists of the Hong Kong media about the identity of a participant in the WPP. Egan's conviction was later quashed upon appeal. The Court of Appeal, by a majority, ruled that the finding of fact by the trial judge that Egan believed the secretary was in the WPP was not supported and should be reversed. The Court of Appeal also ruled that even if Egan had such a belief, he had not actually disclosed to Chow that the secretary was in the WPP when answering her enquiry nor did he have the intention to do so (*Secretary for Justice v Kevin Egan,* CACC 248/2006). An application for further appeal by the prosecution was dismissed by the Court of Final Appeal, which pointed out problems in the way the trial court analyzed the evidence (*HKSAR v Kevin Egan* (2010) 13 HKCFAR 314).

Despite the final legal outcomes for the first prosecutions under the witness protection law, it is obvious that breaches of the WPO were treated very seriously. In the actions challenging the legality of the ICAC search operation, both the

Court of First Instance and the Court of Appeal said that it is paramount that the identity of the WPP participant is not allowed to pass into the public domain. The Court of Appeal was very concerned about the disclosure, noting that it would put the well-being of the participant in jeopardy, and risk undermining the proceedings in train and debilitating the future efficacy of the WPO *(So Wing Keung v Sing Tao Ltd & Anor* [2005] 2 HKLRD 11).

WPO s 17(1) allows disclosure based on reasonable excuse. But court rulings in this high-profile case did not throw any light on what constitutes reasonable excuse for such disclosure. It remains to be seen whether s 17(1) in effect exerts a blanket and permanent prohibition on public dissemination of any information regarding a participant. Does the provision unnecessarily hinder the media in their reporting of issues of public importance? These questions call for an answer.

In the present case, the name of the arrested secretary was in fact posted on the notice board and outside the courtroom door because a writ of *habeas corpus* was being applied for to release the woman from alleged unlawful detention by the ICAC. The media were there to closely monitor possible ICAC wrongdoings and the judicial scrutiny of any such allegations. But the media had been effectively prevented by both *in-camera* proceedings and WPO s 17(1) from reporting on why the court eventually refused to issue a writ of *habeas corpus* for the woman and commenting on the rationale.

WPO s 17(1) therefore placed the press in a very difficult situation. As such, should both the law and the court make adjustments to accommodate the need to report an issue of such public importance? At the same time, the media should familiarize themselves with the restrictions imposed by WPO s 17(1) and lobby for changes if they find the restrictions unacceptable.

7. Protection of journalistic material

While the law provides some protection for journalistic material, especially relating to search and seizure procedures, it is less clear on covert surveillance of journalistic activities that might result in government interceptions of journalistic material.

7.1 The IGCO regime

Law enforcement officers, authorized by law to enter premises to conduct criminal investigations, must fulfil additional conditions and follow specific procedures laid down in Part XII of the IGCO if their search or seizure involves known or suspected journalistic material (IGCO ss 81–90 and schedule 7).

Journalistic material is defined as any material acquired or created for the purposes of journalism and which is in the possession of a person who acquired or created it for such purposes (IGCO s 82). The protection extends to journalistic materials contained in a computer (IGCO s 88), and those kept by journalists in their homes or vehicles (IGCO s 81).

However, the protection specified in these IGCO provisions does not extend to investigations concerning drug trafficking proceeds or organized or serious crimes (see Drug Trafficking (Recovery of Proceeds) Ordinance s 21(7) and Organized and Serious Crimes Ordinance s 5(8)).

7.1.1 Three tiers for access

The IGCO regime for handling demands for coercive access to journalistic material consists of three tiers. The first tier concerns production orders. If a law enforcement officer wants access to certain material that may involve journalistic material, he or she may apply for a production order in accordance with IGCO s 84, requesting access to the material or to take it from the owner.

The application has to be made to a judge of the Court of First Instance or District Court. The hearing of the application is *inter partes*, that is, the person in possession of the material shall be given a chance to object to the application.

Before a production order is granted, several access conditions have to be met: (a) there are reasonable grounds for believing that an arrestable offence has been committed; (b) the material is likely to be of substantial value to the investigation of the arrestable offence or relevant evidence in proceedings for the arrestable offence; and (c) other methods for obtaining the material have been attempted and have failed, or have not been attempted due to the likelihood of failure or of seriously prejudicing the investigation.

In addition to these access conditions, there is a public-interest requirement: that there are reasonable grounds for believing that it is in the public interest that an order should be granted after considering the benefit likely to accrue to the investigation and the circumstances under which a person in possession of the material holds it. Upon granting of a production order, the person in possession of the journalistic material must produce it or give the applicant access to it within seven days or any other longer period specified.

The second tier concerns *ex parte* applications in accordance with IGCO s 85 for a warrant to enter any premises for the purpose of searching for or seizing journalistic material. Stricter conditions are imposed. Before the application is made to a judge of the Court of First Instance or District Court, it has to be approved by a directorate-level disciplined officer specified in the ordinance, such as a Chief Superintendent or above in the case of the police force.

In granting the warrant, conditions similar to the application of a production order have to be fulfilled. Furthermore, the officer has to prove lack of compliance with a production order, an inability to communicate the request of entry or access to the material to the appropriate persons, or the likelihood that service of a production order may seriously prejudice the investigation.

According to IGCO s 85(6), the material seized has to be sealed pending any application to have the material returned by the person from whom the material was seized or anyone claiming to be the owner. The material can only be unsealed if there is no application within three days or if the judge refuses to grant such an order.

IGCO s 87 governs the application to have the material returned. The hearing is *inter partes* and the judge will make a determination after considering, among other things, the circumstances under which the material was being held at the time of its seizure.

The third tier allows an *ex parte* application in accordance with IGCO s 85 for a warrant and for immediate use of the journalistic material. But the judge has to be satisfied that there may be serious prejudice to the investigation if immediate access to the material is not granted.

In addition, there is an overall public-interest consideration underlying these IGCO provisions. Section 89(2) stipulates that nothing in these provisions shall be construed as requiring a judge to make an order if he considers that, in all the circumstances of the case, it would not be in the public interest to make that order.

7.1.2 **Background and rationales for introducing the IGCO regime**

These provisions, introduced to Hong Kong in 1995, were similar to UK legislation. The aim was to tighten numerous provisions in various laws that granted law enforcement officers powers of entry, search and seizure.

Police officers, for example, in their search of journalistic material can no longer rely solely on PFO s 50(7). This provision stipulates much simpler requirements by allowing a magistrate (not a judge) to issue a warrant for the police to enter any building, vessel, or place to search and seize a newspaper, book, or document if, upon the oath of any person, it appears that there is reasonable cause to suspect such material is likely to be of value to the investigation of crimes, whether committed or about to be committed.

The IGCO provisions were enacted, generally, to provide additional protection to media freedom in anticipation of the 1997 handover. In particular, they were in response to the public outcry caused by an incident in October 1989.

Relying upon the PFO, the police on that occasion in 1989 obtained a warrant from a magistrate and went to the two terrestrial television stations, TVB and ATV, to take away news footage, both unedited and aired, of a scuffle between police and demonstrators. The scuffle took place outside the venue of a National Day reception by the New China News Agency, Beijing's representative in Hong Kong before the 1997 handover. The tapes were returned on the same day by the police, who stated that the footage would not be used as evidence.

It is obvious that this and other such police actions would have a negative effect on media freedom. Journalist organizations and some legislators urged the government to tighten the search and seizure procedures to protect journalistic material. However, it took six years before the IGCO provisions were enacted in 1995.

7.1.3 **Searches of media organizations**

Nonetheless, it is doubtful whether these IGCO provisions offer sufficient protection to journalistic material. There have been three incidents of searches of media organizations, all conducted by the ICAC using search warrants. Two searches related to alleged bribery by *Apple Daily* and *Sudden Weekly* reporters (see section 2.5 of this chapter), and third was the July 2004 search operation (see also section 6.2). Except for the *Sudden Weekly* incident, media organizations challenged these searches.

When investigating the *Apple Daily* reporter bribery case in November 1999, ICAC officers equipped with two warrants, one issued under the POBO and the other issued in accordance with s 85 of the IGCO, searched the premises of *Apple Daily* and seized various documents and materials. *Apple Daily* applied for court orders to prevent the ICAC from using the material and to have the two warrants set aside. The newspaper failed in its application and subsequent appeals.

In refusing *Apple Daily*'s application for leave to appeal to the Court of Final Appeal, Permanent Judge Mr Justice Litton rejected the newspaper's argument that the wording of the s 85 warrant issued was too broad, rendering the warrant void. He stated that it is inevitable that some material seized would upon further examination be found irrelevant to the investigation. He added that the legislation allowed for this possibility and intended to give officers executing warrants some latitude (*Apple Daily Ltd v Commissioner of the Independent Commission Against Corruption* [2000] 1 HKC 295).

After the July 2004 search operation, one of the affected newspapers, *Sing Tao*, and an employee applied to the Court of First Instance to have the search warrants set aside, arguing that in law they never should have been issued. The application also requested the immediate return of the seized material, maintaining that it was not required in the public interest for the ICAC investigations.

The Court of First Instance judge hearing the application attached great importance to press freedom and regarded the issue of a search warrant, constituting the exercise of draconian power, as an investigation tool of last resort (*So Wing Keung v Sing Tao Ltd & Anor*, HCMP 1833/2004). He concluded that the ICAC had failed to demonstrate that a real risk existed among the seven newspapers and the journalists involved of hiding or destroying journalistic material if a production order were served. The judge therefore found for *Sing Tao* and its employee, holding that the ICAC was wrong in fact and in law in seeking the search orders when it could have achieved its legitimate purpose equally well by pursuing less intrusive measures such as the application for a production order.

The ICAC appealed to the Court of Appeal, which dismissed the appeal on the grounds of lack of jurisdiction (*So Wing Keung v Sing Tao Ltd and Anor* [2005] 2 HKLRD 11). The Court of Appeal suggested that the ICAC appeal to the Court of Final Appeal. Nonetheless, the Court of Appeal went on to say that it would have allowed the appeal had it had the necessary jurisdiction. It said that the ICAC acted entirely within the law in seeking the search warrants, and that the issuing of the warrants was also entirely justified.

Freedom of the press in the present case, said the Court of Appeal, must be seen against the fact that serious crimes may have been committed: the newspapers and journalists concerned had been caught up in a possible conspiracy to pervert the course of public justice, and there was *prima facie* evidence that they had breached s 17(1) of the WPO. The application of a production order might seriously prejudice ICAC investigations, since journalists would be alerted and details of the investigation might find their way to persons at the centre of the alleged conspiracy. Moreover, the Court of Appeal opined that the interpretation by the judge in the Court of First Instance that production orders were preferable to search warrants was misleading, and noted that the legislation itself made no such suggestion or assumption.

7.1.4 Review of the IGCO regime

In October 2004, the ICAC announced its decision not to appeal to the Court of Final Appeal. The agency said in a public statement that the decision of the judge in the Court of First Instance had been effectively "overruled" and that the unanimous decision of the Court of Appeal was of high persuasive authority and provided valuable guidance for law enforcement agencies in the handling of journalist material.

After the Court of Appeal ruling in *Sing Tao*, the Legislative Council set up a sub-committee to review the relevant IGCO provisions. In mid-2006, the administration agreed that future applications for coercive access to journalistic material would have to be made to a District Court judge. This new arrangement means that the decision to issue a production order or search warrant could be subject to judicial review. Nonetheless, if there is an imminent risk of serious harm to life and limb, or in cases of utmost sensitivity, search warrant applications may still be made to the Court of First Instance. Under these circumstances, advice has to be sought from the Department of Justice before making such an application.

7.1.5 Applying for production orders

In mid-August 2013, the ICAC went to court to apply for production orders forcing two media organizations to produce tapes and notes for its officers to take away for criminal investigations. This was the first time that a law enforcement agency had resorted to production orders since the enactment of the IGCO provisions in 1995 offering additional protection to journalistic material.

iSun Affairs Weekly published an interview with Lew Mon-hung on 24 January 2013. Commercial Radio conducted follow-up telephone interviews with Lew during a radio programme on 24 and 25 January. Lew was a close ally of Leung Chun Ying, the HKSAR Chief Executive, but the two parted ways soon after Leung assumed office. Lew was later investigated and prosecuted for several offences. The ICAC applied for a production order to demand that *iSun* produce notes, records and/or recordings concerning Lew's interview, and another production order to request Commercial Radio produce the original and unedited sound recordings of Lew's telephone interviews.

During two court hearings held in early September and early October, the ICAC stated that the sole purpose of seeking the production orders was to ensure that the interview reports/recordings published by the two media organizations were a full, accurate and reliable account of what Lew had told reporters. The application regarding Commercial Radio was quickly dismissed by the judge in the first court hearing because the radio station had confirmed that it did not have any unedited records of Lew's interviews other than what was available for download from the station's website. In the second court hearing, the ICAC said it might request more at a later stage of investigation, but the judge indicated that he would not grant the agency an indefinite adjournment of the case. As a result, the ICAC agreed to withdraw its application regarding *iSun*. The court ordered the ICAC to pay the legal costs incurred by *iSun*.

An ICAC spokesman later told the *SCMP* that the ICAC respected the court's decisions and that the agency had always respected press freedom. The spokesman insisted that it was legal and appropriate for the agency to apply for production orders requesting the two media organizations hand over their interview materials.

However, it is submitted that the IGCO scheme was never designed to facilitate double-checking by law enforcement agencies of the accuracy of press reports. Moreover, it is very likely that the ICAC was conducting a fishing expedition for valuable information or evidence against Mr. Lew. In so doing, the ICAC not only jeopardized the neutrality of the press but also caused a chilling effect on press freedom by forcing the press to disclose confidential sources or materials. In addition, the media organizations and journalists affected were put under considerable stress because of the legal proceedings initiated by the ICAC. All of this goes against the original intention of the IGCO scheme of striking a proper balance between the protection of press freedom and the genuine requirements of criminal investigations. Indeed, this proper balance was repeatedly stressed by the judge presiding over this ICAC application for production orders.

Meanwhile, in the UK, law enforcement's reliance on production orders to obtain journalistic materials had obviously become more frequent in recent years. This caused widespread concern among journalists, noting that the police were engaged in fishing expeditions and that the applications for production orders were made on an unfocused and scattergun basis.

In 2012, several media organisations in the UK won a judicial review overturning the granting of production orders to the police (*R. (British Sky Broadcasting Ltd and Others) v Chelmsford Crown Court and Essex Police (interested party)* [2012] 2 Cr.App. R.33). Handing down the judgment, the High Court in the UK noted that although production orders could be of great value in tracing people committing crimes and thus serving the public interest, they should not be granted as a formality.

The police had to provide cogent evidence to prove the access conditions for such an order were fulfilled, which included proof that the evidence sought was of substantial value to the police investigations. In addition, the judge hearing the application also had to assess whether the granting of the production order was compatible with the goal of protecting freedom of expression, bearing in mind the inhibiting effect of production orders on the press.

7.2 Covert surveillance and interception

There have been other incidents reflecting inadequate protection of journalistic material in Hong Kong. They involved interception of phone calls made to an editor and a reporter. The interceptions were made by law enforcement officers in accordance with the Interception of Communications and Surveillance Ordinance (ICSO, Cap 589), which was enacted in August 2006. In his 2009 annual report, the Commissioner on Interception of Communications and Surveillance, who oversees ICSO compliances by law enforcement agencies, treated these incidents as interceptions in which journalistic material was obtained inadvertently.

The ICSO provides a statutory regime to regulate interceptions and covert surveillance operations conducted by law enforcement officers in their prevention or detection of serious crimes or protection of public security. The ordinance requires a law enforcement officer in his or her application for authorization of interception or covert surveillance to state clearly whether journalistic material may be obtained in the operation. This is a factor that the relevant authority has to take into account when considering whether issuing an authorization meets the conditions of necessity and proportionality as stipulated in the ordinance.

Nonetheless, the Commissioner's 2009 report revealed several shortcomings. When told of the likelihood of obtaining journalistic material in the operation, the judge presiding over two applications imposed a set of additional restrictive requirements to be met by the law enforcement agency upon granting the authorization of interception. The requirements were broadly in line with those concerning the interception of information protected by legal professional privilege. The judge presiding over another application, however, did not impose similar conditions, and only revoked the authorization after receiving a report from the law enforcement agency that journalistic material had been obtained.

The ICSO does not require a law enforcement agency to report to the panel judge or the Commissioner when obtaining information likely to be journalistic material through interception or covert surveillance. In addition, the Commissioner had since 2009 refrained from listening to intercepted conversations pending clarification of his authority to do so. In other words, the whole arrangement concerning the protection of journalistic material in interceptions and covert surveillance hinged largely on the honesty of law enforcement officers. The monitoring by the Commissioner was very limited, a situation that the Commissioner himself considered far from satisfactory.

However, the ICSO code of practice was amended in late 2011, requiring law enforcement agencies to notify the Commissioner of operations that are likely to involve journalistic material or where such information had been obtained inadvertently. This means an extension of a practice already applicable to information protected by legal professional privilege. Failure to do so would be treated as non-compliance with the ICSO requirements. In mid-2013, after a two-year review of ICSO, the government reported to LegCo that it was drafting several legislative amendments, including one that would give the Commissioner access to materials produced under interception or surveillance, including journalistic material. As of late 2013, no new amendments had been introduced.

8. Protection of journalistic sources

Hong Kong has no statutory law offering protection against the disclosure of journalistic sources. At common law, journalists do not have an immunity to preserve the confidentiality of their sources. It is up to the judge to decide whether to force journalists to disclose their sources. Since the mid-1990s, Hong Kong courts have rejected two requests for newspapers to disclose the identity of their reporters or sources. In *John Sham v Eastweek Publisher Ltd* [1995] 1 HKC 264, the plaintiff sued *Eastweek* magazine for libel. He initially obtained an order from the High Court seeking the names of the author and editors of the article concerned, but the order was subsequently set aside by the Court of Appeal upholding the "newspaper rule":

> The newspaper rule is a rule of over one hundred years standing. A defendant at the pretrial stage of an action for libel published in a newspaper should not be forced to disclose his source of information. It applies not only to newspapers but also to the news media. The overriding jurisdiction for the rule is the public interest in the free flow of information.

But this kind of protection is very limited, as the rule is applicable neither to the trial period of libel actions nor to any other actions.

In 2000, *Apple Daily* was prosecuted for contempt by publication in its coverage of a court case. (For more on this case, see Chapter 4 Court Reporting and Contempt of Court.) The Secretary for Justice applied to the High Court for an order requiring the newspaper to disclose the name and address of the reporter who wrote the article, with a view to prosecuting the reporter as well (*Secretary for Justice v Apple Daily Ltd & Anor* [2000] 2 HKLRD 704). The application was refused. The court ruled that this was a criminal contempt case and that principles of criminal law should therefore prevail. The newspaper enjoyed the right to silence, and the discovery process used in civil proceedings was not applicable.

Developments in the United Kingdom have been different. The 1981 Contempt of Court Act s 10 stipulates: "No court may require a person to disclose, nor is any person guilty of contempt of court for refusing to disclose, the source of information contained in a publication for which he is responsible, unless it be established to the satisfaction of the court that disclosure is necessary in the interests of justice or national security or for the prevention of disorder or crime." In 1986, the Law Reform Commission of Hong Kong published its "Report on Contempt of Court", recommending the introduction of a Contempt of Court Ordinance with a similar s 10. The Hong Kong government has so far not acted on the recommendations.

Nonetheless, UK courts have repeatedly ordered journalists and news organizations to disclose their confidential sources because judges ruled that such disclosures were considered necessary under s 10 of the Contempt of Court Act. On two occasions, a journalist and several media organizations complained to the

European Court of Human Rights that the UK court decisions ordering disclosure of journalistic sources had violated Article 10 of the European Convention on Human Rights, which protects freedom of expression. The European Court ruled in favour of the journalist and the news organizations.

In *Goodwin v The UK* [1996] ECHR 16 and again in *Financial Times v The UK* [2009] ECHR 2065, the European Court stressed that having regard to the importance of the protection of journalistic sources for press freedom in a democratic society, and the potentially chilling effect that an order for disclosure of a source has on the exercise of that freedom, such an order cannot be compatible with Article 10 unless it is justified by an overriding requirement in the public interest. In particular, ordering disclosure to prevent further leaks of confidential information would only be justified in exceptional circumstances where no reasonable and less invasive alternatives were available to discover the source.

In view of these two European Court of Human Rights decisions, together with UK court decisions in *Ashworth Hospital Authority v MGN* [2002] UKHL 29 and *Mersey Care NHS Trust v Ackroyd* (No. 2) [2007] EWCA Civ 101, the protection of confidential journalistic sources has been strengthened in the UK. Comparatively speaking, Hong Kong lags behind in this area.

9. Conclusion

Since 2011, there has been an apparent rise of tension between the police and the media during dignitary visits and public protests in relation to newsgathering arrangements. For Hong Kong to remain a free and open society, the city's police should highly regard the right to media freedom. Journalists and the public alike should always take pains to resist disingenuous, unreasonable and disproportionate restrictions imposed by government authorities on newsgathering and reporting on the pretext of protecting public order or the rights of others. On the other hand, the right of newsgathering and reporting is not absolute, however, nor should the right be used to fend off valid criticism. Journalists should be constantly vigilant of news coverage activities becoming too aggressive and leading to unjustified infringements of the rights of others. Moreover, existing protections accorded to journalistic material and sources in Hong Kong may need to catch up with the practical demands of journalism.

9

Reporting on the Mainland

Doreen Weisenhaus

FREQUENTLY ASKED QUESTIONS

1. What laws and regulations apply to Hong Kong and international media when reporters cover news stories on the mainland?
2. Do Hong Kong journalists have any special privileges or restrictions as a result of Hong Kong's status as a Special Administrative Region of the PRC? (See sections 4 and 5)
3. Do Hong Kong and foreign journalists travelling to the mainland to report news require any special visa or permit? (See section 4)
4. What do journalists need to know about state secrets laws? (See section 5)
5. What are the Open Government Information regulations and how do they relate to state secrets laws? (See section 7)
6. What should reporters do if they are detained? (See section 6)
7. Do Hong Kong and foreign journalists face potential legal actions from private citizens they report on? (See section 9)

1. Introduction

News events on the mainland of the People's Republic of China are important for both Hong Kong and international media. Many stories, from health scares such as the SARS crisis in 2003 and bird flu outbreaks to those involving incidents of labour unrest, land disputes, mine disasters and the latest economic and political developments, are of vital interest to the world's media, including Hong Kong's. More than 400 international and Hong Kong-based news organizations operate or work on the mainland, with nearly 700 accredited foreign journalists.[1] Media from at least 50 countries have established a presence in China, mostly in Beijing and Shanghai, but some in the southern city of Guangzhou as well. The western provinces — including the megacity Chongqing, the focus of recent massive corruption trials — also have drawn more foreign press. Thousands of foreign journalists descended on China on temporary journalist visas to cover the 2008 Olympics in Beijing.

1. 2012 edition of "Foreign Press in China", provided by the Ministry of Foreign Affairs.

What happens in China, however, has especially unique significance for Hong Kong. For cultural, political, historical and nationalistic reasons, Hong Kong's media now cover the mainland in ways they did not while reporting on the British government during its rule. After the resumption of Chinese sovereignty in 1997, the mainland became a much more important story for the Hong Kong media's audience. With the mainland's proximity facilitating news coverage, Hong Kong reporters regularly head north over the border for stories. But they — like the international press — must also continually keep an eye on the rapidly changing and potentially troublesome legal and regulatory landmines awaiting those who report on the mainland.

This chapter is not intended as an exhaustive examination of PRC laws and regulations that affect newsgathering there. This is not a guide, for example, for Chinese reporters, who are PRC citizens, working for state media. Nor is this an in-depth look at the Internet and government controls over that medium that affect online writers of news and commentary and users of social media, although it does examine some of those aspects. Many excellent publications and research centres deal with these topics.[2] Instead, this chapter focuses on some key laws, regulations and rules that Hong Kong and foreign journalists reporting on the mainland typically face. These journalists usually go to China to cover news that they consider important or dramatic. This means they are often covering stories that the mainland government considers sensitive, and so they are subject to a certain degree of control, which has tightened in recent years.

2. History/Background

Until fairly recently, only foreign media were allowed to maintain bureaus on the mainland. For these international media, which does not include Hong Kong-based news organizations, the Ministry of Foreign Affairs publishes a *Handbook for Foreign Journalists in China,* which outlines the regulations and procedures for accreditation in China, including press cards, bureau licences, visas and residence permits. It provides government contacts and guidelines on applying to interview state leaders and officials of State Council ministries and commissions, Beijing municipal government and provincial governments.[3] (For more details on the

2. Some of these publications include: Hualing Fu and Richard Cullen, *Media Law in the PRC* (Hong Kong: Asia Law & Practice 1996); Sun Xupei, *An Orchestra of Voices: Making the Argument for Greater Speech and Press Freedom in the People's Republic of China* (Westport, CT: Prager 2001); Perry Keller, "Privilege and Punishment: Press Governance in China", 21 *Cardozo Arts & Entertainment Law Journal* 87 (Winter/Spring 2003); *Internet Filtering in China 2012,* Open Net Initiative, https://opennet.net/research/profiles/China. Research centres include: China Media Project, Journalism and Media Studies Centre, the University of Hong Kong, http://cmp.hku.hk; Berkman Center for Internet and Society, Harvard Law School, http://cyber.law.harvard.edu; The China Center, Yale Law School, http://www.yale.edu/chinalaw; Center for Chinese Legal Studies, Columbia Law School, http://web.law.columbia.edu/chinese-legal-studies.

3. The handbook also provides information on purchasing or renting a premise, hiring local employees and service staff, taking Chinese-language courses, paying taxes and finding schools for children.

regulations, see section 4 in this chapter, "Regulating non-mainland reporters in China".)

In 2001, PRC authorities announced that Hong Kong media also could establish bureaus. The Liaison Office of the Central People's Government (LOCPG), Beijing's main representative in Hong Kong, and the Hong Kong and Macau Affairs Office (HKMAO) of the State Council have oversight authority over these bureaus and operations.

The English-language *South China Morning Post* opened its Beijing office as a foreign bureau in the 1990s before the handover; it later added offices in Shanghai, Guangzhou and Shenzhen.[4] In 2004, *Ming Pao*, a leading Chinese-language Hong Kong newspaper, opened its Beijing bureau, which has since closed. Other Hong Kong news organizations with outposts on the mainland include *Hong Kong Commercial Daily* newspaper, Phoenix TV, Television Broadcasts Limited (TVB), Asia Television Limited (ATV), Hong Kong Cable Television Limited (Cable TV), NOW TV, Radio Television Hong Kong (RTHK), and Hong Kong Commercial Broadcasting Company Limited (Commercial Radio).

Some Hong Kong-based media companies chose not to establish bureaus, preferring instead to selectively send reporters to cover specific breaking-news events. Even news organizations with bureaus also will send additional reporters on occasion. Regardless of status, news organizations need to seek permission from the appropriate PRC agencies to cover certain official events, such as the annual meetings of the National People's Congress (NPC) or visits by Hong Kong or other leaders, or to conduct interviews with certain officials, although there was some loosening of these requirements in the lead-up to the 2008 Olympics in Beijing (see section 4 of this chapter).

Not all Hong Kong media are welcomed on the mainland. Next Media Limited, which includes *Apple Daily*, its pro-democracy Chinese-language newspaper that frequently criticizes central authorities, is not permitted to open a bureau or to have its reporters cover many official events. In 2005, for example, *Apple Daily* was barred from accompanying a delegation of Hong Kong Legislative Council members in their unprecedented visit with then Chief Executive Donald Tsang to several mainland cities in the Pearl River Delta. Five years later, the paper's application to send reporters to cover the Shanghai World Expo was denied.

Such denials have not stopped *Apple Daily* from sending journalists unofficially. In 2004, Chinese authorities detained two *Apple Daily* reporters and a photographer who were in Beijing trying to cover the annual sessions of the NPC and its advisory body, the Chinese People's Political Consultative Conference (CPPCC). They were questioned for several hours and then escorted to the airport to return to Hong Kong. In July 2008, shortly before the Beijing Olympics, a senior *Apple Daily* reporter was barred from entering the city and sent back to Hong Kong with his travel documents confiscated.[5] The reporter, who had obtained accreditation

4. The pro-Beijing newspapers *Wen Wei Po* and *Ta Kung Pao* also already had mainland bureaus.
5. "Hong Kong Newspaper Reporter Turned Back on Arrival in Beijing", Reporters Without Borders, 3 July 2008, available at: http://www.unhcr.org/refworld/docid/487de254c.html.

to cover the Olympics, was eventually allowed to travel to Beijing after protests from Hong Kong and international media advocates.

For covering non-official events or breaking news, such as villager unrest and labour disputes or disasters, many Hong Kong media also did not seek official permission, often in violation of PRC reporting regulations, when they entered the mainland or travelled beyond their assigned news bureau in China. For the most part, the reporters successfully brought back a wide range of stories. For example, in February 2012, *Apple Daily* reporters again travelled to China without official permission to report on a suspected SARS-like outbreak in the northern city of Baoding.

But increasingly in recent years, Hong Kong reporters and foreign journalists alike have been hindered or detained and questioned by authorities, and even attacked as they covered volatile news stories or visited sensitive areas, such as the deadly Sichuan earthquake in 2008, "Jasmine Revolution"-style protests in 2011 and the escape of blind activist Chen Guangcheng in 2012 to the US embassy in Beijing.[6] In August 2012, the Foreign Correspondents Clubs of Hong Kong, China and Shanghai issued a joint statement expressing concern over the escalating number of incidents involving violence, intimidation and harassment of their members. They detailed incidents against journalists from Japan, Germany, Poland, US and Hong Kong. The following month, two *Ming Pao* reporters were detained for more than 40 hours with their phones, computers and cameras confiscated by Hunan authorities after interviewing family members of dissident Li Wangyang, who had died under questionable circumstances. Days later, *South China Morning Post* photographer Felix Wong was beaten by Shenzhen police as he covered anti-Japanese protests.

And while there has not been another prosecution of a Hong Kong-based journalist since 2005 when Ching Cheong, a correspondent for *The Straits Times* newspaper in Singapore, was detained in Guangzhou, accused of spying for Taiwan and later convicted, tension and apprehension remain high for Hong Kong journalists working on the mainland. They know they must be vigilant to avoid tripping over China's often-vague laws and regulations. And they remain acutely aware that China continues to be one of the world's worst countries for imprisoning journalists, with 32 in custody as of December 2012.[7]

3. China's legal system and "media law"

Article 35 of the Constitution of the PRC (1982) states:

> Citizens of the People's Republic of China enjoy freedom of speech, of the press, of assembly, of association, of procession and of demonstration.

---

6. For a list of sensitive areas and topics, see the website of Foreign Correspondents Club of China, http://www.fccchina.org/reporters-guide/sensitive-areas-and-topics/.
7. Committee to Protect Journalists 2012 Prison Census, available at: http://cpj.org/imprisoned/2012.php.

Despite the seemingly clear-cut pronouncement of Article 35 of the PRC Constitution,[8] other laws, regulations and practices create a sharply different reality for the media in China, where state control over freedom of expression and of the press is a top political priority.

The first notion to understand is that there is no "media law" as such in China, at least none similar to what is found in Western-style legal systems such as Hong Kong's. What exists on the mainland is a broad regulatory system of administrative and criminal law that enables tight but flexible control and management of the media. Less emphasis is placed on formal law, except for criminal prosecutions, and more on regulation that, as authors Hualing Fu and Richard Cullen note, "relies very heavily on political-managerialism, secondary regulations, ad hoc notices, and administrative practice".[9]

Perry Keller, an academic who has written about China's legal system, further observes:

> Media law in China is more concerned with procedural requirements of approval, registration and supervision than it is with matters of substance, which are typically expressed in general, non-specific terms. The media regulatory system is set up so the [Chinese Communist] Party can use mass communication primarily as an instrument to achieve its political and economic goals.[10]

Numerous entities can make, enforce or administer laws and regulations that affect the media, with varying levels of authority. The most significant are the **National People's Congress** (全國人民代表大會) (NPC) and the **Standing Committee of the NPC** (全國人民代表大會常務委員會), which enact national laws, and the **State Council** (國務院), the top executive and administrative body, which issues administrative regulations.

The State Council is a particularly powerful institution with broad authority to oversee provincial governments, draft budgets and legislative bills and monitor government initiatives. Ministries and other organizations under the State Council can issue governmental orders to implement laws and administrative regulations. The **Ministry of Foreign Affairs** (外交部) and the **Hong Kong and Macau Affairs Office** (港澳事務辦公室), for example, are under the State Council.

Lower-level entities — such as local people's congresses and provincial and local governments — also can issue regulations and orders regarding the media. But only the NPC has the authority to enact criminal laws.

But probably the most influential body in regulating the country's media is the **Publicity Department** (as it is now known in its official English translation, but still referred to as the Propaganda Department in Chinese) of the Chinese Communist Party Central Committee (中共中央宣傳部), which sets media policies, supervises their implementation and issues directives and regulations.[11]

---

8. For the English version of the PRC Constitution, as last amended in 2004, see: http://english.gov.cn/2005-08/05/content_20813.htm.
9. Fu and Cullen, *Media Law in the PRC*, pp. 15–16.
10. Perry Keller (ed.), *Chinese Law and Legal Theory* (Aldershot: Ashgate Publishing, 2001).
11. Keller, "Privilege and Punishment: Press Governance in China", pp. 97–8.

The **Supreme People's Procuratorate** (最高人民檢察院) is the state prosecutorial agency, and it also supervises local procuratorate offices. The **Ministry of Public Security** (公安部) is the police authority; with **Public Security Bureaus** (公安局) in local municipalities, it has the power to detain individuals and execute arrests approved by the procuratorate. The **Ministry of State Security** (國家安全部) is the PRC's chief foreign intelligence agency, which also engages in domestic intelligence and surveillance.

Other important differences exist between China's unique legal system and Hong Kong's common law system. The foundation of PRC law is socialism with a framework that blends a continental European-style civil code system with aspects of the Soviet Marxist/Leninist legal model and traditional Chinese culture.

PRC courts do not follow binding precedent (*stare decisis*) from previous cases, although lower courts frequently try to follow interpretations issued by the **Supreme People's Court** (最高人民法院) (SPC), China's highest court. The president of the SPC is elected by the NPC, which oversees the court, and serves a maximum of two five-year terms. In addition to handling appeals, the SPC has original jurisdiction to hear some cases, supervises the lower courts and gives judicial explanations on the application of laws within the judicial process. In November 2010, the SPC announced it would begin issuing "guiding cases" to "summarize adjudication experiences, unify application of law, enhance adjudication quality, and safeguard judicial justice".[12] Lower courts are expected to "refer" to the guiding cases when adjudicating similar cases. As of 2013, the SPC had issued more than 20 cases, involving mostly criminal, contract and environmental law.[13]

PRC courts also do not have the power to review or nullify a law or regulation of government for contravening the Constitution or for any other reason. Over the years, reformers have campaigned for China to strengthen rule of law by "constitutionalism", enforcing the principles of its Constitution, now into its fourth decade.[14] It was hoped that when Xi Jinping replaced Hu Jintao as China's top leader in March 2013, he would support constitutionalism, but to date, political stability and other non-legal considerations remain the priority.

The absence of conventional media law concepts in China and the inability of its courts to review or challenge laws and regulations adopted by the government to control and manage the media give reformers scant hope that China will deliver on press freedom any time soon.

12. Provisions of the Supreme People's Court Concerning Work on Guiding Cases (No. 51, 26 November 2010). Chinese text can be found at: http://www.law-lib.com/law/law_view.asp?id=342688; English text at: http://cgc.law.stanford.edu/supreme-peoples-court-concerning-work-on-guiding-cases.

13. For English translations and discussions of the cases, see Stanford Law School's China Guiding Cases Project, http://cgc.law.stanford.edu/.

14. "For China to Rise, So Must the Status of Its Constitution", *Caijing Online*, 12 December 2012; Edward Wong and Jonathan Ansfield, "Reformers Aim to Get China to Live up to Its Own Constitution", *The New York Times*, 4 February 2013.

4. Regulating non-mainland reporters in China

As mentioned, journalists who go to the mainland to report for either the foreign press or Hong Kong-based media are subject to numerous reporting regulations and laws. The most common they deal with are the administrative regulations.

4.1 Foreign journalists

For the foreign press, the regulations seek to try to control at least two aspects of journalists' work: one, the nuts and bolts of how they set up their offices and operations on the mainland, and, two, reporting activities.

In 1990, the State Council promulgated "Regulations Concerning Foreign Journalists and Permanent Offices of Foreign News Agencies", which regulated everything from press credentials to restrictions on interviews. In December 2006, the State Council issued new regulations for the temporary relaxation of some of these restrictions for foreign media in advance of the 2008 Olympics in Beijing for the period of 1 January 2007 to 17 October 2008. On the day the temporary regulations were due to expire, the government announced that they would be made permanent.

These latest regulations represented a major shift as foreign journalists were told that they could interview anyone without first having to get prior government permission, as previously required, as long as they had the consent of the individuals or organizations they wanted to interview, and that they could travel anywhere in the country. But increasingly in the years since, despite these regulations, reporters have found themselves hindered or harassed when travelling to sensitive scenes of natural disasters or political unrest (see Appendix A for the full text in English and Chinese of "Regulations of the People's Republic of China on News Coverage by Permanent Office of Foreign Media Organizations and Foreign Journalists").[15] The Ministry of Foreign Affairs (MFA) is responsible for overseeing the foreign press and provides a copy of the regulations, along with its *Handbook for Foreign Journalists in China,* updated regularly, as well as a media guide available online through its International Press Center.[16]

Other aspects of the regulations that remained in effect as of 2013 focused on the mechanics of foreign media operating on the mainland. The three categories affected by the regulations include:

1. "resident foreign journalists" (defined as "career journalists who are dispatched by foreign media organizations to be stationed in China for . . . not less than six months for news coverage and reporting");
2. "foreign journalists for short-term coverage" ("career journalists" staying less than six months); and
3. "permanent offices of foreign media organizations".

15. English text can also be found at: http://ipc.fmprc.gov.cn/eng/wgjzzhzn/t716835.htm and Chinese text at: http://www.gov.cn/zwgk/2008–10/17/content_1124261.htm.

16. International Press Center, Ministry of Foreign Affairs, http://ipc.fmprc.gov.cn/eng/wgjzzhzn/.

When a foreign news organization wants to send one or more resident correspondents, it should submit an application to the Information Department of the MFA and provide the following:

- a written application signed by an executive from the headquarters of the media organization, including information about the position, job description and place of intended residence;
- a profile of each reporter, including a photocopy of the passport, curriculum vitae, journalist certificate and contact information; and
- a copy of the document establishing that the correspondent is a professional reporter in the home country of the media organization, although the regulations give no definitions or standards for what that might be.

After approval of the application, the correspondent has to register with the Information Department within seven days of arrival in China and present his or her passport and an appointment letter signed by the news organization to obtain a foreign press card, which is renewed at the end of each calendar year. If the correspondent plans to be posted outside of Beijing, then he or she should follow the procedures with the relevant local foreign affairs office. To stay in China for more than six months, a resident foreign correspondent must obtain what is known as a "J-1" visa.

To set up a permanent office, foreign news organizations must provide similar information as above for the reporters to be sent, plus the place of their intended residence, the organization's business scope and a copy of the registration certificate issued by its home country. Upon the application's approval, the head of the permanent office should register with the Information Department within seven days of arrival in China and present an appointment letter signed by the foreign news organization and his or her passport, along with the passports of other members.

Any substitute reporters, replacement of bureau chiefs, changes in size of staff or other "important changes" need approval of the Information Department.

Bureaus can be established in several mainland cities, including Beijing, Shanghai, Guangzhou, Chongqing and Shenyang in the northeast province of Liaoning.

Visa and other requirements for foreign press who want to come to China for short-term news coverage, which includes accompanying visiting heads of state, are also addressed.

The regulations further require foreign journalists to work within the scope of authorized journalistic activities, to observe journalistic ethics and "conduct news coverage and reporting activities on an objective and impartial basis". Reporters also cannot engage in activities incompatible with their status or tasks or engage in business activities in China. Foreign reporters and media organizations also are cautioned that they are required to abide by the "laws, regulations and rules of the People's Republic of China".

If a bureau or one of its reporters violates any of the existing regulations, the Information Department may give a warning, suspend their journalistic activities in China or revoke the foreign journalist's card or the news organization's permanent office certificate. But the government is more frequently delaying or declining to renew or issue visas as a way of expressing disapproval over a journalist's or news organization's news coverage. In May 2012, the visa for Melissa Chan, the Beijing correspondent for Al Jazeera's English-language TV channel for the past five years, was not renewed, resulting in the first expulsion of a foreign journalist in more than a decade and the bureau's close.[17] In December 2012, the visa for *New York Times* correspondent Chris Buckley, who had been a reporter in China for 12 years, also was not renewed. According to a survey of its members in 2012 by the Foreign Correspondents Club of China, dozens of foreign journalists reported delays in visa approvals over the previous two years and some reporters said they were told by officials that the delay or denial was due to content of news coverage. Correspondents reported similar results the following year. By the end of 2013, the situation was considered so serious that US Vice President Joseph Biden raised the issue directly with PRC President Xi Jinping.[18]

For additional guidance on the latest developments on reporting on the mainland, journalists can also consult organizations such as the Foreign Correspondents' Club of China[19] and the International Federation of Journalists (IFJ).[20]

4.2 Hong Kong-based reporters

Journalists are not required to obtain local government accreditation or special journalist visas to work in Hong Kong. But when they travel to the mainland for reporting, whether they work for international news organizations based in Hong Kong or for local Hong Kong media companies, they face certain administrative requirements.

Despite the revised regulations, foreign journalists based in Hong Kong still need to apply for journalist visas to report on the mainland and can contact the Commissioner's Office of the Ministry of Foreign Affairs.[21] They also can contact this office to apply to cover major government events such as sessions of the National People's Congress.

As stated earlier in this chapter, Hong Kong media can set up their own bureaus by applying to the Central Government's Liaison Office in Hong Kong. After the application is approved by the HKMAO, the news organization is to register with

17. http://www.fccchina.org/2012/05/08/correspondent-expelled/.
18. http://www.cpj.org/blog/2013/07/in-china-foreign-correspondents-see-worsening-cond.php. Also, David Nakamura and William Wan, "Biden Forcefully Complains to Chinese Leaders about Crackdown on Foreign News Media", *Washington Post*, 5 December 2013.
19. http://www.fccchina.org/reporters-guide/.
20. http://asiapacific.ifj.org/assets/docs/012/222/7661e0c-82f2ade.pdf.
21. For additional resources, contact The Foreign Correspondents Club of Hong Kong, http://www.fcchk.org.

the government's All-China Journalists Association (ACJA). Permanent correspondents of Hong Kong media also must be accredited with HKMAO through the ACJA. Local Hong Kong reporters who are not in mainland bureaus but have PRC passports or home return permits do not need visas to go to the mainland. (A reporter without a PRC passport or Hong Kong permanent ID card who works for local Hong Kong media needs to apply for a visa to enter the mainland.)

As to reporting activities, local reporters were governed for years by what had become known as the "Seven Reporting Rules".[22] First issued by the PRC in 1989, post-Tiananmen, and adjusted several times to reflect a changing reporting climate, the rules required reporters to apply for permission to conduct interviews before going to the mainland and to register with the All-China Journalists Association to obtain a limited-use reporter's identity card. The rules also prohibited Hong Kong news organizations from hiring mainland personnel as correspondents or from bringing radio, television or video equipment onto the mainland without declaring the equipment at customs. Reporters who travelled to the mainland for reporting purposes could not engage in non-journalistic activities. Reporters were also banned from reporting if they used their normal travel documents for family or other visits.

In practice, however, because of the sensitive nature of many stories and their ability to travel to and from the mainland with home return permits, many local reporters often bypassed these rules. The restrictions were not uniformly enforced; at times, however, reporters were detained by public security officers or other government agents and questioned over the lack of accreditation for interviewing. This often resulted in the confiscation of notes and/or film.

Over the years, the Hong Kong Journalists Association repeatedly called for these restrictions to be lifted, saying they were introduced to "screen and control" media organizations and journalists,[23] such as Next Media and Radio Free Asia, a US government-funded broadcaster. In 2002, for example, state security officers detained several *Apple Daily* reporters for periods ranging from a few hours to several days. Two were detained for several days and held in a hostel run by Ministry of State Security. Questioning mostly focused on how the journalists obtained their stories and on their reporting without permission.[24]

But in December 2006, in a move that paralleled changes in rules for foreign journalists covering the 2008 Olympics, the PRC said it also would lift some of these controversial reporting restrictions for Hong Kong and Macau journalists in advance of and during the games. Yet, unlike the relaxed rules for foreign journalists, which became permanent after the Olympics, Beijing did not extend the same rules for Hong Kong and Macau journalists. Instead, in February 2009,

22. *China Reporting Handbook*, Hong Kong Journalists Association (2006).

23. "Questionable Beginnings: Freedom of Expression in Hong Kong One Year After the Handover to China", Joint Report of the Hong Kong Journalists Association and Article 19, June 1998.

24. "The Line Hardens: Tougher Stance on Civil Rights Threatens Freedom of Expression in Hong Kong", Joint Report of the HKJA and Article 19, June 2002.

new rules[25] were issued ("Rules for Hong Kong and Macau Journalists Reporting in Mainland China") that still required journalists to apply in advance to the Central Government's Liaison Office to cover specific stories. If the applications are approved, reporters are issued temporary press cards from ACJA, valid for one month, for each particular assignment. Although a temporary card may be used for repeated trips, it should only be used to travel to the pre-approved destination (see Appendix A for Chinese and English text). The Hong Kong Journalists Association and other journalism groups have issued strong protests over these rules. Furthermore, local journalists have organized marches to protest how Hong Kong journalists are treated when they cover stories on the mainland and to urge the Hong Kong government to intervene with PRC authorities.

5. Secrets, spying and state security

The biggest fear, however, for Hong Kong journalists working on the mainland, whether in bureaus or during reporting trips, is being accused of violating laws relating to state secrets, spying and other offences, especially in light of the Ching Cheong case. These laws are vaguely defined and selectively enforced and can result in long prison sentences. They have been invoked against journalists, academics and others who obtain and use information across a broad range of categories the PRC government considers sensitive, often for information that would not seem "secret" in any other context.

5.1 Key laws and regulations

Key PRC laws in this area that are of most concern to Hong Kong journalists include:

- The Law on Guarding State Secrets 1988, revised in 2010 (保守國家秘密法) ("State Secrets Law");
- The Procedures for the Implementation of the Law on Guarding State Secrets 1990 (保守國家秘密法實施辦法) ("State Secrets Implementation Procedures");
- The revised Criminal Law 1997 (刑法); and
- The State Security Law 1993 (國家安全法) and its Implementation Measures 1994 (國家安全法實施細則).

The **State Secrets Law**, first enacted in 1988 and revised in 2010,[26] replaced the 1951 Provisional Regulation on the Protection of State Secrets. Article 2 of the State Secrets Law declares that state secrets are "matters that have a vital bearing

25. http://news.xinhuanet.com/newscenter/2009-02/06/content_10773947.htm.
26. Chinese-language text can be found at: http://www.gov.cn/flfg/2010-04/30/content_1596420.htm. An unofficial English translation provided by Human Rights in China, is at http://www.hrichina.org/sites/default/files/attachments/story/annex_c_ssl_law_translation.pdf.

on state security and national interests and, as specified by legal procedures, are entrusted to a limited number of people for a given period of time".

Article 9 sets out the broad categories in which state secrets are generated:

(1) secrets concerning major policy decisions on state affairs;
(2) secrets in the building of national defence and in the activities of the armed forces;
(3) secrets in diplomatic activities and in activities related to foreign countries as well as secrets to be maintained as commitments to foreign countries;
(4) secrets in national economic and social development;
(5) secrets in science and technology;
(6) secrets concerning activities for safeguarding state security and the investigation of criminal offences; and
(7) any other matters that are classified as state secrets by the state secret-guarding department.

Article 10 classifies state secrets into three categories by degree of harm (but does not specify which secrets fall into which category):

- **Top secret** (絕密): "those vital state secrets, the divulgence of which will cause *extremely serious harm* to state security and national interests";
- **Highly secret** (機密): "important state secrets, the divulgence of which will cause *serious harm* to state security and national interests"; and
- **Secret** (秘密): "ordinary state secrets, the divulgence of which will cause *harm* to state security and national interests."

The entities that can designate a state secret include the central state organs (such as the ministries of Foreign Affairs, Public Security, and State Security), the Central Military Commission, and local authorities at or above the municipal level (Article 11), but the 2010 amendments permit only central and provincial authorities to designate the highest level of "top secret" (Article 13). The amendments also added time limits to each of the three categories of secrets of a maximum of 30, 20 and 10 years, respectively, unless otherwise specified (Article 15).

Article 48 designates legal responsibility and specifies that violations of the law, including "illegally obtaining or possessing any items bearing state secrets", may be prosecuted in accordance with the law.

The **State Secrets Implementation Procedures** from 1990[27] further define state secrets according to perceived impact. Article 4 states:

> Any matter, which would give rise to any of the following consequences if it were divulged, shall be brought within the scope of a state secret and a specific secrecy grade:
>
> (1) jeopardizes the ability of the national government to maintain stability and defend itself;
> (2) affects the integrity of the nation's unity, solidarity among peoples or social stability;

27. http://www.stats.gov.cn/tjgl/swdcglgg/xgfg/t20041118_402209111.htm.

(3) harms political or economic interests of the nation with respect to the outside world;
(4) affects the safety of any national leader or foreign dignitary;
(5) hinders important national safety or health work;
(6) causes a reduction in the effectiveness or reliability of any measures to protect state secrets;
(7) weakens the nation's economy or technological strength;
(8) causes any national organ to lose its ability to exercise its legal authority.

One critical change in the expansion was that the State Secrets Implementation Procedures shifted the burden of proof to the defendant to show that the secrets did not go beyond designated limits and did not become known to unauthorized persons.

A new draft of the implementation procedures was issued in mid-2012, but as of date of publication had not been adopted. Proposed changes included clarifying the scope of state secrets and enhancing secrecy protection systems.[28]

The 1979 **Criminal Law** prohibited the disclosure of state secrets. In 1997, the Criminal Law[29] was substantially revised and replaced "counter-revolutionary crimes" with offences of endangering national security and inciting to subvert state power as well as broadened the government's power to prosecute offences involving state secrets. In particular, it banned the following activities:

Providing state secrets or intelligence to foreigners

One key provision is Article 111, which deals with the unlawful obtaining or distributing of state secrets and "intelligence", to foreigners, including through espionage. Specifically, it punishes anyone who "steals, spies, buys or unlawfully supplies State secrets or intelligence for an organ, organization or individual outside the territory of China".

The penalty for conviction is harsh — a sentence of between five and ten years of imprisonment. Severe infractions could result in a life sentence; minor infractions could lead to up to five years of imprisonment, criminal detention, supervision or deprivation of political rights.

As noted, the definition of "state secrets" is dealt with somewhat, albeit unsatisfactorily, in the State Secrets Law and the Implementation Procedures. But the definition of "intelligence" is even more vague. According to the "Interpretation on Specific Application of Laws When Hearing Cases of Stealing, Spying, Purchasing, and Illegally Providing State Secrets and Intelligence for Overseas Countries", issued in 2000 by the Supreme People's Court, effective January 2001 (2001 Explanation), the term "intelligence" as used in Article 111 of the Criminal Law refers to items which involve the "security and interests of the nation, but which are not public or which, according to relevant regulations, should not be made public". Observers say the lack of specificity in the language opens the door even wider to prosecution for alleged violations under the law.

28. http://www.chinalaw.gov.cn/article/cazjgg/201205/20120500367762.shtml.
29. English text can be found at: http://www.asianlii.org.

Illegally obtaining state secrets through theft, spying or purchase

Article 282 of the Criminal Law focuses more narrowly on the illegal obtaining of state secrets — "by stealing, spying or buying shall be sentenced to fixed-term imprisonment of not more than three years, criminal detention, public surveillance or deprivation of political rights".

Severe infractions could result in between three to seven years of prison. Someone found to have illegal possession of documents, information, or other materials classified as top secret or secret and who refuses to explain the source or purpose shall be punished by up to three years imprisonment, criminal detention, or supervision.

Using a computer to steal state secrets

Article 287 prohibits anyone who "uses computers to commit . . . financial fraud, theft, embezzlement, misappropriation of public funds and theft of State secrets".

Divulging state secrets intentionally or negligently

Article 398 further sets out restrictions for state personnel, but more important for journalists, it also applies to non-state personnel:

> Any functionary of a State organ who, in violation of . . . State Secrets Law, intentionally or negligently divulges State secrets, if the circumstances are serious, shall be sentenced to . . . not more than 3 years or criminal detention; if the circumstances are especially serious, he shall be sentenced to . . . not less than 3 years but not more than 7 years.
>
> *Any person who is not a functionary of a State organ* commits the crime mentioned in the preceding paragraph shall, in the light of the circumstances, be punished in accordance with the provisions of the preceding paragraph.

Using the Internet to transfer state secrets

The 2001 Explanation included the use of the Internet for transferring state secrets. Those individuals "using the Internet to illegally transmit state secrets or intelligence to a foreign entity, organization or individual shall be prosecuted and punished under the provisions of Article 111 of the Criminal Law; where the promulgation of state secrets through the Internet is particularly serious, they shall be prosecuted and punished under the provisions of Article 398". The government has since issued many regulations involving the Internet.

In 2010, the amended State Secrets Law added Article 28, which specified that Internet and other public information networking operators and service providers must cooperate with public security and state security organs and prosecutors in investigation of cases regarding the leaking of secrets. When information involving leaking of state secrets is found to have been published through the Internet, transmission must be stopped, relevant records must be kept, and reports must be made to the various law enforcement entities; however, information involving leaking of state secrets must be deleted.

Inciting to subvert state power

Article 105 of the Criminal Law prohibits inciting others by spreading rumours or slanders or other means. "The use of rumour mongering or defamation or other means to incite subversion of the national regime or the overthrow of the socialist system shall be punished by a sentence of five years or less of imprisonment, criminal detention, supervision or deprivation of political rights. Criminal leaders or those whose crimes are particularly severe shall be punished by a sentence of five years or more of imprisonment." So far, the crime of subversion has been applied mostly to mainland Chinese journalists, such as in the case of Jiang Weiping, described in the next section. Imposition of the death penalty is possible, although quite rare in state secrets cases. Article 113 of the Criminal Law permits this sentence for the crime of endangering national security "if the crime causes particularly grave harm to the State and the people or if the circumstances are especially serious".

Another law that could affect journalists is the **State Security Law 1993**[30] and its **Implementation Measures** in 1994. Article 4 of the law bans acts by persons and groups inside China acting in concern with those outside the country, including, "plotting to subvert the government, dismember the state and overthrow the socialist system", "stealing, secretly gathering, buying and illegally providing state secrets", and "other disruptive behaviour which jeopardizes national security". The Implementation Measures additionally list "fabricating or distorting facts, publishing or disseminating written or verbal speeches or producing or propagating audio and visual products which endanger state security".

There are other PRC offences under the Criminal Law not necessarily related to state secrets or national security that could mean trouble for journalists trying to get information. They include:[31]

- Bringing unlawful goods or items past customs (Article 154);
- Detaining unlawfully another person (Article 238);
- Concealing, destroying or unlawfully opening another person's mail (Article 252);
- Obstructing or resisting a public security agent or official (Article 277);
- Impersonating a government employee or official (Article 279);
- Stealing or destroying an official document (Article 280); and
- Bribing a government employee or official (Article 389).

5.2 Prosecution of journalists and writers for Hong Kong media

While there are many instances of prosecutions for illegal use of state secrets and spying against PRC journalists and writers publishing on the mainland, the cases of Ching Cheong in 2005 and others beginning more than a decade earlier remain harrowing reminders of how harshly China can deal with those who also write for

30. English text can be found at: http://www.asianlii.org.
31. "Resources Kits for Newsgathering in China", Hong Kong Journalists Association, updated by this author.

or are representatives of Hong Kong media. Because the proceedings and trials are usually held in secret, it is frequently difficult to know exactly which laws or facts have been cited in a prosecution. What is known about some cases include:

- **Xi Yang** (1994). Xi Yang became the first Hong Kong reporter to be charged with violating China's state secrets and security laws. The PRC accused the *Ming Pao* reporter of "spying on major financial and economic state secrets", after he wrote about the People's Bank of China's gold rates, the adjustment of the foreign exchange rate and plans to raise interest rates.[32] Convicted and sentenced to 12 years in prison, Xi was released in 1997 just before the handover and has since emigrated to Canada.
- **Gao Yu** (1994). A prominent mainland journalist, Gao Yu was sentenced to six years for illegally providing "important state secrets" to institutions outside China's borders for articles she wrote for *Mirror Monthly* and *Overseas Chinese Daily*, two Hong Kong-based publications. She was accused of publishing information from documents relating to recent structural reforms and policy decisions made by senior Communist Party officials, some of which had been previously reported in other Hong Kong media, including the pro-Beijing paper *Wen Wei Po*. Gao argued that the information did not involve national security and involved such details as wage system reforms. She was released in 1999 after serving five years. She lives in Beijing and continues to write.
- **Jiang Weiping** (2001). A former correspondent for Xinhua, China's official news agency, Jiang had written for several Hong Kong-based publications, including as a bureau chief in Dalian for *Wen Wei Po*, and as a freelancer for *Qianshao* (Frontline), a magazine on mainland affairs. In particular, Jiang wrote articles for *Qianshao* about alleged corruption involving several high-level officials in northeastern China, including Ma Xiangdong, deputy mayor of Shenyang who lost huge sums of state money gambling and was later executed, and Bo Xilai, then mayor of Dalian who later became governor of the powerful Liaoning province. Jiang was charged with "illegally providing state secrets overseas" and "inciting to subvert state power". After serving five out of a six-year reduced sentence, he was released in 2006, emigrated to Canada in 2009 and published a book in 2010 on Bo Xilai. In 2013, Bo was convicted and sentenced to life in prison for bribery, embezzlement and abuse of power.[33]
- **Xu Zerong** (2002). A Hong Kong permanent resident, Xu (also known as David Tsui) was a co-founder of a Hong Kong-based academic journal,

32. "State Secrets — A Pretext for Repression", Amnesty International, May 1996; Chris Yeung, "China Gives Details of Xi Allegations", *South China Morning Post*, 12 April 1994.
33. Jiang Weiping wrote a personal account of his career and time in prison, available at: http://en.rsf.org/china-my-experience-as-a-journalist-part-10–08-2009,34141.html.

> *China Social Sciences Quarterly*, and a university professor in southern China. He was sentenced to 13 years in prison for "illegally providing state secrets", for sending to someone in Hong Kong some reference materials on the Korean War, which reportedly were not classified as state secrets until after his arrest. Some observers, though, attributed the prosecution to an article the Oxford-educated historian wrote for *Yazhou Zhoukan* (Asia Weekly), a Chinese-language newsweekly in Hong Kong, which discussed support given by the Chinese Communist Party for Malaysian communist insurgency groups in the 1950s and 1960s.[34] Xu was released in June 2011.

As serious as these cases were, however, more worrisome was the arrest of Ching Cheong, the first Hong Kong journalist to be arrested since the handover. The correspondent for *The Strait Times* of Singapore was accused of spying for Taiwan intelligence agencies and providing state secrets, including on military affairs, but Ching's wife said he was entrapped by Chinese authorities to come to Guangzhou to obtain a secret book manuscript about former Chinese leader Zhao Ziyang, removed from office for siding with protesters in Tiananmen Square in 1989. Ching was a permanent resident of Singapore who held a British National Overseas (BNO) passport specific to Hong Kong.

After Ching's arrest, supporters hoped for his expulsion from the mainland; that had happened in the case of Li Shaomin, a former Hong Kong professor and US citizen, convicted in 2001 of spying for Taiwan. Instead, Ching was convicted in 2006 and sentenced to five years in prison. The court judgment accused him of passing state secrets and confidential information, contained in several earlier articles he had written — for which he had been paid HK$300,000 — for a Taiwanese think tank that Beijing said was a front for Taiwanese intelligence agencies.[35] Ching was released in February 2008 on medical parole and he then returned to Hong Kong.

And while the 2004 detention of Zhao Yan, a researcher for *The New York Times*, did not involve Hong Kong, his case highlighted the dangers of Chinese nationals working for the foreign media. Zhao, a former reporter for *China Reform*, a Beijing-based magazine, was charged with "divulging state secrets to foreigners" after *The New York Times* published an article on former president Jiang Zemin's imminent resignation as China's military chief. The newspaper denied that Zhao provided the information for the story, but the government reportedly obtained notes written by Zhao that described a possible leadership dispute over military promotions. In early 2006, even though initial charges were dropped against Zhao, he was not released from custody. New charges of divulging state secrets and fraud were filed against him and he was tried in a closed, one-day hearing in June 2006.

In a surprise development two months later, the court dismissed the state secrets charge, a highly unusual move that implied a clash with prosecutors. The

34. Committee to Protect Journalists, http://www.cpj.or/attacks05/pages05/imprison_05.html.
35. *Ching Cheong* (Second Intermediate People's Ct, Beijing, 2006).

court, however, still convicted Zhao on a lesser, unrelated fraud charge for allegedly receiving money from an official in northeastern China in exchange for promising to help the official avoid legal problems. Zhao, who denied the allegation, was sentenced to three years in prison. Zhao was released in September 2007 after completing the three-year sentence.[36]

For Ching and Zhao, their experiences mirrored what the others had dealt with: intense secrecy surrounding their detention and prosecution, a lack of access to defence lawyers and family members and a substantial prison sentence.

5.3 Some observations and a checklist

Although it is often difficult to know exactly what a state secret is or what journalistic activity might prompt a prosecution, some observations can be made:

State secrets do not have to be about national security

Divorce statistics, national exam questions, interest rates, economic growth figures, criminal investigations, and scientific and technological developments have all been classified at some point as state secrets. A decision in 2013 by the Ministry of Environmental Protection to refuse to turn over results of a national survey on soil pollution because it had deemed the information a "state secret" was heavily criticized.[37]

Publicly available information can still be a state secret

Local newspapers sent outside China, readily available books used in academic research or information about widely known situations such as corruption have been the basis of prosecutions for leaking state secrets. Even documents readily available on the Internet can be a "state secret". In 2009, a property rights advocate was sentenced to two years in prison for possessing a document he downloaded from the Internet that had been issued by the Ministry of Housing and Urban-Rural Development on its policies for handling rental properties. The advocate had been petitioning for the return of property seized by the government years earlier.[38]

Official and internal documents are risky

Reporters should be especially careful if the information they wish to publish comes from official or internal government documents. In 2005, PRC journalist Shi Tao was sentenced to ten years for "illegally divulging state secrets abroad" for emailing the text of internal instructions propaganda authorities had sent to newspapers about coverage of the upcoming fifteenth anniversary of the Tiananmen

36. *Zhao Yan* (Second Intermediate People's Ct, Beijing, 2006). As of 2013, Zhao Yan was living and working as a journalist in New York. He was in the news again in 2012 after claiming he was denied access to a White House press conference with President Obama and Chinese leader Xi Jinping while on assignment for boxun.com, a US-based Chinese-language news site.

37. Li Jing, "Report on Mainland China's Soil Pollution a 'State Secret'", *South China Morning Post*, 26 February 2013.

38. Kristine Kwok, "Petitioner, 70, Jailed over 'State Secret' Downloaded from Net", *South China Morning Post*, 8 November 2009.

Square crackdown.[39] Even if the information contained in the documents is common knowledge or previously published, there are risks. Gao Yu received such information from documents given to her by someone in the general office of the Chinese Communist Party, who had hand-marked the documents secret. And beware that documents can be classified retroactively. Many documents are unmarked, and the prosecution can always take the documents to a secrets protection bureau and have them classified. Reporters for *Yazhou Zhoukan* are instructed to "never take any kind of document from a government or other official even if they made it available to us", according to editor Yau Lop-poon.[40]

Beware of the timing, political nature, and subject of the information

Information about the party and its leaders, particularly in advance of planned actions, can lead to trouble. Zhao Yan was accused of tipping off *The New York Times* about Jiang Zemin's planned resignation from a military position before the event. When authorities could not find evidence of Zhao having provided that information, they reportedly found his research on disputes over military appointments. In 1993, Wu Shishen, a Xinhua editor, was convicted of illegally divulging state secrets after giving to a Hong Kong reporter a speech by Jiang Zemin ahead of its delivery to the fourteenth Party Congress.[41] And one of the documents given to Gao Yu was said to be a speech by Jiang Zemin. Journalists researching issues sensitive to the Chinese leadership have to tread with caution.

Attempts to examine government shortcomings can be hazardous

Bringing public attention, particularly on the Internet, to government shortcomings can prompt prosecutions. The devastating Sichuan earthquake in 2008 that killed tens of thousands of residents including many children trapped inside poorly constructed schools raised many questions about the government's handling of the disaster. Several activists who wrote critical online reports and articles about post-earthquake efforts were charged with violating state secrets and subversion laws, reflecting a growing trend to prosecute those writing outside China's state-controlled media, which receive regular instructions on news coverage. Those included Huang Qi, who had posted on his own website, and Tan Zuoren, who was arrested days after his critical investigation was published online. Hong Kong journalists were physically prevented from covering Tan's 2009 trial in Chengdu.

Harsher penalties are generally given when information is published outside China or given to foreigners

The cases of Xi Yang, Gao Yu and Wu Shishen involved Hong Kong publications, which before the handover were considered "foreign" media. The more recent prosecutions of Shi Tao and others involving overseas websites have elicited long sentences. In addition, the 2001 Explanation makes it clear that "any person who

39. *Shi Tao*, Trial Case No. 29 (Intermediate People's Ct, Changsha, Hunan Province, 2005). Full text of the criminal verdict in Chinese and English can be found at: http://www.globalvoicesonline.org/wp-content/ShiTao_verdict.pdf.

40. Interview, 10 November 2005.

41. Wu Shishen was released in 2005 after serving 12 years in prison.

knows, or should know, that an item which is not marked secret relates to the security and interests of the nation and steals, acquires through spying or buys it for, or illegally supplies it to, a foreigner, shall be prosecuted and punished under Article 111 of the Criminal Law for stealing, acquiring through spying or buying state secrets for, or illegally supplying state secrets to, a foreigner". The case of Shi Tao provoked controversy because of allegations that Yahoo Hong Kong disclosed details of Shi's email account to PRC authorities. In March 2007, Hong Kong's Privacy Commissioner concluded there was "insufficient evidence" that Yahoo Hong Kong turned over the data, which instead was controlled and provided to authorities by a mainland subsidiary. (For more details on the ruling, see Chapter 5 Privacy.)

The status of secrets can change over time

Information not originally designated a state secret can become one at a later time (Article 18). Conversely, state secrets can be declassified as the 2010 amendments to the state secrets law imposed time limits (Article 15), but determining status can be difficult without an official announcement. During the outbreak of SARS in 2003, and of bird flu in 2004, information relating to epidemics on the mainland were considered state secrets, with only the government able to decide what to release and when. In 2005, authorities announced that casualty counts from natural disasters would no longer be classified as state secrets.[42]

Chinese reporters or staff members face more risks

As of 2013, it remained a fact that non-Chinese foreign correspondents generally did not face the same penalties as Chinese journalists and will usually only be expelled. But while the PRC government might not prosecute foreign reporters for their news coverage, it often will go after their Chinese news sources and local Chinese who work for them as news assistants and researchers. Given the harsh punishments frequently imposed on Chinese reporters and sources, the foreign media should think more carefully about ways they can try and protect them. As an added complication, the Chinese government in 2009 issued a code of conduct for Chinese news assistants and translators prohibiting them from conducting independent reporting and obligating them to spread "positive information".[43] Thus, correspondents should be careful not to send Chinese assistants to work independently doing journalist-like duties, such as conducting interviews, because they could be detained even if the correspondent is working nearby. Many international and Hong Kong media also do not identify the mainland stringers they use (but, of course, should credit their efforts whenever possible).

Are Hong Kong journalists becoming more vulnerable?

Until Ching Cheong's case, it was thought that Hong Kong journalists were less susceptible to trouble than mainland PRC journalists. Some believed that Xi Yang

42. Hu Shuli, "Make Transparency the Law", *Caijing*, 17 April 2006.
43. "Freedom of Expression in China, China's Media and Information Controls", 2009 Annual Report to Congress, US-China Economic and Security Review Commission, p. 271; found at: http://www.uscc.gov.

might have received the harsh sentence he did because he had only recently immigrated to Hong Kong from the mainland. But since the 1997 transfer of Hong Kong to PRC sovereignty, its local Chinese residents are now PRC citizens under law. Furthermore, Hong Kong reporters who are Chinese citizens need to remember that even if offences they are accused of committing occur outside China, they can be arrested and prosecuted if they return to the mainland. If Hong Kong writers are hired by an organization in Taiwan, they should be extra careful. As tensions and controls escalate for news coverage on the mainland, Hong Kong journalists are becoming their own unique and potentially vulnerable category. They are neither mainland reporter nor foreign journalist. They can go further in their reporting than their mainland counterparts yet are subject to less protection than foreign journalists.

6. Detention and arrest

As referred to earlier, many news organizations have had reporters and photographers detained, questioned, and harassed, particularly when covering sensitive breaking news stories. In late February 2011, for example, more than a dozen foreign journalists were briefly detained, and at least two assaulted, when they tried to report from the site of a planned "Jasmine Revolution"-style protest on a busy commercial street in Beijing. A week later in Shanghai, at least fifteen reporters were detained for several hours in an underground room while attempting to cover another similar protest. Reporters were subsequently warned that attempting to cover the protests and interview people in public areas without prior permission would violate local rules, and were threatened with punishment, including possible revocation of their journalist visas.[44] Reporters covering other sensitive stories — such as the crackdown on an unlicensed church in Beijing, a spate of self-immolations by Tibetans in western China, and interviews with activists and dissidents — faced ongoing challenges.

Increasingly, journalists, including mainland reporters working for domestic publications, also have been targets of incidents of harassment and violence, making their profession one of China's most dangerous. As noted, the Jasmine protests that swept many countries in early 2011 made Chinese authorities nervous. While attempting to cover one of these protests in Beijing, Bloomberg reporter Stephen Engle was pushed to the ground by several security officers, dragged by one leg, and beaten with a broom handle by a man dressed as a street-cleaner. Two CNN journalists trying to visit the blind legal activist Chen Guangcheng in February 2011 said they were assaulted by guards who threw stones and pushed them away from the entrance to the village in northeast China where the activist

44. "Foreign Journalists Detained in China's 'Jasmine' Protest", Committee to Protect Journalists, 28 February 2011, http://www.cpj.org/2011/02/foreign-journalists-detained-during-chinas-jasmine.php; "China's New Clampdown: Press Freedom in China 2011, International Federation of Journalists", http://asiapacific.ifj.org/assets/docs/062/182/118a93e-f5ef4b6.pdf; and "Media at Risk: Press Freedom in China 2012–2013", IFJ, http://asiapacific.ifj.org/assets/docs/104/080/f463268-b4a3250.pdf.

and his family were then kept under house arrest. In July 2012, a Japanese journalist for the *Asahi Shimbun* newspaper taking photos of police assaulting protesters in Nantong in the eastern coastal province of Jiangsu was himself attacked by more than a dozen officers. In March 2013, two Hong Kong TV cameramen were beaten as they filmed outside the residence of the wife of Liu Xiaobo, the imprisoned Nobel laureate.

When a Hong Kong resident is detained or arrested on the mainland, PRC authorities are required to notify the SAR government, and vice versa, according to a 2001 agreement between the two governments, but there is no agreement allowing Hong Kong authorities to have access to Hong Kong residents held on the mainland.

The **Criminal Procedure Law** (CPL) and related laws and regulations govern detention, arrest and criminal trials. Enacted in 1979, the CPL underwent major revisions in 1996 and 2012.[45] The latest revisions, which went into effect in January 2013, were substantial, with more than 100 amendments offering more due-process protections for criminal suspects and defendants, but also troubling provisions for suspects in cases involving national security, terrorism or major corruption.

The CPL provides that a person can be detained for up to thirty-seven days before police must release him or formally place him under arrest (CPL, Article 89). Arrests are a serious step and must be approved by a people's procuratorate or court (CPL, Articles 78, 85). Once formally arrested, a suspect can be further detained for up to six months before trial to allow additional investigation (CPL, Article 77). But many suspects in politically sensitive cases, such as those of Ching Cheong and Zhao Yan, have been held for longer periods than permitted by law, with pretrial detentions of a year or more. Zhao was held for twenty-two months before his trial in June 2006 (CPL, Article 73).

Individuals can also be detained administratively by public security agents without supervision from a court or other agencies for up to 20 days. In 2005, the Standing Committee of the NPC enacted the Public Security Administration Punishments Law, which provided for review of some of these detention decisions, but also increased the number and types of situations subject to administrative detention to include illegal demonstrations, disturbing social order in the name of religion, privacy invasion, and publication that incites ethnic or national hostility or discrimination.[46]

So what should reporters do if detained? Here are some recommendations:[47]

45. Chinese text of the amended 2012 CPL can be found at: http://www.china.com.cn/policy/txt/2012–03/18/content_24922812.htm; an unofficial English translation of a comparison chart between the 1997 and 2012 versions of CPL at: http://lawprofessors.typepad.com/files/130101-crim-pro-law-as-amended-en.pdf.

46. This law replaced the 1986 Regulations on Administrative Penalties for Public Security, amended in 1994. For English and Chinese texts, see: http://www.lawinfochina.com/display.aspx?lib=law&id=4549&CGid=.

47. Excellent guides on what to do if detained and other reporting tips are provided by the Foreign Correspondents' Club of China ("Reporters' Guide") at: http://www.fccchina.org/reporters-guide/if-you-get-detained/ and the International Federation of Journalists (*Handbook*

Assess the situation

Try to find out who is detaining you because the agency holding you might provide the first clues. If it is the local public security bureau, then perhaps you are being held for reporting violations or because local officials want to know more about the story you are working on, or who you are interviewing. If the Ministry of State Security is involved, then the investigation might centre on state security or state secrets. The local police, however, could also be conducting a criminal investigation. Initial signs that a case is getting serious include whether you are being "interrogated" instead of just being held, the length of time you have been held and whether a formal detention warrant has been issued. An "interrogation" has to occur at the procuratorate's office or the Ministry of Public Security's office and requires at least two witnesses. In PRC law, questioning for a few hours is not regarded as formal detention. Be sure to get the names and badge numbers of any officers detaining or questioning you. And call your editor and others who can assist you.

Ask what offence you are being held for

Ask why you are being held or detained. Different offences — from violations of rule to breaking of laws — trigger different permissible time periods for detentions.

Defend your right to cover a story

Show your copy (Chinese text) of the reporting rules permitting your right to cover a particular story. Always carry proper identification and accreditation documents. If your credentials are confiscated, try to ascertain the identity of the persons withholding them.

Ask to see a detention warrant

When detention becomes formal, a public security agency must produce a detention warrant. Within 24 hours of a person's detention, his or her family is to be notified of the reasons for detention and the place of custody "except where it is impossible to furnish a notice or where crimes endangering state security or crimes of terrorism are suspected and a notice may impede the investigation" (CPL, Article 83). Also, within 24 hours of detention, agents must conduct their interrogations; if they do not find evidence, they are to release the person immediately (CPL, Article 84). Within three days of detention, police must apply for an arrest; however, that time period can be extended (CPL, Article 89).

In the PRC, a detainee has the right to consult a lawyer *after* being interrogated for the first time (CPL, Article 33), but new provisions spell out what the defence attorney can do on the detainee's behalf, such as make a complaint or find out what crimes are being investigated (CPL, Article 36). Historically, a large majority of criminal defendants go to trial without a lawyer;[48] it remains to be seen whether

for Investigative Reporting in China), at: http://asiapacific.ifj.org/assets/docs/012/222/7661e0-82f2ade.pdf, among others.

48. Critics estimate that only 20 to 30 percent get to see a lawyer. Congressional-Executive Commission on China, 2005 Report.

the revised law will change that. But cases involving state security, terrorism or major bribery make the process even more perilous. The investigating agency has the discretion to approve the appointment of a lawyer or even allow a suspect to meet his lawyer (CPL, Article 37). In state secret cases, the defendant is rarely permitted access to counsel, even at the trial, which is usually held in secret. Persons charged with criminal offences are entitled by law to apply for bail (CPL, Articles 64–71), but in practice few have been released before trial.

Be careful if asked to sign a statement

Reporters from Hong Kong and Macau have sometimes been asked to sign a statement as a condition of release, which can be dangerous because these statements could become evidence in a later prosecution. Veteran Hong Kong journalist Wang Jian Min recalled his efforts in 2004 to resist signing a police statement. A senior staff correspondent for *Yazhou Zhoukan*, Wang was detained for three days in Wuhan in central China after investigating reports of official corruption. He was told to sign a statement acknowledging that he was reporting illegally, but Wang would not. Only after he offered authorities an alternative statement admitting that he had come to Wuhan without government permission, and that the advice he received from public security agents was "valuable", was he allowed to leave.

7. Open Government Information

One counter-trend to the secrecy imposed by the Chinese government was the national Regulations on Open Government Information (政府信息公開條例), which went into effect in May 2008, having been adopted a year earlier by the State Council.[49] These were not the first access-to-information regulations in China as several local governments (e.g. Shanghai and Guangzhou) had been experimenting with similar initiatives, but they were the first to mandate compliance across the country.

The OGI regulations set out standards for "citizens, legal persons and other organizations to obtain government information . . . enhance transparency of the work of government, promote administration . . . and bring into full play the role of government information in serving the people's production and livelihood and their economic and social activities" (Article 1).

In addition to requiring government entities to respond to citizen requests for information (Article 13), the regulations also directed them to establish procedures to regularly and clearly disclose government information "on their own initiative" (Articles 9–12) within specific time limits (Article 24), but the information disclosed "may not endanger state security, public security, economic stability and social stability" (Article 8). The information to be disclosed included various financial budgets, development plans, statistics, environmental protection, public health, food and drugs, product quality, urban and rural construction projects

49. Chinese text of the OGI regulations can be found at: http://www.gov.cn/zwgk/2007–04/24/content_592937.htm and an English translation at: http://www.law.yale.edu/documents/pdf/Intellectual_Life/CL-OGI-Regs-English.pdf.

and land use. These topics proved to be fertile areas for citizens, lawyers, NGOs, academics and others as they quickly began making thousands of requests.

Early on, observers pointed out the legal, political and administrative hurdles of the scheme, such as discrepancies between what the national regulations sought and what local rules actually implemented as local governments tried to minimize the release of information.[50] A 2009 survey by Peking University's Center for Public Participation Studies and Support (CPPSS) found that more than half of China's city and provincial governments and most of the State Council's cabinet-level entities failed the requirements for open information.[51] The survey results were not much better the following year. Furthermore, most of the administrative appeals and lawsuits filed to challenge the denied requests also were unsuccessful.

In 2012, the CPPSS survey showed that more ministries and local governments were becoming more transparent,[52] but another study in 2013 by Tsinghua University concluded that most Chinese cities exhibited weak fiscal transparency on budgets, expenditures, debts and revenues.[53] Through a series of interpretations, the Government and the People's Supreme Court have held that Chinese citizens have the right to sue over denied requests, but the scope of standing has been narrowed to those individuals who can prove a personal relevance to the information sought, which would limit the OGI's practical value for journalists.[54]

Some successful court challenges have occurred, including in politically sensitive cases. In October 2012, for example, a Beijing court ordered the Ministry of Health to comply with a consumer's request for minutes of a meeting in which revisions made to the national food safety standard for baby formula and milk products were discussed.[55] This was remarkable in light of the tainted baby formula scandal of 2008, in which six infants died and tens of thousands were hospitalized.

The uneven way in which the OGI regulations have been implemented and enforced nationwide in their first five years of operation leave much room for improvement.[56] Still, in a country with so many restrictions against the free flow of information on the Internet, in state media and in the way it classifies state secrets,

---

50. Hualing Fu, "Can OGI Take Off in China?" Human Rights in China, 1 April 2009, http://www.hrchina.org/content/3704. See also, Liu Wenjing, "Approaching Democracy through Transparency: A Comparative Law Study on Chinese Open Government Information", 26 *American University International Review* 4 (2011), 983–1007.

51. This annual survey is done with several other academic institutions including Tsinghua University and China University of Political Science and Law. See http://www.cppss.cn/.

52. http://www.freedominfo.org/2012/10/chinese-ministries-more-transparent-study-says/.

53. "Cities' Finance Transparency Unsatisfactory", *China Daily*, 23 July 2013.

54. http://www.court.gov.cn/qwfb/sfjs/201108/t20110815_159790.htm.

55. *Zhao Zhengjun v Ministry of Health* (First Intermediate People's Ct, Beijing, 2012). Details can be found at: http://chinaelectionsblog.net/ogi/court-orders-ministry-of-health-to-respond-to-ogi-request/.

56. In addition to Peking University, other institutions and NGOs provide updates on the latest OGI developments, including The China Law Center at Yale Law School, http://www.law.yale.edu/intellectuallife/openinformation.htm; The Carter Center, Global Access to Information Initiative, http://www.chinatransparency.org/; and freedominfo.org at: http://www.freedominfo.org/regions/east-asia/china/.

the OGI has to be seen as progress. This is even truer, considering that Hong Kong's own anaemic administrative code on access to information lacks some of the legal provisions provided by the mainland.

8. Privacy and personal data

A potentially troubling development for journalists working on the mainland involves a growing trend for privacy protection, including for personal data and online information. While China does not have a comprehensive legal framework for privacy, it has been building an expanding web of laws and regulations that addresses aspects of privacy. These include:

- The PRC's 1982 Constitution, which provides undefined, general protection for a citizen's "personal dignity" (Article 38) and personal correspondence (Article 40) and against unlawful searches of a person (Article 37) and of residences (Article 39);
- A 2009 amendment to the Criminal Law (Article 253(A)) that prohibits the illegal sale or other unlawful disclosure to third parties of a citizen's personal data by government entities, officials and employees in the financial, telecommunications, transportation, education and medical sectors or for anyone to steal such information with penalties of up to three years in prison.
- A new Tort Liability Law in 2010 that recognizes individuals' right to privacy and allows them to sue for civil damages for privacy violations, a provision spurred in part to curb Internet "human flesh searches" (mass actions to publish personal information to shame a targeted person).[57]

In one of the more significant recent developments, the National People's Congress Standing Committee in December 2012 issued its "Decision on Strengthening Network Information Protection", the first national legislation on electronic personal data information in China. It established principles for protecting, collecting and using electronic data that is personally identifiable and involves personal privacy and banned the stealing, illegal obtaining, selling or unlawfully providing of "personal electronic information". The law, which went into effect in 2013, also imposed obligations on Internet service providers and others that collect and use the personal data of Chinese citizens to maintain information security.[58]

57. Article 2–"Those who infringe upon civil rights and interests shall be subject to the tort liability according to this Law. Civil rights and interests used in this law shall include the right to life, the right to health, the right to name, the right to reputation, the right to honor, right to self image, right of privacy, marital autonomy, guardianship, ownership, usufruct, security interest, copyright, patent right, exclusive right to use a trademark, right to discovery, equities, right of succession, and other personal and property rights and interests". Full English text of the Tort Liability Law can be found at: http://www.procedurallaw.cn/english/law/201001/t20100110_300173.html.
58. Chinese text at: http://www.gov.cn/jrzg/2012-12/28/content_2301231.htm. English text at: http://chinacopyrightandmedia.wordpress.com. See Graham Greenleaf, "China: NPC Standing

Many observers applauded these laws and other related regulations[59] as important steps toward protecting the privacy interests of Chinese citizens, particularly as the PRC moves toward a more robust online marketplace, but concern remains over how the legal regime might be used in contrary ways. In August 2013, for example, British citizen and former journalist Peter Humphrey and his Chinese-American wife and business partner, Yu Yingzeng, were arrested for illegally acquiring private personal data apparently connected to fraud investigations they were conducting for their long-time corporate risk management firm. Details of the charges were not disclosed but the prosecution was believed to be part of a broader inquiry by the PRC government into possible corruption involving Chinese officials and foreign drug companies.[60]

While cases have yet to be brought against journalists for violating personal data laws, the CCTV image of a handcuffed Humphrey confessing to illegally collecting personal information on Chinese individuals was chilling.

9. Defamation

This chapter basically covers PRC government interaction with the Hong Kong and foreign media, but journalists should be aware that they also face possible legal actions from private citizens over defamation if their works are published on the mainland.[61]

In China, the right to protect personal reputation was first recognized in criminal law in 1979 and is now contained in the revised Criminal Law 1997, Article 246, which states:

> Whoever, by violence or other methods, publicly humiliates another person or invents stories to defame him, if the circumstances are serious, shall be sentenced to fixed-term imprisonment of not more than three years, criminal

Committee Takes a Small Leap Forward", *Privacy Laws and Business International Report,* February 2013.

59. These include those issued by China's Ministry of Industry and Information Technology (MIIT): "Telecommunications and Internet Personal User Data Protection Regulations" (2013), "Information Security Technology — Guidelines for Personal Information Protection Within Public and Commercial Services Information Systems" (2013) and "Several Regulations on Standardising Market Order for Internet Information Services" (2011). See Graham Greenleaf and George Tian, "China Expands Data Protection Through 2013 Guidelines: A 'Third Line' of Personal Information Protection", *Privacy Laws & Business International Report,* April 2013.

60. Jane Perlez, "In China, the Dangers of Due Diligence", *The New York Times,* 13 September 2013.

61. For additional reading on defamation in the PRC, refer to Fu and Cullen, *Media Law in the PRC,* pp. 183–207; Charles Glasser Jr. (ed.), *International Libel and Privacy Handbook,* 3rd ed. (New York: Wiley, 2013), pp. 149–171; X. Chen and P. Ang, "Defamation Litigation and the Press in China", *International Journal of Communications Law and Policy,* 12(2008), 53–91; Benjamin Liebman, "Innovation through Intimidation: An Empirical Account of Defamation Litigation in China", 47 *Harvard International Law Journal,* 47 (2006), 33–177; Yik Chan Chin, "Truth, Fair Comments, Immunity and Public Opinion Supervision: Defenses of Freedom of Expression in Chinese Right to Reputation Lawsuits", 27 February 2013. Available at SSRN: http://ssrn.com/abstract=2225735 or http://dx.doi.org/10.2139/ssrn.2225735.

> detention, public surveillance or deprivation of political rights. The crime mentioned . . . shall be handled only upon complaint, except where serious harm is done to public order or to the interests of the State.

In 1982, the PRC's Constitution provided protection of reputation in Article 38:

> The personal dignity of citizens of the People's Republic of China is inviolable. Insult, libel, false charge, or frame-up directed against citizens by any means is prohibited.

But it was not until 1986, when the NPC passed its first civil code, the **General Principles of the Civil Law (GPCL)**[62], which codified the right of individuals to sue for harm to reputation, that an avalanche of defamation lawsuits fell upon the mainland media. Plaintiffs have included citizens, public officials, celebrities and corporations. The Hong Kong media are typically not the targets of these lawsuits, but potentially they could be.

Key passages in the GPCL include Article 101:

> Citizens and legal persons shall enjoy the right of reputation. The personality of citizens shall be protected by law, and the use of insults, libel or other means to damage the reputation of citizens or legal persons shall be prohibited.

And Article 120:

> If a citizen's right of personal name, portrait, reputation or honour is infringed upon, he shall have the right to demand that the infringement be stopped, his reputation be rehabilitated, the ill effects be eliminated and an apology be made; he may also demand compensation for losses.

Furthermore, the Supreme People's Court has issued several judicial interpretations, based in part on actual defamation cases, to guide the lower courts on the law. These have dealt with such issues as jurisdiction, review, liability, place of infringement, republication and inaccuracies and standards in news reporting.[63]

In the PRC, the media in a defamation case are held to an objective negligence fault standard. The Supreme People's Court established four issues that judges must consider before finding that defamation has been established:[64]

- Was the plaintiff's reputation harmed?
- Did the defendant's actions violate the law?

62. English text can be found at: http://www.china.org.cn/china/LegislationsForm2001–2010/2011–02/11/content_21898337.htm.

63. The judicial explanations and interpretations are officially known as: Several Questions Concerning the Implementation of the PRC, Civil Law General Principles Opinion (1988); the 1993 Reply of the Supreme People's Court to the Questions in the Trial of the Cases Concerning the Right of Reputation (The 1993 Reply), and the 1998 Interpretation of the Supreme People's Court on the Trial of the Case Concerning the Right of Reputation (The 1998 Explanation). Chinese and English texts can be found at: http://chinacopyrightandmedia.wordpress.com/china-media-law-database/.

64. The 1993 Reply.

- Did the defendant's illegal actions cause damage to the plaintiff's reputation?
- Was the defendant at fault?

In general, protection for personal reputation on the mainland is broader than that available under the common law, the system existing in Hong Kong, and has historically included elements of privacy to protect the "personal dignity of citizens", as provided in Article 38 of the PRC Constitution. It remains to be seen how the Tort Liability Law,[65] which went into effect in 2010, will ultimately impact this combined defamation-privacy concept as the new law separately refers to the rights of reputation and privacy. In addition to privacy considerations, defamation can also include insults even if they do not contain false statements of fact. Words such as "bastard", "shameless", "monster", "mad dog", "hooligan", "presumptuous", "rotten", "human scum", and "Mickey Mouse" have been found to be defamatory.[66] Also, unlike in the common law, a defamation action in the PRC can be brought on behalf of a dead person. Relatives who can sue include a spouse, parents, children, siblings, grandparents and grandchildren.[67]

Similarities, however, do exist between defamation cases in the PRC and Hong Kong. Both require a statement that is published and that refers to a particular person who does not necessarily have to be identified by name.

Some of the libel defences in both jurisdictions also share similarities such as **privilege**, which the mainland media also enjoy for quoting or reporting on courts documents, government-issued documents[68] and quasi-governmental proceedings, provided the reports are objective, accurate and do not reveal state secrets.

The defence of **fair comment** for opinion is not established as clearly in the PRC as it is in Hong Kong, but there has been some judicial recognition of it. For the comment to be protected, it generally should be about a matter of public concern, fair (not insult), made in good faith and based on substantially true facts.[69] In what some observers consider an important recent case, a Guangzhou court articulated support for the news media's right to comment on reported facts as one of their "most basic responsibilities" and "in the public interest". *New Express Daily v The Journalist Monthly* (Tianhe Dist, People's Ct, Guangzhou, 2010).[70]

But what is in the "public interest" is not well defined in Chinese cases. For example, are news stories and commentary about public officials or figures in the public interest? The PRC Constitution's Article 41 provides that "citizens have the right to criticize and make suggestions to any state organ or functionary", but that does not necessarily translate into a *New York Times v Sullivan*-type malice standard. Public officials and famous people were among the first to bring

65. Article 2. See http://www.procedurallaw.cn/english/law/201001/t20100110_300173.html.
66. Fu and Cullen, p. 193.
67. The 1993 Reply.
68. The 1998 Explanation. See also Fu and Cullen, p. 202.
69. Glasser, pp. 161–2.
70. Case found at website of Shanghai Xin Wenhui Law firm at: http://www.700210012345.com/bsmrgs/Detail.php?ID=3279.

defamation claims against the media in the 1980s and 1990s. It was not until 2002 that a Shanghai court held that a well-known soccer player was a public figure and therefore should be tolerant of minor factual errors. *Fan Zhiyi v The Oriental Sports Daily* (Jing'an Dist. People's Ct, Shanghai, 2002). But other courts have ruled differently.

With regards to insults and privacy concerns mentioned earlier, truth is not an absolute defence for defamation in the PRC as it is in most common law countries. Defamation is also not a tort of strict liability, meaning that under Chinese law the person bringing a lawsuit needs to prove the underlying facts to sustain the claim.[71] In practice, though, mainland courts still frequently require the media to prove the truth of their statements. In some cases, however, courts have held that when a news story was based on credible sources contributing to a journalist's reasonable belief in the facts, the news organization was not held liable. *Guangzhou Huaqiao Real Estate Development Co. v China Reform Magazine* (Tianhe Dist. People's Ct, Guangzhou, 2004).

As China's civil defamation cases only started in 1986 and their outcomes are not binding on other cases, its defamation law is still not as developed as in common law jurisdictions such as Hong Kong, but it is gradually formulating principles and guidelines to give some predictability in this area of law.

Claimants not satisfied with civil remedies have brought private prosecutions under Article 246 of the Criminal Law. But as more citizens took to the Internet to complain about government misconduct, more local officials turned to local law enforcement to bring controversial public prosecutions against their online critics. This trend escalated to such a degree that central authorities intervened in 2009 (Ministry of Public Security) and 2010 (Supreme People's Procuratorate) to first order restraint and then to impose restrictions on when and how criminal prosecutions could be brought.[72]

The criminal defamation terrain shifted sharply again in September 2013 when the Supreme People's Procuratorate and the Supreme People's Court issued a joint interpretation[73] of Article 246 and other existing law pertaining to online speech to clarify how Internet users were vulnerable to prosecution in cases involving "serious circumstances". The new interpretation includes in its definition of serious circumstances as situations when posts are viewed at least 5,000 times or

71. Article 106 General Principles of the Civil Law and Article 2 of "Some Provisions of Supreme People's Court on Evidence in Civil Litigation" 2001. See also Chin, "Defenses of Freedom of Expression in Chinese Right to Reputation Lawsuits", p. 18, supra note 61.

72. For an excellent and comprehensive summary and analysis of criminal defamation cases in China, see Mei Ning Yan (2011), "Criminal Defamation in the New Media Environment — The Case of the People's Republic of China", *International Journal of Communications Law and Policy* 14.

73. Interpretation concerning Some Questions of Applicable Law When Handling Uses of Information Networks to Commit Defamation and Other Such Criminal Cases, at: http://www.chinacourt.org/law/detail/2013/09/id/146710.shtml. Unofficial English text at: http://chinacopyrightandmedia.wordpress.com/2013/09/06/interpretation-concerning-some-questions-of-applicable-law-when-handling-uses-of-information-networks-to-commit-defamation-and-other-such-criminal-cases/. See "Judicial Move Aims at Online Rumors", *China Daily*, 10 September 2013.

re-posted 500 times or more, which can be low thresholds in a country with 600 million Internet users.

It also defined Article 246's public prosecution requirement of "serious harm to the public order and interests of the state" if a post leads to an upset of social stability, mass protests, ethnic or religious conflict, damage to the nation's image or national interests, or causes "other" damage. The new interpretation makes Internet users, including potentially those in Hong Kong who post on popular mainland microblogs, for example, more vulnerable to penalties of up to three years in prison.

10. Conclusion

The ability of Hong Kong journalists and foreign media to report on the mainland has become more difficult — and more dangerous — in recent years. Despite hopes for a better environment for both groups that appeared to come with some easing of reporting rules in connection with the 2008 Olympics in Beijing, the situation has deteriorated, particularly for Hong Kong journalists.

The deterioration has occurred because of new laws, new rules and newly aggressive tactics against journalists reporting stories deemed sensitive. These developments come in the historical wake of a country that has sometimes used its regulatory powers to punish journalists and publications for stories and points of views it did not like and its prosecutorial powers to convict and silence others, usually in secret.

In 2010, the mainland revised its State Secrets law to make Internet publication of material deemed to be a state secret a more risky proposition. Since 2012, the government has increased use of its administrative power to deny or delay visas to foreign journalists whose coverage it disapproved.

To many, the most alarming development is that the laws and regulations in China governing media — domestic, Hong Kong and foreign — have failed to protect them from increasingly violent and intimidating official misconduct. In recent years, while covering major news stories or local marches and protests, journalists have been beaten, intimidated, harassed and detained, sometimes by undercover police, and have had their equipment, video or notes destroyed or confiscated.

The better environment Hong Kong journalists and foreign media had hoped for has proven elusive.

10

Copyright

Doreen Weisenhaus

FREQUENTLY ASKED QUESTIONS

1. What is copyright and how does it affect journalists? (See section 1)
2. What kinds of works are protected and for how long? To be protected, do works need to be registered? (See sections 1.2 and 2)
3. What constitutes infringement? (See section 5)
4. Can ideas, facts or news be copyrighted? (See section 1.2)
5. Can a journalist refer to a copyrighted work in news reporting, criticism or review? What is fair dealing? (See section 6)
6. What rights do journalists, both media employees and freelancers, have in protecting their own works? (See sections 3, 7 and 12)
7. What special copyright issues involving the Internet and social media do journalists need to know about? (See sections 1.1, 1.2, 5.1, 6.1.3, 8.1, 9.2, 11 and 12)
8. Are parodies permissible under copyright law? (See sections 6.1.3 and 11)
9. Are there any alternatives to traditional copyright regimes? (See section 10)

1. Introduction

Copyright is the exclusive legal right for a limited time period to reproduce, publish, adapt, distribute, perform, sell or transmit original works such as books, computer software, plays, drawings, films, musical compositions and so on. Copyright is part of a larger scheme to protect what is known as intellectual property, which also includes trademarks, patents and designs. In the age of the Internet and multimedia, copyright issues have become increasingly important to journalists in both traditional and new media as works appearing on the Internet are also protected. Journalists today need to understand the concepts of copyright and its implications, particularly as more countries are focusing on enforcement. Journalists should be aware of copyright in two regards: one, in acknowledging the copyrights of other people's works that might affect newsgathering, writing and news production; and two, in protecting a journalist's own works.

1.1 History/Background

Like much of the law in Hong Kong, copyright law here has its origins in the UK, having imported the latter's 1911 Copyright Act and later its 1956 Act. In preparation for the handover to Chinese sovereignty in 1997, Hong Kong was required to localize imported laws. It did so by passing Copyright Ordinance (Cap 528), which came into effect in June 1997 and remains the controlling law. The 1997 ordinance modelled a number of sections after the UK's Copyright, Designs and Patents Act 1988, adopted international standards and norms such as those espoused by the World Trade Organization and World Intellectual Property Organization and addressed new technology, including the then emerging Internet. The ordinance also expanded protection in Hong Kong to original works created anywhere in the world; in the past, such works needed a connection to Hong Kong. These changes made Hong Kong's copyright laws among the most modern of a common law jurisdiction.

Hong Kong has amended its ordinance several times. Criminal sanctions for the use of infringing copies in businesses and the workplace (known as "end-user piracy") were added in 2001. Several of those amendments, particularly relating to the educational use of some copyrighted material such as newspapers and other publications, were suspended at the time after public concern was raised over the amendments' potential impact on educational institutions. Remaining in effect were the amendments imposing criminal penalties over the use of infringing copies of computer software, movies, television dramas and music recordings.

In 2003, Hong Kong relaxed restrictions on parallel importation of computer software, which meant that certain copies of software made outside of Hong Kong could be imported into Hong Kong without obtaining further copyright permission. In 2004, the Copyright Ordinance was amended again to prohibit copy shops from making, selling or possessing illegal copies of books, magazines and other publications.

Additional amendments, enacted in 2007 and 2009, included, among other provisions, making frequent and significant copies of newspapers, magazines, periodicals and books a criminal offence with exemptions for educational establishments; shortening the criminal liability period for parallel imported copyright works, and expanding fair dealing for educational and public administration purposes. The amendments also made company directors or partners responsible for internal management criminally liable for copyright infringement committed by their companies, but that it would be a defence for employees to show they were not in a position to make or influence such decisions.

But government's attempts to introduce legislation to regulate copyright in the digital environment have been less successful. With the growing controversy and worldwide use of peer-to-peer file sharing and other issues involving the Internet, the Hong Kong government conducted a public consultation in 2006–2007 on legal liability for unauthorized uploading and downloading of copyright works and the role of online service providers (OSPs) to help combat Internet piracy. After years of discussions and debates with various stakeholders and the public, the government introduced Copyright (Amendment) Bill 2011, which recommended a number of controversial measures that met considerable resistance and, in June 2012, the bill was removed from the legislative agenda without a vote. As of 2013, no new legislation has been introduced (see further discussion in sections 6.1.3 and 11 below).

1.2 **Overview: What is copyright?**

Copyright is a right belonging to the owner of an original work, which includes literary, musical, dramatic and artistic works (and published editions of these works); sound recordings; film, and broadcasts and cable programmes. Unlike trademarks, patents and designs, which need to be registered with the government to be protected, copyright is an automatic right that emerges when the original work is fixed in a tangible form and requires no registration. The quality of a work is not relevant in determining whether it is entitled to copyright protection. It does not have to be innovative or have artistic or literary value; the work just has to be an original expression, even a simple, bad one such as a short article with grammatical mistakes or a fuzzy snapshot. In short, a work acquires copyright protection upon creation when it is original, no matter the quality, and is in a fixed, physical form.

Facts, news or ideas cannot be protected by copyright; only the expression of them can, such as the precise words written down or a chart with particular information or certain headline fonts. For example, if a newspaper wrote about a news event, it cannot claim copyright over the news event and prevent others from writing about it. But if that newspaper's article and/or photograph about the event were duplicated or reproduced by a competitor that did not get copyright permission or licence, that act could be a copyright violation. Limited reproduction of copyright work is permitted in several exceptions, including for criticism, review and reporting on current events, and is explained below. While mere information or news is not protected under copyright law, copyright could exist in the compilation of news, with protection arising from the skill and labour used to make the compilation, rather than from the content itself. *Apple Daily Ltd v Oriental Press Group Ltd* [2011] 2 HKC 28, citing section 4(1) of the CO, which protects compilations. (See also section 2.1 of this chapter.)

But is there protection for "hot news" beyond copyright law? In a 1918 case, *International News Service v Associated Press*, 248 US 215, the US Supreme Court recognized the tort of "hot news misappropriation" in ruling against a news agency that had rewritten a competitor's news stories to use as its own; the Court held there was a quasi-property right in news while it was still timely. A federal appeals court in 1997 spelled out what was needed for such a claim, including that generating the time-sensitive information came at a cost and that the defendant was a direct competitor "free-riding" on the plaintiff's efforts. *National Basketball Association v Motorola Inc,* 105 F.3d 841 (2d Cir 1997). But in a closely watched case in 2011, the same appeals court rejected a claim of "hot news misappropriation" after several financial firms objected to a website aggregator posting their timely stock recommendations, holding that copyright law pre-empted the claims. *Barclays Capital Inc v TheFlyontheWall.com Inc*, 650 F.3d 876 (2d Cir. 2011). While the doctrine is not dead in the US, it is clear that its use is limited. The doctrine has never been recognized in Hong Kong nor does it seem to be evident in other countries such as the UK or in Europe. Although it has been recognized in India (*M/s Marksman Marketing Private Ltd v Bharti Tele-Ventures Ltd* (Madras HC 2006)), the doctrine was rejected more recently in September 2013. *Akuate Internet Services Private Ltd v Star India Private Ltd* (Delhi HC 2013).

1.3 Sources of law

Article 140 of the Basic Law requires that Hong Kong have laws protecting the achievements, rights and interests of authors of artistic and literary creations. The current law in Hong Kong is the Copyright Ordinance (CO, Cap 528), which became effective June 1997. Hong Kong is bound to follow certain international treaties and agreements affecting copyright; these include the Berne Convention for the Protection of Literary and Artistic Works, the Universal Copyright Convention, the Geneva Convention for the Protection of Producers of Phonograms Against Unauthorized Duplication of Their Phonograms and The World Trade Organization — Agreement on Trade Related Aspects of Intellectual Property Rights.

2. What is protected?

Sections 4 to 10 of the CO set out specific categories of works that are protected. Works created in Hong Kong, as well as works created anywhere in the world, can be protected in Hong Kong. Sections 37 to 88 list permissible exemptions and defences.

2.1 Literary, dramatic and musical works

A literary work is described in section 4 of the CO as any work "written, spoken or sung", provided the work exists in a physical form. The typical items covered of interest to journalists are books, magazine and newspaper articles, as well as computer programs and data compilations such as tables and charts (CO s 4(1)). Regular listings often compiled by magazines and newspapers for entertainment, television/movie schedules, races, restaurants and so on are also protected by copyright. It is arguable that news articles might be considered a compilation under copyright protection if "they contain a variety of information and materials that are indicative of efforts and skill being expended in researches, selection, collation and presentation". *Apple Daily Ltd v Oriental Press Group Ltd* [2011] 2 HKC 28. A letter to the editor, an email and other written communication sent to a news organization are considered copyright material, but the author's act of sending such work implies authorization for at least one use. A musical work refers to music only; the words of a song are considered literary works. A dramatic work includes dance and mime. As with literary works, copyright for musical and dramatic works will exist only if they are written, recorded or in otherwise permanent form.

2.2 Artistic works

Artistic works, as defined in section 5 of the CO, includes photographs, sculpture, collage, works of architecture such as a building or model, paintings, drawings, diagrams, maps, charts, plans, engravings, etchings, lithographs and woodcuts.

2.3 Sound recordings and films

A sound recording, according to CO s 6, is:

> (a) a recording of sounds, from which the sounds may be reproduced; or (b) a recording of the whole or any part of a literary, dramatic or musical work, from which sounds reproducing the work or part may be produced, regardless of the medium on which the recording is made or the method by which the sounds are reproduced or produced.

A film is defined in CO s 7(1) as "a recording on any medium from which a moving image may by any means be produced" and can include any recorded moving image whether it is on film, video or whatever technology can record moving images. Section 7(4) notes that a film will not have copyright if it copies from another film.

2.4 Broadcasts and cable programmes

Section 8 of the CO describes broadcasts as visual images and sounds transmitted wireless for the public to receive in Hong Kong or elsewhere. These broadcasts cover radio and terrestrial and satellite television. Section 9 on cable programmes refers to the sending of sounds, visual images and other information "otherwise than by wireless telegraphy at two or more places in Hong Kong or elsewhere". This does not include video conferences, video telephones and videos-on-demand.

2.5 Published editions

Section 10 of the CO refers to the typographical arrangement of a published edition of a literary, dramatic or musical work. A typographical arrangement includes the layouts, headings, fonts and other aspects of how a published work is presented. And again, copyright will not be extended if the published edition infringes the typographical arrangement of someone else's edition.

3. Who owns a copyright?

3.1 Author

The general rule, as set out in CO s 13, is that the author of a work is the first owner of any copyright in it. Thus, a writer or photographer is the first owner of a copyright in his or her work. But there can be exceptions, for example, for works that are commissioned or done while on the job.

3.2 Employee's works

For works done during the course of employment (CO s 14), the general rule is that the employer owns the copyright, unless the employee has made a different agreement with the employer. In short, the employer has the right to works produced by the employee in the course of his or her employment unless the employer has agreed to give up this right. This holds for reporters, editors, artists, photographers and anyone else who works for newspapers, magazines, television and any other media employer. In 2005, *Oriental Daily News* sued two of its former reporters for alleging passing two photographs, taken by one of them, to rival newspaper, *Apple Daily*, for a story about food poisoning caused by contaminated seafood. The lawsuit said that *Oriental Daily News* had only used one photo but that both photos appeared in other newspapers and websites, including *Apple Daily*.[1]

If, however, the employer uses the work in a way that could not have been reasonably anticipated by both employer and employee at the time the work was produced, the employee is entitled to additional compensation. Using a reporter's newspaper article also on the newspaper's website would be considered foreseeable in today's world, but other commercial uses might not be. If the employee and employer cannot agree on an amount for compensation, then the employee can take the matter to the Hong Kong Copyright Tribunal. (For more details, see section 9.3 in this chapter.)

The copyright for works done outside the employment context that is unrelated to the employee's duties and responsibilities will generally belong to the employee. For example, if an employee is hired as a technology writer for a newspaper and writes a play in his off-duty hours, then the copyright for the play would belong to the employee, not the newspaper.

But be aware that a number of Hong Kong newsrooms have employment contracts that address copyright issues that might be more restrictive for employees. One media group, for example, claims copyright for any work done by an employee regardless of whether it was in connection with the job if it in any way affects or relates to the business of any company or division within the media group. A journalist who has signed an employment contract should review it.

3.3 Commissioned works

When a publication or other media commission an assignment from a freelance writer or photographer, copyright ownership depends on the agreement made between the parties (CO s 15). If no agreement has been made between the author/creator and the person or entity that commissioned the work, then the author/creator will be considered the first owner of the copyright. But regardless of an agreement, the media organization commissioning the assignment has

1. Anita Lam, "Ex-reporters Sued over Copyright", *South China Morning Post*, 28 May 2005.

the exclusive right to use the article, photograph or other works in a reasonable manner and the assigning editor or other company representative can prevent others who might use the work "for any purpose against which he could reasonably take objection" (CO s 15(a) and (b)). In any agreement, the freelancer is advised to specify terms he or she finds acceptable, such as media (e.g. print but not broadcast) or distribution (e.g. Hong Kong only). (For more discussion, see the section 12, "Freelancers: Special issues and a checklist" in this chapter.)

3.4 Government documents

Unlike law in the US, the Hong Kong government owns the copyright for most documents it produces, even articles its officials might write for newspapers (CO s 182). Similar to what is required under UK law, anyone wanting to reproduce government material would have to seek copyright permission or be eligible for a waiver. Often, when the government has posted articles, documents or other materials on its website (http://www.gov.hk), it will also post details of its waiver with the conditions that need to be met.

The waiver typically states that the information within the website may be re-disseminated or reproduced, provided that the government agency that produced the materials is acknowledged as the source and that the reproduction is for non-commercial use. Any commercial use of that material needs written authorization from the agency and, if approved, might require a licence fee. Interestingly, the government also usually posts a disclaimer that it does not accept responsibility for any loss or damage resulting from the use of its information. Publications produced by the Legislative Council are also covered by copyright (CO s 184).

3.5 Special circumstances for authorship

Different medium can have different rules regarding authorships. Sound recordings can have several authors: the person who makes the recording, the person who performs it and the composer. A movie's copyright is not owned by the director who makes the movie but, traditionally under British law applicable in Hong Kong until 1997, by the producer who finances it because of the economic interests underlying copyright. Since 1997, the copyright in a film is owned jointly by the producer and principal director (CO s 11 (2)(b)). For a photograph, it is the person who controlled the arrangements for the taking of the photo and not the person in the photo who owns the copyright, but if the photograph was commissioned, it belongs to the person or entity that commissioned it. If someone gives an interview, he might not own the copyright, but the person who recorded it or wrote it down might.

4. How long is a work protected?

In general, copyright continues for the life of the author/creator plus fifty years (CO s 17). Copyright for a broadcast programme extends fifty years from its airing, a cable programme fifty years from inclusion in the cable service (CO s 21), a sound recording fifty years from its release or making (CO s 18) and a typographical arrangement of a printed edition twenty-five years from the first publishing (CO s 21). After a copyright has expired, a work becomes part of the public domain, which normally means that anyone can copy it.

5. What infringes a copyright?

5.1 Primary infringement

If you do not own the copyright in a work, you cannot copy, publish, adapt, distribute, post on the Internet, broadcast or place in cable service a work or rent copies to the public unless you obtain permission and/or a licence from the owner of the copyright or are using it under one of the permitted defences or exemptions (CO ss 22–29). How can you tell whether you have infringed a copyright?

5.2 A two-step analysis

To sort out this question, Jared Margolis, co-author of *Intellectual Property Rights: Hong Kong SAR and the People's Republic of China*,[2] suggests a two-step analysis. He recommends that first, you examine the work in question to see if it is even protected under the law and then determine whether infringement has occurred.

Step 1: Is it a work covered under law?

To be covered, the work must belong to a category listed in the Copyright Ordinance and must be an original, tangible expression. Is the work in question a literary, artistic, dramatic or musical work as defined by the ordinance? Is it a book, painting, play or musical composition, for example? Is it a film, sound recording, broadcast or cable programme? If yes (that the work belongs in one of these categories), is it original? As only original work is protected, you need to determine just how original this is. (Note that countries have varying requirements for originality for the work to qualify for copyright protection.) The author says you should:

> . . . (E)xamine it to determine if it reaches the required threshold of originality. The manner of determination of the originality threshold varies somewhat according to the class of work involved. Very little originality is required to establish copyright subsistence (however, if there is only the bare minimum of originality,the scope of protection will be consequently limited).[3]

Step 2: Is there infringement?

After determining that the item is in a protected category and has sufficient originality, Margolis suggests then looking at both the original item and the one in question for a "feature by feature comparison". More original aspects of the former will be entitled to greater protection.

2. Michael D. Pendleton, Peter Garland, and Jared R. Margolis, *Intellectual Property Rights: Hong Kong SAR and the People's Republic of China*, 2nd ed. (Hong Kong: Butterworth Asia 2003).
3. Ibid.

5.3 Infringement: Copying must be substantial

The general rule is that for a work to be infringed, a *substantial* part must be taken (CO s 22 (3)(a)). But what does substantial mean? It is not defined in the ordinance. But do not think that substantial refers only to quantity, the amount of what is taken. That, of course, will be relevant. But more important is the *quality* of what is taken (*Ladbroke (Football) v William Hill (Football)* [1964] 1 WLR 272). A typical example given is a musician who copies a quite short but memorable musical snippet from someone else's song. There are few court cases in Hong Kong on copyright infringement involving the media. One notable case is *Oriental Press Group Ltd v Apple Daily Ltd* [1999] 4 HKC 131. The *Apple Daily* newspaper reproduced a smaller version of the front page of a rival publication, *Oriental Sunday* magazine, which had exclusive coverage, including a photograph, of a visibly pregnant movie star. The reproduction was indeed substantial — an entire front cover, though smaller in size. *Apple Daily* had not sought *Oriental*'s consent to run the photograph and layout and the court observed that it was unlikely that *Oriental* would have given a licence had it been asked to do so and ruled for *Oriental Sunday*.

Another relevant Hong Kong case is *Lam Tai Hing v Koo Chih Ling, Linda* [1993] 2 HKC 1, which centred on whether a medical questionnaire substantially copied another questionnaire. The court found that even though there were major differences between the questionnaires, infringement can incur if the part copied was an "important part of the work even if it was a smaller part than the balance which was not so copied".

5.4 Secondary infringement

Secondary infringement, as described in sections 30 to 34 of the CO, happens with the exporting, importing and possessing of unauthorized copies or providing the means to make unauthorized copies, for other than private use.

6. Exemptions and defences

Sections 37 to 88 of the CO set out permitted acts that will not be considered infringement, provided that they not "conflict with a normal exploitation of a work by a copyright owner and unreasonably prejudice the legitimate interests of the copyright owner" (CO s 37(3)). The permitted acts are included on what is known as an "exhaustive" list, meaning that if something is not on the list, it is not allowed without obtaining copyright permission. This is an approach similar to that taken in Australia and Singapore. The US has a more liberal, non-exhaustive approach, which means that it will consider more possible permissible acts, even if not listed, provided they are reasonable.

6.1 Fair dealing

The most important defence for journalists is fair dealing. Hong Kong's Copyright Ordinance, like the laws of the US and UK, among others, recognizes the public interest in having exceptions for copyright, especially for journalists who need to cover news, disseminate information and offer opinions to the public. Fair dealing[4] permits the use of copyright material for the limited purposes of criticism, reviews and covering the news — as well as for research and private study and for education — as long as certain conditions are met.

6.1.1 Criticism, review and news

Of particular interest to journalists is the use of fair dealing for criticism, reviews and the reporting of current events. CO s 39 establishes that copying a portion of a copyright work for the purposes of criticism, reviews and reporting of current events can be permissible as long as proper acknowledgement is given. Acknowledgement, however, is not required for the reporting of current events by means of a sound recording, film, broadcast or cable programme. The law does not specify the exact usage that is permitted but will consider what is reasonable for the purposes of criticism, reviews and reporting news. So if you are reviewing a play or book and reproduce only the parts necessary to illustrate your comments, that use would likely be considered reasonable. Be careful when reproducing copyrighted photographs and images as their use must clearly relate to criticism, reviews or reporting and be proportionate to that purpose.

This defence is not meant to give a green light for a publication to usurp a scoop of a competing publication under the guise of reporting "news" by copying articles, headlines or photographs. In the case mentioned earlier, *Oriental Press Group v Apple Daily*, the court rejected an argument by *Apple Daily* that it was merely bringing news of interest to its readers when it reproduced the front page of rival *Oriental Sunday*, which had exclusive coverage of the pregnant movie star. While this case was not about fair dealing per se and dealt primarily with assessing damages, it showed that the courts had little tolerance for the reproduction of a competitor's material.

---

4. Many common law countries feature fair dealing exemptions in their copyright laws including the UK, Canada and Australia. Fair dealing is different from the fair use exemption found in US copyright law, which does not restrict the exemption only to specific categories of protected works. Instead, in determining whether the use made of a work in any particular case is a fair use, the factors to be considered shall include (1) the purpose and character of the use, whether use is of a commercial nature or is for non-profit educational purposes; (2) the nature of the copyrighted work; (3) the amount and substantiality of the portion used and (4) the effect of the use upon the potential market for or value of the copyrighted work. Copyright Act 1976, 17 U.S.C. s 107.

6.1.2 Research, private study and educational establishments

Fair dealing also permits copying for research and private study. CO s 38 lists these factors to be considered as to whether fair dealing applies: (a) the purpose and nature of the dealing; (b) the nature of the work; and (c) the amount and substantiality of the portion dealt with in relation to the work as a whole. Copyright (Amendment) Ordinance 2007 expanded protection for educational establishments and students (CO s 41A), which permits, for example, scans and photocopies to a reasonable extent for teaching purposes, if there is no licensing scheme authorizing the copying (s 45). Many schools have entered into licence agreements with the Hong Kong Reprographic Rights Licensing Society and the Hong Kong Copyright Licensing Association. The amended Ordinance also addresses the issue of placing copyright works on an Intranet for teaching purposes, which requires the teaching establishment to adopt appropriate security measures (such as log-in username and password) and to ensure works are stored for a limited period of time, up to 12 months (s 41A(5)).

6.1.3 Parodies

Hong Kong copyright law does not provide an exemption or defence for parody (a literary or musical work that closely imitates another work for comic effect or ridicule) or pastiche (a work that imitates the style of another work or is a hodgepodge of selections from other works). Under current law, the creator of a parody would either have to get permission from copyright holders to use their works or demonstrate that the parody constitutes "criticism" of a work within the fair dealing context and provide proper acknowledgement.

The Internet has proven to be fertile ground for parodies and "mashups" of popular works. "To ease the concern of some netizens", the Hong Kong government said it considered adding a parody exemption to the Copyright (Amendment) Bill 2011, but declined to do so, indicating the difficulties of constructing a legal definition of parody and concern for copyright owners.[5] It also referred to the UK's several consultations since 2006 on possible changes to its copyright law, which likewise did not provide a parody exemption, stating, "the UK experience demonstrates that the issue on parody is by no means straightforward".[6]

In December 2012, the UK government announced its plans to provide some legislative leeway for parody, so as to permit content creators more flexibility, in part, as acknowledgment of the "growing trend for user-generated, often non-commercial, parody content on YouTube and similar websites".[7] As support for its decision, the UK government cited the European Union Copyright Directive[8]

5. "Copyright Exception for Parody", Commerce and Economic Development Bureau, Intellectual Property Department, November 2011, LC Paper No. CB(1)385/11–12(04).

6. Ibid.

7. "Modernising Copyright: A Modern, Robust and Flexible Framework", HM Government, Intellectual Property Office, at: http://www.ipo.gov.uk/response-2011-copyright-final.pdf.

8. EU Copyright Directive (2001/29/EC).

allowing parody exception, and laws in Australia, Canada, France, Germany and the Netherlands permitting parodies. When Canada approved its Copyright Modernization Act in 2012, it provided protection for parodies in two ways: (1) by expanding fair dealing to cover parodies as well as satires, and (2) by creating a new exemption for non-commercial, user-generated content on blogs, video-sharing websites and the like that do not affect the market for the original material.[9] In 2013, the Hong Kong government conducted a consultation to consider options to deal with parody in copyright law, including clarifying existing provisions and/or introducing a criminal exemption or fair dealing exception.[10] (See also section 11 below)

6.2 Incidental inclusion

If a protected work is included in an incidental way, such as taking a photograph of someone walking in front of a billboard or building purely incidentally, then copyright will not be infringed (CO s 40). But a musical work, even a small portion, will not be regarded as "incidental" if inclusion is "deliberate" (s 40(3)).

6.3 Public records

Section 58 of the CO deals with the use of public records. This section clearly allows a reporter to write down or get a copy of public records without violating copyright. The section sets out that "material which is comprised in public records which are open to public inspection may be copied, and a copy may be supplied to any person without infringement of copyright". Public records are defined as:

> the records of any nature or description which have been made, received or acquired in the course of proceedings of the Legislative Council, judicial proceedings or executive transaction, together with exhibits and other material evidence which form part of or are annexed to or are otherwise related to any record, which are or are required to be in the custody of, or which may be transferred to or be acquired by, any department of the Government.

7. Moral rights

Moral rights represent the non-economic interests in copyright protection, of concern to many individual writers and creators (CO ss 89–100).

9. More information can be found on the Canadian government website at: http://balanced-copyright.gc.ca/eic/site/crp-prda.nsf/eng/home.

10. The Hong Kong government received more than 2,400 submissions, including one from the Journalism and Media Studies Centre, University of Hong Kong, authored by Prof. Peter Yu, a leading US expert in international intellectual property and communications law. ("Digital Copyright and the Parody Exception: Accommodating the Needs and Interests of Internet Users", 15 November 2013.) It was the third such submission by the JMSC in consultations for digital copyright reforms being considered by the government. See also LC Paper No. CB(1)516/13-14(03).

7.1 Paternity right

What if your name was left off something you created? Can you demand that you be identified as the author, otherwise known as a paternity right? Under CO s 89, the author of a literary work or a director of a film has this right. But for journalists in Hong Kong, this right is limited. CO s 91(5) says "the right does not apply in relation to any work made for the purpose of reporting current events" and CO s 91(6) says "the right does not apply in relation to the publication in a newspaper, magazine or similar periodical; or an encyclopaedia, dictionary, yearbook or other collective work of reference of a literary, dramatic, musical or artistic work made for the purposes of such publication". In other words, you do not have the right to a byline on a story if you are writing about current news events or if your writing, regardless of content, is for a newspaper, magazine or reference text.

7.2 Integrity right

A related right — an integrity right — is the chance to object when your work is changed in a way that distorts, mutilates or otherwise harms your reputation, otherwise known as "derogatory treatment". CO s 92 says that you have the right to challenge these edits and changes, that is, unless again you are a journalist in Hong Kong. The same restrictions apply for an integrity right as for a paternity right. If you are reporting about current events or if the work is published by a newspaper, magazine or similar periodical or in a reference book, you cannot object to changes in your work (CO s 93). You do, however, also have the right not to have a work "falsely attributed" to you (CO s 96).

8. Infringing copies in the workplace

What about how you use your computer at your place of employment? You may want to pay close attention to some of these issues as you can face possible criminal penalties for violations. The Copyright Ordinance has been amended several times (in 2001, 2007 and 2009) to toughen penalties for those who knowingly possess or use infringing copies of protected works in a business setting. The amended law made it a crime to make or use unauthorized copies of computer software, movies, musical recordings and TV dramas (CO s 118). Violators can face up to four years in prison and a HK$50,000 fine (s 119). It is a defence for the person charged to prove that his employer provided the infringing copy for use in the course of his employment (s 118 (3)(A)). Unauthorized copies of newspapers, magazines, periodicals and books can give rise to both criminal penalties and civil liability (s 119B). A number of media companies have distributed notices to their employees warning them to comply with copyright law and have laid out specific guidelines to follow in the workplace. Be aware that some of the company guidelines are broader than what is prohibited by law. Please check with your company for their policies. Common areas are as follows.

8.1 Software

A user is generally allowed to make a back-up copy of software, assuming the original copy was properly obtained (CO s 60). Also, a user can make adaptations to software to make it compatible at work, provided the manufacturer has no restrictions (s 61). But again, check with office policy regarding software on company computers. One media company specifically spells out that its employees cannot copy or modify software in their office computers without company authorization, cannot install any software for personal use and cannot copy for personal use any software from the office computer. Some even prohibit the downloading of any software from the Internet for screensavers or other use onto the office computer.

8.2 Photocopies of newspapers, magazines, books, and other publications

Check with the legal department of your media company to see if they have licensing agreements with publishers and other producers of copyright work for books, magazines, newspapers and the like. Some companies have negotiated a collective licensing agreement with the Hong Kong Reprographic Rights Licensing Society that allows the making of copies of publications covered by the agreement, provided certain conditions are met such as a set percentage of works that may be copied.

Frequent and significant copying of these publications "resulting in a financial loss" to the copyright holder would constitute an offence (s 119B). To avoid liability under the ordinance, copying would need to stay under certain limits, sometimes referred to as a "safe harbour". For newspapers, magazines and periodicals, the total number of "infringing pages" made for distribution or distributed within any 14-day period must not exceed 500. For books and academic journals, the total value of infringing copies made for distribution or distributed within any 180-day period must not exceed HK$6,000 (CO Schedule 1AA). Statutory defences include: the user made a request for a licence but failed to receive a timely response; the user could not obtain commercially available copies and could not obtain a licence on reasonable commercial terms, and the user did not know that the copies he made or distributed infringed copyright (s 119B).

8.3 Electronic copies

Making electronic copies — the scanning or storing of information in the computer or faxing — of a protected work is also prohibited without copyright permission unless for private study or research. If doing research for a news story, the protected work can be accessed but should not reproduced unless it is fair dealing within the meaning of CO s 39, on which, however, there is very little case law.

9. Remedies

9.1 Civil

For general copyright infringement, the copyright owner can pursue civil remedies such as asking a court for an injunction to stop the unauthorized use of the work, an order to deliver the infringing copies and/or damages (CO ss 107, 109). In particularly egregious cases, the court may consider additional damages beyond normal damages (CO s 108).

For copyright infringement of moral rights — paternity and integrity — an action can be filed for breach of statutory duty owed to the author or director (CO s 114). For the integrity right — derogatory treatment of a work (CO s 92) — the court may require a disclaimer disassociating the author/creator from the altered work.

9.2 Criminal

A person faces a maximum fine of HK$50,000 and up to four years in prison if he makes, imports, exports, possesses for trade or business or distributes an infringing copy of a protected work. A person who makes, sells, imports, exports or possesses for trade or business equipment to infringe copies faces a maximum fine of HK$500,000 and up to eight years in prison (CO ss 118, 119). The Hong Kong Customs and Excise Department handles prosecution of these cases. In 2005, a Hong Kong man became the first person in the world convicted for distributing protected movies on the Internet using BitTorrent technology (CO s 118(1)(f)) (*HKSAR v Chan Nai Ming* [2005] 4 HKLRD 142). The Court of Final Appeal confirmed the conviction of Chan Nai Ming of attempting to commit an offence of distributing an infringing copy of a copyright work, namely three films. Using the BitTorrent technology, a number of individuals downloaded copies of films that were duplicates of infringing copies from Chan's computer, which acted as the initial "seeder". The two issues before the CFA were: (1) what constituted a "copy" capable of distribution under s 118(1)(f); and (2) whether Chan's conduct constituted illegal "distribution" under the law. The defendant argued that a copy could only exist as something stored in a physical tangible object and so a digital/electronic copy could not be distributed unless the storage device was itself physically transferred, which did not happen in this case. The CFA rejected the defendant's arguments and held that electronic copies distributed via the Internet could be infringing and that illegal distribution did not require a physical transfer nor active conduct by the defendant. By keeping his computer connected to the BitTorrent network, the defendant ensured that copies of the films would be transferred to downloaders, according to the court (*Chan Nai Ming v HKSAR* [2007] 2 HKLRD 486).

9.3 Copyright Tribunal

A Copyright Tribunal was established to handle copyright licensing issues (CO ss 169–176). Of particular interest to journalists who are employees of media companies is the tribunal's jurisdiction (CO s 14) for "use of work outside reasonable contemplation" (see section 3.2 in this chapter, "Employee's works"). The tribunal can determine the amount of compensation owed the employee if there is a dispute between the journalist and the employer.

Enquiries can be made to the Clerk to the Copyright Tribunal, 25/F, Wu Chung House, 213 Queen's Road East, Wanchai, Hong Kong. Telephone: 852–2961–6813.

10. A non-traditional approach to copyright: Creative Commons

Founded in 2001 by then Stanford professor Larry Lessig as a non-traditional approach to copyright, Creative Commons, a non-profit organization, provides a simple, user-friendly template from which copyright holders can choose terms in their licences. These include: attribution (giving credit), non-commercial use (sharing for non-commercial purposes), no derivative works (no alterations or adaptations allowed) and share alike (any subsequent sharing of work must be subject to the same licence terms) or a combination. A Creative Commons licence is not a replacement for copyright but a standardized method for users to modify their own copyright terms.[11] In 2008, Hong Kong became the 50th jurisdiction to localize the Creative Commons licences.[12] As of 2011, more than 400 million works carried CC licences. For more information on the Hong Kong scheme, contact http://hk.creativecommons.org.

11. The Internet: Special issues

Copyright law applies to works on the Internet (CO s 26), but the medium also has its own unique aspects, issues and implications. For example, a work is considered fixed when it is on a computer memory and a work's appearance on the World Wide Web is a reproduction. How to handle those reproductions in the copyright context is an issue the Hong Kong government, like other governments around the world, is grappling with. After years of debate and discussion that started with a public consultation launched in 2006, the government introduced the Copyright (Amendment) Bill 2011, which introduced a series of measures, including creating a technology-neutral exclusive right for copyright owners to communicate their works to the public through any mode of electronic transmission, with criminal sanctions against those who make unauthorized communication of copyright works to the public. It also proposed establishing a "safe harbour" for online service providers to limit their liability for copyright infringement if they complied with a Code of Practice specifying how to respond when notified of acts

11. http://creativecommons.org.
12. Hosted by the Journalism and Media Studies Centre at the University of Hong Kong (HKU), the public lead is Professor Ying Chan and legal leads are Associate Professors Alice Lee and Yahong Li at the Faculty of Law, HKU.

of online piracy. Many Internet users raised concerns that the law would further restrict parodies (see section 6.1.3) or other creative derivative works, with some calling the bill "the Article 23 of the Internet", a reference to proposed national security laws that prompted huge protests before being withdrawn in 2003 (see Chapter 7 Official Secrets and Sedition). In June 2012, the government removed its proposed digital copyright amendments from the legislative agenda without a vote and said it would study a copyright exemption for parodies, among other possible changes, for the bill's next version. (See also section 6.1.3.)

11.1 **Linking**

Another worry that Internet users had over the Copyright (Amendment) Bill was whether linking to other websites would expose them to liability under the proposed law. The government responded that as long as users did not control the content, they would not face liability, adding that, "a hyperlink is not a copyright work".[13] A key feature of many websites is to provide easy linking to other websites. Hyperlinks refer to a website using a few words (usually underlined or in a different colour) or an image or icon that when clicked takes the viewer to a different website. In general, a website does not need permission to simply link to another website, but it can get into trouble if it uses material, even a small amount, or images from the second website to make the hyperlink. In 2004, the *Ming Pao* newspaper in Hong Kong threatened legal action against Google after the US search engine launched its Hong Kong news website, which used news summaries and some photos from a number of Chinese newspapers and provided hyperlinks to their websites, including *Ming Pao*'s. The newspaper agreed to drop any possible legal action after Google stopped using summaries from *Ming Pao* or even providing a link.

11.2 **Deep linking/framing**

What happens if a website in providing a link takes the viewer beyond the home page of another website to an inside page, otherwise known as "deep linking"?

As of 2013, there has not been any case law on this point in Hong Kong, although deep linking has remained quite prevalent on the Internet. Some experts though believe that deep linking can be troubling legally. Deep linking allows the viewer to bypass possible advertising and other material that the linked website might want visitors to see. And it can create a moral rights problem if the deep link goes to an inside page that does not identify the creator/author of the work.

Early court cases on this issue include ones from Scotland (*Shetland Times Ltd v Dr Jonathan Wills*, [1997] SLT 669) and the US (*Ticketmaster Corp v Microsoft Corp*, No 97-3055DDP (CD Cal 1997)), in which the parties settled with the agreement to link but not deep link. But in 2000, another case established that deep linking,

13. "Online Copyright Claims Rejected", Hong Kong Information Services Department, 24 April 2012, http://www.news.gov.hk/en/categories/finance/html/2012/04/20120424_190120.shtml.

at least in the US, was permissible (*Ticketmaster v Tickets.com* 99-CV-07654 (CD Ca)), although a court in 2006 disallowed an unauthorized link to a webcast (*Live Nation Motor Sports Inc v Davis* WL79311 (N.D. Tex 2006)). In 2003, Germany's high court held that deep linking did not violate copyright (*Holtzbrinck v Paperboy*, I ZR 259/00), while other European courts have ruled differently. Many advocates say the Web's inherent nature of information sharing indicates an implied licence to link to specific pages, but to be sure, it might be prudent to just link to the homepage or obtain permission for the deep link. Be aware that some websites are posting notices that permission must be obtained for links, but courts have not ruled on the enforceability of these notices.

Likewise, there have not been any Hong Kong cases involving framing — the placing on one website some elements, often visual, from a second, unrelated website, but these cases seem to be clearer examples of copyright infringement. In a US case, the website Total News provided links to news sites that when clicked caused content from those news sites to appear on Total News's site. The case was settled, as many of these cases are, with Total News agreeing to stop framing (*Washington Post v Total News Inc.* 97 Civ 1190 SDNY 1997).

In 2003 and 2007, a US federal appeals court approved the use of "thumbnails" (reduced image of graphics) to deep link to other websites, finding the use "transformative"; *Kelly v Arriba Soft Corp*, 336 F.3rd 811 (9th Cir. 2003); *Perfect 10 v Amazon.com*, 487 F.3rd 701 (9th Cir. 2007).

11.3 **Derivative liability**

Suppose your website provides a link to another website that has content in violation of copyright or other illegal content? You might be held liable as well if it is determined you knew or had reason to know your link encouraged infringement by directing users to the infringing website. Make sure you know what is on the other side of your link.

11.4 **Bloggers and social media**

Non-commercial users such as bloggers, who keep web diaries of thoughts, observations and links to other websites, are also subject to copyright laws. If a blogger provides links to other websites and/or use quotes from them, adding some commentary would better ensure that the links and quotes could be considered fair dealing. Likewise, users of social media such as Facebook, Twitter and YouTube are not immune from copyright laws, although there has been no case law involving social media and copyright in Hong Kong. In the UK, for example, tweets that reproduce even part of a sentence from a copyright work might face potential liability for copyright violation.[14] News media trolling Facebook, Twitter and other social media sites for images of newsworthy events need to remember that just

14. Observers say that recent European Court of Justice cases, which the UK is obligated to follow, "have suggested that rather than look for skill, judgment or labour in putting words together, there must be an assessment of whether the author has exercised creative choices . . . in arranging

because photographs and videos are posted does not mean they are in the public domain. Twitter's terms of service indicate that users are merely granting a licence for the website to use the photos or videos.

11.5 Protecting own works on Internet

What if you discover an article you have written or a photograph you have taken has been posted on a website without your permission or knowledge when you did not want it distributed in that manner? Hong Kong's CO was one of the first laws to say that a copyright owner can prevent his or her works from being distributed without permission on the Internet (CO s 26(2)). If you find a website that has wrongfully taken your article and passed it off as someone else's, you also have some remedies although enforcement can be problematic. The Hong Kong Intellectual Property Department recommends requesting the Internet Service Provider (ISP) hosting the offending website to remove the infringing material.

If the website is in the US, the department advises contacting the American Society of Journalists and Authors (www.asja.org) for a copy of the "takedown" guidelines under the US Digital Millennium Copyright Act 1998. To find details of the ISP, including who to contact about your complaint, the department suggests using Network Solutions (www.networksolutions.com), a large registrar of domain names, and sending the ISP the following information:

- your physical or electronic signature;
- identification of the copyright works claimed to be infringed (or a representative list of such works);
- identification of the material claimed to be infringing (e.g. filenames on the server) together with sufficient information to allow the ISP to locate them;
- sufficient information to allow the ISP to contact the complainant;
- a statement that you believe in good faith that the identified material is not authorized by you;
- a statement that the information in the notification is accurate under penalty of perjury and that you are authorized to act on your own behalf as the infringed party.

While Hong Kong copyright law does not provide "takedown" instructions, the department says providing a similar request and information to the local ISP "is still a good option".

words, images or sounds." Luke Scanlon, "Twitter and the Law: Ten Legal Risks", *The Guardian*, 10 August 2012.

12. Freelancers: Special issues and a checklist

Freelancers in particular should be vigilant about safeguarding their rights. In addition to general copyright considerations discussed elsewhere in this chapter, other special matters affect freelancers. They often confront copyright issues on a piece-by-piece basis with media companies with varying copyright policies and practices. These issues include:

Proposals/Query letters

As previously mentioned, ideas, facts, concepts and general topics are not protected by copyright, so your proposal or query letter about a proposed article can be at risk. A publisher or media company might like the idea you present, but not you as the author, and assign your proposal to someone else.

Some writers groups such as the US-based Authors Guild[15] suggest that before you submit a proposal, you might send a preliminary letter alerting the publisher that you would like to present an idea (on X topic) and that if they use the idea, even without giving you the assignment, they will provide reasonable compensation and appropriate credit. If they agree to consider your proposal under those conditions, you will send it. Another method, the guild recommends, is to send a preliminary letter with the proposal itself in a smaller, separate envelope inside; if the publisher's representatives open the second envelope, they are agreeing to conditions specified in the letter. Such precautions are not typical for Hong Kong and might be of little practical use. On the other hand, if you submitted a completed article on speculation to a publication, which then used parts or all of your work without your consent, you would have a stronger claim because actual original expression is protected. In general, however, your best bet for preserving your ideas is to establish ongoing relationships with reputable media outlets.

Agreements/Contracts

When a publication or other media company commissions an assignment from you, copyright ownership depends on the agreement you make with it (see section 3.3 in this chapter, "Commissioned works"). If no agreement has been made between you and the media outlet that commissioned the work, then you will be considered the first owner of the copyright.

If you do sign an agreement for an assignment, be sure to be clear which rights you as a freelancer are granting to the media company and which ones you are retaining or obtaining. For example, if you grant first publication rights, it means you are giving the publication the right to be the first to publish that particular work. "One-time rights" means you are selling for one-time use but not necessarily the first one. You might want to control the terms for exclusivity (that you can sell to other publications simultaneously), number of uses (how many times a publication can print the article), duration (rights expire after a certain time), languages

15. Kay Murray and Tad Crawford, *The Writer's Legal Guide: An Authors Guild Desk Reference* (New York: Allworth Press; Authors Guild 2013), 4th ed.

(e.g. English-only but not Chinese), distribution (e.g. Hong Kong only), electronic rights and so on.[16]

If authorship and the right to review changes are important to you, make sure those terms are included in the agreement. You are not entitled to a byline or to object to changes in your text if your assignment is writing about current news events or if your writing, regardless of content, is for a newspaper, magazine, encyclopaedia, reference text, or other collective works of reference (CO ss 91, 92).

A typical freelance contract for a Hong Kong newspaper or magazine might require the freelancer to grant the right to publish the work for the first time in print and online, to publish exclusively in Hong Kong, to store as part of its database and archives in all formats (print, digital and electronic) and to promote your works to third parties for republication, reprint and reproduction (for this latter, they would normally share any royalties received).

A written contract before production of freelance work can clarify issues you consider important. In 2003, a freelance journalist lost a HK$50,000 claim against the Hong Kong government for brochures she produced for InvestHK, the government's investment-promotion agency. Merle Linda Wolin and InvestHK had a verbal agreement in which she was paid to design, provide content and produce seven brochures. After the government printed an eighth brochure using elements from the other brochures without permission, Wolin signed a deal for which she received HK$30,000 to assign copyright to InvestHK. She later discovered that a ninth brochure had been printed without disclosure at the time of the deal. In Small Claims Tribunal, the agency conceded it did not tell Wolin about the ninth brochure, but said it thought the agreement had transferred copyright retroactively. The tribunal rejected Wolin's request for additional payment.

Reasonable use

Without a contract, a publisher has no right to make other use of your works beyond the presumed one-time use. But regardless of an agreement, the media company that commissioned the assignment has the exclusive right to use your works in a reasonable manner and the assigning editor or other company representative can prevent others who might use the work "for any purpose against which he could reasonably take objection" (CO s 15(a) and (b)).

Internet

In addition to controlling whether a print media organization can use your works online, you also want to protect from third parties using your work on the Internet without seeking copyright permission (see section 11.5 "Protecting own works on Internet" in this chapter.)

16. Other freelance contract terms that are not copyright-related include fees, expenses, due date, payment terms and cancellation fees. For further discussion and sample freelance contracts/letters, suggestions are offered by such writers groups as the Authors Guild in the US (http://www.authorsguild.org), the UK-based Creators' Rights Alliance (http://www.londonfreelance.org), the Professional Writers Association of Canada (http://www.writers.ca) and the International Federation of Journalists (http://www.ifj.org).

13. For more information

For inquiries on Hong Kong copyright law, contact the Intellectual Property Department, Hong Kong SAR, 24/F and 25/F, Wu Chung House, 213 Queen's Road East, Wanchai, Hong Kong. 852-2961-6901. Enquiry@ipd.gov.hk.

11

Obscenity and Indecency

Yan Mei Ning

FREQUENTLY ASKED QUESTIONS

1. Can a newspaper publish a photograph of a person in the nude? Would the newspaper evade or reduce its liability by obscuring private body parts? (See sections 3 and 4)
2. Is it mandatory for newspapers and magazines to send their articles to the Obscene Articles Tribunal for classification before publication? (See section 2.2.1)
3. Under what circumstances are publications required by law to be put in wrappers and to print statutory warnings that such publications cannot be sold to people under 18 years of age? (See section 2)
4. Is mere possession of obscene publications unlawful? Under what circumstances are possession and import of obscene publications unlawful? (See section 2)
5. Is the law governing obscenity and indecency in an online environment different from that regulating print media? (See sections 2.4 and 3.3)
6. Is it unlawful to publish or possess child pornography in Hong Kong? If so, is the law applicable to online child pornography and computer-generated images? (See section 6)

1. Introduction

Hong Kong's obscenity law not only regulates adult magazines and audio-visual materials, but also polices the city's mainstream print media. Indeed, criminal prosecutions of Hong Kong newspapers and magazines arise mainly from the publication of indecent or obscene content. Like its counterparts in many parts of the world, Hong Kong's obscenity law has been controversial and has brought uncertainty to the daily operations of the Hong Kong press.

Some groups and parents have, however, criticized the city's obscenity law as too lax, and have lobbied for tougher measures to be introduced to curb indecent and objectionable content in mass-circulation print media. Complaints and dissatisfaction towards obscenity law have since the mid-1990s been compounded by the rising popularity of online content and the related regulatory dilemma. In an attempt to reform obscenity law, the HKSAR government has conducted two public consultations since 2000, and the latest round only finished in mid-2012. As of late 2013, legislative changes had yet to be announced.

2. The statutory regime under the COIAO

The enactment of the Control of Obscene and Indecent Articles Ordinance (COIAO, Cap 390) in 1987 aimed at reducing the amount of offensive matter displayed at newsstands and access by juveniles to indecent material. According to the Court of Final Appeal, the COIAO restricts freedom of speech in the interest of the community as a whole (*Oriental Daily Publisher Ltd v Commissioner for Television and Entertainment Licensing Authority* [1998] 4 HKC 505).

The ordinance imposes restrictions via the introduction of: (a) a classification scheme to identify obscene articles, the publication of which are prohibited, and indecent articles, which are for an adult audience only and the publication of which is subjected to specific requirements or conditions; and (b) a prosecution system that imposes criminal sanctions on the publication of obscene articles, and on the publication of indecent articles to juveniles or in contravention of specific requirements or conditions (*Three Weekly v Obscene Articles Tribunal & Anor* [2007] 3 HKC 425). The COIAO also restricts the public display of indecent matter, a topic that will not be covered in this chapter.

2.1 Definition of obscene and indecent articles

The COIAO, as indicated by its title, controls indecent and obscene articles. The term "article" is broadly defined to mean "anything consisting of or containing material to be read or looked at or both read or looked at, any sound recording, and any film, video-tape, disc or other record of a picture or pictures" (COIAO s 2(1)). In practice, the ordinance targets print media, both adult and mainstream, and adult audio-visual materials. The term "article" also covers free gifts included in adult publications and comic books such as sex toys or swords. For the application of the COIAO to the digital environment such as contents on the Internet and in mobile phones, see section 2.4 of this chapter.

On the other hand, films for public screening purposes, videotapes or laser disc of these films, and videos shown on buses, trains, at piers, and in other public places are instead regulated by the Film Censorship Ordinance (FCO, Cap 392). Likewise, sound and television broadcasts are governed by the Communications Authority Ordinance (Cap 616), Broadcasting (Miscellaneous Provisions) Ordinance (Cap 391), and Broadcasting Ordinance (Cap 562).

Similar to the laws of many other jurisdictions, the COIAO does not give precise definitions of "obscenity" and "indecency". Instead, COIAO s 2(2) describes both terms by reference to suitability for publication, stipulating that "a thing is obscene if by reason of obscenity it is not suitable to be published to any person"; and "a thing is indecent if by reason of indecency it is not suitable to be published to a juvenile".

Juvenile refers to a person under the age of 18. Publication includes the distribution, circulation, sale, hiring, or lending of the article to the public or a section of the public. In addition, COIAO s 2(3) states that obscenity and indecency for the purpose of the ordinance include "violence, depravity and repulsiveness", but again does not define those terms.

2.2 The Obscene Articles Tribunal

The COIAO provides for the establishment of the Obscene Articles Tribunal (OAT or the Tribunal), a judicial body under the Judiciary that is central to the classification scheme, as well as integral to the prosecution of offences under the COIAO. Under the Objectionable Publications Ordinance that preceded the COIAO, a single magistrate, who was often an expatriate, decided whether a publication was objectionable. There were complaints that the rulings were often too liberal, skewed towards Western tradition, and did not reflect the prevailing moral standard of the Hong Kong community. The classification scheme and the OAT were introduced under the COIAO to address such concerns.

2.2.1 Classification

An author, printer, manufacturer, publisher, importer, or distributor may voluntarily submit an article to the OAT for classification prior to its public release. Since pre-publication classifications are optional, they do not act as compulsory censorship but provide a relatively convenient means of ascertaining the nature of an article before publication. In practice, newspapers and news magazines do not submit their articles for classification, due both to the belief in media freedom and to time constraints in the production process. Instead, reporters and editors exercise their editorial judgment in assessing whether the content of their publications would contravene the ordinance.

The COIAO is enforced by the Office of Film, Newspaper and Article Administration (OFNAA), a government agency that replaced the Television and Entertainment Licensing Authority (TELA) in April 2012, Customs and Excise Department, and the police. Officials from these departments and the Secretary for Justice may also submit any articles suspected to have violated the COIAO to the OAT for post-publication classification.

Interim hearing in private

The OAT consists of a presiding magistrate and two or more lay adjudicators selected from a panel. Upon the submission of an article, the Tribunal is to provide an interim classification within five days. Lay adjudicators are recruited through open invitation and appointed by the Chief Justice. Their inclusion is designed to allow for community participation and to reflect public standards of morality, decency, and propriety in the classification process. Lay adjudicators, as compared to a single magistrate, are expected to be more representative of the views of the Hong Kong Chinese majority.

The interim hearing is conducted in private, without the attendance of the applicant. The result is then published in one English-language newspaper and one Chinese-language newspaper. If no request for review is lodged within five days of the interim classification taking effect, the classification will be confirmed as final.

Full hearing in public

Upon a request for review of an interim classification, a full public hearing will be conducted by the OAT, consisting of a presiding magistrate and four or more adjudicators not involved in the original interim classification. The COIAO stipulates that the Tribunal is required at both the interim and full hearings to identify the part or parts of an article that are obscene or indecent (see ss 14 and 15). A party may appeal on a point of law to the Court of First Instance within fourteen days of the OAT decision. The Tribunal may also reconsider, upon request or on its own initiative, articles previously classified.

Class I, II, and III articles

According to COIAO s 8, articles may be classified into Class I, II, and III. Class I articles are neither obscene nor indecent and may be published without restriction. Class II articles are indecent, and the OAT may impose conditions relating to their publication. In addition, COIAO s 24(1) details restrictions on the publication of indecent articles, which include the sealing of articles in wrappers and the display of a warning notice stating that these articles must not be published or sold to persons under the age of 18. Class III are obscene articles, which are prohibited from publication.

It is important not to confuse the classification of articles under the COIAO with that of films under the FCO. Compulsory censorship is required for all films intended for public exhibition, which are then classified into Category I (suitable for all ages), Category IIA (not suitable for children), Category IIB (not suitable for young persons and children), and Category III (for persons aged 18 or above).

Items not subject to classification

Although the term "article" has been broadly defined, not all items are susceptible to classification. In *Kailey Enterprises Ltd v Obscene Articles Tribunal* [1995] 3 HKC 235, the court held that the OAT did not have the jurisdiction to classify a bronze statue called "New Man" depicting a nude male because it was not an article within the meaning of the ordinance, noting that the COIAO did not envisage the control of sculpture or censorship of works of art by a system of classification. Meanwhile, COIAO s 8(2) stipulates that the OAT shall refuse an application to make a classification if it is of the opinion that the article may be child pornography (see also section 6 of this chapter).

2.2.2 **Determination**

The OAT performs two different and separate tasks — classification and determination. In the latter, the OAT determines in open court whether an article referred by a court or magistrate in the course of any civil or criminal proceedings is indecent or obscene (COIAO s 29). The OAT has exclusive jurisdiction in determining whether an article is obscene or indecent. Nonetheless, if a person admits in any court proceedings that the article is obscene or indecent, the court or magistrate may accept that admission and find accordingly against the person, and the OAT is not required to make any determination.

2.2.3 Guidance set out in section 10 of the COIAO

In its classification or determination, the OAT must follow the guidance set out in COIAO s 10, having regard to: standards of morality, decency and propriety that are generally accepted by reasonable members of the community; the dominant effect of an article as a whole; the class or age of the potential audience; and whether the article has an honest purpose or whether its content is merely camouflage designed to render acceptable any part of it.

In the course of these considerations, expert opinion is admissible. However, such expert evidence has to be based on research, whether academic or commercial, but not purely personal values or feelings (*Hui Siu Yan, Edward v Obscene Articles Tribunal* [1994] 1 HKC 627). On another occasion, the Tribunal decided not to give much weight to the evidence given by an academic who was an experienced editor because of lack of survey findings (OAT proceedings transcript: OAT/GOT/772/2002/Review). The possibility of harm does not need to be proved before indecency can be established, even though the purpose of the COIAO is to safeguard the community against harm (*East Touch Publisher Ltd v Television and Entertainment Licensing Authority* [1996] 3 HKC 195).

2.3 The COIAO offences

As in many Western countries, the mere possession of obscene or indecent publications is not a crime in Hong Kong. The COIAO only bans acts which lead to the spreading of obscene/Class III articles amongst the public or cause indecent/Class II articles accessible to minors. There are two parallel sets of offences, one for articles not submitted to OAT classification before distribution or sale while the other for OAT classified articles. Any person who publishes, possesses or imports for the purpose of publication any obscene article is subject to a maximum fine of HK$1,000,000 and imprisonment of three years (COIAO s 21).

Possession for the purpose of publication applies to two situations: (a) when a person possesses an article with the intention of manufacturing or reproducing a copy of it for publication; and (b) in the absence of evidence to the contrary, a person possesses more than two copies of an article in circumstances that give rise to a reasonable suspicion that he or she intends to publish it (COIAO s 32). The above criminal sanctions are applicable to the same acts concerning Class III articles (COIAO s 26), even in cases of interim classification (COIAO s 25).

A person who publishes an indecent article to a juvenile or in violation of the statutory requirements stipulated in s 24(1) faces a maximum fine of HK$400,000 and imprisonment of twelve months on first conviction, and a fine of HK$800,000 and imprisonment of twelve months on a subsequent conviction. The same criminal sanctions are applicable to those who publish Class II articles contravening conditions imposed by the OAT (COIAO s 27). A person also commits an offence if he or she possesses for publication any indecent article contravening statutory requirements or conditions imposed by the OAT (COIAO s 27A).

The COIAO s 28 stipulates the defence of public good, which is available for the above-mentioned offences if the OAT finds that the publication of an article is in the interests of science, literature, art, learning, or any other object of general concern. Expert evidence is admissible in establishing or negating the defence of public good.

2.4 Application of the COIAO to the digital environment

Because the COIAO was written before the advent of the Internet, no reference was made to the law's applicability to the Web. Nonetheless, the ordinance has been used since 1996 to prosecute obscene and indecent publications on the Internet, resulting in convictions. The applicability of the COIAO to the Internet was challenged in *HKSAR v Cheung Kam Keung* [1998] 2 HKC 156, where the court held that the definition of "article" in the COIAO is very wide, and that the term "disc or other record" could cover the graphic computer files complained of in that court prosecution.

In *HKSAR v Hiroyuki Takeda* [1998] 3 HKC 411, the court dismissed an appeal against a sentence for committing offences of publishing obscene pictures on the Internet. The aggravating factors considered by the court were the publication of pictures showing heterosexual and homosexual acts with children on the Internet free to anyone without safeguards, and that these pictures could potentially reach a very wide audience both locally and internationally, including children and mentally unstable people. Section 3.3 of this chapter gives an account of law enforcement agencies' handling of the online dissemination of the Edison Chen sex photographs in early 2008. See also section 9 of Chapter 12 for the regulation of online media.

3. Notable COIAO prosecutions of mass-circulation print media

In recent years, there have been several notable prosecutions of popular magazines and mainstream newspapers for contravening the COIAO. As mentioned, the ordinance controls not only the content of adult publications and audio-visual materials but also the mass-circulation print media. Many Chinese-language newspapers in Hong Kong are tabloids. Quite a number of them have sex pages that often serve as advertisements for brothels. At times, vulgar language and sexually explicit pictures can also be found in news reports.

Sex pages in newspapers became more explicit in the 1990s. During the same period, several daily newspapers expanded into media groups. The latter have launched popular magazines in which salacious and intrusive stories about celebrities and entertainers are the staple diet. The city has also seen a rapid growth in chain convenience stores where popular magazines are prominently displayed.

3.1 Several prosecutions against Next Media Group

In 2002, a Hong Kong actress, Pauline Chan, committed suicide in Shanghai. *Next Magazine*, a popular weekly from Next Media Group, published a photograph of her bloodstained body in a mortuary there. The publication of the photograph drew strong criticism, particularly from Chan's family and Hong Kong entertainers. The photograph was subsequently classified as Class II, and the magazine was fined HK$5,000.

Another incident again involved *Next Magazine* and its sister publication, the *Apple Daily* newspaper. In 2003, they published several photographs depicting child molestation by a private tutor, which were later classified as Class II articles. The two publications failed in their legal challenges to the OAT's classifications and were each fined HK$25,000 in 2008.

A different publication of Next Media Group, *Easy Finder*, was a popular magazine targeting teens and youths. In September 2004, the magazine was fined a record HK$250,000 for publishing an indecent article without a wrapper and warning notice, contrary to COIAO s 24. The article contained photographs and text depicting two youths' cruelty to dogs and cats. On appeal to the Court of First Instance, the prosecution agreed that a fine of HK$250,000 was excessively high, as the highest fine previously imposed had been only HK$100,000. The fine was ultimately reduced to HK$25,000 (*HKSAR v Easy Finder Ltd*, HCMA 1010/2004).

3.1.1 *Easy Finder* publication of Gillian Chung photographs taken in dressing room

In August 2006, *Easy Finder* published photographs of pop idol Gillian Chung showing her upper body wearing only a bra as she was trying on outfits in a private dressing room in preparation for a concert in a resort in Malaysia. The magazine did not disclose who had taken the photographs and how they were taken, although it appeared that a hidden camera was used. The incident caused widespread condemnation.

While media intrusion was the main concern, the TELA received more than 2,800 complaints from the public alleging that the photographs were indecent and should not be widely available on newsstands. Upon submission by TELA for a post-publication classification, the OAT classified the photographs and the accompanying text as Class II. The magazine applied for a review of the classification but failed to convince the OAT. The interim classification was therefore confirmed as final. In late 2008, the magazine was fined HK$30,000 for publishing an indecent article without proper wrapper and warning notice contravening COIAO s 24(1).

3.1.2 Complaints against *Sharp Daily*

The launching of *Sharp Daily* in September 2011 signified the entry of Next Media Group into the city's highly competitive free daily newspaper market. The newspaper quickly came under fire from sectors of the community and was banned by some schools. By early 2012, the TELA received 209 complaints from the public alleging that *Sharp Daily* contained content that was indecent, obscene, and promoted violence and gambling. The OAT issued Class II classifications in relation to 20 published articles, including an allegedly erotic novelette serialized in the newspaper. Eventually, *Sharp Daily* was prosecuted and fined in March 2012 for HK$110,000 for 11 articles published. In October 2013, Next Media Group folded *Sharp Daily*, admitting the free newspaper had lost millions of dollars.

3.2 Publication by *Eastweek* and *Three Weekly* of Carina Lau's nude photograph

Two other prominent incidents concerned the publication of an identical photograph. They resulted in the arrests of editorial staff and the subsequent jailing of a chief editor. In October 2002, *Eastweek* published exclusively a photograph of a topless Carina Lau, a well-known Hong Kong actress. Showing her in a distressed state, the photograph had been taken under duress when Lau was kidnapped a decade earlier. Although her eyes and nipples were pixelated, strong hints were given in the accompanying text revealing her identity. *Eastweek* claimed that the photograph had been sent to it by an anonymous source, and that it was in the public interest to publish the photograph to warn young girls about the dark side of the entertainment industry.

The magazine sold out within hours, but also sparked public condemnation with leading entertainers participating in large-scale demonstrations. Lau also turned up and spoke at one protest meeting. However, it was only years later, in 2008, that the actress publicly admitted to being the victim. Within days of publication of the nude photograph, the TELA received more than 1,000 complaints, and *Eastweek*'s owner quickly closed down the magazine as a gesture of remorse. Two days after *Eastweek*'s publication, another popular magazine, *Three Weekly*, published a follow-up story printing the same photograph of Carina Lau but in a smaller size.

Upon submission by the TELA for a post-publication classification, the OAT classified the pages of both magazines showing the photograph as Class III articles. Arrests and prosecutions followed. Both magazines launched legal challenges to the OAT classifications that lasted for several years. The *Eastweek* and *Three Weekly* were eventually fined HK$20,000 and HK$100,000, respectively, for publishing an obscene article. Two editors, one from each magazine, pleaded guilty to charges of publishing an obscene article and were sentenced to a Community Service Order. The conviction of another editor from *Eastweek* was quashed upon appeal because of irregularities in the police investigation (*HKSAR v Lee Sin Sau* [2009] 6 HKC 441).

The chief editor of *Eastweek,* Mong Hong Ming, pleaded guilty in late 2008 to a charge of publishing an obscene article and was given a suspended sentence of six months. The prosecution applied for review of Mong's sentence. In May 2009, the Court of Appeal removed the suspension order but reduced Mong's jail sentence to five months (*Secretary for Justice v Mong Hon Ming* [2009] 3 HKC 481). Thus Mong became the first editor jailed for a COIAO offence.

In the Court of Appeal's view, Mong had committed a uniquely serious offence calling for condign punishment: "The very idea that any responsible member of the press would contemplate publishing, under the guise of public interest, for that is all it was, a story of this kind, illustrated by photograph of a half-naked woman, taken when she was a victim of abuse, almost defies belief." Moreover, the Court of Appeal regarded Mong's remorse as "extremely shallow", noting that Mong only admitted guilt six years after the incident, having exhausted all legal manoeuvres, and that he managed to secure a lenient sentence at trial by giving the false mitigation that he was away from Hong Kong when the photograph was published.

3.3 Dissemination of Edison Chen's sex photographs

In Hong Kong's recent history, the most spectacular display of explicit sex photographs on the Web and in mass-circulation print media occurred in early 2008. Hundreds of photographs taken by Hong Kong pop idol Edison Chen showing him having sex with a variety of partners (one being Gillian Chung, while some others were well-known actresses or celebrities) were leaked onto the Web. For more than two weeks, batch after batch of sex photographs emerged. They attracted immense attention from millions of Internet users in Hong Kong and mainland China, who widely circulated the photographs online.

The incident brought to the forefront the chronic problem of regulating online pornography. The police quickly arrested a man for disseminating an obscene article online. In an attempt to put the situation under control, senior police officers further warned the public that even mere possession of the sex photographs might attract criminal liability. This was certainly a misinterpretation of the COIAO provisions, and soon turned into a fight for online freedom of expression.

Some Internet users quickly organized themselves and staged protests outside the police headquarters to support the arrested man. The police faced further criticisms when *Ming Pao*, a daily newspaper, submitted several of Chen's sex photographs to the OAT for classification. The photograph relied on by the police to make the arrest was classified as indecent and not obscene. The police dropped the charge against the man and released him, by which time he had already been in custody for about two weeks. The police came under severe criticism for their COIAO enforcement in the incident.

Meanwhile, many mainstream newspapers followed this saga closely and reproduced, on a daily basis on their front pages, some of Chen's sex photographs with private body parts pixelated. The TELA did not take action against the newspapers. Two popular magazines, *Next Magazine* and *Oriental Sunday*, even came up with special editions of the sex photographs. The TELA submitted the two special editions to the OAT for post-publication classification. The OAT first classified the publications as Class I articles but later re-classified them as Class II articles upon a review request from the TELA. The two magazines were eventually fined HK$35,000 and HK$30,000, respectively, for publishing indecent articles without proper wrappers and warning notices contrary to COIAO s 24(1).

3.4 Effectiveness of the COIAO being questioned

To some sectors of the community and parents, the above-mentioned prosecutions illustrated that the COIAO had failed to maintain public decency and protect minors. They complained that prosecutions had been too few and that the punishments handed down were often too lenient to have any deterrent effect. In *Secretary for Justice v Hong Kong Daily News Ltd* [2007] 1 HKC 563, it was revealed that the *Hong Kong Daily News* had 47 previous convictions for the same offence of publishing indecent articles without proper wrappers and warning notices contrary to s 24(1), but the fines ranged from only HK$3,000 to HK$80,000.

The newspaper applied for sentence review of several s 24(1) convictions in relation to photographs published in the newspaper's sex page. Dismissing the application, the Court of Appeal noted that the sentence handed down by the court would be far greater had the prosecution targeted the accompanying text. In the court's opinion: "The text is written in the unmistakable style of a pornographic magazine and had, it goes almost without saying, no place whatsoever in a daily newspaper."

Another illustration comes from the Next Media Group, which owns *Apple Daily, Next Magazine, Easy Finder, Sharp Daily* and some other publications. The group had more than 100 previous convictions for COIAO offences, with the highest fine of HK$50,000. Months after *Easy Finder*'s publication of photographs showing Gillian Chung in a private dressing room, the owner of the Group, Jimmy Lai, apologized only when asked about his views on a television talk show. After this incident and several COIAO convictions, *Easy Finder* survived and changed its name to *Face* in May 2008. In a similar move, *Eastweek,* which was closed down soon after the 2002 Carina Lau incident, resumed publication after a new owner took over its operations.

4. Controversies arising from COIAO regime and their impact on print media

The COIAO has attracted criticism from both ends of the spectrum. Some press groups and parents complain that the ordinance has not done enough to curb indecent content. Others, however, maintain that media freedom has been unduly restricted by the COIAO. Since its enactment, the ordinance has troubled journalists working for mainstream print media. Given the elusive definitions of indecency and obscenity, it is not easy for editors to anticipate what kinds of content might attract criminal sanctions. The COIAO regime is so complicated that it looks more like a maze. The operations of the OAT have been far from transparent and accountable, and its decisions not consistent enough. Over the years, these problems have been repeatedly exposed in legal challenges brought by local print media.

4.1 OAT operations: Questions of transparency and accountability

The OAT is entrusted with an exclusive role to decide on the nature of an article, i.e. whether it is Class I, II, or III, a function that higher courts cannot usurp. In several cases, however, judges from higher courts were critical of how the OAT had acted.

4.1.1 Lax approach and arbitrariness in classification

Two recent notable cases occurred in early 2007. They concerned the OAT's interim classification as Class II articles of several editions of *CU Student Press* containing a sex/gender column and a Sunday supplement published by *Ming Pao* in the form of a parody of the *CU Student Press*' sex/gender column. *CU Student Press* is a campus newspaper published by students of the Chinese University of Hong Kong, while *Ming Pao* is a mainstream daily newspaper with middle-class readers as the target audience.

The sex/gender column was a new item added to *CU Student Press* to allow more discussion of taboo topics. The column drew criticism, however, and came to the attention of the TELA when it ran a survey asking readers whether they had sexual fantasies about their parents and siblings and towards animals. Both *CU Student Press* and *Ming Pao* sought judicial review of the OAT interim classifications.

Ming Pao succeeded in its judicial review, and the OAT interim classification was quashed (*Ming Pao Newspaper Ltd & Anor v Obscene Articles Tribunal & Anor*, HCAL 96/2007, HCAL101/2007). Handing down the judgment, Justice Johnson Lam held that the OAT was wrong in assuming that what was submitted for classification was one article and for making an interim classification without distinguishing among the different articles included. He said such a practice would lead to a gross distortion of the character of the articles, and it also cast doubt on whether the OAT had applied properly the guidance stipulated in s 10 of the COIAO.

These two cases also exposed another defect of OAT operations. To prepare for its judicial review application, *Ming Pao* approached the OAT for further details of the interim classification. Three months later, the newspaper received a form from OAT recording its decision with only five Chinese characters scribbled on it. The direct English translation is: "picture, stick into the lower part of the body". In his judgment, Justice Lam said he could not gather the exact meaning of these five Chinese characters.

In the case of *CU Student Press*, one OAT form also consisted of only five Chinese characters meaning "text and pictures". The judge stated that the OAT had only paid lip service to its statutory duty to identify which part was indecent. Nor did entries on other forms convey any meaning concerning the part or parts identified as indecent. The OAT's interim classifications on *CU Student Press* were therefore quashed for failing to apply s 10 guidance and for failing to comply with the legal requirement of identifying which part of the article was indecent.

Justice Lam said these two cases served as a reminder that even in making an interim classification, the OAT is answerable to the courts. He observed that the exemption from a duty to give reasons for interim classifications had unwittingly caused the Tribunal to adopt a lax approach. The judge stressed that there is no room for arbitrariness or slackness, because the OAT is given the task for protecting the public interest in the preservation of public morals and in controlling the dissemination of indecent and obscene materials while OAT decisions also have bearing on the freedom of expression, a fundamental right cherished by Hong Kong society.

4.1.2 **Refusal to reveal names of adjudicators**

The above two cases of *Ming Pao* and *CU Student Press* revealed major flaws in OAT operations. It is regrettable for the OAT to adopt such a lax approach. Since the OAT sits in private in its interim classifications, the publications being classified cannot send representatives to the proceedings or argue before the OAT. However, this is not the first time that the transparency and accountability of the OAT has been called into question.

In *Eastern Express Publisher Ltd v Obscene Articles Tribunal* [1995] 5 HKPLR 247, the now defunct *Eastern Express* appealed against a decision by the OAT not to reveal the names of adjudicators who sat for an interim classification of an article from the newspaper. The judge hearing the case found no compelling reason to withhold the identity of adjudicators and remarked that such a practice was contrary to the interests of justice and not for the common good.

4.1.3 **Failure to give adequate reasons**

Another case criticizing the lack of accountability in the OAT's operations went all the way to the Court of Final Appeal (*Oriental Daily Publisher Ltd v Commissioner for Television and Entertainment Licensing Authority* [1998] 4 HKC 505). As mentioned, the OAT is not required to give reasons for any interim classification. There is, however, no such express provision in the COIAO for final classification or determination.

In 1996, the *Oriental Daily News* was prosecuted for publishing indecent articles without proper wrappers and warning notices contrary to COIAO s 24(1). The case involved photographs showing nude female bodies with the nipples obscured by pixelation. In determining that the articles were indecent, the OAT gave reasons that were in essence a recitation of COIAO s 10 without elaboration. The newspaper appealed, complaining that the OAT failed to give adequate reasons for its determination. The argument did not prevail in either the High Court or the Court of Appeal. The Court of Appeal held that the concepts of obscenity and indecency are notoriously abstract and involve value judgments difficult to express. Moreover, the indecency of the articles was overwhelmingly clear and the photographs spoke for themselves.

The Court of Final Appeal reversed the earlier rulings, holding that the reasons given were inadequate to discharge the OAT's duty to give reasons. They were conclusions rather than reasons. Under the common law, the requirements of fairness demand that the Tribunal should give reasons. The Tribunal should take a positive attitude towards such a duty, and not regard it as an additional burden.

Chief Justice Li described at great length various benefits resulting from giving reasons, which included ensuring that decisions are made on proper grounds, providing future guidance, promoting and enhancing the consistency of decisions, and engendering public confidence in the work of the Tribunal. Where there is a duty to give reasons, he said, it must be discharged with adequate reasons. The reasons given should show that the OAT has addressed the substantial issues before it and show why it has come to its decision. Unless the content of the articles virtually speak for themselves, merely reciting the statutory guidelines would not normally be adequate. Difficulties in expressing concepts of obscenity and indecency might have been exaggerated.

Apparently, the OAT has not improved its practices much since this Court of Final Appeal ruling in 1998. It took another decade before another judge had a further opportunity to examine the issue of OAT accountability in the *CU Student Press* and *Ming Pao* cases in 2008.

4.2 The early 1990s: Several OAT decisions that affected press operations

Since the early days of the COIAO, OAT decisions have at times caused much confusion. Two other appeals lodged by *Eastern Express* vividly illustrate the kind of unreasonable and unacceptable interference that the OAT could impose on the daily operations of the mainstream media (*Eastern Express Publisher Ltd v Obscene Articles Tribunal* [1995] 5 HKPLR 247). Ruling on the appeals, a High Court judge sharply criticized the OAT, saying, "These cases have, in my view, involved a great waste of time, money and valuable resources."

An advertisement in *Eastern Express* depicting Michelangelo's statue of David was determined to be indecent by the OAT in 1995. The Tribunal maintained that it was not appropriate for the newspaper to publish a photograph of a statue of a wholly naked male body with the penis fully exposed. In allowing the appeal by *Eastern Express*, the judge noted that he had never, until then, heard any sensible person suggest that the statue of David was indecent. He considered the OAT conclusion "totally incomprehensible" and one that could not have been reached reasonably given that the advertisement was published on an inside page of a serious English-language newspaper and was clearly intended to be read by normal, reasonable adults.

Another appeal concerned an article in *Eastern Express* featuring the wide availability of pornographic comic books to children. The article contained drawings depicting youth sex. The OAT classified the article as Class II, refuting the argument that the publication was for the public good. The High Court, however, pointed out that the OAT failed to appreciate that the publication was in a serious newspaper not likely to attract the attention of juveniles.

The judge also questioned why the OAT only mentioned the pictures but not the text. He concluded that the OAT had not given sufficient consideration to the newspaper's argument that the article — the pictures and the text taken together — was for the honest purpose of warning parents of dangers of which they might be unaware.

4.3 Since the mid-1990s: The unresolved problem of nude photographs

Indeed, local print media have faced the persistent danger of prosecutions directed at photographs, regardless of accompanying text. In 1993, *Ming Pao Weekly* published an article accompanied by four photographs (*Po Wai Loui & Anor v Obscene Articles Tribunal* [1995] 1 HKC 51). One photograph featured a nude pose by the singer Madonna and was captioned "the daring style of Madonna".

The OAT classified the photograph and its caption as indecent. The magazine was prosecuted for contravening COIAO s 24(1) by not having a proper wrapper and warning notice. The High Court dismissed a judicial review application from the magazine, holding that the photograph alone formed an article for the purpose of the COIAO and that the OAT could consider the photograph independent of the text.

The Court of Appeal, however, allowed an appeal by the magazine, ruling that the ordinance requires the OAT to examine a photograph illustrating a text in the light of that text and that the photograph alone does not constitute an article. Justice Godfrey stated that it was clear from COIAO s 10(1)(b) and (e) that the legislature expressly contemplated that articles, part of which might, standing on their own, have been considered obscene or indecent, would not be so considered when read or taken in context. He remarked: "To deprive a publisher of the possible benefit of that context by entertaining a submission of part only of an article appeared to me to be both illegal and a disguised threat to freedom of speech and expression."

Despite this Court of Appeal ruling, photographs have continued to be singled out for prosecution. In *Ming Pao Newspapers Ltd v Commissioner for Television and Entertainment Authority* [1997] 7 HKPLR 314, the OAT determined as indecent a photograph published in *Ming Pao* showing the front view of a naked woman. The full outline of the woman's breasts was clearly visible with nipples obscured by pixelation. The photograph accompanied a news story about a shop in Melbourne, Australia, welcoming nude customers on its anniversary.

An appeal from *Ming Pao* was allowed on the grounds that the OAT had been unduly restrictive in requiring that the photograph must provide further illustration or explanation to the text in order to have an honest purpose under s 10 of the COIAO. The use of a photograph to attract readers' attention to the news item being reported can be an honest purpose, the court said, except in the case of excessive and unnecessary nudity.

A crucial issue has remained unresolved: Does nudity equate with indecency or even obscenity? In *Oriental Daily Publisher Ltd v Commissioner for Television and Entertainment Licensing Authority* [1998] 4 HKC 505, Chief Justice Li said he did not consider the articles concerned obviously indecent, and noted: "I venture to suggest that if these photographs are considered indecent, the OAT would be coming close to holding that photographs of semi-naked females are *per se* indecent according to community standards. If that is the tribunal's reason, it should so explain."

In practice, mass-circulation newspapers and magazines are sold without wrappers to readers of all ages, and their editors regularly resort to pixels to obscure nipples of semi-naked females shown in photographs. However, as seen in the *Ming Pao* case concerning a nude customer's photograph, this technique does not always protect a newspaper from prosecution.

More recently, in a determination concerning the publication by two daily newspapers of topless photographs of model Kelly Brook taken by photographers while she was on holiday, the OAT says: "To avoid doubt, we wish to state that we are using the standards of moralities, decency and propriety that are generally accepted by reasonable members of the community. We find that it is indecent to expose the naked body of a woman and her breasts, despite the obscuring of the nipples in such fashion as adopted by the two articles. The body and breasts are given a large and prominent position, and the effect is further enhanced by the vivid language of the younger generation used to describe them" (*Commissioner for Television and Entertainment Licensing Authority v Oriental Daily Publisher Ltd & Anor* [2008] 1 HKC 192).

Apparently, OAT classifications have pressured editors to overact. In late 2008, the Chinese edition of *National Geographic* carried several computer-generated images of a naked Neanderthal woman. The publisher was cautious enough to put the edition in a wrapper coupled with a statutory warning notice so to avoid any violation of the COIAO. Commenting on this incident, the *South China Morning Post* in an editorial entitled "The Tribunal's Arbitrariness Makes an Ass of Us All" warned of the chilling effect that some OAT decisions can create.

4.4 Into the 2000s: Use of obscenity law to protect privacy?

To further complicate matters, the OAT has in recent years taken invasion of privacy into consideration when deciding whether an article is indecent or obscene. Obvious examples include Carina Lau's nude photograph in 2002 and Gillian Chung's photographs in 2006.

Three Weekly not only obscured Lau's eyes but also covered a large part of her breasts with a banner written with words "not acceptable by any standard", but the OAT came up with an interim classification as a Class III article. The magazine applied for a review of the interim classification.

In the review proceedings, the OAT noted that invasion of privacy and injury to the dignity of the person photographed are not relevant or legal factors for its consideration when making classification of the article, and that invasion of privacy or injury to the dignity *per se* is not sufficient to make an article Class II or Class III. However, when considering standards of morality, decency and propriety, the OAT opined, it must take into account the article's particular characteristics and all the circumstances, including but not limited to the fact that the article may involve the invasion of privacy and injury to the dignity of the person photographed and each case must be decided on its own merits. The interim classification was confirmed.

This approach of the OAT was upheld by the Court of Appeal in mid-2007: "The task of the OAT is to look at the intrinsic nature of the article in question from the vantage point of the reader so as to ascertain whether the reader or potential reader would be repelled or whether there would be aroused any revulsion. These circumstances could include the invasion of privacy and affront to dignity." (*Three Weekly v Obscene Articles Tribunal & Anor* [2007] 3 HKC 425)

In relation to Gillian Chung's photographs, *Easy Finder* argued in the OAT review proceedings that a photograph that is not indecent in itself should not become indecent simply because it has invaded privacy (*Easy Finder v Commissioner for Television and Entertainment Licensing Authority* OAG000164/2006). Rejecting the argument, the OAT followed Justice Lam's reasoning in *Three Weekly* that sometimes the obscenity or indecency lies in the publication of matters that a reasonable and decent person in our community would regard as undue invasion of privacy. The Tribunal further noted that this is a moral issue, and that according to contemporary community standards of morality, decency and propriety, reporting based on peeping at female bodies is an act that violates the moral standard generally accepted by the community.

A detailed examination of these two high-profile cases, however, may render the OAT classifications debatable. The report by *Three Weekly* following up on *Eastweek's* exclusive focused more on how the photograph was sent to media organizations and did not show Carina Lau's breasts. In the 2006 Gillian Chung incident, some might argue that *Easy Finder* was intrusive in publishing the photographs, but the entertainer was wearing a bra and no bare breast was shown. In sum, the photographs showing Lau and Chung are not indecent or obscene in a traditional sense. It is quite obvious that the invasion of privacy and the fact that the person being photographed was a not willing participant played a more crucial role in these OAT classifications.

The Hong Kong Law Reform Commission recommended in 2004 an expansion of privacy protection by proposing two statutory privacy torts. The Commission further recommended in 2006 that criminal sanctions should be introduced to punish certain acts of surveillance and covert filming. These legislative proposals met with strong oppositions from local media. As of late 2013, the HKSAR government has not acted on the proposals. Instead, the COIAO regime has taken an active role in curbing media intrusion. This trend poses greater difficulties for editors of mainstream print media in their assessment of what exactly the OAT would regard as indecent or even obscene.

4.5 Issues of comparables and consistency

The Sun and *Oriental Daily News*, two high-circulation sister dailies, have complained bitterly about OAT classifications. The topless photographs of model Kelly Brooks that they published in late 2005 with nipples obscured were classified as Class II articles by the OAT, whilst the same photographs published by *Apple Daily*, the two newspapers' main rival, were classified as Class I articles. The two newspapers applied for judicial review of the OAT classifications.

Dismissing the applications, the court rejected the newspapers' argument based on comparables (*The Sun News Publisher Ltd & Anor v Commissioner for Television and Entertainment Licensing Authority*, HCAL50/2006, 77/2006). The judge noted that the *Apple Daily* article had not used the same headings and captions. He added that any comparison would involve speculation, because all Class I articles that the two newspapers relied on were interim classifications for which the OAT was not required to give any reasons.

Also, *Eastweek* and *Three Weekly* in their review proceedings maintained that Carina Lau's nude picture and the related content should not be classified as Class III because some other articles, having more explicit contents, were only classified as Class I and II. The OAT rejected their use of comparables, noting that the content and nature of each article was different (*Eastweek v Commissioner for Television and Entertainment Licensing Authority*, OAT proceedings transcript: OAT/GOT/772/2002/Review; *Three Weekly v TELA*, OAT/GOT/775/2002).

In early 2007, three Chinese-language newspapers, *Wen Wei Po*, *Ta Kung Pao*, and *Sing Pao*, published the same photograph showing a nude female soldier. Upon OAT's classification of these articles as Class II, the three newspapers were prosecuted for publishing indecent articles without proper wrappers and warning notices contrary to COIAO s 24(1). *Wen Wei Po* and *Ta Kung Pao* pleaded guilty and paid the fines, but *Sing Pao* pleaded not guilty.

In the trial, the photograph was referred to the OAT for determination. This time, the OAT decided that the photograph was neither indecent nor obscene, and as a result, the prosecution against *Sing Pao* was dropped. When a legislator queried in the Legislative Council the OAT decisions in this case and in the case of Kelly Brooks' photographs, the authorities did not directly address the issue of consistency but apparently blamed the public's lack of understanding of the OAT's functions. This example is not unique. As mentioned, in early 2008, the OAT classified the two special editions of Edison Chen's sex photographs as Class I articles, but the same publications were classified as Class II articles upon review.

In September 2003, *Open Magazine*, a current affairs monthly specializing in China reporting, was fined HK$5,000 for publishing an indecent article without proper wrapper and warning contrary to COIAO s 24(1). It concerned a news story with photographs illustrating the cooking and tasting of human foetus soup by Taiwanese businessmen in mainland China. Three years later, the Taiwan edition of *Next Magazine* on sale in Hong Kong was fined HK$20,000 for publishing an obscene article when it came up with a story on the same topic illustrated with several photographs. These two incidents reflect not only the issue of comparables, but also the wide variety of topics, in addition to nudity and invasion of privacy, that might fall foul of the COIAO classification scheme.

Indeed, it is difficult for editors to predict how lay adjudicators will decide. As mentioned, the COIAO does not give precise definitions of obscenity and indecency. While the COIAO stipulates that the OAT shall have regard to the s 10 guidance, which is quite vague, in deciding whether an article is indecent or obscene, it does not require the OAT to follow previous decisions. Moreover, the administration considered it inappropriate to devise a set of classification guidelines for lay adjudicators to follow.

4.6 Problems with the adjudicator system

Other problems have existed in the adjudicator system for some years. The Director of Audit, who monitors the cost-effectiveness of government and public authority operations, revealed in his 2004 report that no new adjudicator had been appointed since 1996, pending the outcome of the 2000 review of the COIAO. As a result, by December 2003, the total number of adjudicators had dropped from 174 to 102 while those in the age group of 21 to 30 had dropped from 15 percent in 1997 to 1 percent.

Not only was the panel of adjudicators aging, but the bulk of the OAT's work had been taken up by 21 adjudicators who were more active than the rest. Some lay adjudicators were keener in attending OAT sittings than others. Doubts were expressed regarding the representativeness of adjudicators, and questions were also raised over whether the few eager ones in fact held conservative views. In response, recruitment of new adjudicators was stepped up, and the number of adjudicators increased to around 300 by September 2006.

Meanwhile, the problem of OAT adjudicators working under tight deadlines had been raised as early as 1997. In recent years, the OAT's annual caseload has amounted to some 70,000 articles. Most of these articles are adult VCDs and DVDs seized on the black market. OAT adjudicators do not go through the entire content of this hardcore pornography. In practice, they deal with the articles by their titles and only watch the first few scenes when determining whether these articles should be banned or restricted to adults. As such, adjudicators perform their job in a speedy manner. However, it is problematic to adopt the same approach in OAT classification of articles from mainstream newspapers. The Tribunal has habitually targeted photographs without paying adequate attention to the accompanying text.

4.7 Confusion caused by OAT's dual functions

The OAT is required to perform the dual functions of classification and determination. It is common for OFNAA (which replaced TELA in April 2012), upon receiving public complaints about a publication, to submit it to the OAT for post-publication classification. If the publication concerned is later prosecuted for a COIAO offence but the publication disputes the classification, the magistrate or the judge will during trial refer the publication to the OAT, which determines whether it is indecent or obscene, depending on the offence charged. This arrangement has been subject to criticism for some years and challenged on two grounds. First, does the earlier classification prejudice the subsequent determination? Second, the dual processes of classification and determination seem confusing and overlapping.

In the case of *Ming Pao Weekly*, Justice Godfrey, *obiter*, remarked that it is not necessary for a photograph to be classified prior to the initiation of the prosecution for obscenity: "If the submission for classification was made for the purpose of influencing the result of the criminal proceedings, it was an illegitimate exercise of power for an ulterior or collateral motive. The classification would be struck down on that ground as well." (*Po Wai Loui & Anor v Obscene Articles Tribunal* [1995] 1 HKC 51)

A decade later, the OAT's dual functions were again challenged in *Mong Hon Ming v Anthony Yuen*, HCAL 137/2004. Handing down the judgment, Justice Hartmann maintained that it was in the public interest to obtain an interim classification so as to prevent copy-cat publishing by newspapers or magazines of Carina Lau's nude photograph, thus protecting the actress from further exploitation.

Justice Hartmann explained in detail the major differences between the two processes of classification and determination. The OAT when exercising its jurisdiction to classify articles is a different body, possessed of different powers and subject to different procedures and rules of evidence, from when it is exercising its jurisdiction to determine whether an article is indecent or obscene in respect of criminal prosecutions. Moreover, the OAT in the determinative process will be composed of new lay adjudicators. As a professional judicial officer, the presiding magistrate will be able to give directions designed to counteract any prejudice, even an indirect residual prejudice, that Mong Hon Ming, editor of *Eastweek*, might suffer.

Justice Johnson Lam also decided against *Three Weekly* when the magazine challenged the OAT's dual functions. In a postscript to his judgment, Justice Lam nonetheless suggested that there should be a review of possible measures to confine post-publication submission for classification to proper cases, and to remove any appearance of classification as a pre-action ruling for the benefit of the prosecution, or an attempt to influence the determination process (*The Three Weekly Ltd v Obscene Articles Tribunal & Anor*, HCAL42/2003).

Further appeal by *Three Weekly* was dismissed by the Court of Appeal. The Appeal Committee of the Court of Final Appeal later dismissed the magazine's application for leave to final appeal. The Court of Appeal upheld the ruling of Mr Justice Hartmann in *Mong Hon Ming*, noting that the OAT is unique for having both an administrative and a judicial function in relation to the same subject matter, namely, obscenity and indecency (*Three Weekly Lt v Obscene Articles Tribunal & Anor* [2007] 3 HKC 425). The Court of Appeal stressed that the courts have consistently held that these two functions are entirely separate and distinct. It also agreed that post-publication classifications can serve the purpose of stopping any copycat re-publication, but it sided with Justice Lam in saying that care should be taken to ensure that different panels of the OAT should sit in the exercise of its different functions in relation to the same article, to avoid giving any impression of bias.

4.8 Not in line with obscenity law developments overseas

Enacted in 1987, the COIAO was not a Hong Kong invention but was modelled on obscenity laws from Britain and New Zealand. The classification scheme originated in New Zealand, where an indecent publication tribunal was established in 1963. However, newspapers in New Zealand have largely been subject to their own editorial policies. In the past few decades, only one issue of a newspaper was banned, and an issue of another student newspaper was classified as objectionable.

Australia also has a classification scheme, but it targets adult publications, not newspapers or news magazines. Furthermore, the classification schemes in these two countries have improved over the years. A two-tier classification scheme was introduced, detailed classification guidelines have been devised, and most classification officers are well-qualified full-time appointees.

In England and Wales, no classification has been introduced. The authorities have since the late 1970s refrained from using the Objectionable Publications Act to prosecute publications, except for hardcore pornography and books glorifying illegal activities such as the taking of dangerous drug. The mainstream press there, including tabloids, is therefore not under any threat of prosecutions for publishing indecent or obscene content.

Traditionally, obscenity laws restrict media freedom for the purpose of protecting public morals. Their implementation has nonetheless been controversial because it can be difficult to gauge whether the restrictions are justified. Community standards over what is obscene or indecent vary with time, place, and culture, and wide disparities can exist between the public standards of the community and the private taste of individuals. Fundamental differences of opinions exist as to whether pornography is harmful and to whom.

Moreover, there is often the danger that the authorities will curb the free flow of information and the right to freedom of expression under the pretext of protecting public morals. Excessive measures adopted in the name of protecting children, juveniles, and society could result in undue restrictions on what adults may read, hear, or see. In a modern pluralistic society, it is widely acknowledged that there can be many sets of community standards. The consideration of preservation of public morals therefore carries less weight than the need to prevent demonstrable harm.

Most Western countries have in recent years adopted a more liberal attitude towards pornography and have concentrated their efforts on combating child pornography and extreme pornography. The UK, for example, enacted legislation in 2008 criminalizing the possession of extreme pornographic material — pornographic images that are grossly offensive, disgusting, or otherwise of an obscene character and that portray an extreme act in an explicit and realistic manner. The latter specifically refers to bestiality, necrophilia, and acts that threaten a person's life or are likely to result in serious injury to a person's anus, breasts, or genitals. Indeed, the COIAO has not kept up with obscenity law developments overseas.

5. Reviews of the COIAO

In 2000, the HKSAR government published a consultation paper entitled "Protection of Youth from Obscene and Indecent Materials" (2000 Consultation Paper). This was in response to growing dissatisfaction over the amount of indecent material available in the popular press, as reflected in a 1998 TELA-commissioned survey of Hong Kong residents on the operation of the COIAO. More than 60 percent of the respondents said that articles advertising prostitution should not be published in newspapers and Class I magazines. Over 50 percent of respondents cited protection of juveniles from exposure to indecent publication as the primary reason for their objection.

5.1 The 2000 Review

The 2000 Consultation Paper reviewed the COIAO and proposed major changes to the ordinance and its related regulatory mechanism, in an attempt to enhance control over indecent publications. Many legislative proposals contained in the 2000 Consultation Paper were not well received. The media industry in particular expressed deep concern over the proposed "serial publication order", which aimed at tackling the problem of sex pages in newspapers.

The industry also had major reservations about the introduction of a new two-tier classification system, fearing that the classification process would become less independent and more prone to influence by the administration. The HKSAR government announced in January 2004 that it had given up these legislative proposals. As reasons, it cited divided public opinion and the enhanced operation of the COIAO resulting from effective law enforcement and public education.

5.2 The 2008 Review

In the wake of the 2006 Gillian Chung incident, however, the administration promised to review whether COIAO provisions needed to be strengthened, in particular in relation to repeat offenders, so as to enhance the deterrent effect of the ordinance. The 2008 Edison Chen sex photographs saga intensified calls for a review of the COIAO. In November that year, a consultation paper entitled "Healthy Information for a Healthy Mind" (2008 Consultation Paper) was published, signifying the launch of another review consisting of two rounds of public consultation.

The 2008 Consultation Paper was written in an open-ended format with many options proposed. A number of the proposals are noteworthy. The idea of having a two-tier classification scheme with an independent classification board to deal with interim classifications was again raised. If implemented, the OAT will only deal with appeals and determinations. The consultation paper also asked whether a detailed set of classification guidelines should be provided for the future classification board, and which agency should be responsible for drafting the guidelines.

Another proposal involved the selection of adjudicators from the list of jurors so as to make the OAT more representative. One proposal of great significance was to replace existing Class II articles with new Class IIA articles (restricted to persons above 15 years old) and Class IIB articles (restricted to persons above 18 years old). The 2008 Consultation Paper also raised the issue of whether law enforcement agencies should seek post-publication classification of an article before laying a charge.

In view of the Edison Chen incident, the 2008 Consultation Paper came up with several proposals tightening regulation concerning the dissemination of indecent and obscene articles on the Internet. They included a mandatory requirement for Internet service providers (ISPs) to provide filtering software, and the imposition of additional requirements on local ISPs, such as the provision of warnings when displaying indecent material and the installation of an access control system to authenticate the age of Internet users. Other proposals included asking ISPs to include terms in their service contracts prohibiting customers from publishing indecent or obscene articles and to adopt measures to limit the bandwidth of repeat offenders.

5.2.1 **Responses from the Judiciary**

In a high-profile response to the 2008 Consultation Paper, the Judiciary complained that review of the COIAO was long overdue and that the adjudicator system was highly problematic. The Judiciary noted that if all adjudicators held the same view but different from that of the presiding magistrate in a classification or determination, then the magistrate would be in a minority and would have to submit to the majority view. The Judiciary considered such a scenario inappropriate and undesirable. In addition, when appointing lay adjudicators, the administration first sent out invitations for self-nomination to potential candidates. The Chief Justice found that this arrangement made it difficult for him to identify suitable candidates and to vet nominations.

The Judiciary also voiced its strong and clear oppositions to the OAT's dual functions in its submission to the 2008 Review. The Judiciary maintained that it is highly unsatisfactory for the OAT to perform both administrative and judicial functions, and proposed removing the classification function from the Judiciary. It further expressed concern that the exercise of an administrative function by a judicial body may undermine the fundamental principle of judicial independence. The submission also noted that the OAT has been criticized for lack of transparency in its interim classification. When performing its classification function, the OAT operates as an administrative body and the principle of open justice in judicial proceedings does not apply. The public, however, may not understand and accept this. In addition, the OAT has given the public the impression that the Tribunal handles appeals against its own decisions.

5.2.2 The second round of public consultation conducted in 2012

The 2008 Review composed of two rounds, and the second round was launched in April 2012. The HKSAR government noted that the first round of public consultation confirmed general support for retaining the COIAO regulatory regime and the imposition of heavier penalties on offenders to enhance the deterrent effect of the COIAO. The 2012 Consultation Paper therefore contained concrete proposals to increase penalties for obscene and indecent article offences. The proposals also took into account indecent articles published by *Sharp Daily*, a free newspaper launched by the Next Media Group in late 2011 (see also section 3.1.2).

How to reform the OAT was the other major issue. The 2012 Consultation Paper put forward two reform options to alleviate serious concerns expressed by the Judiciary regarding the OAT's performance of both administrative and judicial functions. The first option is for the HKSAR government to set up a statutory classification board and a statutory appeal panel to carry out the administrative classification function of the OAT. The Judiciary will no longer be involved in the classification of articles. This largely follows the practices of regulating indecent and obscene publications in Australia, New Zealand, and Germany.

The second option is to abolish the OAT's administrative classification function altogether. This is in line with practices in the United Kingdom, the United States, and Canada. In adopting either option, the revamped OAT will be a purely judicial body performing only the judicial determination function. It will be led by a presiding magistrate, and the adjudicators may be retained or replaced by a jury system.

As a result of strong opposition from the ISPs, the HKSAR government backed down on its proposed regulatory measures in the 2008 Consultation Paper to clamp down on online dissemination of indecent and obscene articles. The 2012 Consultation Paper only proposed a regular review of the existing co-regulatory framework and updating the self-regulatory code of practice promulgated in 1997 (see also section 9 of Chapter 12), as well as stepping up publicity and public education. The two rounds of the 2008 Review have been completed, but as of late 2013, the HKSAR had not announced any legislative proposals amending the COIAO.

6. Child pornography

The COIAO does not deal with child pornography. The Prevention of Child Pornography Ordinance (PCPO, Cap 579) was enacted in 2003, imposing a total ban on child pornography, including its production, publication, copying, importing, exporting, or possession. When reviewing sentencing guidelines for the offence of possession of child pornography, the Court of Appeal reiterated that the aim of the PCPO is principally the protection of children from being exploited and abused for the purpose of pornography, and noted that this exploitation is of the worst kind because many victims were well under the age of 16 and were depicted in the most adult of sexual activity and conduct, in states of distress, or were even involved in sadism and bestiality (see *Secretary for Justice v Man Kwong Choi & Anor* [2008] 5 HKLRD 519).

According to PCPO s 2(1)(a), "child pornography" includes the pornographic depiction not only of a real child but also of an adult who pretends to be a child. "Virtual child pornography" composed of computer-generated images is also prohibited. The highest penalty for the offence of publishing child pornography is a fine of HK$2 million and a prison term of eight years (PCPO s 3).

This piece of legislation mainly targets paedophiles. In November 2006, however, *Easy Finder* became the first media organization prosecuted for publishing child pornography. It published photographs of a 14-year-old female singer wearing a wet T-shirt and a skin-colour bra underneath, which led to police investigation. Also prosecuted were its editor and printer. Acquitting the three accused, the magistrate found that the photographs in question did not depict the singer's breast in a sexual manner or context, and the prosecution had therefore not proved beyond reasonable doubt that the photographs amounted to "pornographic depiction" as stipulated in the ordinance. The subsequent appeal by the prosecution was also dismissed *(HKSAR v Easy Finder Limited & Ors* [2008] 4 HKLRD 555).

7. Conclusion

In sum, the existing COIAO regime needs to be reformed. There should be a statutory scheme that is more transparent and accountable and provides greater consistency and predictability. In addition, it should adequately take into account the right to freedom of expression and the free flow of information, not only in print media but also on the Web. Two opposing camps of distinct concerns exist — one criticizing the city's mass-circulation print media for sexual and violent content and their alleged corrupting influence on minors in particular and on the community in general, and the other focusing on the inhibiting effect of the COIAO regime on freedom of expression. Such a dichotomy is not conducive to reform.

Bad taste or vulgar content certainly offends sectors of the community, but more should be required to attract criminal sanctions. The outcome of the reform should not simply be the introduction of harsher measures and more severe penalties. A delicate balance has to be struck between media freedom and the prevention of demonstrable harm, so that a somewhat protective environment can be secured for child development while ample room is allowed for artistic and literary advancement and the exploration of new ideas.

The new arrangements should be in line with trends in a modern pluralistic society. The main aim of obscenity law should no longer be the policing of public morals. Obscenity law should instead concentrate more on combating extreme and child pornography. Meanwhile, media freedom is not absolute. In lobbying for a less intimidating COIAO, the city's mainstream print media need to convince the public by practising genuine self-regulation. The announcements made by *Apple Daily* in August 2012 and by *The Sun* in late 2012 that they would scrap their sex pages were a move in the right direction.

12

Media Regulation in the Age of Convergence

Yan Mei Ning

FREQUENTLY ASKED QUESTIONS

1. Do I need a licence to start a newspaper? How about an online newspaper? (See sections 2 and 9)
2. If something published in a newspaper leads to prosecution, who can be held liable? (See section 2)
3. What is meant by media self-regulation? How does it differ from statutory regulation? (See sections 2–5 and 7)
4. What are the major reasons for licensing broadcasting services? Why are television and radio stations subject to more rules than the print media? (See sections 1, 3 and 7)
5. How are broadcast journalists affected by statutory regulation? (See section 4)
6. What is meant by media convergence, and what impact does that trend have on regulation? In view of convergence, should there be any differences in the regulation of print, broadcast, and online media? (See sections 1 and 9)

1. Introduction

Principles and practices of Hong Kong media regulation broadly follow those of Western countries. First, media organizations enjoy media freedom in their daily operations subject to general media laws such as defamation, contempt of court, copyright, and obscenity. In general, the HKSAR government does not impose prior restraint on publications or exercise censorship on media content.

The Emergency Regulations Ordinance (Cap 241), however, governs measures on occasions of emergency and public danger. At such times, censorship or the control and suppression of publications and communications can be introduced by the Chief Executive (CE) acting after consultation with the Executive Council, a constitutional arrangement since colonial days for assisting the CE in policymaking, known formally as Chief Executive in Council (CE in C) if he considers it desirable in the public interest to do so.

Second, there are significant differences in the government's treatment of print, broadcast, and online media. Print and online media are largely left to self-regulation, but broadcast media are subject to licensing and detailed regulation. Broadcast journalists, unlike their print counterparts, are obliged to follow statutory codes of practice in their daily reporting routines.

Since the 1990s, however, there has been ongoing integration among the industries for broadcast media, telecommunications and computers, both in terms of technological developments and business operations. This trend of convergence has made the distinct regulatory regimes applied to print, broadcast, and online media highly inappropriate. Many governments around the world have realized that major transformations in media policies and regulatory measures are needed to cope with various innovations and challenges.

In Hong Kong, media convergence is best illustrated by the fact that most newspapers now have their own websites with some even carrying news reports in animated and video forms, and such items are readily accessible to all members of the public around the clock.

This chapter will outline the existing regulation and self-regulation of print, broadcasting, and online media in Hong Kong, with a focus on content regulation, a topic with which journalists should be familiar. While this chapter will also provide some overview on media ownership and fair competition, detailed discussion of these topics is beyond its scope.

2. Regulation of the print media

In line with common law traditions, Hong Kong does not have a Press Law detailing rights and responsibilities of the press. The repeal in 1987 of the Control of Publications Consolidation Ordinance (COPCO) brought an end to the colonial practice of imposing draconian rules on local print media. Controls and suppressive measures — such as a mandatory deposit for starting and operating a newspaper, wide inspection powers by the government of media organizations, and strict rules governing printing presses — no longer exist. The COPCO was replaced by the Registration of Local Newspapers Ordinance (ROLNO, Cap 268), which stipulates a relatively straightforward scheme of registration for newspapers.

2.1 Registration of newspapers

According to the ROLNO, any newspapers printed or produced in Hong Kong, whether for sale or free distribution, must be registered with the Registrar of Newspapers (the Registrar). A "newspaper" is defined as any paper or other publication available to the general public that contains news, intelligence, occurrences, or any remarks, observations, or comments on these or any other matter of public interest, and that is published at intervals not exceeding six months. The schedule to the ROLNO lists the types of publications excluded from the definition of newspaper, such as academic journals, cartoons, sales catalogues, and advertisements.

Registering a newspaper requires the furnishing of its particulars and those of its proprietor, printer, publisher and editor, and payment of an annual fee. As of September 2013, the registration fee is HK$905 and the annual renewal fee is HK$680. A copy of the newspaper has to be duly delivered to the Registrar on every day that it is published or on the following day. The copy should bear the signature, full name, and address of the printer or publisher, or his or her representative.

Distribution of newspapers for sale must be done through distributors licensed by the Registrar. Moreover, the Printed Documents (Control) Regulations (Cap 268C) require all printed documents, including local newspapers, to bear the name and the full address of the printer. The printer must retain for six months one copy of each newspaper printed and produce it to the Registrar upon request.

The ROLNO s 15 stipulates that the proprietor, printer, publisher, and editor of a newspaper have vicarious responsibility for any offence relating to the publication of matter contained in the newspaper. If prosecuted, the defendant can only be exempted from liability if he or she proves that the publication occurred without his or her authority, consent, or knowledge, and that the publication did not arise from want of due care or caution on his or her part.

By contrast, section heads, individual reporters, photographers, and sub-editors do not face vicarious liability. Usually, they are accountable only to their aspects of involvement in the preparation of news stories. Reporters and photographers are liable for offences committed in person during the newsgathering process. (For more detail, see Chapter 8 Other Restrictions on Newsgathering and Reporting.)

Proprietors are free to start as many newspapers or magazines as they like. No licence or prior government permission is required. The only existing restriction is on cross-media ownership. According to the Broadcasting Ordinance (BO, Cap 562), newspaper proprietors and their associates are barred from owning and operating any domestic television programme services, whether free or paid, but the CE in C can lift the ban.

2.2 Self-regulation of the print media

Newspapers and magazines in Hong Kong are largely left to self-regulation. The Hong Kong Press Council (HKPC), the first self-regulatory body for the Hong Kong print media, came into existence in 2000. In the past decade or so, however, the intrusive practices and objectionable content of some newspapers and magazines have become increasingly prominent and have attracted severe criticism from sectors of the public. Doubts have been raised concerning the sincerity and effectiveness of media self-regulation.

2.2.1 Origin of the Hong Kong Press Council

The origin of the HKPC can be traced to 1999 when the sub-committee on privacy of the Law Reform Commission of Hong Kong (LRC) published its *Consultation Paper on the Regulation of Media Intrusion* (1999 consultation paper), which sparked a major debate in Hong Kong over media self-regulation. The consultation paper recommended that a "Press Council for the Protection of Privacy" (statutory press council) be created by law to curb unwarranted media intrusion into privacy. According to the proposal, the HKSAR government would exert significant influence over the appointment of members to the proposed "statutory press council".

The body would have wide powers to regulate newspapers and magazines, as it would draft and revise for them a code of conduct for privacy-related matters (privacy code); receive complaints about alleged breaches of the "privacy code"; initiate its own investigations; conduct conciliations; and rule on alleged breaches. It could reprimand the newspaper found to have violated the "privacy code"; require it to publish an apology, correction or the findings of the body; or impose a fine. The maximum fine would be HK$500,000 for a first breach and HK$1,000,000 for subsequent breaches. Failure to publish apologies, corrections, or other matters as required would also be liable to fines.

These recommendations met with severe opposition from local media establishments and journalist organizations, which feared that media freedom would be jeopardized. The media sector acted promptly to strengthen self-regulation. In June 2000, four journalist groups — the Hong Kong Journalists Association (HKJA), the Hong Kong Federation of Journalists (HKFJ), the Hong Kong News Executives Association (NEA), and the Hong Kong Press Photographers' Association (HKPPA) — jointly devised the Journalists' Code of Professional Ethics. In July 2000, 11 newspapers, together with the NEA and the HKFJ, formed the HKPC.

Defending press freedom, promoting professional and ethical standards of local newspapers, and handling public complaints of media intrusion into privacy were the HKPC's major objectives. In July 2001, the council extended its remit to cover complaints related to prurience, indecency, and sensationalism. The council attained the status of a charitable organization in 2009. Its funding comes from subscriptions of member newspapers and public donations.

The council has both corporate members and public members. The former category comes from the member newspapers, the NEA, and the HKFJ, while the latter constitutes at any time more than half of the total membership. The HKPC constitution also stipulates that both its chairman and vice-chairman should come from the non-press sector. Professor Edward Chen, then president of Lingnan University, and Arthur Garcia, a retired judge and the territory's first ombudsman, were elected as the first chairman and vice-chairman, respectively. Professor Joseph Chan, a renowned communications scholar, has been the HKPC chairman since 2007.

2.2.2 **First decade of the Hong Kong Press Council**

At the outset, the HKPC was successful. It was formed within a relatively short period bringing together most of Hong Kong's daily newspapers. It also incorporated public members who were reputable and representative of a cross-section of the community. Serving as an excellent public relations exercise, the formation of the council sent a clear message to the community — that the print media were subjecting themselves to self-regulation, and any proposals for statutory regulation should therefore be shelved.

A decade later, however, an effective media self-regulatory regime has not been firmly established in Hong Kong. Two major requirements necessary for success are lacking: the existence of an industry-wide binding code of practice for journalists, and the creation of an independent body with adequate funding to enforce the code.

Although public perceptions of the Hong Kong media in recent years have been quite negative as reflected by polls, the HKPC received a total of only 319 complaints of media malpractice between September 2000 and December 2010. There were only 15 in 2003 and 16 in 2010. The highest number, 47, was recorded in 2007. The actual number dealt with by the HKPC was even smaller. A substantial proportion of the complaints concerned inaccuracy of news reports, which fell outside the remit of the council.

The HKPC upheld very few complaints, only six in 2007, for example, and two in 2010. Moreover, many complaints were directed at non-member media organizations, which mostly ignored the rulings of the HKPC and refused to publish any correction or apology. Indeed, three influential local newspapers enjoying wide circulation — *Oriental Daily News*, *Apple Daily*, and *The Sun* — have refused to join the council.

The HKPC unsuccessfully lobbied for a statutory qualified privilege to protect its statements and findings on complaints concerning non-members from defamation lawsuits. It was sued for defamation in 2003 by *Next Magazine*, a non-member and a sister publication of *Apple Daily*, after the council publicly reprimanded the magazine for publishing nude photographs of a teenage schoolgirl taken by herself.

The two major frontline journalist organizations, the HKJA and the HKPPA, also chose not to join the council. The HKJA does not favour the idea of a press council, arguing that it would have a chilling effect on media freedom and could ultimately affect media diversity.

As a follow-up to its 1999 consultation paper, the LRC published a report in 2004 entitled *Privacy and Media Intrusion* (see also Chapter 5 Privacy). In the report, the LRC proposed the creation by law of a commission (statutory commission) to deal with complaints of unjustifiable infringements of privacy by newspapers and magazines. The jurisdiction of the "statutory commission" would cover all local newspapers and magazines.

When a complaint against a publication is upheld, the "statutory commission" would have the power to advise, warn, or reprimand the publisher, or to require it to publish a correction or the commission's findings and decisions. If the publisher failed to comply with the ruling, the "statutory commission" would apply to the court for an order requiring the publisher to take the specified action and to bear the costs of the application incurred by the "statutory commission". The commission's members would enjoy immunity from civil suits, but not the commission itself.

The LRC report was silent, however, on whether the "statutory commission" would replace or co-exist with the HKPC. The HKSAR government has so far not acted on the "statutory commission" proposal.

3. Statutory regulation of broadcast media

Unlike the print media, broadcast media in Hong Kong are subject to licensing and detailed statutory regulation. Traditional rationales given for stricter control over the broadcast media include the scarcity of frequency spectrum, and the pervasiveness and intrusiveness of radio and television.

The Communications Authority Ordinance (CAO, Cap 616) was enacted in mid-2011 after long delay. It signified an important move to set up a single regulator, the Communications Authority (CA), to regulate Hong Kong's electronic communications sector. Coming into operation on 1 April 2012, the CA administers and enforces the BO, Telecommunications Ordinance (TO, Cap 106), and Unsolicited Electronic Messages Ordinance (UEMO, Cap 593). Upon the establishment of the CA, the Broadcasting Authority (BA), previously in charge of regulating licensed television and radio broadcasters, was dissolved.

The CA consists of ten part-time non-official members, a public official, and the Director-General of Communications (DG Com). Ambrose Ho, a non-official member and a senior barrister, became the first CA chairman. With the exception of the DG Com, all CA members are appointed by the Chief Executive. The DG Com, a public official and an ex-officio member of the CA, heads a new government department: the Office of the Communications Authority (OFCA). Serving as the executive arm of the CA, the OFCA also came into being on 1 April 2012 by merging and replacing the former Office of the Telecommunications Authority and the Television and Entertainment Licensing Authority (TELA).

3.1 The Broadcasting Ordinance and television programmes

The regulation of television in Hong Kong underwent major changes in 2000 with the enactment of the BO, which replaced the formerly separate regulation of terrestrial (or known as free-to-air), cable, satellite television and video-on-demand services contained in different legislation.

To cope with technological advances, the BO introduced a "transmission and technology neutral" regulatory regime which was supposedly flexible enough to embrace any new services made possible by convergence. This is done by grouping television programme services provided in or uplinked from Hong Kong into four categories, each of which belongs to a separate type of licence and is subject to different regulatory rules based on its characteristics, pervasiveness, and degree of influence.

3.1.1 Domestic free television licences

The first category is "domestic free television programme service" (domestic free), which is for reception by the public free of charge in Hong Kong by an audience of more than 5,000 specified premises, and primarily targets Hong Kong. Specified premises mean any domestic premises or hotel room. Having the widest viewer penetration, "domestic free" is supposed to be more pervasive and influential than other categories and is therefore subject to the strictest regulation.

As of late 2013, the two terrestrial television stations, Asia Television Limited (ATV) and Television Broadcasts Limited (TVB), are the only holders of this category of licence. This duopoly has existed for many years, with TVB dominating the Hong Kong television market and ATV in enormous financial difficulties.

3.1.2 New free television licence saga

Meanwhile, several operators currently offering pay TV services want a share of the free TV market. In late 2009 and early 2010, the HKSAR government received three applications for a "domestic free" licence from Fantastic Television Limited; Hong Kong Television Entertainment Company Limited, and City Telecom (Hong Kong) Limited (see also section 9 of this chapter). The BA, before its dissolution, recommended the HKSAR government to approve the three applications and granted them each a free TV licence. As for ATV and TVB, they have all along expressed objections and reservations, and have since then in turn sought judicial review actions.

In mid-October 2013, the HKSAR government announced the long-awaited decision on the granting of new "domestic free" licences. The CE in C decided that only Fantastic Television Limited and Hong Kong Television Entertainment Company Limited were to be granted a licence, while Hong Kong Television Network Limited (HKTVN) failed in its application. Previously known as City Telecom (Hong Kong) Limited, HKTVN adopted its current name in late 2012.

It was widely perceived that the HKSAR government had played on the safe side by granting two new licences to sister companies of the existing "domestic pay" licensees, namely, Cable TV and NOW TV. Free-to-air television is always seen as highly influential because of its audience reach. Not allowing HKTVN, an ambitious and relatively new television operator, to enter the free television market would avoid political uncertainty and any immediate major impact on incumbent operators, i.e. TVB and ATV.

However, the CE in C decision drew widespread condemnation. Large-scale protests and demonstrations followed. Many television viewers were unhappy that their choices of television programmes would continue to be very limited. They felt they deserved better television. Many people working in television, film and other creative industries were also dismayed because the highly unsatisfactory status quo of Hong Kong's free television remained largely unchanged.

There were also bitter complaints of unfair treatment of HKTVN, lack of transparency and accountability of the CE in C in its licence-granting decision, and little sign of rationality in the HKSAR government's broadcasting policy. In sum, the refusal to grant HKTVN a "domestic free" licence sparked off social movements demanding more viewing choices and greater accountability in government decisions.

Meanwhile, the CE and his top aides refuted the accusation that political considerations were behind the refusal to grant HKTVN a "domestic free" licence. They maintained that the decision was reached after all relevant factors were carefully considered and that the confidentiality of the CE in C decision-making process must be maintained. In early 2014 HKTVN sought a judicial review challenging the decision.

3.1.3 Other categories of television licences

The second category is "domestic pay television programme service" (domestic pay), which is for reception by the public, on payment of a subscription, in Hong Kong by an audience of more than 5,000 specified premises, and primarily targets Hong Kong. As of late 2013, Hong Kong Cable Television Limited (Cable TV), PCCW Media Limited (offering services to viewers as NOW TV), and TVB Pay Vision were holders of this category of licence.

The third category is "non-domestic television programme service" (non-domestic), which does not primarily target Hong Kong. In deciding whether a service primarily targets Hong Kong, factors taken into consideration include whether the service can be received in Hong Kong; whether advertising and subscription revenues come mainly from Hong Kong; the language of the service; the nature and size of the audiences targeted by the service, and whether the service is actively marketed in Hong Kong. There were more than a dozen "non-domestic" licensees, with Phoenix TV, a Hong Kong-based broadcaster serving mainland China, Hong Kong and other Chinese markets, the best-known.

The last category is "other licensable television programme service" (other licensable), which is further divided into two sub-categories: for reception in Hong Kong, whether free or by subscription, by an audience of not more than 5,000 specified premises (the licence requirement may be waived upon application if the service is for a single housing estate); or in hotel rooms. The former sub-category caters to niche markets. A licensee and its associates may apply for more than one licence, with an upper limit of 200,000 specified premises.

Subsequent to the enactment of the BO, the BA in June 2001 issued new generic codes of practice on television programme standards (TV Programme Code) and on advertising standards (TV Advertising Code); see also section 4. These codes have since been updated and amended from time to time.

The CA (taking over from the BA) deals with complaints from the public on alleged breaches of the codes and adjudicates on them. If the CA finds a breach, it may give advice or a warning to the broadcaster concerned. In case of serious breaches, the CA may impose a fine. Furthermore, it may direct a licensee to include a correction or an apology in its television programme service. These regulatory powers of the CA mark the major difference between broadcast and print media in Hong Kong.

3.2 The Telecommunications Ordinance and sound broadcasting

The BO, for the time being, regulates only television programme services. Regulation of sound broadcasting (radio) is beyond the remit of the BO and still comes under TO Part IIIA. Hong Kong Commercial Broadcasting Company Limited (Commercial Radio) and Metro Broadcast Corporation Limited (Metro

Broadcast), each operating three channels, are two holders of a sound broadcasting licence offering analogue sound broadcasting. Three new licences for offering digital audio broadcasting (DAB) services were granted in early 2011 (see also section 6.2).

Statutory provisions regulating sound broadcasting licences are quite similar to those for the "domestic free" licences in the BO. A licensee has to observe licence conditions and several codes of practice, including the Radio Code of Practice for Programme Standards (Radio Programme Code) and the Radio Code of Practice for Advertising Standards (Radio Advertising Code).

Meanwhile, Radio Television Hong Kong (RTHK) has for years been operating seven analogue radio channels and a television section, and launched DAB services in late 2011. No sound broadcasting licence is required for RTHK because it has been and will remain a government department. The broadcaster has nonetheless voluntarily observed codes of practice issued by the BA (now the CA) and is subject to its monitoring.

4. Broadcast journalism: Regulation and self-regulation

The TV Programme Code and the Radio Programme Code contain specific rules for the presentation of news and interviews for "domestic free", "domestic pay", and sound broadcasting. Broadcast journalists working for these licensees must abide by the rules stipulated in the codes, though the CA (formerly the BA) would not punish journalists personally for any violations but may issue sanctions against the licence holder.

4.1 Rules on accuracy and impartiality

The most detailed regulation is on impartiality and fairness. First, broadcast news should be presented with accuracy and due impartiality. Second, morbid, sensational, or alarming details not essential to factual reporting should be avoided. Third, in the case of television news, pictures should be carefully selected to ensure fairness: they should not be misleading or sensational. Fourth, sound effects, expressions, and other techniques characteristically associated with radio news should be reserved for the announcement of news.

Fifth, commentary and analysis should be clearly distinguished from news. Sixth, every effort should be made to eliminate "manufactured" incidents provoked by the presence of television cameras. Seventh, correction of factual errors should be made as soon as practicable. In some cases, it might require a print version. Lastly, no *bona fide* news programmes may be sponsored. Moreover, no advertising matter should be offered as news or included in a news programme or newsreel.

4.1.1 Two illustrations of BA's handling of inaccurate news reports

By 2011 the largest fine imposed to date for programme code violations was on ATV in relation to an inaccurate news story it broadcasted over two days in July of that year. ATV reported that former Chinese leader Jiang Zemin had died after a long illness, which turned out to be untrue. The broadcaster later retracted the story and made a public apology.

Receiving only 45 public complaints, the BA nevertheless noted that the incident had aroused serious public concern. In November 2011, the BA imposed a fine of HK$300,000 on ATV after finding the broadcaster in breach of the TV Programme Code for its inaccurate news report and the belated correction. In a rare move, the BA also regretted publicly that ATV had acted irresponsibly to the regulator's inquiry. (See more on a further investigation of ATV in section 7.1.2 of this chapter.)

The BA's response was noticeably milder for a similar error committed earlier by several other broadcasters. In November 2002, the BA upheld complaints by members of the public against Cable TV, Commercial Radio, and Metro Broadcast and advised the stations to more closely observe the statutory codes. No warnings or fines were handed down.

In that instance, the broadcasters erroneously reported in their news bulletins the death of singer Roman Tam, who was then critically ill and died soon after. The BA noted that the stations had not exercised adequate due diligence in reporting the news, and that the programmes did not meet the high standards of accuracy required by the codes of news reports.

4.1.2 **Due impartiality requirement for factual programmes**

The requirement of due impartiality is not confined to news programmes but is extended to any factual programmes dealing with matters of public policy or controversial issues of public importance in Hong Kong, with the exception of personal view programmes. Factual programmes are widely defined as non-fiction programmes based on material facts. They range from news, current affairs programmes, and personal view programmes, to documentaries and investigative reports.

In ensuring due impartiality, licensees are required to present opposing views even-handedly in their programmes. Furthermore, programmes should not be slanted by the concealment of facts or by misleading emphasis. Every reasonable effort must be made to ensure that the factual content of programmes is accurate.

Achieving due impartiality does not entail equal time or absolute neutrality, nor does it mean that principal opposing views must be expressed in a single programme. The codes allow due impartiality to be achieved over time. The licensees are supposed to exercise their own judgment. Meanwhile, programme hosts should encourage the widest possible airing of views. They should also be alert to the danger of unsubstantiated allegations made in live programmes and correct factual errors to the best of their knowledge.

4.1.3 Complaints against *ATV Focus*

In September 2012, the CA received an exceptionally high number of public complaints against five episodes of *ATV Focus,* totalling 42,000. The episodes consisted of negative comments on huge protests staged at the time in Hong Kong against the introduction of national education.

Looking into the complaints, the CA said the programme did give the public a strong impression of an editorial representing the stance of ATV. The CA, however, sided with ATV in classifying *ATV Focus* as a personal view programme. The CA noted that the existing TV Programme Code does not expressly prohibit a licensee from expressing its views in a personal view programme and is silent on the format and the presentation of such type of programmes.

The CA concluded that the five episodes had violated several rules set out in the TV Programme Code for personal view programmes, which include: (a) failing to provide suitable opportunity for responses; (b) failing to allow a broad range of views to be expressed on the issue of national education; and (c) providing inaccurate or misleading content.

But ATV was only given a warning by the CA to observe more closely the relevant provisions in the TV Programme Code. No fines were imposed. An OFCA officer told Legislative Councillors that a huge number of complaints do not necessarily attract harsh CA sanctions. Meanwhile, mindful of serious public concern, the CA launched a public consultation in late 2013 to review provisions of the TV programme code regulating editorial and personal view programmes.

4.2 Rules on fairness

The codes also set out a number of rules on fairness in relation to factual programmes. Generally speaking, the licensees have a responsibility to avoid unfairness to individuals or organizations featured in factual programmes. Programme items that are based on extracts of court proceedings or other matters of public record must be presented fairly and accurately.

In reports of criminal cases when proceedings have commenced, care should be taken to avoid presentations that are likely to prejudice a fair trial, including any pre-judgment of the issues in the case, and in particular of the guilt or innocence of the accused; any discussion of the merits or facts of the case that may prejudice the relevant legal proceedings; any comment relating to the character or conduct of the accused; and any comment or report that tends to impair the impartiality of the court.

The BA (now the CA) can investigate complaints lodged by the public even if the Secretary for Justice decides not to take action against a licensee for contempt of court. (For more on contempt of court actions, see Chapter 4 Court Reporting and Contempt of Court.) This again represents a major difference between broadcast and print media.

In the use of interviews, the codes require that editing should not distort or misrepresent the views of interviewees. Moreover, licensees should not misrepresent views of interviewees by broadcasting a previously recorded interview and presenting it as the interviewee's current views. When necessary to avoid confusion, viewers should be informed of the date the interviews were conducted. References to missing participants, whether they are unable or unwilling to attend the programme, should be made in a detached and factual manner. Care should be taken to ensure that their views are not misrepresented.

As for "dramatized" reconstruction based on actual events, the codes require careful labelling to prevent fictional elements being mistaken for fact. Meanwhile, two rules have been devised in relation to right of reply. First, licensees should take special care when their programmes are capable of adversely affecting the reputation of individuals, companies, or other organizations. All reasonable care should be taken to ensure that facts are fairly and accurately presented. Second, where a factual programme reveals evidence of iniquity or incompetence, or contains a damaging critique of an individual or organization, those criticized should be given an appropriate and timely opportunity to respond.

Licensees are also required to introduce a mechanism for presenters of news and factual programmes to disclose any potential conflict of interest in relation to their commercial dealings that may call into question the fairness or impartiality of the programmes. The licensees should then exercise editorial judgment and decide whether a presenter should refrain from discussion of relevant topics or whether a disclosure announcement should be made. Licensees also need to handle complaints from the public on such matters. Meanwhile, detailed rules have also been devised for personal view programmes to prevent views that are biased, partial, or based on false evidence.

4.3 Rules on privacy

Besides impartiality and fairness, the codes also stipulate rules to protect privacy. First, licensees should avoid causing additional anxiety or distress when interviewing, filming, or recording people who are already extremely upset or under stress. Furthermore, people in a state of distress should not be put under pressure to provide interviews. Funerals, for example, may under normal circumstances be covered with the permission of the family. Children should not be questioned to elicit views on private family matters, or asked for expression of opinions on matters likely to be beyond their judgment. Reporting of sexual offences against children should avoid identification of the child.

4.4 Self-regulation

Some broadcasters or their news departments have devised their own codes or guidelines for self-regulatory purposes. The most comprehensive is the "Producers' Guidelines" issued by RTHK, which are modelled closely upon the British Broadcasting Corporation's "Editorial Guidelines" (formerly known as "Producers' Guidelines"). These guidelines do not elaborate on how to deal with breaches, however.

5. More on content regulation of broadcast media

The television industry is subject to very detailed content regulation, which is not confined to news reports and factual programmes. Although the BA (now the CA) and the HKSAR government do not preview television programmes or censor their contents, the BO does contain inhibiting provisions.

BO s 36 empowers the Chief Secretary for Administration to apply for a court order prohibiting the inclusion of a television programme if the Secretary reasonably believes it is likely to incite hatred against any groups of persons defined by race, colour, sex, or religion, nationality or ethnic or national origins; to result in a general breakdown in law and order; or to gravely damage public health or morals.

Moreover, television advertisements of a religious or political nature, or concerned with any industrial dispute, are prohibited (BO schedules 4–7). Meanwhile, the BO prohibits subliminal messages and interference with the programming independence of licensees (BO ss 22–23).

Generally, content regulation is achieved through licensee compliance with statutory provisions, codes of practice, and licence conditions. "Domestic free" programmes are subject to the most stringent and detailed content regulation because they are accessible free of charge to the majority of Hong Kong television viewers and may therefore be very influential.

BO schedule 4 stipulates that a "domestic free" licensee is required to broadcast no fewer than five hours a day. The maximum advertising time allowed for each clock hour between 5 p.m. and 11 p.m. is 10 minutes. In the other hours of the day, the maximum advertising time allowed is 18 percent of total programme time.

BO s 19 stipulates that the BA (now the CA) may require a "domestic free" licensee to include without charge any educational television programme for schools supplied by the HKSAR government. Granted the right to use frequency spectrum, which is a valuable public asset, ATV and TVB have an obligation to provide a mix of programmes as required. Their "domestic free" licences contain many positive programme requirements, which specify, for example, the minimum duration a licensee has to allocate for news, current affairs, and documentary programmes.

5.1 Programme scheduling and standards for domestic free television

The TV Programme Code and the TV Advertising Code set out principles and rules on such matters as scheduling, general programme standards, taste and decency, protection of children, fairness and impartiality, and advertising. A licensee has to make editorial judgments in accordance with the codes.

In deciding whether a television programme complies with the codes, the BA (now the CA) gives consideration to factors such as type of licences; type, context, and merits of the programme; time of the day and circumstances under which the programme is shown, and the target audience; and whether clear and appropriate information about the programme has been given to the audience.

The TV Programme Code stipulates a "family viewing hour policy" for "domestic free", meaning that nothing unsuitable for children should be shown on any day between 4 p.m. and 8:30 p.m. Furthermore, programmes not suitable for children must be classified into parental guidance (PG) and mature (M) categories. The M category can only be shown between 11:30 p.m. and 6 a.m. Aural and visual advice on the classification of programmes should be given before the start of the programme. The classification symbol should be shown on the screen during the programme as required.

The BA, for example, gave advice to TVB in June 2003 to observe more closely the TV Programme Code in relation to violence upon complaints concerning scenes of goat killing in a programme. The imposition of fines is much less frequent.

ATV was fined HK$210,000 in October 2004 for three episodes of the programme *Catering Specialist II.* Ruling that the episodes had given undue prominence to the sponsoring restaurants that amounted to advertising for the restaurants concerned, the BA considered this a "blatant contravention" of the TV Advertising Code in relation to rules governing indirect advertising and undue prominence.

In March 2011, TVB was fined HK$120,000 for breaching the TV Programme Code that prohibits mingling programme and advertising material or embedding advertising material within programme content, and giving undue prominence to products and services of a commercial nature. The BA ruled that the showing of 41 segments related to a film entitled *The Jade and the Pearl* in a total of 28 broadcast days in two TVB infotainment programmes were gratuitous and amounted to promotion for the film.

On that occasion, the BA fined TVB another HK$40,000 for breaching TV Programme and Advertising codes by broadcasting a variety show that the regulator regarded as a tailor-made programme with an obvious intention to promote the same film, which was jointly produced by TVB, Shaw Brothers (Hong Kong), and others. Unhappy with these rulings, TVB nevertheless said that it would not lodge an appeal, complaining that the procedure was too time-consuming.

BA adjudications have from time to time drawn criticism. Two such adjudications occurred in early 2007. The first concerned a complaint of TVB showing on a Sunday afternoon *An Autumn's Tale,* a local award-winning movie. The BA found the complaint substantiated and advised the station to follow more closely the TV Programme Code.

The regulator said that the unedited version of the movie contained both offensive expressions, which should not be shown at any time, and coarse expressions, which should not be shown on a Sunday afternoon when large numbers of children and young people might be viewing. The BA decision sparked heated debate. TVB argued that any editing in compliance with the ruling would do injustice to the movie. Other critics challenged the adjudication as over-protective and conservative, ignoring the artistic context of the expressions.

The other adjudication concerned "Gay Lovers", produced by RTHK's flagship documentary programme *Hong Kong Connection*. The episode focused on same-sex couples and their desire for legalized marriage. The BA ruled that the programme was unfair, partial, and biased towards homosexuality with the effect of promoting homosexual marriage, and strongly advised RTHK to follow more closely the TV Programme Code in relation to: (a) the policy on family viewing hours, (b) the likely effects of television materials on children, and (c) the impartiality requirement of factual programmes. RTHK expressed disappointment, calling for public debate on the adjudication because it would affect future production of current affairs programmes.

An interviewee appearing in "Gay Lover" sought judicial review, and the High Court in May 2008 quashed the BA adjudication (*Cho Man Kit v Broadcasting Authority* (2008) HCAL 69/2007). The court ruled that the BA had misunderstood the TV Programme Code, resulting in an impermissible restriction on freedom of speech, and that the restriction was founded on a discriminatory factor, namely that homosexuality may be offensive to certain viewers. This incident represents a rare occasion in which the court intervened and overturned a BA adjudication.

Other earlier BA adjudications also highlighted problems of content regulation and the possible adverse impact such regulation could have on broadcasting freedom. In October 2001, the RTHK programme *Headliner* used characteristics of the Taliban regime to satirize the Chief Executive's annual Policy Address. The BA considered the complaints against the programme justified. It advised RTHK to observe more closely the TV Programme Code, noting that the programme as a whole "has failed to strike a fair balance among different viewpoints on the Policy Address, even allowing for the fact that most viewers were unlikely to take a serious view of the political satire".

RTHK expressed disappointment with the verdict, complaining that the BA had over-simplified the principle of impartiality. The broadcaster also disagreed with the BA's classification of *Headliner* as a current affairs programme, noting that the programme contained fictitious and non-factual segments. It further proposed the expansion of the TV Programme Code to include a category for satirical programmes to allow for diversity and creativity. As of late 2013, the CA had not taken up RTHK's suggestion.

5.2 Requirements for other types of television programmes

The other three categories, i.e. "domestic pay", "non-domestic", and "other licensable", are subject to less stringent content regulation. However, BO s 20 requires the provision of mandatory locking devices to these television programme services, with the exception of services to hotel rooms and "non-domestic" free-to-air services. Generally speaking, "domestic pay" is allowed more leeway by the TV Programme Code in relation to sex and violence, use of language, and protection of children, but is subject to the same rules as "domestic free" regarding impartiality and fairness, indirect advertising, and protection of privacy.

The TV Programme Code contains few rules for "non-domestic" licensees other than the general guidance that "the licensee should have respect for the cultural, religious and racial sensitivities of the intended recipient countries or places". This can be traced to the "open sky policy" practised by Hong Kong and many other countries.

Under the "open sky policy", it is for the originating country to ensure programme content compliance, and a recipient country generally does not impose restrictions on incoming satellite television. Nevertheless, as there may be different rules and regulations in different countries, the HKSAR government can only remind television operators uplinked from Hong Kong of the need to respect laws and customs in recipient countries.

Also due to the "open sky policy", BO schedule 3 clearly stipulates that satellite television uplinked elsewhere, not primarily targeting Hong Kong, and not charging a fee for viewing, is not regarded as a television programme service and is therefore exempt from licensing or regulation. However, licensing is required if the incoming satellite television service is on a subscription basis.

5.3 Notable BA adjudications on radio programme content

As mentioned, sound broadcasting services, all free of charge and accessible to the majority of the Hong Kong population, are required to fulfil detailed requirements on programme standards. In June 2006, the BA handed down the most severe penalties so far against a sound broadcaster for breaching the Radio Programme Code.

Two programme hosts of the Commercial Radio programme *So Fab* invited listeners to an Internet poll on the "Hong Kong female artistes whom I would most want to indecently assault". In addition to the imposition of a fine of HK$140,000 on Commercial Radio, the BA also invoked for the first time its power to order the broadcaster to include a public apology made by a member of senior management in its sound broadcasting.

The TO s 13M mirrors BO s 36, which empowers the Chief Secretary for Administration to apply for a court order prohibiting a sound broadcasting licensee to broadcast any programme or advertisement if the Secretary reasonably believes it is likely to incite hatred against any groups of persons defined by race, colour, sex, religion, nationality, or ethnic or national origins; to result in a general breakdown in law and order; or to gravely damage public health or morals. Furthermore, Radio Advertising Code para 28 provides that no advertisement of a political nature shall be broadcast except with prior approval of the BA (now the CA).

The debate on the ban on political advertising was brought to the forefront in August 2010 when the BA handed down two rulings against Commercial Radio. The first ruling concerned an appeal to "March for Universal Suffrage" broadcast several times on Commercial Radio during late April and early May that year. The appeal was made by Legislative Council member Emily Lau, who bought airtime to rally the public to join an upcoming march in support of universal suffrage. Holding Lau's appeal to be an advertisement of a political nature, the BA imposed a fine of HK$30,000 on Commercial Radio for breaching para 28 of the Radio Advertising Code.

The second ruling concerned two episodes of the radio programme *Night Rider 18* broadcast on Commercial Radio in early 2010. The programme was sponsored by the Democratic Alliance for the Betterment and Progress of Hong Kong, a major political party in Hong Kong. The BA found that the two episodes had the objective effect of promoting the image and interests of the sponsor and constituted "advertisements of a political nature", and imposed a fine of HK$30,000 on Commercial Radio for breaching paras 28 and 50 of the Radio Advertising Code. Para 50 requires a broadcaster to make clear announcements if any programme, or part of a programme, is sponsored, supplied, or suggested by an advertiser. After the BA's adjudication, Commercial Radio suspended the programme.

Some legislators and political activists maintained that the ban on political advertising is outdated and should be abolished or modified. Meanwhile, the HKSAR government was criticized for promoting its political reform proposal by airing "Announcements in the Public Interest", seen by some people as a means of getting around the ban on political advertising in broadcast media.

An adjudication made by the BA in 2003 is also worth mentioning. It concerned two episodes of Commercial Radio's phone-in programme, *Tea Cup in the Storm*. One of the programme hosts, Albert Cheng, challenged some high-ranking HKSAR officials for failing their duties and dubbed one of them a "dog-like official". The BA in its adjudication concluded that Cheng had not taken special care in the use of language that was capable of adversely affecting the reputation of the interviewees. It also ruled that Cheng had repeatedly interrupted the interviewees' attempts to respond and had deprived them of their right of reply. As such, the interviewees had not been treated fairly.

Commercial Radio was given a warning for each episode of the programme to observe more closely the Radio Programme Code on the right of reply. Commercial Radio disputed the BA's adjudication, maintaining that the host had not intended to infringe on anyone's right to speak, and that ample time had been given for responses.

This BA adjudication attracted more than 8,000 complaints, and some members of the public doubted the real motive behind the adjudication since Cheng had adopted an aggressive and provocative broadcasting style over the past nine years. The HKSAR government rejected any link of this BA decision to a potential clampdown on broadcasting freedom in Hong Kong. Commercial Radio, nevertheless, soon replaced Cheng and dropped this popular phone-in programme (see more on Cheng in section 6.2).

5.4 Two decades of BA adjudications

Between March 1990 and August 2010, the BA reached a total of 1,244 decisions on public complaints against broadcasting content, amongst which, 413, 412, 145, 100, and 91 concerned TVB, ATV, HKCTV, Commercial Radio, and RTHK respectively. Most common was for the BA to give "advice" to the broadcaster in question to follow the relevant provision(s) of the code(s) closely, amounting to 424.

There were 296 instances of "serious advice". The BA also issued 151 "warnings" and 93 "serious warnings". In the past two decades, the BA imposed financial sanctions on broadcasters breaching the codes on only 45 occasions and only once did the BA demand that the broadcaster make a public apology (see also BA ruling on Commercial Radio's *So Fab* programme in section 5.3 above).

As mentioned, some BA adjudications have been subject to widespread public criticism for inducing a chilling effect on broadcasting freedom and even leading to censorship in disguise. The HKSAR government nevertheless did not take the opportunity to shape the CA to address longstanding problems faced by the BA.

Calls for an independent secretariat and a full-time chairman have been ignored. The CA does not satisfy the general requirements of a regulatory body, namely, independence, transparency, accountability, and competence. All non-official CA members, including the chairman, are part-timers handpicked by the administration. Like its predecessor, the CA depends heavily upon government officials for administrating detailed content regulation.

6. Technical regulations and digital terrestrial broadcasting

Regulation of broadcast media in Hong Kong also involves technical aspects. In the case of television, rules and arrangements concerning technical matters are provided in the BO, licence conditions, and in the "Generic Code of Practice on Television Technical Standards". BO s 18 requires a "domestic free" licensee to enable the reception of the service throughout Hong Kong within a specified time period to the satisfaction of the BA (now the CA). The same provision requires a "domestic pay" licensee to provide service to parts of Hong Kong as specified in the licence.

6.1 Transition to digital terrestrial television

In recent years, the most important issue regarding technical regulation has been the transition to digital terrestrial broadcasting. The HKSAR government in 2000 conducted a public consultation on the introduction of digital terrestrial television (DTT), but met with severe opposition from ATV and TVB, particularly with the choice of DTT standard. The objections were so vigorous that the HKSAR government conducted a second consultation in 2003 with concessions made. More negotiations were followed by further concessions.

Finally, the CE in C in July 2004 adopted a plan to implement DTT. The finalized plan places no restrictions on the maximum number of multiplexes each operator is allowed. (A multiplex, by deploying DTT compression technology, carries several television programme services on the same frequency channel.) The original proposal of restricting an operator to two multiplexes was dropped.

ATV and TVB share one multiplex in transmitting their simulcasting services during the transition. On top of that, they were each given one multiplex for launching their new high definition television broadcasting services. The remaining two multiplexes will be assigned at a later stage. This amended multiplex allocation favours existing terrestrial broadcasters and is likely to have an adverse impact on media plurality and diversity.

ATV and TVB eventually launched DTT broadcasting in phases from the end of 2007. Simulcasting of digital and analogue television is offered during the transitional period, with the HKSAR government planning to switch off analogue television services in five years' time, i.e. at the end of 2012.

By May 2011, the coverage of DTT was extended to over 95 percent of the population. The DTT penetration nonetheless stood at about 63 percent in March 2011 and the take-up rate for DTT slowed down. The proposed date for switching off analogue television services has therefore been deferred to the end of 2015 so as to allow more time for ATV and TVB to expand their DTT coverage to at least 98 percent of the population and for more viewers to take up DTT viewing.

6.2 Introduction of digital audio broadcasting

Sound broadcasting is likewise subject to technical regulation. Technical trials for digital audio broadcasting (DAB) were first conducted in Hong Kong in 1998. Nonetheless, the HKSAR government in its 2000 and 2003 consultation papers only promoted the development of DTT and preferred to leave the launching of DAB services entirely to interested private enterprises. It was almost a decade later, in late 2009, that the HKSAR government endorsed the development of DAB and decided to release one of the four multiplexes suitable for DAB services.

In March 2011, three DAB licences, for a period of 12 years subject to a mid-term review, were granted to Digital Broadcasting Corporation Hong Kong Limited (DBC) (formerly known as Wave Media), Metro Broadcast, and Phoenix U Radio Limited. DBC was the most prominent DAB operator. Headed by Albert Cheng, DBC was widely regarded as a comeback for Cheng (and possibly his style of broadcasting) following his departure from Commercial Radio in 2004.

The HKSAR government has also assigned five DAB channels to RTHK. According to plan, a total of 18 free-to-air DAB channels were to be available to the Hong Kong public by late 2012. Besides 24-hour sound broadcasting, DAB channels will also offer ancillary visual services. The BA issued new codes of practice to regulate these new ancillary visual services and advertising. On the other hand, DAB services will not be subject to any positive programme requirements.

Several aspects of DAB development in Hong Kong are noteworthy. As mentioned, it took a decade before the HKSAR government changed its mind and started promoting DAB services. Amongst the two incumbent analogue sound broadcasters, only Metro Broadcast was willing to venture into DAB. Commercial Radio withdrew its DAB licence application, stating that it would opt for improving webcasting and reception via mobile phones.

Indeed, online radio broadcasting has gained considerable popularity since 2000. This makes it more difficult to convince incumbent broadcasters to invest in DAB transmission facilities and to persuade listeners to buy DAB radio sets. More significantly, DAB services are now seen as a supplement to rather than a replacement for existing analogue broadcasting services. Upon granting the DAB licences, the HKSAR government made it clear that it currently had no plan to switch off analogue AM/FM radio services.

A further twist occurred in October 2012 when DBC closed down its operations. Cheng, as a prominent co-founder of the station, blamed several DBC investors for failing to live up to their financial commitments because of political pressure from Beijing, an accusation openly refuted by one major investor. The CA imposed a fine of HK$80,000 on DBC in November for interruption of services.

The CA further suggested in mid-December 2012 to suspend the station's licence for 30 days. DBC was given 28 days to respond. The feuding DBC investors came to a truce before the deadline and the station resumed broadcasting in late January 2013. Cheng, however, left DBC to launch a new webcasting venture of his own.

Another DAB operator, Phoenix U Radio, apparently encountered problems in the rolling out of its services. The launch of the station's second and third channels was delayed. In August 2013, the station again applied to postpone the launch of its third channel and was given one extra year by the CA.

Indeed, performances of DBC and Phoenix U Radio did not live up to their licence conditions. This together with the decision by Commercial Radio not to apply for a DAB licence, and the increasing popularity of webcasting via reception by mobile phones (the operation of which does not require any licence) raised further queries about traditional sound broadcasting licensing in the age of convergence.

7. Licensing and ownership regulation of broadcast media

In addition to regulation of programme content and technical matters, there are very comprehensive regulations governing licensing and ownership of broadcast media, and the structure of broadcasting industry.

7.1 Television programme service licences

BO s 5 stipulates that it is illegal to provide a broadcasting service without a licence or not in accordance with licence conditions. Any breach may result in a fine of up to HK$1 million and a prison term of up to five years. Licences for "domestic free" and "domestic pay" are granted by the CE in C with recommendations from the BA (now the CA), while licences for "non-domestic" and "other licensable" are granted by the BA (now the CA).

Licences can be renewed, suspended, or revoked. BO s 21 provides that a licensee and any person in control of the licensee shall be a fit and proper person, taking into account business and criminal records, etc.

The "domestic free" licences for ATV and TVB were last renewed for a period of 12 years from December 2003 to November 2015. A mid-term review of their performance was conducted in early 2010. As "domestic free" licensees, ATV and TVB are required to implement approved plans on capital investment and programme development.

The BO only governs the provision of television programme services. For transmission of these services, the licensees still need to obtain telecommunications licences under the TO or to hire licensed telecommunications facilities.

7.1.1 **Residency requirement**

The BO stipulates ownership rules, including residency requirements and cross-media ownership restrictions. To encourage investment in the broadcasting industry, the present regulatory regime does not restrict foreign ownership. Instead, residency requirements are imposed on the licensees.

Again, "domestic free" licensees are subject to the strictest residency requirements. A "domestic free" licensee must be a company incorporated in Hong Kong and should not be a subsidiary of a corporation. This is to ensure that the licensee remains an independent entity with management and control free from interference from other companies.

The company must also fulfil the specified residency requirement set out in BO s 8 to ensure that it is more likely to have the best interests of Hong Kong at heart. Except with prior approval by the BA (now the CA), the majority of the company's directors and principal officers, including the principal officer in charge of the selection, production or scheduling of television programmes, must be "ordinarily resident" in Hong Kong and must have been so for at least seven continuous years. For an individual, "ordinarily resident" means that he is currently residing in Hong Kong for at least 180 days a year or 300 days in any two consecutive years.

For a company, "ordinarily resident" means that the control and management of the company is *bona fide* exercised in Hong Kong, and the majority of its directors who actively participate in the company (if the number is two, then the rule applies to both of them) are currently "ordinarily resident" in Hong Kong and have been so for at least seven continuous years.

According to BO schedule 1 part 3, prior written approval of the BA (now the CA) is required for those voting controllers who do not satisfy the above-mentioned residency requirement (i.e. unqualified voting controllers) to hold, acquire, or exercise 2 percent or more of the total voting control of the licensee company.

Furthermore, except for matters otherwise specified, votes cast by unqualified voting controllers on a poll at any general meeting of the licensee company shall be attenuated to 49 percent of the total voting control of the licensee company in accordance with the formula stipulated in the BO.

7.1.2 **Investigation of ATV**

The investigation of ATV was notable in recent years as it highlighted the exercise of regulatory power by the BA (now CA) over local television stations' ownership and governance. In June 2011, the BA received a complaint alleging that Wong Ching, a mainland Chinese businessman, was actively involved in ATV's day-to-day operations in violation of his undertaking not to do so. Wong became ATV's major investor in early 2010, but he did not satisfy the residency requirement and was neither a shareholder, director nor principal officer of ATV. The BA also took into account wide public concerns after ATV's erroneous Jiang Zemin death report as to whether Wong had interfered with the ATV news department.

The BA began its investigation on ATV in July 2011 to see if there had been breaches of licence conditions and violations of BO statutory requirements. The BA sent a draft report on the investigation to ATV in March 2012 detailing the provisional findings and proposed sanctions. But ATV sought judicial review to compel the CA (BA was dissolved in April 2012) to disclose identities of confidential interviewees upon whose evidence the CA relied and to quash a CA decision concerning the release of the report.

The CA eventually published the investigation report in August 2013, soon after ATV's legal challenges were dismissed by the Appeal Committee of the Court of Final Appeal. The CA report concluded that Wong had been exercising *de facto* control of ATV and that Wong and ATV were respectively in breach of his non-control undertaking and a licence condition. The CA imposed a fine of HK$ 1 million on ATV.

The CA also found that James Shing, ATV's Executive Director, was no longer a "fit and proper person" for the purpose of s 21 of the BO because Shing seldom made decisions and permitted Wong to exercise unduly interference in the station's management and operations. The CA therefore issued a direction to ATV requiring Shing cease to act as a person exercising control of ATV including being a director.

The CA further directed ATV to: a) ensure Wong would refrain from exercising *de facto* control of ATV; b) take immediate actions to prevent similar situations from happening again; and c) submit a report to CA within three months on how to improve its corporate governance. Nonetheless, the CA found ATV was still a "fit and proper person" and refrained from revoking its licence.

7.1.3 **Rules on cross-media ownership**

In addition to the residency requirement, the BO imposes restrictions on cross-media ownership to minimize conflicts of interest and editorial uniformity among licensees, and to prevent formation of monopolies in the media market. Again, "domestic free" licensees are subject to stricter rules than the other three categories of licensees.

The BO stipulates that a "disqualified person" shall not hold a "domestic free" licence or exercise control of it. BO schedule 1 part 2 defines a "disqualified person" as a licensee of any of the four categories of television programme services, a sound broadcasting licensee, advertising agencies, and proprietors of local newspapers, including people exercising control of any of the above and their associates.

People exercising control of a corporation include its directors or principal officers, those who own or control more than 15 percent of its voting shares, or any person who has been formally assured that the affairs of the corporation have to be conducted in accordance with his or her wishes. The meaning of associate is even wider, covering relatives or business partners.

The CE in C may nonetheless lift the "cross-media ownership" restrictions for a public interest reason, after considering factors such as the effect on competition in the relevant service market, the extent to which viewers will be offered more diversified television programme choices, the impact on the development of the broadcasting industry, and the overall benefit to the economy.

7.1.4 Less strict ownership rules applicable to other types of licensees

Comparatively speaking, with regard to residency requirements and cross-media ownership rules, the BO imposed lesser restrictions on the other three categories of licensees. Apart from several differences, a "domestic pay" licensee is subject to similar ownership rules as a "domestic free" licensee.

First, a "domestic pay" licensee can be a subsidiary of a corporation. Second, no restriction is imposed on voting control of "unqualified voting controllers". Third, a "non-domestic" licensee may at the same time hold a "domestic pay" licence. As for the "non-domestic" and "other licensable" licensees, they are not subject to any cross-media ownership rules and are only required to have at least one director or principal officer to satisfy the stipulated residency requirement.

7.1.5 Competition rules

In revamping its broadcasting regulatory regime in 2000, the HKSAR government followed the prevailing worldwide trend by opting for further ownership deregulation. Fair competition clauses, formerly incorporated only in licences, were for the first time included in legislation aimed at providing a level playing field for both incumbent licensees and new entrants.

BO s 13 applies to all players in the market and deals with anti-competitive practices generally. It forbids a licensee from engaging in conduct that has the purpose or effect of preventing, distorting or substantially restricting competition in a television programme service market. BO s 14 is a specific provision prohibiting a dominant licensee from abusing its position. A dominant licensee is one that is able to act without significant competitive restraint from its competitors and customers. To facilitate the implementation of the competition provisions, the BA promulgated in 2001 two documents — "Guidelines to the Application of the Competition Provisions of the BO" and "Competition Investigation Procedures".

In mid-2012, the Legislative Council enacted the Competition Ordinance (CO, Cap 619). This legislation is to be implemented in phases from 2013. The first conduct rule and the second conduct rule specified in the CO would replace BO ss 13 and 14, respectively. The CA, however, has concurrent jurisdiction with the Competition Commission (CC) in handling competition matters regarding TV licensees and sound broadcasting licensees, and a memorandum will govern any transfer of cases between the CA and the CC (see CO ss 159–161).

In September 2013, the CA for the first time determined that a TV licensee had violated the anti-competitive provisions. Previously, eight other complaints of anti-competitive practices had all been dismissed by the former BA as unsubstantiated. This decision by the CA could bring significant changes to the HK television industry by breaking the effective monopoly that TVB has long enjoyed.

In late 2009, ATV lodged a complaint with the then BA that certain clauses in TVB's contracts with TV artists and some informal policies and practices pursued by TVB had the purpose or effect of preventing, distorting and substantially restricting competition, thus violating ss 13 and 14 of the BO. After a full investigation lasting for two years, the CA concluded that four of the ATV allegations were substantiated.

The CA investigations showed that TVB had hired a significant proportion of Hong Kong TV artists and some 90 percent of Hong Kong singers. Many of them, however, were not full-time TVB employees; they only worked for TVB occasionally or on one-off basis. Even so, their exclusive contracts with TVB contained harsh and unreasonable terms. Some clauses prevented them from working with other TV stations. Other clauses barred them from speaking Cantonese in public or private functions where footages would be aired by TV stations other than TVB.

The CA announced that TVB had to pay a fine of HK$900,000 for its violations of the BO anti-competitive provisions, that it must end such practices and policies, that it must within three months inform all those affected of its abandonment of the anti-competitive measures, and that it must submit a full written report to the CA within four month detailing the remedies it had taken. TVB disagreed with the CA findings and denied that it had adopted any anti-competitive policies or practices. In mid-October 2013, the broadcaster lodged an appeal to the CE in C against the CA decision.

7.1.6 **Doubts about regulatory effectiveness**

Since 2000, questions have been raised over the effectiveness of regulating Hong Kong television, particularly in respect of competition rules and cross-media ownership restrictions. The BA dealt with a total of nine competition complaints. The regulator ruled eight complaints unsubstantiated.

The CE in C has lifted the ban on cross-media ownership on a number of occasions. The granting of a "domestic pay" licence to Galaxy in 2000 has been the most controversial. Galaxy was then a wholly-owned subsidiary of TVB, which has dominated Hong Kong television market for decades.

In October 2013, sister companies of the other two "domestic pay" licencees, Cable TV and NOW TV, were each granted a "domestic free" licence. In other words, all three big players — TVB, NOW TV and Cable TV — are to offer both free and pay television. The differentiation between "domestic free" and "domestic pay" licences in the BO and the imposition of cross-media ownership restrictions on them seem to be superfluous. It is also worrisome that the Hong Kong television market might become too concentrated, and the welfare of viewers and new entrants to the television market may not be properly protected.

7.2 Sound broadcasting licences

Licences for establishing and operating sound broadcasting services are granted by the CE in C under TO Part IIIA with recommendations from the BA (now the CA). The licensee must be a company incorporated in Hong Kong and should not be a subsidiary of a corporation. It has to observe residency requirements and cross-media ownership restrictions largely similar to those of "domestic free" licensees.

The rationales behind these strict rules are stated in the licence: the radio frequency spectrum assigned to a licensee is not the property of the licensee but that of the community, and the licensee has to make proper use of the frequency in the best interests of the whole community and accept regulation as necessary and justified because radio programmes go freely into homes and may be readily listened to by children and adults.

Licences for Commercial Radio and Metro Broadcast to provide analogue sound broadcasting services were last renewed in mid-2003 for a period of 12 years from August 2004 to August 2016 with a mid-term review conducted in mid-2010. As mentioned, three DAB licences were granted in early 2011.

Sound broadcasters were previously only required to abide by competition clauses in their licence. But once the CO comes into operation, licensed sound broadcasters, like licensed television operators, will be subject to the first and second conduct rules stipulated in the ordinance.

7.2.1 Prosecutions for illicit broadcasting

In recent years, Hong Kong has seen the emergence and persistence of pirate broadcasting. The sudden departure of Albert Cheng and several other prominent programme hosts from Commercial Radio in 2004 and 2005 led to allegations of self-censorship by radio stations. To promote broadcasting freedom, some activists launched web-based radio stations and called for the introduction of community radio.

A couple of web-based radio stations also started illicit terrestrial sound broadcasting to assert their right to broadcast. On air since October 2005, Citizens' Radio has been the most active unlicensed broadcaster offering FM broadcasting on a sporadic basis. The police and officers from the Office of Telecommunications Authority (now dissolved and absorbed into the OFCA) raided the station and seized its transmitting equipment in August 2006.

Six defendants including Ocean Technology Limited, the company that owns Citizens' Radio, were prosecuted on 14 charges contravening TO ss 8(1) and 20 between July 2005 and October 2006 (*Secretary for Justice v Ocean Technology Ltd & Ors* [2009] 1 HKC 271). These provisions make it an offence to establish or maintain any means of telecommunications save under and in accordance with a licence granted by the CE in C. The maximum penalty for summary conviction can be a jail term of two years and a fine of HK$50,000 whilst that for an indictment conviction can be a jail term of five years and a fine of HK$100,000.

The magistrate hearing the case declared the relevant legislative provisions unconstitutional and dismissed all charges against the accused. The decision was however reversed by the Court of Appeal, and leave to appeal to the Court of Final Appeal was refused. The case was sent back to the magistrate's court, and the defendants were eventually convicted and fined a total of HK$42,000 on 14 charges.

Citizens' Radio and other unlicensed broadcasters have continued their illicit broadcasting in defiance of further raids and threats of prosecution. Meanwhile, several prominent legislators and political activists who appeared as guests at an outdoor public forum staged by Citizens' Radio in April 2008 were prosecuted for their participation in illicit broadcasting contravening TO s 23. The provision prohibits, among other things, the delivery of any message for transmission by illegal means.

The defendants were convicted at the trial and the case went all the way to the Court of Final Appeal. In November 2012, the Court of Final Appeal by a majority of four to one quashed the convictions, ruling that the mere act of speaking into a microphone did not constitute "delivering a message". The court, however, declined to rule on the constitutionality of Hong Kong's broadcasting regulatory regime (*HKSAR v Wong Yuk Man and Others* [2012] HKCFA 68).

7.2.2 **New guidelines and criteria for licence applications**

In another development, Ocean Technology Limited in September 2005 submitted to the BA an application for a sound broadcasting licence, shortly before Citizen's Radio started its illicit broadcasting. The plan was to launch a non-commercial FM venture with local communities as the target audience.

Ocean Technology complained that there were no procedures or forms available for any licence application that had not been invited by the government, and its application received little attention from the BA. Months later, the regulator decided behind closed doors not to support the application. In December 2006, the CE in C rejected the application upon the BA's recommendation. Ocean Technology found it too costly to seek a judicial review of this CE in C decision.

Instead, when prosecuted for illicit broadcasting, Ocean Technology and other defendants took the opportunity to challenge the constitutionality of Hong Kong's broadcasting licensing regime. The defendants complained, amongst other things, that the licensing regime lacks clarity and certainty and was not "provided by law" as required by Article 16(3) of the Hong Kong Bill of Rights, and that there was no provision in the TO to regulate the discretion of the CE in C in the awarding of a sound broadcasting licence. As mentioned, the defendants were eventually convicted.

The HKSAR government nonetheless went on to amend the TO, introducing ss 13C and 13CA in 2010. Section 13C sets out a list of matters that the CE in C must have regard to when exercising discretion on whether to grant a sound broadcasting licence. Factors such as public opinion, the applicant's financial soundness and ability to maintain the service, the quality and technical viability of the proposed service, and speed of service roll-out are included in the list. Section 13CA authorizes the BA (now the CA) to issue guidelines for licence applicants on what the regulator would do upon receiving an application.

In contrast to what was experienced by Ocean Technology Limited, Albert Cheng's Wave Media made an application in January 2008 and was soon granted a licence by the CE in C in July 2008. With backing from several top leaders of Hong Kong's political and business circles, Wave Media planned to invest HK$140 million to launch an AM channel. In fact, the CE in C has so far granted sound broadcasting licences only to commercial radio stations.

The new TO s 13C indicates that a successful applicant has to be a major commercial enterprise with sound financial, technical, and management capabilities. Meanwhile, a new s 13B was also introduced to the TO in 2010, posing another hurdle for licence applicants. It stipulates that an application for a licence may be entertained only if the BA (now the CA) is satisfied that the radio frequency the applicant proposes to use is available as of the date of application, and that the frequency is suitable for use in providing the proposed broadcasting service. Relying on this new provision, the BA in late 2010 rejected another sound broadcasting licence application by Ocean Technology Limited.

7.2.3 **Calls for diversity versus the scarcity rationale**

These new TO provisions, coupled with the HKSAR government's long-standing practice of licensing only commercial radio stations, are at odds with calls for plurality and diversity in Hong Kong's sound broadcasting scene. When rejecting the licence application of Ocean Technology Limited in 2005, the HKSAR government indicated that it had no intention of introducing community broadcasting.

This position was slightly changed in late 2010; RTHK was given a new task of experimenting with community broadcasting for a period of three years with a budget of HK$45 million when the HKSAR government announced its decision not to turn RTHK into an independent public broadcaster.

In sum, the HKSAR government has exhibited little enthusiasm for community broadcasting or public service broadcasting. At least in the near future, Hong Kong listeners will not be able to experience the mix of commercial, public service, and community radio broadcasting that is common in many Western cities nowadays.

Worse yet, both the HKSAR courts and the administration are still resorting to the scarcity rationale as a major reason for the licensing and strict control of sound broadcasting. The Court of Appeal noted in the Citizens' Radio ruling that due to radio spectrum scarcity and problems caused by unrestricted access to the spectrum, there could be no right to the airwaves, and the requirement to obtain a licence to broadcast was not an unjustifiable restriction on the right to freedom of expression (*Secretary for Justice v Ocean Technology Ltd & Ors* [2009] 1 HKC 271).

The Court of Appeal also found support in the *Red Lion* ruling made by the Supreme Court of the United States in the 1960s: without government control, the medium would be of little use because none of the competing voices could be clearly and predictably heard (*Red Lion Broadcasting Co. v Federal Communications Commission,* 395 U.S. 367 (1969)).

As mentioned earlier, the Court of Final Appeal when hearing the appeal by Citizen's Radio guests did not rule on the constitutionality of Hong Kong's licensing regime for broadcast media. Four local judges, however, agreed that a licensing regime helps to prevent chaos and potential dangers caused by broadcasting (*HKSAR v Wong Yuk Man and Others* [2012] HKCFA 68).

The scarcity rationale, though influential and widely employed by countries around the world to justify regulating broadcast media, has been subject to challenge for years. Critics argue that the so-called scarcity is artificially created by governments and doubt whether it can be used as a valid justification for licensing broadcast media, particularly with the advent of digital technology. The new TO s 13B nevertheless reinforces the scarcity rationale.

8. RTHK as a public broadcaster

RTHK has been a government department since its inception. It operates a number of radio channels. For years, however, RTHK has had no television channel of its own, relying on very limited time slots allocated by the two terrestrial television stations. There has been an ongoing debate since the mid-1980s on whether RTHK should be turned into a fully independent public broadcaster equipped with its own television channels.

After the 1997 handover, the editorial independence of RTHK has increasingly come under attack by the pro-Beijing camp for programmes that ridiculed or criticized the Chief Executive in Hong Kong and Chinese leaders in Beijing. The BA's adjudication over the programme *Headliner* (see section 5.1) has added further constraints to RTHK production.

In 2005, the role of RTHK was again hotly debated. Donald Tsang, who later became the Chief Executive, remarked in his election campaigns that RTHK should refrain from producing such programmes as those on horse racing. Soon after Tsang's remarks, RTHK cut its live broadcast of horse racing but maintained that the decision had in fact been made some time ago with thorough discussions among its staff. In response to public criticism, the broadcaster also suggested revisiting the proposal of turning RTHK into an independent corporation.

In early 2006, the Chief Executive appointed a seven-member committee to review the city's public service broadcasting (PSB). The stated objective was to arrive at a clear policy framework that would provide both the vision and specific plans for future development of PSB in Hong Kong. The review was generally regarded as long overdue.

The committee released its review report in early 2007. It supported the strengthening of PSB provision in Hong Kong and recommended the establishment of a Hong Kong Public Broadcasting Corporation, a statutory body independent of the government but to be funded primarily from public funds in its initial years. The committee stressed that the corporation should enjoy a fresh start and did not favour transforming RTHK into a public broadcaster.

The CE in C announced a decision in September 2009 that RTHK would remain a government department but at the same time serve as the city's public broadcaster. In other words, the HKSAR government ruled out the possibility of RTHK becoming independent.

After another round of public consultation, the RTHK was given a new Charter. The HKSAR government announced in late 2010 a package of new arrangements for the broadcaster, including new posts and the construction of a new building. RTHK was also assigned three digital television channels, including one high-definition channel to transmit core RTHK programmes and one standard-definition channel re-transmitting China Central Television programmes from the mainland. All three channels were launched in early 2014.

In September 2011, the HKSAR government appointed a new Director of Broadcasting who was a senior government official with no experience in broadcasting. The Director's job is to head RTHK and has for decades been promoted from within RTHK. Two months later, two talk-show hosts at the station were informed that their contracts would not be renewed. Indeed, with these pledges from the HKSAR administration of modernizing and strengthening RTHK in the pipeline, the broadcaster's editorial independence remains a question of great concern.

9. Regulation and self-regulation of online media

In Hong Kong and many Western countries, a light-handed regulatory approach has been adopted in respect of online media so as to encourage innovation and promote freedom of expression. The online media are subject only to general media laws and self-regulation.

In particular, online media content has to abide by the Control of Obscene and Indecent Articles Ordinance (COIAO, Cap 390). Only upon public complaints, however, will any COIAO breaches be investigated. Established on 1 April 2012 to take over most of the duties of the former TELA, the Office of Film, Newspaper and Article Administration (OFNAA) is the government department responsible for such investigations.

The OFNAA works with the Hong Kong Internet Services Providers Association to implement a self-regulatory code of practice that was promulgated in 1997. The HKSAR government put forward proposals in 2000 and again in 2008 to tighten the control of online media content and to step up the responsibilities of internet service providers, but most of these proposals were met with strong oppositions and were stalled. As of late 2013, results of a further round of consultation have not been announced (see section 5.2.2 of Chapter 11 Obscenity and Indecency).

Also, the proposal made by the Electoral Affairs Commission in 2011 to extend election guidelines to cover online media was subject to severe criticism and eventually dropped (see section 3.3 of Chapter 8). And to help combat online copyright violations, the Hong Kong government introduced Copyright (Amendment) Ordinance 2011 in which it proposed establishing a "safe harbour" of limited liability for ISPs. As a condition, ISPs have to comply with a code of practice which set out specific conduct expected of them if notified of online piracy. The bill was withdrawn a year later after public objections to a number of the bill's provisions. (For more discussion, see Chapter 10 Copyright.) No new legislation has been introduced as of late 2013.

Several problematic issues regarding the regulation of online media have become apparent. First, Hong Kong law does not require the registration of websites, but the ROLNO defines the term "newspaper" broadly. According to TELA (now OFNAA), an online newspaper without hard copies is required to register. This is despite the fact that the ROLNO requirements are largely designed for conventional newspapers.

Second and more problematic has been the provision of television services over the Internet. In line with the prevalent practice in the late 1990s, BO schedule 3 clearly stipulates that services provided on the Internet are not regarded as "television programme services" and are therefore not subject to broadcasting licensing or regulation by the government. Development of IPTV technology has since made the provision of subscription television over the Internet possible.

The IPTV-based NOW TV has become Hong Kong's largest pay television operator. Its holding company, PCCW Media Limited, voluntarily applied for and was granted a "domestic pay" licence, as a result of which NOW TV is regulated by the BO. That has not been the case for another IPTV operator, Hong Kong Broadband Network, which has so far not applied for a "domestic pay" licence and is not subject to any licensing or regulation by the BO. Instead, its holding company, City Telecom (Hong Kong) Limited, has applied for a "domestic free" licence (see section 3.1.2 of this chapter).

Third, questions also arise as to whether mobile television comes under the BO. In early 2007, the BA rejected an appeal concerning a complaint against four 3G mobile service operators for offering broadcasting services without a licence, thus breaching BO s 5. The BA concluded that the mobile television services offered by these operators were not licensable under existing laws.

In July 2010, China Mobile Hong Kong Corporation Limited obtained a 15-year licence from the Telecommunications Authority (now dissolved and taken over by the CA) to offer broadcast-type mobile Television services in Hong Kong. These new services involve the wireless transmission of audio-visual content for reception by mobile phones or other portable devices.

The HKSAR government considers mobile television different from conventional free-to-air television and maintains that more flexibility should be allowed for operators. Broadcast-type mobile television services are therefore not regulated by the BO but are subject to a light-handed regulatory approach similar to that enjoyed by the online media.

Fourth, disparities also exist between the regulation of television news and web-published news videos. The latter are only subject to general media law. News videos appearing on websites need not abide by the TV Programme Code, which imposes tighter regulatory measures than the COIAO.

This is best illustrated by Next Media Animation (NMA), a relatively new venture of the Next Media Group. The group used to publish only print media, including *Apple Daily* and *Next Magazine*. The NMA re-enacts news stories using animation, quite often in a sensational and salacious manner, and became famous worldwide in 2009 by animating golfer Tiger Wood's extramarital affairs and marital breakup.

All these issues go beyond the regulation of online media. Indeed, improvements to the existing regulatory regimes are much needed in view of new services made possible by convergence. As media convergence continues, should a single mode of regulation be applied to all kinds of media? In view of the rapid growth in media outlets and platforms and the importance of freedom of expression, should a light-handed approach to content regulation be adopted regardless of the medium?

Meanwhile, the enactment of the CAO itself has not brought any major changes to licensing and regulatory arrangements for broadcasting and telecommunications services. It is for the CA to conduct a comprehensive review of the existing regulatory regimes and to recommend legislative changes to update and rationalize the existing TO and BO. Very likely, new legislation governing electronic communications will be enacted to replace the BO, the TO, and the UEMO.

In sum, there will be plenty of regulatory issues waiting for the CA to tackle. It is also paramount that the CA devises new, consistent rationales on media regulation relevant to the information age.

10. Conclusion

To conclude, numerous possible changes are in the pipeline concerning the regulation of electronic media. It is uncertain, however, exactly what measures the HKSAR government will eventually introduce to tackle disparities existing between the regulation of print, broadcast, and online media. It is also far from clear that the HKSAR government is committed to media plurality and diversity so that Hong Kong people may enjoy a healthy mix of commercial, public service, and community media.

Meanwhile, while media self-regulation has been the norm for Hong Kong's print and online media, an effective mechanism has yet to emerge. Public criticism deploring the misbehaviour of newspapers and magazines continues to lend support to more statutory regulation of mass media. For self-regulation to prevail, Hong Kong journalists and media organizations must take media freedom more seriously and refrain from abusing it.

Appendix A: Excerpts of Key Statutes and Regulations

HONG KONG[1]

Basic Law of the Hong Kong Special Administrative Region of the People's Republic of China (Basic Law)

Article 1
The Hong Kong Special Administrative Region is an inalienable part of the People's Republic of China.

Article 2
The National People's Congress authorizes the Hong Kong Special Administrative Region to exercise a high degree of autonomy and enjoy executive, legislative and independent judicial power, including that of final adjudication, in accordance with the provisions of this Law.

Article 4
The Hong Kong Special Administrative Region shall safeguard the rights and freedoms of the residents of the Hong Kong Special Administrative Region and of other persons in the Region in accordance with law.

Article 5
The socialist system and policies shall not be practised in the Hong Kong Special Administrative Region, and the previous capitalist system and way of life shall remain unchanged for 50 years.

Article 8
The laws previously in force in Hong Kong, that is, the common law, rules of equity, ordinances, subordinate legislation and customary law shall be maintained, except for any that contravene this Law, and subject to any amendment by the legislature of the Hong Kong Special Administrative Region.

Article 23
The Hong Kong Special Administrative Region shall enact laws on its own to prohibit any act of treason, secession, sedition, subversion against the Central

1. The Hong Kong ordinances used in this appendix were reproduced with the permission of the Government of Hong Kong Special Administrative Region.

People's Government, or theft of state secrets, to prohibit foreign political organizations or bodies from conducting political activities in the Region, and to prohibit political organizations or bodies of the Region from establishing ties with foreign political organizations or bodies.

Article 27

Hong Kong residents shall have freedom of speech, of the press and of publication; freedom of association, of assembly, of procession and of demonstration; and the right and freedom to form and join trade unions, and to strike.

Article 28

The freedom of the person of Hong Kong residents shall be inviolable.

No Hong Kong resident shall be subjected to arbitrary or unlawful arrest, detention or imprisonment. Arbitrary or unlawful search of the body of any resident or deprivation or restriction of the freedom of the person shall be prohibited. Torture of any resident or arbitrary or unlawful deprivation of the life of any resident shall be prohibited.

Article 29

The homes and other premises of Hong Kong residents shall be inviolable. Arbitrary or unlawful search of, or intrusion into, a resident's home or other premises shall be prohibited.

Article 30

The freedom and privacy of communication of Hong Kong residents shall be protected by law. No department or individual may, on any grounds, infringe upon the freedom and privacy of communication of residents except that the relevant authorities may inspect communication in accordance with legal procedures to meet the needs of public security or of investigation into criminal offences.

Article 39

The provisions of the International Covenant on Civil and Political Rights, the International Covenant on Economic, Social and Cultural Rights, and international labour conventions as applied to Hong Kong shall remain in force and shall be implemented through the laws of the Hong Kong Special Administrative Region...

Bill of Rights Ordinance (Cap 383)

Article 10

Equality before courts and right to fair and public hearing

All persons shall be equal before the courts and tribunals. In the determination of any criminal charge against him, or of his rights and obligations in a suit at law, everyone shall be entitled to a fair and public hearing by a competent, independent and impartial tribunal established by law. The press and the public may be excluded from all or part of a trial for reasons of morals, public order (ordre public) or national security in a democratic society, or when the interest of the private lives of the parties so requires, or to the extent strictly necessary in the opinion of the court in special circumstances where publicity would prejudice the interests of justice; but any judgment rendered in a criminal case or in a suit at law shall be made public except where the interest of juvenile persons otherwise requires or the proceedings concern matrimonial disputes or the guardianship of children.

Article 14
Protection of privacy, family, home, correspondence, honour and reputation

(1) No one shall be subjected to arbitrary or unlawful interference with his privacy, family, home or correspondence, nor to unlawful attacks on his honour and reputation.
(2) Everyone has the right to the protection of the law against such interference or attacks.

Article 16
Freedom of opinion and expression

(1) Everyone shall have the right to hold opinions without interference.
(2) Everyone shall have the right to freedom of expression; this right shall include freedom to seek, receive and impart information and ideas of all kinds, regardless of frontiers, either orally, in writing or in print, in the form of art, or through any other media of his choice.
(3) The exercise of the rights provided for in paragraph (2) of this article carries with it special duties and responsibilities. It may therefore be subject to certain restrictions, but these shall only be such as are provided by law and are necessary —
    (a) for respect of the rights or reputations of others; or
    (b) for the protection of national security or of public order (ordre public), or of public health or morals.

Control of Obscene and Indecent Articles Ordinance (Cap 390)

Section 2
Interpretation

(2) For the purposes of this Ordinance —
    (a) a thing is obscene if by reason of obscenity it is not suitable to be published to any person; and
    (b) a thing is indecent if by reason of indecency it is not suitable to be published to a juvenile.
(3) For the purposes of subsection (2), "obscenity" (淫褻) and "indecency" (不雅) include violence, depravity and repulsiveness.
(4) For the purposes of this Ordinance, other than section 24(1E) and (1F), a person publishes an article if he, whether or not for gain —
    (a) distributes, circulates, sells, hires, gives or lends the article to the public or a section of the public;

(b) in the case of an article —
(i) consisting of or containing material to be looked at; or
(ii) that is a sound recording or a film, video-tape, disc or other record of a picture or pictures, shows, plays or projects that article to or for the public or a section of the public.

(5) For the purposes of subsection (4) —
(a) "article" (物品) includes anything which is intended to be used, either alone or as one of a set, for the purpose of manufacturing or reproducing an article; and
(b) "person" (人、人士) and "public" (公眾人士) include, respectively, a person having the control or management of anything which is or purports to be a club, and the members of that club.

(6) For the purposes of this Ordinance, in determining whether any matter publicly displayed is indecent —
(a) there shall be disregarded any part of that matter which is not exposed to view; and
(b) account may be taken of the effect of juxtaposing one thing with another.

(7) Any matter which is displayed in or so as to be visible from —
(a) any public street or pier, or public garden; and
(b) any place to which the public have or are permitted to have access (whether on payment or otherwise) except a place to which the public are permitted to have access only on payment which is or includes payment for a display of indecent matter, shall for the purposes of this Ordinance be deemed to be matter publicly displayed.

Section 8
Jurisdiction

(1) In relation to any article, or any matter publicly displayed, referred to it by a court or magistrate under Part V a Tribunal may determine for the purposes of this Ordinance whether
(a) the article is obscene or indecent;
(b) the matter is indecent; or
(c) the ground of defence under section 28 is proved in respect of the publication of an article or the public display of any matter.

(2) In relation to any article submitted to it under section 13, a Tribunal shall refuse an application to make a classification if it is of the opinion that the article may be child pornography within the meaning of section 2(1) of the Prevention of Child Pornography Ordinance (Cap 579), and may in any other case —
(a) refuse an application to make a classification in respect of any article if it considers that article cannot be adequately described for the purpose of giving notice of classification under section 19; or
(b) make a classification that the article is —
(i) a Class I article if it is of the opinion that the article is neither obscene nor indecent;

(ii) a Class II article if it is of the opinion that the article is indecent; or
(iii) a Class III article if it is of the opinion that the article is obscene; and
(c) in respect of any classification that an article is a Class II article and at the time of making that classification, impose conditions relating to the publication of that article.

Section 10
Guidance to Tribunal

(1) In determining whether an article is obscene or indecent or whether any matter publicly displayed is indecent, or in classifying an article, a Tribunal shall have regard to —
(a) standards of morality, decency and propriety that are generally accepted by reasonable members of the community, and in relation thereto may, in the case of an article, have regard to any decision of a censor under section 10 of the Film Censorship Ordinance (Cap 392) in respect of a film within the meaning of section 2(1) of that Ordinance;
(b) the dominant effect of an article or of matter as a whole;
(c) in the case of an article, the persons or class of persons, or age groups of persons, to or amongst whom the article is, or is intended or is likely to be, published;
(d) in the case of matter publicly displayed, the location where the matter is or is to be publicly displayed and the persons or class of persons, or age groups of persons likely to view such matter; and
(e) whether the article or matter has an honest purpose or whether its content is merely camouflage designed to render acceptable any part of it.
(2) The opinion of an expert as to any of the matters to which a Tribunal must or may have regard under subsection (1) may be admitted in any proceedings before a Tribunal either to establish or negative that matter.

Section 24
Restrictions on publishing indecent article

(1) A person shall not publish an indecent article —
(a) where —
(i) the article has no cover or packaging or the covers or packaging is not indecent, unless the article (together with its covers or packaging, if any) is sealed in a transparent wrapper;
(ii) either the front cover or back cover of the article or both such covers are indecent (whether or not the article has any packaging and whether or not the packaging is indecent), unless the article (together with the covers, and packaging if any) is sealed in a completely opaque wrapper; or
(iii) the packaging of the article is indecent (whether or not the article has any cover and whether or not the covers are indecent), unless the article (together with the covers, if any, and the packaging) is sealed in a completely opaque wrapper;

(b) where the article is an article —
(i) described in paragraph (a)(i), unless the article bears; or
(ii) described in paragraph (a)(ii) or (iii), unless the article and the completely opaque wrapper each bears, a notice which is in the form specified in subsection (1D) and is displayed in accordance with subsection (1C); and
(c) unless the article, and its transparent wrapper or completely opaque wrapper, as the case may be, comply with the relevant requirements in subsections (1A) and (1B).

(1A) Subject to subsections (1B) and (1C), where an indecent article is published —
(a) if it is an article which is sealed in a completely opaque wrapper, nothing other than the name of the article, its date of publication, issue number and selling price shall be displayed on its completely opaque wrapper; or
(b) if it is an article which is sealed in a transparent wrapper, nothing shall be displayed on its transparent wrapper.

(1B) Where an indecent article is published —
(a) it shall have —
(i) where it has no packaging, printed either on its front cover or back cover;
(ii) where it has any packaging, (whether or not it has any covers) printed on its packaging; or
(iii) where it has no cover or packaging, printed on a label affixed to the article and which occupies the whole article; and
(b) where it is sealed in a completely opaque wrapper, it shall have in addition to the requirement in paragraph (a) printed on either side of the completely opaque wrapper, clearly and conspicuously, the name, the full address of place of business and the telephone number of the publisher.

(1C) Where an indecent article is published, the notice referred to in subsection (1) shall be displayed so that it is easily noticeable —
(a) (i) on both the front and back covers of the article;
(ii) on the packaging of the article if the article has no cover; or
(iii) on a label affixed to the article and which occupies the whole article if the article has no cover or packaging; and
(b) on both sides of its completely opaque wrapper where the article (together with its covers or packaging, if any) is sealed in a completely opaque wrapper.

(1D) The notice referred to in subsection (1) shall be in the following form —
"WARNING: THIS ARTICLE CONTAINS MATERIAL WHICH MAY OFFEND AND MAY NOT BE DISTRIBUTED, CIRCULATED, SOLD, HIRED, GIVEN, LENT, SHOWN, PLAYED OR PROJECTED TO A PERSON UNDER THE AGE OF 18 YEARS.
警告：本物品內容可能令人反感；不可將本物品派發、傳閱、出售、出

租、交給或出借予年齡未滿18歲的人士或將本物品向該等人士出示、播放或放映。";

and the following shall apply in respect of the notice —

(a) the letters and characters constituting the notice shall occupy at least —

(i) (A) 20% of each cover of the article;

(B) 20% of the packaging of the article if the article has no cover; or

(C) 20% of a label affixed to the article and which occupies the whole article if the article has no cover or packaging; and

(ii) 20% of each side of its completely opaque wrapper where the article (together with its covers or packaging, if any) is sealed in a completely opaque wrapper;

(b) the letters and characters referred to in paragraph (a) shall be of a colour which contrasts with the colour of the background upon which they are printed;

(c) the area within which the notice is displayed shall not contain anything other than the letters and characters constituting the notice.

(1E) (a) (i) In case the publisher and the printer of the indecent article are the same person, that person; or

(ii) in any other case, the publisher of the article, shall ensure that the requirements of subsections (1A), (1B), (1C) and (1D) are complied with.

(b) Subject to subsection (3), any publisher or printer, as the case may be, who contravenes paragraph (a), whether or not he knows that the article is an indecent article, commits an offence and is liable to a fine of $400,000 and to imprisonment for 12 months on his first conviction, and to a fine of $800,000 and to imprisonment for 12 months on a second or subsequent conviction.

(c) Any person who is not the publisher of an indecent article but wilfully or knowingly allows his name to be printed on it or its completely opaque wrapper (as may be appropriate) as the publisher of it, commits an offence and is liable to a fine at level 5 and to imprisonment for 6 months.

(1F) In subsection (1E), with respect to an indecent article —

"the publisher" (出版人) means the person who causes, manages or controls the printing, manufacturing or reproduction of it, as the case may be;

"the printer" (印刷人) means the person who prints, manufactures or reproduces it, as the case may be.

(2) Subject to subsection (3), any person who contravenes subsection (1), whether or not he knows that the article is an indecent article, commits an offence and is liable to a fine of $400,000 and to imprisonment for 12 months

on his first conviction, and to a fine of $800,000 and to imprisonment for 12 months on a second or subsequent conviction.

(3) It shall be a defence to a charge under this section to prove that the article the subject of the charge is, or was at the time the offence is alleged to have been committed, classified as a Class I article.

Section 25
Offences in relation to interim classification

Where an article is classified as a Class III article by virtue only of an interim classification, any person who publishes that article, whether or not he knows it has been so classified, commits an offence and is liable to a fine of $1,000,000 and to imprisonment for 3 years.

Section 26
Prohibition on publishing Class III article

Any person who —

(a) publishes;
(b) possesses for the purpose of publication;
(c) imports for the purpose of publication,

any article classified by a Tribunal, other than by virtue only of an interim classification, as a Class III article, whether or not he knows it has been so classified, commits an offence and is liable to a fine of $1,000,000 and to imprisonment for 3 years.

Article 27
Restriction on publishing Class II article

Where, in relation to any article classified as a Class II article, a Tribunal has imposed conditions under section 8(2)(c), any person who publishes that article otherwise than in accordance with those conditions, whether or not he knows it has been so classified or that those conditions have been imposed, commits an offence and is liable to a fine of $400,000 and to imprisonment for 12 months on his first conviction, and to a fine of $800,000 and to imprisonment for 12 months on a second or subsequent conviction.

Article 28
Defence of public good

It shall be a defence to a charge under this Part in respect of the publication of an article or the public display of matter if that publication or display, as the case may be, is found by a Tribunal to have been intended for the public good on the ground that such publication or display was in the interests of science, literature, art or learning, or any other object of general concern.

Copyright Ordinance (Cap 528)

Section 4
Literary, dramatic and musical works

(1) In this Part-"dramatic work" includes a work of dance or mime; "literary work" means any work, other than a dramatic or musical work, which is written, spoken or sung, and accordingly includes —
   (a) a compilation of data or other material, in any form, which by reason of the selection or arrangement of its contents constitutes an intellectual creation, including but not limiting to a table;
   (b) a computer program; and
   (c) preparatory design material for a computer program; "musical work" means a work consisting of music, exclusive of any words or action intended to be sung, spoken or performed with music.

(2) Copyright does not subsist in a literary, dramatic or musical work unless and until it is recorded, in writing or otherwise; and references in this Part to the time at which such a work is made are to the time at which it is so recorded.

(3) It is immaterial for the purposes of subsection (2) whether the work is recorded by or with the permission of the author; and where it is not recorded by the author.

Section 14
Employee works

(1) Where a literary, dramatic, musical or artistic work, or a film, is made by an employee in the course of his employment, his employer is the first owner of any copyright in the work subject to —
   (a) any agreement to the contrary; and
   (b) subsection (2).

(2) Subject to any agreement to the contrary, where such work is exploited by his employer or by someone else with the employer's permission in a way that could not reasonably have been contemplated by the employer and the employee at the time of making the work, the employer shall pay an award to the employee in respect of such exploitation at such amount as agreed between the employer and the employee or failing an agreement, as determined by the Copyright Tribunal.

Section 15
Commissioned works

(1) Where a work is made on the commission of a person and there is an agreement between the author and the commissioner of the work which expressly provides for the entitlement to the copyright, copyright in the commissioned work belongs to the person who is entitled to the copyright under the agreement.

(2) Notwithstanding subsection (1) and sections 13 and 103, the person who commissioned the work —

(a) has an exclusive licence to exploit the commissioned work for all purposes that could reasonably have been contemplated by the author and the person who commissioned the work at the time the work was commissioned; and
(b) has the power to restrain any exploitation of the commissioned work for any purpose against which he could reasonably take objection.

Section 39
Criticism, review and news reporting

(1) Fair dealing with a work for the purpose of criticism or review, of that or another work or of a performance of a work, if it is accompanied by a sufficient acknowledgement, does not infringe any copyright in the work or, in the case of a published edition, in the typographical arrangement.
(2) Fair dealing with a work for the purpose of reporting current events, if (subject to subsection (3)) it is accompanied by a sufficient acknowledgement, does not infringe any copyright in the work.
(3) No acknowledgement is required in connection with the reporting of current events by means of a sound recording, film, broadcast or cable programme.

Section 58
Public records

(1) Material which is comprised in public records which are open to public inspection may be copied, and a copy may be supplied to any person without infringement of copyright.
(2) In this section "public records" (公共紀錄) means the records of any nature or description which have been made, received or acquired in the course of proceedings of the Legislative Council, judicial proceedings or executive transaction, together with the exhibits and other material evidence which form part of or are annexed to or are otherwise related to any record, which are or are required to be in the custody of, or which may be transferred to or be acquired by, any department of the Government.

Section 89
Right to be identified as author or director

(1) The author of a copyright literary, dramatic, musical or artistic work, and the director of a copyright film, has the right to be identified as the author or director of the work in the circumstances mentioned in this section; but the right is not infringed unless it has been asserted in accordance with section 90.
(2) The author of a literary work (other than words intended to be sung or spoken with music) or a dramatic work has the right to be identified whenever —
    (a) the work is published commercially, performed in public, broadcast or included in a cable programme service; or
    (b) copies of a film or sound recording including the work are issued or made available to the public,

and that right includes the right to be identified whenever any of those events occur in relation to an adaptation of the work as the author of the work from which the adaptation was made.

(3) The author of a musical work, or a literary work consisting of words intended to be sung or spoken with music, has the right to be identified whenever —
   (a) the work is published commercially, performed in public, broadcast or included in a cable programme service;
   (b) copies of a sound recording of the work are issued or made available to the public; or
   (c) a film of which the sound-track includes the work is shown in public or copies of such a film are issued or made available to the public, and that right includes the right to be identified whenever any of those events occur in relation to an adaptation of the work as the author of the work from which the adaptation was made.

(4) The author of an artistic work has the right to be identified whenever —
   (a) the work is published commercially or exhibited in public, or a visual image of it is broadcast or included in a cable programme service;
   (b) a film including a visual image of the work is shown in public or copies of such a film are issued or made available to the public; or
   (c) in the case of a work of architecture in the form of a building or a model for a building, a sculpture or a work of artistic craftsmanship, copies of a graphic work representing it, or of a photograph of it, are issued or made available to the public.

(5) The author of a work of architecture in the form of a building also has the right to be identified on the building as constructed or, where more than one building is constructed to the design, on the first to be constructed.

(6) The director of a film has the right to be identified whenever the film is shown in public, broadcast or included in a cable programme service or copies of the film are issued or made available to the public.

(7) The right of the author or director under this section is —
   (a) in the case of commercial publication or the issue or making available to the public of copies of a film or sound recording, to be identified in or on each copy or, if that is not appropriate, in some other manner likely to bring his identity to the notice of a person acquiring a copy;
   (b) in the case of identification on a building, to be identified by appropriate means visible to persons entering or approaching the building; and
   (c) in any other case, to be identified in a manner likely to bring his identity to the notice of a person seeing or hearing the performance, exhibition, showing, broadcast or cable programme in question,

   and the identification must in each case be clear and reasonably prominent.

(8) If the author or director in asserting his right to be identified specifies a pseudonym, initials or some other particular form of identification, that form must be used; otherwise any reasonable form of identification may be used.

(9) This section has effect subject to section 91.

Section 90
Requirement that right be asserted

(1) A person does not infringe the right conferred by section 89 (right to be identified as author or director) by doing any of the acts mentioned in that section unless the right has been asserted in accordance with the following provisions so as to bind him in relation to that act.

(2) The right may be asserted generally, or in relation to any specified act or description of acts —

(a) on an assignment of copyright in the work, by including in the instrument effecting the assignment a statement that the author or director asserts in relation to that work his right to be identified; or (b) by instrument in writing signed by the author or director.

(3) The right may also be asserted in relation to the public exhibition of an artistic work —

(a) by securing that when the author or other first owner of copyright parts with possession of the original, or of a copy made by him or under his direction or control, the author is identified on the original or copy, or on a frame, mount or other thing to which it is attached; or

(b) by including in a licence by which the author or other first owner of copyright authorizes the making of copies of the work a written statement signed by or on behalf of the person granting the licence that the author asserts his right to be identified in the event of the public exhibition of a copy made in pursuance of the licence.

(4) The persons bound by an assertion of the right under subsection (2) or (3) are —

(a) in the case of an assertion under subsection (2)(a), the assignee and anyone claiming through him, whether or not he has notice of the assertion;

(b) in the case of an assertion under subsection (2)(b), anyone to whose notice the assertion is brought;

(c) in the case of an assertion under subsection (3)(a), anyone into whose hands that original or copy comes, whether or not the identification is still present or visible;

(d) in the case of an assertion under subsection (3)(b), the licensee and anyone into whose hands a copy made in pursuance of the licence comes, whether or not he has notice of the assertion.

(5) In an action for infringement of the right the court shall, in considering remedies, take into account any delay in asserting the right.

Section 91
Exemption to right conferred by Section 89

(1) The right conferred by section 89 (right to be identified as author or director) is subject to the following exceptions.

(2) The right does not apply in relation to the following descriptions of work-

(a) a computer program;
(b) the design of a typeface;
(c) any computer-generated work.

(3) The right does not apply to anything done by or with the authority of the copyright owner where copyright in the work originally vested in the author's employer by virtue of section 14(1) (employee works).

(4) The right is not infringed by an act which by virtue of any of the following provisions would not infringe copyright in the work —
(a) section 39 (fair dealing for certain purposes), so far as it relates to the reporting of current events by means of a sound recording, film, broadcast or cable programme;
(b) section 40 (incidental inclusion of work in an artistic work, sound recording, film, broadcast or cable programme);
(c) section 41(3) (examination questions);
(d) section 54 (Legislative Council and judicial proceedings);
(e) section 55(1) or (2) (statutory inquiries);
(f) section 66 or 75 (acts permitted on assumptions as to expiry of copyright, etc.).

(5) The right does not apply in relation to any work made for the purpose of reporting current events.

(6) The right does not apply in relation to the publication in —
(a) a newspaper, magazine or similar periodical; or
(b) an encyclopaedia, dictionary, yearbook or other collective work of reference,

of a literary, dramatic, musical or artistic work made for the purposes of such publication or made available with the consent of the author for the purposes of such publication.

(7) The right does not apply in relation to —
(a) a work in which Government copyright or Legislative Council copyright subsists; or
(b) a work in which copyright originally vested in an international organization by virtue of section 188,

unless the author or director has previously been identified as such in or on published copies of the work.

Section 92
Right to object to derogatory treatment of work

The author of a copyright literary, dramatic, musical or artistic work, and the director of a copyright film, has the right in the circumstances mentioned in this section not to have his work subjected to derogatory treatment.

(2) For the purposes of this section–
(a) "treatment" (處理) of a work means any addition to, deletion from or alteration to or adaptation of the work, other than —
(i) a translation of a literary or dramatic work; or

(ii) an arrangement or transcription of a musical work involving no more than a change of key or register; and

(b) the treatment of a work is derogatory if it amounts to distortion or mutilation of the work or is otherwise prejudicial to the honour or reputation of the author or director,

and in the following provisions of this section references to a derogatory treatment of a work are construed accordingly.

(3) In the case of a literary, dramatic or musical work the right is infringed by a person who —

(a) publishes commercially, performs in public, broadcasts or includes in a cable programme service a derogatory treatment of the work; or

(b) issues or makes available to the public copies of a film or sound recording of, or including, a derogatory treatment of the work.

(4) In the case of an artistic work the right is infringed by a person who —

(a) publishes commercially or exhibits in public a derogatory treatment of the work, or broadcasts or includes in a cable programme service a visual image of a derogatory treatment of the work;

(b) shows in public a film including a visual image of a derogatory treatment of the work or issues or makes available to the public copies of such a film; or

(c) in the case of —

(i) a work of architecture in the form of a model for a building;

(ii) a sculpture; or

(iii) a work of artistic craftsmanship,

issues or makes available to the public copies of a graphic work representing, or of a photograph of, a derogatory treatment of the work.

(5) Subsection (4) does not apply to a work of architecture in the form of a building; but where the author of such a work is identified on the building and it is the subject of derogatory treatment he has the right to require the identification to be removed.

(6) In the case of a film, the right is infringed by a person who —

(a) shows in public, broadcasts or includes in a cable programme service a derogatory treatment of the film; or

(b) issues or makes available to the public copies of a derogatory treatment of the film.

(7) The right conferred by this section extends to the treatment of parts of a work resulting from a previous treatment by a person other than the author or director, if those parts are attributed to, or are likely to be regarded as the work of, the author or director.

(8) This section has effect subject to sections 93 and 94 (exceptions to and qualifications of right).

Section 93
Exemption to right conferred by Section 92

(1) The right conferred by section 92 (right to object to derogatory treatment of work) is subject to the following exceptions.

(2) The right does not apply to a computer program or to any computer-generated work.

(3) The right does not apply in relation to any work made for the purpose of reporting current events.

(4) The right does not apply in relation to the publication in —

(a) a newspaper, magazine or similar periodical; or

(b) an encyclopaedia, dictionary, yearbook or other collective work of reference,

of a literary, dramatic, musical or artistic work made for the purposes of such publication or made available with the consent of the author for the purposes of such publication.

Nor does the right apply in relation to any subsequent exploitation elsewhere of such a work without any modification of the published version.

(5) The right is not infringed by an act which by virtue of section 66 or 75 (acts permitted on assumptions as to expiry of copyright, etc.) would not infringe copyright.

(6) Subject to subsection (7), the right is not infringed by anything done for the purpose of —

(a) avoiding the commission of an offence; or

(b) complying with a duty imposed by or under an enactment.

(7) Where the author or director is identified at the time of the relevant act under subsection (6) or has previously been identified in or on published copies of the work, subsection (6) has effect only if there is a sufficient disclaimer.

Crimes Ordinance (Cap 200)

Section 2
Treason

(1) A person commits treason if he —

(a) kills, wounds or causes bodily harm to Her Majesty, or imprisons or restrains Her;

(b) forms an intention to do any such act as is mentioned in paragraph (a) and manifests such intention by an overt act;

(c) levies war against Her Majesty —

(i) with the intent to depose Her Majesty from the style, honour and royal name of the Crown of the United Kingdom or of any other of Her Majesty's dominions; or

(ii) in order by force or constraint to compel Her Majesty to change Her measures or counsels, or in order to put any force or constraint

upon, or to intimidate or overawe, Parliament or the legislature of any British territory;
(d) instigates any foreigner with force to invade the United Kingdom or any British territory;
(e) assists by any means whatever any public enemy at war with Her Majesty; or
(f) conspires with any other person to do anything mentioned in paragraph (a) or (c).

(2) Any person who commits treason shall be guilty of an offence and shall be liable on conviction on indictment to imprisonment for life.

Section 3
Treasonable Offences

(1) Any person who forms an intention to effect any of the following purposes, that is to say —
(a) to depose Her Majesty from the style, honour and royal name of the Crown of the United Kingdom or of any other of Her Majesty's dominions;
(b) to levy war against Her Majesty within the United Kingdom or any British territory in order by force or constraint to compel Her Majesty to change Her measures or counsels, or in order to put any force or constraint upon, or to intimidate or overawe, Parliament or the legislature of any British territory; or
(c) to instigate any foreigner with force to invade the United Kingdom or any British territory,

and manifests such intention by an overt act or by publishing any printing or writing, shall be guilty of an offence and shall be liable on conviction upon indictment to imprisonment for life.

(2) It shall be no defence to a charge under this section that any act proved against the person charged amounts to treason under section 2; but no person convicted or acquitted of an offence under this section shall afterwards be prosecuted for treason under section 2 upon the same facts.

Section 4
Trial limitations

(1) A person shall not be prosecuted for any offence under section 2 or 3 unless the prosecution is commenced within 3 years after the offence is committed.
(2) This section does not apply to cases in which the overt act alleged is the killing of Her Majesty, or a direct attempt to endanger the life of Her Majesty.
(3) The procedure on trials for treason or misprision of treason shall be the same as the procedure on trials for murder.

Section 9
Seditious Intention

(1) A seditious intention is an intention —

(a) to bring into hatred or contempt or to excite disaffection against the person of Her Majesty, or Her Heirs or Successors, or against the Government of Hong Kong, or the government of any other part of Her Majesty's dominions or of any territory under Her Majesty's protection as by law established;
(b) to excite Her Majesty's subjects or inhabitants of Hong Kong to attempt to procure the alteration, otherwise than by lawful means, of any other matter in Hong Kong as by law established; or
(c) to bring into hatred or contempt or to excite disaffection against the administration of justice in Hong Kong; or
(d) to raise discontent or disaffection amongst Her Majesty's subjects or inhabitants of Hong Kong; or
(e) to promote feelings of ill-will and enmity between different classes of the population of Hong Kong; or
(f) to incite persons to violence; or
(g) to counsel disobedience to law or to any lawful order.

(2) An act, speech or publication is not seditious by reason only that it intends —
(a) to show that Her Majesty has been misled or mistaken in any of Her measures; or
(b) to point out errors or defects in the government or constitution of Hong Kong as by law established or in legislation or in the administration of justice with a view to the remedying of such errors or defects; or
(c) to persuade Her Majesty's subjects or inhabitants of Hong Kong to attempt to procure by lawful means the alteration of any matter in Hong Kong as by law established; or
(d) to point out, with a view to their removal, any matters which are producing or have a tendency to produce feelings of ill-will and enmity between different classes of the population of Hong Kong.

Section 10
Sedition Offences

(1) Any person who —
(a) does or attempts to do, or makes any preparation to do, or conspires with any person to do, any act with a seditious intention; or
(b) utters any seditious words; or
(c) prints, publishes, sells, offers for sale, distributes, displays or reproduces any seditious publication; or
(d) imports any seditious publication, unless he has no reason to believe that it is seditious,

shall be guilty of an offence and shall be liable for a first offence to a fine of $5000 and to imprisonment for 2 years, and for a subsequent offence to imprisonment for 3 years; and any seditious publication shall be forfeited to the Crown.

(2) Any person who without lawful excuse has in his possession any seditious publication shall be guilty of an offence and shall be liable for a first offence to a fine of $2000 and to imprisonment for 1 year, and for a subsequent offence to imprisonment for 2 years; and such publication shall be forfeited to the Crown.

(3) Where any person has been convicted of an offence under subsection (1) or (2) in respect of any seditious publication, the court may order the seizure and forfeiture of any copies of the seditious publication in the possession of —
  (a) the person convicted; or
  (b) any other person named in the order, if the court is satisfied by evidence on oath that the copies are in the possession of the other person for the use of the person convicted.

(4) Any copies seized under subsection (3) shall be disposed of as the court may direct; but no copies shall be destroyed until the expiration of the period within which an appeal may be lodged or, if an appeal is lodged, until the appeal has been finally determined or abandoned.

(5) In this section —
"seditious publication" (煽動刊物) means a publication having a seditious intention;
"seditious words" (煽動文字) means words having a seditious intention.

Section 156
Anonymity of complainants

(1) Subject to subsection (9)(a), after an allegation is made that a specified sexual offence has been committed no matter likely to lead members of the public to identify any person as the complainant in relation to that allegation shall either be published in Hong Kong in a written publication available to the public or be broadcast in Hong Kong except as authorized by a direction given in pursuance of this section.

(2) If, before the commencement of a trial at which a person is charged with a specified sexual offence, he or another person against whom the complainant may be expected to give evidence at the trial applies to a judge for a direction in pursuance of this subsection and satisfies the judge —
  (a) that the direction is required for the purpose of inducing persons to come forward who are likely to be needed as witnesses at the trial; and
  (b) that the conduct of the applicant's defence at the trial is likely to be substantially prejudiced if the direction is not given,

the judge shall direct that subsection (1) shall not, by virtue of the accusation alleging the offence aforesaid, apply in relation to the complainant.

(3) If after the commencement of a trial at which a person is charged with a specified sexual offence a new trial of the person for that offence is ordered, the commencement of any previous trial at which he was charged with that offence shall be disregarded for the purposes of subsection (2).

(3A) A direction that subsection (1) shall not apply in relation to such complaint or such matter as is specified in the direction may be given, where it is necessary for the purpose of seeking information which may lead to the arrest of a person responsible for an alleged specified sexual offence, or is for any other reason in the public interest —

(a) by a police officer of the rank of Senior Superintendent or above, where the complainant consents in writing to such a direction being given; or

(b) by the Secretary for Justice in any other case,

and notice of any such direction shall be published in the Gazette.

(4) If at a trial at which a person is charged with a specified sexual offence the judge or, as the case may be, the District Judge, magistrate or juvenile court, is satisfied that the effect of subsection (1) is to impose a substantial and unreasonable restriction upon the reporting of proceedings at the trial and that it is in the public interest to remove or relax the restriction, the judge or, as the case may be, the District Judge, magistrate or juvenile court, shall direct that subsection (1) shall not apply to such matter relating to the complainant as is specified in the direction; but a direction shall not be given in pursuance of this subsection by reason only of an acquittal of a defendant at the trial.

(5) If a person who has been convicted of an offence and given notice of an appeal to the Court of Appeal against the conviction, or notice of an application for leave so to appeal, applies to the Court of Appeal for a direction in pursuance of this subsection and satisfies the Court —

(a) that the direction is required for the purpose of obtaining evidence in support of the appeal; and

(b) that the applicant is likely to suffer substantial injustice if the direction is not given,

the Court shall direct that subsection (1) shall not, by virtue of such allegation of a specified sexual offence as is specified in the direction, apply in relation to a complainant so specified.

(6) Subsection (5) shall apply in relation to a conviction of an offence tried summarily as mentioned in section 155(3), and, in so applying for references to the Court of Appeal there shall be substituted references to a judge and the reference to notice of an application for leave to appeal shall be omitted.

(7) For the purposes of this section an allegation of a specified sexual offence is made if —

(a) it is made to a police officer; or

(b) a complaint is made to or an information is laid before a magistrate alleging that a person has committed a specified sexual offence against the complainant; or

(c) a person appears before a magistrate or a court charged with a specified sexual offence against the complainant; or

(d) a person is committed for trial at the Court of First Instance on a charge alleging a specified sexual offence against the complainant; or

(e) an indictment charging a person with a specified sexual offence against the complainant is preferred before the Court of First Instance,

and references in this section to an allegation of a specified sexual offence shall be construed accordingly.

(8) In this section —

"broadcast" (廣播) means a broadcast by wireless telegraphy of sound or visual images intended for general reception;

"complainant" (申訴人), in relation to an allegation of a specified sexual offence, means the person against whom the offence is alleged to have been committed; and

"written publication" (書刊) includes a film, a sound track and any other record in permanent form but does not include an indictment or other document prepared for use in particular legal proceedings.

(9) Nothing in this section —

(a) prohibits the publication or broadcasting, in consequence of an allegation of a specified sexual offence, of matter consisting only of a report of legal proceedings other than proceedings at, or intended to lead to, or on an appeal arising out of, a trial at which a person is charged with that offence; or

(b) affects any prohibition or restriction imposed by virtue of any other enactment upon a publication or broadcast,

and a direction in pursuance of this section does not affect the operation of subsection (1) at any time before the direction is given.

Criminal Procedure Ordinance (Cap 221)

Section 123
Criminal proceedings may be held in camera and non-disclosure of identity of witnesses in certain cases

(1) Notwithstanding any other law but subject to the provisions of the Hong Kong Bill of Rights Ordinance (Cap 383), if it appears to a court that it is necessary so to do in the interests of justice or public order or security, the court may order that the whole of the proceedings before it in respect of any offence or, having regard to the reason for making such an order, any appropriate part of such proceedings shall take place in a closed court.

(1A) (a) Notwithstanding the making of an order under subsection (1) in respect of certain proceedings and subject to paragraph (b), such an order shall not apply to the following matters in those proceedings —

(i) the arraignment of the accused person;

(ii) the reading of the summary of facts with respect to the accused person;

(iii) the delivery of verdict by a jury or a court (as the case may be);

(iv) the pronouncement of sentence by a court.

(b) Where the court is satisfied that in the special circumstances of the case, the non-application of an order made under subsection (1) to the matter referred to in paragraph (a)(ii) will prejudice the interests of justice or public order or security, the court may determine that such an order shall apply to that matter referred to in paragraph (a)(ii).

(1B) (a) A person aggrieved by an order made under subsection (1) may appeal to the Court of Appeal, if the Court of Appeal grants leave, against such an order and the decision of the Court of Appeal shall be final.

(b) On an application for leave to appeal under this subsection, the Court of Appeal shall have power to give such directions as appear to it to be appropriate and, without prejudice to the generality of this paragraph, power —

(i) to order the production in court of any transcript or note of proceedings or other document;

(ii) to give directions as to persons who are to be parties to the appeal or who may be parties to it if they wish and as to service of documents on any person.

(c) Subject to any rules of court made by virtue of paragraph (e), any party to an appeal under this subsection may give evidence before the Court of Appeal orally or in writing.

(d) On the hearing of an appeal under this subsection the Court of Appeal shall have power —

(i) to stay any proceedings in any other court until after the appeal is disposed of;

(ii) to confirm, reverse or vary the order complained of; and

(iii) to make such order as to costs as it thinks fit.

(e) Without prejudice to the generality of section 54 of the High Court Ordinance (Cap 4) and section 9, rules of court may make in relation to criminal proceedings satisfying specified conditions special provision as to practice and procedure to be followed in relation to criminal proceedings taking place in closed court and appeals from orders made under subsection (1) and may in particular, but without prejudice to the generality of this paragraph, provide that paragraph (c) shall not have effect.

(f) Notwithstanding any other law but subject to the provisions of the Hong Kong Bill of Rights Ordinance (Cap 383), if it appears to the Court of Appeal that it is necessary so to do in the interests of justice or public order or security, the Court of Appeal may order that the whole of the hearing of an appeal under this subsection or, having regard to the reason for making such an order, any appropriate part of such hearing shall take place in a closed court.

Criminal Procedure (Appeal Against Discharge) Rules (Cap 221F)

Rule 6
Restrictions on reports of appeals

(1) Unless the Court of Appeal, on the application of the respondent, otherwise directs, no person shall publish in Hong Kong a written report, or broadcast in Hong Kong a report, of any proceedings on an appeal containing any matter other than that permitted by paragraph (3).

(2) Notwithstanding paragraph (1), a report of proceedings on an appeal containing matter other than that permitted by paragraph (3) may be published where the Court of Appeal either disallows the appeal or allows the appeal but does not quash the acquittal of the respondent and order him to be tried.

(3) A report of proceedings on appeal may contain —
   (a) the identity of the court and the names of the judges thereof;
   (b) such details concerning the proceedings on the application under section 16 to which the appeal relates as may lawfully be published or broadcast in accordance with the Criminal Procedure (Applications under Section 16) Rules (Cap 221 sub. leg.);
   (c) the grounds of the appeal or a summary thereof;
   (d) the names of counsel and solicitors engaged in the proceedings;
   (e) any decision of the Court of Appeal on the disposal of the appeal and, in the event of the Court of Appeal determining that the respondent is to be tried, the charge upon which he is to be tried;
   (f) where the proceedings on appeal are adjourned, the date to which they are adjourned;
   (g) whether legal aid was granted to the respondent.

Defamation Ordinance (Cap 21)

Section 3
Admissibility in evidence, in mitigation of damages in action for defamation, of apology

In any action for defamation it shall be competent to the defendant (after notice in writing of his intention to do so duly given to the plaintiff within a reasonable time before the trial of the cause) to give in evidence in mitigation of damages that he made or offered an apology to the plaintiff for such defamation before the commencement of the action, or as soon afterwards as he had an opportunity of doing so in case the action has been commenced before there was an opportunity of making or offering such apology.

Section 4
Right of defendant in action for libel to plead absence of malice, etc. and apology

In an action for a libel contained in any newspaper it shall be competent to the defendant to set up as a defence that the libel was inserted in the newspaper without actual malice and without gross negligence, and that before the commencement of the action, or at the earliest opportunity afterwards, he inserted in the newspaper a full apology for the libel, or if the newspaper in which the libel appeared is ordinarily published at intervals exceeding 1 week, had offered to publish the said apology in any newspaper to be selected by the plaintiff in the action: and to such defence to the action it shall be competent to the plaintiff to reply generally denying the whole of such defence:

Provided that it shall not be competent to any defendant in such action to set up any defence as aforesaid without at the same time making a payment of money into court by way of amends, and every such defence so filed without such payment into court shall be deemed a nullity and may be treated as such by the plaintiff in the action.

Section 13
Privilege of newspaper report of proceedings in court

(1) A fair and accurate report in any newspaper or broadcast of proceedings publicly heard before any court shall, if published contemporaneously with such proceedings, be privileged:
Provided that nothing in this section shall authorize the publication of any blasphemous or indecent matter.

(2) Any report in a newspaper, and any broadcast report, of committal proceedings in a case where publication is permitted by virtue only of section 87A(5) and (6) of the Magistrates Ordinance (Cap 227), published as soon as practicable after it is so permitted, shall be treated for the purposes of subsection (1) as having been published or broadcast contemporaneously with the committal proceedings.

Section 14
Qualified privilege of newspapers

(1) Subject to the provisions of this section, the publication in a newspaper or the broadcasting of any such report or other matter as is mentioned in the Schedule shall be privileged unless the publication is proved to be made with malice.

(2) In an action for libel in respect of the publication of any such report or matter as is mentioned in Part II of the Schedule, the provisions of this section shall not be a defence if it is proved that the defendant has been requested by the plaintiff to publish in the manner in which the original publication was made a reasonable letter or statement by way of explanation or contradiction, and has refused or neglected to do so, or has done so in a manner not adequate or not reasonable having regard to all the circumstances.

(3) Nothing in this section shall be construed as protecting the publication of any matter the publication of which is prohibited by law, or of any matter which is not of public concern and the publication of which is not for the public benefit.

Section 22
Broadcast statements

For the purposes of law and slander, the broadcasting of words shall be treated as publication in permanent form.

Section 25
Unintentional defamation

(1) A person who has published words alleged to be defamatory of another person may, if he claims that the words were published by him innocently in relation to that other person, make an offer of amends under this section; and in any such case —
  (a) if the offer is accepted by the party aggrieved and is duly performed, no proceedings for libel or slander shall be taken or continued by that party against the person making the offer in respect of the publication in question (but without prejudice to any cause of action against any other person jointly responsible for that publication);
  (b) if the offer is not accepted by the party aggrieved, then, except as otherwise provided by this section, it shall be a defence, in any proceedings by him for libel or slander against the person making the offer in respect of the publication in question, to prove that the words complained of were published by the defendant innocently in relation to the plaintiff and that the offer was made as soon as practicable after the defendant received notice that they were or might be defamatory of the plaintiff, and has not been withdrawn.

(2) An offer of amends under this section must be expressed to be made for the purposes of this section, and must be accompanied by an affidavit specifying the facts relied upon by the person making it to show that the words in question were published by him innocently in relation to the party aggrieved; and for the purposes of a defence under subsection (1)(b) no evidence, other than evidence of facts specified in the affidavit, shall be admissible on behalf of that person to prove that the words were so published.

(3) An offer of amends under this section shall be understood to mean an offer —
  (a) in any case, to publish or join in the publication of a suitable correction of the words complained of, and a sufficient apology to the party aggrieved in respect of those words;
  (b) where copies of a document or record containing the said words have been distributed by or with the knowledge of the person making the offer, to take such steps as are reasonably practicable on his part for notifying persons to whom copies have been so distributed that the words are alleged to be defamatory of the party aggrieved.

(4) Where an offer of amends under this section is accepted by the party aggrieved —

(a) any question as to the steps to be taken in fulfilment of the offer as so accepted shall in default of agreement between the parties be referred to and determined by the Court of First Instance, whose decision thereon shall be final;

(b) the power of the court to make orders as to costs in proceedings by the party aggrieved against the person making the offer in respect of the publication in question, or in proceedings in respect of the offer under paragraph (a), shall include power to order the payment by the person making the offer to the party aggrieved of costs on an indemnity basis and any expenses reasonably incurred or to be incurred by that party in consequence of the publication in question,

and if no such proceedings as aforesaid are taken, the Court of First Instance may, upon application made by the party aggrieved, make any such order for the payment of such costs and expenses as aforesaid as could be made in such proceedings. (Amended 25 of 1998 s. 2)

(5) For the purposes of this section words shall be treated as published by one person (in this subsection referred to as the publisher) innocently in relation to another person if and only if the following conditions are satisfied, that is to say —

(a) that the publisher did not intend to publish them of and concerning that other person, and did not know of circumstances by virtue of which they might be understood to refer to him; or

(b) that the words were not defamatory on the face of them, and the publisher did not know of circumstances by virtue of which they might be understood to be defamatory of that other person,

and in either case that the publisher exercised all reasonable care in relation to the publication; and any reference in this subsection to the publisher shall be construed as including a reference to any servant or agent of his who was concerned with the contents of the publication.

(6) Subsection (1)(b) shall not apply in relation to the publication by any person of words of which he is not the author unless he proves that the words were written by the author without malice.

Section 26
Justification

In an action for libel or slander in respect of words containing 2 or more distinct charges against the plaintiff, a defence of justification shall not fail by reason only that the truth of every charge is not proved if the words not proved to be true do not materially injure the plaintiff's reputation having regard to the truth of the remaining charges.

Section 27
Fair comment

In an action for libel or slander in respect of words consisting partly of allegations of fact and partly of expression of opinion, a defence of fair comment shall not fail by reason only that the truth of every allegation of fact is not proved if the expression of opinion is fair comment having regard to such of the facts alleged or referred to in the words complained of as are proved.

Section 28
Limitation on privilege at election

A defamatory statement published by or on behalf of a candidate in any election to the Legislative Council or to a District Council shall not be deemed to be published on a privileged occasion on the ground that it is material to a question in issue in the election, whether or not the person by whom it is published is qualified to vote at the election.

Schedule
Newspaper statements having qualified privilege

Part I
Statements privileged without explanation or contradiction

1. A fair and accurate report of any proceedings in public of the legislature of any part of the Commonwealth outside Hong Kong.
2. A fair and accurate report of any proceedings in public of an international organization of which the Government of Hong Kong or Her Majesty's Government in the United Kingdom is a member, or of any international conference to which the Government of Hong Kong or Her Majesty's Government in the United Kingdom sends a representative.
3. A fair and accurate report of any proceedings in public of an international court.
4. A fair and accurate report of any proceedings before a court exercising jurisdiction throughout any part of the Commonwealth outside Hong Kong or of any proceedings before a court-martial of the Chinese People's Liberation Army held outside Hong Kong.
5. A fair and accurate report of any proceedings in public of a body or person appointed to hold a public inquiry by the Government or legislature of any part of the Commonwealth outside Hong Kong.
6. A fair and accurate copy of or extract from any register kept in pursuance of any Ordinance which is open to inspection by the public, or of any other document which is required by the law of Hong Kong to be open to inspection by the public.
7. A notice or advertisement published by or on the authority of any court within Hong Kong or any judge or officer of such a court.

Part II
Statements privileged subject to explanation or contradiction

8. A fair and accurate report of the findings or decision of any of the following associations, or of any committee or governing body thereof, that is to say–
   (a) an association formed in Hong Kong for the purpose of promoting or encouraging the exercise of or interest in any art, science, religion or

learning, and empowered by its constitution to exercise control over or adjudicate upon matters of interest or concern to the association, or the actions or conduct of any persons subject to such control or adjudication;

(b) an association formed in Hong Kong for the purpose of promoting or safeguarding the interests of any trade, business, industry or profession, or of the persons carrying on or engaged in any trade, business, industry or profession, and empowered by its constitution to exercise control over or adjudicate upon matters connected with the trade, business, industry or profession, or the actions or conduct of those persons;

(c) an association formed in Hong Kong for the purpose of promoting or safeguarding the interests of any game, sport or pastime to the playing or exercise of which members of the public are invited or admitted, and empowered by its constitution to exercise control over or adjudicate upon persons connected with or taking part in the game, sport or pastime,

being a finding or decision relating to a person who is a member of or is subject by virtue of any contract to the control of the association.

9. A fair and accurate report of the proceedings at any public meeting held in Hong Kong, that is to say, a meeting bona fide and lawfully held for a lawful purpose and for the furtherance or discussion of any matter of public concern, whether the admission to the meeting is general or restricted.

10. A fair and accurate report of the proceedings at any meeting or sitting in any part of Hong Kong of —

(a) any body, board or authority formed or constituted under the provisions of any Ordinance or of any committee appointed by such body, board or authority;

(b) (Repealed 47 of 1997 s. 10)

(c) any commission, tribunal, committee or person appointed for the purposes of any inquiry by Letters Patent, Act of Parliament, Ordinance, by Her Majesty, by the Governor or by the head of any department of Government;

(d) any other tribunal, board, committee or body constituted by or under, and exercising functions under, an Ordinance,

not being a meeting or sitting admission to which is denied to representatives of newspapers and other members of the public.

11. A fair and accurate report of the proceedings at a general meeting of any company or association constituted, registered or certified by or under any Ordinance or Act of Parliament or incorporated by Royal Charter, not being a private company within the meaning of the Companies Ordinance, Chapter 32.

12. A copy or fair and accurate report or summary of any notice or other matter issued for the information of the public by or on behalf of any Government department, or by or on behalf of the Commissioner of Police.

13. A copy or fair and accurate report or summary of any notice or other matter issued for the information of the public by or on behalf of the Consumer Council.

14. A copy or fair and accurate report or summary of any report made or published under section 16 or 16A of The Ombudsman Ordinance (Cap 397).
15. A copy of a fair and accurate report or summary of any report prepared and supplied for the purposes of section 30 of the Mandatory Provident Fund Schemes Ordinance (Cap 485) or prepared and published under section 32 of that Ordinance.

Disability Discrimination Ordinance (Cap 487)

Section 46
Vilification

(1) It is unlawful for a person, by any activity in public, to incite hatred towards, serious contempt for, or severe ridicule of, another person with a disability or members of a class of persons with a disability.

(1A) For the purposes of subsection (1), it is immaterial whether a person is actually incited, by an activity, to-
- (a) hatred towards;
- (b) serious contempt for; or
- (c) severe ridicule of,

another person with a disability or members of a class of persons with a disability.

(2) Nothing in this section renders unlawful-
- (a) a fair report of an activity in public;
- (b) an activity in public that-
  - (i) is a communication or the distribution or dissemination of any matter; and
  - (ii) consists of a publication which is subject to a defence of absolute privilege in proceedings for defamation; or
- (c) an activity in public done reasonably and in good faith, for academic, artistic, scientific or research purposes in the public interest, including discussions about and expositions of any matter.

(3) In this section and section 47, activity in public (公開活動) includes-
- (a) any form of communication to the public, including speaking, writing, printing, displaying notices, broadcasting, screening and playing of tapes or other recorded material;
- (b) any conduct (not being a form of communication referred to in paragraph (a)) observable by the public, including actions and gestures and the wearing or display of clothing, signs, flags, emblems and insignia;
- (c) the distribution or dissemination of any matter to the public

Interpretation and General Clauses Ordinance (Cap 1)

Section 3
Definition of "public place"

. . . "public place" (公眾地方、公眾場所) means —

(a) any public street or pier, or any public garden; and
(b) any theatre, place of public entertainment of any kind, or other place of general resort, admission to which is obtained by payment or to which the public have or are permitted to have access;

Section 82
Meaning of "Journalistic Material"

(1) Subject to subsection (2), in this Part "journalistic material" (新聞材料) means any material acquired or created for the purposes of journalism.
(2) Material is only journalistic material for the purposes of this Part if it is in the possession of a person who acquired or created it for the purposes of journalism.
(3) A person who receives material from someone who intends that the recipient shall use it for the purposes of journalism is to be taken to have acquired it for those purposes.

Section 83
Power to enter and search or seize

A provision in any Ordinance which confers on, or authorizes the issue of a warrant conferring on, any person the power to enter any premises and to search the premises or any person found on the premises or to seize any material (whether of a general or particular kind and whether or not the word "material" is used in that provision) shall not, in the absence of an express provision to the contrary, be construed as conferring, or authorizing the issue of a warrant conferring, a power to enter premises where such entry is for the purpose of searching for or seizing material which is known or suspected to be journalistic material.

Section 84
Application for production order in respect of journalistic material

(1) A person on whom there is or may be conferred under a provision in any Ordinance, being a provision to which section 83 applies, the power to enter any premises and to search the premises or any person found on the premises or to seize any material, may apply to a judge of the Court of First Instance or District Court for an order under subsection (2) in relation to material which is known or suspected to be journalistic material.
(2) If on an application under subsection (1) a judge is satisfied that the conditions in subsection (3) are fulfilled he may make an order that the person who appears to be in possession of journalistic material specified in the application shall —
    (a) produce it to the applicant to take away; or
    (b) give the applicant access to it,

    not later than the end of the period of 7 days from the date of the order or the end of such longer period as the order may specify.
(3) The conditions to be fulfilled for the purposes of subsection (2) are that —
    (a) there are reasonable grounds for believing —
        (i) that an arrestable offence has been committed;

(ii) that there is material which consists of or includes material known or suspected to be journalistic material on premises specified in the application;

(iii) that the material is likely to be —

(A) of substantial value to the investigation of the arrestable offence; or

(B) relevant evidence in proceedings for the arrestable offence;

(b) but for section 83 the applicant would be or could have been authorized under the provision mentioned in subsection (1) to enter onto the premises specified in the application and to search the premises or a person found on the premises or to seize the material specified in the application;

(c) other methods of obtaining the material —

(i) have been tried and failed; or

(ii) have not been tried because they were unlikely to succeed or would be likely to seriously prejudice the investigation; and

(d) there are reasonable grounds for believing that it is in the public interest that an order should be granted, having regard to —

(i) the benefit likely to accrue to the investigation; and

(ii) the circumstances under which a person in possession of the material holds it.

(4) An application for an order under subsection (2) shall be made inter partes.

(5) Any person who without reasonable cause fails to comply with an order made under subsection (2) commits an offence and is liable to a fine at level 6 and to imprisonment for 1 year.

Section 85

Application for warrant to seize journalistic material

(1) A person on whom there is or may be conferred under a provision in any Ordinance, being a provision to which section 83 applies, the power to enter any premises and to search the premises or any person found on the premises or to seize any material, may apply to a judge of the Court of First Instance or District Court for the issue of a warrant under subsection (3) authorizing him to enter those premises for the purpose of searching for or seizing material which is known or suspected to be journalistic material.

(2) An application for a warrant under this section shall not be made unless it has been approved by a person specified in Schedule 7 to be a directorate disciplined officer.

(3) If on an application under subsection (1) a judge —

(a) is satisfied —

(i) that the conditions specified in section 84(3)(a), (c) and (d)(i) are fulfilled; and

(ii) that one of the further conditions set out in subsection (5) is also fulfilled; or

(b) is satisfied that an order under section 84 relating to the material has not been complied with, he may, subject to subsection (4), issue a warrant authorizing the applicant to enter onto the premises and to search the premises and any person found on the premises and to seize any material.

(4) A warrant issued under subsection (3) shall not authorize any entry, search or seizure other than such entry, search or seizure as, but for section 83, would be or could have been authorized under the provision mentioned in subsection (1).

(5) The further conditions mentioned in subsection (3)(a)(ii) are —
   (a) that it is not practicable to communicate with any person entitled to grant entry to the premises to which the application relates;
   (b) that while it might be practicable to communicate with a person entitled to grant entry to the premises, it is not practicable to communicate with any person entitled to grant access to the material;
   (c) that service of notice of an application for an order under section 84(2) may seriously prejudice the investigation.

(6) Subject to subsection (7), it shall be a term of any warrant issued under this section that a person who seizes journalistic material pursuant to the warrant shall seal the material upon seizure and shall hold the sealed material until otherwise authorized or required under section 87.

(7) Subsection (6) shall not apply where the judge is satisfied that there may be serious prejudice to the investigation if the applicant is not permitted to have immediate access to the material.

(8) Any person empowered by a warrant issued under this section may —
   (a) use such force as may be necessary to enter the premises specified in the warrant;
   (b) on the premises, seize such material, including journalistic material, as may be found and as but for section 83 he would be or could have been authorized under the provision mentioned in subsection (1) to take possession of;
   (c) detain for a reasonable period any person found on the premises who may have such material in his possession or under his control and who if not so detained may prejudice the purpose of the search.

Section 86
Further provision for warrants under section 85

(1) A warrant issued under section 85, other than a warrant to which subsection (7) of that section applies, shall —
   (a) specify the name of the applicant and the court issuing the warrant;
   (b) contain a statement setting out —
      (i) the terms of the warrant applying by virtue of subsection (6) of that section;
      (ii) the rights conferred under section 87 to apply within a specified period for the immediate return of journalistic material seized under the warrant, and the consequences provided for in that section of not so applying.

(2) A person executing or seeking to execute such a warrant shall —
  (a) where the occupier of the premises being entered is present, supply the occupier with a copy of the warrant;
  (b) where the occupier of the premises is not present but some other person who appears to be in charge of the premises is present, supply that person with a copy of the warrant;
  (c) if there is no person present who appears to be in charge of the premises, leave a copy of the warrant in a prominent place on the premises.

(3) Where pursuant to such a warrant material is seized which is required to be sealed and held, the person executing the warrant shall make an endorsement on the warrant setting out details of such material and shall return the warrant to the court from which it was issued.

Section 87
Procedure in relation to sealed material

(1) A person from whom journalistic material has been seized pursuant to a warrant issued under section 85, other than a warrant to which subsection (7) of that section applies, or a person claiming to be the owner of such material, may within 3 days of such seizure apply to the court from which the warrant was issued for an order under subsection (2).

(2) On an application under subsection (1), unless the judge is satisfied that it would be in the public interest that the material be made use of for the purposes of the investigation, he shall order that the material be immediately returned to the person from whom it was seized; and in making a determination under this subsection the judge shall have regard to, among other things, the circumstances under which the material was being held at the time of its seizure.

(3) If on an application under subsection (1) the judge determines not to grant an order under subsection (2), or where no application has been made under subsection (1) within the period specified in that subsection, the material may be unsealed.

(4) For the purpose of determining an application under subsection (1) a judge may require the person who seized the material to produce it to the judge for examination by him.

(5) An application for an order under subsection (1) shall be made inter partes.

Judicial Proceedings (Regulation of Reports) Ordinance (Cap 287)

Section 3
Restriction on publication of reports of judicial proceedings

(1) It shall not be lawful to print or publish, or cause or procure to be printed or published —
  (a) (Repealed 68 of 1995 s. 6)

(b) in relation to any judicial proceedings for dissolution of marriage, for nullity of marriage, or for judicial separation, any particulars other than the following, that is to say —
   (i) the names, addresses and occupations of the parties and witnesses;
   (ii) a concise statement of the charges, defences and counter-charges in support of which evidence has been given;
   (iii) submissions on any point of law arising in the course of the proceedings, and the decision of the court thereon;
   (iv) the summing-up of the judge and the finding of the jury (if any) and the judgment of the court and observations made by the in giving judgment.

(2) Any person who contravenes the provisions of subsection (1) shall be guilty of an offence and shall be liable to a fine of eight thousand dollars and to imprisonment for four months:
Provided that no person, other than a proprietor, editor, master printer or publisher, shall be liable to be convicted under this section.

(3) A prosecution under this section shall not be instituted except by or with the consent of the Secretary for Justice.

(4) Nothing in this section shall apply to the printing of any pleading, transcript of evidence or other document for use in connection with any judicial proceedings or the communication thereof to persons concerned in the proceedings, or to the printing or publishing of any notice or report in pursuance of the directions of the court; or to the printing or publishing of any matter in any separate volume or part of any bona fide series of law reports which does not form part of any other publication and consists solely of reports of proceedings in courts of law, or in any publication of a technical character bona fide intended for circulation among members of the legal or medical profession.

Section 4
Innocent publication and distribution

A person shall not be guilty of contempt of court on the ground that he has published any matter calculated to interfere with the course of justice in connection with any proceedings pending or imminent at the time of publication if at that time, having taken all reasonable care, he did not know and had no reason to suspect that the proceedings were pending, or that such proceedings were imminent, as the case may be.

(2) A person shall not be guilty of contempt of court on the ground that he has distributed a publication containing such matter as is mentioned in subsection (1) if at the time of distribution, having taken all reasonable care, he did not know that it contained any such matter as aforesaid and had no reason to suspect that it was likely to do so.

(3) The proof of any fact tending to establish a defence afforded by this section to any person in proceedings for contempt of court shall lie upon that person.

Section 5
Publication of information relating to proceedings in private

(1) The publication of information relating to proceedings before any court sitting in private shall not of itself be contempt of court except in the following cases, that is to say —
   (a) where the proceedings relate to the wardship or adoption of an infant or wholly or mainly to the guardianship, custody, maintenance or upbringing of an infant, or rights of access to an infant;
   (b) where the proceedings are brought under Part II, IV or IVA of the Mental Health Ordinance (Cap 136);
   (c) where the court sits in private for reasons of national security during that part of the proceedings about which the information in question is published;
   (d) where the information relates to a secret process, discovery or invention which is in issue in the proceedings;
   (e) where the court, having power to do so, expressly prohibits the publication of all information relating to the proceedings or of information of the description which is published.

(2) Without prejudice to subsection (1), the publication of the text or a summary of the whole or part of an order made by a court sitting in private shall not of itself be contempt of court except where the court, having power to do so, expressly prohibits the publication.

(3) Nothing in this section shall be construed as implying that any publication is punishable as contempt of court which would not be so punishable apart from this section.

Juvenile Offenders Ordinance (Cap 226)

Section 20A
Restriction on reports of proceedings in juvenile courts and power of other courts to prohibit certain reports

(1) Subject to subsection (2) no person shall —
   (a) publish a written report or broadcast a report of any proceedings in a juvenile court or on appeal from a juvenile court —
      (i) revealing the name, address or school; or
      (ii) including any particulars calculated to lead to the identification,

   of any child or young person concerned in the proceedings, either as being the person against or in respect of whom the proceedings are taken or as being a witness therein; or
   (b) publish in a written report any picture or broadcast any picture as being or including a picture of any child or young person so concerned in any such proceedings.

(2) The court may, if satisfied that it is in the interests of justice so to do, by order dispense with the requirements of subsection (1) to such extent as may be specified in the order.

(3) In any proceedings in any court, other than proceedings to which subsection (1) applies, the court may direct that, except in so far as the court may otherwise permit, no person shall publish any of the matters specified in subsection (1) in respect of the proceedings before it.

(4) If a report or picture is published or broadcast in contravention of subsection (1) or of a direction of a court under subsection (3), the following persons —

(a) in the case of publication of a written report or picture as part of a newspaper or periodical publication, any proprietor, editor, publisher or distributor thereof;

(b) in the case of a publication of a written report or picture otherwise than as part of a newspaper or periodical publication, the person who publishes or distributes it;

(c) in the case of a broadcast of a report or picture, any person who transmits or provides the programme in which the report or picture is broadcast and any person having functions in relation to the programme corresponding to those of the editor of a newspaper or periodical publication,

shall be guilty of an offence and shall be liable on conviction to a fine of $10000 and to imprisonment for 6 months.

(5) Proceedings for an offence under this section shall not be instituted except with the consent of the Secretary for Justice.

(6) Subsections (1) and (3) shall be in addition to, and not in derogation from, the provisions of any other Ordinance with respect to the publication of reports of judicial proceedings.

(7) In this section —

"broadcast" (廣播) means sounds or visual images broadcast by wireless telegraphy or by means of a high frequency distribution system over wire or other paths provided by a material substance and intended for general reception;

"publish" (發表), in relation to a report, means publish the report, either by itself or as part of a newspaper or periodical, for distribution to the public.

Magistrates Ordinance (Cap 227)

Section 87A
Committal hearing reporting restrictions

(1) No person shall publish in Hong Kong a written report, or broadcast in Hong Kong a report, of any committal proceedings in Hong Kong containing any matter other than that permitted by subsection (7).

(2) Notwithstanding subsection (1), a magistrate shall, on an application for the purpose made with reference to any committal proceedings by the accused or one of the accused, as the case may be, order that subsection (1) shall not apply to reports of those proceedings, and any such order shall be entered in the Magistrate's Case Register.

(3) If the accused is not represented at any preliminary inquiry by counsel or by a solicitor, the magistrate shall, immediately before taking depositions of witnesses, explain to the accused the restrictions on reports of committal

proceedings imposed by subsection (1) and inform him of his right to apply to the court for an order removing those restrictions.

(4) Where a magistrate has made an order under subsection (2) removing the restrictions on reports of committal proceedings and has adjourned those proceedings to another day, he shall, at the beginning of the adjourned hearing of the proceedings, state that the order has been made.

(5) Notwithstanding subsection (1) a report of committal proceedings containing matter other than that permitted by subsection (7) may be published or broadcast —

(a) where the magistrate determines not to commit the accused for trial, after he has so determined;

(b) where the magistrate commits the accused or any of the accused for trial, after the conclusion of his trial or, as the case may be, the trial of the last to be tried.

(6) Notwithstanding subsection (1), where at any time during committal proceedings the magistrate assumes power to deal with the offence summarily under section 91 or 92, a report of so much of the committal proceedings containing any such matter as takes place before the magistrate assumes such power may be published or broadcast, after the magistrate has assumed power, as part of a report of the summary trial.

(7) A report of committal proceedings published or broadcast without any order under subsection (2) and before the time specified in subsections (5) and (6) may contain —

(a) the identity of the court and the name of the magistrate;

(b) the names, addresses, occupations and ages of the parties and witnesses;

(c) the offence, or a summary thereof, with which the accused is charged;

(d) the names of counsel and solicitors engaged in the proceedings;

(e) any decision of the magistrate to commit the accused for trial, and any decision of the magistrate on the disposal of the case of any defendants not committed;

(f) where the magistrate commits the accused for trial, the charge, or a summary thereof, on which he is committed and the court to which he is committed;

(g) where the committal proceedings are adjourned, the date and places to which they are adjourned;

(h) (Repealed 56 of 1994 s. 11)

(i) whether legal aid was granted to the accused.

(8) If a report is published or broadcast in contravention of this section, the following persons —

(a) in the case of publication of a written report as part of a newspaper or periodical publication, any proprietor, editor, publisher or distributor thereof;

(b) in the case of a publication of a written report otherwise than as part of a newspaper or periodical publication, the person who publishes or distributes it;

(c) in the case of a broadcast of a report, any person who transmits or provides the programme in which the report is broadcast and any person having functions in relation to the programme corresponding to those of the editor of a newspaper or periodical publication,

shall be guilty of an offence and shall be liable on conviction to a fine of $10000 and to imprisonment for 6 months.

(9) Proceedings for an offence under this section shall not be instituted otherwise than by or with the consent of the Secretary for Justice.

(10) Subsection (1) shall be in addition to, and not in derogation from, the provisions of any other Ordinance with respect to the publication of reports and proceedings of magistrates' and other courts.

Official Secrets Ordinance (Cap 521)

Section 18
Information resulting from unauthorized disclosures or information entrusted in confidence

(1) A person who comes into possession of any information, document or other article in circumstances mentioned in subsection (2) commits an offence if he discloses it without lawful authority and knowing, or having reasonable cause to believe, that —

(a) it is protected against disclosure by any of sections 13 to 17; and

(b) it has come into his possession as mentioned in subsection (2).

(2) The circumstances referred to in subsection (1) are where any information, document or other article protected against disclosure by any of sections 13 to 17 has come into a person's possession as a result of it having been —

(a) disclosed (whether to him or another) by a public servant or government contractor without lawful authority;

(b) entrusted to him by a public servant or government contractor on terms requiring it to be held in confidence or in circumstances in which the public servant or government contractor could reasonably expect that it would be so held; or

(c) disclosed (whether to him or another) without lawful authority by a person to whom it was entrusted as mentioned in paragraph (b).

(3) In the case of information or a document or article protected against disclosure by sections 13 to 16, a person does not commit an offence under this section unless —

(a) the disclosure by him is damaging; and

(b) he makes it knowing, or having reasonable cause to believe, that it would be damaging.

(4) The question whether a disclosure of information or of a document or other article is damaging shall be determined for the purposes of subsection (3) as it would be determined in relation to a disclosure of that information, document or article by a public servant in contravention of section 14, 15 or 16.

(5) A person does not commit an offence under this section in respect of information or a document or other article that has come into his possession as a result of it having been disclosed —
  (a) as mentioned in subsection (2)(a) by a government contractor; or
  (b) as mentioned in subsection (2)(c),

unless that disclosure was by a British national or Hong Kong permanent resident or took place in Hong Kong.

(6) For the purposes of this section, information or a document or article is protected against disclosure by any of sections 13 to 17 if —
  (a) it relates to security or intelligence, defence or international relations or is such as is mentioned in section 16(1)(b); or
  (b) it is information or a document or article to which section 17 applies,

and information or a document or article is protected against disclosure by sections 13 to 16 if it falls within paragraph (a).

(7) No person shall be convicted for both an offence under this section and an offence under any of sections 13 to 17 in relation to the disclosure by him of any information or document or other article.

Section 21
Authorized disclosures

(1) For the purposes of this Part, a disclosure by —
  (a) a public servant; or
  (b) a person, not being a public servant or government contractor, in whose case a notification for the purposes of section 13(1) is in force,

is made with lawful authority if, and only if, it is made in accordance with his official duty.

(2) For the purposes of this Part, a disclosure by a government contractor is made with lawful authority if, and only if, it is made —
  (a) in accordance with an official authorization; or
  (b) for the purposes of the functions by virtue of which he is a government contractor and without contravening an official restriction.

(3) For the purposes of this Part, a disclosure by any other person is made with lawful authority if, and only if, it is made —
  (a) by a public servant for the purposes of his functions as such; or
  (b) in accordance with an official authorization.

(4) It is a defence for a person charged with an offence under any of sections 13 to 20 to prove that at the time of the alleged offence he believed that he had lawful authority to make the disclosure in question and had no reasonable cause to believe otherwise.

(5) In this section "official authorization" (正式授權) and "official restriction" (正式限制) mean, subject to subsection (6), an authorization or restriction duly given or imposed by a public servant or government contractor or by or on behalf of a prescribed body or a body of a prescribed class.

(6) In relation to section 20, "official authorization" (正式授權) includes an authorization duly given by or on behalf of the territory, State or organization concerned or, in the case of an organization, a member of it.

Personal Data (Privacy) Ordinance (Cap 486)

Section 18
Data access request

(1) An individual, or a relevant person on behalf of an individual, may make a request —
  (a) to be informed by a data user whether the data user holds personal data of which the individual is the data subject;
  (b) if the data user holds such data, to be supplied by the data user with a copy of such data.

Section 61
News

(1) Personal data held by a data user —
  (a) whose business, or part of whose business, consists of a news activity; and
  (b) solely for the purpose of that activity (or any directly related activity), are exempt from the provisions of —
    (i) data protection principle 6 and sections 18(1)(b) and 38(i) unless and until the data are published or broadcast (wherever and by whatever means);
    (ii) sections 36 and 38(b).

(2) Personal data are exempt from the provisions of data protection principle 3 in any case in which —
  (a) the use of the data consists of disclosing the data to a data user referred to in subsection (1); and
  (b) such disclosure is made by a person who has reasonable grounds to believe (and reasonably believes) that the publishing or broadcasting (wherever and by whatever means) of the data (and whether or not they are published or broadcast) is in the public interest.

(3) In this section —
"news activity" (新聞活動) means any journalistic activity and includes —
  (a) the —
    (i) gathering of news;
    (ii) preparation or compiling of articles or programmes concerning news; or
    (iii) observations on news or current affairs,
  for the purpose of dissemination to the public; or
  (b) the dissemination to the public of —
    (i) any article or programme of or concerning news; or
    (ii) observations on news or current affairs.

Section 64
Offences for disclosing personal data obtained without consent from data users (amended 2012)

(1) A person commits an offence if the person discloses any personal data of a data subject which was obtained from a data user without the data user's consent, with an intent —
  (a) to obtain gain in money or other property, whether for the benefit of the person or another person; or
  (b) to cause loss in money or other property to the data subject.
(2) A person commits an offence if —
  (a) the person discloses any personal data of a data subject which was obtained from a data user without the data user's consent; and
  (b) the disclosure causes psychological harm to the data subject.
(3) A person who commits an offence under subsection (1) or (2) is liable on conviction to a fine of HK$1,000,000 and to imprisonment for 5 years.
(4) In any proceedings for an offence under subsection (1) or (2), it is a defence for the person charged to prove that—
  (a) the person reasonably believed that the disclosure was necessary for the purpose of preventing or detecting crime;
  (b) the disclosure was required or authorized by or under any enactment, by any rule of law or by an order of a court;
  (c) the person reasonably believed that the data user had consented to the disclosure; or
  (d) the person—
    (i) disclosed the personal data for the purpose of a news activity as defined by section 61(3) or a directly related activity; and
    (ii) had reasonable grounds to believe that the publishing or broadcasting of the personal data was in the public interest.

Schedule 1 (Data Protection Principles)
Principle 1 — purpose and manner of collection of personal data

(1) Personal data shall not be collected unless —
  (a) the data are collected for a lawful purpose directly related to a function or activity of the data user who is to use the data;
  (b) subject to paragraph (c), the collection of the data is necessary for or directly related to that purpose; and
  (c) the data are adequate but not excessive in relation to that purpose.
(2) Personal data shall be collected by means which are —
  (a) lawful; and
  (b) fair in the circumstances of the case.
(3) Where the person from whom personal data are or are to be collected is the data subject, all practicable steps shall be taken to ensure that —
  (a) he is explicitly or implicitly informed, on or before collecting the data, of —

(i) whether it is obligatory or voluntary for him to supply the data; and
(ii) where it is obligatory for him to supply the data, the consequences for him if he fails to supply the data; and

(b) he is explicitly informed —
(i) on or before collecting the data, of —
(a) the purpose (in general or specific terms) for which the data are to be used; and
(b) the classes of persons to whom the data may be transferred; and
(ii) on or before first use of the data for the purpose for which they were collected, of —
(a) his rights to request access to and to request the correction of the data; and
(b) the name and address of the individual to whom any such request may be made,

unless to comply with the provisions of this subsection would be likely to prejudice the purpose for which the data were collected and that purpose is specified in Part VIII of this Ordinance as a purpose in relation to which personal data are exempt from the provisions of data protection principle 6.

Principle 2 — accuracy and duration of retention of personal data

(1) All practicable steps shall be taken to ensure that —
(a) personal data are accurate having regard to the purpose (including any directly related purpose) for which the personal data are or are to be used;
(b) where there are reasonable grounds for believing that personal data are inaccurate having regard to the purpose (including any directly related purpose) for which the data are or are to be used–
(i) the data are not used for that purpose unless and until those grounds cease to be applicable to the data, whether by the rectification of the data or otherwise; or
(ii) the data are erased;
(c) where it is practicable in all the circumstances of the case to know that —
(i) personal data disclosed on or after the appointed day to a third party are materially inaccurate having regard to the purpose (including any directly related purpose) for which the data are or are to be used by the third party; and
(ii) that data were inaccurate at the time of such disclosure, that the third party —
(a) is informed that the data are inaccurate; and
(b) is provided with such particulars as will enable the third party to rectify the data having regard to that purpose.

(2) Personal data shall not be kept longer than is necessary for the fulfilment of the purpose (including any directly related purpose) for which the data are or are to be used.

Principle 3 — use of personal data

Personal data shall not, without the prescribed consent of the data subject, be used for any purpose other than —

(a) the purpose for which the data were to be used at the time of the collection of the data; or

(b) a purpose directly related to the purpose referred to in paragraph (a).

Principle 4 — security of personal data

All practicable steps shall be taken to ensure that personal data (including data in a form in which access to or processing of the data is not practicable) held by a data user are protected against unauthorized or accidental access, processing, erasure or other use having particular

regard to —

(a) the kind of data and the harm that could result if any of those things should occur;

(b) the physical location where the data are stored;

(c) any security measures incorporated (whether by automated means or otherwise) into any equipment in which the data are stored;

(d) any measures taken for ensuring the integrity, prudence and competence of persons having access to the data; and

(e) any measures taken for ensuring the secure transmission of the data.

Principle 5 — information to be generally available

All practicable steps shall be taken to ensure that a person can —

(a) ascertain a data user's policies and practices in relation to personal data;

(b) be informed of the kind of personal data held by a data user;

(c) be informed of the main purposes for which personal data held by a data user are or are to be used.

Principle 6 — access to personal data

A data subject shall be entitled to —

(a) ascertain whether a data user holds personal data of which he is the data subject;

(b) request access to personal data —

  (i) within a reasonable time;

  (ii) at a fee, if any, that is not excessive;

  (iii) in a reasonable manner; and

  (iv) in a form that is intelligible;

(c) be given reasons if a request referred to in paragraph (b) is refused;

(d) object to a refusal referred to in paragraph (c);

(e) request the correction of personal data;

(f) be given reasons if a request referred to in paragraph (e) is refused; and

(g) object to a refusal referred to in paragraph (f).

Prevention of Bribery Ordinance (Cap 201)

Section 30
Offence to disclose identity, etc. of persons being investigated

(1) Any person who knowing or suspecting that an investigation in respect of an offence alleged or suspected to have been committed under Part II is taking place, without lawful authority or reasonable excuse, discloses to —

(a) the person who is the subject of the investigation (the "subject person") the fact that he is so subject or any details of such investigation; or

(b) the public, a section of the public or any particular person the identity of the subject person or the fact that the subject person is so subject or any details of such investigation,

shall be guilty of an offence and shall be liable on conviction to a fine of $20000 and to imprisonment for 1 year.

(2) Subsection (1) shall not apply as regards disclosure of any of the descriptions mentioned in that subsection where, in connection with such investigation —

(a) a warrant has been issued for the arrest of the subject person;

(b) the subject person has been arrested whether with or without warrant;

(c) the subject person has been required to furnish a statutory declaration or a statement in writing by a notice served on him under section 14(1)(a) or (b);

(d) a restraining order has been served on any person under section 14C(3);

(e) the residence of the subject person has been searched under a warrant issued under section 17; or

(f) the subject person has been required to surrender to the Commissioner any travel document in his possession by a notice served on him under section 17A.

(3) Without affecting the generality of the expression "reasonable excuse" in subsection (1) a person has a reasonable excuse as regards disclosure of any of the descriptions mentioned in that subsection if, but only to the extent that, the disclosure reveals —

(a) any unlawful activity, abuse of power, serious neglect of duty, or other serious misconduct by the Commissioner, the Deputy Commissioner or any officer of the Commission; or

(b) a serious threat to public order or to the security of Hong Kong or to the health or safety of the public.

Public Order Ordinance (Cap 245)

Section 2
Interpretation

(1) In this Ordinance, unless the context otherwise requires — "closed area" (禁區) means any area or place declared to be a closed area by order under section 36; "designated public area" (指定公眾地點) means an area designated as a designated public area by the Chief Executive under section 10

(Added 67 of 1980 s. 2; Amended 13 of 1999 s. 3); "meeting" (集會) means any gathering or assembly of persons convened or organized for the purpose of the discussion of issues or matters of interest or concern to the general public or a section thereof, or for the purpose of the expression of views on such issues or matters, and includes any gathering or assembly of persons whether or not previously convened or organized at which any person assumes or attempts to assume control or leadership thereof for any such purpose; but does not include any gathering or assembly of persons convened or organized exclusively —

(a) for social, recreational, cultural, academic, educational, religious or charitable purposes, or as a conference or seminar bona fide intended for the discussion of topics of a social, recreational, cultural, academic, educational, religious, charitable, professional, business or commercial character;
(b) for the purpose of a funeral;
(c) for the purposes of any public body; or
(d) for the purpose of carrying out any duty or exercising any power imposed or conferred by any Ordinance; "offensive weapon" (攻擊性武器) means any article made, or adapted for use, or suitable, for causing injury to the person, or intended by the person having it in his possession or under his control for such use by him or by some other person; "procession" (遊行) means a procession organized as such for a common purpose, and includes any meeting held in conjunction with such procession; "public gathering" (公眾聚集) means a public meeting, a public procession and any other meeting, gathering or assembly of 10 or more persons in any public place; "public meeting" (公眾集會) means any meeting held or to be held in a public place; "public place" (公眾地方) means any place to which for the time being the public or any section of the public are entitled or permitted to have access, whether on payment or otherwise, and, in relation to any meeting, includes any place which is or will be, on the occasion and for the purposes of such meeting, a public place; "public procession" (公眾遊行) means any procession in, to or from a public place; "society" (社團) means any club, company, partnership, association or body of persons.

(2) In this Ordinance the expressions "public safety", "the protection of public health" and "the protection of rights and freedoms of others" are interpreted in the same way as under the International Covenant on Civil and Political Rights as applied to Hong Kong. "National security" (國家安全) means the safeguarding of the territorial integrity and the independence of the People's Republic of China.

Section 17B
Disorder in public places

(1) Any person who at any public gathering acts in a disorderly manner for the purpose of preventing the transaction of the business for which the public gathering was called together or incites others so to act shall be guilty of an offence and shall be liable on conviction to a fine of $5000 and to imprisonment for 12 months.

(2) Any person who in any public place behaves in a noisy or disorderly manner, or uses, or distributes or displays any writing containing, threatening, abusive or insulting words, with intent to provoke a breach of the peace, or whereby a breach of the peace is likely to be caused, shall be guilty of an offence and shall be liable on conviction to a fine of $5000 and to imprisonment for 12 months.

Section 36
Closed areas

(1) The Chief Executive may, where he reasonably believes that it is necessary for the protection of national security or public safety, or the protection of public order or public health, by order declare any area or place to be a closed area.

(2) An order made under subsection (1) shall come into force at such time as may be specified therein or, if no time is so specified, immediately upon the making thereof by the Chief Executive and shall be published in the Gazette as soon as may be reasonably practicable after the making thereof.

(3) The Commissioner of Police and such other person as may be authorized in any order made under subsection (1) may cause a closed area to be closed by the erection of barriers or otherwise.

Section 49
Power to require identification

(1) Where a member of Her Majesty's forces acting in the course of his duty or a police officer reasonably believes that it is necessary for the purpose of preventing, detecting or investigating any offence for which the sentence is fixed by law or for which a person may (on a first conviction for that offence) be sentenced to imprisonment, the member or officer may require any person to produce proof of his identity for inspection, and any person who fails to comply with any such requirement commits an offence and is liable on summary conviction to a fine of $10,000 and to imprisonment for 6 months.

Section 50A
Obstruction

Any person who obstructs —

(a) any member of Her Majesty's forces;
(b) any officer or member of the Government Flying Service; or
(c) any other person,

exercising any powers or performing any duties conferred or imposed on him by this Ordinance or by any orders, directions, requirements or notices made thereunder shall be guilty of an offence and shall be liable on summary conviction to a fine of $1000 and to imprisonment for 6 months.

Summary Offences Ordinance (Cap 228)

Section 2
Interpretation

"public meeting" (公眾聚會) includes any meeting in a public place and any meeting which the public or a section thereof are permitted to attend, whether on payment or otherwise;

"public officer," (公職人員) or "public department," (公共機關) extends to and includes the Chief Executive and every officer or department invested with or performing duties of a public nature, whether under the immediate control of the Chief Executive or not;

"public place" (公眾地方) includes all piers, thoroughfares, streets, roads, lanes, alleys, courts, squares, archways, waterways, passages, paths, ways and places to which the public have access either continuously or periodically, whether the same are the property of the Government or of private persons.

Section 4
Nuisances committed in public places, etc.

Any person who without lawful authority or excuse —

(30) trespasses or allows any beast to trespass upon or in any messuage, tenement, cemetery or land vested in or under the control or management of any public officer or department whatsoever;

shall be liable to a fine of $500 or to imprisonment for 3 months.

Section 7
Prohibition on taking photographs, etc., in court

(1) Any person who —

(a) takes or attempts to take in any court any photograph, or with a view to publication makes or attempts to make in any court any portrait or sketch, of any person, being a judge of the court or a juror or a witness in or a party to any proceeding before the court, whether civil or criminal; or

(b) publishes any photograph, portrait or sketch taken or make in contravention of the foregoing provisions of this section or any reproduction thereof,

shall be liable to a fine of $250.

Section 22
Falsely pretending to be or be able to influence a public officer

(1) Any person who, by any act or omission and whether or not with intent to procure any valuable thing, falsely pretends that he is a public officer or is able to procure any public officer to do or refrain from doing any act or thing in connection with the duty of such public officer shall be liable to a fine of $1000 or to imprisonment for 6 months.

(2) In any proceedings for an offence under subsection (1) consisting of falsely pretending to be a public officer, it shall be presumed, until the contrary is proved, that the defendant was not a public officer at the material time.

Witness Protection Ordinance (Cap 564)

Section 17 (Offences)

(1) A person shall not, without lawful authority or reasonable excuse, disclose information —
  (a) about the identity or location of a person who is or has been a participant or who has been considered for inclusion in the witness protection programme; or
  (b) that compromises the security of such a person.

(4) A person who contravenes
  (a) subsection (1) commits an offence and is liable on conviction on indictment to imprisonment for 10 years;

PEOPLE'S REPUBLIC OF CHINA[2]

Constitution[3]

中华人民共和国宪法

Article 1

(1) The People's Republic of China is a socialist state under the people's democratic dictatorship led by the working class and based on the alliance of workers and peasants.

(2) The socialist system is the basic system of the People's Republic of China. Disruption of the socialist system by any organization or individual is prohibited.

第一条

中华人民共和国是工人阶级领导的、以工农联盟为基础的人民民主专政的社会主义国家。

社会主义制度是中华人民共和国的根本制度。禁止任何组织或者个人破坏社会主义制度。

---

2. Sources for the Chinese and English text of PRC laws and regulations include the PRC's Central People's Government, Supreme People's Court, Ministry of Foreign Affairs, State Council, Hong Kong and Macau Affairs Office of the State Council and the Xinhua News Agency. Some English translations were also provided by Asian Legal Information Institute (http://www.asianlii.org); the Congressional-Executive Commission on China; Human Rights in China, an NGO based in New York and Hong Kong; The China Center, Yale Law School; and the Journalism and Media Studies Centre at the University of Hong Kong.

3. The text is based on the 1982 Constitution, as amended in 1988, 1993, 1999 and 2004. English text can be found at: http://english.people.com.cn/constitution/constitution.html.

Article 5

(1) The People's Republic of China governs the country according to law and makes it a socialist country ruled by law.
(2) The state upholds the uniformity and dignity of the socialist legal system.
(3) No laws or administrative or local rules and regulations may contravene the Constitution.
(4) All state organs, the armed forces, all political parties and public organizations and all enterprises and institutions must abide by the Constitution and the law. All acts in violation of the Constitution or the law must be investigated.
(5) No organization or individual is privileged to be beyond the Constitution or the law.

第五条

中华人民共和国实行依法治国，建设社会主义法治国家。
国家维护社会主义法制的统一和尊严。

一切法律、行政法规和地方性法规都不得同宪法相抵触。一切国家机关和武装力量、各政党和各社会团体、各企业事业组织都必须遵守宪法和法律。一切违反宪法和法律的行为，必须予以追究。

任何组织或者个人都不得有超越宪法和法律的特权。

Article 33

(1) All persons holding the nationality of the People's Republic of China are citizens of the People's Republic of China.
(2) All citizens of the People's Republic of China are equal before the law. Every citizen enjoys the rights and at the same time must perform the duties prescribed by the Constitution and the law.
(3) The State respects and preserves human rights.

第三十三条

凡具有中华人民共和国国籍的人都是中华人民共和国公民。
中华人民共和国公民在法律面前一律平等。任何公民享有宪法和法律规定的权利，同时必须履行宪法和法律规定的义务。
国家尊重和保障人权。

Article 35

Citizens of the People's Republic of China enjoy freedom of speech, of the press, of assembly, of association, of procession and of demonstration.

第三十五条

中华人民共和国公民有言论、出版、集会、结社、游行、示威的自由。

Article 38

The personal dignity of citizens of the People's Republic of China is inviolable. Insult, libel, false accusation or false incrimination directed against citizens by any means is prohibited.

第三十八条

中华人民共和国公民的人格尊严不受侵犯。禁止用任何方法对公民进行侮辱、诽谤和诬告陷害。

Article 40

Freedom and privacy of correspondence of citizens of the People's Republic of China are protected by law. No organization or individual may, on any ground, infringe upon citizens' freedom and privacy of correspondence, except in cases where, to meet the needs of state security or of criminal investigation, public security or procuratorial organs are permitted to censor correspondence in accordance with procedures prescribed by law.

第四十条

中华人民共和国公民的通信自由和通信秘密受法律的保护。除因国家安全或者追查刑事犯罪的需要，由公安机关或者检察机关依照法律规定的程序对通信进行检查外，任何组织或者个人不得以任何理由侵犯公民的通信自由和通信秘密。

Article 41

(1) Citizens of the People's Republic of China have the right to criticize and make suggestions regarding any state organ or functionary. Citizens have the right to make to relevant state organs complaints or charges against, or exposures of, any state organ or functionary for violation of the law or dereliction of duty; but fabrication or distortion of facts for purposes of libel or false incrimination is prohibited.

(2) The state organ concerned must deal with complaints, charges or exposures made by citizens in a responsible manner after ascertaining the facts. No one may suppress such complaints, charges and exposures or retaliate against the citizens making them.

(3) Citizens who have suffered losses as a result of infringement of their civic rights by any state organ or functionary have the right to compensation in accordance with the law.

第四十一条

中华人民共和国公民对于任何国家机关和国家工作人员，有提出批评和建议的权利；对于任何国家机关和国家工作人员的违法失职行为，有向有关国家机关提出申诉、控告或者检举的权利，但是不得捏造或者歪曲事实进行诬告陷害。

对于公民的申诉、控告或者检举，有关国家机关必须查清事实，负责处理。任何人不得压制和打击报复。

由于国家机关和国家工作人员侵犯公民权利而受到损失的人，有依照法律规定取得赔偿的权利。

Criminal Law (Revised) 1997

中华人民共和国刑法

Article 105 (2)

Subversion by spreading rumours, slanders and other means

Whoever incites others by spreading rumours or slanders or any other means to subvert the State power or overthrow the socialist system shall be sentenced to fixed-term imprisonment of not more than five years, criminal detention, public surveillance or deprivation of political rights; and the ringleaders and the others who commit major crimes shall be sentenced to fixed-term imprisonment of not less than five years.

第一百零五条（第二款）

以造谣、诽谤或者其他方式煽动颠覆国家政权、推翻社会主义制度的，处五年以下有期徒刑、拘役、管制或者剥夺政治权利；首要分子或者罪行重大的，处五年以上有期徒刑。

Article 111

State secrets obtained through spying or providing to foreign entity, organization or personnel

Whoever steals, spies into, buys or unlawfully supplies State secrets or intelligence for an organ, organization or individual outside the territory of China shall be sentenced to fixed-term imprisonment of not less than five years but not more than 10 years; if the circumstances are especially serious, he shall be sentenced to fixed-term imprisonment of not less than 10 years or life imprisonment; if the circumstances are minor, he shall be sentenced to fixed-term imprisonment of not more than five years, criminal detention, public surveillance or deprivation of political rights.

第一百一十一条

为境外的机构、组织、人员窃取、刺探、收买、非法提供国家秘密或者情报的，处五年以上十年以下有期徒刑；情节特别严重的，处十年以上有期徒刑或者无期徒刑；情节较轻的，处五年以下有期徒刑、拘役、管制或者剥夺政治权利。

Article 246

Criminal defamation

Whoever, by violence or other methods, publicly humiliates another person or invents stories to defame him, if the circumstances are serious, shall be sentenced to fixed-term imprisonment of not more than three years, criminal detention, public surveillance or deprivation of political rights. The crime mentioned…shall be handled only upon complaint, except where serious harm is done to public order or to the interests of the State.

第二百四十六条【侮辱罪、诽谤罪】

以暴力或者其他方法公然侮辱他人或者捏造事实诽谤他人，情节严重的，处三年以下有期徒刑、拘役、管制或者剥夺政治权利。前款罪，告诉的才处理，但是严重危害社会秩序和国家利益的除外。

Article 282

Acquiring state secrets through theft, espionage or purchase and possession

Whoever unlawfully obtains State secrets by stealing, spying or buying shall be sentenced to fixed-term imprisonment of not more than three years, criminal detention, public surveillance or deprivation of political rights; if the circumstances are serious, he shall be sentenced to fixed-term imprisonment of not less than three years but not more than seven years.

Whoever unlawfully holds the documents, material or other objects classified as "strictly confidential" or "confidential" State secrets and refuses to explain their sources and purposes shall be sentenced to fixed-term imprisonment of not more than three years, criminal detention or public surveillance.

第二百八十二条

以窃取、刺探、收买方法，非法获取国家秘密的，处三年以下有期徒刑、拘役、管制或者剥夺政治权利；情节严重的，处三年以上七年以下有期徒刑。

非法持有属于国家绝密、机密的文件、资料或者其他物品，拒不说明来源与用途的，处三年以下有期徒刑、拘役或者管制。

State Secrets Law (Law on Guarding State Secrets 1988, revised 2010)

保守国家秘密法

Article 2

State secrets shall be matters that have a vital bearing on state security and national interests and, as specified by legal procedure, are entrusted to a limited number of people for a given period of time.

第二条

国家秘密是关系国家安全和利益，依照法定程序确定，在一定时间内只限一定范围的人员知悉的事项。

Article 4

The work of guarding state secrets (hereinafter referred to as "secret-guarding work") shall be carried out in line with the principles of active prevention of leaks, emphasizing priorities, and management according to the law, so that the security of state secrets is protected while the rational use of information and resources is facilitated.

Matters requiring disclosure by laws or administrative regulations shall be disclosed in accordance with the law.

第四条

第保守国家秘密的工作（以下简称保密工作），实行积极防范、突出重点、依法管理的方针，既确保国家秘密安全，又便利信息资源合理利用。

法律、行政法规规定公开的事项，应当依法公开。

Article 9
In accordance with the provisions of Article 2 of this Law, state secrets shall include the following:

(1) secrets concerning major policy decisions on state affairs;
(2) secrets in the building of national defence and in the activities of the armed forces;
(3) secrets in diplomatic activities and in activities related to foreign countries as well as secrets to be maintained as commitments to foreign countries;
(4) secrets in national economic and social development;
(5) secrets concerning science and technology;
(6) secrets concerning activities for safeguarding state security and the investigation of criminal offences; and
(7) other matters that are classified as state secrets by the national department for the administration and management of state secret-guarding.

Secrets of political parties that conform with the provisions of Article 2 of this Law shall be state secrets.

第九条
下列涉及国家安全和利益的事项，泄露后可能损害国家在政治、经济、国防、外交等领域的安全和利益的，应当确定为国家秘密：
（一） 国家事务重大决策中的秘密事项；
（二） 国防建设和武装力量活动中的秘密事项；
（三） 外交和外事活动中的秘密事项以及对外承担保密义务的秘密事项；
（四） 国民经济和社会发展中的秘密事项；
（五） 科学技术中的秘密事项；
（六） 维护国家安全活动和追查刑事犯罪中的秘密事项；
（七） 经国家保密行政管理部门确定的其他秘密事项。
政党的秘密事项中符合前款规定的，属于国家秘密。

Article 10
State secrets are classified into three categories: “top secret”, “highly secret”, and “secret”.

Secrets classified as “top secret” are the most vital state secrets, the divulgence of which will cause extremely serious harm to state security and national interests; secrets classified as “highly secret” are important state secrets, the divulgence of which will cause serious harm to state security and national interests; and secrets classified as “secret” are ordinary state secrets, the divulgence of which will cause harm to state security and national interests.

第十条
国家秘密的密级分为绝密、机密、秘密三级。

绝密级国家秘密是最重要的国家秘密，泄露会使国家安全和利益遭受特别严重的损害；机密级国家秘密是重要的国家秘密，泄露会使国家安全和利益遭受严重的损害；秘密级国家秘密是一般的国家秘密，泄露会使国家安全和利益遭受损害。

Article 28

Internet and other public information networking operators and service providers must cooperate with public security, state security, and procuratorate organs in investigation of cases regarding leaking of secrets; when information involving leaking of state secrets is found to have been published through the Internet and other public information networks, transmission must stop immediately, relevant records must be kept, and reports must be made to public security organs, state security organs, or the departments for the administration and management of guarding state secrets; information involving leaking of state secrets must be deleted as required by public security organs, state security organs, or the departments for the administration and management of guarding state secrets.

第二十八条

互联网及其他公共信息网络运营商、服务商应当配合公安机关、国家安全机关、检察机关对泄密案件进行调查；发现利用互联网及其他公共信息网络发布的信息涉及泄露国家秘密的，应当立即停止传输，保存有关记录，向公安机关、国家安全机关或者保密行政管理部门报告；应当根据公安机关、国家安全机关或者保 密行政管理部门的要求，删除涉及泄露国家秘密的信息。

Procedures for the Implementation of the Law on Guarding State Secrets 1990[4]

保守国家秘密法实施办法

Article 4

Any matter which would give rise to any of the following consequences if it were divulged, shall be brought within the scope of a state secret and a specific secrecy grade:

(1) jeopardizes the ability of the national government to maintain stability and defend itself;
(2) affects the integrity of the nation's unity, solidarity among peoples or social stability;
(3) harms political or economic interests of the nation with respect to the outside world;
(4) affects the safety of any national leader or foreign dignitary;
(5) hinders important national safety or health work;
(6) causes a reduction in the effectiveness or reliability of any measures to protect state secrets;
(7) weakens the nation's economy or technological strength;
(8) causes any national organ to lose its ability to exercise its legal authority.

4. In May 2012, the State Council published a draft of revised implementation measures for the law on state secrets, asking for public comments until June 2012. The Chinese text of the draft is here: http://www.chinalaw.gov.cn/article/cazjgg/201205/20120500367762.shtml

第四条
某一事项泄露后会造成下列后果之一的，应当列入国家秘密及其密级的具体范围（以下简称保密范围）：
（一）危害国家政权的巩固和防御能力；
（二）影响国家统一、民族团结和社会安定；
（三）损害国家在对外活动中的政治、经济利益；
（四）影响国家领导人、外国要员的安全；
（五）妨害国家重要的安全保卫工作；
（六）使保护国家秘密的措施可行性降低或者失效；
（七）削弱国家的经济、科技实力；
（八）使国家机关依法行政职权失去保障。

Interpretation on Specific Application of Laws When Hearing Cases of Stealing, Spying, Purchasing, and Illegally Providing State Secrets and Intelligence for Overseas Countries (2001) (Supreme People's Court)

关于审理为境外窃取、刺探、收买、非法提供国家秘密、情报案件具体应用法律若干问题的解释(最高人民法院)

Article 1
The term "intelligence" in Article 111 of the Criminal Law refers to items which involve the security and interests of the nation, but which are not public or which, according to relevant regulations, should not be made public.

第一条
刑法第一百一十一条规定的"国家秘密"，是指《中华人民共和国保守国家秘密法》第二条、第八条以及《中华人民共和国保守国家秘密法实施办法》第四条确定的事项。

Article 5
Any person who knows, or should know, that an item which is not marked secret relates to the security and interests of the nation and steals, acquires through spying or buys it for, or illegally supplies it to, a foreigner, shall be prosecuted and punished under the provisions of Article 111 of the Criminal Law for stealing, acquiring through spying or buying state secrets for, or illegally supplying state secrets to, a foreigner.

第五条
行为人知道或者应当知道没有标明密级的事项关系国家安全和利益，而为境外窃取、刺探、收买、非法提供的，依照刑法第一百一十一条的规定以为境外窃取、刺探、收买、非法提供国家秘密罪定罪处罚。

Article 6
Anyone using the Internet to illegally transmit state secrets or intelligence to a foreign entity, organization or individual shall be prosecuted and punished under the provisions of Article 111 of the Criminal Law; where the promulgation of state secrets through the Internet is particularly serious, they shall be prosecuted and punished under the provisions of Article 398 of the Criminal Law.

第六条

通过互联网将国家秘密或者情报非法发送给境外的机构、组织、个人的，依照刑法第一百一十一条的规定定罪处罚；将国家秘密通过互联网予以发布，情节严重的，依照刑法第三百九十八条的规定定罪处罚。

State Security Law 1993
国家安全法

Article 4

Any organization or individual that has committed any act endangering the State security of the People's Republic of China shall be prosecuted according to law. "Act endangering State security" as referred to in this Law means any of the following acts endangering the State security of the People's Republic of China committed by institutions, organizations or individuals outside the territory of the People's Republic of China, or, by other persons under the instigation or financial support of the afore-mentioned institutions, organizations or individuals, or, by organizations or individuals within the territory in collusion with institutions, organizations or individuals outside the territory:

(1) plotting to subvert the government, dismember the State or overthrow the socialist system;
(2) joining an espionage organization or accepting a mission assigned by an espionage organization or by its agent;
(3) stealing, secretly gathering, buying, or unlawfully providing State secrets;
(4) instigating, luring or bribing a State functionary to turn traitor; or
(5) committing any other act of sabotage endangering State security.

第四条

任何组织和个人进行危害中华人民共和国国家安全的行为都必须受到法律追究。本法所称危害国家安全的行为，是指境外机构、组织、个人实施或者指使、资助他人实施的、或者境内组织、个人与境外机构、组织、个人相勾结实施的下列危害中华人民共和国国家安全的行：

（一）阴谋颠覆政府，分裂国家，推翻社会主义制度的；
（二）参加间谍组织或者接受间谍组织及其代理人的任务的；
（三）窃取、刺探、收买、非法提供国家秘密的；
（四）策动、勾引、收买国家工作人员叛变的；
（五）进行危害国家安全的其他破坏活动的。

Measures for the Implementation of State Security Law (1994)
国家安全法实施细则

Article 7

As used in Article 4 of the Law on State Secrets, "collude" to carry out actions which will jeopardize national security, refers to any actions of organizations or individuals within the borders of China:

(1) plotting or carrying out together with foreign entities, organizations or individuals activities which jeopardize national security;
(2) accepting financing from foreign entities, organizations or individuals to facilitate or carry out activities which jeopardize national security;
(3) establishing affiliation with, obtaining aid from, assisting or carrying out with foreign entities, organizations or individuals activities which jeopardize national security.

第七条

《国家安全法》第四条所称“勾结”实施危害国家安全的行为，是指境内组织、个人的下列行为：

(一)与境外机构、组织、个人共同策划或者进行危害国家安全活动的；
(二)接受境外机构、组织、个人的资助或者指使，进行危害国家安全活动的；
(三)与境外机构、组织、个人建立联系，取得支持、帮助，进行危害国家安全活动的。

Article 8

The following actions shall constitute “other disruptive activities which jeopardize national security” under Article 4 of the Law on National Security:

(1) organizing, plotting or implementing terrorist activities which jeopardize national security;
(2) fabricating or distorting facts, disseminating or spreading writing or speech or producing or transmitting audio/visual productions that jeopardize national security;
(3) taking advantage of established social groups or enterprise organizations to carry out activities which jeopardize national security;
(4) taking advantage of religions to carry out activities which jeopardize national security;
(5) producing dissension among peoples or inciting division among peoples in a manner which jeopardizes national security; and
(6) any foreign individual who, in violation of relevant regulations, does not listen to dissuasion, and without authorization meets with personnel in China who has activities which jeopardize national security, or who are under significant suspicion of having activities which jeopardize national security.

第八条

下列行为属于《国家安全法》第四条所称“危害国家安全的其他破坏活动”：

(一)组织、策划或者实施危害国家安全的恐怖活动的；
(二)捏造、歪曲事实，发表、散布文字或者言论，或者制作、传播音像制品，危害国家安全的；
(三)利用设立社会团体或者企业事业组织，进行危害国家安全活动的；
(四)利用宗教进行危害国家安全活动的；
(五)制造民族纠纷，煽动民族分裂，危害国家安全的；
(六)境外个人违反有关规定，不听劝阻，擅自会见境内有危害国家安全行为或者有危害国家安全行为重大嫌疑的人员的。

Regulations of the People's Republic of China on News Coverage by Permanent Offices of Foreign Media Organizations and Foreign Journalists (2008) (Decree No. 537, State Council)

Article 1

These Regulations are formulated for the purpose of facilitating news coverage and reporting activities carried out by permanent offices of foreign media organizations and foreign journalists in the territory of the People's Republic of China in accordance with law and promoting international exchange and dissemination of information.

Article 2

The term "permanent offices of foreign media organizations" in these Regulations means branch offices established by foreign media organizations in China for the purpose of news coverage and reporting.

The term "foreign journalists" in these Regulations includes resident foreign journalists and foreign journalists for short-term news coverage. The term "resident foreign journalists" means career journalists who are dispatched by foreign media organizations to be stationed in China for a period of not less than six months for news coverage and reporting. The term "foreign journalists for short-term news coverage" means career journalists who stay in China for a period of less than six months for news coverage and reporting.

Article 3

China follows a basic State policy of opening up to the outside world, protects the lawful rights and interests of permanent offices of foreign media organizations and foreign journalists in accordance with law, and facilitates their news coverage and reporting activities carried out in accordance with law.

Article 4

Permanent offices of foreign media organizations and foreign journalists shall abide by the laws, regulations and rules of China, observe the professional ethics of journalism, conduct news coverage and reporting activities on an objective and impartial basis, and shall not engage in activities which are incompatible with the nature of the organizations or the capacity as journalists.

Article 5

The Ministry of Foreign Affairs of the People's Republic of China (hereinafter referred to as the Foreign Ministry) is the competent authority in charge of the affairs concerning permanent offices of foreign media organizations and foreign journalists. The Information Office of the State Council and other competent departments are, within their respective functions and duties, responsible for the relevant affairs concerning permanent offices of foreign media organizations and foreign journalists.

The foreign affairs offices of the local people's governments are entrusted by the Foreign Ministry with the handling of affairs concerning permanent offices of foreign media organizations and foreign journalists in their respective administrative areas. The information offices and other competent departments of the local people's governments are, within their respective functions and duties, responsible for the relevant affairs concerning permanent offices of foreign media organizations and foreign journalists in their respective administrative areas.

Article 6

A foreign media organization that intends to establish a permanent office in China or dispatch a resident journalist to China shall seek the approval of the Foreign Ministry.

Article 7

A foreign media organization that applies for the establishment of a permanent office in China shall submit the following documents to the Foreign Ministry directly or through a Chinese diplomatic mission abroad:

(1) a written application signed by a principal officer in charge of the headquarters of the media organization;
(2) a profile of the media organization;
(3) profiles of the head of the permanent office to be established and the journalists and staff members to be dispatched; and
(4) a copy of the document certifying that the media organization is established in its home country.

Article 8

Upon approval of the application for the establishment of a permanent office in China, the head of the permanent office to be established shall, within 7 working days from the date of his arrival in China, register with the Foreign Ministry by presenting his passport for the issue of the Certificate for Permanent Office of Foreign Media Organization in China; where the permanent office of a foreign media organization to be established is based in a place other than Beijing, the head thereof shall, within 7 working days from the date of his arrival in China, register with the foreign affairs office of the local people's government entrusted by the Foreign Ministry by presenting his passport for the issue of the Certificate for Permanent Office of Foreign Media Organization in China.

Article 9

A foreign media organization that applies for the dispatch of a resident journalist to China shall submit the following documents to the Foreign Ministry directly or through a Chinese diplomatic mission abroad:

(1) a written application signed by an officer in charge of the headquarters of the media organization;
(2) a profile of the journalist to be dispatched; and
(3) a copy of the document certifying the professional activities of the said journalist in the home country of the media organization.

Where two or more foreign media organizations intend to dispatch one and the same resident journalist, they shall submit separate applications in accordance with the provisions of the preceding paragraph and specify in their respective applications other foreign media organizations for which the said journalist works concurrently.

Article 10

Upon approval of the application for the dispatch of a resident journalist to China, the resident journalist dispatched shall, within 7 working days from the date of his arrival in China, register with the Foreign Ministry by presenting his passport for the issue of the Press Card (R); where a resident foreign journalist is to reside in a place other than Beijing, he shall, within 7 working days from the date of his arrival in China, register with the foreign affairs office of the local people's government entrusted by the Foreign Ministry by presenting his passport for the issue of the Press Card (R).

After being issued the Press Card (R), the foreign journalist shall register with the public security authority of his place of residence for the issue of a resident permit.

Article 11

Where the permanent office of a foreign media organization intends to change its name, place of residence, etc., it shall submit a written application to the Foreign Ministry for approval before going through the necessary procedures accordingly.

The permanent office of a foreign media organization shall notify the Foreign Ministry in writing of the change of its head, office address, etc. within 7 working days after the change is made. The permanent office of a foreign media organization based in a place other than Beijing shall notify in writing the foreign affairs office of the local people's government entrusted by the Foreign Ministry of the change of its head, office address, etc. within 7 working days after the change is made.

Article 12

Where the Press Card (R) of a resident foreign journalist needs to be extended upon expiration, he shall, prior to the expiration, apply to the Foreign Ministry or the foreign affairs office of the local people's government entrusted by the Foreign Ministry for extension and go through the necessary procedures accordingly. If he fails to do so, he shall be deemed to have automatically waived his status as a resident foreign journalist and his Press Card (R) shall be cancelled accordingly.

Article 13

Where the permanent office of a foreign media organization intends to terminate its operation in China, it shall notify the Foreign Ministry of its intention 30 days prior to the termination and, within 7 working days from the date of the termination, register with the Foreign Ministry or the foreign affairs office of the local people's government entrusted by the Foreign Ministry for the cancellation of its Certificate for Permanent Office of Foreign Media Organization in China and the Press Cards (R) of its resident journalists.

Where the permanent office of a foreign media organization does not have any resident journalists for ten consecutive months or more, it shall be deemed to have automatically terminated its operation and its Certificate for Permanent Office of Foreign Media Organization in China shall be cancelled accordingly.

Where a resident foreign journalist stays in China for less than six months annually on an accumulative basis, his Press Card (R) shall be cancelled.

The permanent office of a foreign media organization shall, before the departure of a resident journalist, register with the Foreign Ministry or the foreign affairs office of the local people's government entrusted by the Foreign Ministry for the cancellation of his Press Card (R).

Article 14

The cancellation of the Certificate for Permanent Office of Foreign Media Organization in China and the Press Card (R) shall be made public.

The Journalist Visa of a resident foreign journalist whose Press Card (R) is cancelled automatically becomes invalid ten days after the date of cancellation.

A resident foreign journalist whose Press Card (R) is cancelled shall, within ten days from the date of cancellation, present the relevant certifying documents to the public security authority of his place of residence to apply for the alteration of his visa or resident permit.

Article 15

A resident foreign journalist or a foreign journalist for short-term news coverage shall apply for the Journalist Visa with a Chinese diplomatic mission abroad or a visa agency authorized by the Foreign Ministry.

Article 16

Where a foreign journalist is to travel to China with the head of State, head of government, head of legislative body, members of the royal family or senior government officials of a country, the foreign ministry or relevant department of the country concerned shall apply to a Chinese diplomatic mission abroad or a visa agency authorized by the Foreign Ministry of China for the Journalist Visa on behalf of the journalist.

Article 17

A foreign journalist who intends to interview organizations or individuals in China needs to obtain their prior consent.

A foreign journalist shall carry and present his Press Card (R) or Journalist Visa for Short Visit when conducting news coverage activities.

Article 18

The permanent office of a foreign media organization or a foreign journalist may, through organizations providing services to foreign nationals, hire Chinese citizens to do auxiliary work. Organizations providing services to foreign nationals are designated by the Foreign Ministry or the foreign affairs offices of the local people's governments entrusted by the Foreign Ministry.

Article 19

For the needs of news coverage and reporting, the permanent office of a foreign media organization or a foreign journalist may, on a short-term basis, bring into, install and use radio communications equipment in China after completing the application and approval procedures in accordance with law.

Article 20

Where a foreign national engages in news coverage or reporting activities in China without obtaining a Press Card (R) or Journalist Visa for Short Visit or without holding a valid one, the public security authority shall order him to stop the news coverage or reporting activities and shall handle the case in accordance with the relevant law.

Article 21

Where the permanent office of a foreign media organization or a foreign journalist violates the provisions of these Regulations, the Foreign Ministry shall give it/him a warning, order it/him to suspend or terminate its/his operational activities and, if the circumstances are serious, revoke the Certificate for Permanent Office of Foreign Media Organization in China, Press Card (R) or Journalist Visa.

Article 22

The permanent office of a foreign media organization or a foreign journalist that violates the provisions of other laws, regulations or rules of China shall be dealt with in accordance with law. If the circumstances are serious, the Foreign Ministry shall revoke the Certificate for Permanent Office of Foreign Media Organization in China, Press Card (R) or Journalist Visa.

Article 23

These Regulations shall be effective as of October 17, 2008. The Regulations Concerning Foreign Journalists and Permanent Offices of Foreign News Agencies promulgated by the State Council on January 19, 1990 shall be repealed simultaneously.

中华人民共和国外国常驻新闻机构和外国记者采访条例（第537号国务院令）

第一条

为了便于外国常驻新闻机构和外国记者在中华人民共和国境内依法采访报道，促进国际交往和信息传播，制定本条例。

第二条

本条例所称外国常驻新闻机构，是指外国新闻机构在中国境内设立、从事新闻采访报道业务的分支机构。

本条例所称外国记者包括外国常驻记者和外国短期采访记者。外国常驻记者是指由外国新闻机构派遣，在中国境内常驻6个月以上、从事新闻采访报道业务的职业记者；外国短期采访记者是指在中国境内停留期不超过6个月、从事新闻采访报道业务的职业记者。

第三条
中国实行对外开放的基本国策，依法保障外国常驻新闻机构和外国记者的合法权益，并为其依法从事新闻采访报道业务提供便利。

第四条
外国常驻新闻机构和外国记者应当遵守中国法律、法规和规章，遵守新闻职业道德，客观、公正地进行采访报道，不得进行与其机构性质或者记者身份不符的活动。

第五条
中华人民共和国外交部（以下简称外交部）主管外国常驻新闻机构和外国记者事务。国务院新闻办公室和其他部门在各自职责范围内负责外国常驻新闻机构和外国记者有关事务。

地方人民政府外事部门受外交部委托，办理本行政区域内外国常驻新闻机构和外国记者事务。

地方人民政府新闻办公室和其他部门在各自职责范围内负责本行政区域内外国常驻新闻机构和外国记者有关事务。

第六条
外国新闻机构在中国境内设立常驻新闻机构、向中国派遣常驻记者，应当经外交部批准。

第七条
外国新闻机构申请在中国境内设立常驻新闻机构，应当直接或者通过中国驻外使领馆向外交部提交以下材料：
（一）由该新闻机构总部主要负责人签署的书面申请；
（二）该新闻机构情况介绍；
（三）拟设立机构的负责人、拟派遣的常驻记者以及工作人员情况介绍；
（四）该新闻机构在所在国设立的证明文件副本。

第八条
在中国境内设立常驻新闻机构的申请经批准后，该常驻新闻机构负责人应当自抵达中国之日起7个工作日内，持本人护照到外交部办理外国常驻新闻机构证；其中，驻北京市以外地区的常驻新闻机构，其负责人应当自抵达中国之日起7个工作日内，持本人护照到外交部委托的地方人民政府外事部门办理外国常驻新闻机构证。

第九条
外国新闻机构申请向中国派遣常驻记者，应当直接或者通过中国驻外使领馆向外交部提交以下材料：
（一）由该新闻机构总部负责人签署的书面申请；
（二）拟派遣记者情况介绍；
（三）拟派遣记者在所在国从事职业活动的证明文件副本。
两个以上外国新闻机构派遣同一名常驻记者的，应当依照前款规定分别办理申请手续，并在各自的书面申请中注明该记者所兼职的外国新闻机构。

第十条

向中国派遣常驻记者的申请经批准后，被派遣的外国记者应当自抵达中国之日起7个工作日内，持本人护照到外交部办理外国常驻记者证；其中，驻北京市以外地区的常驻记者，应当自抵达中国之日起7个工作日内，持本人护照到外交部委托的地方人民政府外事部门办理外国常驻记者证。

外国记者办理外国常驻记者证后，应当到居住地公安机关办理居留证。

第十一条

外国常驻新闻机构变更机构名称、常驻地区等事项，应当向外交部提交书面申请，经批准后办理变更手续。

外国常驻新闻机构变更负责人、办公地址等事项，应当在变更后7个工作日内书面告知外交部；其中，驻北京市以外地区的常驻新闻机构变更负责人、办公地址等事项，应当在变更后7个工作日内书面告知外交部委托的地方人民政府外事部门。

第十二条

外国常驻记者证有效期届满需要延期的，外国常驻记者应当提前向外交部或者外交部委托的地方人民政府外事部门提出申请，办理延期手续；逾期不办理的，视为自动放弃外国常驻记者资格，其外国常驻记者证将被注销。

第十三条

外国常驻新闻机构拟终止业务的，应当在终止业务30日前告知外交部，并自终止业务之日起7个工作日内到外交部或者外交部委托的地方人民政府外事部门办理外国常驻新闻机构证及其常驻记者的外国常驻记者证注销手续。

外国常驻新闻机构连续10个月以上无常驻记者，视为该机构已经自动终止业务，其外国常驻新闻机构证将被注销。

外国常驻记者在中国境内居留时间每年累计少于6个月的，其外国常驻记者证将被注销。

外国常驻新闻机构应当在其常驻记者离任前到外交部或者外交部委托的地方人民政府外事部门办理该记者外国常驻记者证注销手续。

第十四条

外国常驻新闻机构证、外国常驻记者证被注销后，应当向社会公布。

外国常驻记者证被注销的记者，其记者签证自注销之日起10日后自动失效。

外国常驻记者证被注销的记者，应当自外国常驻记者证被注销之日起10日内持相关证明，到居住地公安机关申请办理签证或者居留证变更登记。

第十五条

外国记者常驻或者短期采访，应当向中国驻外使领馆或者外交部授权的签证机构申请办理记者签证。

第十六条

外国记者随国家元首、政府首脑、议长、王室成员或者高级政府官员来中国访问，应当由该国外交部或者相关部门向中国驻外使领馆或者外交部授权的签证机构统一申请办理记者签证。

第十七条
外国记者在中国境内采访，需征得被采访单位和个人的同意。
外国记者采访时应当携带并出示外国常驻记者证或者短期采访记者签证。

第十八条
外国常驻新闻机构和外国记者可以通过外事服务单位聘用中国公民从事辅助工作。外事服务单位由外交部或者外交部委托的地方人民政府外事部门指定。

第十九条
外国常驻新闻机构和外国记者因采访报道需要，在依法履行报批手续后，可以临时进口、设置和使用无线电通信设备。

第二十条
外国人未取得或者未持有有效的外国常驻记者证或者短期采访记者签证，在中国境内从事新闻采访报道活动的，由公安机关责令其停止新闻采访报道活动，并依照有关法律予以处理。

第二十一条
外国常驻新闻机构和外国记者违反本条例规定的，由外交部予以警告，责令暂停或者终止其业务活动；情节严重的，吊销其外国常驻新闻机构证、外国常驻记者证或者记者签证。

第二十二条
外国常驻新闻机构和外国记者违反中国其他法律、法规和规章规定的，依法处理；情节严重的，由外交部吊销其外国常驻新闻机构证、外国常驻记者证或者记者签证。

第二十三条
本条例自2008年10月17日起施行。1990年1月19日国务院公布的《外国记者和外国常驻新闻机构管理条例》同时废止。

Guidelines for Hong Kong and Macau Journalists Reporting in Mainland China (Hong Kong Macau Affairs Office, State Council, 6 February 2009)[5]

Article 1
These Guidelines are made for the convenience of Hong Kong and Macau journalists so they could report in mainland China in accordance with the law.

Article 2
The Hong Kong and Macau journalists referred to in these Guidelines must be Hong Kong or Macau residents, and must be professional journalists doing news reporting for news organizations legally registered in Hong Kong or Macau, and that are published, distributed, operated as permitted by the Hong Kong and

5. Unofficial English translation provided by the Journalism and Media Studies Centre (JMSC), the University of Hong Kong (HKU). Official Chinese text can be found at: http://news.xinhuanet.com/newscenter/2009–02/06/content_10773947.htm.

Macau Special Administrative Governments. News organizations include newspapers, publications, radio stations, television stations and news agencies.

Article 3

Hong Kong and Macau journalists shall abide by the laws, regulations and rules of China, observe professional ethics of journalism, conduct news reporting activities on an objective and impartial basis, and shall not engage in activities which are incompatible with the nature of the organization or the role of journalists.

Article 4

Hong Kong and Macau news organizations which have established bureaus or dispatched correspondents in mainland China will conduct their affairs in accordance to existing regulations.

Article 5

Hong Kong and Macau journalists reporting in mainland China must obtain a [temporary] press pass, as issued by the All-China Journalists Association, from the Liaison Office of the Central People's Government in the HKSAR or Macau SAR.

Article 6

Hong Kong and Macau journalists wishing to interview organizations or individuals in China need to obtain their prior approval, and must carry and show their correspondent press pass or [temporary] press pass.

Article 7

Hong Kong and Macau journalists may hire mainland Chinese residents, through service units as designed by the Chinese authorities, to carry out assistance work.

Article 8

Hong Kong and Macau journalists may temporarily bring in, set up and use radio communication equipment after completing application procedures for approval in accordance with the law.

Article 9

These Guidelines are subject to interpretation of the State Council's Hong Kong and Macau Affairs Office.

Article 10

These Guidelines come into force the day of publication.

香港澳门记者在内地采访办法
国务院港澳事务办公室

第一条

为了便于香港和澳门记者在内地依法采访报道，制定本办法。

第二条

本办法所称香港和澳门记者必须是香港或者澳门居民，并在香港或者澳门依法注册的，香港或者澳门特区政府核准出版、发行、经营的时事类报纸、刊物以及电台、电视台、通讯社等新闻机构从事新闻报道工作的职业记者。

第三条

香港和澳门记者应当遵守国家法律、法规和规章，遵守新闻职业道德，客观、公正地进行采访报道，不得进行与其机构性质或者记者身份不符的活动。

第四条

香港和澳门新闻机构在内地设立常驻记者站及派遣常驻记者事宜，按照现行办法办理。

第五条

香港和澳门记者来内地采访，需向中央人民政府驻香港特别行政区联络办公室或中央人民政府驻澳门特别行政区联络办公室领取由中华全国新闻工作者协会制发的港澳记者采访证。

第六条

香港和澳门记者在内地采访，需征得被采访单位和个人的同意，采访时应当携带并出示港澳新闻机构常驻内地记者证或港澳记者采访证。

第七条

港澳记者可以通过有关部门指定的服务单位聘用内地居民从事辅助工作。

第八条

香港和澳门记者因采访报道需要，在依法履行报批手续后，可以临时进口、设置和使用无线电通信设备。

第九条

本办法由国务院港澳事务办公室负责解释。

第十条

本办法自公布之日起实施。

Guidelines for Applying for a "Hong Kong and Macau Journalist Press Card"[6]

In accordance to the rules under the "Guidelines for Hong Kong and Macau Journalists Reporting in Mainland China" issued by the State Council's Hong Kong and Macau Affairs Office on February 6, 2009, in order to carry out reporting in mainland China, Hong Kong journalists must obtain from the Liaison Office of the Central People's Government in the HKSAR a "Hong Kong and Macau Journalist Press Card" issued in the name of All-China Journalists Association.

The procedures for obtaining the "Hong Kong and Macau Journalist Press Card" are as follows:

6. Unofficial English translation provided by the JMSC, HKU. Chinese text at: http://www.locpg.hk/big5/hwzn/200902/t20090209_3681.asp.

1. Download the "Hong Kong and Macau Journalist Press Card Registration Form" from the website of the Liaison Office of the Central People's Government in the HKSAR (www.locpg.hk), fill out all required information in the form; can make a copy of the form for record;
2. Submit the completed "Hong Kong and Macau Journalist Press Card Registration Form" to the person in charge of your organization for signature; the form must also provide the contact details of the journalist responsible for this reporting assignment;
3. Fax in advance the "Hong Kong and Macau Journalist Press Card Registration Form" to 23087396, and send the electronic copy of a recent colour photo (320x240, 100–200KB, JPG, no hat) of the journalist applying for the press card to locpg_media@hotmail.com.

When the "Hong Kong and Macau Journalist Press Card" is produced someone will contact the journalist to collect the card. The validity of the press card is 30 days.

"港澳記者採訪證"辦證指引

按照國務院港澳辦2009年2月6日公佈的《香港澳門記者在內地採訪辦法》的有關規定，香港記者赴內地採訪，需向中央人民政府駐香港特別行政區聯絡辦公室領取由中華全國新聞工作者協會制發的"港澳記者採訪證"。

領取"港澳記者採訪證"的具體程序如下：

1、登陸中聯辦網站(www.locpg.hk)下載《港澳記者採訪證登記表》，按照表格上的內容逐項填寫，該表可自行複印備用；

2、將已填妥的《港澳記者採訪證登記表》交機構負責人簽名，並注明負責此項採訪的記者的聯絡方式；

3、提前將《港澳記者採訪證登記表》傳真至23087396，同時將申領採訪證的記者的近期免冠彩色照片電子版（320×240圖元以上，100–200KB，JPG格式）寄往電子郵箱locpg_media@hotmail.com。

"港澳記者採訪證"製作完成後將有專人通知記者前來領取。採訪證有效期為30天。

Open Government Information Regulations (Effective 1 May 2008) (State Council)

中华人民共和国政府信息公开条例（2008年5月1日生效）（国务院）

Article 2

"Government information" referred to in these Regulations means information made or obtained by administrative organs in the course of exercising their responsibilities and recorded and stored in a given form.

第二条

本条例所称政府信息，是指行政机关在履行职责过程中制作或者获取的，以一定形式记录、保存的信息。

Article 8

The government information disclosed by administrative organs may not endanger state security, public security, economic security and social stability.

第八条

行政机关公开政府信息，不得危及国家安全、公共安全、经济安全和社会稳定。

Article 9

Administrative organs should disclose on their own initiative government information that satisfies any one of the following basic criteria:

(1) Information that involves the vital interests of citizens, legal persons or other organizations;
(2) Information that needs to be extensively known or participated in by the general public;
(3) Information that shows the structure, function and working procedures of and other matters relating to the administrative organ; and
(4) Other information that should be disclosed on the administrative organ's own initiative according to laws, regulations and relevant state provisions.

第九条

行政机关对符合下列基本要求之一的政府信息应当主动公开：
（一）涉及公民、法人或者其他组织切身利益的；
（二）需要社会公众广泛知晓或者参与的；
（三）反映本行政机关机构设置、职能、办事程序等情况的；
（四）其他依照法律、法规和国家有关规定应当主动公开的。

Article 10

People's governments at the county level and above and their departments should determine the concrete content of the government information to be disclosed on their own initiative within their scope of responsibility in accordance with the provisions of Article 9 of these Regulations, and emphasize disclosure of the following government information:

(1) Administrative regulations, rules, and regulatory documents;
(2) Plans for national economic and social development, plans for specific projects, plans for regional development and related policies;
(3) Statistical information on national economic and social development;
(4) Reports on financial budgets and final accounts;
(5) Items subject to an administrative fee and the legal basis and standards therefor;
(6) Catalogues of the government's centralized procurement projects, their standards and their implementation;
(7) Matters subject to administrative licensing and their legal bases, conditions, quantities, procedures and deadlines and catalogues of all the materials that need to be submitted when applying for the administrative licensing, and the handling thereof;

(8) Information on the approval and implementation of major construction projects;
(9) Policies and measures on such matters as poverty assistance, education, medical care, social security and job creation and their actual implementation;
(10) Emergency plans for, early warning information concerning, and counter measures against sudden public events;
(11) Information on the supervision and inspection of environmental protection, public health, safe production, food and drugs, and product quality.

第十条
县级以上各级人民政府及其部门应当依照本条例第九条的规定，在各自职责范围内确定主动公开的政府信息的具体内容，并重点公开下列政府信息：
（一）行政法规、规章和规范性文件；
（二）国民经济和社会发展规划、专项规划、区域规划及相关政策；
（三）国民经济和社会发展统计信息；
（四）财政预算、决算报告；
（五）行政事业性收费的项目、依据、标准；
（六）政府集中采购项目的目录、标准及实施情况；
（七）行政许可的事项、依据、条件、数量、程序、期限以及申请行政许可需要提交的全部材料目录及办理情；
（八）重大建设项目的批准和实施情况；
（九）扶贫、教育、医疗、社会保障、促进就业等方面的政策、措施及其实施情况；
（十）突发公共事件的应急预案、预警信息及应对情况；
（十一）环境保护、公共卫生、安全生产、食品药品、产品质量的监督检查情况。

Article 11
The government information to be emphasized for disclosure by the people's governments at the level of cities divided into districts and the county level people's governments and their departments should also include the following contents:

(1) Important and major matters in urban and rural construction and management;
(2) Information on the construction of social and public interest institutions;
(3) Information on land requisition or land appropriation, household demolition and resettlement, and the distribution and use of compensation or subsidy funds relating thereto; and
(4) Information on the management, usage and distribution of social donations in funds and in kind for emergency and disaster relief, special care for families of martyrs and military service personnel, and assistance to poverty stricken and low income families.

第十一条
设区的市级人民政府、县级人民政府及其部门重点公开的政府信息还应当包括下列内容：
（一）城乡建设和管理的重大事项；
（二）社会公益事业建设情况；

（三）征收或者征用土地、房屋拆迁及其补偿、补助费用的发放、使用情况；
（四）抢险救灾、优抚、救济、社会捐助等款物的管理、使用和分配情况。

Article 12

People's governments at the township (town) level should determine the concrete content of the government information to be disclosed on their own initiative within their scope of responsibility in accordance with the provisions of Article 9 of these Regulations, and emphasize disclosure of the following government information:

(1) Information on the implementation of rural work policies of the state;
(2) Information on fiscal income and expenses and the management and use of various specialized funds;
(3) Overall township (town) land use plans and information on the verification of land to be used by farmers for their primary residences;
(4) Information on land requisition or land appropriation, household demolition and resettlement, and the distribution and use of compensation or subsidy funds therefor;
(5) Information on township (town) credits and debts, fund raising and labour levies;
(6) Information on the distribution of social donations in funds and in kind for emergency and disaster relief, special care for families of martyrs and military service personnel, and assistance to poverty stricken and low income families;
(7) Information on contracting, leasing and auctioning of township and town collectively owned enterprises and other township and town economic entities; and
(8) Information on implementation of the family planning policy.

第十二条

（镇）人民政府应当依照本条例第九条的规定，在其职责范围内确定主动公开的政府信息的具体内容，并重点公开下列政府信息：
（一）贯彻落实国家关于农村工作政策的情况；
（二）财政收支、各类专项资金的管理和使用情况；
（三）乡（镇）土地利用总体规划、宅基地使用的审核情况；
（四）征收或者征用土地、房屋拆迁及其补偿、补助费用的发放、使用情况；
（五）乡（镇）的债权债务、筹资筹劳情况；
（六）抢险救灾、优抚、救济、社会捐助等款物的发放情况；
（七）乡镇集体企业及其他乡镇经济实体承包、租赁、拍卖等情况；
（八）执行计划生育政策的情况。

Article 13

In addition to government information disclosed by administrative organs on their own initiative provided for in Articles 9, 10, 11 and 12, legal persons or other organizations may, based on the special needs of such matters on their own production, livelihood and scientific and technological research, also file requests with departments of the State Council, local people's governments at all levels and departments under local people's governments at the county level and above to obtain relevant government information.

第十三条

除本条例第九条、第十条、第十一条、第十二条规定的行政机关主动公开的政府信息外，公民、法人或者其他组织还可以根据自身生产、生活、科研等特殊需要，向国务院部门、地方各级人民政府及县级以上地方人民政府部门申请获取相关政府信息。

Article 24

After receiving requests for open government information, administrative organs should reply to the requests on-the-spot to the extent possible. If an on-the-spot reply is not possible, administrative organs should provide a reply within 15 business days from receiving a request. If an extension of the time limit for replying to a request is needed, the agreement of the responsible person in charge of the office for open government information work should be obtained and the requester notified. The maximum extension of the time limit for replying to a request may not exceed 15 business days.

If the requested government information involves the rights and interests of a third party, the time needed by administrative organs to seek the opinion of the third party shall not be counted against the time limit provided in Paragraph 2 of this Article.

第二十四条

行政机关收到政府信息公开申请，能够当场答复的，应当当场予以答复。

行政机关不能当场答复的，应当自收到申请之日起15个工作日内予以答复；如需延长答复期限的，应当经政府信息公开工作机构负责人同意，并告知申请人，延长答复的期限最长不得超过15个工作日。

申请公开的政府信息涉及第三方权益的，行政机关征求第三方意见所需时间不计算在本条第二款规定的期限内。

Appendix B:
Searching for Public Records of Courts

Chan Pui-king and Vivian Kwok[1]

Three main types of court records are available to the public: case filings, case details and judgments.

Case Filings

To cover court news, journalists can start examining the case filings from the courts. A record is filed whenever a case is brought to a court. Because there is no central registry in Hong Kong, you must go to the registry of the relevant court to check the case filing. Not all filings are open to the public. For example, in the High Court (Court of First Instance and Court of Appeal) and the District Court, only filings on civil actions are open. Case filing includes a Daily Cause List and a Cause Book.

A **Daily Cause List** is the daily schedule of court cases and is posted on the notice board at the reception or lobby of every court and tribunal. It lists the cases to be heard that day, the courtroom and judge, the start time of the trial or proceeding and the nature of the offences. The daily cause list is also available online on the judiciary's website at: www.judiciary.gov.hk/en/crt_lists/daily_caulist.htm and is posted by 6 p.m., the preceding business day. Court reporters check the list to decide which court to attend and which news to cover.

Filings can be searched in the **Cause Book**. The case filings of each court are classified by different subjects and are arranged by date and bound in the cause book. A typical page of a cause book shows the action number (i.e. the case number) of the cases, filing dates, names and addresses of plaintiffs and defendants, names of the solicitors for both sides and the nature of the cases.

The cause books of the District Court are classified as:

---

1. Chan Pui-king, an honorary lecturer at the Journalism and Media Studies Centre at the University of Hong Kong and former editor-in-chief of *Next Magazine*, is a leading expert on access to information in Hong Kong. Vivian Kwok is editor-in-chief and associate publisher of *Bloomberg Businessweek* (Chinese) and former deputy editor-in-chief at *Next Magazine*, former news editor at *Forbes* and former senior enterprise reporter at *South China Morning Post* where she broke front-page investigative stories on university scandals, land deals and a secret agreement between the Hong Kong government and developers. Her series about private clubs in Hong Kong won a Society of Publishers in Asia award for investigative reporting in 2011.

- Civil Action
- Distraint Case[2]
- Tax Claim
- Employee's Compensation
- Equal Opportunities Action
- Miscellaneous Proceedings
- Personal Injuries Action

Cases of the High Court are classified as:

- Civil Action
- Miscellaneous Proceedings
- Bankruptcy Proceedings
- Company Winding-up Proceedings
- Personal Injuries Action
- Administrative Law Proceedings
- Admiralty Action
- Commercial Action
- Construction and Arbitration Proceedings
- Application to Set Aside a Statutory Demand
- Bill of Sale Registration
- Application for Interim Order (Bankruptcy)
- Stop Notice

The most important information we can get from the cause book is the action number. For instance, if you want to write an article about the controversial 2004 lawsuit of *Lo Siu Lan and Another v Hong Kong Housing Authority*, you may wish to look at the writ of her "Application for Leave to Apply for Judicial Review". (In December 2004, Lo Siu Lan, a 67-year-old woman who received public assistance and lived in public housing, filed a judicial review on the listing of 180 shopping malls and 79,000 parking spaces on Hong Kong Stock Exchange by the Hong Kong Housing Authority. She wanted the Housing Authority to halt the $23 billion REIT[3] listing. Her legal action argued that the assets were undervalued and rents for public housing tenants would rise after sale.)

But how can you find the writ? First, you have to find out the action number of the case by inspecting the appropriate cause book. In Lo Siu Lan's case, you can go to the High Court Registry to look for the **Administrative Law Proceedings Cause Book** in December 2004. (Keep in mind that cause books are classified by subject and you can ask registry officers for help if you are not sure about the classification of the case.) From the cause book, you will notice the action number of Lo's case is **HCAL 154/2004**, and you can further search for the **writ of summons**

2. Distraint cases are actions in which the government takes possession of property for sale towards settlement of an unpaid tax bill.

3. Real Estate Investment Trust (REIT) is a security that sells like a stock on an exchange and invests in real estate directly.

thereafter (for some big cases, you may luckily find the action number quoted from news articles and thus need not to search the cause book).

Case Details

The **Writ of Summons** is used to start a civil action arising from a breach of contract, fraud, damages for personal injury or death, damage to property due to a breach of duty, and generally for all actions involving disputed facts. The court issues the writ of summons to the defendant as a notification of the claim against him. The original is sent to the defendant. A duplicate is filed in the Court, and it is open to the public.

The writ of summons of the judicial review filed by Lo Siu Lan shows the names and addresses of the applicants, the factual background of the listing of Links, the statutory framework of Lo's application, the relief sought and other information such as the names of the legal representatives for both sides.

Like Lo's case, the details of most civil cases heard in the District Court, the High Court and the Final Court of Appeal can be found in the writ of summons.

Each civil and criminal case has its own **Case File** to contain every legal document in it, but files are restricted only to the parties involved.

How to Search for Case Filings and Case Details

As the **Cause Book** is not available online, you must go in person to a court registry to inspect it and pay a HK$18 search fee for each cause book inspected. (A cause book contains approximately two months of records.)

There is no public access to the **Case File**. Only the plaintiff, the defendant and their lawyers are allowed access. Journalists cannot examine the file unless with the approval of the judge or if the litigants and their attorneys are willing to show you. (Rules of the District Court (Cap 336H) O 63 r 4; Rules of the High Court (Cap 4A) O 63 r 4)

The **Writ of Summons** can be inspected at the registry of the respective court and is located by its case number. An inspection of the writ costs HK$18; photocopying is allowed at HK $0.5 per page.

Case filings and case details records of different court are summarized[4] as follows:

Court of Final Appeal			
Records	**Format**	**Costs**	**Availability**
Daily Cause List	Information sheet	Free	Court notice board/website
Cause Book	Book	$18 search fee	Open to public at the Registry
Notice of Appeal	Document	$18 search fee	Open to public at the Registry
Case File	File	$18 search fee	Restricted to the parties involved or with court approval

4. Source: http://www.judiciary.gov.hk/en/other_info/access_info/pdf/access_to_info.pdf.

High Court			
Daily Cause List	Information sheet	Free	Court notice board/website
Cause Book	Book	$18 search fee	Open to public at the Registry
Writ of Summons	Document	$18 search fee	Open to public at the Registry
Case File	File	$18 search fee	Restricted to the parties involved or with court approval

District Court			
Daily Cause List	Information sheet	Free	Court notice board/website
Civil Action Register	Book	$18 search fee	Open to public at the Registry
Writ of Summons	Document	$18 search fee	Open to public at the Registry
Case File	File	$18 search fee	Restricted to the parties involved or with court approval

Probate Registry			
Probate Action File	File	$18 search fee	Restricted to the parties involved
Probate Action Book	Book	$18 search fee	Open to public at the Registry

Family Court			
Daily Cause List	Information sheet	Free	Court notice board/ Judiciary website
Divorce Registry	Book	$18 search fee	Restricted to parties involved or their lawyers with court approval

Lands Tribunal			
Daily Cause List	Information sheet	Free	Tribunal notice board/ Judiciary website
Tribunal Case Register	Book	$18 search fee	Open to public at the Registry
Tribunal case files	File	$18 search fee	Restricted to the concerned parties of the proceedings

Magistracies' Courts			
Daily Cause List	Information sheet	Free	Court notice board/ Judiciary website

Small Claims Tribunal			
Daily Cause List	Information sheet	Free	Tribunal notice board/ Judiciary website
Case File	File	$18 search fee	Restricted to the parties concerned

Labour Tribunal			
Daily Cause List	Information sheet	Free	Tribunal notice board/ Judiciary website
Case File	File	Varies	Restricted to Labour Tribunal's approval

Coroner's Court			
Weekly Cause List	Information sheet	Free	Notice board
Daily Cause List	Web	Free	Judiciary website
Autopsies and police investigation reports	Report	$18 search fee	Restricted to parties concerned and subject to Coroner's investigation reports approval

Obscene Articles Tribunal			
Daily Cause List	Information sheet	Free	Tribunal notice board/ Judiciary website
Register of Notices	Book	$33 search fee	Open to public at the Registry
Articles kept in Tribunal repository	Magazines, periodicals, videotapes, LD, CD-ROMs	$420	For viewing in repository, accompanied by Tribunal staff

Transcripts of proceedings

In most court actions or proceedings that are tried or heard with witnesses, an official shorthand note or recording is taken of any evidence given orally in court and of any judgment delivered. A party to the action can request a transcript and must pay costs, which can be considerable. Court rules permit journalists and other non-parties to obtain transcripts in proceedings in District Court or High Court, except for closed proceedings, such as for matrimonial cases. Because costs can be prohibitive, you might try to obtain a copy from one of the parties. ("Nothing in this rule shall be construed as prohibiting the supply of transcripts to persons not parties to the proceedings." Rules of the District Court (Cap 336H) O 68 r 2; Rules of the High Court (Cap 4A) O 68 r 2.)

Judgments

Among all legal records, judgments are the easiest to search.

A judgment is the formal decision made by a court following legal proceedings. A judgment prepared by a judge will either be read out in open court or circulated in printed form to all the parties involved in the case.

In addition to stating the result of the suit and the reasons behind a judicial decision, judgment also tells you who sued whom for what and contains an elaborate account of the background of each party, their relationship and dispute.

Since 1998, there have been internal guidelines in the Judiciary on keeping records of different categories of judgments in the Judiciary Library and for uploading on the website. However, as these guidelines are not public, we do not specifically know what kind of judgment is open for public inspection and who is responsible for deciding whether a judgment shall be open or closed, as they sometimes are.

Searching for judgments of District Court, High Court and the Final Court of Appeal is much easier than finding judgments from the Magistrates' Court and Tribunals.

Any person wanting to inspect court records in Magistrates' Court has to apply to the relevant Registrar or magistrate's clerk by giving good and sufficient reason pursuant to s 35A(1) of the Magistrates Ordinance (Cap 227). To inspect judgments of Tribunal cases, non-parties have to apply to the relevant registrar for approval.

The Court of Final Appeal, the High Court, and the District Court are more open; you can retrieve most of their judgments online or from the High Court Library.

Searching Judgments Online

Judgments from the Court of Final Appeal (since its establishment in 1997), Court of Appeal of the High Court, Court of First Instance of the High Court, District Court, Family Court and Lands Tribunal which delivered between 1946 and 1948 and from 1966 onwards are available free of charge at www.judiciary.gov.hk/en/legal_ref/judgments.htm, the **Legal Reference System**, an online database of the Judiciary.

It is faster and easier to get the judgment if you know the case number of the suit. For instance, if you input the case number FACV00012/2000 into the search engine, two results will be found. They are:

1	*Albert Cheng and Another v Tse Wai Chun Paul*	Date of Judgment: 13/11/2000
2	*Albert Cheng and Another v Tse Wai Chun Paul*	Date of Judgment: 17/01/2001

These judgments, by the Court of Final Appeal, refer to the landmark libel case involving Albert Cheng (former Legislative Council member and former radio talk-show host) and Lam Yuk Wah (former radio-talk show co-host), who were both sued by a well-known solicitor, Tse Wai Chun Paul.

The first judgment, issued 13 November 2000, gives considerable details about the litigation. From the judgment, we know the case centred on an on-air discussion between Cheng and Lam, the two hosts of the popular radio programme, "Teacup in a Storm", about a tourist escort who had been arrested and jailed in the Philippines for allegedly trafficking drugs. Tse Wai Chun, legal adviser for the Tourist Industry Rescue Group, had worked for the release of the escort, who was eventually released. After returning to Hong Kong, the escort received suggestions from others that he should seek compensation from his former employer, but Tse advised him not to do so. In their radio programme, the hosts commented on Tse's advice and raised questions about his intention. Tse filed a defamation suit against them and the broadcasting company.

The hosts lost at trial and appealed to the Court of Appeal, which also ruled against them. Cheng and Lam appealed further to the Court of Final Appeal and won the case in 2000. From the judgment, we are able to know the background of the case and above all, the reasons explaining why Cheng and Lam won the lawsuit.

In 2001, the second judgment you see, the Court of Final Appeal ordered Tse to pay the appellants' costs in the appeal.

Now you understand how informative a judgment is. Even if you do not know the court case number, you can still find the judgment by using the names of the parties involved. As in the case of Albert Cheng versus Tse Wai Chun, you can either input "Albert Cheng" or "Tse Wai Chun Paul", to do a simple or advanced search. The database then will show you all the cases involving them or mentioning their names. You have to examine the results to look for a particular case.

For instance, if you go to "Advanced Search" and input *"Albert Cheng"*, you will find 19 records, such as:

> *Toppan Printing Co v Chinese United Press Ltd and Another* 13/05/2005
> *Jademan (Holdings) Ltd v Francis Leung Pak To and Others* 16/02/1989

If you search *"Tse Wai Chun, Paul"*, you can access 30 records, such as:

> *A Solicitor v The Law Society of Hong Kong* 18/02/2004
> *Tse Wai Chun Paul v Solicitors Disciplinary Tribunal and Another* 11/09/2002

You also can retrieve judgments from the **Hong Kong Legal Information Institute** (**HKLII**), a free information system developed by the Faculty of Law and the Department of Computer Science of the University of Hong Kong, with assistance from the Australasian Legal Information Institute (AustLII). Go to the website, http://www.hklii.hk, and click on "All HKLII Databases", you may find the following records:

- Court of Final Appeal judgments, from 1997 onwards
- Court of Appeal judgments, from 1946 onwards
- Court of First Instance judgments, from 1946 onwards
- District Court judgments, from 1946 onwards
- Family Court judgments, from 1973 onwards
- Lands Tribunal judgments, from 1982 onwards
- Miscellaneous Courts and Tribunals judgments, from 2005 onwards

Just like the database of the Judiciary, you can search a particular judgment by specifying the name of the plaintiff or the defendant. Records in HKLII are provided by the Judiciary of the Hong Kong government.

Other services for retrieving cases online are commercial vendors such as Westlaw (Thomson Reuters, http://www.westlaw.com) and Lexis (LexisNexis Group, Reed Elsevier, http://www.lexis.com). They have the added benefits of providing editorial summaries, known as "headnotes", on the decisions, commentaries, legal journals and other editorial products and services. Check with your media company to see if they have subscriptions to this service. If you are a university student, check with your university library.

Searching Judgments from Judiciary Library

The Judiciary Library has a collection of some 56,000 judgments of Hong Kong since 1946–1948 and 1966 onwards. The judgments are kept in bound volumes, arranged by year. Cases are arranged by folio number (i.e. case number). You can find the case number in advance from the online catalogue (http://library.judiciary.gov.hk). You can either input the name of the judge, case number, or date of judgment, etc., to find the judgment you want. Should you know nothing of the above information, simply do a keyword search like typing in "Albert Cheng" or "Tse Wai Chun" and you will retrieve entries about them showing the case number, case name, judgment date, case nature, names of the judges, call number and where the judgment is filed (e.g. High Court Library, District Court Library or Court of Final Appeal Library).

The collection of judgments at the High Court Library is the same as those judgments on the Judiciary website. The judgments on the Judiciary website were uploaded from the Library collection, which by itself is not complete because the systematic depositing of judgments from the District Court upwards began only in 1998.

Judiciary libraries' principal patrons are members of the Judiciary. Journalists and others who have valid reasons to use the libraries' facilities may apply for a reader's card at a fee of HK$220 per year.

Library	Location
High Court Library	LG4/F, High Court, 38 Queensway
Court of Final Appeal Library	No. 1 Battery Path, Central, Hong Kong
District Court Library	Room 1212, Wanchai Law Courts, Wanchai Tower, 12 Harbour Road

Searching Judgment from Legal Journals

While it is convenient to retrieve a judgment online, not all judgments can be found there, especially those of the early years. You have to look them out from legal journals. Two main legal journals contain most of the judgments, which are *Hong Kong Cases* and *Hong Kong Law Reports & Digest.*

Hong Kong Cases, published by Butterworths Asia, is a bi-weekly loose-leaf periodical. Cases are edited in alphabetical order according to the case name (such as *Chan Sai Hung v Well Develop. Ltd.*) and there is a subject index (such as Banking and Finance, Road Traffic, Tort, etc.) to classify different cases in each volume.

The journal was first published in 1946. Since 1996, the publication occasionally has provided briefs of cases in Chinese. Libraries usually bind the periodical quarterly and there are separate bound volumes that contain cases during 1946–72, 1973–76, and 1977–79.

Hong Kong Law Reports & Digest is published by Thomson Sweet and Maxwell Asia. Cases are filed in alphabetical order and can be searched by subject index. The publication started in 1905; until 1995, it was published by the government and considered official; usually judges admit only its version of judgments to be cited in court documents.

The publishers of the two journals have contracts with the Judiciary, and get the judgments directly from the judges. The publications cover almost all years. They cover most of the cases in the Court of Final Appeal, the Court of Appeal, the High Court, and the District Court. Minor cases tried in the Magistracy and the tribunals are usually not included. Each publisher has its own editorial board which selects cases for inclusion.

Searching judgment from these journals, you can start with the name of the person or company involved as plaintiff, defendant or respondent. It is easier if you know when the judgment was delivered.

First, check the index book. There is a consolidated index that you can use to locate a specific case and all cases relating to a specific person.

The Consolidated Index to All Reported Hong Kong Decisions (published by Butterworths Asia) covers all decisions contained in *Hong Kong Cases, Hong Kong Law Reports & Digest*, and other reports.

The Index consists of five parts: table of cases reported; Hong Kong decisions referred to; other decisions referred to; subject index and legislation referred to.

As an example, if you want to check on Tse Wai Chun, Paul, the *Consolidated Index of All Reported Hong Kong Decisions* has the following:

> *Tse Wai Chun Paul v Solicitors Disciplinary Tribunal* [CA] [2002] 2 HKC 1
> *Tse Wai Chun v Solicitors Disciplinary Tribunal & Another* [CFI] [2002] 3 HKLRD 712

You can then locate a particular case through the reference keys. For example, in the citation [2002] 3 HKLRD 712, **2002** is the year of the report, **3** is the volume number, **HKLRD** is the abbreviation of the name of the reference (*Hong Kong Law Reports & Digest*), and **712** is the page on which the case starts.

There are five other court report publications, updated regularly, covering certain types of cases:

The Hong Kong Court of Final Appeal Reports are authorized reports published by Sweet & Maxwell Asia four times a year as loose-leaf publications and every year as bound volumes. Cases are in alphabetical order.

District Court law reports (published by the government since 1953) contain cases heard from the District Court. Trademark cases were included in 1962 and 1963 volumes. A selection of decisions by the Taxing Master for the year 1968 was included in 1969 volume. Inland Revenue Board of Review decisions were found in 1972 and 1973 volumes. The reports incorporate the Hong Kong Land Tribunal law reports from 1981 onwards.

Inland Revenue Board of Review decisions (published by the government) does not provide the names of the parties, only case numbers. The first two volumes cover 1968–82 and 1982–87. Since then, the decisions have been published yearly.

Hong Kong Conveyancing and Property Reports, which contain the decisions of all courts dealing with these topics, are published annually by Butterworths Asia.

They include cases deemed to be of most practical relevance to people in the industry. Cases are in alphabetical order.

Hong Kong Tax Cases (published by the government) contains all cases taken to the courts under the Inland Revenue Ordinance, the Estate Duty Ordinance and the Stamp Duty Ordinance. This journal does not give the names of the parties involved, only the case numbers. The reports are not published regularly; the most recent issue was in 1993.

You may find the above journals at the following libraries.

Library	**Location**	**Online Catalogue**
High Court Library	LG4/F., High Court, 38 Queensway, Hong Kong	http://library.judiciary.gov.hk/
The University of Hong Kong Libraries	University of Hong Kong, Pokfulam, Hong Kong	http://library.hku.hk/
Run Run Shaw Library, City University of Hong Kong	City University of Hong Kong, Tat Chee Avenue, Kowloon	http://lib.cityu.edu.hk/
The Chinese University of Hong Kong Library	The Chinese University of Hong Kong, Shatin	http://library.cuhk.edu.hk/screens/opacmenu.html/
Hong Kong Central Library	66 Causeway Road, Causeway Bay	http://www.hkpl.gov.hk/hkcl/eng/home/index.html

Appendix C: Judicial Practice Directions: Hearings in Chambers in Civil Proceedings

Judicial Practice Direction 25.1

Chambers Hearings in Civil Proceedings in the High Court, the District Court, the Family Court and the Lands Tribunal

1. This Practice Direction governs hearings in chambers in civil proceedings in the High Court, the District Court, the Family Court and the Lands Tribunal regulating when such hearings are to be open to the public and when such hearings are not open to the public, as the case may be. A hearing open to the public is one where the hearing is open to the press and the public to attend. A hearing not open to the public is a closed one where the press and the public are excluded from attending.
2. All chambers hearings (interlocutory or otherwise) shall be held in public except in the instances set out in paragraphs 3, 4(a) and 5.
3. Where statutory provision(s) specifically require proceedings to be not open to the public, such as those listed in **Schedule 1**, such proceedings shall not be open to the public in accordance with the provisions.
4. (a) The proceedings listed in **Schedule 2** would usually not be open to the public. In relation to such proceedings, it is considered that having regard to their nature, one or more of the reasons for excluding the press and the public laid down in Article 10 of the Hong Kong Bill of Rights Ordinance, Cap. 383 ("Article 10") are usually satisfied. Accordingly, such proceedings would usually not be open to the public.
   (b) However, if in a particular case, the court is of the view that none of the reasons in Article 10 is satisfied in the circumstances of the case concerned, the court may, whether upon a party's application (as to which see paragraph 7) or on its own motion, order that the hearing be open to the public.
5. At any stage of any proceedings other than those governed by paragraphs 3 and 4 above, where the court is of the view that one or more of the reasons in Article 10 are satisfied, it may, whether upon a party's application (as to which see paragraph 7) or on its own motion, order that a chambers hearing open to the public be closed to the public for the whole or part of the hearing.

6. Where the court has made an order referred to in paragraph 4(b) or paragraph 5, it may subsequently revoke or vary such an order.
7. Any party to an inter partes application who wishes to apply for an order referred to in paragraph 4(b) or paragraph 5 shall, as soon as practicable, and in any case not less than 2 clear days before the hearing apply in writing to the court with grounds in support thereof, giving notice to all other parties to the application. Any party who opposes the application shall state his grounds in opposition which shall reach the court and the party who has applied for the order no later than the day before the hearing. Such application will be dealt with by the court on paper unless the court directs that an oral hearing be held.
8. This Practice Direction is without prejudice to the court's powers to adjourn the hearing of any summons or other application from chambers into court and subsequently from court into chambers pursuant to Order 32 rule 18 of the Rules of the High Court and Rules of the District Court.

Summons or notice

9. The party filing a summons or notice for hearing in chambers should specify therein, in accordance with this Practice Direction, whether the hearing is to be open to the public or not open to the public.

Daily Cause List

10. Where any chambers hearing is not to be open to the public, such hearing will be listed as "In chambers (not open to the public)".

Order

11. An order made by the court at a hearing in chambers not open to the public should be so stated expressly therein.

Exceptions

12. For the avoidance of doubt, this Practice Direction does not apply to proceedings under Orders 115 to 119 of the Rules of the High Court.

Rights of Audience

13. The existing rights of audience of solicitors in chambers hearings shall continue to apply, whether the chambers hearings are open to the public or not open to the public.
14. The existing rights of persons entitled to appear before a master in chambers and a taxing master as provided for in Practice Directions PD14.1 and paragraph 3 of PD27 shall continue to apply, whether the chambers hearings are open to the public or not open to the public.
15. This Practice Direction will take effect on 18 July 2005.

(Issued 31 May 2005 by the Judiciary of the Hong Kong SAR)

Schedule 1

Types of proceedings *required* by legislation to be not open to the public, including the following:

Adoption Rules (Cap 290A), rule 4, on all proceedings under the Adoption Ordinance.

Patent Ordinance (Cap 514), s 130(s), on all appeals under the Ordinance concerning a patent application which has not been published.

Schedule 2

Types of proceedings *usually* not open to the public by reason of their nature, including the following:

(1) Matters relating to children and applications for financial provisions and ancillary relief

Rules of the High Court (Cap 4A): Order 54, on applications for writ of *habeas corpus and subjiciendum* on behalf of a minor; Order 90, on applications relating to minors, and Order 121, on all applications under the Child Abduction and Custody Ordinance (Cap 512).

Guardianship of Minors Ordinance (Cap 13), s 23, on all applications under the Ordinance.

Separation and Maintenance Orders Ordinance (Cap 16), on all applications under the Ordinance except judgment summonses.

Matrimonial Causes Ordinance (Cap 179), on all applications relating to children under the Ordinance, and s 52(3), on questions of sexual capacity in proceedings for nullity of marriage.

Matrimonial Causes Rules (Cap 179A), on all applications relating to children under the Rules, and r. 81, on applications for ancillary relief or questions arising thereon having been referred or adjourned to a judge.

Maintenance Orders (Reciprocal Enforcement) Ordinance (Cap 188), on all applications under the Ordinance except judgment summones.

Domestic Violence Rules (Cap 189A), r. 8, on all proceedings under the Ordinance.

Matrimonial Proceedings and Property Ordinance (Cap 192), s. 2A, s 25, on all applications under the Ordinance except judgments summones.

Rules of the District Court (Cap 336H), order 90, on applications relating to minors.

Parent and Child Ordinance (Cap 429), s 8(3), on applications for declaration of parentage, legitimacy or legitimation.

Human Reproductive Technology Ordinance (Cap 561), s 35 (3) and (4), on questions as to whether a person is or is not the parent of a child.

(2) Matters relating to disability, e.g., mental disability, infancy

Rules of the High Court (Cap 4A), Order 32, rule 9, on applications for leave to institute proceedings under s 69 of the Mental Health Ordinance (Cap 136); and Order 80, on applications relating to persons under disability.

Employees' Compensation Ordinance (Cap 282), s 6A, on applications relating to apportionment of compensation in fatal cases; s 6H(6), on applications relating to the disposal of compensation apportioned to dependants, etc, and s 13, on applications relating to distribution of compensation, etc.

Rules of the District Court (Cap 336H), Order 80, on applications relating to persons under disability.

(3) Matters relating to ex parte applications for injunctions or orders of a restraining or compulsory nature

Rules of the High Court (Cap 4A), Order 29, on ex parte applications for injunction; Order 30, on ex parte applications for receiver and injunction; Order 44A, on ex parte applications for prohibition order and for taking security/attachment of property, and Order 51, on ex parte applications for the appointment of receiver by way of equitable execution.

Landlord and Tenant (Consolidation) Ordinance (Cap 7), s 77, 85, 91, on ex parte applications for warrant of distress and order to break open outer doors and windows.

Rules of the District Court (Cap 336H), Order 29, on ex parte applications for injunction, and Order 30, on ex parte applications for receiver and injunction, Order 44A, on ex parte applications for prohibition order, and Order 51, on ex parte applications for the appointment of receiver by way of equitable execution.

(4) Matters relating to companies winding-up and bankruptcy

Rules of the High Court (Cap 4A), Order 29, on applications for order restraining presentation or advertisement of winding up petition

Bankruptcy Ordinance (Cap 6), s 13, on applications to appoint interim receiver for protection of estate, and s 27, on applications to arrest debtor.

Bankruptcy Rules (Cap 6A), r 48, on applications to set aside statutory demands; r 82A, on applications for public examination of bankrupt pursuant to s 19 of the Ordinance, and r 87B, on applications for inquiry into bankrupt's conduct pursuant to s 29 of the Ordinance.

Companies Ordinance (Cap 32), s 193, on applications for appointment of provisional liquidator; s 199(1)(e) and (f), on applications by liquidator to sanction compromise; s 221(1), on applications for an order for private examination, and s 224, on applications to arrest absconding contributory or officer.

Companies (Winding-up) Rules (Cap 32H), r. 5(2), on private examinations conducted pursuant to s 221 of the Ordinance and directed to be held in chambers; r 50 and 51, on applications for consideration of report pursuant to s 191(2) and 222 of the Ordinance., and r 58, on summonses returnable in the first instance in chambers for consideration of report in applications pursuant to s 1681, 275, 276 and 358(2) of the Ordinance.

(5) Matters relating to intellectual property

Copyright (Border Measures) Rules (Cap 4F), s 5, on proceedings under sections 136, 137, 139 and 140 of the Copyright Ordinance (Cap 528) relating to detention and disclosures of information.

Trademark (Border Measures) Rules (Cap 362F), r 5, on proceedings under sections 30B, 30C, 30D, 30E and 30F of the Trade Descriptions Ordinance (Cap 362) relating to detention and disclosures of information.

Registered Design Ordinance (Cap 522), s 58(2), on all appeals under the Ordinance concerning an application for registration of a design.

(6) Matters relating to arbitration

Rules of the High Court (Cap 4A), Order 73, on all applications under the Arbitration Ordinance (Cap 341).

Arbitration Ordinance (Cap 341), s 2D, on all proceedings under the Ordinance in the High Court and Court of Appeal.

(7) Matters relating to representation in legal proceedings

Rules of the High Court (Cap 4A), Order 5, r 6(3) and Order 12, r 1(2A)(a), on applications by company for leave to be represented by director, and Order 67, on applications by solicitors for a declaration of having ceased to act.

Legal Aid Ordinance (Cap 91), s 26, on appeals from decision of Director of Legal Aid to Registrar of High Court.

Rules of the District Court (Cap 336H), Order 67, on applications by solicitors for a declaration of having ceased to act.

(8) Matters relating to trustees

Rules of the High Court (Cap 4A), Order 85, r 2, on applications by a trustee for directions, include a Beddoe Order.

Administration of Trust Funds Rules (Cap 29a), r 6, on applications by trustee under the Ordinance relating to administration of funds.

Judicial Trustee Rules (Cap 29B), r 12, on applications to obtain from judicial trustee information or explanation required for properly giving directions, or for the purpose of explaining the nature of the directions.

(9) Matters relating to obtaining evidence for foreign court

Rules of the High Court (Cap 4A), Order 70, on applications to obtain evidence for foreign court.

Judiciary Practice Direction 25.2

Reports on hearings held in chambers not open to the public

1. Proceedings held in chambers not open to the public are those where the press and the public are excluded from attending. Practitioners are reminded of the provisions of Practice Direction 25.1 dated 31st May 2005 governing chambers hearings in civil proceedings in the High Court, the District Court, the Family Court and the Lands Tribunal.
2. No report should be made of any proceedings (including the judgment) held in chambers not open to the public without the authority of the master or the judge before whom the proceedings were conducted. If the master or the judge considers that proceedings should be open for reporting or the judgment should be released for publication he should afford the parties an opportunity to make representations upon the matter before so declaring.
3. This Practice Direction shall take effect on 18 July 2005 and supersedes the previous undated Practice Direction 25.1 (which contained two paragraphs).

(Dated this 31st day of May 2005.)

Appendix D: The Code on Access to Information

The Code on Access to Information is an administrative regulation and can be found on the Hong Kong SAR government website, http://www.access.gov.hk/en/index.htm.

Departments that must comply with the Code:

Annex A of the Code refers to the departments to which the code applies. The departments are:

Agriculture, Fisheries and Conservation Department
All registries and administrative offices of courts and tribunals for which the Judiciary Administrator has responsibility
Architectural Services Department
Audit Commission
Auxiliary Medical Service (department)
Buildings Department
Census and Statistics Department
Civil Aid Service (department)
Civil Aviation Department
Civil Engineering and Development Department
Civil Service Bureau
Commerce and Economic Development Bureau
Companies Registry
Constitutional and Mainland Affairs Bureau
Correctional Services Department
Customs and Excise Department
Department of Health
Department of Justice
Development Bureau
Drainage Services Department
Education Bureau
Electrical and Mechanical Services Department
Environment Bureau

Environmental Protection Department
Financial Services and the Treasury Bureau
Fire Services Department
Food and Environmental Hygiene Department
Food and Health Bureau
General Office of the Chief Executive's Office
Government Flying Service
Government Laboratory
Government Logistics Department
Government Property Agency
Highways Department
Home Affairs Bureau
Home Affairs Department
Hong Kong Auxiliary Police Force
Hong Kong Monetary Authority
Hong Kong Observatory
Hong Kong Police Force
Housing Department
Immigration Department
Independent Commission Against Corruption
Information Services Department
Inland Revenue Department
Innovation and Technology Commission
Intellectual Property Department
Invest Hong Kong
Joint Secretariat for the Advisory Bodies on Civil Service and Judicial Salaries and Conditions of Service
Labour Department
Land Registry
Lands Department
Labour and Welfare Bureau
Legal Aid Department
Leisure and Cultural Services Department
Marine Department
Office of the Commissioner of Insurance
Office of the Communications Authority
Offices of the Chief Secretary for Administration and the Financial Secretary
Official Receiver's Office
Planning Department
Post Office
Radio Television Hong Kong
Rating and Valuation Department
Registration and Electoral Office
Secretariat of the Public Service Commission

Secretariat, Commissioner on Interception of Communications and Surveillance
Security Bureau
Social Welfare Department
Student Financial Assistance Agency
Trade and Industry Department
Transport and Housing Bureau
Transport Department
Treasury
University Grants Committee Secretariat
Water Supplies Department

Public Bodies in Schedule 1 of Ombudsman Ordinance that have adopted Code on Access to Information or similar guide

Airport Authority	Auxiliary Medical Services	Civil Aid Service
Consumer Council	Employees Retraining Board	Equal Opportunities Commission
Estate Agents Authority	Financial Reporting Council	Hong Kong Arts Development Council
Hong Kong Housing Authority	Hong Kong Housing Society	Hong Kong Sports Institute Limited
Hospital Authority	Kowloon-Canton Railway Corporation	Mandatory Provident Fund Schemes Authority
Privacy Commissioner for Personal Data	Securities and Futures Commission	The Hong Kong Examinations and Assessment Authority
Urban Renewal Authority	Vocational Training Council	West Kowloon Cultural District Authority

Examples of the kinds of files and records kept by a department

Administration Branch

(A) General Administration		
Accidents	Conferences, Meetings & Seminars	Statistics
Accommodation	Correspondence	Stores & Equipment
Associations & Clubs	Department Reports	Sundries
Authorization	Electronic Data Interchange	Translation
Bilingualism	Identity Cards & Passes	Transport
Certificates Departmental	Office Automation	Uniforms
Circulars Ordinances & Regulations	Printing Matters	Visits
Committees & Boards	Publicity & Publications	Welfare
Communication	Security	
Complaints	Stationary	

(B) Personnel & Establishment		
Administration	Establishment Committee	Leave Passage
Allowances & Pay	Establishment & Strength	Medical & Dental Facilities
Appointments & Related Matters	Establishment Reviews	Staff Appraisal
Conduct & Discipline	Estimates	Staff Relations
Creation of Posts	Housing Benefits	Training

(C) Accounts		
Advances & Deposits	Fees & Charges	Vote & Allocation
Cheque	Queries	Vouchers & Demand Notes
Estimates	Revenue	
Expenditure	Salaries & Allowances	

Annex B: Definition of a Record

Record **may include a document in writing and —**

(a) any book, map, plan, graph or drawing;

(b) any photograph;

(c) any label, marking or other writing which identifies or describes anything of which it forms part, or to which it is attached by any means whatsoever;

(d) any diskette, tape, sound-track or other device in which sounds or other data (not being visual images) are embodied so as to be capable (with or without the aid of some other equipment) of being reproduced therefrom;

(e) any film, negative, tape, microfilm, microfiche, CD-ROM or other device in which one or more visual images are embodied so as to be capable (with or without the aid of some other equipment) of being reproduced therefrom; and

(f) anything whatsoever on which is marked any words, figures, letters or symbols which are capable of carrying a definite meaning to persons conversant with them.

Annex C: Application for Access to Information

(This form can be completed either in English or Chinese. Please read the notes below before writing.)

Applicant's Particulars

Name *Mr/Mrs/Miss ______________________ #HK I/D No. ______________

Correspondence Address ______________________________________

Tel. No. ______________________________ Fax No. ______________

* Please delete as appropriate

Fill in only if personal information is required

Information Requested

To: Access to Information Officer

____

(Name of department)

Details of information requested (Please be as specific as possible: it will help us identify clearly what you are looking for. Use a separate sheet if necessary.)

____

____

____

____

Signature ______________________________ **Date** ______________

Notes

1. A charge reflecting the cost of reproducing the records concerned may be levied. The department will advise you in advance of any such charge.
2. You may be asked to provide additional information to help us meet your request. The department may not be able to process your application if you do not provide sufficient information.
3. The information provided will be used for processing your application for access to information. It may be divulged to other departments/agencies for the same purpose.
4. For correction of or access to personal data contained in this application, please contact the Access to Information Officer of the department concerned.

Appendix E: Useful Organizations, Online Publications and Websites

Many organizations, online publications and websites provide timely and comprehensive information on developments concerning the intersections of law, journalism and freedom of expression. The following is a sampling.

Journalists' and writers' associations

Association of European Journalists, http://www.aej.org

Authors Guild (US), http://www.authorsguild.org

Creators Rights Alliance (UK), http://creatorsrights.org.uk

Foreign Correspondents' Club of China, http://www.fccchina.org

Foreign Correspondents' Club, Hong Kong, http://fcchk.org

Hong Kong Journalists Association, http://www.hkja.org.hk

International Federation of Journalists, http://www.ifj.org

Professional Writers Association of Canada, http://www.pwac.ca

Non-government organizations

Amnesty International (monitors human rights violations, including against journalists), http://www.amnesty.org

Article 19 (monitors and advocates free expression/media laws globally), http://www.article19.org

Asian Legal Information Institute (free legal research in Asia, part of Worldlii.org), http://www.asianlii.org

Committee to Protect Journalists (promotes global defence of press freedom), http://www.cpj.org

Creative Commons (alternative copyright licensing scheme), http://creativecommons.org

Freedom House (annual reports on press freedom worldwide), http://www.freedomhouse.org

Freedominfo.org (monitors freedom of information laws worldwide), http://www.freedominfo.org

Hong Kong Legal Information Institute (free Hong Kong legal research, part of World Legal Information Institute), http://www.hklii.hk

Human Rights in China, http://www.hrichina.org

IFEX (global network of free expression groups), http://www.ifex.org/

Open Net Initiative (monitors Internet censorship, filtering, surveillance), https://opennet.net

Privacy International (monitors privacy rights, laws and developments), https://www.privacyinternational.org

Reporters Committee for Freedom of the Press (provides free legal assistance to US journalists), http://www.rcfp.org

Reporters Without Borders (annual World Press Freedom index), http://www.rsf.org

World Legal Information Institute (free legal research), http://www.worldlii.org

Centres and Universities

Journalism and Media Studies Centre, The University of Hong Kong, http://jmsc.hku.hk
China Media Project, http://cmp.hku.hk/
Media Law Project, http://medialawproject.com

Berkman Center for Internet & Society, Harvard Law School, http://cyber.law.harvard.edu
Digital Media Law Project (US Internet caselaw), http://www.dmlp.org/

Center for Global Communication Studies, Annenberg School of Communication, University of Pennsylvania, http://www.global.asc.upenn.edu

Centre for Media and Communications Law, University of Melbourne, http://www.law.unimelb.edu.au/cmcl/
Media & Arts Law Review, http://www.law.unimelb.edu.au/cmcl/publications/media-and-arts-law-review

Center for Chinese Legal Studies, Columbia Law School, http://web.law.columbia.edu/chinese-legal-studies

Center for Public Participation Studies and Support, Peking University, http://www.cppss.cn

Center for Socio-Legal Studies, Programme in Comparative Media Law and Policy, Oxford University, http://pcmlp.socleg.ox.ac.uk

The China Center, Yale Law School, http://www.yale.edu/chinalaw

Governments and courts

Hong Kong

Bilingual Laws Information System, Department of Justice, Hong Kong, http://www.legislation.gov.hk

Hong Kong Special Administrative Region government, http://www.gov.hk

Privacy Commissioner for Personal Data, Hong Kong, http://www.pcpd.org.hk/

The Judiciary, Hong Kong, http://www.judiciary.gov.hk

Europe, UK

European Court of Human Rights, http://www.echr.coe.int

Information Commissioner's Office (oversees UK's FOI and personal data laws) http://www.ico.org.uk/

Ministry of Justice, United Kingdom, http://www.justice.gov.uk

The Judiciary, http://www.judiciary.gov.uk/

PRC

Central People's Government, PRC (English text), http://english.gov.cn

Ministry of Foreign Affairs, International Press Center, PRC (English text), http://ipc.fmprc.gov.cn/eng

National People's Congress, PRC (English text), http://www.npc.gov.cn/englishnpc/news

State Council, Legislative Affairs Office, PRC, http://www.chinalaw.gov.cn

Supreme People's Court, PRC, http://www.court.gov.cn

US

US-China Economic and Security Review Commission, http://www.uscc.gov

References

Books and articles

Banisar, David, "Freedom of Information around the World", *Freedominfo.org Global Survey*, July 2006, http://www.freedominfo.org/documents/global_survey2006.pdf.

Barendt, Eric, and Hitchens, Lesley, *Media Law: Cases and Materials* (Harlow, UK: Longman, 2000).

Berthold, Mark, and Wacks, Raymond, *Hong Kong Data Privacy Law: Territorial Regulation in a Borderless World*, second edition (Hong Kong: Sweet and Maxwell Asia, 2003).

Blanton, Thomas, "The World's Right to Know", *Foreign Policy*, July/August 2002.

Chan, Johannes, "Freedom of the Press: The First Ten Years in the Hong Kong Special Administrative Region", *Asia Pacific Law Review*, Vol. 15, No. 2 (2007).

Chan, Johannes, "National Security and the Unauthorized and Damaging Disclosure of Protected Information", in Fu Hualing, Carole J. Petersen, and Simon N. M. Young (eds.), *National Security and Fundamental Freedoms: Hong Kong's Article 23 under Scrutiny* (Hong Kong: Hong Kong University Press, 2005), pp. 251–276.

Chan, Johannes, and Leung, Kenneth, W. Y., "Silencing the Press? 1997 and After", 24 July 2000 (a paper presented at the 35th Anniversary Conference of the School of Journalism and Communication of the Chinese University of Hong Kong).

Chan, Joseph Man, Lee, Paul Siu-nam, and Lee, Chin-chuan, *Hong Kong Journalists in Transition* (Hong Kong: Hong Kong Institute of Asia-Pacific Studies, Chinese University of Hong Kong, 1996).

Chan, Yuen-ying, "A Scholar's View: The State Media Have an Iron Grip and Grand Plans", *Global Asia*, Summer 2010.

Chan, Yuen-ying, "The English-Language Media in Hong Kong", in Kingsley Bolton (ed.), *Hong Kong English: Autonomy and Creativity* (Hong Kong: Hong Kong University Press, 2002).

Chan, Yuen-ying, "The Market Dictates the News in Hong Kong", *Journalism Asia 2005* (Southeast Asian Press Alliance Annual Report).

Chen, Albert H. Y., *An Introduction to the Legal System of the People's Republic of China* (Hong Kong: Lexis Nexis 2004).

Chen, Xiaoyan, and Ang, Peng Hwa, "Defamation Litigation and the Press in China", *International Journal of Communications Law & Policy*, Issue 12, pp. 53–91 (2008).

China Reporting Handbook (Hong Kong: Hong Kong Journalists Association, 2006).

Clark, David, "Sedition and Article 23", *Hong Kong's Basic Law: Problems and Prospects*, Faculty of Law, University of Hong Kong, 1990.

Crone, Tom, *Law and the Media* (revising authors, P. Alberstat, T. Cassells, and E. Overs), fourth edition (Oxford: Focal Press, 2002).

Duff, Peter, Findlay, Mark, Horwarth, Carla, and Chan, Tsang-Fai, *Juries: A Hong Kong Perspective* (Hong Kong: Hong Kong University Press, 1992).

Evans, Rob, "Fare Disclosure", *The Guardian*, 2 January 2006.

Fu, Hualing, "The National Security Factor: Putting Article 23 of the Basic Law in Perspective", *Judicial Independence and the Rule of Law in Hong Kong*, p. 76.

Fu, Hualing, and Cullen, Richard, *Media Law in the PRC* (Hong Kong: Asia Law and Practice, 1996).

Fu, Hualing, Petersen, Carole J., and Young, Simon N. M. (eds.), *National Security and Fundamental Freedoms: Hong Kong's Article 23 under Scrutiny* (Hong Kong: Hong Kong University Press, 2005).

Glasser, Charles J. Jr., *International Libel & Privacy Handbook: A Global Reference for Journalists, Publishers, Webmasters and Lawyers*, third edition (New York: Wiley-Bloomberg Press, 2013).

Glofcheski, Rick, *Tort Law in Hong Kong*, third edition (Hong Kong: Sweet and Maxwell Asia, 2012).

Google Transparency Report, http://www.google.com/transparencyreport/.

Halsbury's Laws of Hong Kong, second edition 2011, Media and Communications (255).

Hanna, Mark, and Dodd, Mike, *McNae's Essential Law for Journalists*, 21st edition (Oxford: Oxford University Press, 2012).

Hong Kong Journalists Association, *Annual Reports*: 2002, 2005, 2007–2013.

Keller, Perry (ed.), *Chinese Law and Legal Theory* (Aldershot; Burlington, VT: Ashgate Publishing, 2001).

Keller, Perry, "Privilege and Punishment: Press Governance in China", 21 *Cardozo Arts & Entertainment Law Journal* 87 Winter/Spring 2003.

Liebman, Benjamin, "Innovation Through Intimidation: An Empirical Account of Defamation Litigation in China", 47 *Harvard International Law Journal* 33 (Winter 2006).

Media and Arts Law Review, Centre for Media and Communications Law, Melbourne Law School.

Murray, Kay and Crawford, Tad, *The Writer's Legal Guide: An Authors Guild Desk Reference*, fourth edition (New York: Allworth Press, 2013).

Pearson, Mark, *Blogging & Tweeting Without Getting Sued: A Global Guide to the Law for Anyone Writing Online* (Sydney: Allen and Unwin, 2012).

Pearson, Mark, and Polden, Mark, *The Journalist's Guide to Media Law*, fourth edition (Sydney: Allen and Unwin, 2011).

Pendleton, Michael D., Garland, Peter, and Margolis, Jared R., *Intellectual Property Rights: Hong Kong SAR and the People's Republic of China*, second edition (Hong Kong: Butterworths Asia, 2003).

"Questionable Beginnings: A Report on Freedom of Expression in Hong Kong SAR One Year after the Change of Sovereignty", Joint Report of the Hong Kong Journalists Association and Article 19, June 1998.

Resources Kit for Newsgathering in China (Hong Kong: Hong Kong Journalists Association, 1995).

Robertson, Geoffrey, and Nicol, Andrew, *Robertson & Nicol on Media Law*, fifth edition (London: Sweet and Maxwell 2007).

Selby, Stephen, "Writers and the Web", HKSAR, http://www.ipd.gov.hk/eng/intellectual_property/study_aids/writing_for_the_web.htm.

Shane, Scott, "Increase in the Number of Documents Classified by the Government", *The New York Times*, 3 July 2005.

Siegel, Paul, *Communication Law in America*, third edition (Lanham MD: Rowman and Littlefield, 2011).

Stephenson, Paul, Kwan, Alisa, and Ellis, David, *Cyberlaw in Hong Kong* (Hong Kong: Butterworths Asia, 2001).

Sun Xupei, *An Orchestra of Voices: Making the Argument for Greater Speech and Press Freedom in the People's Republic of China* (Westport, CT: Prager, 2001).

The First Amendment Handbook, Reporters Committee for Freedom of the Press, http://www.rcfp.org/first-amendment-handbook.

"The Line Hardens — Tougher Stance on Civil Rights Threatens Freedom of Expression in Hong Kong", Joint Report of the Hong Kong Journalists Association and Article 19, June 2002.

Trager, Robert, Russomanno, Joseph, and Dente Ross, Susan, *The Law of Journalism and Mass Communication,* second edition (Washington, DC: Sage-CQ Press, 2010).

Tsang, Stephen, ed., *Judicial Independence and the Rule of Law in Hong Kong* (Basingstoke: Palgrave, 2001).

Weaver, David H., and Wilhoit, G. Cleveland, *The American Journalist in the 1990s* (Mahwah, NJ: Lawrence Erlbaum Associates, 1996).

Wei, Luo, and Liu, Joan, *A Complete Research Guide to the Laws of the People's Republic of China (PRC)* (2003).

Weisenhaus, Doreen, "Article 23 and Freedom of the Press", *National Security and Fundamental Freedoms: Hong Kong's Article 23 under Scrutiny,* pp. 277–301.

Weisenhaus, Doreen, "Communication Law and Policy: Asia", in Wolfgang Donsbach (ed.), *The International Encyclopedia of Communication* (Malden, MA: Blackwell Publishing, 2008, revised 2012).

Weisenhaus, Doreen, "Hong Kong Free Press: Overshadowed by Beijing", *IPI Global Journalist* (First quarter 2005).

Weisenhaus, Doreen, "Hong Kong Media Ownership Trends: A Case Study of Conglomeration, Expansion and the Rise of the Market Principle", in Indrajit Banerjee and Madanmohan Rao (eds), *Media and Development in Asia: Regional Perspectives* (Singapore: AMIC Asian Communication Series, 2008).

Weisenhaus, Doreen, "Media Law Education for Journalists in Hong Kong", *Asia Pacific Media Educator* (December 2004).

Weisenhaus, Doreen, "Newsgathering Practices: Hong Kong Journalists' Views and Use of Controversial Techniques", *Global Media Journal,* Vol. 4, Issue 7 (2005).

Wesley-Smith, Peter, *An Introduction to the Hong Kong Legal System,* third edition (Oxford: Oxford University Press, 1998).

World Press Freedom Annual Reports (Reports without Borders), http://www.rsf.org.

"World Press Freedom Review 2005 (China)", International Press Institute, http://www.freemedia.at.

Wright, Clare, McAuliffe, Will, and Gamvros, Anna, "Copyright, Moral Rights and Patents", *Internet Law in Hong Kong* (Hong Kong: Thomson Sweet and Maxwell Asia, 2003).

Yan, Mei Ning, "Criminal Defamation in the New Media Environment — The Case of the People's Republic of China", 14 *International Journal of Communications Law & Policy* 1 (2011).

Yan, Mei Ning, "Freedom of Expression and the Right of Journalists to Cover Protests and Demonstrations: Hong Kong and Beyond", 33(3) *Hong Kong Law Journal* 613 (2003).

Yan, Mei Ning, "Media Photography in Hong Kong Streets: The Impact of Proposed Privacy Torts", 11 *Media and Art Law Review* 161 (2006).

Yan, Mei Ning, "Regulating Online Pornography in Mainland China and Hong Kong", in Mark McLelland and Vera Mackie (eds.) *The Routledge Handbook of Sexuality Studies in East Asia* (forthcoming).

Yan, Mei Ning, "Search Warrant Versus Production Order: The Hong Kong Experience in Protecting Journalists' Material", 10(2) *Media and Art Law Review* 117 (2005).

Yan, Mei Ning, "Tackling Media Intrusion: Recent Experience and Debates from Hong Kong", 12(5) *Communications Law* 169 (2007).

Yan, Mei Ning, "The First Five Years of the Hong Kong Press Council: A Case-study of the Desirability and Feasibility of Media Self-regulation", 33 (1& 2) *Media Asia* 13 (2007).

Yan, Mei Ning, "The Role of Academic Research in Media Policy-making: The Case-study of Hong Kong", 2 *International Journal of Communication* 396 (2008).

Youm, Kyu, "Cameras in the Courtroom in the Twenty-First Century: The US Supreme Court Learning from Abroad?" *Brigham Young University Law Review* (2012).
Young, Simon, and Ghai, Yash (eds.) *Hong Kong's Court of Final Appeal: The Development of Law in China's Hong Kong* (Cambridge: Cambridge University Press, 2013).

Government documents, submissions and others

Briefing papers on broadcasting prepared by the administration for Legislative Council's Panel on Information Technology and Broadcasting (http://www.cedb.gov.hk/ctb/eng/broad/info-legco.htm).
Chairman's reports and press releases, Hong Kong Press Council (2001–2013).
Civil Liability for Invasion of Privacy, Law Reform Commission of Hong Kong (2004).
Competition Investigation Procedures, Communications Authority (revised 2012).
Complaint and enquiry case notes, Office of the Privacy Commissioner for Personal Data (http://www.pcpd.org.hk/english/casenotes/case.html)
Complaints on broadcasting services (http://www.coms-auth.hk/en/complaints/handle/broadcasting_services/index.html)
Congressional Executive Commission on China, US (http://www.cecc.gov).
Consultation on Digital Broadcasting: Mobile Television and Related Issues, Commerce, Industry and Technology Bureau, HKSAR (2006).
Consultation on the Establishment of the Communications Authority, Commerce, Industry and Technology Bureau, HKSAR (2007).
Consultation Paper on Civil Liability for Invasion of Privacy, Subcommittee on Privacy, Law Reform Commission of Hong Kong (1999).
Consultation Paper on the Regulation of Media Intrusion, Subcommittee on Privacy, Law Reform Commission of Hong Kong (1999).
Consultation Paper on the Review of the Control of Obscene and Indecent Articles Ordinance, 2nd round, Commerce and Economic Development Bureau, HKSAR (2011).
Consultation Paper on Stalking, Constitutional and Mainland Affairs Bureau, HKSAR (2011).
Contempt of Court, Law Reform Commission of Hong Kong (1986).
Contempt of Court, UK Law Reform Commission Consultation Paper No. 209 (2012).
Contempt of Court: Scandalising the Court, UK Law Reform Commission Report No. 335 (2012).
Copyright for Journalists, HKSAR (http://www.info.gov.hk, 2000).
Country Reports on Human Rights Practices, US State Department (2005).
Digital Terrestrial Broadcasting in Hong Kong: A Consultation Paper, Information Technology and Broadcasting Bureau, HKSAR (2000).
Follow-up Review of the Television and Entertainment Licensing Authority's Control of Obscene and Indecent Articles. Audit Commission, HKSAR (2004).
Force Procedures Manual, Chapter 39 (Police, Public and Media Relations), HKSAR.
Generic Code of Practice on Television Advertising Standards, Communications Authority, HKSAR (2013).
Generic Code of Practice on Television Programme Standards, Communications Authority, HKSAR (2013).
Generic Code of Practice on Television Technical Standards, Communications Authority, HKSAR (2012).
Guidance Note for Those Interested in Applying for Licences to Establish and Maintain in Hong Kong a Broadcasting Service under Part IIIA of the Telecommunications Ordinance (Cap 106), Communications Authority (revised 2012)
Guidelines to the Application of the Competition Provisions of the Broadcasting Ordinance, Communications Authority, HKSAR (revised 2012).
Healthy Information for a Healthy Mind, Commerce and Economic Development Bureau, HKSAR (2008)

Hong Kong Bar Association's Views on the National Security (Legislative Provisions) Bill 2003, 11 April 2003, para. 105–111.

Interim Report No. 14, *Review of the Classification System of Advisory and Statutory Bodies in the Public Sector,* Annex 4, July 2005, LC Paper No. CB(2)2176/04–05(04) (prepared by the Home Affairs Bureau, HKSAR government).

Legal System in Hong Kong, 4th ed., Department of Justice (2008) (http://www.doj.gov.hk/eng/legal/index.html).

Legislative Council briefs on the Broadcasting Bill and related broadcasting policy decisions (see http://www.citb.gov.hk/ctb/eng/broad/info-legco.htm).

Legislative Council brief on *Protection of Youth from Obscene and Indecent Materials: The 2000 Review of the Control of Obscene Articles Ordinance* (2000).

Legislative Council's Panel on Security briefing papers and meeting minutes concerning search and seizure of journalistic material (2004–6).

Legislative Council papers and the *Hansard* on the passage of the Undesirable Medical Advertisements (Amendment) (No. 2) Bill 2004.

Licences for sound broadcasting and television programme services (http://www.cedb.gov.hk/ctb/eng/broad/licences.htm).

Major Incident Manual, Chapter 11 (The Media and VIPs), HKSAR.

The News Media Meets "New Media": Rights, Responsibilities and Regulation in the Digital Age, New Zealand Law Reform Commission (2011).

Policy decisions arising from the 1998 Review of Television Policy, HKSAR (1998).

Practice Statement on Regulation of Obscene and Indecent Material, Hong Kong Internet Service Providers Association (revised 2003).

Privacy and Media Intrusion, Law Reform Commission of Hong Kong (2004).

Privacy: The Regulation of Covert Surveillance, Law Reform Commission of Hong Kong (2006).

Protection of Youth from Obscene and Indecent Materials: The 2000 Review of the Control of Obscene Articles Ordinance, HKSAR (2000).

Public Consultation Paper on Pilot Project for Community Involvement Broadcasting Service, Radio Television Hong Kong (2011).

Public Consultation Paper on the New Radio Television Hong Kong: Fulfilling its Mission as a Public Service Broadcaster, Commerce and Economic Development Bureau, HKSAR (2009).

Radio Code of Practice on Advertising Standards, Communications Authority, HKSAR (2013).

Radio Code of Practice on Advertising Standards, Communications Authority, HKSAR (2012).

Radio Television Hong Kong: New Developments in Public Service Broadcasting, Legislative Council brief, Commerce and Economic Development Bureau/Radio Television Hong Kong (2011).

Reform of the Law Relating to the Protection of Personal Data, Law Reform Commission of Hong Kong (1994).

Regulating the Interception of Communications, Law Reform Commission of Hong Kong (1996).

Report of the Broadcasting Review Board, Hong Kong Government (1985).

Report on Review of Public Service Broadcasting in Hong Kong, Committee on Review of Public Service Broadcasting (2007).

Report on the Review of Hong Kong's Competition Policy, Competition Policy Review Committee (2006).

Review of Advisory and Statutory Bodies, Legislative Council Secretariat, LC Paper No. CB(2)2176/04–05(05).

Review of Certain Provisions of Copyright Ordinance, Commerce, Industry and Technology Bureau, HKSAR (December 2004).

Review of Television Policy, HKSAR (1998).

Review of the Television Environment, HKSAR (1998).

Second Consultation Paper on Digital Terrestrial Broadcasting in Hong Kong, Commerce, Industry and Technology Bureau, HKSAR (2003).

Stalking, Law Reform Commission of Hong Kong (2000).

Glossary of Legal Terms

Adjudication: When a court determines the facts, decides on the appropriate law, applies the law to the facts and reaches a result.

Arrestable offence: An offence for which the suspected offender may be arrested without an arrest warrant; these offences are those for which the sentence is fixed by law or for which a person may under or by virtue of any law be sentenced to imprisonment for a term exceeding 12 months, and an attempt to commit any such offence. See section 3 of the Interpretation and General Clauses Ordinance (IGCO), Cap 1.

Arraignment: The proceeding in which a defendant can plead guilty or not guilty to pending charges.

Bail: The release of a person arrested or imprisoned with or without security for his appearance at a later date.

Barrister: A lawyer who is a specialist in advocacy, litigation and legal advice and has the right to appear in any court in Hong Kong.

The Basic Law: Hong Kong's "mini-Constitution", in effect since 1997, which establishes the essential fundamental political and legal principles, defines the powers and duties of the government and guarantees specific rights of Hong Kong citizens.

Bind over: A judge, a District Judge or a magistrate has the power to bind over to keep the peace, and power to bind over to be of good behaviour, a person who or whose case is before the court, by requiring the person to enter into his or her own recognizances or to find sureties or both, and committing him or her to prison if the person does not comply. See section 109I of Criminal Procedure Ordinance, Cap 221. Recognizance is a formal agreement to pay a sum of money to the authorities if he or she fails to follow the court's instruction to keep peace or to behave well. A surety is a person who gives security for another.

Breach of confidence claim: A civil action that claims the unauthorized disclosure of confidential information.

Burden of proof: The obligation to prove allegations presented in a legal action. Also, standard of proof. In a criminal case, the government must prove beyond a reasonable doubt.

Bylaw: Subsidiary legislation made under or by virtue of any ordinance and having legislative effect in Hong Kong used mainly for rules made by statutory bodies like the Mass Transit Railway or the Airport Authority.

Case law: In a common law system, case law refers to the body of law established through court rulings.

Chief Executive: The head of government for the executive branch in Hong Kong, replacing the post of Governor after the 1997 handover to Chinese sovereignty.

Chief Executive in Council: Chief Executive acting after consultation with the Executive Council, Hong Kong, a constitutional arrangement since colonial days for assisting the Chief Executive in policymaking. See section 3 of IGCO.

Committal proceeding: In cases involving more serious crimes, the Magistrates' Court conducts a preliminary hearing to determine whether there is sufficient evidence to commit the accused for trial before a jury.

Committed for trial: A person is committed to trial with a view to his or her being tried before the Court of First Instance; or admitted to bail to appear and stand his or her trial before the Court of First Instance.

Common law: Non-legislative, "judge-made" law, which relies on binding precedent, following the rulings of previous cases. Can also refer to one of two major types of legal systems in the world.

Contempt of court: The wrongful interference with the administration of justice; a criminal offence. Can also include civil contempt to enforce court orders; violators can still face jail sentence.

Convergence: The term describes the trend and the process of an ongoing integration of three industries, namely, electronic media (broadcast media), communications technologies (telecommunications) and information technologies (computer) in terms of their technological developments, business operations and regulatory measures. Convergence is made possible because of advances in digital and compression technologies.

Copyright: The exclusive legal right for a limited time period to reproduce, publish, adapt, distribute, perform, sell or transmit original work such as books, computer software, plays, drawings, films, musical compositions, and so on.

Court of Final Appeal: The highest court in Hong Kong.

Damages: Money award ordered by the court for the defendant to pay the successful claimant in a civil action for loss or injury.

Data subject: The individual who is the subject of personal data, as defined in the Personal Data (Privacy) Ordinance, Cap 486.

Data user: The person or organization that controls the collection, holding, processing or use of the personal data of an individual, as defined in the Personal Data (Privacy) Ordinance.

Defamation: A statement that has the ability to damage the reputation of the person or body to which it refers.

Deregulation: The move away from state regulation. Instead of relying on statutory laws and codes designed for the broadcast media, more emphasis is placed on the operation of market forces and industry self-regulation. As such, the term "deregulation" is closely associated with terms like "self-regulation," "co-regulation" and "re-regulation."

***Ex parte* application of a search warrant:** (Latin for "from one side") When a law enforcement officer applies to the court for a search warrant to search for and seize journalistic material, the judge hearing the application may issue the warrant if he or she is satisfied that the requirements stipulated in the IGCO provisions are fulfilled. The affected party, that is, the person possessing the journalistic material, is not notified of the application nor given a chance to argue against it.

Fair comment: One of the defences in a libel action. A prominent Hong Kong case defining this defence is *Cheng v Tse* [2000] 3 HKLRD 418. This defence is now more commonly referred to as "honest comment".

Fair dealing: A defence in a copyright infringement claim, which permits the limited use of a protected work for the public interest, especially for journalists who need to cover news, disseminate information and offer opinions to the public. Fair dealing permits the use of copyright material for the limited purposes of criticism, reviews and covering the news — as well as for private research and study and education — as long as certain conditions are met.

Habeas corpus: (Latin for "you should have the body") A writ of seeking the production of a person held in custody.

High Court: The Court of First Instance and the Court of Appeal in Hong Kong.

Honest comment: A defence to defamation previously known as "fair comment".

House of Lords: Formerly, the highest court in the United Kingdom until the Constitutional Reform Act 2005 established a new Supreme Court as the final court of appeal in England, Wales and Northern Ireland, which became operational in 2009, and abolished the appellate jurisdiction of the House of Lords. It remains the upper house of the UK Parliament.

In camera: (Latin for "in a chamber") Court proceedings held in private without the public or press.

Indictable offence: Refers to a crime that can be tried "on indictment" which means with a jury following committal for trial.

Injunction: A court order that prohibits or compels a specific act or activity.

Intellectual property rights: Legal protection given to copyright, trademark and patents.

***Inter partes* application of a production order or an order to have seized material return:** (Latin for "between parties") Before the judge comes up with a decision whether to issue the relevant court order, both the law enforcement officer in charge and the person possessing the journalistic material are given a chance to present their arguments to the court.

Journalistic material: Any material acquired or created for the purposes of journalism and is in possession of a person who acquired or created it for such purposes.

Judgment: The formal decision made by a court following legal proceedings.

Judicial review: A court review of a decision by a lower court, tribunal, public agency or public official.

Jurisdiction: The power, right, or authority to interpret and apply the law or the power or right to exercise authority.

Justification: One of the defences in a defamation action, otherwise known as "truth".

Juvenile: A person under the age of sixteen who has certain legal rights.

Law Reform Commission: A government-appointed body whose lawyer and non-lawyer members conduct studies on aspects of law at the request of the Secretary for Justice or the Chief Justice or on its own initiative, with a view to recommending changes in the law.

Legislation: Law made by the Legislative Council, otherwise known as an "ordinance", and subsidiary legislation made under the authority of an ordinance.

Legislative Council: Also known as "LegCo", the Hong Kong body that enacts laws; examines and approves budgets, taxation and public expenditures; and monitors the work of the executive branch of government.

Libel: A defamatory statement in written or more permanent form.

Licensing: The commonest means so far for a government to regulate the broadcasting industry within its jurisdiction. A broadcaster must obtain a licence from the government or the relevant regulatory body before it can operate and its operation must follow the conditions set out in the licence.

Limitation period: A specified period within which a civil action can be brought. Less often there is such a limitation on the period for bringing a prosecution for a criminal offence.

Malice: Usually means either an intention to hurt, or an improper motive. Its presence may increase damages, or defeat a defence. In a qualified privilege defence in a defamation case, malice is established by showing that the defamer had a motive that the law does not recognize as proper. In the defence of fair comment in a libel case, the only form of malice now recognized in Hong Kong is the absence of honest belief in the comment made.

Moral rights: The non-economic interests in copyright protection in an original work such as a paternity right (the right to be identified as an author) and integrity right (the right to object when your work is changed in a way that distorts, mutilates or otherwise harms your reputation).

News activity: The gathering of news, preparation or compiling of articles or programs concerning news, observations on news or current events and the dissemination to the public of news or observations on news or current events, as defined in the Personal Data (Privacy) Ordinance.

Ordinance: A law passed by the Legislative Council.

Personal data: Any data relating directly or indirectly to a living individual, from which it is practicable for the identity of the individual to be directly or indirectly ascertained and in a form which access to or processing of the data is practicable.

Precedent: The rulings of higher courts that lower courts must follow in common law jurisdictions.

Prima facie: (Latin for "on its face") Usually refers to evidence that is sufficient on its face unless other evidence is produced to show otherwise.

Privilege: A defamation defence that is absolute or qualified for statements resulting from certain events, documents or statements.

Privy Council: A UK-based appeals court that serves as the final appeals court for some former British colonies such as Jamaica. It served in this capacity for Hong Kong until 1997 when Hong Kong's own Court of Final Appeal was established.

Public domain: After the copyright period pertaining to a work has expired, anyone is free to copy that work without permission or paying a licensing fee.

Public interest defence: One of the defences in a libel action, originally a variant of qualified privilege (see next entry), to protect responsible journalism on matters of public interest.

Qualified privilege: One of the defences in a libel action for publication under a legal, moral or social duty under common law or for statutory privilege as provided by Defamation Ordinance, Cap 21.

Sedition: A crime of incitement to resist or insurrect against lawful authority; usually in words or acts.

Slander: A defamatory statement by the spoken word.

Solicitor: A lawyer who can deal with most legal matters, including giving legal advice, drafting documents, registering companies, property sales etc, and can represent clients in courts other than the Court of First Instance and above.

Solicitor-advocate: A solicitor with a prerequisite number of years' experience who can apply for the right to appear before the High Court and the Court of Final Appeal.

Stare decisis: (Latin for "standing by things decided") Also known as precedent, see above.

Statute: Enacted law by the Legislative Council, otherwise known as an "ordinance".

Strict liability: Liability imposed without the showing of intent of the party. For example, for strict liability in contempt of court, it is not necessary for the prosecution to prove that the media *intended* to interfere with the administration of justice or the courts, only that the act occurred; also true of civil liability for defamation.

***Sub judice* rule:** (Latin for "under a judge") Refers to the time period after the commencement of a case during which certain details cannot be publicly discussed until the case is concluded.

Subpoena: (Latin for "under penalty") Refers to a court order compelling someone to attend court to give testimony or evidence.

Subsidiary legislation: Law made under the authority of an ordinance, by a minister or some other public authority, including rules, bylaws and other regulations needed to implement an ordinance.

Tort: A private or civil wrong or injury (except breach of contract) for which money damages may be awarded. One type of tort involving the media is defamation.

Writ of summons: Used to start a civil action arising usually from a breach of contract, fraud, damages for personal injury or death and damage to property due to a breach of duty.

Index

(Index entries marked with asterik (*) indicate inclusion in the Glossary, 409–414. For lists of cases and statutes with page references, see xxvii–xlvi.)